Women's Voices, Feminist Visions

Women's Voices, Feminist Visions

Classic and Contemporary Readings

SUSAN M. SHAW and JANET LEE

Oregon State University

MAYFIELD PUBLISHING COMPANY

Mountain View, California

London • Toronto

Library of Congress Cataloging-in-Publication Data
Women's voices, feminist visions : classic and contemporary readings /
[edited by] Susan M. Shaw and Janet Lee.
    p.   cm.
  Includes bibliographical references and index.
ISBN 0-7674-1814-X
    1. Women's studies.   2. Feminism.   I. Shaw, Susan M. (Susan Maxine), 1960–
II. Lee, Janet, 1954–
HQ1180.W689 2001
305.42—dc21   00-065379

Manufactured in the United States of America

10   9   8   7   6   5   4   3   2   1

Mayfield Publishing Company
1280 Villa Street
Mountain View, California 94041

Sponsoring editor, Serina Beauparlant; production editor, Carla White Kirschenbaum; manuscript editor, Jennifer Gordon; text designer, Joan Greenfield; cover designer, Jeanne Schreiber; art editor, Rennie Evans; manufacturing manager, Randy Hurst; photo researcher, Brian Pecko; signing rep, Simone Rico. The text was set in 10/12 Book Antiqua by G&S Typesetters and printed on 45# Chromotone Matte by Banta Book Group.

Cover image: Judith Rothschild. Interior, 1970. Oil on canvas. 40 × 60.5 in. Gift of The Judith Rothschild Foundation, 1999. Photo © The Phillips Collection, Washington, D.C.

Photo Credits: p. 8, © Corbis; p. 53, © Bettmann/Corbis; p. 113, © AFP/Corbis; p. 150, © Corbis; p. 186, © Bettmann/Corbis; p. 230, © Bettmann/Corbis; p. 273, Courtesy National Council of Jewish Women; p. 311, Courtesy Dawn M.C. Cuellar; p. 366, © Jane Scherr; p. 397, Photo © J. Cleland, Courtesy Phyllis Lyon and Del Martin; P. 438, © Peter Turnley/Corbis; p. 488, Library of Congress; p. 525, © Neil Preston/Corbis

Preface

We decided to create this book after finding our students were increasingly not reading the assigned material in our introductory women's studies course. Our students found the texts to be mostly inaccessible, or alternatively, they enjoyed reading the more testimonial first-person accounts included in some texts but were not getting the theoretical framework necessary to make sense of these more experiential readings. We were tired of creating packets of readings, and students were tired of having to access alternative readings on top of purchasing a textbook. This book was crafted to include a balance of recent contemporary readings with historical and classic pieces as well as both testimonial and more theoretical essays that would speak to the diversity of women's experiences. Each chapter has an introduction that provides an overview of the topic and provides a framework for the readings that follow. Additionally, each chapter provides a variety of learning activities, activist profiles, ideas for activism, and other sidebars that can engage students with the material in various ways.

Although students of women's studies in the early 2000s are in many ways like the students who have preceded them, they are also characterized by certain distinctions from the students of the 1980s and 1990s. Many of today's students come to our classes believing the goals of the Women's Movement have already been accomplished, and, although most will say they believe in gender equity of some sort, few identify with feminism as a political theory or social movement. Even among students who are supportive of feminist thought, there is a distinct sense of a "third wave" of feminism that reflects the interests of young women who have come of age benefiting from the gains made by their feminist foremothers. Moreover, as women's studies has become institutionalized on college campuses and is fulfilling baccalaureate core requirements, more students are being exposed to women's studies than ever before. Many of these students "choose" women's studies from a menu of options and come to the discipline with varying levels of misunderstanding and resistance. Some of these students have been influenced by the backlash efforts of the 1980s and 1990s and by conservative religious ideologies that seek a return to traditional gender relations. All of these distinctions call for a new, relevant, and accessible introductory women's studies text.

As is typical of contemporary students, students in women's studies today are the kind of visual learners who often prefer reading and interacting in front of a computer screen or watching video clips to reading traditional texts. They are unlikely to wade through long, dense, theoretical readings because they deem them "boring" and "irrelevant." We know from experience that a large percentage of students in introductory women's studies classes only read a fragment of the required readings and that our required readings end up as "fragmented texts."

Our intention in this book is to address these challenges by presenting a student-friendly text that provides short, accessible readings reflecting the diversity of women's experiences and offering a balance of classic/contemporary and theoretical/experiential pieces. The goal is to start where students are rather than where we hope they might be and to provide a text that enriches their thinking, encourages them to read, and relates to their everyday experiences. We have chosen accessible articles that we hope are readable. They are relatively short, to the point, and interesting in terms of both topics and writing styles. Although most articles are quite contemporary, we have also included several earlier classic articles that are "must-reads." And although the articles we have chosen cover the breadth of issues and eras in women's studies, we hope students will read them and enjoy reading them because of their accessibility, style of presentation, and relevance to their lives. Many are written by young feminists, many are testimonial in format, and, on the whole, they avoid dense, academic theorizing. The cartoons, we hope, bring humor to this scholarship.

We also structure opportunities for students to reflect on their learning throughout the text, and, in this sense, the book is aimed at "teaching itself." It includes not only articles and introductions but also a number of features designed to engage students in active learning around the content. For example, we address students' tendencies to lose interest by creating a format that presents smaller, self-contained, more manageable pieces of knowledge that hold together through related fields and motifs that are woven throughout the larger text as boxes. This multiple positioning of various forms of scholarship creates independent but related pieces that enable students to read each unit in its entirety and make connections between the individual units and the larger text. We see this subtext as a way to address students' familiarity and comfort with contemporary design, multiple windows (as on web pages), and "sound bytes." By also presenting material in these familiar formats, we intend to create a student-friendly text that will stimulate their interest. We encourage them to actually read the text and then be actively engaged with the material.

Pedagogy is imbedded within the text itself. In addition to the textual narrative, we include in each chapter learning activities, questions for discussion that help students explore chapter themes critically, activism ideas that provide students with examples and opportunities for the practical implementation of the content, and suggestions for further reading. Instructors will be able to utilize the various pedagogical procedures suggested in the text itself to develop teaching plans for their class sessions. By embedding the pedagogy within the text, we are creating a classroom tool that enables a connection between content and teaching procedure, between assigned readings and classroom experience. Thus, students and instructors should experience the text as both a series of manageable units of information and a holistic exploration of the larger topics.

We hope that this text will address the needs and concerns of students and instructors alike by speaking to students where they are in relation to feminist issues.

Our hope is that the innovations included in this book will invite students into productive dialogue with feminist ideas and encourage personal engagement in feminist work.

Like other women's studies text-readers, this book covers the variety of issues that we know instructors address in the introductory course. We do not isolate race and racism and other issues of difference and power as separate topics, but thoroughly integrate them throughout the text into every issue addressed. We have also chosen not to present groups of chapters in parts or sections but to let the individual chapters stand alone. Pragmatically, this facilitates instructors being able to decide how they want to organize their own courses. At the same time, however, the chapters do build on each other. For example, after introducing students to women's studies, Chapter 2 presents the systems of privilege and inequality that form the context of women's lives and then Chapter 3 explores the social construction of gender, building on the previous chapter by introducing the plurality of sex/gender systems. The following chapters then examine how sex/gender systems are expressed and maintained in social institutions.

ACKNOWLEDGMENTS

Writing a textbook is inevitably a community project, and without the assistance of a number of people this project would have been impossible. We would particularly like to thank our graduate assistant Dawn M. C. Cuellar for the many hours of tedious library and Internet research she put into this book. Our office coordinator, Lisa Lawson, also provided invaluable help with the clerical tasks of preparing a manuscript. Additionally, we thank our graduate teaching assistants for their input at various stages throughout the writing and editing process—Janet Armentor, Sriyanthi Gunewardena, Fabiola Sanchez-Sandoval, and Susan Wood.

We also would like to acknowledge the work of the many reviewers who provided insights and suggestions that strengthened our work: Amber Ault, Oakland University; Suzanne Bergeron, University of Michigan, Dearborn; Jill Bystydzienski, Iowa State University; Suzanne Cherrin, University of Delaware; Carolyn DiPalma, University of South Florida; Susan Goldstein, Diablo Valley College; Patricia L. Hartman, California University of Pennsylvania; Mazie Hough, University of Maine; Patricia Langley, University of Illinois, Springfield; Amy Lind, Arizona State University; and Sujata Moorti, Old Dominion University.

Finally, we want to thank Serina Beauparlant, our editor at Mayfield Publishing Company. Serina pushed, supported, challenged, and cajoled us at every step along the way to create an innovative, accessible, and useful introductory text. She is a wonderful editor, whose constant encouragement was key to the completion of this book.

Contents

CHAPTER 4: SEX, POWER, AND INTIMACY   145

CHAPTER 7: FAMILY SYSTEMS, FAMILY LIVES   268

CHAPTER 10: RESISTING VIOLENCE AGAINST WOMEN   395

CHAPTER 11: STATE, LAW, AND SOCIAL POLICY   435

CHAPTER ONE

Women's Studies: Perspectives and Practices

WHAT IS WOMEN'S STUDIES?

Women's studies is the examination of women's experiences that recognizes our achievements and addresses our status in society. Women's studies puts women (in all our diversity) at the center of inquiry and focuses on our reality as subjects of study. This is different than the traditional enterprise of women as objects of study. Being the objects of study means that researchers theorize about women's lives without women's input, placing women in a subordinate position to men. Instead, women as subjects of study implies both active agency on women's part and a challenge to male domination and other systems of inequality like racism and classism. In other words, when we are subjects of study as in women's studies courses, our experiences and voices have informed analyses about our lives. This means that all women, across all our differences, are included. It also means that traditional notions regarding men as "humans" and women as "others" must be challenged and transcended. This confusion of maleness with humanity, which puts men at the center and relegates women to outsiders in society, is called *androcentrism*. By making women the subjects of study, we assume that our opinions and thoughts about our own experiences are central in understanding human society generally. Adrienne Rich's "Claiming an Education" articulates this demand for women as subjects of study. It also encourages you as a student to take seriously your right to be taken seriously.

Women's studies also involves the study of gender as a central aspect of human existence. Gender concerns what it means to be a woman or a man in society. Gender involves the way society creates, patterns, and rewards our understandings of femininity and masculinity. In other words, *gender* can be defined as the way society organizes understandings of sexual difference. Women's studies explores our gendered existence: what it means to be feminine and masculine and how this interacts with other aspects of our identity, such as our race, ethnicity, socioeconomic status, and sexuality.

1

SYLVIA   by Nicole Hollander

Reprinted with permission.

HOW DID WOMEN'S STUDIES COME ABOUT?

Women's studies emerged as women and concerned men noticed the absence, mis-representation, and trivialization of women in the higher education curriculum as well as the ways women were systematically excluded from many positions of power and authority as college faculty and administrators. This was especially true for women of color. In the late 1960s and early 1970s, students and faculty be-gan demanding that the knowledge learned and shared in colleges around the country be more inclusive of women's issues, and they asked to see more women in leadership positions on college campuses. It was not unusual, for example, for entire courses in English or American literature to include not one novel written by a woman. Literature was full of men's ideas about women—ideas that often continued to stereotype women and justify their subordination. History courses often taught only about men in wars and as leaders, and sociology courses pri-marily addressed women in the context of marriage and the family. Similarly, en-tire departments often consisted exclusively of men with perhaps a small minority of (usually White) women in junior or part-time positions. Although there have been important changes on most college campuses as women's issues are slowly integrated into the curriculum and advances have been made in terms of women in leadership positions, these problems still do, unfortunately, exist in higher edu-cation today.

It is important to note that making women subjects of study involves two strategies that together result in changes in how colleges do business. First, it re-balanced the curriculum. Women as subjects of study were integrated into existing curricula, and whole courses about women were offered. This shifted the focus on men and men's lives in the traditional academic curriculum and gave some atten-tion to women's lives and concerns. Second, it resulted in a transformation of the existing curriculum. People began questioning the nature of knowledge, how knowledge is produced, and the applications and consequences of knowledge in wider society. Although the first strategy was an "add women and stir" approach, the second involved a serious challenge to traditional knowledge and its claims to truth. In this way, women's studies aimed not only to create programs of study where students might focus on women's issues and concerns but also to integrate a perspective for looking at things that would challenge previously unquestioned knowledge. This perspective questions how such knowledge reflects women's lives and concerns, how it maintains patterns of male privilege and power, and how the consequences of such knowledge affect women.

Women's studies as a discipline has its origins in the women's movement and is often named as its academic wing. The demand to include women as subjects of study in higher education in the late 1960s and early 1970s was facilitated by a broad societal movement in which organizations and individuals (both women and men) focused on such issues as work and employment, family and parenting, sexuality, reproductive rights, and violence against women. The objective was to improve women's status in society and therefore the conditions of women's lives. The women's movement emerged at a moment of widespread social turmoil as various social movements questioned traditional social and sexual values, racism, poverty and other inequities, and U.S. militarism. These social movements, including the women's movement and the civil rights movement, struggled for the rights of people of color, women, the poor, gays and lesbians, the aged and the young, and the disabled.

Two aspects of the women's movement—a commitment to personal change and to societal change—have helped establish women's studies. In terms of the personal, the women's movement involved women asking questions about the cultural meanings of being a woman in U.S. society. Intellectual perspectives that became central to women's studies as a discipline were created from the everyday experiences of women both inside and outside the movement. Through consciousness-raising groups and other situations where women came together to talk about their lives, women realized that they were not alone in their experiences. Problems they thought to be personal (like working outside the home all day and then coming home to work another full day taking care of the domestic tasks that are involved with being a wife and mother) were actually part of a much bigger picture of masculine privilege and female subordination. Women began to make connections and coined the notion "the personal is political" to explain how things taken as personal or idiosyncratic have broader social, political, and economic causes and consequences. In other words, situations that we are encouraged to view as personal are actually part of broader cultural patterns and arrangements. Note that the idea that the personal is political has relevance for men's lives too. In his essay "Shame, Guilt, and Responsibility," Allan Johnson discusses the issue of masculine privilege and entitle-ment. He emphasizes that men need to understand the connections between patterns of gender in societal institutions and their personal experience of privilege and entitlement. The term *patriarchy* can be defined as a system in which men dominate because power and authority is in the hands of adult men. However, it is important to remember that many men are supporters of women's rights and that many of the goals of the women's movement do benefit men as well.

In terms of societal change, the women's movement continues to be successful in bringing about various legal and political changes that increase women's status in society. These changes have laid the foundation for the increased power of

How Much Progress Have We Made?

In 1992 the AAUW Educational Foundation published *How Schools Shortchange Girls,* a landmark report providing overwhelming evidence that girls were often ignored in the classroom and neglected in the curriculum. This report brought gender equity to the forefront of educational reform.

Six years later, on the verge of a new millennium, *Gender Gaps: Where Schools Still Fail Our Children* examines how far the nation has come toward educational equity. What is different for girls in America's schools? What gaps still need to be addressed?

Based on an analysis of approximately 1,000 research documents published between 1990 and 1998, *Gender Gaps* reveals good news and bad news. Girls have made great strides in education and probably receive a fairer education today than in 1992. While gender gaps in areas such as math and science have narrowed, other gaps—some favoring boys and some favoring girls— have persisted or emerged. For girls, an equitable education is in many respects still an elusive goal, in sight yet out of reach.

. . .

WHAT THE RESEARCH REVEALS

How Are Girls Doing in Math and Science? *In 1992* How Schools Shortchange Girls *found that girls enrolled in fewer advanced math and science courses than boys and did not perform as well as boys on standardized tests. What's happened since then?*

. . .

Girls' participation is improving in some academic areas where it previously lagged, particularly in math and science. The increase in girls' enrollments is welcome news. But the number of classes taken doesn't tell the whole story. Girls are still not taking higher-level courses in science and computer science in the same numbers as boys.

What Is the Impact of Technology in Schools? *Since 1992 school districts have invested millions in wiring schools for computer technology. In 1996, 65 percent of U.S. public schools had access to the Internet. What is the impact of this technology on gender equity and education?*

. . .

A discouraging new gap is emerging, as computer science becomes the new "boys' club." The failure to include girls in advanced-level computer science courses threatens to make women bystanders in the technological 21st century. Some say computer access may one day bridge the educational gap between wealthy and poor students. But little attention has been given to how computer technology is affecting the educational gap between girls and boys. The goal should not simply be to "fix" girls to think like boys. Instead, we need to assess the role of computer technology in schools to ensure that it promotes equity and collaboration among all students.

What Happens in the Classroom? Teachers and Testing *In 1992* How Schools Shortchange Girls *documented dramatic differences in the quality and quantity of classroom attention that boys and girls receive. Are students today receiving a fairer and better education?*

. . .

Excellent education—education that meets high standards—requires equitable teaching. But teachers, because they receive little or no training in equity from schools of education, are unprepared. Teaching materials, such as computers and textbooks, also need attention. While textbooks have become more gender-conscious, many still place female characters in stereotypical roles that reinforce biases. Computer technology in the classroom also runs the risk of exacerbating rather than diminishing inequities.

High-stakes tests, those that determine college scholarships, admissions, and course credit, magnify gender gaps between girls and boys bound for college. For reasons that continue not to be entirely clear, girls consistently earn better grades than boys, but score lower on standardized tests.

Are Students at Risk? *The 1992 report called attention to the "evaded curriculum," tough issues facing students such as pregnancy, violence, and harassment that are rarely discussed in school. Do girls and boys face different risks? Why do some students succeed in the face of such risks while others do not?*

. . .

Girls are more vulnerable than boys to some risks. Girls confront widespread sexual violence and harassment that interferes with their ability to learn, both within the family and within the schools. Schools limit gender equity when they fail to confront or discuss risk factors for students.

The teen pregnancy rate has declined slowly but steadily from 1991 (when 62 percent of all pregnant women were teens) to 1996 (when 55 percent were teens). The number of teen births has also dropped. However, the decline is not consistent across all racial and ethnic groups. It is unclear whether school interventions have contributed to the decline in pregnancy and birth rates. Most troubling, school sex education programs tend to place primary responsibility for teen pregnancy on girls, while boys' sexual behavior goes relatively unmodified and unchecked.

Rather than try to provide students a risk-free environment—an impossible task—youth workers today focus more on building students' coping skills so they can withstand stress and weather crises. Such a "resiliency" approach builds on the social and cultural strengths and resources of students and their communities. School programs have the potential to help students develop strengths to overcome risks and succeed.

Are Students Prepared for the Work Force? *Since 1992 some school districts have launched School-to-Work and other career preparation programs to give students a taste of "real world" careers. Have these programs encouraged girls and boys to pursue fields considered nontraditional for their sex?*

. . .

Students still face gender barriers when they prepare to enter the work force. School-to-Work and other new career preparation programs have pledged to recruit boys and girls into nontraditional fields, but have achieved limited success. Simply offering boys and girls the same menu of career choices without actively encouraging them to consider nontraditional fields does little to change the status quo.

Ironically, some programs that make conscious efforts to interest girls and boys in nontraditional fields face resistance from students themselves who have entrenched ideas about what careers are appropriate for them. While boys tend toward careers in business,

(continued)

(continued)

managerial, technical, and engineering careers, girls cluster in the social sciences, health services, and education. . . .

The channeling of students into "gender-appropriate fields" reinforces gender inequities in the work force. In today's economy, women cluster in only 20 of the more than 400 job categories, and two out of three minimum-wage earners are women.

CONCLUSION

Have schools made progress toward equity since 1992? In critical areas such as math and science, the answer for girls is a definitive *yes,* although as *Gender Gaps* makes clear, some troubling gaps remain. The field of public education is ever-changing. And so, even as we narrow historic gaps, new ones emerge; technology is the prime example.

In the 21st century, America's public schools will have to serve the needs of an increasingly diverse student body. Gender equity research and practice will have to take into account the unique needs of diverse populations of girls entering the public schools. Even as girls narrow many gaps in math and science, new disciplines—like computer science, biotechnology, and environmental science—could produce new gender gaps. For girls to achieve economic independence and participate fully in the boom industries of the 21st century, educators will need to ensure that girls are included in these fields. Similarly, as we enter a more information-based global economy, boys will need to be encouraged to pursue and develop communication skills.

For all students to achieve in school, educators, parents, and policymakers must develop strategies to address the different learning styles of all students. We must give all public school students, both girls and boys, the chance to learn, excel, and achieve educationally.

. . .

Source: "Executive Summary," *Gender Gaps: Where Schools Still Fail Our Children* (AAUW Educational Foundation, 1998), pp. 1–8.

women in higher education. Remember that although women have been present on college campuses since the nineteenth century, they have been a small minority of faculty and administrators. Not until the 1960s did political and legal changes improve women's status in society and help remove legal obstacles to their full participation in higher education as faculty and students. This struggle continues today.

These legal changes include the passage of the Equal Pay Act in 1963 that sought equal pay for individuals performing the same work, Title VII of the 1964 Civil Rights Act that forbade workplace discrimination, and the creation of the Equal Employment Opportunity Commission (EEOC) to enforce antidiscrimination laws in the early 1970s. Affirmative action as a legal mechanism to combat discrimination was first utilized in 1961 and was extended to women in 1967. In terms of legal changes directly aimed at higher education, Title IX of the Education Amendments Act of 1972 supported equal education and forbade gender discrimination in schools. This included women's access to sports in the context of schooling.

These legal changes were accompanied by a small, although significant, increase in women running for political office and taking positions of authority in government, business, education, science, and the arts. Women were becoming visible and active in all societal institutions. In addition, the gains women were making in U.S. society were being mirrored by women's gains in other Western societies. These societal changes strengthened the demand for alternative educational models: Not only was it the right thing to include women in college life, it was illegal to prevent their participation.

WHAT WERE THE ORIGINS OF WOMEN'S RIGHTS ACTIVISM IN THE UNITED STATES?

Although the women's movement of the 1960s and 1970s (often termed the *second wave*) facilitated women's studies on college campuses, earlier in the nineteenth century there was a first wave of activity organized around women's issues. The reading by Sheila Ruth titled "Feminist Activism: Historical Context" explains the origins of this movement and the themes involved. Women had few legal, social, and economic rights in nineteenth-century U.S. society. They had no direct relationship to the law outside of their relationships as daughters or wives; in particular, married women lost property rights upon marriage. Women were also mostly barred from higher education until women's colleges started opening later in the nineteenth century.

Most early women's rights activists (then it was referred to as "woman's" rights) in the United States had their first experience with social activism in the abolition movement, the struggle to free slaves. These activists included such figures as Elizabeth Cady Stanton, Lucretia Mott, Susan B. Anthony, Sojourner Truth, Sarah M. and Angelina Grimké, Henry Blackwell, Frederick Douglass, and Harriet Tubman. Many abolitionists became aware of inequities elsewhere in society. Some realized that to improve women's status a separate social movement was required. In this way, for many abolitionists, their experiences with abolition inspired their desire to improve the conditions of women's lives.

Although English philosopher Mary Wollstonecraft's book *A Vindication of the Rights of Woman* (1792) is seen as the first important expression of the demand for women's equality, the beginning of the women's movement in the United States is usually dated to the Seneca Falls Convention of 1848. This convention was conceived as a response to the experience of Lucretia Mott and Elizabeth Cady Stanton, who as delegates to the world Anti-Slavery Convention in London in 1840, were refused seating, made to sit behind a curtain, and not allowed to voice their opinions because they were women. Their experience fueled the need for an independent women's movement in the United States and facilitated the convention at Seneca Falls, New York, in July 1848. An important document, the "Declaration of Sentiments and Resolutions," came out of this convention. Authored primarily by Elizabeth Cady Stanton, it used the language of the U.S. Declaration of Independence and included a variety of demands to improve women's status in the family and in society. Woman's suffrage, the right of women to vote, was included. Other conventions occurred across the country, and national organizations were

Activist Profile: Susan B. Anthony

Born in Massachusetts in 1820, Susan B. Anthony grew up in a Quaker family in which she learned justice and activism. In the 1840s she became involved with the temperance movement, campaigning for stricter liquor laws to address the ill effects of drunkenness on families. In 1853, she was denied the right to speak at the New York Sons of Temperance meeting because she was a woman. That year she joined with Elizabeth Cady Stanton in founding the Women's State Temperance Society. The society gathered 28,000 signatures urging the state legislature to pass a law limiting the sale of liquor, but, because most of the signatures were from women and children, the legislature rejected the petition. As a result of this experience, Anthony realized that women needed the vote in order to have political influence.

From that point on, Anthony campaigned vigorously for women's suffrage. In 1866, she and Stanton founded the American Equal Rights Association and in 1868 began to publish *The Revolution,* with the masthead "Men, their rights, and nothing more; women, their rights, and nothing less." In 1872, Anthony was arrested in Rochester, New York, for voting. At her trial, the judge ordered the jury to find her guilty, and then he fined her $100 plus court fees. Although she refused to pay, he did not imprison her, thereby denying her the opportunity to appeal and force the issue before the Supreme Court.

In 1877 she gathered 10,000 signatures from twenty-six states, but Congress ignored them. She appeared before every Congress from 1869 to 1906 to ask for passage of a suffrage amendment. Even in her senior years, Anthony remained active in the cause of suffrage, presiding over the National American Women Suffrage Association from 1892 to 1900. Anthony died in 1906, fourteen years before American women won the vote with the Nineteenth Amendment, also known as the Susan B. Anthony Amendment.

> **Learning Activity: The National Women's Hall of Fame**
>
> Visit the National Women's Hall of Fame at *www.greatwomen.org*. Follow the links to the exercise "Winning the Right to Vote," and find out when your state ratified the Nineteenth Amendment. Then follow the links to play the "Name Game." See how well you know the women in the hall of fame. Finally, follow the links to the 1998 inductees. Who are they and why were they inducted? What do you think is the significance of having a national women's hall of fame?

organized to promote women's rights generally and suffrage in particular. These organizations included the National Woman Suffrage Association (NWSA) formed in 1869 and the National American Woman Suffrage Association (NAWSA) in 1890. NAWSA was formed from the merging of NWSA and the American Woman Suffrage Association. These organizations fought for women's political personhood—a struggle that continues today. The "Anthony Amendment," the women's suffrage amendment, was introduced into Congress in 1878; it took another forty-two years for this amendment to be ratified as the Nineteenth Amendment in 1920, granting women the right to vote.

WHAT IS THE STATUS OF WOMEN'S STUDIES ON COLLEGE CAMPUSES TODAY?

Over the past twenty-five or thirty years women's studies has steadily become institutionalized, or established as a regular custom, on many college campuses. From a scattering of courses (often taught for free by committed faculty when colleges did not want to spend money on these courses) have come whole programs and departments with minors and majors of study and graduate degrees at both the masters and doctorate levels. Although most campuses have adopted women's studies, some have gone with gender studies and others with feminist studies. These different names reflect different perspectives concerning knowledge about and for women.

Professors of women's studies might only teach women's studies, or they might do most of their work in another department like anthropology or history. This illustrates the multidisciplinary nature of women's studies: It can be taught from the point of view of many different disciplines. For the most part, however, women's studies is *interdisciplinary*; that is, it combines knowledge from and methodologies of disciplines across the humanities and the social and biological sciences in its analysis.

A list of the goals or objectives of women's studies might look like this:

- To understand the social construction of gender and the intersection of gender with other systems of inequality in women's lives
- To learn about the status of women in society and ways to improve that status through individual and collective action for social change.

- To experience how institutions in society affect individual lives and to be able to think critically about the role of patterns of privilege and discrimination in women's lives
- To improve writing and speaking skills, gain new insights, and empower self and others

WHAT DOES WOMEN'S STUDIES HAVE TO DO WITH FEMINISM?

Women's studies is generally associated with feminism as a paradigm for understanding self and society. Although there are many definitions of feminism and some disagreement concerning a specific definition, there is agreement on two core principles underlying any concept of feminism. First, feminism concerns equality and justice for all women, and it seeks to eliminate systems of inequality and injustice in all aspects of women's lives. Because feminism is politics of equality, it anticipates a future that guarantees human dignity and equality for all people, women and men. Second, feminism is inclusive and affirming of women; it celebrates women's achievements and struggles and works to provide a positive and affirming stance toward women and womanhood. Feminism is a personal perspective as well as a social movement.

Put this way, feminism is hardly a radical notion. Indeed, a recent study found that a large number of women (more than 90 percent who were asked) said they believed women should be paid comparably to men for the work that they do, that women deserve equal rights in society, and that sexism still exists. However, very few of these same women (only 16 percent) said they considered themselves feminists.

Other kinds of feminism, although they embrace the two core concepts listed above, vary in terms of their explanations for understanding the social organization of gender and their solutions for the problem. Sheila Ruth mentions these in her article and makes the distinction between liberal feminism and radical feminism. Liberal feminists believe in the viability of the present system and work within this context for change in such public areas as education and employment.

Thank a Feminist

Thank a feminist if you agree that …

- Women should have the right to vote.
- Women should have access to contraceptives.
- Women should have the right to work outside the home.
- Women should receive equal pay for equal work.
- Women should have the right to refuse sex, even with their husbands.
- Women should be able to receive a higher education.
- Women should have access to safe, legal abortion.
- Women should be able to participate in sports.
- Women should be able to hold political office.
- Women should be able to choose any career that interests them.
- Women should be free from sexual harassment in the workplace.
- Women should be able to enter into legal and financial transactions.
- Women should be able to study issues about women's lives and experiences.

One hundred years ago, none of these statements was possible for women in the United States. Only through the hard work and dedication of women in each decade of the twentieth century did these rights become available to women.

Imagine a world without feminism. If you are a woman, you would not be in college. You would not be able to vote. You could not play sports. Contraception is illegal. So is abortion. You're expected to marry and raise a family. If you must work, the only jobs available to you are in cleaning or clerical services. And you have no legal protection on the job if your boss pressures you for sex or makes lewd comments. Your husband can force you to have sex, and, if you were sexually abused as a child, most likely no one will believe you if you tell. If you are sexually attracted to women, you are considered mentally ill and may be subjected to an array of treatments for your illness.

Today, young women who claim, "I'm not a feminist, but …" benefit from the many gains made by feminists through the twentieth century. So, the next time you go to class or vote or play basketball, thank a feminist!

Liberal feminists attempt to remove obstacles to women's full participation in public life. Strategies include education, federal and state policies, and legal statutes.

Although liberal feminists want a piece of the pie, radical feminists, on the other hand, want a whole new pie. Radical feminists recognize the oppression of women as a fundamental political oppression wherein women are categorized as inferior based upon their gender. It is not enough to remove obstacles; rather, deeper, more transformational changes need to be made in societal institutions (like the government or media) as well as in people's heads. Patriarchy, radical feminists believe, shapes how women and men think about the world, their place in it, and their relationships with one another as well as the social institutions in which it is embedded. Radical feminists assert that reformist solutions like those liberal feminism would enact are problematic because they work to maintain rather than undermine the system. Not surprisingly, although the focus of liberal feminism is on the public sphere, the focus of this radical approach is the private sphere of everyday individual consciousness and change. Radical feminist off-shoots include lesbian feminism, which focuses on how compulsory heterosexuality (the cultural norm that assumes and requires heterosexuality) and heterosexual privilege (the rights and privileges of heterosexuality, such as legal marriage and being intimate in public) affect women's lives. It also includes ecofeminism, a perspective that focuses on the association of women with nature and the environment and the simultaneous relationships among patriarchy, global economic expansion, and environmental degradation.

In addition, Ruth writes about Marxist feminism, a perspective that uses economic explanations from traditional Marxist theory to understand women's oppression. For Marxist feminists, the socioeconomic inequities of the class system are the major issues. Ruth also mentions socialist feminism, a perspective that integrates both Marxist and radical feminism. Socialist feminists use the insights of class analysis alongside radical feminist explanations of gender oppression. Socialist feminists seek to understand the workings of capitalist patriarchal institutions and societies. All these feminist approaches have been critiqued by the perspectives of women of color, who require that these approaches be inclusive of *all* women's lives. Similarly, some feminists have utilized a postmodern perspective to emphasize that truth is a relative concept and that identity is more multifaceted than we often imagine. This approach pays attention to differences among women and avoids using the term *woman* because that may imply that all women share similar or universal characteristics. It emphasizes that women actively construct or shape their lives in the context of various social systems and often in the face of serious constraints.

Feminists recognize both the similarities and differences in women's status worldwide. Women's status in developing and nonindustrialized countries is often very low, especially in societies where strict religious doctrines govern gendered behaviors. Although women in various countries around the world tend to be in subordinate positions, the form this subordination takes varies. As a result, certain issues, like the ability of women to maintain subsistence agriculture and feed their families—matters of personal survival—take priority over the various claims to autonomy that characterize women's issues in the West. What are considered feminist issues in the United States are not necessarily the most important concerns of women in other parts of the world. It is important to understand this in order to avoid overgeneralizing about feminism's usefulness globally, even though the notion of global feminism is real and useful for political alliances across national borders. Nonetheless, global feminism underscores the similarities women share across the world and seeks strategies that take into account the interdependence of women globally. And, as communication technologies have advanced, the difficulties of organizing women in all parts of the world have lessened. International feminist groups have worked against militarism, global capitalism, and racism, and they have worked for issues identified by local women. This action culminated in the United Nations Fourth World Conference on Women held in Beijing, China, in 1995. More than 30,000 women attended the Beijing conference, and 181 governments signed the "Platform for Action." This platform is a call for concrete action to include the human rights of women and girls as part of universal human rights, thus eradicating poverty of women, removing the obstacles to women's full participation in public life and decision making, eliminating all forms of violence against women, ensuring women's access to educational and health services, and promoting actions for women's economic autonomy.

Many writers now refer to a current "third wave" of feminist activity that has its origins in the early 1990s. Third wave feminists are typically young adults who are part of generation X, those born after 1960. Coming of age during the Reagan years of the 1980s, they grew up with feminism as well as the resistance or backlash to it. Indeed, many third wave feminists are the children of second wave parents (activists of the 1960s and 1970s). Third wave issues focus on sexuality and identity and tend not to have arisen from a mass-based social movement. For these reasons, many believe that third wave feminism is better understood as a generational aspect of contemporary feminism (that is, young adults responding to what they see as the outdated issues of the second wave) and that it represents a transitional period in the movement rather than a new feminist perspective as such. Nonetheless, contemporary third wave activity has been important in fueling feminist activism, especially through "riot grrl" punk rock band performances and other musical and artistic forms, various "rags" or "zines" (consciousness-raising magazines produced locally and usually shared electronically), and the use of electronic information and entertainment technologies generally. Third wave feminists understand the need for theory and practice that take into account the globalization of economic markets, technologies, and the workplace as well as global information systems.

WHAT ARE THE MYTHS ASSOCIATED WITH FEMINISM?

Feminism suffers from an image problem, one that has grown in proportion to feminist progress, and there has been an institutionalized backlash to the gains feminism has achieved. For example, certain groups who believe they would lose from a redistribution of power have worked hard to discredit and destroy the feminist movement and brand feminists in negative ways. This perspective is known as anti-feminism. Although such anti-feminist activity includes conservative groups and politicians, it also involves women who claim to be feminists yet are resistant to its core principles. These women include such successful female academics as Christina Hoff Summers, Camille Paglia, and Daphne Patai, and such third wave "feminist" voices as Katie Roiphe and Rene Denfield. The reading by Deborah Rhode, an excerpt from *Speaking of Sex: The Denial of Gender Inequality*, focuses on the backlash that denies the existence of gender inequality despite the concrete realities of women's lives.

One result of this backlash has been the coining of the term *postfeminism* by those who recognize feminism as an important perspective but believe its time has passed, and it is now obsolete. "We're already liberated" is the stance they take. Like other broad generalizations, there is some truth to this: Things have improved for some women in some areas. Although generally it is accurate to say that women's status in the United States at the end of the twentieth century is markedly improved, we still have a long way to go to reach equality. In terms of the issues of poverty, violence, pornography, and HIV/AIDS (to name just a few), things are worse for many women than they ever have been. There are still many areas in which women's status might be enhanced, and, for the majority of the world's women, life is very difficult indeed.

The idea that women have achieved equality is reinforced by the capitalist society in which we live. Surrounded by consumer products, we are encouraged to confuse liberation with the freedom to purchase these products or to choose among a relatively narrow range of choices. Often personal style is mistaken for personal freedom as the body becomes a focus for fashion, hair, piercing, exercise, and so forth. We are often encouraged to confuse such freedoms of expression with freedom in the sense of equality and social justice. Of course, popular culture and the mass media play a large part in this. We are encouraged to enjoy the freedoms that, in part, feminism has brought, without recognition of this struggle or allegiance to maintaining such freedoms. Phyllis Chesler makes this point in the essay "Your Legacy," reminding us of the responsibilities associated with the freedoms we often take for granted.

Many people, groups, and institutions have attempted to discredit feminism (and therefore women's studies) in other ways. Feminism has been associated with angry, hostile women who have an axe to grind and no sense of humor; it is declared that feminists hate men and selfishly want to create new systems of power *over* men; all feminists are said to be lesbians, women who choose romantic relationships with other women; and feminism is dismissed as a White, middle-class movement.

Yes, I Am

"I'm proud to be a lifelong [feminist]. It's as natural as breathing, feeling, and thinking. Never go back, never apologize, and never forget we're half the human race."
—Bella Abzug, former congresswoman

"It is from feminism that all of the many other things that I am flow. I am a mother and a mate, an activist, a mistake-maker, rule-breaker, Gloria-worshipping, Oprah-loving, risk-taker. I am a feminist, and my God and my feminism are compatible and powerful. I am a feminist, and sometimes I disappoint my feminism, and sometimes I walk hand in hand with it. I celebrate every feminist who stood strong, who took the chance, risked, and leapt."
—Kathy Najimy, actor

"This is what comes to mind when I think about feminism: a female infant placed in a wooden bucket, floating down the river. Slowly, the bucket sinks. A peasant couple in Northern China were discovered to have drowned five of their daughters this way. The victims' only fault was that they were girls."
—Anchee Min, author

"I'm not ashamed of [being feminist]. A lot of women are. It's difficult to be in the workforce, in any position of power, and not be a feminist. We have to be twice as intelligent to be in the same positions as men. On top of that, I'm a Black woman, so in my career, I've had to walk a very thin line. When I am assertive, men equate that with being antimale. Strong-mindedness intimidates most men. I've had many brothers say, 'You're a helluva woman.

I hope you can find a man who can deal with you!' So much of the support I've gotten has been from women. Women have the spine, they feel where I'm coming from."
—Sandra St. Victor, vocalist

"In my native Dominican Republic, I run into women who shake their heads disapprovingly and say, 'Yo no soy feminista, pero, sí creo …' The subtext of the phrase is: I am a feminist, but I don't want to have to fight for what I believe in. By refusing to claim their feminism openly, these women make the burden all the harder for the rest of us who are willing to pay the price."
—Julia Alvarez, author

"Feminism saved my life. It's a simple fact. If there had not been a women's movement and a lesbian and gay rights movement, there's no question I'd be dead. I was on my way as it was. I deeply believe that I got picked up by a wave of history that had the possibility of allowing me to see my life in a different way and survive. There was no other voice that could say to you, 'Yes, you're an incest survivor, but you're not a monster.' There was no other voice that could say to you, 'Yes, you come out of this enormous, broken, working-class family, and that is not the problem.' There was no other voice that could say, 'Yes, you're a lesbian, but you're not crazy.' The women's movement was it. That's where my source of sanity originated. I can still remember the feeling of being lifted up out of this confusion and despair and self-destruction—just lifted up. It's been the fuel of my life."
—Dorothy Allison, author

"Every woman who has achieved success in the working world in the last quarter century owes that success in some measure to the feminist movement. My mother taught us to respect and pay homage to those whose efforts benefited us. My life has been indelibly marked by the civil rights and feminist movements, so in addition to acknowledging my debt to the civil rights movement, I am a feminist out of respect for the efforts of those who fought for equal rights for women in every sphere.

"There are few monuments to the early feminists who revolutionized society. Their most important and enduring monument should be the gratitude of women whose minds, lives, and futures were made safe by feminists. We owe them our gratitude and a commitment to continue the equal rights struggle."
—Ruth Simmons, president, Smith College

Each of these myths can easily be shattered. First, although there are some feminists who respond, some would say rightly, to societal injustices with anger, most feminists work patiently with little resentment. Men as a social group demonstrate much more anger than women, feminists included. Even though men's rage comes out in numerous acts of violence, wars, school shootings, and so on, men's anger is seen merely as a human response to circumstance. Note the androcentrism at work here. Because a few angry feminists get much more publicity than the majority of those resigned to the status quo, a better question might be why women are not more angry, given the levels of injustice against women both in the United States and worldwide. We should also ask why women's anger provokes such a negative response. The cause of the relatively intense reaction to women's anger is grounded in a societal mandate against female anger that works to keep women from resisting their subordination—that is, it keeps them passive. Anger is seen as destructive and inappropriate, going against what we imagine to be feminine. As a result, organized expressions of anger are interpreted as hostile.

Second, it is often said that feminists hate men. It is accurate to say that, in their affirmation of women and their desire to remove systems of inequality, feminists ask that men understand how gender privilege works in men's lives. Many men are more than willing to do this because the same social constructions of masculinity that privilege men also limit them. The demand for the examination of gender privilege is not synonymous with hating men, and thus we might ask why these different concepts are so easily conflated. A more interesting question is why men are not accused more often of hating women. Certainly the world is full of *misogyny,* the hatred of women, and every day we see examples of the ways misogyny influences, and sometimes destroys, the lives of women. The reality, of course, is that most feminists are in relationships with men, and some feminists *are* men. Some men eagerly call themselves pro-feminist because feminism is a perspective on life (even though some would argue that just as people of color are better prepared to understand racial inequality, so women are in a better place to understand how gender works). Nonetheless, the man-hating myth works to prevent many women who want to be in relationships with men from claiming feminism. They are encouraged to avoid a political stance that suggests antagonism toward men.

Feminists often respond to the declaration that they hate men with the observation that the statement illustrates a hypersensitivity about the possibility of exclusion and loss of power on the part of men. Only in a patriarchal society would the inclusion of women be interpreted as a potential threat or loss of men's power. It is a reflection of the fact that we live in a competitive patriarchal society that it is assumed that the feminist agenda is one that seeks to have power over men. And only in an androcentric society where men and their reality is center stage would it be assumed that an inclusion of one group must mean the exclusion of another. In other words, male domination encourages the idea that affirming women means hating men and interprets women's request for power sharing as a form of taking over. This projection of patriarchal mentality equates someone's gain with another's loss.

Third, feminists are accused of being lesbians in an effort to discredit feminism and prevent women both from joining the movement and from taking women's studies classes. Feminism affirms women's choices to be and love whomever they choose. Although some lesbians are feminists, many lesbians are not feminists, and many feminists are heterosexual. Feminists do not interpret an association with lesbianism as an insult. Nonetheless, *homophobia,* the societal fear or hatred of lesbians and gay men, functions to maintain this as an insult. There is considerable fear associated with being called a lesbian, and this declaration that all feminists are lesbians serves to keep women in line, apart from one another, and suspicious of feminism and women's studies. Note that this myth is related to the above discussion on men-hating because it is assumed that lesbians hate men too. Again, although lesbians love women, this does not necessitate a dislike of men.

Fourth, feminism has been critiqued as a White, middle-class perspective that has no relevance to the lives of women of color. The corollary of this is that women's studies is only about the lives of White, bourgeois young women. This critique is important because throughout the history of the women's movement there have been examples of both blatant and subtle racism, and White women have been the ones to hold most of the positions of power and authority. Similarly, working-class women have been underrepresented. This is also reflected in the discipline of women's studies as faculty and students have often been disproportionately White and economically privileged. Much work has been done to transform the women's movement into an inclusive social movement that has relevance for all people's lives. Women's studies departments and programs today are often among the most diverse units on college campuses, although most still have work to do. It is absolutely crucial that the study of women as subjects both recognizes and celebrates diversity and works to transform all systems of oppression in society. This is the theme of bell hooks's article "Revolutionary Feminism: An Anti-Racist Agenda." She emphasizes that any call to sisterhood must involve a commitment on the part of White women to examine White privilege and understand the interconnections among gender, race, and class domination.

bell hooks's essay is followed by JeeYeun Lee's "Beyond Bean Counting." Lee shares her experience of women's studies and her observations about inclusion. She recalls how she lamented the absence of information about Asian American women in her first feminist studies course but at the same time was profoundly exhilarated by the class. She recognizes the efforts feminists have made to deal with issues of race even though work remains to be done. She also notes how social movements that affirm struggles over race and ethnicity can still be exclusionary in terms of sexual orientation. She uses the term *queer* in this essay as a way to affirm and celebrate her lesbianism. Her hope is for solidarity among all groups.

The first and second waves of the women's movement have had a profound impact on the lives of American women, and, although great strides have been made toward equality, real problems remain. Women continue to face discrimination and harassment in the workplace, domestic violence, rape and abuse, inequities in education, poverty, racism, and homophobia. Women's studies provides a forum for naming the problems women face, analyzing the root causes of these problems, envisioning a just and equitable world, and developing strategies for change. As you read the following articles, keep these questions in mind: What does the author identify as problems women face? What does the author suggest is the root of these problems? What strategies does the author suggest for bringing about change to improve the lives of women?

Claiming an Education

Adrienne Rich

For this convocation, I planned to separate my remarks into two parts: some thoughts about you, the women students here, and some thoughts about us who teach in a women's college. But ultimately, those two parts are indivisible. If university education means anything beyond the processing of human beings into expected roles, through credit hours, tests, and grades (and I believe that in a women's college especially it *might* mean much more), it implies an ethical and intellectual contract between teacher and student. This contract must remain intuitive, dynamic, unwritten; but we must turn to it again and again if learning is to be reclaimed from the depersonalizing and cheapening pressures of the presentday academic scene.

The first thing I want to say to you who are students, is that you cannot afford to think of being here to *receive* an education; you will do much better to think of yourselves as being here to *claim* one. One of the dictionary definitions of the verb "to claim" is: *to take as the rightful owner; to assert in the face of possible contradiction.* "To receive" is *to come into possession of; to act as receptacle or container for; to accept as authoritative or true.* The difference is that between acting and being acted-upon, and for women it can literally mean the difference between life and death.

One of the devastating weaknesses of university learning, of the store of knowledge and opinion that has been handed down through academic training, has been its almost total erasure of women's experience and thought from

the curriculum, and its exclusion of women as members of the academic community. Today, with increasing numbers of women students in nearly every branch of higher learning, we still see very few women in the upper levels of faculty and administration in most institutions. Douglass College itself is a women's college in a university administered overwhelmingly by men, who in turn are answerable to the state legislature, again composed predominantly of men. But the most significant fact for you is that what you learn here, the very texts you read, the lectures you hear, the way your studies are divided into categories and fragmented one from the other—all this reflects, to a very large degree, neither objective reality, nor an accurate picture of the past, nor a group of rigorously tested observations about human behavior. What you can learn here (and I mean not only at Douglass but any college in any university) is how *men* have perceived and organized their experience, their history, their ideas of social relationships, good and evil, sickness and health, etc. When you read or hear about "great issues," "major texts," "the mainstream of Western thought," you are hearing about what men, above all white men, in their male subjectivity, have decided is important.

Black and other minority peoples have for some time recognized that their racial and ethnic experience was not accounted for in the studies broadly labeled human; and that even the sciences can be racist. For many reasons, it has been more difficult for women to comprehend our exclusion, and to realize that even the sciences can be sexist. For one thing, it is only within the last hundred years that higher education has grudgingly been opened up to women at all, even to white, middle-class women. And many of us have found ourselves

---

This talk was given at the Douglass College Convocation, September 6, 1977, and first printed in *The Common Woman*, a feminist literary magazine founded by Rutgers University women in New Brunswick, New Jersey.

poring eagerly over books with titles like *The Descent of Man; Man and His Symbols; Irrational Man; The Phenomenon of Man; The Future of Man; Man and the Machine; From Man to Man; May Man Prevail?; Man, Science and Society;* or *One-Dimensional Man*—books pretending to describe a "human" reality that does not include over one-half the human species.

Less than a decade ago, with the rebirth of a feminist movement in this country, women students and teachers in a number of universities began to demand and set up women's studies courses—to *claim* a woman-directed education. And, despite the inevitable accusations of "unscholarly," "group therapy," "faddism," etc., despite backlash and budget cuts, women's studies are still growing, offering to more and more women a new intellectual grasp on their lives, new understanding of our history, a fresh vision of the human experience, and also a critical basis for evaluating what they hear and read in other courses, and in the society at large.

But my talk is not really about women's studies, much as I believe in their scholarly, scientific, and human necessity. While I think that any Douglass student has everything to gain by investigating and enrolling in women's studies courses, I want to suggest that there is a more essential experience that you owe yourselves, one which courses in women's studies can greatly enrich, but which finally depends on you, in all your interactions with yourself and your world. This is the experience of *taking responsibility toward your selves.* Our upbringing as women has so often told us that this should come second to our relationships and responsibilities to other people. We have been offered ethical models of the self-denying wife and mother; intellectual models of the brilliant but slapdash dilettante who never commits herself to anything the whole way, or the intelligent woman who denies her intelligence in order to seem more "feminine," or who sits in passive silence even when she disagrees inwardly with everything that is being said around her.

Responsibility to yourself means refusing to let others do your thinking, talking, and naming for you; it means learning to respect and use your own brains and instincts; hence, grappling with hard work. It means that you do not treat your body as a commodity with which to purchase superficial intimacy or economic security; for our bodies and minds are inseparable in this life, and when we allow our bodies to be treated as objects, our minds are in mortal danger. It means insisting that those to whom you give your friendship and love are able to respect your mind. It means being able to say, with Charlotte Brontë's *Jane Eyre:* "I have an inward treasure born with me, which can keep me alive if all the extraneous delights should be withheld or offered only at a price I cannot afford to give."

Responsibility to yourself means that you don't fall for shallow and easy solutions—predigested books and ideas, weekend encounters guaranteed to change your life, taking "gut" courses instead of ones you know will challenge you, bluffing at school and life instead of doing solid work, marrying early as an escape from real decisions, getting pregnant as an evasion of already existing problems. It means that you refuse to sell your talents and aspirations short, simply to avoid conflict and confrontation. And this, in turn, means resisting the forces in society which say that women should be nice, play safe, have low professional expectations, drown in love and forget about work, live through others, and stay in the places assigned to us. It means that we insist on a life of meaningful work, insist that work be as meaningful as love and friendship in our lives. It means, therefore, the courage to be "different"; not to be continuously available to others when we need time for ourselves and our work; to be able to demand of others—parents, friends, roommates, teachers, lovers, husbands, children—that they respect our sense of purpose and our integrity as persons. Women everywhere are finding the courage to do this, more and more, and we are finding that courage both in our study of women in the past who possessed it, and in each other as we look to other women for comradeship, community, and challenge. The difference between a life lived actively, and a life of passive drifting and dispersal of energies, is an immense difference. Once we begin to feel committed to our lives, responsible to ourselves, we can never again be satisfied with the old, passive way.

Now comes the second part of the contract. I believe that in a women's college you have the right to expect your faculty to take you seriously. The education of women has been a matter of debate for centuries, and old, negative attitudes about women's role, women's ability to think and take leadership, are still rife both in and outside the university. Many male professors (and I don't mean only at Douglass) still feel that teaching in a women's college is a second-rate career. Many tend to eroticize their women students—to treat them as sexual objects—instead of demanding the best of their minds. (At Yale a legal suit [*Alexander* v. *Yale*] has been brought against the university by a group of women students demanding a stated policy against sexual advances toward female students by male professors.) Many teachers, both men and women, trained in the male-centered tradition, are still handing the ideas and texts of that tradition on to students without teaching them to criticize its antiwoman attitudes, its omission of women as part of the species. Too often, all of us fail to teach the most important thing, which is that clear thinking, active discussion, and excellent writing are all necessary for intellectual freedom, and that these require *hard work*. Sometimes, perhaps in discouragement with a culture which is both antiintellectual and antiwoman, we may resign ourselves to low expectations for our students before we have given them half a chance to become more thoughtful, expressive human be-

ings. We need to take to heart the words of Elizabeth Barrett Browning, a poet, a thinking woman, and a feminist, who wrote in 1845 of her impatience with studies which cultivate a "passive recipiency" in the mind, and asserted that "women want to be made to *think actively*: their apprehension is quicker than that of men, but their defect lies for the most part in the logical faculty and in the higher mental activities." Note that she implies a defect which can be remedied by intellectual training; *not* an inborn lack of ability.

I have said that the contract on the student's part involves that you demand to be taken seriously so that you can also go on taking yourself seriously. This means seeking out criticism, recognizing that the most affirming thing anyone can do for you is demand that you push yourself further, show you the range of what you *can* do. It means rejecting attitudes of "take-it-easy," "why-be-so-serious," "why-worry-you'll-probably-get-married-anyway." It means assuming your share of responsibility for what happens in the classroom, because that affects the quality of your daily life here. It means that the student sees herself engaged *with* her teachers in an active, ongoing struggle for a real education. But for her to do this, her teachers must be committed to the belief that women's minds and experience are intrinsically valuable and indispensable to any civilization worthy [of] the name; that there is no more exhilarating and intellectually fertile place in the academic world today than a women's college—*if* both students and teachers in large enough numbers are trying to fulfill this contract. The contract is really a pledge of mutual seriousness about women, about language, ideas, methods, and values. It is our shared commitment toward a world in which the inborn potentialities of so many women's minds will no longer be wasted, raveled-away, paralyzed, or denied.

Letter One
Your Legacy

Phyllis Chesler

Here I sit, head bent, writing you an intimate letter. I sense your presence, even though I don't know your name. I envision you as a young woman, possibly a young man, somewhere between the ages of eighteen and thirty-five, but you may also be a decade older—or younger—than that. You may not yet be born.

Perhaps I am trying to speak to my own younger self. When I was coming of age—a process which is still far from over—no one ever spoke strong truths to me in a loving voice. When I was your age, I did not know what I needed to know in order to understand my life—anybody's life. Perhaps, in writing to you, I wish to correct that, to make amends.

In the past, Niccolò Machiavelli wrote a letter such as mine to a prince, Sun Tzu to a king, Virginia Woolf to a gentleman, Rainer Maria Rilke to a male admirer. This letter is for you. You are either poor or rich; you are any or all the colors of the human rainbow, all shades of luck and character. You are my heir. This letter is your legacy. Without your conscious intervention, that legacy may again lie dormant for one hundred years. Or longer.

I imagine you are a person who wants to know why evil exists. People commit evil deeds because we, the good people, do not stop them. To quote Edmund Burke: "All that is necessary for the forces of evil to win in the world is for enough good men to do nothing." Ah, Burke, evil also triumphs when good *women* do nothing.

Men alone are not responsible for patriarchy; women are also their willing, even ardent, collaborators.

Perhaps you believe you can "have it all": a brilliant career, a loving, life-long marriage, healthy children/no children, enough money, and happiness too. If you're anything like I was, you probably believe that whatever awful things may have happened to women in the past, or still are happening to "other" women today, cannot happen to you.

Darling, I don't want to frighten you away, but I don't want to waste your time either, so I can't pretend that simply because you or I *want* it to be so that in fact women and men are equal.

Even when men and women do exactly the same thing, it means something different. The father who changes a diaper is often seen as a hero; not so the mother who is, after all, only doing what she's expected to do. This is not true in reverse. The woman who succeeds in a man's world—although she is not expected to do so—is rarely treated as a conquering hero. She is, more often, seen as an aggressive bitch. She may well be aggressive—but no more than her male colleagues are. Some women try to prove their worth by outdoing their male colleagues in tough, anti-female behavior. Some women feel compelled to behave in "feminine" or "maternal" ways to appease those who would otherwise punish them for stepping so far out of line.

Thus, unlike her male counterparts, the chief judge pours her own coffee, and the police officer may not use what she's learned on the job to stop her husband from beating her; whatever she's learned at work can't over-ride what she's learned all her life about being a woman. The female employee—not her male counterpart—is still expected to buy the gifts, take the coats, bake the cookies for an office party, babysit her employer's child. Hardly gang-rape, but sexism nevertheless.

Yes, the world is different now than it was when I was your age. In only thirty years, a visionary feminism has managed to seriously challenge, if not transform, world consciousness. Some astronauts, army officers, ministers, *prime* ministers, and senators are women—there are women's studies programs too, and you can't open a newspaper without reading about some man on trial for rape or sexual harassment. But the truth is women are still far from free. We're not even within striking range.

Fundamentalist passions are threatening to destroy what feminists have accomplished. Three examples immediately come to mind.

The right to an abortion remains under an increasingly bloody siege.

Although we now understand that rape is epidemic and has lasting consequences, we are, as yet, unable to stop it. Today, in Algeria, Bangladesh Bosnia, Guatemala, Haiti, Rwanda, rape has become a systematic, full-fledged weapon—not merely a spoil—of war. In an era of ethnic cleansing, rape is a form of gender cleansing.

We remain separate and unequal—segregated both by race and gender. In the 1950s and 1960s, brave, young, African-American school children were confronted with adult faces contorted with rage, verbal abuse, turned backs, and hate-filled hearts when they integrated previously all-white schools. Today, brave young women are facing similar fury and danger for trying to integrate traditionally male-only military schools such as the Citadel in South Carolina.

In 1995, heroic nineteen-year-old Shannon Faulkner, the first woman ever to enroll in the previously all-male institution, faced the hate alone; she (and many young men) left after a few weeks. In September of 1996, four women were admitted. By December, two women, Kim Messer and Jeanie Mentavlos, and seventy-five men had quit. While all first-year cadets endured sadistic ritual hazing and harassment, the female cadets were singled out and, in addition to all else, subjected to vulgar songs about masturbation, obscene pictures, sexual-ized physical intimidation, and death threats. One was also set on fire. Like Faulkner, they were "hated out."

The most extraordinary legal victories are only scraps of paper until human beings test them on the ground. As I write, twenty-four young women have been accepted as cadets at the Citadel. Like their African-American counterparts, the women will not be deterred—but they will pay a high price.

As feminists, we learned that one cannot do such things alone, only together.

I want you to know what our feminist gains are, and why you must not take them for granted. (Although it is your right to do so—we fought for that too.) I also want you to know what remains to be done. I want you to see your place in the historical scheme of things, so you may choose whether and how to stand your ground in history.

Hear me: It may be 1998 but, in my view, we are still living in the 1950s. The poet Sylvia Plath (God/dess rest her soul) is about to put her head in the oven again. I am saying that we have not come far enough. We are also still living in the 1930s, and that great writer, Virginia Woolf, is slowly making her way down to the sea, about to drown herself. No, we are still living in 1913. The sculptor, Camille Claudel, who assisted her lover, Auguste Rodin, on some of his works, is—even as we speak—trussed up and on her way to a lunatic asylum. Claudel was imprisoned in one by her own mother and brother, Paul (the poet). The family condemned her to languish there for thirty years. She died in captivity, in 1943.

I often want to discreetly remove Rodin's august name and replace it with Camille Claudel's in various museums around the world—but then, I'm also the one who wants to behead the statue of Perseus who stands, triumphantly, at the top of the steps at the Metropolitan Museum in New York, holding aloft Medusa's severed head. Her honor demands it, her snaky locks tempt me to it.

There's a worthy precedent for such an action. Did you know that in 1914, while British suffragists were jailed, beaten, and force-fed (they went on hunger strikes) for demanding the vote, suffragist Polly Richardson marched into a London museum and swung an ax at Diego Velázquez's *Rokeby Venus*. Society howled. Velázquez's perfect woman is a reclining nude, and vain too; we observe Venus observing herself (and us) in a mirror. Perhaps this was Richardson's way of saying: My Lords, this portrait mocks real women who are, in fact, powerless. How does it feel to have something *you* value mutilated and destroyed?

Some say that Plath, Woolf, and Claudel were "mad" geniuses who'd have ended up the same sad way even if they'd each been nourished in a woman-loving family and culture.

How can such cynics be so sure?

Although many a sane woman has, in the past, been locked away in a loony bin, I am not saying that madness itself is a myth. Madness is real. Neither ideology nor good friends can save a woman from it. Still, the accumulation of daily slights and humiliations that most women must learn to absorb, to "not see," does have a way of calling down more than the usual number of demons.

I am thinking about the demands for perfection to which most girls and women are routinely subjected, combined with the lack of rewards—in fact, the grave *punishments* that most women must endure in order to survive. I am no longer talking only about educated white women of genius with whom you may be most familiar, but about all women, of all colors, in all lines of work. So many women are deprived, punished, forced to walk a far narrower line that most men ever are. Our genius does not save us, nor does our obedience.

Dutiful women, rebellious women, "mad" geniuses too, so many of us are systematically ground down and "disappeared," rendered invisible, forced to sink out of sight for centuries at a time. We lose touch with one another in our own lifetimes.

If we cannot see each other, we cannot see ourselves.

You must stand on our feminist shoulders in order to go further than we did.

Confinement distorts character. Centuries of women have been swallowed whole and doomed to such darkness that, like prisoners, we instinctively come to fear the light; it is blinding, unnatural. We fear standing up, we take small and careful steps when we do, we stumble, and we look to our jailors for protection.

Stand up as early as you can in life. Take up as much space in the (male) universe as you need to. Sit with your legs apart, not together. Climb trees. Climb mountains too. Engage in group sports. Dress comfortably. Dress as you wish.

How do we stop injustice?

We begin by speaking truth to power. That child who told the emperor he was naked is one of ours.

We begin by daring to remain connected to those whom prejudice silences, renders less than human.

We begin, of course, by fighting back.

Towards that end, you must move beyond words. You must act. Do not hesitate because your actions may not be perfect enough, or beyond criticism. "Action" is how you put your principles into practice. Not just publicly, or towards those more powerful than you, but also privately, towards those less fortunate than you. Not just towards those who are (safely) far away, but towards those with whom you live and work.

If you're on the right track, you can expect some pretty savage criticism. Trust it. Revel in it. It is the truest measure of your success.

Those who endure small humiliations—daily—say that the most lasting and haunting harm resides in growing accustomed to such treatment, in large part because others insist that you do. After all, *they* have. What's so special about you? "So, your boss asked you and not your male colleagues to make coffee at the meeting—big deal. At least you *have* a job." "So, your husband keeps forgetting his promise to help out with the housework—At least you *have* a husband."

Always implied, but unspoken: "It could be worse." But things could also be better. That will not happen if you do not act heroically.

Telling a rape survivor that she's "exaggerating the trauma in order to get attention" is not useful. Nor is asking her: "Why did you go out with that guy in the first place?"

Comments like these shame a woman into silence and inaction. They imply that there is nothing she can do or say that will change anything so she might as well give up and accept things as they are. Such comments forbid her to storm the gates of power. In a sense, this kind of gatekeeping constitutes bystander behavior. Survivors of serious atrocities say they are haunted by those who heard their screams but turned their backs, closed their doors, remained neutral, refused to take any stand other than an opportunistic one.

One cannot remain a bystander without becoming complicit. Morally, one must "take sides." But, once a person takes the side of anyone who's suffered a grave injustice, listens to her, believes what she says, tries to help her— that quiet act of humanity and courage will be viewed as a traitorous act.

Commit such treason as often as you can.

Women's hearts, men's hearts, are irretrievably broken when people default on the dream of a common, moral humanity (we are all connected, what happens to one happens to all) and do nothing.

I think such interventions are possible when we are inspired by a larger vision, guided by a great dream. Not otherwise.

Women do not need a room of their own. Feminists, both men and women, need a very large continent of our own. Nothing less will do.

Feminist Activism
Historical Context

Sheila Ruth

WHEN DID THE WOMEN'S MOVEMENT BEGIN?

It is often asked: When did the women's movement begin? Some *her*storians attempt to fix the origins of feminist ideas in relatively recent times—specifically, in the Enlightenment and the French Revolution, in the drive for the abolition of slavery, or in the American civil rights and war resistance movements. These attempts have a certain logic, but they can be misleading. They tend to focus attention not on one movement but on many: on eighteenth-, nineteenth-, or twentieth-century movements, each with a discernible starting point, each built around distinct goals, and each with separate and char-acteristic political attitudes, personalities, and strategies. A traditional reading in this vein might be summed up as follows:

> The first stirrings of the women's movement were felt with the publication of Mary Woll-stonecraft's *A Vindication of the Rights of Woman* in 1792. The women's rights movement in the United States was born during the drive for abolition, particularly in the activities and writings of the Grimké sisters in the 1830s. It culminated in the winning of the vote in 1920; and then, because women had exhausted themselves in the fight for suffrage, it died, until Betty Friedan's *The Feminine Mystique* brought it back to life in 1963.

A way of looking at the women's movement more accurately is simply that of women moving toward greater strength and freedom both in their awareness and in their sociopolitical position. This has been happening through the centuries, often for individuals, sometimes collectively. It has progressed, and it has receded; it has sometimes been subterranean, and sometimes it crests into waves of activism. It has expressed itself in many ways: in poetry, in marches on courthouses, or in the quiet but sturdy resistance of women in their households. It has been expressed in various contexts—political, economic, psychological, or even physical—and it is not easily confined to one model. From this perspective, no discernible "beginning" to the women's movement exists. . . .

Such an approach has manifold value. First, it reveals the universality of women's concerns. It reveals the startling continuity over time of feminist issues, values, goals, and challenges and, in so doing, allows us to see that each wave of activism is not separate and anomalous, destined for an end or for limited achievement at best, but rather is an integral part of a progressive development. Finally, this approach affords us a context for evaluating challenges not only to feminist goals but also to the very legitimacy of feminism as a world movement.

KEY THEMES OF WOMEN'S MOVEMENT

For centuries, in groups and as individuals, women have spoken out consistently on certain key issues. Although they may reflect the character of the times and the issues prominent in their age, the goals of feminist women's efforts have been remarkably consistent: They have to do with the *quality* of life for women and for the entire human community.

. . .

Again and again in poetry, political treatises, personal letters, speeches, and social analyses, we see these themes reiterated: the folly of grossly distorting women's physical, emotional, and intellectual development; the injustice of denying to half the world's population their rights, opportunities, and contributions; the great need for humanitarian treatment of the young, the sick, and the powerless in the face of the insensitive and selfish values of traditional masculist institutions; the unlikeliness of peace and harmony in a world permeated with the aggressiveness and arrogance of martial power values.

The consistency of the themes in our history underscores the continuity of the movement, the character of feminist concerns, and, it would appear, the legitimacy of our claims. Feminist analysis is not transitory, but rather is part of the mainstream of ongoing political thought, although it has not been perceived or treated that way.

. . .

JUST A DISAPPOINTED FEW

The contention that feminists are not of the majority of women or are not like "normal" women bears looking at, first, because it is an attack so often made, and second, because it raises the question of how accurately feminists may claim to represent women's concern. The argument is phrased in various ways: "Feminists are just a bunch of losers who couldn't make it in the man-woman world." "Feminism is just a white middle-class movement." "Feminists are just a bunch of bored, selfish middle-class women trying to get more for themselves when there is *real* oppression in the world that affects millions of people." Let us consider those charges one by one.

. . .

A White Middle-Class Movement

To a movement that proposes to speak to all women, a movement in which the term *sisterhood* is of first priority, the charge that we are composed of and concerned with only a small part of the female community, and that part the more privileged segment, is a serious matter.

. . .

Certainly, a great deal of writing and activism originated with middle-class women (some from working-class backgrounds). An examination of history reveals, however, that almost all movements for liberation and change have originated among those people who appear privileged beyond the means of those most sorely oppressed. It was they who had the education and training to see beyond their condition to reasons and alternatives; they who could articulate issues and instigate strategies for change; they who had the time and the wherewithal to act. The themes *liberté, egalité* and *fraternité* of the French Revolution originated among the well-educated, well-placed philosophers of the Enlightenment, not among the wretched poor who suffered most and most needed change, and to whom help eventually flowed. Marx and Lenin were intellectuals, and although they hoped for a rising of the masses, Lenin ultimately came to believe in the necessity of an educated vanguard of leadership.

Although the movement may appear to have been instigated by the white middle class (and even this appearance is misleading), it was not meant to be a movement *of* the white middle class. That is, it was not about only the white middle class, nor is it today. Obviously, ending violence against women is the concern of every woman on the globe. The drive for jobs and occupational equity certainly concerns working-class and poor women as much as it does middle-class women. Opening skilled and semiskilled unions to women, reforming clerical and secretarial occupations, and expanding women's place in government-funded poverty relief projects are all goals of the feminist movement. Securing the right of women to control our own bodies affect poor women even more than it does the affluent. Welfare reform *in favor of women and their children* has long been a feminist goal. The extinction of racism, homophobia, and other forms of bigotry is a major feminist target.

Where the women's movement originally erred was not in its intentions, but in individuals' failure to see; this was a result of lack of development, lack of sufficient perceptiveness. Like much of the society around us, feminists need greater sensitivity to *difference* and to the difference in our lives that difference makes. This has led many of us to lump all women into one category—woman—and to assume that female experience is always the same. . . .

Tension arises over strategies and issues and between black and white, gay and straight, moderate and radical feminists—but diversity and interchange are creative. The ultimate values have stood.

A Diversion from "Real" Oppression

Feminists have been told that the movement, being about "peripheral" and "trivial" matters, dangerously diverts resources away from "real" problems that are far more serious than that of women. That charge is neither new nor unique to our times. When Abigail Adams—a young, intelligent, spunky woman of the emerging republic—wrote to her husband to "remember the ladies," she met with little success. Husband John, at that time a young firebrand in the cause of liberty but eventually the second president of the United States, cautioned her to be patient, for *more important matters* were at stake. In a letter to his compatriot James Sullivan, Adams revealed that although good reasons existed to consider the rights of "the ladies," it was consciously decided *not* to ensure the rights of women citizens in the new society because it would be impractical and raise too many problems.[1] The egalitarian founders of the new republic were too busy, it seems, to open such a messy can of worms as rights of women.

. . .

The charge of triviality is a constant in women's history and should not surprise us. Reducing women's suffering to trivia is not only an enduring masculist perspective but a misogynist strategy as well. To the sane and right-minded, it is self-evident that denial of autonomy and freedom, denial of political, economic, and educational equity, and daily exploitation and violence are as destructive in women's lives as in men's. A revolution that advances only the position of men cannot justly be called a revolution for human rights. Similarly, "affirmative action" that guarantees jobs for men but not for women cannot claim to be a program for "equal" human rights. When political activists demand parity for the poor, the colonized, and the oppressed, they must remember that more than half of those poor, colonized, and oppressed are female and that women are doubly tyrannized in being exploited even within their own subgroups, *as women,* by men. History shows that, when all is said and done, women's movement has been a drive to free all women from the tyranny of misogyny and all humanity from the tyrannies of masculism—hardly trivial.

. . .

ENLIGHTENMENT THEMES

The eighteenth century was a period of tremendous upheaval and change both in its social organization and in the philosophical themes that developed out of it. The major issues focused on what rights people should have in society and in government. Certain ideas, although hotly debated and often maintained more in principle than in fact, came to occupy a central position in political philosophy. New importance was given to the ancient idea of *natural human worth*—that is, the value of the individual, which was held to be cosmic in its source (Nature or God) and prior to any privilege or status that could be bestowed by "civilized" society. Men were said to be equal in that value, brothers to one another, rational, and essentially good. Education for all, freedom of opportunity, and the exercise of reason were seen as supplying the major ingredients of

progress and harmonious community. Privilege, hereditary wealth and power, and unearned status were represented as villainous. Authority unchecked and exercised without consent was tyranny. Human excellence was composed of rationality, responsibility, emotional and physical health, independence, and tolerance. These were the major ideals of the political thought that we later called the Enlightenment. Although there was often great controversy over how these ideals might be instituted, the values themselves were taken as fundamental by a very large portion of the intelligentsia.

Note that *men* were said to be equal in worth. "All *men* are created equal"—not women. It was left to thinkers like Mary Wollstonecraft to remind the great liberal egalitarians that all they had said regarding worth, rights, opportunity, and freedom, as well as the condition and potential of the poor and oppressed and uneducated, could and should be applied to women also. . . .

HUMAN RIGHTS AND ABOLITION

. . .

[W]omen learned much from their work in the abolition movement. It was a combination of the Quaker conviction in the equality of people and the Enlightenment commitment to human liberty that they brought against slavery, and it was not a far distance from the rights of slaves to the rights of women. Many women learned for the first time about the effectiveness of political organization, and they experienced the potential and the joy of female unity and assertiveness. They learned to say openly, "Me, too." As women came to see clearly the hypocrisy and cruelty of black oppression, they gained the insight to recognize it in the lives of all women and the strength to reject the absurdity and meanness of masculist values, behavior, and rules.

Presenting so well the analogy between the oppression and liberation of blacks and that of women is the speech of Sojourner Truth at a rights convention in Ohio in 1851. An ex-slave who had become a lecturer and a preacher, Truth was described by the convention's president, Frances Gage, as an "almost Amazon form, which stood nearly six feet high, head erect, and eyes piercing the upper air like one in a dream." Truth's "Ain't I a woman?" speech is a most powerful and stirring statement of masculist injustice and irrationality.

THEMES OF THE FIRST HALF OF THE TWENTIETH CENTURY

The first half of the twentieth century saw the people of the world drawing closer together, albeit painfully. The rise of industrialism, the need for increased trade, the Great War, the rise of Marxism, and other factors all brought internationalistic questions to the foreground and forced reexamination of many issues. People had to place themselves in a wider context and reconsider the limits of authority; the sources of government; the uses of knowledge; the concepts of community, social responsibility, and freedom; and even the nature of happiness. During this period the social sciences—sociology, psychology, and anthropology—were evolving, and they, too, were raising new questions: What have we learned about what is desirable and undesirable in our own society, and how should we change it for the better? What does the new study of human behavior tell us about possibilities for the future of life and society? What are the proper limits of science in changing our lives? That is, what should we not or could we not tamper with? What part of us comes from nature (and is therefore unchangeable), and what part originates somewhere else?

The debate over women's issues was affected by the emerging intellectual models. A belief, prevalent among many feminists and nonfeminists alike, is that the women's movement simply died in 1920 with the passage of the Nineteenth Amendment and the winning of suffrage. It is claimed that because the move-

ment narrowed in the latter part of the nineteenth century from very wide-ranging concerns to a total involvement in suffrage, and because the winning of that goal required a Herculean effort, when it was won, activists simply folded in exhaustion. This argument has some basis. Certainly, political activity on a scale of the preceding seven decades did diminish. One could look for reasons in the Depression of the 1930s, in the political turmoil of the entire world during that same decade, and in the vast energy output in World War II during the 1940s. Such monumental events, coupled with the belief that suffrage created the opportunity to cure all women's ills, might indeed have led to a decrease in organized activism.

. . .

In the first half of the twentieth century, America's economic system underwent tremendous changes, as did women's participation in it. After World War I, women moved into the public workplace in growing numbers on every level. Frequently, as they grew in numbers, they organized. Women were particularly active in the trade union movement. In the professions, organizations such as Business and Professional Women (BPW) not only supported women in gaining better educational and business opportunities but also lobbied—and still do—for other women's goals in the legislatures and with presidential commissions.

Given all this activity, it is clearly not the case that exhausted women let their movement die. It is more accurate to say that many suffrage activists moved into different areas of activity and that new feminist women expressed their values through these different models. The movement—less centralized, less political, less visible in some ways, even less populous—was nonetheless alive.

THE SECOND HALF AND THE SECOND WAVE

Although women's issues as a major focus of public discussion receded in importance during the 1940s, conditions that would change this continued to ferment. The Depression had had a negative effect on women's position in the economy. What jobs existed had gone to men, and women lost ground in education, professional status, work rights, and salary. During World War II, however, conditions changed. Positions left empty by men gone to war and jobs in the burgeoning industrial sector had to be filled by women. Laboring in factories and offices, managing small businesses, running farms, teaching college, and building tanks, women did very well. Jobs that, until then, had been deemed "for men only" were effectively accommodated by women, and they learned an unforgettable lesson: There is no masculine or feminine occupation.

From 1945 on, even immediately after the war, when many women lost their jobs to returning veterans, the number and percentage of working women of all kinds—married and unmarried, young and mature, parent and nonparent—increased dramatically, and the realities of women's lives changed. But what changed very little, and what eventually was to cause much of the conflict that crystallized in the 1950s and exploded in the 1960s, was the cultural mythology, the projected ideals of femininity and the "place" of women. Except for the brief wartime appearance of the patriotic Rosie the Riveter, America's dream-girl image never adjusted to women's new realities and changing needs. In fact, the gap between myth and reality widened. In the late 1940s and 1950s, popular culture stressed the vision of the virginal, naïve girl-next-door and the softly pliant housewife in cotton dress and spike heels tending single-mindedly to family and home. On the surface, at least, it was a time of traditional values and "togetherness."

Betty Friedan, in *The Feminine Mystique*, credits the wars, especially the Korean War, for this period of retrenchment. Disillusioned and emotionally exhausted, people (particularly men) craved the security and nurturance of a stable family and home, and they retreated to the familiar comforting arrangement of marriage, or

at least the image of it, and to the concept of the nurturing, tender wife-mother. This is at least partly true.

Again, however, one must be careful not to oversimplify, and one must seek explanations for women's situation with an eye to events in the wider culture. A period of apparent quiescence, the 1950s nevertheless harbored the seeds of turmoil. Although the decade was known for a kind of apathy toward political and national events, it also saw the Cold War, the second "red scare," and McCarthy and McCarthyism. It may have had "the corporation man" and the man in gray flannel, but it also had Jack Kerouac and anticonformist Beatniks. It was a day in 1955 when Rosa Parks refused to go to the back of the bus that touched off the civil rights movement. These and other events were as much a part of the personal history of the new feminist women of the 1960s as were the television images of the superwife.

Somewhere between the opposing realities, between prom gowns and Rosa Parks, between affluence and Vietnam, between maternal admonitions of sexual purity and the realities of displaced homemakers, the feminists of the second wave emerged alive and kicking.

Early in the 1950s Simone de Beauvoir's book *The Second Sex* had appeared in English in the United States, offering a profound philosophical analysis not only of certain aspects of injustice toward women, such as economic and political discrimination, but of the whole distorted conceptualization of femaleness in a patriarchal world. In 1963 Betty Friedan published *The Feminine Mystique,* treating the hidden disappointment and unhappiness of many American women in male-female relationships, in the structures of marriage and motherhood, in their lives, and exploding the cultural myth of the happy homemaker. These and other writings in novels, newspapers, and magazines were part of a widening examination of women's lives, not only among academics but among a growing number of ordinary women.

In the mid-to-late 1960s, civil rights activism and opposition to the Vietnam war generated scores of activist groups and organizations on college campuses all over the United States. Women's participation in these activities and groups had a variety of consequences. Just as their ill treatment by many men in the abolitionist movement made nineteenth-century women reflect upon their own circumstances, discrimination and misogyny in twentieth-century activism had the same effect—young women began to question society and politics not only from a class or racial perspective but from a *female* perspective, a gender perspective. Furthermore, they found that concepts and strategies learned in a drive for international or racial justice could be employed in a drive for *women's* justice, and increasingly they were. Finally, as many women activists were students, they carried the perspectives, terminology, ideas, values, attitudes, and expectations they had developed in social activism into their studies and their writing. What emerged was the feminist analysis of the "women's liberation movement," as it was called in the early years of the second wave.

. . .

THE SECOND WAVE— THEMES AND THEORIES

Although there are issues upon which most feminists agree, there are others upon which there is great difference: in philosophic orientation, strategy, and treatment. These issues, which can generate conflict, are internal themes of contemporary feminism developed during and since the early 1960s. Because they have a strong effect on the strategies that movement leaders choose, because they often determine how we articulate our concerns, and because opponents of feminism often seize upon them to split unity among women, these issues deserve our careful attention.

In the introduction to the first edition of the book *Feminist Frameworks,* Alison Jaggar and Paula Rothenberg (Struhl) outline four basic feminist frameworks or theoretical orientations: (1) *liberal* feminism (some call it *moderate* feminism), which essentially seeks opportunities for women's advancement in the existent society through institutional changes in education and the workplace; (2) *Marxist* feminism, which locates the source of women's oppression in the general problems of a capitalist society and the remedy, therefore, in its dissolution; (3) *radical* feminism, which locates the source of women's oppression not in any particular economic system, but in the nature and implications of gender (perhaps even sex) itself; and (4) *socialist* feminism, an amalgam of the last two, which holds both economic and gender/sex factors equally responsible.

. . .

The word *radical* is a relative term. Where anyone is placed on the spectrum of radical-to-conservative has at least as much to do with the person doing the placing as it does with the person described. Yet there have been strong differences of opinion among feminists regarding a number of issues: strategy (for example, militancy, demonstrations, and strikes versus painstaking political or legal action), procedural rules (for example, complete separatism versus male participation), and even language (for example, reform versus revolution).

Some theoreticians have associated moderation or conservatism with the women's rights organizations aimed basically at securing equality for women and men through institutional reform. They have reserved the term *radical* for those groups that wish to go beyond institutional reform, beyond equality, to bring about profound changes in the culture as well as a complete redefinition of gender itself. It has been said that moderate feminists want to secure for women a piece of the pie; radical feminists want to change the pie. We must, however, use even this characterization with care, for clearly there is overlap. Radical feminists usually support institutional reform, and moderate or conservative activists realize that even small changes in society beget profound alterations in our lives.

The differences between radicals and moderates are based in their general philosophical orientation, ethical priorities, interpretation of causes, cultural vision, and even temperament. Compare, for example, the sharp differences in the tone, attitudes, explanatory constructs, strategies, and goals of the following documents.

Radical feminism recognizes the oppression of women as a fundamental political oppression wherein women are categorized as an inferior class based upon their sex. It is the aim of radical feminism to organize politically to destroy this sex class system. . . .

A political power institution is set up for a purpose. We believe that the purpose of male chauvinism is primarily to obtain psychological ego satisfaction, and that only secondarily does this manifest itself in economic relationships. For this reason we do not believe that capitalism, or any other economic system, is the cause of female oppression, nor do we believe that female oppression will disappear as a result of a purely economic revolution. The political oppression of women has its own class dynamic; and that dynamic must be understood in terms previously called "nonpolitical"—namely the politics of the ego.[2]   —*Ann Koedt, "Politics of the Ego"*[3]

We, men and women who hereby constitute ourselves as the National Organization for Women, believe that the time has come for a new movement toward true equality for all women in America, and toward a fully equal partnership of the sexes, as part of the worldwide revolution of human rights now taking place within and beyond our national borders.

The purpose of NOW is to take action to bring women into full participation in the mainstream of American society now, exercising all the privileges and responsibilities thereof in truly equal partnership with men. . . .

We realize that women's problems are linked to many broader questions of social justice; their solution will require concerted action by many groups. Therefore, convinced that human rights for all are indivisible, we expect to give active support to the common cause of equal rights for all those who suffer discrimination and deprivation, and we call upon other organizations committed to such goals to support our efforts toward equality for women.

—*National Organization for Women, Statement of Purpose, 1966*[4]

INTO THE FUTURE: THE NEXT WAVE

Feminists must decide many issues for the future. We are feeling the full brunt of an antifeminist, antiwoman backlash, not only in the United States but all over the world. A strong wave of political and economic conservatism has reversed many of the hard-won victories of the past: Affirmative action, comparable worth, and professional upward-mobility programs lie almost in tatters. The religious right has sworn absolute enmity to women's reproductive liberty, and they are making progress. Increasing numbers of women and their children are poor, homeless, and hungry. The earth we have vowed to protect is being devoured for its resources. All over the world, war, famine, and political repression hit women worst.

Fewer young women today are actively involved in politics or social activism. Indeed, they seem less aware, less concerned, than they were 20 years ago.

Yet some observers of society see the possibilities of the worm turning. Consider the renewed discussion of civil rights for all in the federal government, renewed awareness of social discrimination on American campuses, renewed vigor of pro-choice activities in response to the relentless attacks upon our personal freedom. It is possible to see seeds of rebirth in the present that will flourish in the next century, just as the worst repressions of the

1950s gave birth to the energy of the 1960s. This is already visible. The "women's vote" was considered a major factor in the last presidential election, as were the issues of reproductive and sexual freedom, and educational and work opportunities for the next generation.

We are the ones who can decide how the energy of the new millennium will be employed. What shall we do? Where shall we put our greatest efforts? What should be our priorities? How can we revitalize the energy, optimism, and power of women's movement, and where shall we take it?

. . .

In 1977 Barbara Jordan, legislator and political leader, gave the keynote speech at the First National Women's Conference in Houston. She said:

> If Americans were asked to differentiate or distinguish between what characterized other countries and what characterizes us, we would say our high regard for the individual. That's the thing which makes us different.
>
> We endorse personal and political freedom as a national right of human pride. Human rights are more than abstractions, particularly when they are limited or non-existent. . . .
>
> Women are human. We know our rights are limited. We know our rights are violated. We need a domestic human rights program. . . .
>
> At a time when this country is drifting, if it is not shifting to the right, civil rights and affirmative action efforts are lagging.
>
> Not making a difference is a cost we cannot afford. . . .
>
> The cause of equal and human rights will reap what is sown November 18th through November 21st, 1977.
>
> What will you reap?
> What will you sow?[5]

Nearly 20 years have passed since Jordan's words were spoken, and, extraordinarily, the country is *still* drifting, if not shifting to the right; civil and human rights are still lagging; and not making a difference is still a cost we cannot afford. Indeed, the only thing that we must change about Jordan's comments is this: the cause of equality will reap what is sown *today* and tomorrow and thereafter—by all of us and each of us.

What will *you* sow?

NOTES

1. Alison M. Jaggar and Paula Rothenberg Struhl, eds., *Feminist Frameworks* (New York: McGraw-Hill, 1978), pp. xii–xiii. The second edition of *Feminist Frameworks* (McGraw-Hill, 1984) maintains the concept of "frameworks," or categories, but develops and deepens them.
2. *ego:* We are using the classical definition rather than the Freudian—that is, the sense of individual self as distinct from others. [Footnote in original source.]
3. "Politics of the Ego" was adopted as the manifesto of the New York Radical Feminists at its founding meeting in December 1969.
4. Reprinted in Aileen S. Kraditor, ed., *Up from the Pedestal* (Chicago: Quadrangle, 1968), pp. 363ff.
5. Keynote speech, First Plenary Session, the First National Women's Conference, November 19, 1977. Reported in Helene Mandelbaum, ed., *The Spirit of Houston* (Washington, DC: National Commission on the Observance of International Women's Year, 1978), p. 223.

Revolutionary Feminism
An Anti-Racist Agenda

bell hooks

Throughout the more than twenty years that I have spent writing feminist theory, I have consistently worked to make a clear distinction between revolutionary feminist politics and the more widely accepted version of feminism that has as its primary agenda achieving for white women of privileged classes social and economic equality with men of their class. In my first book, *Ain't I a Woman: Black Women and Feminism,* I suggested that the movement of masses of white women, particularly those from privileged-class backgrounds, into the workforce was not sanctioned simply by feminist thinking but by the very white supremacist capitalist patriarchal economic system that movement claimed to want to dismantle. Coming in the wake of civil rights struggle, of black power movements which were demanding cultural revolution, a sharing of the nation's material resources as well as an end to white supremacy, contemporary white women's liberation movement was easily co-opted to serve the interests of white patriarchy by reconsolidating white power, by keeping resources all in the family.

It should have come as no surprise to any of us that those white women who were mainly concerned with gaining equal access to domains of white male privilege quickly ceased to espouse a radical political agenda which included the dismantling of patriarchy as well as an anti-racist, anti-classist agenda. No doubt white patriarchal men must have found it amusing and affirming that many of the white women who had so vehemently and fiercely denounced domination were quite happy to assume the role of oppressor and/or exploiter if it meant that they could wield power equally with white men. Nor should it have surprised

us that those individual white women who remained true to the radical and/or revolutionary vision of feminist politics, who had been among the vanguard of the struggle, were soon marginalized as feminist politics entered the mainstream. For example, many of the radical white women who struggled to establish women's studies in colleges and universities throughout the United States did not have doctoral degrees and were soon let go as patriarchal academic legitimation became more important than sisterhood and solidarity. Often to stay within this system individual white women were compelled to complete further graduate study, a process which was usually depoliticizing, which rewarded abandoning of radical feminist practice.

No critical intervention renewed the spirit of radical feminism that had been sorely diminished by patriarchal co-optation more than the insistence on the part of black women and other women of color that white women interrogate their racial identity and racial privilege. Ironically, many white women appropriated the discourse of race to advance their careers, drawing from the scholarship and critical thinking of black women even as they then bashed us for insisting that any meaningful feminist movement would necessarily have an anti-racist agenda. This bashing is most vehemently expressed in the work of self-proclaimed "white power-feminists" who would have everyone believe that there is no undermining of feminist politics when the central goal of the movement is to allow individual white women access to ruling-class wealth and power. It is this opportunistic appropriation of feminist thinking that consistently corrupts feminist politics, sending the clear message to disenfranchised poor and working-class women and men of all races that feminist movement is not for them. Given this message and the white supremacist agenda that is perpetuated by white power-feminism, it is not surprising that people of color who do not understand the history of the movement, who may not have access to revolutionary feminist thought and praxis, usually see feminism as a threat and do not see the uses these opportunistic white women have made of it. If people of color naively allow our understanding of feminist politics to be shaped by mass media which focus only on white power-feminism then we become complicit, denying ourselves and our diverse communities access to a resistance struggle that would provide strategies for challenging sexist exploitation and oppression in our lives.

To many black folks feminism continues to be seen as synonymous with bourgeois white women. As a consequence any black woman who uses the term risks being seen as a race traitor. The dismissal of black female voices that advocate feminist politics has intensified with the resurgence of narrow nationalist thinking that either invests in supporting the maintenance of patriarchal gender role or insists that embracing an Afrocentric worldview will necessarily return black females and males to an idyllic location where gender hierarchies do not exist. Again and again in my work I have had to reiterate that the racism of white women should be militantly challenged but that it should not act as a barrier preventing black women and men from engaging feminist politics. Even though Karl Marx was clearly racist in his thinking, this has never stopped black folks who seek to radicalize their consciousness around the issue of class from engaging Marxism. Surely it is patriarchal condescension that leads black folks, particularly sexist black men, to assume that black females are incapable of embracing revolutionary feminism in ways that would enhance rather than diminish black liberation, despite the continued overt racism and racist agendas of those groups of white women who can most easily lay claim to the

term "feminism" and project their conservative and reactionary agendas. Often this condescension merely masks allegiance to sexism and patriarchal thinking in black life. Certainly, the labeling of black women who engage feminist thinking as race traitors is meant to prevent us from embracing feminist politics as surely as white power-feminism acts to exclude our voices and silence our critiques. In this case, both groups are acting to protect and maintain the privileges, however relative, that they receive in the existing social structure.

It is usually materially privileged white women who identify as feminists, and who have gained greater social equality and power with white men in the existing social structure, who resist most vehemently the revolutionary feminist insistence that an anti-racist agenda must be at the core of our movement if there is ever to be solidarity between women and effective coalitions that cross racial boundaries and unite us in common struggle. These are the women who are determined to leave the issue of race behind. Recently white women producers of an ABC news story on feminist movement went in search of radical/revolutionary feminists to appear on their show. I was called, then dismissed as inappropriate because I would raise the issue of race and racism, thereby—according to them—changing the subject. Similar silencing occurs in predominantly black public settings when race is the topic and black females approach these discussions from a feminist standpoint. We are seen as derailing or shifting the focus, not adding to the depth and complexity of our understanding. In such settings we are usually bashed into silence. Given these contexts it is no wonder that there are few black women who choose to publicly advocate revolutionary feminist politics. Indeed, the black female who engages issues of gender, even perhaps challenges sexism, can gain a hearing as long as she does not encourage black folks to embrace revolutionary feminism. Individual radical black women feminists who gain a public hearing usually do so by turning their backs on black constituencies, focusing their attention on white audiences. Often anti-feminist backlash is the excuse they give for not struggling to promote feminist politics in diverse black communities. Yet usually when one examines the history of their engagement, there is no record of any meaningful attempt to educate black communities for critical consciousness when it comes to the issue of feminism. Unfortunately the individual black women who do address gender issues in black settings tend to espouse liberal or conservative politics. They present the same old reformist social-equality white women's liberation agenda in blackface. Like their white female counterparts, these opportunistic black women are primarily concerned with gaining access to privilege within the existing structure.

Revolutionary feminist thinkers must consistently challenge white power-feminism so that our radical agendas are not completely erased by those white women who continue to support racism and white supremacy. Increasingly, more and more individual white revolutionary feminist activists are critiquing the racism of their white peers with the same militancy as their women-of-color peers. Let's be clear. It was individual black women and women of color who were and remain at the forefront of the struggle to maintain an anti-racist revolutionary feminist agenda. It is a meaningful and powerful expression of solidarity and sisterhood that individual radical white women are daring to challenge courageously the racism of their peers. The essays in the collection *The Coming of Black Genocide,* a reprinting of articles from *Bottomfish Blues,* is a fine example. Described in the introduction as an underground Amazon publication, it has two main themes: to "radically challenge white women's complicity in both the on-going Black Genocide and the patriarchy's war against women." Reiterating the analysis first given by black women thinkers, myself included (who are never acknowledged or cited in this text), the anonymous authors courageously make connections between white supremacist perpetuation of black genocide and the women's movement for white equality. Their analysis is worth quoting at length:

> If the just-starting women's liberation movement had survived it would have divided white society, and would have seriously endangered the plans for Black Genocide. Born out of the sparks from Black liberation, with its own revolutionary pulse, women's liberation would have been guerilla movement behind enemy lines. It might have sabotaged the machinery of genocide. Just as the student antiwar movement did to the invasion of Vietnam. . . . The power structure neutralized women's liberation by smothering it under the "neutra-sweet" women's movement for white equality. And then pretended that they were both the same thing.

It is unfortunate that the revolutionary feminist thinkers who wrote these essays do not identify the work of those black women who write about race in ways that mask the debt they owe to black women and women-of-color thinkers often do so because they are working within structures that affirm competition, that encourage folks to make it appear that their ideas always come from some space of original thought. The ethic of competition does not place value on collaboration or dialectical exchange. It does not create an atmosphere where individuals who have white privilege and authority in relation to the discourse of race and racism can link their work to anti-racist struggle by repudiating the need to erase, render invisible, and/or devalue the work of non-white peers.

Honoring the engagement with black peers that enhanced her capacity to break with white supremacist thinking and fully commit to anti-racist struggle Segrest shares:

> Lenny taught me that fascism was about isolation, about political movements deliberately breaking down the human bonds between people so that they give blind allegiance to a leader or an ideology. Reverend Lee showed me how to go after the lost, to defy the isolation imposed by denial, terror and ideologies of hate. But I was lost myself, and I found myself, in part

at least, in the acts of searching out others. It made me a different person—but not a better person—than either of my parents. To differentiate myself, I have had to accept the gifts they gave me, which paradoxically, I could not do until I was sure I am my own person. "When people have to choose, they go with their own race," my mother had said, but she was wrong. It is not a matter of choosing one race or family and betraying one another. The choice is for justice! community! humanity! the glimpse that we are all one organism. . . .

It is this understanding of revolutionary interdependency that must be shared if we are to reclaim a vision of feminist sisterhood that proudly acknowledges feminist commitment

to anti-racist struggle. Advocates of revolutionary feminist movement are among that group of women and men who do not despair about the capacity of white folks to divest of white supremacy because we have engaged in resistance and seen the reality of solidarity emerge in the context of mutual commitment and struggle. These stories must be told to counter the mounting despair, to counter the claims of white power-feminism. There will be no feminist revolution without an end to racism and white supremacy. When all women and men engaged in feminist struggle understand the interlocking nature of systems of domination, of white supremacist capitalist patriarchy, feminist movement will regain its revolutionary progressive momentum.

READING 5

Beyond Bean Counting

Jee Yeun Lee

I came out as a woman, an Asian American and a bisexual within a relatively short span of time, and ever since then I have been guilty of the crime of bean counting, as Bill Clinton oh-so-eloquently phrased it. Every time I am in a room of people gathered for any reason, I automatically count those whom I can identify as women, men, people of color, Asian Americans, mixed-race people, whites, gays and lesbians, bisexuals, heterosexuals, people with disabilities. So when I received the call for submissions for this anthology, I imagined opening up the finished book to the table of contents and counting beans; I then sent the call for submissions to as many queer Asian/Pacific American women writers as I knew.

Such is the nature of feminism in the 1990s: an uneasy balancing act between the imperatives of outreach and inclusion on the one hand, and the risk of tokenism and further marginalization on the other. This dynamic has in-

delibly shaped my personal experiences with feminism, starting from my very first encounter with organized feminism. This encounter happened to be, literally, Feminist Studies 101 at the university I attended. The content of the class was divided into topics such as family, work, sexuality and so forth, and for each topic we studied what various feminist paradigms said about it: "liberal feminism," "social feminism," "radical feminism" and "feminism and women of color."

Taking this class was an exhilarating, empowering and very uneasy experience. For the first time I found people who articulated those murky half-formed feelings that I could previously only express incoherently as "But that's not fair!" People who agreed, sympathized, related their own experiences, theorized, helped me form what I had always known. In seventh grade, a teacher made us do a mock debate, and I ended up arguing with Neil Coleman about whether women or men were better cooks. He said more men were professional chefs, therefore men were better. I responded that more women cooked in daily life, therefore women were better. He said it was quality that mattered, not quantity, and left me standing there with nothing to say. I knew there was something wrong with his argument, something wrong with the whole issue as it was framed, and felt extremely betrayed at being made to consent to the inferiority of my gender, losing in front of the whole class. I could never defend myself when arguments like this came up, invariably with boys who were good at debates and used to winning. They left me seething with resentment at their manipulations and frustrated at my speechlessness. So to come to a class that addressed these issues directly and gave me the words for all those pent-up feelings and frustrations was a tremendously affirming and empowering experience.

At the same time, it was an intensely uncomfortable experience. I knew "women of color" was supposed to include Asian American women, but I could not find any in the class readings. Were there no Asian American feminists? Were there none who could write in English? Did there even exist older Asian American women who were second or third generation? Were we Asian American students in the class the first to think about feminism? A class about women, I thought, was a class about me, so I looked for myself everywhere and found nothing. Nothing about Asian American families, immigrant women's work patterns, issues of sexuality and body image for Asian women, violence against Asian American women, Asian American women in the seventies feminist movement, nothing anywhere. I wasn't fully conscious then that I was searching for this, but this absence came out in certain feelings. First of all, I felt jealous of African American and Chicana feminists. Their work was present at least to some degree in the readings: They had research and theories, they were eloquent and they *existed*. Black and Chicana women in the class could claim them as role

models, voices, communities—I had no one to claim as my own. My emerging identification as a woman of color was displaced through the writings of black and Chicana women, and I had to read myself, create my politics, through theirs; even now, to a certain extent, I feel more familiar with their issues than those of Asian American women. Second, I felt guilty. Although it was never expressed outright, I felt that there was some pressure on me to represent Asian American issues, and I could not. I felt estranged from the Asian American groups on campus and Asian American politics and activism in general, and guilty about this ignorance and alienation.

Now mind you, I'm still grateful for this class. Feminism was my avenue to politics: It politicized me; it raised my consciousness about issues of oppression, power and resistance in general. I learned a language with which I could start to explain my experiences and link them to larger societal structures of oppression and complicity. It also gave me ways that I could resist and actively fight back. I became interested in Asian American politics, people of color politics, gay/lesbian/bisexual politics and other struggles because of this exposure to feminism. But there is no excuse for this nearly complete exclusion of Asian/Pacific American women from the class. Marginalization is not simply a politically correct buzzword, it is a material reality that affects people's lives—in this case, my own. I would have been turned off from feminism altogether had it not been for later classes that dealt specifically with women of color. And I would l like to name names here: I went to Stanford University, a bastion of privilege that pretends to be on the cutting edge of "multiculturalism." Just under twenty-five percent of the undergraduate population is Asian/Pacific American, but there was no mention of Asian/Pacific American women in Feminist Studies 101. All the classes I took on women of color were taught by graduate students and visiting professors. There was, at that time, only one woman of color on the feminist studies faculty. I regret that I realized the political import of these facts only after I left Stanford.

I understand that feminists in academia are caught between a rock and a hard place—not too many of us hold positions of decision-making power in universities. And I must acknowledge my gratitude for their struggles in helping to establish feminist studies programs and produce theories and research about women, all of which create vital opportunities and affirmation. But other women's organizations that are not constrained by such explicit forces are also lily-white. This obviously differs from group to group, and I think many of them are very conscientious about outreach to historically marginalized women. But, for instance, in 1992 and 1993, at the meetings I attended of the Women's Action Coalition (WAC) in New York City, out of approximately two hundred women usually fewer than twenty women of color were present.

But this is not a diatribe against feminism in general. I want to emphasize that the feminism that I and other young women come to today is one that is at least sensitive to issues of exclusion. If perhaps twenty years ago charges of racism, classism and homophobia were not taken seriously, today they are the cause of extreme anguish and soul-searching. I am profoundly grateful to older feminists of color and their white allies who struggled to bring U.S. feminist movements to this point. At the same time, I think that this current sensitivity often breeds tokenism, guilt, suspicion and self-righteousness that have very material repercussions on women's groups. I have found these uneasy dynamics in all the women's groups I've come across, addressed to varying degrees. At one extreme, I have seen groups that deny the marginalizing affects of their practices, believing that issues of inclusion really have nothing to do with their specific agendas. At the other extreme, I have seen groups ripped apart by accusations of political correctness, immobilized by guilt, knowing they should address a certain issue but not knowing how to begin, and still wondering why "women of color just don't come to our meetings." And tokenism is alive and well in the nineties. Those of us who have been aware of our tokenization often become suspicious and tired of educating others, wondering if we are invested enough to continue to do so, wondering if the overall goal is worth it.

In this age when "political correctness" has been appropriated by conservative forces as a derogatory term, it is extremely difficult to honestly discuss and confront any ideas and practices that perpetuate dominant norms—and none of us is innocent of such collusion. Many times, our response is to become defensive, shutting down to constructive critiques and actions, or to individualize our collusion as solely a personal fault, as if working on our individual racist or classist attitudes would somehow make things better. It appears that we all have a lot of work to do still.

And I mean *all*. Issues of exclusion are not the sole province of white feminists. I learned this very vividly at a 1993 retreat organized by the Asian Pacifica Lesbian Network. It has become somewhat common lately to speak of "Asian and Pacific Islanders" or "Asian/Pacific Americans" or, as in this case, "Asian Pacifica." This is meant to be inclusive, to recognize some issues held in common by people from Asia and people from the Pacific Islands. Two women of Native Hawaiian descent and some Asian American allies confronted the group at this retreat to ask for more than lip service in the organization's name: If the group was seriously committed to being an inclusive coalition, we needed to educate ourselves about and actively advocate Pacific Islander issues. And because I don't want to relegate them to a footnote, I will mention here a few of these issues: the demand for sovereignty for Native Hawaiians, whose government was illegally overthrown by the U.S. in 1893; fighting stereotypes of women and men that are different from those of Asian people; decrying U.S. imperialist possession and occupation of the islands of Guam, the Virgin Islands, American Samoa, the Marshall Islands, Micronesia, the Northern Mariana Islands and several others.

This was a retreat where one would suppose everyone had so much in common—after all, we were all queer API women, right? Any such myth was effectively destroyed by the realities of our experiences and issues: We were women of different ethnic backgrounds, with very different issues among East Asians, South Asians, Southeast Asians and Pacific Islanders; women of mixed race and heritage; women who identified as lesbians and those who identified as bisexuals; women who were immigrants, refugees, illegal aliens or second generation or more; older women, physically challenged women, women adopted by white families, women from the Midwest. Such tangible differences brought home the fact that no simplistic identity politics is *ever* possible, that we had to conceive of ourselves as a coalition first and foremost; as one woman on a panel said, our identity as queer API women must be a *coalitional* identity. Initially, I thought that I had finally found a home where I could relax and let down my guard. This was true to a certain degree, but I discovered that this was the home where I would have to work the hardest because I cared the most. I would have to be committed to push myself and push others to deal with all of our differences, so that we *could* be safe for each other. And in this difficult work of coalition, one positive action was taken at the retreat: We changed the name of the organization to include "bisexual," thus becoming the Asian Pacifica Lesbian and Bisexual Network, a name that people started using immediately.

All this is to say that I and other young women have found most feminist movements today to be at this point, where there is at least a stated emphasis on inclusion and outreach with the accompanying risk of tokenism. I firmly believe that it is always the margins that push us further in our politics. Women of color do not struggle in feminist movements simply to add cultural diversity, to add the viewpoints of different kinds of women. Women of color feminist theories challenge the fundamental premises of feminism, such as the very definition of "women," and call for recognition of the constructed racial nature of *all* experiences of gender. In the same way, heterosexist norms do not oppress solely lesbians, bisexuals and gay men, but affect all of our choices and non-choices; issues posed by differently abled women question our basic assumptions about body image, health care, sexuality and work; ecofeminists challenge our fundamental ideas about living on and with the earth, about our interactions with animals, plants, food, agriculture and industry. Many feminists seem to find the issues of class the most difficult to address; we are always faced with the fundamental inequalities inherent to late-twentieth-century multinational capitalism and our unavoidable implication in its structures. Such an overwhelming array of problems can numb and immobilize us, or make us concentrate our energies too narrowly. I don't think that we have to address everything fully at the same time, but we *must* be fully aware of the limitations of our specific agendas. Progressive activists cannot afford to do the masters' work for them by continuing to carry out oppressive assumptions and exclusions.

These days, whenever someone says the word "women" to me, my mind goes blank. What "women"? What is this "women" thing you're talking about? Does that mean me? Does that mean my mother, my roommates, the white woman next door, the checkout clerk at the supermarket, my aunts in Korea, half of the world's population? I ask people to specify and specify, until I can figure out exactly what they're talking about, and I try to remember to apply the same standards to myself, to deny myself the slightest possibility of romanticization. Sisterhood may be global, but who is in that sisterhood? None of us can afford to assume anything about anybody else. This thing called "feminism" takes a great deal of hard work, and I think this is one of the primary hallmarks of young feminists' activism today: We realize that coming together and working together are by no means natural or easy.

Shame, Guilt, and Responsibility

Allan G. Johnson

With just enough exceptions to prove the rule,[1] men have taken almost no responsibility for patriarchy. Some men confuse taking responsibility with being sensitive to women. They offer emotional support and tolerate women's anger and frustration around gender issues. Men can be sensitive, however, without doing anything to challenge or undermine their male privilege or to define gender issues as *men's* issues, especially to other men. Even sensitive men can be drawn to the path of least resistance that defines problems such as housework, workplace discrimination, sexual harassment, and violence as women's issues. This makes it easy for men to see themselves as "good guys"— loving helpers, loyal supporters, or valiant defenders who help women in a patient and caring way. What these men often don't do is the work of taking the initiative: of deciding what needs to be said, asked, listened to, discussed, fought over, attended to, and cared for; of overcoming the status quo's foot-dragging inertia. When women get tired or confused or distracted by the everyday details of their lives, the responsibility these men take often lies dormant until the next time a woman feels compelled to risk making trouble by raising a "women's issue." And when women express anger at always having to carry the burden of figuring out patriarchy and doing something about it, these sensitive and supportive men often react as if they're being unfairly criticized or even attacked, their exceptional and seemingly generous efforts unappreciated, their supposed immunity from reproach unfairly snatched away.

. . . What's going on here, however, isn't men taking responsibility and being punished for their trouble. In my experience, men who take responsibility for patriarchy are the last men most feminist women want to attack. More often than not, [these] men present the appearance of taking responsibility without the substance, *because they don't have a clear sense of what taking responsibility actually means or what there is to take responsibility for.* They may claim to be on women's side because doing the right thing makes them feel good about themselves or because they value their relationships with women and fear women's displeasure and anger, but this merely avoids taking responsibility. It's a stance that dominant groups often take, and women and other minorities rightly distrust it and feel insulted by its implicit condescension.

Why do men avoid taking responsibility for patriarchy? In the simplest sense, most men don't realize that patriarchy exists and therefore don't know there's any responsibility for them to take in the first place. Also, the path of least resistance for members of any dominant group is to see themselves as not *having* to do anything. The status quo is organized in their image and in their gender interests. It reflects maleness in its highest ideals and images. Why, then, change it? Why question, much less give up, what they've got and risk *men's* disapproval, anger, and rejection, not to mention feeling disempowered, diminished, and "softened" to a position of equality with women? And why should they do this when they may not feel terribly good about their own lives in the first place?

Many men feel threatened by the idea of taking responsibility not only because they would have to give up a great deal of what they've been taught to value, but also because they would have to confront what they have given up *already* in order to participate in an oppressive system. There is among men in modern industrial patriarchies an enormous pool of loss, pain, and grief, some of which . . . is tied to the lost relationship between younger and older men. But this reflects a much deeper loss traceable to the portion of men's humanity that they give up as part of their *solidarity* with older men and the patriarchal society whose interests they both identify with. For men to feel their deep and deadening disconnection from their own and other people's lives is potentially so painful and frightening that most men simply don't want to know about it.

Perhaps the most important barrier to men taking responsibility, however, is their reluctance to expose themselves to the ocean of guilt and shame they believe awaits them if they acknowledge that patriarchy and male privilege exist.[2] The negative power of guilt and shame is especially significant for men who are otherwise most sympathetic to women and most likely to oppose patriarchy. These are the men who are most aware of male privilege and the price women pay in order for men to have it, which also makes them most prone to feeling blameworthy. They're in this trap because . . . both women and men often confuse individuals with systems and often place blame where it doesn't belong. Add to this the fact that men routinely confuse guilt and blame with taking responsibility, and it's understandable why even men sympathetic to gender justice avoid going very far down the road of taking responsibility.

. . .

Dominant groups typically show the least tolerance for allowing themselves to feel guilt and shame. I suspect that women, for example, are more likely to feel guilty over criticizing a man for his male privilege and making him feel bad than he is for being criticized. Privilege, after all, should exempt one from having to feel such things. This means that sooner or later, dominant groups experience reminders of their potential for feeling guilt as an affront that infringes on their sense of entitlement to a life unplagued by concern for how their privilege affects other people. The right to deny that

privilege exists is an integral part of privilege itself. So men can be quick to complain about "being made to feel guilty" without actually *feeling guilty.* . . .

. . . [F]ighting social oppression with blame and guilt psychologizes and individualizes something that's rooted in *systems.* The individualistic model relies on the false notion that systems produce bad consequences solely because bad people with bad motives participate in them. The vast majority of men, like women, were born into patriarchy and have grown up knowing little else. They are not, individually or collectively, patriarchy; they do *participate* in it, however, and that's where both the responsibility for how things are and the power to do something about it lie.

The guilt strategy also doesn't work because it disempowers people to act for change. Fear can get people to look at what's going on as a way to survive. Guilt, on the other hand, typically has just the opposite effect. For every man whose guilt has spurred him to dig deeper into the reality of patriarchy, there are thousands more who'd rather dig a deep hole of denial to hide in. To make men feel guilty simply because they are men puts them in a box with no way out, which all but ensures they'll never make a move toward changing themselves or anything else. They're far more likely to detach themselves from whatever the guilt is about ("I wasn't there; I never knew; it never even happened"); or angrily defend themselves against the unfairness of being blamed simply for being male; or get off the hook by saying they're sorry; or seem to change their ways, promising to be more careful in the future.

. . .

To take responsibility for patriarchy, men will have to claim, embrace, and own it without guilt or shame. Men can't hide behind arguments that patriarchy is about someone else, that others benefit from it more or suffer from it less, or that we're the exceptional nice guys who never hurt anyone. We can't pass off the enormous complexity of patriarchy to bad parenting or flawed personalities. We can't hide behind the damage we do to ourselves as we participate in patriarchy ("Leave me alone; it hurts me, too"), for how we damage our own lives doesn't remove responsibility for how patriarchy destroys the lives of others. Suicide doesn't balance homicide, just as men's abuse of themselves and one another doesn't balance men's abuse of women. Men can't hold out until women agree to take care of men's wounds along with their own or even to stop blaming men individually or collectively, fairly or not. And we can't take refuge in issues of race or class by reducing patriarchy to the power of upper-class white males. Men privileged by race and class are in a better position to benefit from core patriarchal values, but they don't have a monopoly on identifying with and defending them. Patriarchy is about all of us.

. . .

. . . To the extent that feminist work is about *patriarchy,* men have the potential to contribute a great deal of experience and analytical perspective. In this sense, feminist work has as much to do with men as it does with women. This doesn't mean that men should presume to tell women how to liberate themselves from gender oppression, but it does mean that men have something to say to other men—and occasionally to women—about *male* privilege and the male-dominated, male-centered, male-identified system that underlies and enforces it.

. . .

. . . It's hard work, not only because no one likes to focus on human suffering or give up privilege or risk feeling guilty, but also because the path of least resistance in a male-centered system is for men to focus on themselves and their own needs and concerns, not on women and gender oppression.

. . .

The tendency of men to focus on themselves as victims rather than on patriarchy is nowhere more evident than in the mythopoetic men's movement.[3] This is most closely associated with the work of Robert Bly, Sam Keen, and various Jung-inspired writers and activists. . . .

As such, the mythopoetic men's movement does more harm than good by encouraging men to pursue private solutions to what are social problems. Drumming, chanting, and storytelling may help men feel more connected to one another and to a mythic essence of manhood, but it does nothing to illuminate or transform the patriarchal system that creates the wounds they want to heal. . . .

. . .

A key step for men who want to participate in change is to connect their inner lives to the outer reality of patriarchy, to go beyond vague attributions to "society" to a clearer understanding of how social systems work and how our participation affects them. If the new men's movement is to be part of the solution rather than merely a self-absorbed, increasingly entrenched part of the problem, men are going to have to learn how to take responsibility for this social system that bears their name. Becoming part of the solution involves a fundamental moral choice about whether to use gender privilege to further that privilege or to join women in taking responsibility for the patriarchal legacy. Either men empower themselves to move toward taking their share of responsibility or they make way for those who will. Until men begin to share seriously in the emotional, intellectual, and practical aspects of struggling with our legacy, not only will change be seriously limited, but men and women will continue to feel at odds with one another, because in fact they *will be* at odds.

Men's alternatives aren't appealing, but neither are the alternatives for women or racial and ethnic minorities trying to deal with oppression. Like all dominant groups, men are often stuck in a state of arrested development that can wrap them in an almost childlike obliviousness, grandiosity, and sense of entitlement in relation to women.[4] This insulates them from the adult responsibility to know what's going on and to move toward doing something about it, a responsibility that includes coming to terms with the reality of privilege and the oppression that supports it. Gender oppression has forced many women to grow up in order to survive and work for something better for us all. It demands nothing less from men.

NOTES

1. See, for example, the work of Arthur Brittan, Harry Brod, Robert Connell, Michael Kaufman, Michael Kimmel, Joseph Pleck, Jon Snodgrass, and John Stoltenberg.
2. See, for example, Robert Bly, *Iron John: A Book About Men* (Reading, Mass.: Addison-Wesley, 1990); Farrell, *Myth of Male Power;* and Sam Keen, *Fire in the Belly: On Being a Man* (New York: Bantam, 1991).
3. See Kay Leigh Hagan, ed., *Women Respond to the Men's Movement* (San Francisco: HarperCollins, 1992); and Michael S. Kimmel, ed., *The Politics of Manhood: Profeminist Men Respond to the Mytho-poetic Movement (And the Mythopoetic Leaders Respond)* (Philadelphia: Temple University Press, 1995).
4. See Ellyn Kaschak, *Engendered Lives* (New York: Basic Books, 1992), 74.

READING 7

Denials of Inequality

Deborah L. Rhode

Americans' most common response to gender inequality is to deny its dimensions. A widespread perception is that once upon a time, women suffered serious discrimination, but those days are over. Barriers have been coming down, women have been moving up, and full equality is just around the corner. If anything, many men believe that women are now getting undeserved advantages. In a series of recent articles with titles like "The Decline and Fall of the White Male," commentators air their view that "merit is out," "special privileges" are in, and the only group that can't claim equal protection under law is white men. "Pale males eat it again," announces a character in Michael Crichton's popular film *Disclosure.* This perspective is widely shared. According to recent polls, close to half of all men think that they are subject to unfair penalties for advantages that others had in the past. Two-thirds of men and three-quarters of male business leaders do not believe that women encounter significant discrimination for top positions in business, professions, or government.

Such views are difficult to square with the facts. White males account for about 40 percent of the population but about 95 percent of senior managers, 90 percent of newspaper editors, 80 percent of the *Forbes* list of richest Americans, and 80 percent of congressional legislators. Significant sex-based disparities in employment salaries and status persist, even when researchers control for objective factors such as education, experience, and hours worked. As *Newsweek's* article "White Male Paranoia" points out, the pale male certainly appears to be "holding his own (and most of everybody else's) in the world of hard facts"; it's only in the "world of images and ideas . . . [that] he's taking a clobbering."

What explains this gap between popular perceptions and concrete data on gender inequality? Part of the explanation lies with selective perception. Men often deny bias because they fail to recognize it. They usually don't need to, it does not significantly affect their lives. As with race, part of the privilege of dominance is the privilege of accepting without noticing its benefits.

. . .

For obvious reasons, women are more sensitive to gender inequality than men are, but some perceptual blinders persist among both sexes. Not all women encounter all forms of bias, and those who lack personal experience sometimes fail to appreciate collective problems. What sociologists label the "Queen Bee Syndrome" is common among some professionally successful women. Their attitude is, "I managed, why can't you?"

Many women also are unable to see patterns of discrimination because important parts of the picture are missing or murky. Salary, hiring, and promotion data that compare similarly qualified men and women are hard to come by, and the most overt sexism has gone underground. As a 1989 Supreme Court case revealed, male employers may still penalize a woman who they think needs courses in "charm school." But that is no longer what they say in mixed company or in personnel records. Moreover, gender is only one of the characteristics, and not always the most important one, that disadvantages women. Race, ethnicity, class, disability, and sexual orientation often overshadow or interact with gender.

. . .

Self-interest complicates the process. For some men, the increasing unacceptability of sexism, coupled with the inconvenience of eliminating it, encourages various strategies of self-deception. These techniques frequently surface on issues of household work. Employed men, who average only half as much time as employed women on family tasks, generally manage not to notice the disparity. In one recent poll, over two-thirds of surveyed husbands reported that they shared childrearing duties equally with their wives, an assessment wildly inconsistent with that of most wives and virtually all reported research.

Moreover, even men who acknowledge disparities often view women's extra tasks as matters of personal choice, not joint responsibility. Rather than accept an equal division of cleaning, cooking, or childcare obligations, some men redefine their share as unnecessary; they don't mind a little mess or a fast-food dinner, and their infants will do just fine with

extra time among their "friends" at daycare. Other men seem not to notice when some of their assigned tasks need doing, or else mismanage key parts of the job. Rather than broadcast constant reminders of complaints, many women simply pick up pieces that their partners don't even realize have been dropped. As one wife wearily noted, "I do my half, I do half of [my husband's half], and the rest doesn't get done."

. . .

Part of what keeps men, and often women, from recognizing that gap is their choice of reference groups. Where gender appears to be a relevant characteristic, most individuals compare themselves to members of their own sex. In assessing domestic burdens, husbands look to other husbands or their own fathers rather than to wives. From this perspective, unequal divisions of labor become easy to rationalize because they remain the norm rather than the exception.

Women also tend to compare their family burdens to those of members of their own sex. As a result, many wives deny that their husbands do less than their "fair share" around the home, even when responsibilities are grossly unequal. Cultural attitudes reinforce such perceptions. As Anna Quindlen notes, "When men do the dishes it's called helping. When women do dishes, that's called life." Most women are not fully aware of how much time they or their partners spend on family work and generally believe that their arrangements are far more equal than they truly are.

This is not to imply that women totally fail to notice gender inequalities in household burdens. How much help they receive (or don't receive) from their male partners shows up in opinion surveys as one of the greatest sources of resentment. Yet even women who are most resentful often do not expect an equal division of household work. It is only their partner's refusal to help with particular jobs or his inability to justify refusing, that triggers conflict. And for many women, avoiding conflict is more important than achieving equality. They, like their male counterparts, use selective perception as a form of self-protection.

Similar patterns operate in other contexts. According to workplace surveys, even when women recognize gender discrimination as a problem or where objective evidence points to that conclusion, most individuals still do not believe that they personally have been targets. Although many critics denounce feminism for encouraging women to exaggerate their own victimization, recent research finds that individuals generally are reluctant to see themselves in that light. Acknowledging vulnerability carries a cost: it erodes individuals' sense of control and self-esteem, and involves the unpleasantness of identifying a perpetrator. Many women understandably are unwilling to alienate men whose approval is important personally and professionally.

Although some individuals enjoy nursing grievances and claiming the moral leverage of victim status, most do not. As Hillary Clinton once noted, "Who wants to walk around constantly with clenched fists?" Particularly where women feel powerless to avoid inequality, they are likely to avoid acknowledging it.

DISCUSSION QUESTIONS FOR CHAPTER ONE

1. Why are you taking a women's studies course?

2. What are your expectations, fears, anxieties, and hopes about taking a women's studies class?

3. Why did women's studies emerge in the academic community?

4. What are negative stereotypes of feminism? Where do they come from? How do these stereotypes serve to perpetuate the dominant social order?

5. Do you think on the whole equality has been achieved? Why or why not? Are there places where you see room for improvement or the need for drastic change?

SUGGESTIONS FOR FURTHER READING

Douglas, Susan J. "I'm Not a Feminist, But. . . ." *Where the Girls Are: Growing Up Female with the Mass Media.* New York: Times Books, 1995.

Griffin, Gail B. "Orphans of the Storm: The F-Word and the Post-Feminist Generation." *Calling: Essays on Teaching in the Mother Tongue.* Pasadena: Trilogy, 1992.

hooks, bell. "Educating Women: A Feminist Agenda." *Feminist Theory: From Margin to Center.* Boston: South End, 1984.

———. *Teaching to Transgress: Education as the Practice of Freedom.* New York: Routledge, 1994.

Maher, Frances A., and Mary Kay Thompson Tetreault. *The Feminist Classroom: An Inside Look at How Professors and Students Are Transforming Higher Education for a Diverse Society.* New York: Basic Books, 1994.

CHAPTER TWO

Systems of Privilege and Inequality in Women's Lives

As women, we are as different as we are alike. Although we share some conditions, including having primary responsibility for children and being victims of male violence, our lives are marked by difference. This is a result of the varying conditions of women's existence in communities around the world and the societies in which these communities are embedded. We inhabit different cultures whose norms or cultural expectations prescribe different ways of acting as women and different sanctions if these norms are broken. It is therefore important to recognize difference and avoid using "woman" as a universal or homogeneous category that assumes sameness.

In the United States, women's lives are also marked by difference. This difference is illustrated by the material conditions of our lives, the values and cultures of the communities in which we live, and even the geographic region of the country we inhabit. In particular, we are different in terms of race and ethnicity, religion, age, looks, sexual orientation, socioeconomic status, and ability. Just as it is important to question the homogenizing notions of sameness in terms of the category "woman" across societies, it is also important to understand that these universalizing tendencies work against our understanding of women in the United States as well. Often we tend to think of women in comparison to a *mythical norm*: White, middle-class, heterosexual, abled, thin, and a young adult. Women not fitting these categories often tend to be considered different. The important question to ask, however, is, different from what? Such a question reveals how difference gets constructed against what people think of as normal. And what is perceived as normal is that which those in power are able to define as normal.

It is important to recognize that the meanings associated with differences are socially constructed. These social construcions would not be problematic were they not created against the notion of the mythical norm. Being a lesbian would not be a "difference" that invoked cultural resistance if it were not for compulsory heterosexuality, the notion that everyone should be heterosexual and have relationships with the opposite sex. This concept is illustrated in "The Social Construction of Disability" by Susan Wendell. She makes the case that *ableism*, discrimination against the mentally and physically disabled, is a direct result of social factors that actively create standards of normality against which ability/disability is constructed. In this chapter we focus on differences among women and explore the ways systems of privilege and inequality are created out of these differences.

Figure 2.1: Intersecting Axes of Privilege, Domination, and Oppression

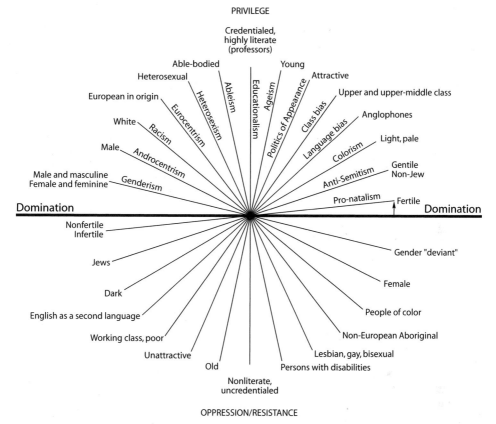

Source: Kathryn Pauly Morgan, "Describing the Emperor's New Clothes: Three Myths of Educational (In)Equality." *The Gender Question in Education: Theory, Pedagogy & Politics,* Ann Diller et al., eds. Boulder, CO: Westview, 1996.

DIFFERENCE, HIERARCHY, AND SYSTEMS OF OPPRESSION

Society recognizes the ways people are different and assigns group membership based upon these differences; at the same time society also ranks the differences. Male is placed above female, thin above fat, economically privileged above poor, and so forth. These rankings of groups and their members create a hierarchy where some ways of being, like being abled or heterosexual, are valued more than others, like being disabled or gay or lesbian. In this way, rankings occur against societal notions of the mythical norm.

The hierarchical ranking of these differences is constructed through social processes such that patterns of difference become systems of inequality and privilege. Inequality for some and privilege for others is the consequence of these processes. *Privilege* can be defined as special advantages people have by virtue of their status or position in society. In "White Privilege and Male Privilege," Peggy McIntosh

Learning Activity: Unpack Your Knapsack

Peggy McIntosh lists a number of ways that she experiences White privilege. Based on your various nontarget statuses, make lists of the ways you experience the following categories of privilege:

White	Male	Heterosexual
Middle or Upper Class	Young	Able-bodied

writes that White privilege is the "invisible package of unearned assets" that White people can count on cashing in every day. And, as McIntosh explains, it is easier to grant that others are disadvantaged than to admit being overprivileged. Men might be supportive of women's rights but balk at the suggestion that their personal behavior is in need of modification. Whites might be horrified by the stories of racial injustice but still not realize that such taken-for-granted White privilege is part of the problem.

Systems that facilitate privilege and inequality, subordination and domination, include: *racism* based upon racial/ethnic group membership (African American, Asian American, Latino/a, Native American—note this also includes anti-Semitism, or discrimination against Jews and those of Semitic descent), *sexism* based upon gender, *classism* associated with socioeconomic status, *heterosexism,* concerning sexual orientation, *ageism* relating to age, *looksism,* concerning body size and looks, and *ableism,* about physical and mental ability. Systems of oppression can be defined as systems that discriminate and privilege based upon perceived or real differences among people. Given this, sexism discriminates and privileges on the basis of gender, resulting in gender stratification, racism discriminates and privileges on the basis of racial and ethnic differences, and so forth for classism, heterosexism, ageism, looksism, and ableism.

Every woman is in multiple places vis-à-vis these systems. She might not have access to race and gender privilege because she is African American and a woman; she might have access to heterosexual privilege because she is heterosexual and class privilege because she lives in a family that is financially secure. This is the *confluence,* the flowing together of various identities. As Patricia Hill Collins explains in "Toward a New Vision," it is not as useful to think of these various identities as being stacked or arranged in a cumulative manner. Lives are not experienced as "Here I'm a woman, here I'm abled, here I'm poor," as if all our various statuses are all stacked up; we experience ourselves as ordinary people who struggle daily with the inequities in our lives and who usually take the privileges for granted. Various identities concerning these systems of equality and privilege are usually thoroughly blended.

Systems of inequality like racism, sexism, and classism interconnect and work together to enforce inequality and privilege, each mostly supporting the other. As Babba Copper explains in her article on ageism, age discrimination is very much connected to sexism as well as to looksism. Women learn to "age pass," that is, we do not want to be mistaken for 40 when we are in our 30s, or mistaken for 70 when

Learning Activity: Hate Crimes Based on Sexual Orientation

Hate crimes are a national problem. In the 1990s almost every state in the nation experienced hate crimes based on sexual orientation. Many of the crimes have been documented by the Human Rights Campaign, the largest lesbian and gay political organization in the United States, with 300,000 members. Data collected by the FBI indicate that 1,102 hate crimes based on sexual orientation were reported to local law enforcement agencies in 1997. The National Coalition of Anti-Violence Programs reported 2,552 incidents of bias based on sexual orientation in 1998—in only sixteen cities/jurisdictions. The Human Rights Campaign's document, "A Decade of Violence: Hate Crimes Based on Sexual Orientation," lists many of the incidents reported throughout the '90s. Five incidents are related from our home state, Oregon:

- July 14, 1991, Eugene, OR. Police arrested a 28-year-old woman and 21-year-old man for allegedly attacking a gay man outside a bar while using offensive language about his sexual orientation.

- September 26, 1992, Salem, OR. A lesbian and gay man died after a firebomb was thrown into their apartment. Three men and one woman, all under the age of 23, were charged in connection with the murders.

- October 27, 1992, Eugene, OR. A conservative activist holding a sign in support of Oregon's anti-gay ballot measure was attacked by two men who apparently mistook him for a gay activist.

- December 8, 1994, Medford, OR. Two prominent lesbian activists, who had been domestic partners for many years, were killed by a man who said he thought their lifestyle was sick.

- February 2, 1998, Corvallis, OR. A gay high school student was allegedly beaten by three youths who used anti-gay epithets. Two teenagers were charged with third-degree assault and first-degree intimidation.

Go to the web page of the Human Rights Campaign at *www.hrc.org* and find the "Decade of Violence" document. Look up your state and see what hate crimes based on sexual orientation occurred near you. How do you feel about these crimes happening in your state? Do you think there should be national hate crime legislation?

only 60. This is part of the pursuit for youth and beauty that encourages women to participate as agents of ageism as we fulfill the expectations of gender. Similarly, Suzanne Pharr writes about the ways homophobia functions as a weapon of sexism. *Homophobia* is the fear and dislike of lesbians and gay men. Pharr emphasizes that homophobia functions as a threat to keep women apart from one another and under male power, thus reinforcing sexism.

Another way that systems of inequality and privilege are maintained is by coercion and force. The best example of this is *hate crimes,* crimes whose motive is hate and bigotry and whose perpetrators are most likely heterosexual White males. There has been a substantial increase in hate crimes in the last decade, especially against people of color and lesbians and gay men, although it may be that improved reporting systems are also increasing our awareness of hate crimes. It is

Learning Activity: Combating Hate

Many web pages provide valuable information about hate, hate crimes, and hate groups in the United States. Go to the Southern Poverty Law Center's homepage at *www.splcenter .org*. Click on "Intelligence Center" and then on "Hate Incidents." Put in your state to see a list of hate crimes where you live. You may also want to visit these websites as well: *www.wiesenthal.com, www.adl.org, www.stopthehate.org,* and *www.hatewatch.org.* Using information from these sites, make a list of ways you can help stop hate.

important to emphasize that gender as a category is omitted from many hate crime statutes despite the fact that women suffer from crimes of misogyny. Women are often hurt and killed because they are women. Hate crimes against women also involve a form of *sexual terrorism,* the threat of rape and sexual assault that controls a woman's life whether or not she is actually raped or assaulted.

Although hate crimes vary in the amount of terror and violence they involve, all leave women feeling vulnerable and victimized. Here are some examples. In 1994 the White neighbors of a Black woman in a Los Angeles suburb burned a cross on her lawn, kicked her children, hanged and gassed her pets, and placed "White power" signs on her property. In Oklahoma City, following the bombing of the federal building, an Iraqi refugee in her mid-20s miscarried her near-term baby after an attack on her home in which assailants pounded on her door, broke windows, and screamed anti-Islamic epithets. In Minneapolis in 1996, an African American lesbian found a note reading "Hate Nigger Faggots" at her door. After a burned cross was left outside her door, she decided to move. These are just a few examples of a widespread problem.

INSTITUTIONS

Institutions are social organizations that involve established patterns of behavior organized around particular purposes. They function through social norms and established rules and/or laws. Major institutions in our society include the family, marriage, the economy, government and criminal justice systems, religion, education, science, health and medicine, mass media, the military, and sports. Usually patterns of rules and practices implicit in major societal institutions have a historical component and reflect political, military, legal, and socioeconomic decisions made over decades and centuries. Although institutions are intended to meet the needs of society generally, or people in particular, they meet some people's needs better than others. These social organizations are central in creating systems of inequality and privilege because they pattern and structure differences among women in relatively organized ways. Institutions are important channels for the perpetuation of what Hill Collins calls "structures of domination and subordination."

Marilyn Frye focuses on the institutional aspect of systems of inequality and privilege in her article "Oppression." She emphasizes that people who suffer under systems of inequality are oppressed by these systems. Frye goes on to explain the difference between being oppressed and being limited and writes that a fundamental aspect of oppression is the double bind: All potential options have limitations. She uses the metaphor of a birdcage to explain the networks of related barriers that function in systems of oppression. One wire might be like an individual-level prejudice; a bird could just move around it and escape. But a birdcage involves patterns of wires, systematically arranged so that escape is thwarted. The wires of the cage symbolically become institutionalized into a system of oppression.

Institutions encourage the channeling of various systems of gendered inequality to all aspects of women's lives. In terms of the patterning of resources and practices, three institutional functions support systems of inequality and privilege. First, institutions assign various roles to women and men and are also places of employment where people perform gendered work. Educational institutions, for example, employ a considerable number of women. However, as the prestige of the teaching position increases, the number of White males in these positions increases, along with higher salaries. Also, it is very difficult for openly lesbian teachers to find employment in schools, and many states are attempting to pass laws preventing lesbians and gay men from teaching in state-funded educational establishments.

Second, institutions distribute resources and extend privileges differentially to different groups. Sports are a good example of this. As an institution, athletics has traditionally been male dominated. Men's sports are more highly valued than women's sports and are a major focus for sports entertainment. Compared to men's professional sports, women's are grossly underrepresented. Despite Title IX of the 1972 Educational Amendments Act, which barred discrimination in education, many colleges still are not in compliance and spend considerably more money on men's sports than on women's. Female athletes on some campuses complain that men receive better practice times in shared gymnasiums and more up-to-date equipment. And, within women's sports, some are more "White" than others. Examples that immediately come to mind are gymnastics, ice skating, equestrian sports, tennis, and golf (all relatively expensive sports). In addition, most women's sports—outside of basketball, volleyball, and track—are dominated by White women. In this way, sports and athletics are an example of an institution where resources are inequitably distributed.

Another blatant example of inequitable distribution concerns the economic system. Other than inherited wealth, the major way our economic system distributes resources is in terms of remuneration for the work that we do. Women tend to work in jobs that are heavily occupied by women; examples include clerical work, service and retail sales, and semiprofessional occupations like teaching and nursing. These jobs are undervalued in our society, contributing to the fact that a woman's average salary generally for all occupations is about 77 percent of a man's wage. Some women work under deplorable conditions at minimum wage levels; some work with hazardous chemicals or have to breathe secondhand smoke throughout their workday. Old women and women of color own a tiny percentage of the wealth in this society—another example of the inequitable distribution of resources.

Third, major institutions in society are interconnected and work to support and maintain one another. Often this means that personnel are shared among major institutions; more likely it means that these institutions mutually support one another in terms of the ways they fulfill (or deny) the needs of people in society. For example, close ties to economic institutions include the military (through the military-industrial complex), the government (corporate leaders often have official positions in government and rely on legislative loopholes and taxation systems to maintain corporate profits), health and medicine (with important ties to pharmaceutical companies), the media (whose content is controlled in part by advertising), and sports (through corporate sponsorship).

IDEOLOGY AND LANGUAGE

In addition to distributing resources and practices, institutions produce messages that shape our understandings of gender. Importantly, ideas and values (like stereotypes and jokes) or sets of beliefs (often called ideologies) provide the rationale for injustice. Hill Collins calls this the "symbolic dimension" of systems of domination and subordination. For example, the media often reinforce stereotypes about women like dumb blondes, passive Asian Americans, or pushy African Americans. Another example of gendered messages comes from the institution of religion. This institution is especially powerful because it implies the notion of divine sanction. Traditional religious texts tell stories (for example, Eve's behavior that led to the banishment from the Garden of Eden or the chaste role of the Virgin Mary) that convey important messages about moral thought and behavior as well as women's place in society. These messages tend to be strongly gendered and often support different behaviors for women and men. A central code of much religious teaching is that women should be subordinate to men in their spiritual and everyday lives.

An example of an ideology that is supported by various institutions and that affects women's lives is the bootstrap myth concerning economic success. Propagated by the economic system, it paints economic success as a result of hard work and ambition. All people, if properly motivated and willing to work hard, can pull themselves up by their bootstraps. Given this set of ideas, those individuals who are not able to provide for their families must have deficiencies. Perhaps they were unmotivated, did not work hard enough, or were not smart enough. Such ideas encourage blaming the poor for their poverty rather than understanding the wider societal forces that shape people's existence and maintain classism. Notice that a particular ideology need not be supported unanimously for it to influence society. Many would disagree vehemently with the bootstrap myth, yet, still, this is a key part of the ideology of capitalist countries. In this way, institutions perpetuate sets of ideas and practices and use them to justify the institution.

Activist Profile: Fannie Lou Hamer

She began life in Mississippi in 1917 as the granddaughter of slaves and the daughter of sharecroppers, but Fannie Lou Hamer was to become one of the most important leaders of the civil rights movement in the United States. Although Hamer became a sharecropper herself, by 1962 she'd had enough of the second-class life of the segregated South. She joined seventeen other African Americans taking a bus to the county seat to register to vote. On the way home, they were stopped by police and arrested. After Hamer returned home, she was visited by the plantation owner, who told her that if she insisted on voting, she would have to get off his land, which she did that same day.

The next year, when Hamer joined other civil rights workers in challenging the "Whites only" policy at a bus terminal diner, she was arrested and jailed. The police ordered two other African American prisoners to beat her with a metal-spiked club. Hamer was blinded in one eye from the beating and suffered permanent kidney damage.

In 1964, Hamer helped organize the Mississippi Freedom Democratic Party (MFDP) to challenge the all-White Mississippi delegation to the Democratic Convention. Hamer spoke to the credentials committee of the convention, and although her live testimony was preempted by a presidential press conference, it was aired by national networks in its entirety later that evening. The MFDP and the credentials committee reached a compromise, giving voting and speaking rights to two MFDP delegates and seating the others as honored guests. Hamer responded, "We didn't come all this way for two seats when all of us is tired." In 1968 the Mississippi Democratic Party did seat an integrated delegation.

Throughout her life, Hamer continued to work for justice, supporting Head Start for Black schools and jobs for poor African Americans, opposing the Vietnam War, and helping to convene the National Women's Political Caucus in the 1970s.

Hamer died in 1977 and was buried in Mississippi. Her tombstone reads, "I am sick and tired of being sick and tired."

Classism is also addressed in the article by Donna Langston titled "Tired of Playing Monopoly?" Here she explains how class is not just about socioeconomic status, that is, how much wealth you have access to or how much you earn. She writes,

> Class is also culture. As a result of the class you were born into and raised in, class is your understanding of the world and where you fit in; it's composed of ideas, attitudes, values, and language; class is how you think, feel, act, look, dress, talk, move, walk; class is what stores you shop at, restaurants you eat in; class is the schools you attend, the education you attain; class is the jobs you will work at throughout your adult life. Class even determines when we marry and become mothers.

Stereotypes and ideologies that support systems of inequality involve prejudices. *Prejudice* means, literally, to prejudge and involves making premature judgments without adequate information or with inaccurate information. Often these ideas support systems of inequality and privilege because prejudice is often adopted when there is no other basis for understanding. For example, many White people have little contact with people of color, and many young people do not interact on an everyday basis with old people. As a result, there is a lack of accurate information, and stereotypes or images from television or the movies are used instead. This kind of ignorance and misinformation breeds prejudice. In "Something About the Subject Makes It Hard to Name," Gloria Yamato writes about different kinds of prejudice: aware/blatant, aware/covert, unaware/unintentional, and unaware/self-righteous. In this article she emphasizes that much prejudice comes from misinformation and is very often unintentional. She also notes that social norms against racism have pushed some racism underground.

Prejudices are *internalized* (assimilated, integrated, or incorporated into our thoughts and behavior) by all of us. If we are members of the target group, the group against whom the prejudice is aimed, it can lead to low self-esteem, self-loathing, and shame. Sadly, it can mean individuals are encouraged to believe they are not worthy of social justice and therefore are less likely to seek equality. Although members of target groups may internalize negative messages, members of nontarget groups, groups (often part of the mythical norm) against whom the prejudice is not aimed, also internalize these messages as well as messages about their own privilege. This can encourage or justify hostility against target groups.

Internalizing oppression means that we not only police ourselves, but we also police one another, encouraging compliance with institutions that may oppress. When individuals direct the resentment and anger they have about their situation onto those who are of equal or of lesser status, this process is called *horizontal hostility*. As a strategy, it is similar to the military notion of "divide and conquer" where groups are encouraged to fight with one another in order to avoid alliances that might collaboratively overpower an enemy. Babba Copper remarks on this horizontal conflict when she writes about woman-to-woman ageism and the ways women compete "for the crumbs of social power."

Language, or the symbolic means by which we communicate, is a central aspect of what makes us human. It is an incredibly sophisticated process of symbols that

Ideas for Activism

- Find out how your university ensures access for people with disabilities. If some structures on your campus are inaccessible, advocate with your administration to create accessibility.
- Plan a celebration of Black women during Black History Month.
- Find out what programs your university offers to recruit and retain students and faculty of color. If programs are not in place, advocate with your administration to develop such programs.
- Find out if your university's antidiscrimination policy includes sexual orientation as a protected classification, and find out if your university provides benefits for domestic partners. If not, advocate with your administration to include sexual orientation in its policy and/or to provide domestic partner benefits.

we learn at an early age and mostly take for granted unless we are confronted with trying to communicate in a language not our own. Because language not only allows us to name the objects of our experience but also to typify them (experience them as similar to something of a similar type), it creates as well as reflects our reality. It shapes as well as expresses thought. And because language helps us sort and anticipate our experiences, it has a primary influence on our lives.

The English language is structured in such a way that it maintains sexism and racism. In "Gender Stereotyping in the English Language," Laurel Richardson explains how the English language helps shape our understandings of gender and limits women's options for self-definition. This article encourages us to think about the ways that language shapes our reality and helps structure the everyday realities of women's lives. When you grow up knowing twenty different words synonymous with *slut,* you learn something powerful about gender. The English language also maintains racism. For example:

> Some may blackly (angrily) accuse me of trying to blacken (defame) the English language, to give it a black eye (a mark of shame) by writing such black words (hostile). They may denigrate (to cast aspersions; to darken) me by accusing me of being black hearted (malevolent), of having a black outlook (pessimistic, dismal) on life, of being a blackguard (scoundrel)—which will certainly be a black mark (detrimental act) against me. Some may black-brow (scowl) at me and hope that a black cat crosses in front of me because of this black deed. I may become a black sheep (one who causes shame or embarrassment because of deviation from the expected standards), who will be black-balled (ostracized) by being placed on a black list (list of undesirables) in an attempt to blackmail (to force or coerce into a particular action) me to retract my words. . . . The preceding is of course a white lie (not intended to cause harm), meant only to illustrate some examples of racist terminology in the English language.*

---

*Robert B. Moore, "Racism in the English Language." Excerpted in *Experiencing Race, Class, and Gender in the U.S.*, Virginia Cyrus, ed. (Mountain View, CA: Mayfield, 1993), p. 152.

In this chapter we focus on the social construction of difference and how systems of inequality and privilege based upon these differences function and are maintained. A next step is to consider how to effect change to improve the conditions of women's lives. Several of the readings focus on this. In particular, Peggy McIntosh suggests we recognize our privilege and work on our internalized prejudices and privileges. Babba Copper writes about identifying and acknowledging sources of inequality and specifically the ways we have been taught to hate old women and deny them power. She hopes for alliances across our differences. Patricia Hill Collins echoes this and writes about the necessity of developing empathy for others as well as creating coalitions around common causes. Suzanne Pharr points out the homophobia of the women's movement and its failure to achieve solidarity when the rights of all women are not recognized. Donna Langston presents ways to challenge classism that involve confronting the behavior in ourselves, making demands on behalf of poor communities, and learning from the skills and strengths of working-class people. Similarly, Gloria Yamato has good ideas for Whites who want to be allies to people of color. The message in all these articles is the need to recognize difference, to understand how the meanings associated with difference get translated into privilege and inequality, and to celebrate those differences through coalitions and other expressions of personal and social concern.

Toward a New Vision
Race, Class, and Gender as Categories of Analysis and Connection

Patricia Hill Collins

The true focus of revolutionary change is never merely the oppressive situations which we seek to escape, but that piece of the oppressor which is planted deep within each of us.

—*Audre Lorde,* Sister Outsider, *123*

Audre Lorde's statement raises a troublesome issue for scholars and activists working for social change. While many of us have little difficulty assessing our own victimization within some major system of oppression, whether it be by race, social class, religion, sexual orientation, ethnicity, age or gender, we typically fail to see how our thoughts and actions uphold someone else's subordination. Thus, white feminists routinely point with confidence to their oppression as women but resist seeing how much their white skin privileges them. African-Americans who possess eloquent analyses of racism often persist in viewing poor White women as symbols of white power. The radical left fares little better. "If only people of color and women could see their true class interests," they argue, "class solidarity would eliminate racism and sexism." In essence, each group identifies the type of oppression with which it feels most comfortable as being fundamental and classifies all other types as being of lesser importance.

Oppression is full of such contradictions. Errors in political judgment that we make concerning how we teach our courses, what we tell our children, and which organizations are worthy of our time, talents and financial support flow smoothly from errors in theoretical analysis about the nature of oppression and activism. Once we realize that there are few pure victims or oppressors, and that each one of us

derives varying amounts of penalty and privilege from the multiple systems of oppression that frame our lives, then we will be in a position to see the need for new ways of thought and action.

. . .

[This discussion] addresses this need for new patterns of thought and action. I focus on two basic questions. First, how can we reconceptualize race, class and gender as categories of analysis? Second, how can we transcend the barriers created by our experiences with race, class and gender oppression in order to build the types of coalitions essential for social exchange? To address these question[s] I contend that we must acquire both new theories of how race, class and gender have shaped the experiences not just of women of color, but of all groups. Moreover, we must see the connections between these categories of analysis and the personal issues in our everyday lives, particularly our scholarship, our teaching and our relationships with our colleagues and students. As Audre Lorde points out, change starts with self, and relationships that we have with those around us must always be the primary site for social change.

How Can We Reconceptualize Race, Class and Gender as Categories of *Analysis?*

To me, we must shift our discourse away from additive analyses of oppression (Spelman 1982; Collins 1989). Such approaches are typically based on two key premises. First, they depend on either/or, dichotomous thinking. Persons, things and ideas are conceptualized in terms of their opposites. For example, Black/White, man/woman, thought/feeling, and fact/opinion are defined in oppositional terms. Thought and feeling are not seen as two different and interconnected ways of approaching truth that can coexist in scholarship and teaching. Instead, feeling is defined as antithetical to reason, as its opposite. In spite of the fact that we all have "both/and" identities, (I am both a college professor and a mother—I don't stop being a mother when I drop my child off at school, or forget everything I learned while scrubbing the toilet), we persist in trying to classify each other in either/or categories. I live each day as an African-American woman— a race/gender specific experience. And I am not alone. Everyone has a race/gender/class specific identity. Either/or, dichotomous thinking is especially troublesome when applied to theories of oppression because every individual must be classified as being either oppressed or not oppressed. The both/and position of simultaneously being oppressed and oppressor becomes conceptually impossible.

A second premise of additive analyses of oppression is that these dichotomous differences must be ranked. One side of the dichotomy is typically labeled dominant and the other subordinate. Thus, Whites rule Blacks, men are deemed superior to women, and reason is seen as being preferable to emotion. Applying this premise to discussions of oppression leads to the assumption that oppression can be quantified, and that some groups are oppressed more than others. I am frequently asked, "Which has been most oppressive to you, your status as a Black person or your status as a woman?" What I am really being asked to do is divide myself into little boxes and rank my various statuses. If I experience oppression as a both/ and phenomenon, why should I analyze it any differently?

Additive analyses of oppression rest squarely on the twin pillars of either/or thinking and the necessity to quantify and rank all relationships in order to know where one stands. Such approaches typically see African-American women as being more oppressed than everyone else because the majority of Black women experience the negative effects of race, class and gender oppression simultaneously. In essence, if you add together separate oppressions, you are left with a grand oppression greater than the sum of its parts.

I am not denying that specific groups experience oppression more harshly than others— lynching is certainly objectively worse than being held up as a sex object. But we must be careful not to confuse this issue of the saliency of one type of oppression in people's lives with a theoretical stance positing the interlocking nature of oppression. Race, class and gender may all structure a situation but may not be equally visible and/or important in people's self-definitions. In certain contexts, such as the antebellum American South and contemporary South America, racial oppression is more visibly salient, while in other contexts, such as Haiti, El Salvador and Nicaragua, social class oppression may be more apparent. For middle class White women, gender may assume experiential primacy unavailable to poor Hispanic women struggling with the ongoing issues of low paid jobs and the frustrations of the welfare bureaucracy. This recognition that one category may have salience over another for a given time and place does not minimize the theoretical importance of assuming that race, class and gender as categories of analysis structure all relationships.

In order to move toward new visions of what oppression is, I think that we need to ask new questions. How are relationships of domination and subordination structured and maintained in the American political economy? How do race, class and gender function as parallel and interlocking systems that shape this basic relationship of domination and subordination? Questions such as these promise to move us away from futile theoretical struggles concerned with ranking oppressions and towards analyses that assume race, class and gender are all present in any given setting, even if one appears more visible and salient than the others. Our task becomes redefined as one of reconceptualizing oppression by uncovering the connections among race, class and gender as categories of analysis.

1. INSTITUTIONAL DIMENSION OF OPPRESSION

Sandra Harding's contention that gender oppression is structured along three main dimensions—the institutional, the symbolic, and the individual—offers a useful model for a more comprehensive analysis encompassing race, class and gender oppression (Harding 1986). Systemic relationships of domination and subordination structured through social institutions such as schools, businesses, hospitals, the work place, and government agencies represent the institutional dimension of oppression. Racism, sexism and elitism all have concrete institutional locations. Even though the workings of the institutional dimension of oppression are often obscured with ideologies claiming equality of opportunity, in actuality, race, class and gender place Asian-American women, Native American men, White men, African-American women, and other groups in distinct institutional niches with varying degrees of penalty and privilege.

Even though I realize that many . . . would not share this assumption, let us assume that the institutions of American society discriminate, whether by design or by accident. While many of us are familiar with how race, gender and class operate separately to structure inequality, I want to focus on how these three systems interlock in structuring the institutional dimension of oppression. To get at the interlocking nature of race, class and gender, I want you to think about the antebellum plantation as a guiding metaphor for a variety of American social institutions. Even though slavery is typically analyzed as a racist institution, and occasionally as a class institution, I suggest that slavery was a race, class, gender specific insti-

tution. Removing any one piece from our analysis diminishes our understanding of the true nature of relations of domination and subordination under slavery.

. . .

A brief analysis of key American social institutions most controlled by elite White men should convince us of the interlocking nature of race, class and gender in structuring the institutional dimension of oppression. For example, if you are from an American college or university, is your campus a modern plantation? Who controls your university's political economy? Are elite White men over represented among the upper administrators and trustees controlling your university's finances and policies? Are elite White men being joined by growing numbers of elite White women helpmates? What kinds of people are in your classrooms grooming the next generation who will occupy these and other decision-making positions? Who are the support staff that produce the mass mailings, order the supplies, fix the leaky pipes? Do African-Americans, Hispanics or other people of color form the majority of the invisible workers who feed you, wash your dishes, and clean up your offices and libraries after everyone else has gone home?

If your college is anything like mine, you know the answers to these questions. You may be affiliated with an institution that has Hispanic women as vice-presidents for finance, or substantial numbers of Black men among the faculty. If so, you are fortunate. Much more typical are colleges where a modified version of the plantation as a metaphor for the institutional dimension of oppression survives.

2. THE SYMBOLIC DIMENSION OF OPPRESSION

Widespread, societally-sanctioned ideologies used to justify relations of domination and subordination comprise the symbolic dimension of oppression. Central to this process is the use of stereotypical or controlling images of diverse race, class and gender groups. In order to assess the power of this dimension of oppression, I want you to make a list, either on paper or in your head, of "masculine" and "feminine" characteristics. If your list is anything like that compiled by most people, it reflects some variation of the following:

Masculine	*Feminine*
aggressive	passive
leader	follower
rational	emotional
strong	weak
intellectual	physical

Not only does this list reflect either/or dichotomous thinking and the need to rank both sides of the dichotomy, but ask yourself exactly which men and women you had in mind when compiling these characteristics. This list applies almost exclusively to middle class White men and women. The allegedly "masculine" qualities that you probably listed are only acceptable when exhibited by elite White men, or when used by Black and Hispanic men against each other or against women of color. Aggressive Black and Hispanic men are seen as dangerous, not powerful, and are often penalized when they exhibit any of the allegedly "masculine" characteristics. Working class and poor White men fare slightly better and are also denied the allegedly "masculine" symbols of leadership, intellectual competence, and human rationality. Women of color and working class and poor White women are also not represented on this list, for they have never had the luxury of being "ladies." What appear to be universal categories representing all men and women instead are unmasked as being applicable to only a small group.

It is important to see how the symbolic images applied to different race, class and gender groups interact in maintaining systems of domination and subordination. If I were to ask you to repeat the same assignment, only this time, by making separate lists for Black men, Black women, Hispanic women and Hispanic men, I

suspect that your gender symbolism would be quite different. In comparing all of the lists, you might begin to see the interdependence of symbols applied to all groups. For example, the elevated images of White womanhood need devalued images of Black womanhood in order to maintain credibility.

. . .

Assuming that everyone is affected differently by the same interlocking set of symbolic images allows us to move forward toward new analyses. Women of color and White women have different relationships to White male authority and this difference explains the distinct gender symbolism applied to both groups. Black women encounter controlling images such as the mammy, the matriarch, the mule and the whore, that encourage others to reject us as fully human people. Ironically, the negative nature of these images simultaneously encourages us to reject them. In contrast, White women are offered seductive images, those that promise to reward them for supporting the status quo. And yet seductive images can be equally controlling. Consider, for example, the views of Nancy White, a 73-year old Black woman, concerning images of rejection and seduction:

> My mother used to say that the black woman is the white man's mule and the white woman is his dog. Now, she said that to say this: we do the heavy work and get beat whether we do it well or not. But the white woman is closer to the master and he pats them on the head and lets them sleep in the house, but he ain't gon' treat neither one like he was dealing with a person. (Gwaltney, 148)

Both sets of images stimulate particular political stances. By broadening the analysis beyond the confines of race, we can see the varying levels of rejection and seduction available to each of us due to our race, class and gender identity. Each of us lives with an allotted portion of institutional privilege and penalty, and with varying levels of rejection and seduction inherent in the symbolic images applied to us. This is the context in which we make our choices. Taken together, the institutional and symbolic dimensions of oppression create a structural backdrop against which all of us live our lives.

3. THE INDIVIDUAL DIMENSION OF OPPRESSION

Whether we benefit or not, we all live within institutions that reproduce race, class and gender oppression. Even if we never have any contact with members of other race, class and gender groups, we all encounter images of these groups and are exposed to the symbolic meanings attached to those images. On this dimension of oppression, our individual biographies vary tremendously. As a result of our institutional and symbolic statuses, all of our choices become political acts.

Each of us must come to terms with the multiple ways in which race, class and gender as categories of analysis frame our individual biographies. I have lived my entire life as an African-American woman from a working class family and this basic fact has had a profound impact on my personal biography. Imagine how different your life might be if you had been born Black, or White, or poor, or of a different race/class/gender group than the one with which you are most familiar. The institutional treatment you would have received and the symbolic meanings attached to your very existence might differ dramatically from what you now consider to be natural, normal and part of everyday life. You might be the same, but your personal biography might have been quite different.

I believe that each of us carries around the cumulative effect of our lives within multiple structures of oppression. If you want to see how much you have been affected by this whole thing, I ask you one simple question— who are your close friends? Who are the people with whom you can share your hopes, dreams,

vulnerabilities, fears and victories? Do they look like you? If they are all the same, circumstance may be the cause. For the first seven years of my life I saw only low income Black people. My friends from those years reflected the composition of my community. But now that I am an adult, can the defense of circumstance explain the patterns of people that I trust as my friends and colleagues? When given other alternatives, if my friends and colleagues reflect the homogeneity of one race, class and gender group, then these categories of analysis have indeed become barriers to connection.

I am not suggesting that people are doomed to follow the paths laid out for them by race, class and gender as categories of analysis. While these three structures certainly frame my opportunity structure, I as an individual always have the choice of accepting things as they are, or trying to change them. As Nikki Giovanni points out, "we've got to live in the real world. If we don't like the world we're living in, change it. And if we can't change it, we change ourselves. We can do something" (Tate 1983, 68). While a piece of the oppressor may be planted deep within each of us, we each have the choice of accepting that piece or challenging it as part of the "true focus of revolutionary change."

How Can We Transcend the Barriers Created by Our Experiences with Race, Class and Gender Oppression in Order to Build the Types of Coalitions Essential for Social Change?

Reconceptualizing oppression and seeing the barriers created by race, class and gender as interlocking categories of analysis is a vital first step. But we must transcend these barriers by moving toward race, class and gender as categories of connection, by building relationships and coalitions that will bring about social change. What are some of the issues involved in doing this?

1. DIFFERENCES IN POWER AND PRIVILEGE

First, we must recognize that our differing experiences with oppression create problems in the relationships among us. Each of us lives within a system that vests us with varying levels of power and privilege. These differences in power, whether structured along axes of race, class, gender, age or sexual orientation, frame our relationships. African-American writer June Jordan describes her discomfort on a Caribbean vacation with Olive, the Black woman who cleaned her room:

> . . . even though both "Olive" and "I" live inside a conflict neither one of us created, and even though both of us therefore hurt inside that conflict, I may be one of the monsters she needs to eliminate from her universe and, in a sense, she may be one of the monsters in mine (1985, 47).

Differences in power constrain our ability to connect with one another even when we think we are engaged in dialogue across differences. . . .

In extreme cases, members of privileged groups can erase the very presence of the less privileged. When I first moved to Cincinnati, my family and I went on a picnic at a local park. Picnicking next to us was a family of White Appalachians. When I went to push my daughter on the swings, several of the children came over. They had missing, yellowed and broken teeth, they wore old clothing and their poverty was evident. I was shocked. Growing up in a large eastern city, I had never seen such awful poverty among Whites. The segregated neighborhoods in which I grew up made White poverty all but invisible. More importantly, the privileges attached to my newly acquired social class position allowed me to ignore and minimize the poverty among Whites that I did encounter. My reactions to those children made me realize how confining phrases such as "well, at least they're not Black," had become

for me. In learning to grant human subjectivity to the Black victims of poverty, I had simultaneously learned to demand White victims of poverty. By applying categories of race to the objective conditions confronting me, I was quantifying and ranking oppressions and missing the very real suffering which, in fact, is the real issue.

One common pattern of relationships across differences in power is one that I label "voyeurism." From the perspective of the privileged, the lives of people of color, of the poor, and of women are interesting for their entertainment value. The privileged become voyeurs, passive onlookers who do not relate to the less powerful, but who are interested in seeing how the "different" live. Over the years, I have heard numerous African-American students complain about professors who never call on them except when a so-called Black issue is being discussed. The students' interest in discussing race or qualifications for doing so appear unimportant to the professor's efforts to use Black students' experiences as stories to make the material come alive for the White student audience. Asking Black students to perform on cue and provide a Black experience for their White classmates can be seen as voyeurism at its worst.

Members of subordinate groups do not willingly participate in such exchanges but often do so because members of dominant groups control the institutional and symbolic apparatuses of oppression. Racial/ethnic groups, women, and the poor have never had the luxury of being voyeurs of the lives of the privileged. Our ability to survive in hostile settings has hinged on our ability to learn intricate details about the behavior and world view of the powerful and adjust our behavior accordingly. I need only point to the difference in perception of those men and women in abusive relationships. Where men can view their girlfriends and wives as sex objects, helpmates and a collection of stereotypes categories of voyeurism—women must be attuned to every nuance of their partners' behavior. Are women "naturally" better in relating to people with more power than themselves, or have circumstances mandated that men and women develop different skills? . . .

Coming from a tradition where most relationships across difference are squarely rooted in relations of domination and subordination, we have much less experience relating to people as different but equal. The classroom is potentially one powerful and safe space where dialogues among individuals of unequal power relationships can occur. . . .

2. COALITIONS AROUND COMMON CAUSES

A second issue in building relationships and coalitions essential for social change concerns knowing the real reasons for coalition. Just what brings people together? One powerful catalyst fostering group solidarity is the presence of a common enemy. African-American, Hispanic, Asian-American, and women's studies all share the common intellectual heritage of challenging what passes for certified knowledge in the academy. But politically expedient relationships and coalitions like these are fragile because, as June Jordan points out:

> It occurs to me that much organizational grief could be avoided if people understood that partnership in misery does not necessarily provide for partnership for change: When we get the monsters off our backs all of us may want to run in very different directions (1985, 47).

Sharing a common cause assists individuals and groups in maintaining relationships that transcend their differences. Building effective coalitions involves struggling to hear one another and developing empathy for each other's points of view. The coalitions that I have been involved in that lasted and that worked have been those where commitment to a specific issue mandated collaboration as the best strategy for addressing the issue at hand.

. . .

. . . None of us alone has a comprehensive vision of how race, class and gender operate as categories of analysis or how they might be used as categories of connection. Our personal biographies offer us partial views. Few of us can manage to study race, class and gender simultaneously. Instead, we each know more about some dimensions of this larger story and less about others. . . . Just as the members of the school had special skills to offer to the task of building the school, we have areas of specialization and expertise, whether scholarly, theoretical, pedagogical or within areas of race, class or gender. We do not all have to do the same thing in the same way. Instead, we must support each other's efforts, realizing that they are all part of the larger enterprise of bringing about social change.

3. BUILDING EMPATHY

A third issue involved in building the types of relationships and coalitions essential for social change concerns the issue of individual accountability. Race, class and gender oppression form the structural backdrop against which we frame our relationship—these are the forces that encourage us to substitute voyeurism . . . for fully human relationships. But while we may not have created this situation, we are each responsible for making individual, personal choices concerning which elements of race, class and gender oppression we will accept and which we will work to change.

One essential component of this accountability involves developing empathy for the experiences of individuals and groups different than ourselves. Empathy begins with taking an interest in the facts of other people['s] lives, both as individuals and as groups. If you care about me, you should want to know not only the details of my personal biography but a sense of how race, class and gender as categories of analysis created the institutional and symbolic backdrop for my personal biography. How can you hope to assess my character without knowing the details of the circumstances I face?

Moreover, by taking a theoretical stance that we have all been affected by race, class and gender as categories of analysis that have structured our treatment, we open up possibilities for using those same constructs as categories of connection in building empathy. For example, I have a good White woman friend with whom I share common interests and beliefs. But we know that our racial differences have provided us with different experiences. So we talk about them. We do not assume that because I am Black, race has only affected me and not her or that because I am a Black woman, race neutralizes the effect of gender in my life while accenting it in hers. We take those same categories of analysis that have created cleavages in our lives, in this case, categories of race and gender, and use them as categories of connection in building empathy for each other's experiences.

Finding common causes and building empathy is difficult, no matter which side of privilege we inhabit. Building empathy from the dominant side of privilege is difficult, simply because individuals from privileged backgrounds are not encouraged to do so. For example, in order for those of you who are White to develop empathy for the experiences of people of color, you must grapple with how your white skin has privileged you. This is difficult to do, because it not only entails the intellectual process of seeing how whiteness is elevated in institutions and symbols, but it also involves the often painful process of seeing how your whiteness has shaped your personal biography. Intellectual stances against the institutional and symbolic dimensions of racism are generally easier to maintain than sustained self-reflection about how racism has shaped all of our individual biographies. Were and are your fathers, uncles, and grandfathers really more capable than mine, or can their accomplishments be explained in part by the racism members of my family experienced? Did your

mothers stand silently by and watch all this happen? More importantly, how have they passed on the benefits of their whiteness to you?

These are difficult questions, and I have tremendous respect for my colleagues and students who are trying to answer them. Since there is no compelling reason to examine the source and meaning of one's own privilege, I know that those who do so have freely chosen this stance. They are making conscious efforts to root out the piece of the oppressor planted within them. To me, they are entitled to the support of people of color in their efforts. Men who declare themselves feminists, members of the middle class who ally themselves with anti-poverty struggles, heterosexuals who support gays and lesbians, are all trying to grow, and their efforts place them far ahead of the majority who never think of engaging in such important struggles.

Building empathy from the subordinate side of privilege is also difficult, but for different reasons. Members of subordinate groups are understandably reluctant to abandon a basic mistrust of members of powerful groups because this basic mistrust has traditionally been central to their survival. As a Black woman, it would be foolish for me to assume that White women, or Black men, or White men or any other group with a history of exploiting African-American women have my best interests at heart. These groups enjoy varying amounts of privilege over me and therefore I must carefully watch them and be prepared for a relation of domination and subordination.

Like the privileged, members of subordinate groups must also work toward replacing judgments by category with new ways of thinking and acting. Refusing to do so stifles prospects for effective coalition and social change. Let me use another example from my own experiences. When I was an undergraduate, I had little time or patience for the theorizing of the privileged. My initial years at a private, elite institution were difficult, not because the course work was challenging (it was, but that wasn't what distracted me) or because I had to work while my classmates lived on family allowances (I was used to work). The adjustment was difficult because I was surrounded by so many people who took their privilege for granted. Most of them felt entitled to their wealth. That astounded me.

I remember one incident of watching a White woman down the hall in my dormitory try to pick out which sweater to wear. The sweaters were piled up on her bed in all the colors of the rainbow, sweater after sweater. She asked my advice in a way that let me know that choosing a sweater was one of the most important decisions she had to make on a daily basis. Standing knee-deep in her sweaters, I realized how different our lives were. She did not have to worry about maintaining a solid academic average so that she could receive financial aid. Because she was in the majority, she was not treated as a representative of her race. She did not have to consider how her classroom comments or basic existence on campus contributed to the treatment her group would receive. Her allowance protected her from having to work, so she was free to spend her time studying, partying, or in her case, worrying about which sweater to wear. The degree of inequality in our lives and her unquestioned sense of entitlement concerning that inequality offended me. For a while, I categorized all affluent White women as being superficial, arrogant, overly concerned with material possessions, and part of my problem. But had I continued to classify people in this way, I would have missed out on making some very good friends whose discomfort with their inherited or acquired social class privileges pushed them to examine their position.

Since I opened with the words of Audre Lorde, it seems appropriate to close with another of her ideas. . . .

Each of us is called upon to take a stand. So in these days ahead, as we examine ourselves and each other, our works, our fears, our differences, our sisterhood and survivals, I urge you to tackle what is most difficult for us all, self-scrutiny of our complacencies, the idea that since each of us believes she is on the side of right, she need not examine her position (1985).

I urge you to examine your position.

REFERENCES

Butler, Johnnella. 1989. "Difficult Dialogues." *The Women's Review of Books* 6, no. 5.

Collins, Patricia Hill. 1989. "The Social Construction of Black Feminist Thought." *Signs.* Summer 1989.

Harding, Sandra. 1986. *The Science Question in Feminism.* Ithaca, New York: Cornell University Press.

Gwaltney, John Langston. 1980. *Drylongso: A Self-Portrait of Black America.* New York: Vintage.

Lorde, Audre. 1984. *Sister Outsider.* Trumansberg, New York: The Crossing Press.

———. 1985 "Sisterhood and Survival." Keynote address, conference on the Black Woman Writer and the Diaspora, Michigan State University.

Jordan, June. 1985. *On Call: Political Essays.* Boston: South End Press.

Spelman, Elizabeth. 1982. "Theories of Race and Gender: The Erasure of Black Women." *Quest* 5: 36–32.

Tate, Claudia, ed. 1983. *Black Women Writers at Work.* New York: Continuum.

Oppression

Marilyn Frye

It is a fundamental claim of feminism that women are oppressed. The word 'oppression' is a strong word. It repels and attracts. It is dangerous and dangerously fashionable and endangered. It is much misused, and sometimes not innocently.

The statement that women are oppressed is frequently met with the claim that men are oppressed too. We hear that oppressing is oppressive to those who oppress as well as to those they oppress. Some men cite as evidence of their oppression their much-advertised inability to cry. It is tough, we are told, to be masculine. When the stresses and frustrations of being a man are cited as evidence that oppressors are oppressed by their oppressing; the word 'oppression' is being stretched to meaninglessness; it is treated as though its scope includes any and all human experience of limitation or suffering, no matter the cause, degree or consequence. Once such usage has been put over on us, then if ever we deny that any person or group is oppressed, we seem to imply that we think they never suffer and have no feelings. We are accused of insensitivity; even of bigotry. For women, such accusation is particularly intimidating, since sensitivity is one of the few virtues that has been assigned to us. If we are found insensitive, we may fear we have no redeeming traits at all and perhaps are not real women. Thus are we silenced before we begin: the name of our situation drained of meaning and our guilt mechanisms tripped.

But this is nonsense. Human beings can be miserable without being oppressed, and it is perfectly consistent to deny that a person or group is oppressed without denying that they have feelings or that they suffer. . . .

The root of the word 'oppression' is the element 'press'. *The press of the crowd; pressed into military service; to press a pair of pants; printing press; press the button.* Presses are used to mold things or flatten them or reduce them in bulk, sometimes to reduce them by squeezing out the gasses or liquids in them. Something pressed is something caught between or among forces and barriers which are so related to each other that jointly they restrain, restrict or prevent the thing's motion or mobility. Mold. Immobilize. Reduce.

The mundane experience of the oppressed provides another clue. One of the most characteristic and ubiquitous features of the world as experienced by oppressed people is the double bind—situations in which options are reduced to a very few and all of them expose one to penalty, censure or deprivation. For example, it is often a requirement upon oppressed people that we smile and be cheerful. If we comply, we signal our docility and our acquiescence in our situation. We need not, then, be taken note of. We acquiesce in being made invisible, in our occupying no space. We participate in our own erasure. On the other hand, anything but the sunniest countenance exposes us to being perceived as mean, bitter, angry or dangerous. This means, at the least, that we may be found "difficult" or unpleasant to work with, which is enough to cost one one's livelihood; at worst, being seen as mean, bitter, angry or dangerous has been known to result in rape, arrest, beating and murder. One can only choose to risk one's preferred form and rate of annihilation.

Another example: It is common in the United States that women, especially younger women, are in a bind where neither sexual activity nor sexual inactivity is all right. If she is heterosexually active, a woman is open to censure and punishment for being loose, unprincipled or a whore. The "punishment" comes in the form of criticism, snide and embarrassing remarks, being treated as an easy lay by men, scorn from her more restrained female friends. She may have to lie and hide her behavior from her parents. She must juggle the risks of unwanted pregnancy and dangerous contraceptives. On the other hand, if she refrains from heterosexual activity, she is fairly constantly harassed by men who try to persuade her into it and pressure her to "relax" and "let her hair down"; she is threatened with labels like "frigid," "uptight," "man-hater," "bitch" and "cocktease." The same parents who would be disapproving of her sexual activity may be worried by her inactivity because it suggests she is not or will not be popular, or is not sexually normal. She may be charged with lesbianism. If a woman is raped, then if she has been heterosexually active she is subject to the presumption that she liked it (since her activity is presumed to show that she likes sex), and if she has not been heterosexually active, she is subject to the presumption that she liked it (since she is supposedly "repressed and frustrated"). Both heterosexual activity and heterosexual nonactivity are likely to be taken as proof that you wanted to be raped, and hence, of course, weren't *really* raped at all. You can't win. You are caught in a bind, caught between systematically related pressures.

Women are caught like this, too, by networks of forces and barriers that expose one to penalty, loss or contempt whether one works outside the home or not, is on welfare or not, bears children or not, raises children or not, marries or not, stays married or not, is heterosexual, lesbian, both or neither. Economic necessity; confinement to racial and/or sexual job ghettos; sexual harassment; sex discrimination; pressures of competing expectations and judgments about *women, wives* and *mothers* (in the society at large, in racial and ethnic subcultures and in one's own mind); dependence (full or partial) on husbands, parents or the state; commitment to political ideas; loyalties to racial or ethnic or other "minority" groups; the demands of self-respect and responsibilities to others. Each of these factors exists in complex tension with every other, penalizing or prohibiting all of the apparently available options. And nipping at one's heels, always, is the endless pack of little things. If one dresses one way, one is subject to the assumption that one is advertising one's sexual availability; if one dresses another way, one appears to "not care about oneself" or to be "unfeminine." If one uses "strong language," one invites categorization as a whore or slut; if one does not, one invites categorization as a "lady"—one too delicately constituted to cope with robust speech or the realities to which it presumably refers.

The experience of oppressed people is that the living of one's life is confined and shaped by forces and barriers which are not accidental or occasional and hence avoidable, but are systematically related to each other in such a way as to catch one between and among them and restrict or penalize motion in any direction. It is the experience of being caged in: all avenues, in every direction, are blocked or booby trapped.

Cages. Consider a birdcage. If you look very closely at just one wire in the cage, you cannot see the other wires. If your conception of what is before you is determined by this myopic focus, you could look at that one wire, up and down the length of it, and be unable to see why a bird would not just fly around the wire any time it wanted to go somewhere. Furthermore, even if, one day at a time, you myopically inspected each wire, you still could not see why a bird would have trouble going past the wires to get anywhere. There is no physical property of any one wire, *nothing* that the closest scrutiny could discover, that will reveal how a bird could be inhibited or harmed by it except in the most accidental way. It is only when you step back, stop looking at the wires one by one, microscopically, and take a macroscopic view of the whole cage, that you can see why the bird does not go anywhere; and then you will see it in a moment. It will require no great subtlety of mental powers. It is perfectly *obvious* that the bird is surrounded by a network of systematically related barriers, no one of which would be the least hindrance to its flight, but which, by their relations to each other, are as confining as the solid walls of a dungeon.

It is now possible to grasp one of the reasons why oppression can be hard to see and recognize: one can study the elements of an oppressive structure with great care and some good will without seeing the structure as a whole, and hence without seeing or being able to understand that one is looking at a cage and that there are people there who are caged, whose motion and mobility are restricted, whose lives are shaped and reduced.

. . .

As the cageness of the birdcage is a macroscopic phenomenon, the oppressiveness of the situations in which women live our various and different lives is a macroscopic phenomenon. Neither can be *seen* from a microscopic perspective. But when you look macroscopically you can see it—a network of forces and barriers which are systematically related and which conspire to the immobilization, reduction and molding of women and the lives we live.

READING 10

Gender Stereotyping in the English Language

Laurel Richardson

Everyone in our society, regardless of class, ethnicity, sex, age, or race, is exposed to the same language, the language of the dominant culture. Analysis of verbal language can tell us a great deal about a people's fears, prejudices, anxieties, and interests. A rich vocabulary on a particular subject indicates societal interests or obsessions (e.g., the extensive vocabulary about cars in America). And different words for the same subject (such as *freedom fighter* and *terrorist, passed away* and *croaked, make love* and *ball*) show that there is a range of attitudes and feelings in the society toward that subject.

It should not be surprising, then, to find differential attitudes and feelings about men and women rooted in the English language. Although the English language has not been completely analyzed, six general propositions concerning these attitudes and feelings about males and females can be made.

First, in terms of grammatical and semantic structure, women do not have a fully autonomous, independent existence; they are part of man. The language is not divided into male and female with distinct conjugations and declensions, as many other languages are. Rather, *women* are included under the generic *man.* Grammar books specify that the pronoun *he* can be used generically to mean *he* or *she.* Further, *man,* when used as an indefinite pronoun, grammatically refers to both men and women. So, for example, when we read *man* in the following phrases we are to interpret it as applying to both men and women: "man the oars," "one small step for man, one giant step for mankind," "man, that's tough," "man overboard," "man the toolmaker," "alienated man," "garbageman." Our rules of etiquette complete the grammatical presumption of inclusivity. When two persons are pronounced "man and wife," Miss Susan Jones changes her entire name to Mrs. Robert Gordon (Vanderbilt, 1972). In each of these correct usages, women are a part of man; they do not exist autonomously. The exclusion of women is well expressed in Mary Daly's ear-jarring slogan "the sisterhood of man" (1973:7–21).

However, there is some question as to whether the theory that *man* means everybody is carried out in practice (see Bendix, 1979; Martyna, 1980). For example, an eight-year-old interrupts her reading of "The Story of the Cavemen" to ask how we got here without cavewomen. A ten-year-old thinks it is dumb to have a woman post*man.* A beginning anthropology student believes (incorrectly) that all shamans ("witch doctors") are males because her textbook and professor use the referential pronoun *he.*

But beginning language learners are not the only ones who visualize males when they see the word *man.* Research has consistently demonstrated that when the generic *man* is used, people visualize men, not women (Schneider & Hacker, 1973; DeStefano, 1976; Martyna, 1978; Hamilton & Henley, 1982). DeStefano, for example, reports that college students choose silhouettes of males for sentences with the word *man* or *men* in them. Similarly, the presumably generic *he* elicits images of men rather than women. The finding is so persistent that linguists doubt whether there actually is a semantic generic in English (MacKay, 1983).

Man, then, suggests not humanity but rather male images. Moreover, over one's lifetime, an educated American will be exposed to the prescriptive *he* more than a million times (MacKay, 1983). One consequence is the exclusion of women in the visualization, imagination, and thought of males and females. Most likely this linguistic practice perpetuates in men their feelings of dominance over and responsibility for women, feelings that interfere with the development of equality in relationships.

Second, in actual practice, our pronoun usage perpetuates different personality attributes and career aspirations for men and women. Nurses, secretaries, and elementary school teachers are almost invariably referred to as *she;* doctors, engineers, electricians, and presidents as *he.* In one classroom, students referred to an unidentified child as *he* but shifted to *she* when discussing the child's parent. In a faculty discussion of the problems of acquiring new staff, all architects, engineers, security officers, faculty, and computer programmers were referred to as

he; secretaries and file clerks were referred to as *she.* Martyna (1978) has noted that speakers consistently use *he* when the referent has a high-status occupation (e.g., doctor, lawyer, judge) but shift to *she* when the occupations have lower status (e.g., nurse, secretary).

Even our choice of sex ascription to nonhuman objects subtly reinforces different personalities for males and females. It seems as though the small (e.g., kittens), the graceful (e.g., poetry), the unpredictable (e.g., the fates), the nurturant (e.g., the church, the school), and that which is owned and/or controlled by men (e.g., boats, cars, governments, nations) represent the feminine, whereas that which is a controlling forceful power in and of itself (e.g., God, Satan, tiger) primarily represents the masculine. Even athletic teams are not immune. In one college, the men's teams are called the Bearcats and the women's teams the Bearkittens.

Some of you may wonder whether it matters that the female is linguistically included in the male. The inclusion of women under the pseudogeneric *man* and the prescriptive *he,* however, is not a trivial issue. Language has tremendous power to shape attitudes and influence behavior. Indeed, MacKay (1983) argues that the prescriptive *he* "has all the characteristics of a highly effective propaganda technique": frequent repetition, early age of acquisition (before age 6), covertness (*he* is not thought of as propaganda), use by high-prestige sources (including university texts and professors), and indirectness (presented as though it were a matter of common knowledge). As a result, the prescriptive affects females' sense of life options and feelings of well-being. For example, Adamsky (1981) found that women's sense of power and importance was enhanced when the prescriptive *he* was replaced by *she.*

Awareness of the impact of the generic *man* and prescriptive *he* has generated considerable activity to change the language. One change, approved by the Modern Language Association, is to replace the prescriptive *he* with the plural *they*—as was accepted practice before the 18th century. Another is the use of *he or she*. Although it sounds awkward at first, the *he or she* designation is increasingly being used in the media and among people who have recognized the power of the pronoun to perpetuate sex stereotyping. When a professor, for example, talks about "the lawyer" as "he or she," a speech pattern that counteracts sex stereotyping is modeled. This drive to neutralize the impact of pronouns is evidenced further in the renaming of occupations: a policeman is now a police officer, a postman is a mail carrier, a stewardess is a flight attendant.

Third, linguistic practice defines females as immature, incompetent, and incapable and males as mature, complete, and competent. Because the words *man* and *woman* tend to connote sexual and human maturity, common speech, organizational titles, public addresses, and bathroom doors frequently designate the women in question as *ladies*. Simply contrast the different connotations of *lady* and *woman* in the following common phrases:

Luck, be a lady (woman) tonight.
Barbara's a little lady (woman).
Ladies' (Women's) Air Corps.

In the first two examples, the use of *lady* desexualizes the contextual meaning of *woman*. So trivializing is the use of *lady* in the last phrase that the second is wholly anomalous. The male equivalent, *lord*, is never used; and its synonym, *gentleman*, is used infrequently. When *gentleman* is used, the assumption seems to be that certain culturally condoned aspects of masculinity (e.g., aggressivity, activity, and strength) should be set aside in the interests of maturity and order, as in the following phrases:

A gentlemen's (men's) agreement.
A duel between gentlemen (men).
He's a real gentleman (man).

Rather than feeling constrained to set aside the stereotypes associated with *man*, males frequently find the opposite process occurring.

The contextual connotation of *man* places a strain on males to be continuously sexually and socially potent, as the following examples reveal:

I was not a man (gentleman) with her tonight.
This is a man's (gentleman's) job.
Be a man (gentleman).

Whether males, therefore, feel competent or anxious, valuable or worthless in particular contexts is influenced by the demands placed on them by the expectations of the language.

Not only are men infrequently labeled *gentlemen*, but they are infrequently labeled *boys*. The term *boy* is reserved for young males, bellhops, car attendants, and as a putdown to those males judged inferior. *Boy* connotes immaturity and powerlessness. Only occasionally do males "have a night out with the boys." They do not talk "boy talk" at the office. Rarely does our language legitimize carefreeness in males. Rather, they are expected, linguistically, to adopt the responsibilities of manhood.

On the other hand, women of all ages may be called *girls*. Grown females "play bridge with the girls" and indulge in "girl talk." They are encouraged to remain childlike, and the implication is that they are basically immature and without power. Men can become men, linguistically, putting aside the immaturity of childhood; indeed, for them to retain the openness and playfulness of boyhood is linguistically difficult.

Further, the presumed incompetence and immaturity of women are evidenced by the linguistic company they keep. Women are categorized with children ("women and children first"), the infirm ("the blind, the lame, the women"), and the incompetent ("women, convicts, and idiots"). The use of these categorical designations is not accidental happenstance; "rather these selectional groupings are powerful forces behind the actual expressions of language and are based on distinctions which are not regarded as trivial by the speakers of the language" (Key, 1975:82). A total language analysis of categorical groupings is not available, yet it seems likely that women tend to be included in groupings that designate incompleteness, ineptitude, and immaturity. On the other hand, it is difficult for us to conceive of the word *man* in any categorical grouping other than one that extends beyond humanity, such as "Man, apes, and angels" or "Man and Superman." That is, men do exist as an independent category capable of autonomy; women are grouped with the stigmatized, the immature, and the foolish. Moreover, when men are in human groupings, males are invariably first on the list ("men and women," "he and she," "man and wife"). This order is not accidental but was prescribed in the 16th century to honor the worthier party.

Fourth, in practice women are defined in terms of their sexual desirability (to men); men are defined in terms of their sexual prowess (over women). Most slang words in reference to women refer to their sexual desirability to men (e.g., *dog, fox, broad, ass, chick*). Slang about men refers to their sexual prowess over women (e.g., *dude, stud, hunk*). The fewer examples given for men is not an oversight. An analysis of sexual slang, for example, listed more than 1,000 words and phrases that derogate women sexually but found "nowhere near this multitude for describing men" (Kramarae, 1975:72). Farmer and Henley (cited in Schulz, 1975) list 500 synonyms for *prostitute,* for example, and only 65 for *whoremonger.* Stanley (1977) reports 220 terms for a sexually promiscuous woman and only 22 for a sexually promiscuous man. Shuster (1973) reports that the passive verb form is used in reference to women's sexual experiences (e.g., *to be laid, to be had, to be taken*), whereas the active tense is used in reference to the male's sexual experience (e.g., *lay, take, have*). Being sexually attractive to males is culturally condoned for women and being sexually powerful is approved for males. In this regard, the slang of the street is certainly not countercultural; rather it perpetuates and reinforces different expectations in females and males as sexual objects and performers.

Further, we find sexual connotations associated with neutral words applied to women. A few examples should suffice. A male academician questioned the title of a new course, asserting it was "too suggestive." The title? "The Position of Women in the Social Order." A male tramp is simply a hobo, but a female tramp is a slut. And consider the difference in connotation of the following expressions:

It's easy.
He's easy.
She's easy.

In the first, we assume something is "easy to do"; in the second, we might assume a professor is an "easy grader" or a man is "easygoing." But when we read "she's easy," the connotation is "she's an easy lay."

In the world of slang, men are defined by their sexual prowess. In the world of slang and proper speech, women are defined as sexual objects. The rule in practice seems to be: If in doubt, assume that *any* reference to a woman has a sexual connotation. For both genders, the constant bombardment of prescribed sexuality is bound to have real consequences.

Fifth, women are defined in terms of their relations to men; men are defined in terms of their relations to the world at large. A good example is seen in the words *master* and *mistress.* Originally these words had the same meaning—"a person who holds power over servants." With the demise of the feudal system, however, these words took on different meanings. The masculine variant metaphorically refers to power over something; as in "He is the master of his trade"; the feminine variant metaphorically (although probably not in actuality) refers to power over a man sexually, as in "She is Tom's mistress." Men are defined in terms of their power in the occupational world, women in terms of their sexual power over men.

The existence of two contractions for Mistress (*Miss* and *Mrs.*) and but one for Mister (*Mr.*) underscores the cultural concern and linguistic practice: women are defined in relation to men. Even a divorced woman is defined in terms of her no-longer-existing relation to a man (she is still *Mrs. Man's Name*). But apparently the divorced state is not relevant enough to the man or to the society to require a label. A divorced woman is a *divorcee,* but what do you call a divorced man? The recent preference of many women to be called *Ms.* is an attempt to provide for women an equivalency title that is not dependent on marital status.

Sixth, a historical pattern can be seen in the meanings that come to be attached to words that originally were neutral: those that apply to women acquire obscene and/or debased connotations but no such pattern of derogation holds for neutral words referring to men. The processes of *pejoration* (the acquiring of an obscene or debased connotation) and *amelioration* (the reacquiring of a neutral or positive connotation) in the English language in regard to terms for males and females have been studied extensively by Muriel Schulz (1975).

Leveling is the least derogative form of pejoration. Through leveling, titles that originally referred to an elite class of persons come to include a wider class of persons. Such democratic leveling is more common for female designates than for males. For example, contrast the following: *lord–lady (lady); baronet–dame (dame); governor–governess (governess).*

Most frequently what happens to words designating women as they become pejorated, however, is that they come to denote or connote sexual wantonness. *Sir* and *mister,* for example, remain titles of courtesy, but at some time *madam, miss,* and *mistress* have come to designate, respectively, a brothelkeeper, a prostitute, and an unmarried sexual partner of a male (Schulz, 1975:66).

Names for domestic helpers, if they are females, are frequently derogated. *Hussy,* for example, originally meant "housewife." *Laundress, needlewoman, spinster* ("tender of the spinning wheel"), and *nurse* all referred to domestic occupations within the home, and all at some point became slang expressions for prostitute or mistress.

Even kinship terms referring to women become denigrated. During the 17th century, *mother* was used to mean "a bawd"; more recently *mother* (*mothuh f——*) has become a common derogatory epithet (Cameron, 1974). Probably at some point in history every kinship term for females has been derogated (Schulz, 1975:66).

Terms of endearment for women also seem to follow a downward path. Such pet names as Tart, Dolly, Kitty, Polly, Mopsy, Biddy, and Jill all eventually became sexually derogatory (Schulz, 1975:67). *Whore* comes from the same Latin root as *care* and once meant "a lover of either sex."

Indeed, even the most neutral categorical designations—*girl, female, woman, lady*—at some point in their history have been used to connote sexual immorality. *Girl* originally meant "a child of either sex"; through the process of semantic degeneration it eventually meant "a prostitute." Although *girl* has lost this meaning, *girlie* still retains sexual connotations. *Woman* connoted "a mistress" in the early 19th century; *female* was a degrading epithet in the latter part of the 19th century; and when *lady* was introduced as a euphemism, it too became deprecatory. "even so neutral a term as *person,* when it was used as substitute for *woman,* suffered [vulgarization]" (Mencken, 1963: 350, quoted in Schulz, 1975:71).

Whether one looks at elite titles, occupational roles, kinship relationships, endearments, or age-sex categorical designations, the pattern is clear. Terms referring to females are pejorated—"become negative in the middle instances and abusive in the extremes" (Schulz, 1975:69). Such semantic derogation, however, is not evidenced for male referents. *Lord, baronet, father, brother, nephew, footman, bowman, boy, lad, fellow, gentleman, man, male,* and so on "have failed to undergo the derogation found in the history of their corresponding feminine designations" (Schulz, 1975:67). Interestingly, the male word, rather than undergoing derogation, frequently is replaced by a female referent when the speaker wants to debase a male. A weak man, for example, is referred to as a *sissy* (diminutive of *sister*), and an army recruit during basic training is called a *pussy*. And when one is swearing at a male, he is referred to as a *bastard* or a *son-of-a-bitch*—both appellations that impugn the dignity of a man's mother.

In summary, these verbal practices are consistent with the gender stereotypes that we encounter in everyday life. Women are thought to be a part of man, nonautonomous, dependent, relegated to roles that require few skills, characteristically incompetent and immature, sexual objects, best defined in terms of their relations to men. Males are visible, autonomous and independent, responsible for the protection and containment of women, expected to occupy positions on the basis of their high achievement or physical power, assumed to be sexually potent, and defined primarily by their relations to the world of work. The use of the language perpetuates the stereotypes for both genders and limits the options available for self-definition.

REFERENCES

Adamsky, C. 1981. "Changes in pronominal usage in a classroom situation." *Psychology of Women Quarterly* 5:773–79.

Bendix, J. 1979. "Linguistic models as political symbols: Gender and the generic 'he' in English." In J. Orasanu, M. Slater, and L. L. Adler, eds., *Language, sex and gender: Does la différence make a difference?* pp. 23–42. New York: New Academy of Science Annuals.

Cameron, P. 1974. "Frequency and kinds of words in various social settings, or What the hell's going on?" In M. Truzzi, ed., *Sociology for pleasure*, pp. 31–37. Englewood Cliffs, N.J.: Prentice-Hall.

Daly, M. 1973. *Beyond God the father.* Boston: Beacon Press.

DeStefano, J. S. 1976. Personal communication. Columbus: Ohio State University.

Hamilton, N., & Henley, N. 1982. "Detrimental consequences of the generic masculine usage." Paper presented to the Western Psychological Association meetings, Sacramento.

Key, M. R. 1975. *Male/female language.* Metuchen, N.J.: Scarecrow Press.

Kramarae, Cheris. 1975. "Woman's speech: Separate but unequal?" In Barrie Thorne and Nancy Henley, eds., *Language and sex: Difference and dominance,* pp. 43–56. Rowley, Mass.: Newbury House.

MacKay, D. G. 1983. "Prescriptive grammar and the pronoun problem." In B. Thorne, C. Kramarae, and N. Henley, eds., *Language, gender, and society,* pp. 38–53. Rowley, Mass.: Newbury House.

Martyna, W. 1978. "What does 'he' mean? Use of the generic masculine." *Journal of Communication* 28:131–38.

Martyna, W. 1980. "Beyond the 'he/man' approach: The case for nonsexist language." *Signs* 5:482–93.

Mencken, H. L. 1963. *The American language.* 4th ed. with supplements. Abr. and ed. R. I. McDavis. New York: Knopf.

Schneider, J., & Hacker, S. 1973. "Sex role imagery in the use of the generic 'man' in introductory texts: A case in the sociology of sociology." *American Sociologist* 8:12–18.

Schulz, M. R. 1975. "The semantic derogation of women." In B. Thorne and N. Henley, eds., *Language and sex: Difference and dominance,* pp. 64–75. Rowley, Mass.: Newbury House.

Shuster, Janet. 1973. "Grammatical forms marked for male and female in English." Unpublished paper. Chicago: University of Chicago.

Stanley, J. P. 1977. "Paradigmatic woman: The prostitute." In D. L. Shores, ed., *Papers in language variation.* Birmingham: University of Alabama Press.

Vanderbilt, A. 1972. *Amy Vanderbilt's etiquette.* Garden City, N.Y.: Doubleday.

Homophobia
A Weapon of Sexism

Suzanne Pharr

Homophobia—the irrational fear and hatred of those who love and sexually desire those of the same sex. Though I intimately knew its meaning, the word homophobia was unknown to me until the late 1970s, and when I first heard it, I was struck by how difficult it is to say, what an ugly word it is, equally as ugly as its meaning. Like racism and anti-Semitism, it is a word that calls up images of loss of freedom, verbal and physical violence, death.

In my life I have experienced the effects of homophobia through rejection by friends, threats of loss of employment, and threats upon my life; and I have witnessed far worse things happening to other lesbian and gay people: loss of children, beatings, rape, death. Its power is great enough to keep ten to twenty percent of the population living lives of fear (if their sexual identity is hidden) or lives of danger (if their sexual identity is visible) or both. And its power is great enough to keep the remaining eighty to ninety percent of the population trapped in their own fears.

. . .

Homophobia works effectively as a weapon of sexism because it is joined with a powerful arm, heterosexism. Heterosexism creates the climate for homophobia with its assumption that the world is and must be heterosexual and its display of power and privilege as the norm. Heterosexism is the systemic display of homophobia in the institutions of society. Heterosexism and homophobia work together to enforce compulsory heterosexuality and that bastion of patriarchal power, the nuclear family. The central focus of the rightwing attack against women's liberation is that women's equality, women's self-determination, women's

control of our own bodies and lives will damage what they see as the crucial societal institution, the nuclear family. The attack has been led by fundamentalist ministers across the country. The two areas they have focused on most consistently are abortion and homosexuality, and their passion has led them to bomb women's clinics and to recommend deprogramming for homosexuals and establishing camps to quarantine people with AIDS. To resist marriage and/or heterosexuality is to risk severe punishment and loss.

It is not by chance that when children approach puberty and increased sexual awareness they begin to taunt each other by calling these names: "queer," "faggot," "pervert." It is at puberty that the full force of society's pressure to conform to heterosexuality and prepare for marriage is brought to bear. Children know what we have taught them, and we have given clear messages that those who deviate from standard expectations are to be made to get back in line. The best controlling tactic at puberty is to be treated as an outsider, to be ostracized at a time when it feels most vital to be accepted. Those who are different must be made to suffer loss. It is also at puberty that misogyny begins to be more apparent, and girls are pressured to conform to societal norms that do not permit them to realize their full potential. It is at this time that their academic achievements begin to decrease as they are coerced into compulsory heterosexuality and trained for dependency upon a man, that is, for economic survival.

There was a time when the two most condemning accusations against a woman meant to ostracize and disempower her were "whore" and "lesbian." The sexual revolution and changing attitudes about heterosexual behavior may have led to some lessening of the power of the word *whore,* though it still has strength as a threat to sexual property and prostitutes are stigmatized and abused. However, the word *lesbian* is still fully charged and carries with it the full threat of loss of power and privilege, the threat of being cut asunder, abandoned, and left outside society's protection.

To be a lesbian is to be *perceived* as someone who has stepped out of line, who has moved out of sexual/economic dependence on a male, who is woman-identified. A lesbian is perceived as someone who can live without a man, and who is therefore (however illogically) against men. A lesbian is perceived as being outside the acceptable, routinized order of things. She is seen as someone who has no societal institutions to protect her and who is not privileged to the protection of individual males. Many heterosexual women see her as someone who stands in contradiction to the sacrifices they have made to conform to compulsory heterosexuality. A lesbian is perceived as a threat to the nuclear family, to male dominance and control, to the very heart of sexism.

Gay men are perceived also as a threat to male dominance and control, and the homophobia expressed against them has the same roots in sexism as does homophobia against lesbians. Visible gay men are the objects of extreme hatred and fear by heterosexual men because their breaking ranks with male heterosexual solidarity is seen as a damaging rent in the very fabric of sexism. They are seen as betrayers, as traitors who must be punished and eliminated. In the beating and killing of gay men we see clear evidence of this hatred. When we see the fierce homophobia expressed toward gay men, we can begin to understand the ways sexism also affects males through imposing rigid, dehumanizing gender roles on them. The two circumstances in which it is legitimate for men to be openly physically affectionate with one another are in competitive sports and in the crisis of war. For many men, these two

experiences are the highlights of their lives, and they think of them again and again with nostalgia. War and sports offer a cover of all-male safety and dominance to keep away the notion of affectionate openness being identified with homosexuality. When gay men break ranks with male roles through bonding and affection outside the arenas of war and sports, they are perceived as not being "real men," that is, as being identified with women, the weaker sex that must be dominated and that over the centuries has been the object of male hatred and abuse. Misogyny gets transferred to gay men with a vengeance and is increased by the fear that their sexual identity and behavior will bring down the entire system of male dominance and compulsory heterosexuality.

If lesbians are established as threats to the status quo, as outcasts who must be punished, homophobia can wield its power over all women through lesbian baiting. Lesbian baiting is an attempt to control women by labeling us as lesbians because our behavior is not acceptable, that is, when we are being independent, going our own way, living whole lives, fighting for our rights, demanding equal pay, saying no to violence, being self-assertive, bonding with and loving the company of women, assuming the right to our bodies, insisting upon our own authority, making changes that include us in society's decision-making; lesbian baiting occurs when women are called lesbians because we resist male dominance and control. And it has little or nothing to do with one's sexual identity.

To be named as lesbian threatens all women, not just lesbians, with great loss. And any woman who steps out of role risks being called a lesbian. To understand how this is a threat to all women, one must understand that any woman can be called a lesbian and there is no real way she can defend herself: there is no way to credential one's sexuality. ("The Children's Hour," a Lillian Hellman play, makes this point when a student asserts two teachers are lesbians and they have no way to disprove it.) She may be married or divorced, have children, dress in the most feminine manner, have sex with men, be celibate—but there are lesbians who do all those things. *Lesbians look like all women and all women look like lesbians.* There is no guaranteed method of identification, and as we all know, sexual identity can be kept hidden. (The same is true for men. There is no way to prove their sexual identity, though many go to extremes to prove heterosexuality.) Also, women are not necessarily born lesbian. Some seem to be, but others become lesbians later in life after having lived heterosexual lives. Lesbian baiting of heterosexual women would not work if there were a definitive way to identify lesbians (or heterosexuals).

We have yet to understand clearly how sexual identity develops. And this is disturbing to some people, especially those who are determined to discover how lesbian and gay identity is formed so that they will know where to start in eliminating it. (Isn't it odd that there is so little concern about discovering the causes of heterosexuality?) There are many theories: genetic makeup, hormones, socialization, environment, etc. But there is no conclusive evidence that indicates that heterosexuality comes from one process and homosexuality from another.

We do know, however, that sexual identity can be in flux, and we know that sexual identity means more than just the gender of people one is attracted to and has sex with. To be a lesbian has as many ramifications as for a woman to be heterosexual. It is more than sex, more than just the bedroom issue many would like to make it: it is a woman-centered life with all the social interconnections that entails. Some lesbians are in long-term relationships, some in short-term ones, some date, some are celibate, some are married to men, some remain as separate as possible from men, some have children by men, some by alternative insemination, some seem "feminine" by societal standards, some "masculine," some are doctors, lawyers and ministers, some laborers, housewives and writers: what all share in common is a sexual/affec-

tional identity that focuses on women in its attractions and social relationships.

If lesbians are simply women with a particular sexual identity who look and act like all women, then the major difference in living out a lesbian sexual identity as opposed to a heterosexual identity is that as lesbians we live in a homophobic world that threatens and imposes damaging loss on us for being *who we are,* for choosing to live whole lives. Homophobic people often assert that homosexuals have the choice of not being homosexual; that is, we don't have to act out our sexual identity. In that case, I want to hear heterosexuals talk about their willingness not to act out their sexual identity, including not just sexual activity but heterosexual social interconnections and heterosexual privilege. It is a question of wholeness. It is very difficult for one to be denied the life of a sexual being, whether expressed in sex or in physical affection, and to feel complete, whole. For our loving relationships with humans feed the life of the spirit and enable us to overcome our basic isolation and to be interconnected with humankind.

. . .

What does a woman have to do to get called a lesbian? Almost anything, sometimes nothing at all, but certainly anything that threatens the status quo, anything that steps out of role, anything that asserts the rights of women, anything that doesn't indicate submission and subordination. Assertiveness, standing up for oneself, asking for more pay, better working conditions, training for and accepting a nontraditional (you mean a man's?) job, enjoying the company of women, being financially independent, being in control of one's life, depending first and foremost upon oneself, thinking that one can do whatever needs to be done, but above all, working for the rights and equality of women.

In the backlash to the gains of the women's liberation movement, there has been an increased effort to keep definitions man-centered. Therefore, to work on behalf of women must mean to work against men. To love women must mean that one hates men. A very effective attack has been made against the word *feminist* to make it a derogatory word. In current backlash usage, *feminist* equals *man-hater* which equals *lesbian*. This formula is created in the hope that women will be frightened away from their work on behalf of women. Consequently, we now have women who believe in the rights of women and work for those rights while from fear deny that they are feminists, or refuse to use the word because it is so "abrasive."

So what does one do in an effort to keep from being called a lesbian? She steps back into line, into the role that is demanded of her, tries to behave in such a way that doesn't threaten the status of men, and if she works for women's rights, she begins modifying that work. When women's organizations begin doing significant social change work, they inevitably are lesbian-baited; that is, funders or institutions or community members tell us that they can't work with us because of our "man-hating attitudes" or the presence of lesbians. We are called too strident, told we are making enemies, not doing good.

The battered women's movement has seen this kind of attack: the pressure has been to provide services only, without analysis of the causes of violence against women and strategies for ending it. To provide only services without political analysis or direct action is to be in an approved "helping" role; to analyze the causes of violence against women is to begin the work toward changing an entire system of power and control. It is when we do the latter that we are threatened with the label of man-hater or lesbian. For my politics, if a women's social change organization has not been labeled lesbian or communist, it is probably not doing significant work; it is only "making nice."

Women in many of these organizations, out of fear of all the losses we are threatened with, begin to modify our work to make it more acceptable and less threatening to the male-dominated society which we originally set out to change. The work can no longer be radical (going to the root cause of the problem) but instead must be reforming, working only on the symptoms and not the cause. Real change for women becomes thwarted and stopped. The word *lesbian* is instilled with the power to halt our work and control our lives. And we give it its power with our fear.

In my view, homophobia has been one of the major causes of the failure of the women's liberation movement to make deep and lasting change. (The other major block has been racism.) We were fierce when we set out but when threatened with the loss of heterosexual privilege, we began putting on brakes. Our best-known nationally distributed women's magazine was reluctant to print articles about lesbians, began putting a man on the cover several times a year, and writing articles about women who succeeded in a man's world. We worried about our image, our being all right, our being "real women" despite our work. Instead of talking about the elimination of sexual gender roles, we stepped back and talked about "sex role stereotyping" as the issue. Change around the edges for middleclass white women began to be talked about as successes. We accepted tokenism and integration, forgetting that equality for all women, for all people—and not just equality of white middleclass women with white men—was the goal that we could never put behind us.

But despite backlash and retreats, change is growing from within. The women's liberation movement is beginning to gain strength again because there are women who are talking about liberation for all women. We are examining sexism, racism, homophobia, classism, anti-Semitism, ageism, ableism, and imperialism, and we see everything as connected. This change in point of view represents the third wave of the women's liberation movement, a new direction that does not get mass media coverage and recognition. It has been initiated by women of color and lesbians who were marginalized or rendered invisible by the white heterosexual leaders of earlier efforts. The first wave was the 19th and early 20th century campaign for the vote; the second, beginning in the 1960s, focused on the Equal Rights Amendment and abortion rights. Consisting of predominantly white middleclass women, both failed in recognizing issues of equality and empowerment for all women. The third wave of the movement, multi-racial and multi-issued, seeks the transformation of the world for us all. We know that we won't get there until everyone gets there; that we must move forward in a great strong line, hand in hand, not just a few at a time.

We know that the arguments about homophobia originating from mental health and Biblical/religious attitudes can be settled when we look at the sexism that permeates religious and psychiatric history. The women of the third wave of the women's liberation movement know that *without the existence of sexism, there would be no homophobia.*

Finally, we know that as long as the word lesbian can strike fear in any woman's heart, then work on behalf of women can be stopped; the only successful work against sexism must include work against homophobia.

READING 12

White Privilege and Male Privilege

Peggy McIntosh

Through work to bring materials and perspectives from Women's Studies into the rest of the curriculum, I have often noticed men's unwillingness to grant that they are overprivileged in the curriculum, even though they may grant that women are disadvantaged. Denials that amount to taboos surround the subject of advantages that men gain from women's disadvantages. These denials protect male privilege from being fully recognized, acknowledged, lessened, or ended.

Thinking through unacknowledged male privilege as a phenomenon with a life of its own, I realized that since hierarchies in our society are interlocking, there was most likely a phenomenon of white privilege that was similarly denied and protected, but alive and real in its effects. As a white person, I realized I had been taught about racism as something that puts others at a disadvantage, but had been taught not to see one of its corollary aspects, white privilege, which puts me at an advantage.

I think whites are carefully taught not to recognize white privilege, as males are taught not to recognize male privilege. So I have begun in an untutored way to ask what it is like to have white privilege. This paper is a partial record of my personal observations and not a scholarly analysis. It is based on my daily experiences within my particular circumstances.

I have come to see white privilege as an invisible package of unearned assets that I can count on cashing in each day, but about which I was "meant" to remain oblivious. White privilege is like an invisible weightless knapsack of special provisions, assurances, tools, maps, guides, codebooks, passports, visas, clothes, compass, emergency gear, and blank checks.

Since I have had trouble facing white privilege, and describing its results in my life, I saw parallels here with men's reluctance to acknowledge male privilege. Only rarely will a man go beyond acknowledging that women are disadvantaged to acknowledging that men have unearned advantage, or that unearned privilege has not been good for men's development as human beings, or for society's development, or that privilege systems might ever be challenged and *changed.*

I will review here several types or layers of denial that I see at work protecting, and preventing awareness about, entrenched male privilege. Then I will draw parallels, from my own experience, with the denials that veil the facts of white privilege. Finally, I will list forty-six ordinary and daily ways in which I experience having white privilege, by contrast with my African American colleagues in the same building. This list is not intended to be generalizable. Others can make their own lists from within their own life circumstances.

Writing this paper has been difficult, despite warm receptions for the talks on which it is based.[1] For describing white privilege makes one newly accountable. As we in Women's Studies work [to] reveal male privilege and ask men to give up some of their power, so one who writes about having white privilege must ask, "Having described it, what will I do to lessen or end it?"

The denial of men's overprivileged state takes many forms in discussions of curriculum change work. Some claim that men must be central in the curriculum because they have done most of what is important or distinctive in life or in civilization. Some recognize sexism in the curriculum but deny that it makes male students seem unduly important in life. Others agree that certain *individual* thinkers are male oriented but deny that there is any *systemic* tendency in disciplinary frameworks or epistemology to overempower men as a group. Those men who do grant that male privilege takes institutionalized and embedded forms are still likely to deny that male hegemony has opened doors for them personally. Virtually all men deny that male overreward alone can explain men's centrality in all the inner sanctums of our most powerful institutions. Moreover, those few who will acknowledge that male privilege systems have overempowered them usually

end up doubting that we could dismantle these privilege systems. They may say they will work to improve women's status, in the society or in the university, but they can't or won't support the idea of lessening men's. In curricular terms, this is the point at which they say that they regret they cannot use any of the interesting new scholarship on women because the syllabus is full. When the talk turns to giving men less cultural room, even the most thoughtful and fair-minded of the men I know will tend to reflect, or fall back on, conservative assumptions about the inevitability of present gender relations and distributions of power, calling on precedent or sociobiology and psychobiology to demonstrate that male domination is natural and follows inevitably from evolutionary pressures. Others resort to arguments from "experience" or religion or social responsibility or wishing and dreaming.

After I realized, through faculty development work in Women's Studies, the extent to which men work from a base of unacknowledged privilege, I understood that much of their oppressiveness was unconscious. Then I remembered the frequent charges from women of color that white women whom they encounter are oppressive. I began to understand why we are justly seen as oppressive, even when we don't see ourselves that way. At the very least, obliviousness of one's privileged state can make a person or group irritating to be with. I began to count the ways in which I enjoy unearned skin privilege and have been conditioned into oblivion about its existence, unable to see that it put me "ahead" in any way, or put my people ahead, overrewarding us and yet also paradoxically damaging us, or that it could or should be changed.

My schooling gave me no training in seeing myself as an oppressor, as an unfairly advantaged person, or as a participant in a damaged culture. I was taught to see myself as an individual whose moral state depended on her individual moral will. At school, we were not taught about slavery in any depth; we were not taught to see slaveholders as damaged people. Slaves were seen as the only group at risk of being dehumanized. My schooling followed the pattern which Elizabeth Minnich has pointed out: whites are taught to think of their lives as morally neutral, normative, and average, and also ideal, so that when we work to benefit others, this is seen as work that will allow "them" to be more like "us." I think many of us know how obnoxious this attitude can be in men.

After frustration with men who would not recognize male privilege, I decided to try to work on myself at least by identifying some of the daily effects of white privilege in my life. It is crude work, at this stage, but I will give here a list of special circumstances and conditions I experience that I did not earn but that I have been made to feel are mine by birth, by citizenship, and by virtue of being a conscientious law-abiding "normal" person of goodwill. I have chosen those conditions that I think in my case *attach somewhat more to skin-color privilege* than to class, religion, ethnic status, or geographical location, though these other privileging factors are intricately intertwined. As far as I can see, my Afro-American co-workers, friends, and acquaintances with whom I come into daily or frequent contact in this particular time, place, and line of work cannot count on most of these conditions.

1. I can, if I wish, arrange to be in the company of people of my race most of the time.
2. I can avoid spending time with people whom I was trained to mistrust and who have learned to mistrust my kind or me.
3. If I should need to move, I can be pretty sure of renting or purchasing housing in an area which I can afford and in which I would want to live.
4. I can be reasonably sure that my neighbors in such a location will be neutral or pleasant to me.
5. I can go shopping alone most of the time, fairly well assured that I will not be followed or harassed by store detectives.

6. I can turn on the television or open to the front page of the paper and see people of my race widely and positively represented.
7. When I am told about our national heritage or about "civilization," I am shown that people of my color made it what it is.
8. I can be sure that my children will be given curricular materials that testify to the existence of their race.
9. If I want to, I can be pretty sure of finding a publisher for this piece on white privilege.
10. I can be fairly sure of having my voice heard in a group in which I am the only member of my race.
11. I can be casual about whether or not to listen to another woman's voice in a group in which she is the only member of her race.
12. I can go into a book shop and count on finding the writing of my race represented, into a supermarket and find the staple foods that fit with my cultural traditions, into a hairdresser's shop and find someone who can deal with my hair.
13. Whether I use checks, credit cards, or cash, I can count on my skin color not to work against the appearance that I am financially reliable.
14. I could arrange to protect our young children most of the time from people who might not like them.
15. I did not have to educate our children to be aware of systemic racism for their own daily physical protection.
16. I can be pretty sure that my children's teachers and employers will tolerate them if they fit school and workplace norms; my chief worries about them do not concern others' attitudes toward their race.
17. I can talk with my mouth full and not have people put this down to my color.
18. I can swear, or dress in secondhand clothes, or not answer letters, without having people attribute these choices to the bad morals, the poverty, or the illiteracy of my race.

19. I can speak in public to a powerful male group without putting my race on trial.

20. I can do well in a challenging situation without being called a credit to my race.

21. I am never asked to speak for all the people of my racial group.

22. I can remain oblivious to the language and customs of persons of color who constitute the world's majority without feeling in my culture any penalty for such oblivion.

23. I can criticize our government and talk about how much I fear its policies and behavior without being seen as a cultural outsider.

24. I can be reasonably sure that if I ask to talk to "the person in charge," I will be facing a person of my race.

25. If a traffic cop pulls me over or if the IRS audits my tax return, I can be sure I haven't been singled out because of my race.

26. I can easily buy posters, postcards, picture books, greeting cards, dolls, toys, and children's magazines featuring people of my race.

27. I can go home from most meetings of organizations I belong to feeling somewhat tied in, rather than isolated, out of place, outnumbered, unheard, held at a distance, or feared.

28. I can be pretty sure than an argument with a colleague of another race is more likely to jeopardize her chances for advancement than to jeopardize mine.

29. I can be fairly sure that if I argue for the promotion of a person of another race, or a program centering on race, this is not likely to cost me heavily within my present setting, even if my colleagues disagree with me.

30. If I declare there is a racial issue at hand, or there isn't a racial issue at hand, my race will lend me more credibility for either position than a person of color will have.

31. I can choose to ignore developments in minority writing and minority activist programs, or disparage them, or learn from them, but in any case, I can find ways to be more or less protected from negative consequences of any of these choices.

32. My culture gives me little fear about ignoring the perspectives and powers of people of other races.

33. I am not made acutely aware that my shape, bearing, or body odor will be taken as a reflection on my race.

34. I can worry about racism without being seen as self-interested or self-seeking.

35. I can take a job with an affirmative action employer without having my co-workers on the job suspect that I got it because of my race.

36. If my day, week, or year is going badly, I need not ask of each negative episode or situation whether it has racial overtones.

37. I can be pretty sure of finding people who would be willing to talk with me and advise me about my next steps, professionally.

38. I can think over many options, social, political, imaginative, or professional, without asking whether a person of my race would be accepted or allowed to do what I want to do.

39. I can be late to a meeting without having the lateness reflect on my race.

40. I can choose public accommodation without fearing that people of my race cannot get in or will be mistreated in the places I have chosen.

41. I can be sure that if I need legal or medical help, my race will not work against me.

42. I can arrange my activities so that I will never have to experience feelings of rejection owing to my race.

43. If I have low credibility as a leader, I can be sure that my race is not the problem.

44. I can easily find academic courses and institutions that give attention only to people of my race.

45. I can expect figurative language and imagery in all of the arts to testify to experiences of my race.

46. I can choose blemish cover or bandages in "flesh" color and have them more or less match my skin.

I repeatedly forgot each of the realizations on this list until I wrote it down. For me, white privilege has turned out to be an elusive and fugitive subject. The pressure to avoid it is great, for in facing it I must give up the myth of meritocracy. If these things are true, this is not such a free country; one's life is not what one makes it; many doors open for certain people through no virtues of their own. These perceptions mean also that my moral condition is not what I had been led to believe. The appearance of being a good citizen rather than a trouble-maker comes in large part from having all sorts of doors open automatically because of my color.

A further paralysis of nerve comes from literary silence protecting privilege. My clearest memories of finding such analysis are in Lillian Smith's unparalleled *Killers of the Dream* and Margaret Andersen's review of Karen and Mamie Fields' *Lemon Swamp*. Smith, for example, wrote about walking toward black children on the street and knowing they would step into the gutter; Andersen contrasted the pleasure that she, as a white child, took on summer driving trips to the south with Karen Fields' memories of driving in a closed car stocked with all necessities lest, in stopping, her black family should suffer "insult, or worse." Adrienne Rich also recognizes and writes about daily experiences of privilege, but in my observation, white women's writing in this area is far more often on systemic racism than on our daily lives as light-skinned women.[2]

In unpacking this invisible knapsack of white privilege, I have listed conditions of daily experience that I once took for granted, as neutral, normal, and universally available to everybody, just as I once thought of a male-focused curriculum as the neutral or accurate account that can speak for all. Nor did I think of any of these perquisites as bad for the holder. I now think that we need a more finely differentiated taxonomy of privilege, for some of these varieties are only what one would want for everyone in a just society, and others give license to be ignorant, oblivious, arrogant, and destructive. Before proposing some more finely tuned categorization, I will make some observations about the general effects of these conditions on my life and expectations.

In this potpourri of examples, some privileges make me feel at home in the world. Others allow me to escape penalties or dangers that others suffer. Through some, I escape fear, anxiety, insult, injury, or a sense of not being welcome, not being real. Some keep me from having to hide, to be in disguise, to feel sick or crazy, to negotiate each transaction from the position of being an outsider or, within my group, a person who is suspected of having too close links with a dominant culture. Most keep me from having to be angry.

I see a pattern running through the matrix of white privilege, a pattern of assumptions that were passed on to me as a white person. There was one main piece of cultural turf; it was my own turf, and I was among those who could control the turf. I could measure up to the cultural standards and take advantage of the many options I saw around me to make what the culture would call a success of my life. *My skin color was an asset for any move I was educated to want to make.* I could think of myself as "belonging" in major ways and of making social systems work for me. I could freely disparage, fear, neglect, or be oblivious to anything outside of the dominant cultural forms. Being of the main culture, I could also criticize it fairly freely. My life was reflected back to me frequently enough so that I felt, with regard to my race, if not to my sex, like one of the real people.

Whether through the curriculum or in the newspaper, the television, the economic system, or the general look of people in the streets, I received daily signals and indications that my people counted and that others *either didn't exist or must be trying, not very successfully, to be like people of my race.* I was given cultural permission not to hear voices of people of other races or a tepid cultural tolerance for hearing or acting on such voices. I was also raised not to suffer seriously from anything that darker-skinned people might say about my group, "protected," though perhaps I should more accurately say *prohibited,* through the habits of my economic class and social group, from living in racially mixed groups or being reflective about interactions between people of differing races.

In proportion as my racial group was being made confident, comfortable, and oblivious, other groups were likely being made unconfident, uncomfortable, and alienated. Whiteness protected me from many kinds of hostility, distress, and violence, which I was being subtly trained to visit in turn upon people of color.

For this reason, the word "privilege" now seems to me misleading. Its connotations are too positive to fit the conditions and behaviors which "privilege systems" produce. We usually think of privilege as being a favored state, whether earned, or conferred by birth or luck. School graduates are reminded they are privileged and urged to use their (enviable) assets well. The word "privilege" carries the connotation of being something everyone must want. Yet some of the conditions I have described here work to systemically overempower certain groups. Such privilege simply *confers dominance,* gives permission to control, because of one's race or sex. The kind of privilege that gives license to some people to be, at best, thoughtless and, at worst, murderous should not continue to be referred to as a desirable attribute. Such "privilege" may be widely desired without being in any way beneficial to the whole society.

Moreover, though "privilege" may confer power, it does not confer moral strength. Those who do not depend on conferred dominance have traits and qualities that may never develop in those who do. Just as Women's Studies courses indicate that women survive their political circumstances to lead lives that hold the human race together, so "underprivileged" people of color who are the world's majority have survived their oppression and lived survivors' lives from which the white global minority can and must learn. In some groups, those dominated have actually become strong through *not* having all of these unearned advantages, and this gives them a great deal to teach the others. Members of so-called privileged groups can seem foolish, ridiculous, infantile, or dangerous by contrast.

I want, then, to distinguish between earned strength and unearned power conferred systemically. Power from unearned privilege can look like strength when it is, in fact, permission to escape or to dominate. But not all of the privileges on my list are inevitably damaging. Some, like the expectation that neighbors will be decent to you, or that your race will not count against you in court, should be the norm in a just society and should be considered as the entitlement of everyone. Others, like the privilege not to listen to less powerful people, distort the humanity of the holders as well as the ignored groups. Still others, like finding one's staple foods everywhere, may be a function of being a member of a numerical majority in the population. Others have to do with not having to labor under pervasive negative stereotyping and mythology.

We might at least start by distinguishing between positive advantages that we can work to spread, to the point where they are not advantages at all but simply part of the normal civic and social fabric, and negative types of advantage that unless rejected will always reinforce our present hierarchies. For example, the positive "privilege" of belonging, the feeling that one belongs within the human circle, as Native Americans say, fosters development and should not be seen as privilege for a few. It is, let us say, an entitlement that none of us should have to earn; ideally it is an *unearned entitlement.* At present, since only a few have it, it is an *unearned advantage* for them. The negative "privilege" that gave me cultural permission not to take darker-skinned Others seriously can be seen as arbitrarily conferred dominance and should not be desirable for anyone. This paper results from a process of coming to see that some of the power that I originally saw as attendant on being a human being in the United States consisted in *unearned advantage* and *conferred dominance,* as well as other kinds of special circumstance not universally taken for granted.

In writing this paper I have also realized that white identity and status (as well as class identity and status) give me considerable power to choose whether to broach this subject and its trouble. I can pretty well decide whether to disappear and avoid and not listen and escape the dislike I may engender in other people through this essay, or interrupt, answer, interpret, preach, correct, criticize, and control to some extent what goes on in reaction to it. Being white, I am given considerable power to escape many kinds of danger or penalty as well as to choose which risks I want to take.

There is an analogy here, once again, with Women's Studies. Our male colleagues do not have a great deal to lose in supporting Women's Studies, but they do not have a great deal to lose if they oppose it either. They simply have the power to decide whether to commit themselves to more equitable distributions of power. They will probably feel few penalties whatever choice they make; they do not seem, in any obvious short-term sense, the ones at risk, though they and we are all at risk because of the behaviors that have been rewarded in them.

Through Women's Studies work I have met very few men who are truly distressed about systemic, unearned male advantage and conferred dominance. And so one question for me and others like me is whether we will be like them, or whether we will get truly distressed, even outraged, about unearned race advantage and conferred dominance and if so, what we will do to lessen them. In any case, we need to do more work in identifying how they actually affect our daily lives. We need more down-to-earth writing by people about these taboo subjects. We need more understanding of the ways in which white "privilege" damages white people, for these are not the same ways in which it damages the victimized. Skewed white psyches are an inseparable part of the picture, though I do not want to confuse the kinds of damage done to the holders of special assets and to those who suffer the deficits. Many, perhaps most, of our white students in the United States think that racism doesn't affect them because they are not people of color; they do not see "whiteness" as a racial identity. Many men likewise think that Women's Studies does not bear on their own existences because they are not female; they do not see themselves as having gendered identities. Insisting on the universal "effects" of "privilege" systems, then, becomes one of our chief tasks, and being more explicit about the *particular* effects in particular contexts is another. Men need to join us in this work.

In addition, since race and sex are not the only advantaging systems at work, we need to similarly examine the daily experience of having age advantage, or ethnic advantage, or physical ability, or advantage related to nationality, religion, or sexual orientation. Professor Marnie Evans suggested to me that in many ways the list I made also applies directly to heterosexual privilege. This is a still more taboo subject than race privilege: the daily ways in which heterosexual privilege makes some persons comfortable or powerful, providing supports, assets, approvals, and rewards to those who live or expect to live in heterosexual pairs. Unpacking that content is still more difficult, owing to the deeper imbeddedness of heterosexual advantage and dominance and stricter taboos surrounding these.

But to start such an analysis I would put this observation from my own experience: the fact that I live under the same roof with a man triggers all kinds of societal assumptions about my worth, politics, life, and values and triggers a host of unearned advantages and powers. After recasting many elements from the original list I would add further observations like these:

1. My children do not have to answer questions about why I live with my partner (my husband).

2. I have no difficulty finding neighborhoods where people approve of our household.

3. Our children are given texts and classes that implicitly support our kind of family unit and do not turn them against my choice of domestic partnership.

4. I can travel alone or with my husband without expecting embarrassment or hostility in those who deal with us.

5. Most people I meet will see my marital arrangements as an asset to my life or as a favorable comment on my likability, my competence, or my mental health.

6. I can talk about the social events of a weekend without fearing most listeners' reactions.

7. I will feel welcomed and "normal" in the usual walks of public life, institutional and social.

8. In many contexts, I am seen as "all right" in daily work on women because I do not live chiefly with women.

Difficulties and dangers surrounding the task of finding parallels are many. Since racism, sexism, and heterosexism are not the same, the advantages associated with them should not be seen as the same. In addition, it is hard to isolate aspects of unearned advantage that derive chiefly from social class, economic class, race, religion, region, sex, or ethnic identity. The oppressions are both distinct and interlocking, as the Combahee River Collective statement of 1977 continues to remind us eloquently.[3]

One factor seems clear about all of the interlocking oppressions. They take both active forms that we can see and embedded forms that members of the dominant group are taught not to see. In my class and place, I did not see myself as racist because I was taught to recognize racism only in individual acts of meanness by members of my group, never in invisible systems conferring racial dominance on my group from birth. Likewise, we are taught to think that sexism or heterosexism is carried on only through intentional, individual acts of discrimination, meanness, or cruelty, rather than

in invisible systems conferring unsought dominance on certain groups. Disapproving of the systems won't be enough to change them. I was taught to think that racism could end if white individuals changed their attitudes; many men think sexism can be ended by individual changes in daily behavior toward women. But a man's sex provides advantage for him whether or not he approves of the way in which dominance has been conferred on his group. A "white" skin in the United States opens many doors for whites whether or not we approve of the way dominance has been conferred on us. Individual acts can palliate, but cannot end, these problems. To redesign social systems, we need first to acknowledge their colossal unseen dimensions. The silences and denials surrounding privilege are the key political tool here. They keep the thinking about equality or equity incomplete, protecting unearned advantage and conferred dominance by making these taboo subjects. Most talk by whites about equal opportunity seems to me now to be about equal opportunity to try to get into a position of dominance while denying that *systems* of dominance exist.

Obliviousness about white advantage, like obliviousness about male advantage, is kept strongly inculturated in the United States so as to maintain the myth of meritocracy, the myth that democratic choice is equally available to all. Keeping most people unaware that freedom of confident action is there for just a small number of people props up those in power and serves to keep power in the hands of the same groups that have most of it already. Though systemic change takes many decades, there are pressing questions for me and I imagine for some others like me if we raise our daily consciousness on the perquisites of being light-skinned. What will we do with such knowledge? As we know from watching men, it is an open question whether we will choose to use unearned advantage to weaken invisible privilege systems and whether we will use any of our arbitrarily awarded power to try to reconstruct power systems on a broader base.

NOTES

I have appreciated commentary on this paper from the Working Papers Committee of the Wellesley College Center for Research on Women, from members of the Dodge seminar, and from many individuals, including Margaret Andersen, Sorel Berman, Joanne Braxton, Johnnella Butler, Sandra Dickerson, Marnie Evans, Beverly Guy-Sheftall, Sandra Harding, Eleanor Hinton Hoytt, Pauline Houston, Paul Lauter, Joyce Miller, Mary Norris, Gloria Oden, Beverly Smith, and John Walter.

1. This paper was presented at the Virginia Women's Studies Association conference in Richmond in April, 1986, and the American Educational Research Association conference in Boston in October, 1986, and discussed with two groups of participants in the Dodge seminars for Secondary School Teachers in New York and Boston in the spring of 1987.

2. Andersen, Margaret, "Race and the Social Science Curriculum: A Teaching and Learning Discussion." *Radical Teacher*, November, 1984, pp. 17–20. Smith, Lillian, *Killers of the Dream*, New York: W. W. Norton, 1949.

3. "A Black Feminist Statement," The Combahee River Collective, pp. 13–22 in G. Hull, P. Scott, B. Smith, Eds., *All the Women Are White, All the Blacks Are Men, But Some of Us Are Brave: Black Women's Studies*, Old Westbury, NY: The Feminist Press, 1982.

READING 13

Something About the Subject Makes It Hard to Name

Gloria Yamato

Racism—simple enough in structure, yet difficult to eliminate. Racism—pervasive in the U.S. culture to the point that it deeply affects all the local town folk and spills over, negatively influencing the fortunes of folk around the world. Racism is pervasive to the point that we take many of its manifestations for granted, believing "that's life." Many believe that racism can be dealt with effectively in one hellifying workshop, or one hour-long heated discussion. Many actually believe this monster, racism, that has had at least a few hundred years to take root, grow, invade our space and develop subtle variations . . . this mind-funk that distorts thought and action, can be merely wished away. I've run into folks who really think that we can beat this devil, kick this habit, be healed of this disease in a snap. In a sincere blink of a well-intentioned eye, presto—poof—racism disappears. "I've dealt with my racism . . . (envision a laying on of hands) . . . Hallelujah! Now I can go to the beach." Well, fine. Go to the beach. In fact, why don't we all go to the beach and continue to work on the sucker over there? Cuz you can't even shave a little piece off this thing called racism in a day, or a weekend, or a workshop.

When I speak of *oppression*, I'm talking about the systematic, institutionalized mistreatment of one group of people by another for whatever reason. The oppressors are purported to have an innate ability to access economic resources, information, respect, etc., while the oppressed are believed to have a corresponding negative innate ability. The flip side of oppression is *internalized oppression*. Members of the target group are emotionally, physically, and spiritually battered to the point that they begin to actually believe that their oppression is deserved, is their lot in life, is natural and right, and that it doesn't even exist. The oppression begins to feel comfortable, familiar enough that when mean ol' Massa lay down de whip, we got's to pick up and whack ourselves and each other. Like a virus, it's hard to beat racism, because by the time you come up with a cure, it's mutated to a "new cure-resistant" form. One shot just won't get it. Racism must be attacked from many angles.

The forms of racism that I pick up on these days are (1) aware/blatant racism, (2) aware/covert racism, (3) unaware/unintentional racism, and (4) unaware/self-righteous racism. I can't say that I prefer any one form of racism over the others, because they all look like an itch needing a scratch. I've heard it said (and understandably so) that the aware/blatant form of racism is preferable if one must suffer it. Outright racists will, without apology or confusion, tell us that because of our color we don't appeal to them. If we so choose, we can attempt to get the hell out of their way before we get the sweat knocked out of us. Growing up, aware/covert racism is what I heard many of my elders bemoaning "up north," after having escaped the overt racism "down south." Apartments were suddenly no longer vacant or rents were outrageously high, when black, brown, red, or yellow persons went to inquire about them. Job vacancies were suddenly filled, or we were fired for very vague reasons. It still happens, though the perpetrators really take care to cover their tracks these days. They don't want to get gummed to death or slobbered on by the toothless laws that supposedly protect us from such inequities.

Unaware/unintentional racism drives usually tranquil white liberals wild when they get called on it, and confirms the suspicions of many people of color who feel that white folks are just plain crazy. It has led white people to believe that it's just fine to ask if they can touch my hair (while reaching). They then exclaim over how soft it is, how it does not scratch their hand. It has led whites to assume that bending over backwards and speaking to me in high-pitched (terrified), condescending tones would make up for all the racist wrongs that distort our lives. This type of racism has led whites right to my doorstep, talking 'bout, "We're sorry/we love you and want to make things right," which is fine, and further, "We're gonna

give you the opportunity to fix it while we sleep. Just tell us what you need. 'Bye!!"— which *ain't* fine. With the best of intentions, the best of educations, and the greatest generosity of heart, whites, operating on the misinformation fed to them from day one, will behave in ways that are racist, will perpetuate racism by being "nice" the way we're taught to be nice. You can just "nice" somebody to death with naïveté and lack of awareness of privilege. Then there's guilt and the desire to end racism and how the two get all tangled up to the point that people, morbidly fascinated with their guilt, are immobilized. Rather than deal with ending racism, they sit and ponder their guilt and hope nobody notices how awful they are. Meanwhile, racism picks up momentum and keeps on keepin' on.

Now, the newest form of racism that I'm hip to is unaware/self-righteous racism. The "good white" racist attempts to shame Blacks into being blacker, scorns Japanese-Americans who don't speak Japanese, and knows more about the Chicano/a community than the folks who make up the community. They assign themselves as the "good whites," as opposed to the "bad whites," and are often so busy telling people of color what the issues in the Black, Asian, Indian, Latino/a communities should be that they don't have time to deal with their errant sisters and brothers in the white community. Which means that people of color are still left to deal with what the "good whites" don't want to . . . racism.

Internalized racism is what really gets in my way as a Black woman. It influences the way I see or don't see myself, limits what I expect of myself or others like me. It results in my acceptance of mistreatment, leads me to believe that being treated with less than absolute respect, at least this once, is to be expected because I am Black, because I am not white. "Because I am (*you fill in the color*), you think, "Life is going to be hard." The fact is life may be hard, but the color of your skin is not the cause of the hardship. The color of your skin may be used as an excuse to mistreat you, but there is no reason or logic involved in the mistreatment. If it seems that your color is the reason, if it seems that your ethnic heritage is the cause of the woe, it's because you've been deliberately beaten down by agents of a greedy system until you swallowed the garbage. That is the internalization of racism.

Racism is the systematic, institutionalized mistreatment of one group of people by another based on racial heritage. Like every other oppression, racism can be internalized. People of color come to believe misinformation about their particular ethnic group and thus believe that their mistreatment is justified. With that basic vocabulary, let's take a look at how the whole thing works together. Meet "the Ism Family," racism, classism, ageism, adultism, elitism, sexism, heterosexism, physicalism, etc. All these ism's are systematic, that is, not only are these parasites feeding off our lives, they are also dependent on one another for foundation. Racism is supported and reinforced by classism, which is given a foothold and a boost by adultism, which also feeds sexism, which is validated by heterosexism, and so it goes on. You cannot have the "ism" functioning without first effectively installing its flip-side, the internalized version of the ism. Like twins, as one particular form of the ism grows in potency, there is a corresponding increase in its internalized form within the population. Before oppression becomes a specific ism like racism, usually all hell breaks loose. War. People fight attempts to enslave them, or to subvert their will, or to take what they consider theirs, whether that is territory or dignity. It's true that the various elements of racism, while repugnant, would not be able to do very much damage, but for one generally overlooked key piece: power/privilege.

. . .

So, what can we do? Acknowledge racism for a start, even though and especially when we've struggled to be kind and fair, or struggled to rise above it all. It is hard to acknowledge the fact that racism circumscribes and pervades our lives. Racism must be dealt with on two levels, personal and societal, emotional and institutional. It is possible—and most effective—to do both at the same time. We must reclaim whatever delight we have lost in our own ethnic heritage or heritages. This so-called melting pot has only succeeded in turning us into fast-food gobbling "generics" (as in generic "white folks" who were once Irish, Polish, Russian, English, etc. and "black folks," who were once Ashanti, Bambara, Baule, Yoruba, etc.). Find or create safe places to actually *feel* what we've been forced to repress each time we were a victim of, witness to or perpetrator of racism, so that we do not continue, like puppets, to act out the past in the present and future. Challenge oppression. Take a stand against it. When you are aware of something oppressive going down, stop the show. At least call it. We become so numbed to racism that we don't even think twice about it, unless it is immediately life-threatening.

Whites who want to be allies to people of color: You can educate yourselves via research and observation rather than rigidly, arrogantly relying solely on interrogating people of color. Do not expect that people of color should teach you how to behave non-oppressively. Do not give into the pull to be lazy. Think, hard. Do not blame people of color for your frustration about racism, but do appreciate the fact that people of color will often help you get in touch with that frustration. Assume that your effort to be a good friend is appreciated, but don't expect or accept gratitude from people of color. Work on racism for your sake, not "their" sake. Assume that you are needed and capable of being a good ally. Know that you'll make mistakes and commit yourself to correcting them and continuing on as an ally, no matter what. Don't give up.

People of color, working through internalized racism: Remember always that you and others like you are completely worthy of respect, completely capable of achieving whatever you take a notion to do. Remember that the term "people of color" refers to a variety of ethnic and cultural backgrounds. These various groups have been oppressed in a variety of ways. Educate yourself about the ways different peoples have been oppressed and how they've resisted that oppression. Expect and insist that whites are capable of being good allies against racism.

Don't give up. Resist the pull to give out the "people of color seal of approval" to aspiring white allies. A moment of appreciation is fine, but more than that tends to be less than helpful. Celebrate yourself. Celebrate yourself. Celebrate the inevitable end of racism.

Tired of Playing Monopoly?

Donna Langston

I. Magnin, Nordstrom, The Bon, Sears, Penneys, K mart, Goodwill, Salvation Army. If the order of this list of stores makes any sense to you, then we've begun to deal with the first question which inevitably arises in any discussion of class here in the U.S.—huh? Unlike our European allies, we in the U.S. are reluctant to recognize class differences. This denial of class divisions functions to reinforce ruling class control and domination. America is, after all, the supposed land of equal opportunity where, if you just work hard enough, you can get ahead, pull yourself up by your bootstraps. What the old bootstraps theory overlooks is that some were born with silver shoe horns. Female-headed households, communities of color, the elderly, disabled and children find themselves, disproportionately, living in poverty. If hard work were the sole determinant of your ability to support yourself and your family, surely we'd have a different outcome for many in our society. We also, however, believe in luck and, on closer examination, it certainly is quite a coincidence that the "unlucky" come from certain race, gender and class backgrounds. In order to perpetuate racist, sexist and classist outcomes, we also have to believe that the current economic distribution is unchangeable, has always existed, and probably exists in this form throughout the known universe; i.e., it's "natural." Some people explain or try to account for poverty or class position by

focusing on the personal and moral merits of an individual. If people are poor, then it's something they did or didn't do; they were lazy, unlucky, didn't try hard enough, etc. This has the familiar ring of blaming the victims. Alternative explanations focus on the ways in which poverty and class position are due to structural, systematic, institutionalized economic and political power relations. These power relations are based firmly on dynamics such as race, gender, and class.

In the myth of the classless society, ambition and intelligence alone are responsible for success. The myth conceals the existence of a class society, which serves many functions. One of the main ways it keeps the working class and poor locked into a class-based system in a position of servitude is by cruelly creating false hope. It perpetuates the false hope among the working class and poor that they can have different opportunities in life. The hope that they can escape the fate that awaits them due to the class position they were born into. Another way the rags-to-riches myth is perpetuated is by creating enough visible tokens so that oppressed persons believe they, too, can get ahead. The creation of hope through tokenism keeps a hierarchical structure in place and lays the blame for not succeeding on those who don't. This keeps us from resisting and changing the class-based system. Instead, we accept it as inevitable, something we just have to live with. If oppressed people believe in equality of opportunity, then they won't develop class consciousness and will internalize the blame for their economic position. If the working class and poor do not recognize the way false hope is used to control them, they won't get a chance to control their lives by acknowledging their class position, by claiming that identity and taking action as a group.

The myth also keeps the middle class and upper class entrenched in the privileges awarded in a class-based system. It reinforces middle- and upper-class beliefs in their own superiority. If we believe that anyone in society really can get ahead, then middle- and upper-class status and privileges must be deserved, due to personal merits, and enjoyed—and defended at all costs. According to this viewpoint, poverty is regrettable but acceptable, just the outcome of a fair game: "There have always been poor people, and there always will be."

Class is more than just the amount of money you have; it's also the presence of economic security. For the working class and poor, working and eating are matters of survival, not taste. However, while one's class status can be defined in important ways in terms of monetary income, class is also a whole lot more—specifically, class is also culture. As a result of the class you are born into and raised in, class is your understanding of the world and where you fit in; it's composed of ideas, behavior, attitudes, values, and language; class is how you think, feel, act, look, dress, talk, move, walk; class is what stores you shop at, restaurants you eat in; class is the schools you attend, the education you attain; class is the very jobs you will work at throughout your adult life. Class even determines when we marry and become mothers. Working-class women become mothers long before middle-class women receive their bachelor's degrees. We experience class at every level of our lives; class is who our friends are, where we live and work even what kind of car we drive, if we own one, and what kind of health care we receive, if any. . . .

Class affects what we perceive as and what we have available to us as choices. Upon graduation from high school, I was awarded a scholarship to attend any college, private or public, in the state of California. Yet it never occurred to me or my family that it made any difference which college you went to. I ended up just going to a small college in my town. It never would have occurred to me to move away from my family for school, because no one ever had and no one would. I was the first person in my family to go to college. I had to figure out from reading college catalogs how to apply—no one in my family could have sat down and said, "Well, you take this test and then you really should think about . . ." Although tests and high school performance had shown I had the ability to pick up white middle-class lingo, I still had quite an adjustment to make—it was lonely and isolating in college. I lost my friends from high school—they were at the community college, vo-tech school, working, or married. I lasted a year and a half in this foreign environment before I quit college, married a factory worker, had a baby and resumed living in a community I knew. . . .

If class is more than simple economic status but one's cultural background as well, what happens if you're born and raised middle class, but spend some of your adult life with earnings below a middle-class income bracket—are you then working-class? Probably not. If your economic position changes, you still have the language, behavior, educational background, etc., of the middle class, which you can bank on. You will always have choices. Men who consciously try to refuse male privilege are still male; whites who want to challenge white privilege are still white. I think those who come from middle-class backgrounds need to recognize that their class privilege does not float out with the rinse water. Middle-class people can exert incredible power just by being nice and polite. The middle-class way of doing things is the standard—they're always right, just by being themselves. Beware of middle-class people who deny their privilege. Many people have times when they struggle to get shoes for the kids, when budgets are tight, etc. This isn't the same as long-term economic conditions without choices. . . .

How about if you're born and raised poor or working class, yet through struggle, usually through education, you manage to achieve a different economic level: do you become middle class? Can you pass? I think some working-class people may successfully assimilate into the middle class by learning to dress, talk, and act middle class—to accept and adopt the middle-class way of doing things. It all depends on how far they're able to go. To succeed in the middle-class world means facing great pressures to abandon working-class friends and ways.

Contrary to our stereotype of the working class—white guys in overalls—the working class is not homogeneous in terms of race or gender. If you are a person of color, if you live in a female-headed household, you are much more likely to be working class or poor. The experience of Black, Latino, American Indian or Asian American working classes will differ significantly from the white working classes, which have traditionally been able to rely on white privilege to provide a more elite position within the working class. Working-class people are often grouped together and stereotyped, but distinctions can be made among the working class, working poor, and poor. Many working-class families are supported by unionized workers who possess marketable skills. Most working-poor families are supported by non-unionized, unskilled men and women. Many poor families are dependent on welfare for their income.

Attacks on the welfare system and those who live on welfare are a good example of classism in action. We have a "dual welfare" system in this country whereby welfare for the rich in the form of tax-free capital gain, guaranteed loans, oil depletion allowances, etc., is not recognized as welfare. Almost everyone in America is on some type of welfare; but, if you're rich, it's in the form of tax deductions for "business" meals and entertainment, and if you're poor, it's in the form of food stamps. The difference is the stigma and humiliation connected to welfare for the poor, as compared to welfare for the rich, which is called "incentives." . . . The "dual welfare" system also assigns a different degree of stigma to programs that benefit women and children, such as AFDC, and programs whose recipients are primarily male, such as veterans' benefits. The implicit assumption is that mothers who raise children do not work and therefore are not deserving of their daily bread crumbs.

Anti-union attitudes are another prime example of classism in action. At best, unions have been a very progressive force for workers, women and people of color. At worst, unions have reflected the same regressive attitudes which are out there in other social structures: classism, racism, and sexism. Classism exists within the working class. The aristocracy of the working class—unionized, skilled workers—have mainly been white and male and have viewed themselves as being better than unskilled workers, the unemployed, and the poor, who are mostly women and people of color. The white working class must commit itself to a cultural and ideological transformation of racist attitudes. The history of working people, and the ways we've resisted many types of oppressions, are not something we're taught in school. Missing from our education is information about workers and their resistance.

Working-class women's critiques have focused on the following issues:

Education: White middle-class professionals have used academic jargon to rationalize and justify classism. The whole structure of education is a classist system. Schools in every town reflect class divisions: like the store list at the beginning of this article, you can list schools in your town by what classes of kids attend, and in most cities you can also list by race. The classist system is perpetuated in schools with the tracking system, whereby the "dumbs" are tracked into homemaking, shop courses and vocational school futures, while the "smarts" end up in advanced math, science, literature, and college-prep courses. If we examine these groups carefully, the coincidence of poor and working-class backgrounds with "dumbs" is rather alarming. The standard measurement of supposed intelligence is white middle-class English. If you're other than white middle class, you have to become bilingual to succeed in the educational system. If you're white middle class, you only need the language and writing skills you were raised with, since they're the standard. To do well in society presupposes middle-class background, experiences and learning for everyone. The tracking system separates those from the working class who can potentially assimilate to the middle class from all our friends, and labels us "college bound."

After high school, you go on to vocational school, community college, or college—public or private—according to your class position. Apart from the few who break into middle-class schools, the classist stereotyping of the working class as being dumb and inarticulate tracks most into vocational and low-skilled jobs. A few of us are allowed to slip through to reinforce the idea that equal opportunity exists. But for most, class position is destiny—determining our educational attainment and employment. Since we must overall abide by middle-class rules to succeed, the assumption is that we go to college in order to "better ourselves"—i.e., become more like them. I suppose it's assumed we have "yuppie envy" and desire nothing more than to be upwardly mobile individuals. It's assumed that we want to fit into their world. But many of us remain connected to our communities and families. Becoming college educated doesn't mean we have to, or want to, erase our first and natural language and value system. It's important for many of us to remain in and return to our communities to work, live, and stay sane.

Jobs: Middle-class people have the privilege of choosing careers. They can decide which jobs they want to work, according to their moral or political commitments, needs for challenge or creativity. This is a privilege denied the working class and poor, whose work is a means of survival, not choice. . . . Working-class women have seldom had the luxury of choosing between work in the home or market. We've generally done both, with little ability to purchase services to help with this double burden. Middle- and upper-class women can often hire other women to clean their houses, take care of their children, and cook their meals. Guess what class and race those "other" women are? Working a double or triple day is common for working-class women. Only middle-class women have an array of choices such as: parents put you through school, then you choose a career, then you choose when and if to have babies, then you choose a support system of working-class women to take care of your kids and house if you choose to resume your career. After the birth of my second child, I was working two part-time jobs—one loading trucks at night—and going to school during the days. While I was quite privileged because I could take my colicky infant with me to classes and the day-time job, I was in a state of continuous semi-consciousness. I had to work to support my family; the only choice I had was between school or sleep: Sleep became a privilege. A white middle-class feminist instructor at the university suggested to me, all sympathetically, that I ought to hire someone to clean my house and watch the baby. Her suggestion was totally out of my reality, both economically and socially. I'd worked for years cleaning other peoples' houses. Hiring a working-class woman to do the shit work is a middle-class woman's solution to any dilemma which her privileges, such as a career, may present her.

Mothering: The feminist critique of families and the oppressive role of mothering has focused on white middle-class nuclear families. This may not be an appropriate model for communities of class and color. Mothering and families may hold a different importance for working-class women. Within this context, the issue of coming out can be a very painful process for working-class lesbians. Due to the homophobia of working-class communities, to be a lesbian is most often to be excommunicated from your family, neighborhood, friends and the people you work with. If you're working class, you don't have such clearly demarcated concepts of yourself as an individual, but instead see yourself as part of a family and community that forms your survival structure. It is not easy to be faced with the risk of giving up ties which are so central to your identity and survival.

. . . .

WAYS TO AVOID FACING CLASSISM

Deny Deny Deny: Deny your class position and the privileges connected to it. Deny the existence or experience of the working class and poor. You can even set yourself up (in your own mind) as judge and jury in deciding who qualifies as working class by your white middle-class standards. So if someone went to college, or seems intelligent to you, not at all like your stereotypes, they must be middle class.

Guilt Guilt Guilt: "I feel so bad, I just didn't realize!" is not helpful, but is a way to avoid changing attitudes and behaviors. Passivity—"Well, what can I do about it, anyway?"—and anger—"Well, what do they want!"—aren't too helpful either. Again, with these responses, the focus is on you and absolving the white middle class from responsibility. A more helpful remedy is to take action. Donate your time and money to local foodbanks. Don't cross picket lines. Better yet, go join a picket line.

HOW TO CHALLENGE CLASSISM

If you're middle class, you can begin to challenge classism with the following:

1. Confront classist behavior in yourself, others and society. Use and share the privileges, like time or money, which you do have.

2. Make demands on working-class and poor communities' issues—anti-racism, poverty, unions, public housing, public transportation, literacy and day care.

3. Learn from the skills and strength of working people—study working and poor people's history; take some Labor Studies, Ethnic Studies, Women Studies classes. Challenge elitism. There are many different types of intelligence: white middle-class, academic, professional intellectualism being one of them (reportedly). Finally, educate yourself, take responsibility and take action.

If you're working class, just some general suggestions (it's cheaper than therapy—free, less time-consuming and I won't ask you about what your mother said to you when you were five):

1. Face your racism! Educate yourself and others, your family, community, any organizations you belong to; take responsibility and take action. Face your classism, sexism, heterosexism, ageism, able-bodiness, adultism. . . .

2. Claim your identity. Learn all you can about your history and the history and experience of all working and poor peoples. Raise your children to be anti-racist, anti-sexist and anti-classist. Teach them the language and culture of working peoples. Learn to survive with a fair amount of anger and lots of humor, which can be tough when this stuff isn't even funny.

3. Work on issues which will benefit your community. Consider remaining in or returning to your communities. If you live and work in white middle-class environments, look for working-class allies to help you survive with your humor and wits intact. How do working-class people spot each other? We have antenna.

We need not deny or erase the differences of working-class cultures but can embrace their richness, their variety, their moral and intellectual heritage. We're not at the point yet where we can celebrate differences—not having money for a prescription for your child is nothing to celebrate. It's not time yet to party with the white middle class, because we'd be the entertainment ("Aren't they quaint? Just love their workboots and uniforms and the way they cuss!"). We need to overcome divisions among working people, not by ignoring the multiple oppressions many of us encounter; or by oppressing each other, but by becoming committed allies on all issues which affect work-ing people: racism, sexism, classism, etc. An injury to one is an injury to all. Don't play by ruling-class rules, hoping that maybe you can live on Connecticut Avenue instead of Baltic, or that you as an individual can make it to Park Place and Boardwalk. Tired of Monopoly? Always ending up on Mediterranean Avenue? How about changing the game?

READING 15

Voices
On Becoming Old Women

Baba Copper

When we ask for a chance to live our old age in comfort, creativity and usefulness, we ask it not for ourselves alone, but for you. We are not a special interest group. We are your roots. You are our continuity. What we gain is your inheritance.

—Irene Pauli, *Some Ironies of Aging*

How can old women define the subjects of age and ageism so that false understanding of these issues does not dominate the interactions between women and keep us forever separate? Aging is a natural and universal personal experience that begins the day we are born. It is a process of challenge—not necessarily growth and development when we are young as opposed to loss and deterioration when we are old—but learning through change. Ageism is the negative social response to different stages in the process of aging and it is a political issue. The ageism that old women experience is firmly embedded in sexism—an extension of the male power to define, control values, erase, disempower, and divide. Woman-to-woman ageism is an aspect of the horizontal conflict that usurps the energies of the colonized—part of the female competition for the crumbs of social power.

How can the same word be used for the experience of teenagers, old women, and the most powerful men in the world? Yet we say that all these are subject to *ageist* attitudes—stereotyping and denigration because of age. But each age group—children, teens, midlife women, old women, old men—have radically different expectations of their due, their rightful social place. For an old woman, ageism is a killer, because her sense of worth has been eroded by a lifelong pursuit of youth/beauty. Age passing—passing for young enough—is part of all female experience. The foundation of lies built into passing and the fear and loathing of female aging are what keep the generations of women—decade by decade—divided from each other.

I believe that age passing is one of the primary learning arenas of female competition, as well as an apprenticeship to hatred of old women. When women pass easily, we gain comfort knowing that we do not have to identify with the woman who, in our view, is not passing. "I am not like her" translates easily into "I am better than her." In our thirties, we do not want to be mistaken for forty. In our forties, we do not want anyone to assume we are fifty. Somewhere in our fifties, the mass of anxieties about age, and the increase of rejection and invisibility we are experiencing, becomes critical. This is often a time when our trained inability to identify with women older than ourselves reaches its climax. Old women cannot rely upon the midlife woman as ally. The midlife woman, in her rage and fear, may unconsciously discharge all kinds of covert aggression against the old woman as the personification of what is threatening her.

Can women afford to ignore issues that surround the aging process? When I have asked younger women what they thought ageism was all about, they talked about the aura of death and decay which permeates age for them, the oppressive power/over of the mythic Mother figure, and the deplorable neglect exhibited by the authorities in making adequate institutional responses to age. None have seen ageism as a problem of prejudice or bigotry on their part. With a righteousness reminiscent of the anchorman on the evening news, most of my young informants have advocated more and better government support for the old. But government subsidies for medicine and institutional care have created a highly profitable industry of geriatric technology, with the elderly aid recipients captive to the modern Grail, longevity. Just staying alive is a false goal. Acceptance of age in women has not kept pace with our increasing life expectancy. It is the quality of that extra time that is important. As long as women allow themselves to be brainwashed into worshiping youth and plasticized beauty, increased life expectancy (and the institutionalized responses to it) will remain a burden for both the young and the old.

How can ageism be defined by women; how can we develop clear vocabulary and theory; can we afford to ignore it? For me these questions are more than rhetorical. I am an old woman living in a highly politicized community of women. I find struggle and change taking place in relation to all the differences between women except age. I need to divert some of that political consciousness toward ageism.

I am an *old* woman. I am sixty-six. Part of the reason I self-identify as *old* is a need to escape the prissy category of "older woman." This label claims descriptive power over women from

eighteen to eighty, depending upon the age and consciousness of the user. . . . After lots of internal arguments, I found a rationalization that made me comfortable with the label. Calling myself an old woman was the radical way out of my dilemma. At sixty-six, it may be presumptuous of me to assume a label that is descriptive of women in their nineties, but I have noticed that many of them avoid the term. Like other words that feminists are reclaiming by proud usage, I would take to myself the word everyone seems to fear. My *real* circumstances would not suffer more than they have from the visual impact of my years. Nobody but radical women would stand there beside me, honest and angry about the distortions that surround the time of life all women dread. I would walk through the door-of-no-return and from the other side name the politics of age instead of waltzing around pretending I am just an "older woman." The lies of age passing would not save me from the stigma of age. In fact, it has been my experience that the invention and practice of feminine lies keep women forever in harness, laboring to be someone who fits in, who pleases, who is chosen, who earns (and therefore deserves) love. I have grown sick of the harness.

. . . .

Young and midlife women tend to see ageism as a continuing oppression of women throughout their lives. The point of view I tried to voice as an old woman sprang from my new experience, which revealed abrupt changes in the degree or intensity of stigma, when, for whatever reasons, one could no longer pass as middle-aged. I am uncomfortable with the absence of differentiation between the kind of ageism I can remember experiencing as a teenager and what I am experiencing in my sixties.

I felt confused. I did not know how to integrate these concepts into my present circumstances. Was the pain over the ageism I experience intensified by the fact that my youth privilege had been augmented by the privileges of being white, able, thin, blond, tall, middle class? And how did all this relate to age passing, for many women try—and some even succeed by the use of repeated plastic surgery—to appear forever middle-aged? For instance, the small, thin old woman—especially one who plays the "cute" social role—does not receive the same direct hostility that big "motherly" women do. Was the pain of ageism relative also, or was there a pall that settled over an old woman (the year varying for different women) which was similar for all whether or not they had been pretty or middle-class?

. . . .

Death is an extremely important subject that our culture has mystified, professionalized, sensationalized—and at the same time, made taboo. Everyone needs to make his or her peace with the meaning of death. However, the assumption that death is a preoccupation, or subject of expertise, of midlife or old women is ageist. I understood that we might want to talk about death. But the old should not be seen as standing with death at their elbow. Nor should they be expected to help others on the subject or allow the subject to be age segregated. Repeatedly, younger women make assumptions about my relationship to death. One woman said that she shared identity with me because she had had many losses of people close to her in her life. She assumed that I had too. In reality, other than the death of my mother when she was ninety-three, no one I loved has ever died.

. . . .

Here it was, that virulent stereotype—the age/death connection. . . . Apparently only old people die. Death does not hover near the cradle, the motorcyle, the toxic workplace, high bridges, or battlefields. But around old women, everyone is reminded that they have given their own possible mortality insufficient attention. Death is a forbidden subject with all but the old, who are expected to bear the burden of this social suppression. Since my own demise is as distant from my conscious mind as it was when I was twenty, I have come to recognize that it is my looks that evoke the age/death connection in others. Death has become a private buzzword for me, warning me of the shoals of ageism before me.

Talking about choice in relation to dying always makes me very nervous. I reminded the group that we were at the beginning of a worldwide demographic boom of old women. It is easy to predict that our society will soon be subject to all kinds of "new looks" at death and dying. I read a clipping from a futurist magazine suggesting that a demise pill be available to the elderly (but not the young, of course). The old are seen as half dead already. Old women, like everyone else, buy into the prevailing concepts surrounding both worth and death—we are as easy to brainwash as the next. When one believes that one has done everything one wants to do, it may be a way of expressing the feeling that what one has to contribute from a wheelchair, for example, is not valuable.

. . . .

How can old women begin to change this? First, we have to name our circumstances more clearly, identifying the root sources of our denigrated place in society. Feminist analysis and the concept of ageism are not used as tools by most old women to explain the increased negative content of our experience. Old women tend to see problems as personal—interpersonal or physical or economic—instead of political. The time of life that should be a final ripening, a meaningful summation, a last chance for all the risks and pleasures of corporeal existence, is all too often deadened by emotional isolation and self-doubts. As the average life expectancy for women keeps creeping upward—almost into the eighties now—the quality of that life-to-be-expected keeps deteriorating.

The "natural alliance" that old women have a right to expect with midlife women will not emerge until all women begin to recognize the pitfalls of age passing. Separating the perspective of the barely-passing older woman from some of my concerns as one-who-no-longer-is-able-to-pass has taken all my confidence and a great deal of hindsight. The midlife woman feels increasing pressure—internal and external—about aging as well as the rejections of ageism. It is natural that she rushes forward to define the problem. In asserting her power over the insights of the old woman—the complaints, the accusations of ageism, the naming of the universal hatred of the Old Woman—she unconsciously silences the inherent radicalism of the only one who can tell her how it really is.

The problem for old women is a problem of power. First, power over the circumstances and directions of our own lives and identity. Second, power as an influence upon the world we live in—the world we have served, in which we have such a large, unrecognized vested interest. This is, of course, the rub. Patriarchal institutions are, without exception, designed to exclude the vision of old women. Most old women have little experience in leadership, influence, or even respect. Mostly, old women know how to serve. The roles reserved and expected of women in old age—grandmothers, self-effacing volunteers to the projects and priorities designed by others, or caretakers of old men—are custom fit to our powerless status.

But there are ways that all women can begin to prepare the way for the empowerment of themselves in the future, when they are old. These changes can first be brought about in the women's community, among lesbians and political women. The first step is for women to recognize that they have been programmed to hate old women and to deny them power. This brainwashing is so subtle that its eradication will take an effort equal to that which we have made and still must expend upon sexism. Further, this brainwashing extends down through our lives, making us fear the processes of our own bodies within time, so that our energies and attention are constantly undermined by ageist competition and self-doubts. These are attitudes and expectations that we can change now, if we decide to. Empowerment of women will come when we identify with women older than we are and not before.

The Social Construction of Disability

Susan Wendell

. . . I maintain that the distinction between the biological reality of a disability and the social construction of a disability cannot be made sharply, because the biological and the social are interactive in creating disability. They are interactive not only in that complex interactions of social factors and our bodies affect health and functioning, but also in that social arrangements can make a biological condition more or less relevant to almost any situation. I call the interaction of the biological and the social to create (or prevent) disability "the social construction of disability."

Disability activists and some scholars of disability have been asserting for at least two decades that disability is socially constructed.

Moreover, feminist scholars have already applied feminist analyses of the social construction of the experience of being female to their analyses of disability as socially constructed. Thus I am saying nothing new when I claim that disability, like gender, is socially constructed. Nevertheless, I understand that such an assertion may be new and even puzzling to many readers, and that not everyone who says that disability is socially constructed means the same thing by it. Therefore, I will explain what I mean in some detail.

I see disability as socially constructed in ways ranging from social conditions that straightforwardly create illnesses, injuries, and poor physical functioning, to subtle cultural factors that determine standards of normality and exclude those who do not meet them from full participation in their societies. I could not possibly discuss all the factors that enter into the social construction of disability here, and I feel sure that I am not aware of them all, but I will try to explain and illustrate the social construction of disability by discussing what I hope is a representative sample from a range of factors.

SOCIAL FACTORS THAT CONSTRUCT DISABILITY

First, it is easy to recognize that social conditions affect people's bodies by creating or failing to prevent sickness and injury. Although, since disability is relative to a person's physical, social, and cultural environment, none of the resulting physical conditions is necessarily disabling, many do in fact cause disability given the demands and lack of support in the environments of the people affected. In this direct sense of damaging people's bodies in ways that are disabling in their environments, much disability is created by the violence of invasions, wars, civil wars, and terrorism, which cause disabilities not only through direct injuries to combatants and noncombatants, but also through the spread of disease and the deprivations of basic needs that result from the chaos they create. In addition, although we more often hear about them when they cause death, violent crimes such as shootings, knifings, beatings, and rape all cause disabilities, so that a society's success or failure in protecting its citizens from injurious crimes has a significant effect on its rates of disability.

The availability and distribution of basic resources such as water, food, clothing, and shelter have major effects on disability, since much disabling physical damage results directly from malnutrition and indirectly from diseases that attack and do more lasting harm to the malnourished and those weakened by exposure. Disabling diseases are also contracted from contaminated water when clean water is not available. Here too, we usually learn more about the deaths caused by lack of basic resources than the (often life-long) disabilities of survivors.

Many other social factors can damage people's bodies in ways that are disabling in their environments, including (to mention just a few) tolerance of high-risk working conditions, abuse and neglect of children, low public safety standards, the degradation of the environment by contamination of air, water, and food, and the overwork, stress, and daily grinding deprivations of poverty. The social factors that can damage people's bodies almost always affect some groups in a society more than others because of racism, sexism, heterosexism, ageism, and advantages of class background, wealth, and education.

Medical care and practices, traditional and Western-scientific, play an important role in both preventing and creating disabling physical damage. (They also play a role in defining disability, . . .) Lack of good prenatal care and dangerous or inadequate obstetrical practices cause disabilities in babies and in the women giving birth to them. Inoculations against diseases such as polio and measles prevent quite a lot of disability. Inadequate medical care of those who are already ill or injured results in unnecessary disablement. On the other hand, the rate of disability in a society increases with improved medical capacity to save the lives of people who are dangerously ill or injured in the absence of the capacity to prevent or cure all the physical damage they have incurred. Moreover, public health and sanitation measures that increase the average lifespan also increase the number of old people with disabilities in a society, since more people live long enough to become disabled.

The *pace of life* is a factor in the social construction of disability that particularly interests me, because it is usually taken for granted by non-disabled people, while many people with disabilities are acutely aware of how it marginalizes or threatens to marginalize us. I suspect that increases in the pace of life are important social causes of damage to people's bodies through rates of accident, drug and alcohol abuse, and illnesses that result from people's neglecting their needs for rest and good nutrition. But the pace of life also affects disability as a second form of social construction, the social construction of disability through expectations of performance.

When the pace of life in a society increases, there is a tendency for more people to become disabled, not only because of physically damaging consequences of efforts to go faster, but also because fewer people can meet expectations of 'normal' performance; the physical (and mental) limitations of those who cannot meet the new pace become conspicuous and disabling, even though the same limitations were inconspicuous and irrelevant to full participation in the slower-paced society. Increases in the pace of life can be counterbalanced for some people by improvements in accessibility, such as better transportation and easier communication, but for those who must move or think slowly, and for those whose energy is severely limited, expectations of pace can make work, recreational, community, and social activities inaccessible.

Let me give a straightforward, personal illustration of the relationship between pace and disability. I am currently just able (by doing very little else) to work as a professor three-quarter time, on one-quarter disability leave. There has been much talk recently about possible increases in the teaching duties of professors at my university, which would not be accompanied by any reduction in expectations for the other two components of our jobs, research and administration. If there were to be such an increase in the pace of professors' work, say by one additional course per term, I would be unable to work more than half-time (by the new standards) and would have to request half-time disability leave, even though there had been no change in my physical condition. Compared to my colleagues, I would be more work-disabled than I am now. Some professors with less physical limitation than I have,

who now work full-time, might be unable to work at the new full-time pace and be forced to go on part-time disability leave. This sort of change could contribute to disabling anyone in any job.

Furthermore, even if a person is able to keep up with an increased pace of work, any increase in the pace of work will decrease the energy available for other life activities, which may upset the delicate balance of energy by which a person manages to participate in them and eventually exclude her/him from those activities. The pace of those other activities may also render them inaccessible. For example, the more the life of a society is conducted on the assumption of quick travel, the more disabling are those physical conditions that affect movement and travel, such as needing to use a wheelchair or having a kind of epilepsy that prevents one from driving a car, unless compensating help is provided. These disabling effects extend into people's family, social, and sexual lives and into their participation in recreation, religious life, and politics.

Pace is a major aspect of expectations of performance; non-disabled people often take pace so much for granted that they feel and express impatience with the slower pace at which some people with disabilities need to operate, and accommodations of pace are often crucial to making an activity accessible to people with a wide range of physical and mental abilities. Nevertheless, expectations of pace are not the only expectations of performance that contribute to disability. For example, expectations of individual productivity can eclipse the actual contributions of people who cannot meet them, making people unemployable when they can in fact do valuable work. There are often very definite expectations about *how* tasks will be performed (not the standards of performance, but the methods). For example, many women with disabilities are discouraged from having children because other people can only imagine caring for children in ways that are impossible for women with their disabilities, yet everything necessary could be done in other ways, often with minor accommodations. Furthermore, the expectation that many tasks will be performed by individuals on their own can create or expand the disability of those who can perform the tasks only in cooperative groups or by instructing a helper.

Expectations of performance are reflected, because they are assumed, in the social organization and physical structure of a society, both of which create disability. Societies that are physically constructed and socially organized with the unacknowledged assumption that everyone is healthy, non-disabled, young but adult, shaped according to cultural ideals, and, often, male, create a great deal of disability through sheer neglect of what most people need in order to participate fully in them.

Feminists talk about how the world has been designed for the bodies and activities of men. In many industrialized countries, including Canada and the United States, life and work have been structured as though no one of any importance in the public world, and certainly no one who works outside the home for wages, has to breast-feed a baby or look after a sick child. Common colds can be acknowledged publicly, and allowances are made for them, but menstruation cannot be acknowledged and allowances are not made for it. Much of the public world is also structured as though everyone were physically strong, as though all bodies were shaped the same, as though everyone could walk, hear, and see well, as though everyone could work and play at a pace that is not compatible with any kind of illness or pain, as though no one were ever dizzy or incontinent or simply needed to sit or lie down. (For instance, where could you rest for a few minutes in a supermarket if you needed to?) Not only the architecture, but the entire physical and social organization of life tends to assume that we are either strong and healthy and able to do what the average young, non-disabled man can do or that we are completely unable to participate in public life.

A great deal of disability is caused by this physical structure and social organization of society. For instance, poor architectural planning creates physical obstacles for people who use wheelchairs, but also for people who can walk but cannot walk far or cannot climb stairs, for people who cannot open doors, and for people who can do all of these things but only at the cost of pain or an expenditure of energy they can ill afford. Some of the same architectural flaws cause problems for pregnant women, parents with strollers, and young children. This is no coincidence. Much architecture has been planned with a young adult, non-disabled male paradigm of humanity in mind. In addition, aspects of social organization that take for granted the social expectations of performance and productivity, such as inadequate public transportation (which I believe assumes that no one who is needed in the public world needs public transportation), communications systems that are inaccessible to people with visual or hearing impairments, and inflexible work arrangements that exclude part-time work or rest periods, create much disability.

When public and private worlds are split, women (and children) have often been relegated to the private, and so have the disabled, the sick, and the old. The public world is the world of strength, the positive (valued) body, performance and production, the non-disabled, and young adults. Weakness, illness, rest and recovery, pain, death, and the negative (devalued) body are private, generally hidden, and often neglected. Coming into the public world with illness, pain, or a devalued body, people encounter resistance to mixing the two worlds; the split is vividly revealed. Much of the experience of disability and illness goes underground, because there is no socially acceptable way of expressing it and having the physical and psychological experience acknowledged. Yet acknowledgement of this experience is exactly what is required for creating accessibility in the public world. The more a society regards disability as a private matter, and people with disabilities as belonging in the private sphere, the more disability it creates by failing to make the public sphere accessible to a wide range of people.

Disability is also socially constructed by the failure to give people the amount and kind of help they need to participate fully in all major aspects of life in the society, including making a significant contribution in the form of work. Two things are important to remember about the help that people with disabilities may need. One is that most industrialized societies give non-disabled people (in different degrees and kinds, depending on class, race, gender, and other factors) a lot of help in the form of education, training, social support, public communication and transportation facilities, public recreation, and other services. The help that non-disabled people receive tends to be taken for granted and not considered help but entitlement, because it is offered to citizens who fit the social paradigms, who by definition are not considered dependent on social help. It is only when people need a different kind or amount of help than that given to 'paradigm' citizens that it is considered help at all, and they are considered socially dependent. Second, much, though not all, of the help that people with disabilities need is required because their bodies were damaged by social conditions, or because they cannot meet social expectations of performance, or because the narrowly-conceived physical structure and social organization of society have placed them at a disadvantage; in other words, it is needed to overcome problems that were created socially.

Thus disability is socially constructed through the failure or unwillingness to create ability among people who do not fit the physical and mental profile of 'paradigm' citizens. Failures of social support for people with disabilities result in inadequate rehabilitation, unemployment, poverty, inadequate personal and medical care, poor communication services, inadequate training and education, poor protection from physical, sexual, and emotional abuse, minimal opportunities for social learning and interaction, and many other disabling situations that hurt people with disabil-

ities and exclude them from participation in major aspects of life in their societies.

. . .

CULTURAL CONSTRUCTION OF DISABILITY

Culture makes major contributions to disability. These contributions include not only the omission of experiences of disability from cultural representations of life in a society, but also the cultural stereotyping of people with disabilities, the selective stigmatization of physical and mental limitations and other differences (selective because not all limitations and differences are stigmatized, and different limitations and differences are stigmatized in different societies), the numerous cultural meanings attached to various kinds of disability and illness, and the exclusion of people with disabilities from the cultural meanings of activities they cannot perform or are expected not to perform.

The lack of realistic cultural representations of experiences of disability not only contributes to the 'Otherness' of people with disabilities by encouraging the assumption that their lives are inconceivable to non-disabled people but also increases non-disabled people's fear of disability by suppressing knowledge of how people live with disabilities. Stereotypes of disabled people as dependent, morally depraved, superhumanly heroic, asexual, and/or pitiful are still the most common cultural portrayals of people with disabilities. Stereotypes repeatedly get in the way of full participation in work and social life. For example, Francine Arsenault, whose leg was damaged by childhood polio and later by gangrene, describes the following incident at her wedding:

> When I got married, one of my best friends came to the wedding with her parents. I had known her parents all the time I was growing up; we visited in each other's homes and I thought that they knew my situation quite well.
>
> But as the father went down the reception line and shook hands with my husband, he said,

"You know, I used to think that Francine was intelligent, but to put herself on you as a burden like this shows that I was wrong all along."

Here the stereotype of a woman with a disability as a helpless, dependent burden blots out, in the friend's father's consciousness, both the reality that Francine simply has one damaged leg and the probability that her new husband wants her for her other qualities. Moreover, the man seems to take for granted that the new husband sees Francine in the same stereotyped way (or else he risks incomprehension or rejection), perhaps because he counts on the cultural assumptions about people with disabilities. I think both the stigma of physical 'imperfection' (and possibly the additional stigma of having been damaged by disease) and the cultural meanings attached to the disability contribute to the power of the stereotype in situations like this. Physical 'imperfection' is more likely to be thought to 'spoil' a woman than a man by rendering her unattractive in a culture where her physical appearance is a large component of a woman's value; having a damaged leg probably evokes the metaphorical meanings of being 'crippled,' which include helplessness, dependency, and pitifulness. Stigma, stereotypes, and cultural meanings are all related and interactive in the cultural construction of disability. . . .

SOCIAL DECONSTRUCTION OF DISABILITY

In my view, then, disability is socially constructed by such factors as social conditions that cause or fail to prevent damage to people's bodies; expectations of performance; the physical and social organization of societies on the basis of a young, non-disabled, 'ideally shaped,' healthy adult male paradigm of citizens; the failure or unwillingness to create ability among citizens who do not fit the paradigm; and cultural representations, failures of representation, and expectations. Much, but perhaps not

all, of what can be socially constructed can be socially (and not just intellectually) deconstructed, given the means and the will.

A great deal of disability can be prevented with good public health and safety standards and practices, but also by relatively minor changes in the built environment that provide accessibility to people with a wide range of physical characteristics and abilities. Many measures that are usually regarded as helping or accommodating people who are now disabled, such as making buildings and public places wheelchair accessible, creating and respecting parking spaces for people with disabilities, providing American Sign Language translation, captioning, and Telephone Devices for the Deaf, and making tapes and Descriptive Video services available for people who are visually impaired, should be seen as preventive, since a great deal of disability is created by building and organizing environments, objects, and activities for a too-narrow range of people. Much more could be done along the same lines by putting people with a wide variety of physical abilities and characteristics in charge of deconstructing disability. People with disabilities should be in charge, because people without disabilities are unlikely to see many of the obstacles in their environment. Moreover, they are likely not to see them *as obstacles* even when they are pointed out, but rather as 'normal' features of the built environment that present difficulties for 'abnormal' people.

Disability cannot be deconstructed by consulting a few token disabled representatives. A person with a disability is not likely to see all the obstacles to people with disabilities different from her/his own, although s/he is likely to be more aware of potential inaccessibility. Moreover, people with disabilities are not always aware of the obstacles in our environment *as obstacles*, even when they affect us. The cultural habit of regarding the condition of the person, not the built environment or the social organization of activities, as the source of the problem, runs deep. For example, it took me several years of struggling with the heavy door to my building, sometimes having to wait until someone stronger came along, to realize that the door was an accessibility problem, not only for me, but for others as well. And I did not notice, until one of my students pointed it out, that the lack of signs that could be read from a distance at my university forced people with mobility impairments to expend a lot of energy unnecessarily, searching for rooms and offices. Although I have encountered this difficulty myself on days when walking was exhausting to me, I interpreted it, automatically, as a problem arising from my illness (as I did with the door), rather than as a problem arising from the built environment having been created for too narrow a range of people and situations. One of the most crucial factors in the deconstruction of disability is the change of perspective that causes us to look in the environment for both the source of the problem and the solutions.

. . .

OBSTACLES TO THE DECONSTRUCTION OF DISABILITY

. . .

Attitudes that disability is a personal or family problem (of biological or accidental origin), rather than a matter of social responsibility, are cultural contributors to disability and powerful factors working against social measures to increase ability. The attitude that disability is a personal problem is manifested when people with disabilities are expected to overcome obstacles to their participation in activities by their own extraordinary efforts. The public adoration of a few disabled heroes who are believed to have 'overcome their handicaps' against great odds both demonstrates and contributes to this expectation. The attitude that disability is a family matter is manifested when the families of people with disabilities are expected to provide whatever they need, even at great personal sacrifice by other family members. Barbara Hillyer describes the strength of expectations that mothers and other caregivers will do whatever is necessary to 'normalize' the lives of family members, especially children, with disabilities—not only providing care, but often doing the work of two people to maintain the illusion that there is nothing 'wrong' in the family.

These attitudes are related to the fact that many modern societies split human concerns into public and private worlds. Typically, those with disabilities and illnesses have been relegated to the private realm, along with women, children, and the old. This worldwide tendency creates particularly intractable problems for women with disabilities; since they fit two 'private' categories, they are often kept at home, isolated and overprotected. In addition, the confinement of people with disabilities in the private realm exploits women's traditional caregiving roles in order to meet the needs of people with disabilities, and it hides the need for measures to make the public realm accessible to everyone.

There also seem to be definite material advantages for some people (people without disabilities who have no disabled friends or relatives for whom they feel responsible) to seeing disability as a biological misfortune, the bad luck of individuals, and a personal or family problem. Accessibility and creating ability cost time, energy, and/or money. Charities for people with disabilities are big businesses that employ a great many non-disabled professionals; these charities depend upon the belief that responding to the difficulties faced by people with disabilities is superogatory for people who are not members of the family—not a social responsibility to be fulfilled through governments, but an act of kindness. Moreover, both the charities and most government bureaucracies (which also employ large numbers of non-disabled professionals) hand out help which would not be needed in a society that was planned and organized to include people with a wide range of physical and mental abilities. The potential resistance created by these vested interests in disability should not be underestimated.

The 'personal misfortune' approach to disability is also part of what I call the 'lottery' approach to life, in which individual good fortune is hoped for as a substitute for social planning that deals realistically with everyone's capabilities, needs and limitations, and the probable distribution of hardship. In Canada and the United States, most people reject the 'lottery' approach to such matters as acute health care for themselves and their families or basic education for their children. We expect it to be there when we need it, and we are (more or less) willing to pay for it to be there. I think the lottery approach persists with respect to disability partly because *fear*, based on ignorance and false beliefs about disability, makes it difficult for most non-disabled people to identify with people with disabilities. If the non-disabled saw the disabled as potentially themselves or as their future selves, they would want their societies to be fully accessible and to invest the resources necessary to create ability wherever possible. They would feel that 'charity' is as inappropriate a way of thinking about resources for people with disabilities as it is about emergency medical care or basic education.

The philosopher Anita Silvers maintains that it is probably impossible for most non-disabled people to imagine what life is like with a disability, and that their own becoming disabled is unthinkable to them. Certainly many people without disabilities believe that life with a disability would not be worth living. This is reflected in the assumption that potential disability is a sufficient reason for aborting a fetus, as well as in the frequent statements by non-disabled people that they would not want to live if they had to use a wheelchair, lost their eyesight, were dependent on others for care, and so on. The belief that life would not be worth living with a disability would be enough to prevent them from imagining their own dis-

ablement. This belief is fed by stereotypes and ignorance of the lives of people with disabilities. For example, the assumption that permanent, global incompetence results from any major disability is still prevalent; there is a strong presumption that competent people either have no major physical or mental limitations or are able to hide them in public and social life.

It seems that the cultural constructions of disability, including the ignorance, stereotyping, and stigmatization that feed fears of disability, have to be at least partly deconstructed before disability can be seen by more people as a set of social problems and social responsibilities. Until that change in perspective happens, people with disabilities and their families will continue to be given too much individual responsibility for 'overcoming' disabilities, expectations for the participation of people with disabilities in public life will be far too low, and social injustices that are recognized now (at least in the abstract), such as discrimination against people with disabilities, will be misunderstood.

To illustrate, let me look briefly at the problem of discrimination. Clearly, when considering whether some action or situation is an instance of discrimination on the basis of ability, the trick is to distinguish ability to do the relevant things from ability to do irrelevant things. But, given that so many places and activities are structured for people with a narrow range of abilities, telling the two apart is not always easy. No one has to walk to be a typist, but if a company is housed in a building that is inaccessible to wheelchairs, and therefore refuses to hire a competent typist who uses a wheelchair because it would be expensive to fix the building, has it discriminated against her on the basis of her disability? Laws may say yes, but people will resist the laws unless they can see that the typist's inability to work in that office is not solely a characteristic of her as an individual. Most people will be ready to recognize refusal to hire her to work in a wheelchair-accessible office, provided she is the most competent typist who applied, as discrimination against her because of her disability; they will regard her disability (like her race) as a personal characteristic irrelevant in the circumstances. But will they be ready to require a company to create wheelchair accessibility so that it can hire her? This is being tested now in the United States by the 1990 Americans with Disabilities Act. Although I expect the Act to have an invaluable educational function, I predict that it will be very difficult to enforce until more people see accessibility as a public responsibility. Only then will they be able to recognize inabilities that are created by faulty planning and organization as irrelevant.

Consider these sentiments expressed in the Burger King case, as described in *The Disability Rag and Resource:*

> When deaf actress Terrylene Sacchetti sued Burger King under the ADA for refusing to serve her when she handed the cashier a written order at the pickup window instead of using the intercom, Stan Kyker, executive vice-president of the California Restaurant Association, said that those "people (with disabilities) are going to have to accept that they are not 100 percent whole and they can't be made 100 percent whole in everything they do in life."

Had a woman been refused service because she used a cane to walk up to the counter, her treatment would, I think, have been recognized at once as discrimination. But since Ms. Sacchetti was refused service because she was unable to perform the activity (ordering food) in the way (orally) that the restaurant required it to be performed, the refusal to serve her was not immediately recognized as discrimination. Indeed, the representative of the restaurant association apparently felt comfortable defending it on the grounds that her individual characteristics were the obstacles to Ms. Sacchetti's being served.

When I imagine a society without disabilities, I do not imagine a society in which every physical and mental 'defect' or 'abnormality' can be cured. On the contrary, I believe the fantasy that someday everything will be 'curable' is a significant obstacle to the social deconstruction of disability. Instead I imagine a fully accessible society, the most fundamental characteristic of which is universal recognition that all structures have to be built and all activities have to be organized for the widest practical range of human abilities. In such a society, a person who cannot walk would not be disabled, because every major kind of activity that is accessible to someone who can walk would be accessible to someone who cannot, and likewise with seeing, hearing, speaking, moving one's arms, working for long stretches of time without rest, and many other physical and mental functions. I do not mean that everyone would be able to do everything, but rather that, with respect to the major aspects of life in the society, the differences in ability between someone who can walk, or see, or hear, and someone who cannot would be no more significant than the differences in ability among people who can walk, see, or hear. Not everyone who is not disabled now can play basketball or sing in a choir, but everyone who is not disabled now can participate in sports or games and make art, and that sort of general ability should be the goal in deconstructing disability.

I talk about accessibility and ability rather than independence or integration because I think that neither independence nor integration is always an appropriate goal for people with disabilities. Some people cannot live independently because they will always need a great deal of help from caregivers, and some people with disabilities, for example the Deaf, do not want to be integrated into non-disabled society; they prefer their own, separate social life. Everyone should, however, have access to *opportunities* to develop their abilities, to work, and to participate in the full range of public and private activities available to the rest of society.

DISCUSSION QUESTIONS FOR CHAPTER TWO

1. How do different forms of prejudice affect your life?

2. How do ideologies undergird institutions? How do these ideologies show up in the institutions that most affect your life?

3. How do institutions maintain gender inequality? Have you experienced gender inequality in particular institutions?

4. How do institutions work together to support and maintain one another?

5. How do hate crimes help maintain systems of inequality? What images of hate crimes do you recall? What effects do these images have on you?

SUGGESTIONS FOR FURTHER READING

Allison, Dorothy. *Trash.* Ithaca, NY: Firebrand, 1989.

Anzaldúa, Gloria. *Borderlands/La Frontera: The New Mestiza.* San Francisco: Aunt Lute, 1987.

Frankenberg, Ruth. *White Women, Race Matters: The Social Construction of Whiteness.* Minneapolis: University of Minnesota Press, 1993.

Lorde, Audre. *Sister Outsider.* Freedom, CA: Crossing Press, 1984.

Penelope, Julia, and Susan J. Wolfe, eds. *The Original Coming Out Stories,* expanded edition. Freedom, CA: Crossing Press, 1989.

CHAPTER THREE

Learning Gender
in a Diverse Society

Recently, while teaching a unit on the social construction of gender in a women's studies class, we asked how many among the large number of women students were identified as tomboys when they were growing up. A sea of hands responded as women remembered their early years as girls who resisted traditional notions of femininity. Then the male students were asked whether they had been called "sissies" when they were young. The whole group laughed as one lone male sheepishly raised his hand and remarked that he'd always been a sissy. Why is it so easy to say you were a tomboy and so difficult to admit to being a sissy? This has a lot to do with the meanings associated with masculinity and femininity and the ways these are ranked in society. In this chapter we focus specifically on gender and sexism, keeping in mind two important points: First, how gender is constructed in connection to other differences among women like race, ethnicity, and class, and second, how sexism as a system of oppression is related to other systems of inequality and privilege.

BIOLOGY AND CULTURE

In Chapter 1 we explained gender as the way society creates, patterns, and rewards our understandings of femininity and masculinity or the process by which roles and appropriate behaviors are ascribed to women and men. Gender, in other words, can be understood as the social organization of sexual difference. Although biological distinctions create female and male humans, society interprets these differences and gives us "feminine" and "masculine" people. These adjectives are intentionally placed in quotation marks to emphasize that notions of femininity and masculinity are socially constructed—created by social processes that reflect the various workings of power in society. Therefore these notions are culturally and historically changeable. There is nothing essential, intrinsic, or static about femininity or masculinity; rather they are social categories that might mean different things in different societies and in different historical periods. Society shapes notions of femininity and masculinity through the subtle interactions between nature and nurture.

The relationship between biology (female/male) and culture (feminine/masculine), however, is more complicated than the assertion that sex is a biological fact

Learning Activity: Tomboys and Sissies

Take an informal poll on your campus. Ask the women if they ever wanted to be a boy when they were growing up. Note their reaction to the question. Then ask why or why not. Also ask the women if they were considered tomboys growing up and how they felt about it if they were. Record responses and observations in a research journal.

Ask men on your campus if they ever wanted to be a girl when they were growing up. Again, note their reaction to the question. Ask why or why not. Then ask if they were considered sissies growing up and, if so, how they felt about it. Record responses and observations.

Once you've completed your poll, compare and contrast the responses you received from women and men. What do you notice? Why do you think responses may have been the way they were? What do responses suggest about gender in American society?

Learning Activity: Speaking of Women and Men

Think about the adjectives we typically use to describe women and men and list these words in the columns below. A couple of examples are provided to get you started

Women	Men
Passive	Active
Nurturing	Strong

What do you notice about the words we use to describe women and men? How does our language reinforce stereotypical notions about women and men?

Think about the words we use to designate women and list these names in the columns below. Also, try to find parallel names for women and men. And think about the profanities we use as well. Again, a couple of examples are provided.

Women	Men
Slut	Stud
Chick	

What do you notice here about the terms we use to name women and men? What is the significance of the words for which you could not identify parallels?

How do you think language plays a role in shaping the ways we think about and "do" gender?

and gender is the societal interpretation of that fact. Although biology may imply some basic physiological facts, culture gives meaning to these in such a way that we must question whether biology can exist except within the society that gives it meaning in the first place. This implies that sex, in terms of raw male or female, is already gendered by the culture within which these physiological facts of biology exist. In other words, although many people make a distinction between biological sex (female/male) and learned gender (feminine/masculine), it is really impossible to speak of a fixed biological sex category outside of the sense that a culture makes of that category.

An example that highlights how biology is connected to culture concerns the processes by which ambiguous sex characteristics in children are handled. When hermaphrodites or "intersex" children are born without distinct genitalia to characterize them as either girls or boys, health professionals and the family make a sex determination. Hormone therapy and surgeries follow to make such a child fit the constructed binary categories our society has created, and gender is taught in accordance with this decision. This is an example of a breakdown in the taken-for-granted tight connection between natural biology and learned gender.

Gender is one of the most important features of a person's identity, shaping social life and informing attitudes, behavior, and the individual's sense of self. This is aptly revealed in Lois Gould's "X: A Fabulous Child's Story." "X" is neither obviously masculine nor feminine, and, as a result, s/he causes much confusion among people who just do not know what to do with an "X." The pervasiveness of

Cathy © 1987 Cathy Guisewite. Reprinted with permission of Universal Press Syndicate. All rights reserved.

Calvin and Hobbes   by Bill Watterson

gender is also a theme of Judith Lorber's article "The Social Construction of Gender." She explains that gender is a process that involves multiple patterns of interaction and is created and re-created constantly in human interaction. Lorber also makes the important point that because gender is so central in shaping our lives, much of what is gendered we do not even recognize; it's made normal and ordinary and occurs on a subconscious level. In other words, the differences between femininity (passive, dependent, intuitive, emotional) and masculinity (strong, independent, in control, out of touch emotionally) are made to seem natural and inevitable despite the fact that gender is a social script that individuals learn. Importantly, many of the skills and practices associated with gender involve privilege and entitlements. They also involve limitations.

In reality, gender is a practice in which all people engage; it is something we perform over and over in our daily lives. In this sense, gender is something that we "do" rather than "have." Through a process of *gender socialization,* we are taught and learn the appropriate thinking and behaviors associated with being a boy or girl in this culture. We actively learn the skills and practices of gender, and most of us become very accomplished in these various performances. For example, in sports, the way that girls tend naturally to throw a ball is often the object of derision. Throwing the way boys do, however, is actually an act that is learned, then performed again and again until it becomes a skill. Girls can learn to throw like boys if they are taught. As Mariah Burton Nelson contends, men are not necessarily better athletes than women; rather, sports as an institution has developed to reflect the particular athletic competencies of men. For example, if long-distance swimming or balance beam (activities where women generally outperform men) were popular national sports, then we might think differently about the athletic capabilities of women and men.

In addition to sports, there are many other major U.S. institutions that support gendered practices. You only need go to a toy store and cruise the very different girls' and boys' aisles to witness the social construction of gender in contemporary U.S. society. What does it mean to get a child-size ironing board instead of a toy gun, and what kinds of behaviors and future roles do these toys help create and

Learning Activity: Performing Gender in the Movies

Many movies offer gender-bending performances. Choose one or more of the following movies to watch. During the movie, record your observations about how the various characters learn and perform gender.

- *Victor/Victoria*
- *Tootsie*
- *Mrs. Doubtfire*
- *To Wong Foo, Thanks for Everything! Julie Newmar*
- *The Adventures of Priscilla, Queen of the Desert*
- *Switch*
- *The Birdcage*
- *Orlando*
- *Shakespeare in Love*

justify? In "Spiking the Punch," Natalie Angier contends that the social context limits how girls and women express their aggression, instead of using their bodies, they use words (as a direct form) and snubbing, sulking, and withdrawing (as indirect forms).

This discussion of gender identity and practices does not imply that all men are ambitious and independent and all women domestic and emotional. However, this discussion clarifies the social norms or shared values associated with the two kinds of human beings our society has created. Gender norms provide the standards or parameters through which thoughts and behaviors are molded. If we created a continuum with "feminine" on one end and "masculine" on the other, we would find mostly women on one end and mostly men on the other, and a mixture in between. This means that women and men learn the practices of gender, internalize the norms associated with masculinity and femininity, are rewarded for appropriate behaviors and sanctioned for inappropriate behaviors, and learn to perform the ones that are expected of them.

There are some people who consider themselves *transgendered*. Identifying oneself as transgendered involves resisting the social construction of gender into two distinct categories, masculinity and femininity, and working to break down these constraining categories. Transgendered people push at the boundaries of gender and help reveal its constructed nature. *Transsexuals* are transgendered people who believe that they are born with the bodies of the wrong sex. Usually they desire to be surgically altered to claim a sex different from the one into which they were born. The terms *transgendered* and *transsexual* are distinct from transvestites, people who dress in the other sex's attire. Being transgendered does not imply being gay. Transgendered identities are about gender performance, whereas homosexual identity is about the expression of sexuality.

Transgendered is also different from androgyny. *Androgyny* can be defined as the lack of gender differentiation; androgynous people display a balanced mixture of recognizable feminine and masculine traits. X in Lois Gould's story is an androgynous child. Transgendered individuals do not want to be constrained by categories of masculinity and femininity and exhibit instead traits that are difficult to label as either masculine or feminine.

It is interesting to note that contemporary ideas about androgyny tend to privilege the "andro" more than the "gyny," with the presentation of androgyny looking a lot more like a young male than a mature female. The trappings of femininity seem to be the first things that are shed when a body tries to redo itself as androgynous. This is related to androcentrism and the ways masculinity more closely approximates our understanding of "human."

MASCULINITY

In contemporary U.S. society, *masculinity* has been constructed from the classical traits of intelligence, courage, and honesty, with the addition of two other key dimensions. One of these revolves around potent sexuality and an affinity for violence: the machismo element. *Machismo* involves breaking rules, sexual potency contextualized in the blending of sex and violence, and contempt for women *(misogyny)*. To be a man is to *not* be a woman. Weakness, softness, and vulnerability are to be avoided at all costs. It is no coincidence that the symbol of male ♂ represents Mars, the Roman god of war. Another dimension of masculinity is the *provider role, composed of ambition, confidence, competence, and strength*. Research by Deborah David and Robert Brannon characterizes four dictates of masculinity that encompass these key dimensions. The dictates include the following: (1) "no sissy stuff," the rejection of femininity; (2) the "big wheel," ambition and the pursuit of success, fame, and wealth; (3) the "sturdy oak," confidence, competence, stoicism, and toughness; and (4) "give 'em hell," the machismo element.* Although these scripts dictate masculinity in a broad sense, there are societal demands that construct masculinity differently for different kinds of men. Middle-class masculinity puts an emphasis on the big wheel dimension, the dictates of White masculinity often involve the sturdy oak, and men of color often become associated with the machismo element. The latter, however, tends not to apply to Asian or Asian American men who are often seen as feminized and less masculine.

Some changes in the social construction of contemporary masculinity have allowed for a downplaying of the machismo element without a loss of sexual potency or societal control: a few small steps made into the land of the feminine. Although the machismo element is still acted out by countless teenage boys and men, it is also avoided by many men who genuinely do not want to be constrained by its demands. Often these men have realized that moving away from the machismo does not necessarily imply a loss of power. In fact, it seems contemporary women may prefer men who are a little more sensitive and vulnerable. In part, these changes have come about as a result of the focus on gender provided by the women's movement. As feminist writer and activist Gloria Steinem once said, gender is a prison for both women and men. The difference, she said, is

---

*Deborah S. David and Robert Brannon, eds. *The Forty-Nine Percent Majority: The Male Sex Role* (Reading, MA: Addison-Wesley, 1976), pp. 13–35.

Activist Profile: Gloria Steinem

Photos and content courtesy of Gloria Steinem

Gloria Steinem didn't set out to become one of the key spokespersons for feminism. Growing up in poverty and with a mentally ill mother, Steinem often found herself in the role of her mother's caretaker. Despite the difficulties at home, she succeeded at school and was eventually accepted to Smith College, where her interest in women's rights began to take hold. After graduating from Smith, Steinem received a fellowship to do graduate studies at the University of Delhi and University of Calcutta, India. While in India, she did some work as a freelance writer and, upon returning to the United States, began a career in journalism.

As a woman in journalism, Steinem was rarely given serious assignments. Her most famous article resulted from a 1963 undercover assignment as a Playboy Bunny. Steinem saw the article as an opportunity to expose sexual harassment, but following its publication she had a difficult time being taken seriously as a journalist, despite the excellent reviews the article received.

She finally got her chance for key political assignments in 1968 when she came on board *New York Magazine* as a contributing editor. One assignment sent her to cover a radical feminist meeting, and following that meeting she moved to the center of the women's movement, co-founding the National Women's Political Caucus and the Women's Action Alliance.

In 1972 she co-founded *Ms.* magazine. Although Steinem believed there should be a feminist magazine, she had not intended to start it herself. Originally, she had thought she'd turn over the editorship once the magazine got on its feet. But with the success of *Ms.*, Steinem became one of the nation's most visible and important proponents of feminism.

The first issue of *Ms.* featured Wonder Woman on the cover, and its entire first printing of 300,000 copies sold out in eight days. Steinem remained editor for fifteen years and is still involved with the magazine today.

The Problem with Promise Keepers

". . . sit down with your wife and say something like this, 'Honey, I've made a terrible mistake. . . . I gave up leading this family, and I forced you to take my place. Now I must reclaim that role.' . . . I'm not suggesting you ask for your role back; I'm urging you to take it back. . . . there can be no compromise here. If you're going to lead, you must lead. . . . Treat the lady gently and lovingly. But lead."
—Tony Evans, leader of Promise Keepers

Promise Keepers posits itself as a Christian men's movement intended to unite men through vital relationships to become godly influences in the world. Sounds great on the surface, doesn't it? Promise Keepers claims it has no political agenda and only desires to help men build meaningful relationships with God, their families, and one another. Admirable goals, no doubt.

But let's look a little deeper. According to a *Washington Post* poll conducted during a Promise Keepers rally in D.C., 60 percent had an unfavorable opinion of feminists, 69 percent favored making divorce harder to obtain, and 94 percent opposed allowing same-sex marriages.

Promise Keepers calls for wives to submit themselves to their husbands and urges husbands to take control of the family back from their wives. They oppose abortion and homosexuality. Promise Keepers founder Bill McCartney was instrumental in the success of Colorado's anti-lesbian and anti-gay legislation, which was eventually ruled unconstitutional by the Supreme Court. McCartney has also been a featured speaker at rallies of the extremist anti-abortion group, Operation Rescue.

At its core, Promise Keepers is about maintenance of patriarchy. Again, examine the words of Promise Keepers leader Tony Evans: "I believe that feminists of the more aggressive persuasion are frustrated women unable to find the proper male leadership. If a woman were receiving the right kind of love and attention and leadership, she would not want to be liberated from that."

Listen carefully and critically to the rhetoric of any group trying to influence people to its way of thinking. Although the rhetoric may suggest the group is doing one thing, the reality may be that the group's agenda is entirely something else. The problem with Promise Keepers is not that it wants to help men be good husbands. The problem is that Promise Keepers wants men to take control and women to submit. They may couch their ideas in language about honor and integrity, but their ideas are really about reinforcing male supremacy.

The National Organization for Women maintains a web page on Promise Keepers. Visit this site at *www.now.org/issues/right/pk.html*.

that for men it's a prison with wall-to-wall carpeting and someone to bring you coffee. Understanding the limitations associated with masculine social scripts has encouraged many men to transform these scripts into more productive ways of living. Many pro-feminist men and men's organizations have been at the forefront of this work.

Some men have responded to the limitations of masculinity by focusing on themselves as victims. This is evident in the mytho-poetic men's movement, discussed in Allan Johnson's essay "Shame, Guilt, and Responsibility" in Chapter 1. Johnson suggests that it does more harm than good by encouraging men to pursue private solutions to social problems. Drumming, chanting, and storytelling may help men feel more connected to one another and to a mythic sense of manhood, but it does little to illuminate or transform the patriarchal system that created the wounds they want to heal.

Other men more overtly express their desire to take back the power they believe they have lost as a result of changes in contemporary notions of femininity and the gains of the women's movement. These include the Promise Keepers, a group of Christian-affiliated men who want to return men to their rightful place in the family and community through a strong re-assertion of traditional gender roles. They believe, that in the family, men are to rule and women are to serve.

FEMININITY

Adjectives associated with traditional notions of femininity include soft, passive, domestic, nurturing, emotional, dependent, sensitive, as well as delicate, intuitive, fastidious, needy, fearful, and so forth. These are the qualities that have kept women in positions of subordination and encouraged them to do the domestic and emotional work of society. Again, no surprise that the symbol of female ♀ represents Venus, the goddess of love. "Doing gender" in terms of femininity involves speaking, walking, looking, and acting in certain ways: in feminine ways. The performative quality involved in being a drag queen (a gay man who is acting out normative femininity), highlights and reveals the taken-for-granted (at least by women) affectations of femininity. Yet, femininity, like masculinity, varies across cultures and groups. For example, due to historical and cultural factors, African American women have not internalized the association of femininity with passivity and dependence characteristic of White women. Asian American women, on the other hand, have to deal with societal stereotypes that construct femininity very much in terms of passivity and dependence: the "exotic gardenia" or "oriental chick" described in Nellie Wong's poem "When I Was Growing Up."

A key aspect of femininity is its bifurcation or channeling into two opposite aspects. These aspects involve the chaste, domestic, caring mother or madonna and the sexy, seducing, fun-loving playmate or whore (known in popular mythology as women you marry and women with whom you have sex). These polar opposites cause tension as women navigate the implications of these aspects of femininity in their everyday lives. This is an example of the double bind that Marilyn Frye wrote about in her article "Oppression" included in Chapter 2. A woman often discovers that neither sexual activity nor sexual inactivity is quite right. If she is too sexually active, she will be censured for being too loose, the whore; if she refrains from sexual activity, she might similarly be censured for being a prude or frigid. Notice there are many slang words for both kinds of women: those who have too much sex and those who do not have enough. This is the double bind: You're damned if you do and potentially damned if you don't. These contradictions and mixed messages serve to keep women in line.

Learning Activity: Walk Like a Man, Sit Like a Lady

One of the ways we perform gender is by the way we use our bodies. Very early, children learn to act their gender in the ways they sit, walk, and talk.

Try this observation research:

- Observe a group of schoolchildren playing. Make notes about what you observe concerning how girls and boys act, particularly how they use their bodies in their play and communication.

- Find a place where you can watch people sitting or walking. A public park or mall may offer an excellent vantage point. Record your observations about the ways women and men walk and sit.

Also try this experiment: Ask a friend of the opposite sex to participate in an experiment with you. Take turns teaching each other to sit and to walk like the opposite sex. After practicing your newfound gender behaviors, write your reflections about the experience.

Unlike contemporary masculinity, which is exhibiting very small steps into the realms of the feminine, femininity has boldly moved into areas that were traditionally off-limits. Today's ideal woman (perhaps from a woman's point of view) is definitely more androgynous than the ideal woman of the past. The contemporary ideal woman might be someone who is smart, competent, and independent, beautiful, thin, and sexy, yet also loving, sensitive, competent domestically, and emotionally healthy. Note how this image has integrated characteristics of masculinity with traditional feminine qualities, at the same time that it has retained much of the feminine social script. The contemporary ideal woman is strong, assertive, active, and independent rather than soft, passive, fearful, delicate, and dependent. The assumption is that she is out in the public world rather than confined to the home. She has not completely shed her domestic, nurturing, and caring dimension, however, or her intuitive, emotional, and sensitive aspects. These attributes are important in her success as a loving and capable partner to a man, as indeed are her physical attributes concerning looks and body size.

To be a modern woman today (we might even say a "liberated woman") is to be able to do *everything:* the superwoman. It is important to ask who is benefiting from this new social script. Women work in the public world (often in jobs that pay less, thus helping employers and the economic system) and yet still are expected to do the domestic and emotional work of home and family as well as stay beautiful. In many ways contemporary femininity tends to serve both the capitalist economic system and individual men better than the traditional, dependent, domestic model.

GENDER RANKING

Gender not only encompasses the socially constructed differences prescribed for different kinds of human beings but also the meanings associated with these dif-

Ideas for Activism

- Be a gender traitor for a day. Act/dress in ways that are not generally considered to be appropriate for your gender.

- Develop and perform on campus a street theater piece about gender performance.

- Plan, create, publish, and distribute a zine challenging traditional gender roles.

- Examine how masculinity is valued above femininity on your campus. Write a letter about your findings to your campus newspaper.

ferences. Recall the sissy/tomboy exercise at the beginning of this chapter. Those traits assigned as feminine are less valued than those considered masculine. It is okay to emulate the masculine and act like a boy, but it is not okay to emulate the feminine. We recently attended a baby shower where the expectant mother was opening gifts. As she pulled a blue sleeper suit from its wrapper, the person who had bought the gift explained that even though the baby's sex was not yet known, she hoped the gift was still appropriate because a girl could still wear blue. The implication was that because a boy ought not to wear pink, a blue sleeper was a more adaptable color and a therefore a safer gift.

Gender ranking sets the stage for sexism. Judith Lorber writes, "When genders are ranked, the devalued genders have less power, prestige, and economic rewards than the valued genders." Just as White is valued above Brown or Black, and young (though not too young) above old, and heterosexual above homosexual, masculinity tends to be ranked higher than femininity. To be male is to have privileges vis-à-vis gender systems; to be female means to be a member of a target group. The social system here that discriminates and privileges on the basis of gender is sexism. It works by viewing the differences between women and men as important for determining access to social, economic and political resources. As defined in Chapter 2, *sexism* is the system that discriminates and privileges on the basis of gender and that results in gender stratification. Given the ranking of gender in our society, sexism works to privilege men and limit women.

Men receive entitlements and privilege in a society that ranks masculinity over femininity. In "What Are Little Boys Made Of?" Michael Kimmel discusses the popular notion that it is actually boys that are suffering the most in our culture. He reframes this debate by encouraging us to look at masculine privilege and entitlement as central in understanding the problems boys face today.

DIVERSE GENDERED EXPERIENCES

Although all women are limited by sexism as a system of power that privileges men over women, the social category "woman," as you recall from Chapter 2, is hardly homogeneous. Gender shapes different women's lives in different ways; women are not affected by gender as a system of privilege and inequality in the same way. Other systems based upon class, race, sexual orientation, and so forth interact with gender to produce different experiences for individual women. In other words, the effects of gender and understandings of both femininity and masculinity are mediated by other systems of power. This is what Virginia Sapiro in "The Plurality of Gender-Based Realities" means when she says that forms of gender-based oppression and exploitation depend in part upon other social characteristics in people's lives. She also makes the important point that gender practices are often a way to enforce other types of inequalities.

For example, African American women are often characterized as promiscuous or matriarchal, and African American men are described as hyperathletic and sexually potent. Jewish women are painted as overly materialistic and overbearing, whereas Jewish men are supposedly very ambitious, thrifty, good at business, yet still tied to their mothers' apron strings. Latinas and Chicanas are stereotyped as sexy and fun loving, and, likewise, Latinos and Chicanos are seen as oversexed, romantic, and passionate. Native American women are portrayed as silent and overworked or exotic and romantic, whereas Native American men are seen as aloof mystics, close to nature, or else as savages and drunks. Asian American women have also been typed as exotic, as well as passive and delicate, at the same time that Asian American men are seen as lacking in masculinity and feminized. All these problematic constructions are created against the norm of Whiteness and work to maintain the privileges of the mythical norm. This concept is illustrated in Nellie Wong's poem. She longed to be White, something she saw as synonymous with being a desirable woman. Although there are ethnic and regional stereotypes for White women (like the Southern belle, sexually liberated Scandinavian, or hot-tempered Irish), for the most part White women tend not to have discreet stereotypes associated with their race. This reflects the fact that White people are encouraged not to see White as a racial category although it is just as racialized as any other racial group. The fact that being White can be claimed the mythical norm strips Whiteness from the historical and political roots of its construction as a racial category.

Diverse gendered experiences (the title of this subsection) implies that the expression of femininity, or the parameters of femininity expected and allowed, is related to the confluence of gender with other systems. Historically, certain women (the poor and women of color) were regarded as carrying out appropriate womanhood when they fulfilled the domestic labor needs of strangers. Upper-class femininity meant that there were certain jobs such women could not perform. This demonstrates the interaction of gender with class and race systems. Old women endure a certain brand of femininity that tends to be devoid of the playmate role and is heavy on the mother aspect. Sexually active old women are violating the norms of femininity set up for them: This shows the influence of ageism in terms of shaping gender norms. Other stereotypes that reveal the interaction of gender with societal systems of privilege and inequality include disabled women's relatively low sexual appetite or lesbians' lack of femininity (they are presumed to want to be like men at the same time that they hate them). In this way the expression of femininity is dependent upon other intersecting systems of inequality and privilege and the beliefs, stereotypes, and practices associated with these systems.

X

A Fabulous Child's Story

Lois Gould

Once upon a time, a baby named X was born. This baby was named X so that nobody could tell whether it was a boy or a girl. Its parents could tell, of course, but they couldn't tell anybody else. They couldn't even tell Baby X, at first.

. . .

The day the Joneses brought their baby home, lots of friends and relatives came over to see it. None of them knew about the secret Xperiment, though. So the first thing they asked was what kind of a baby X was. When the Joneses smiled and said, "It's an X!" nobody knew what to say. They couldn't say, "Look at her cute little dimples!" And they couldn't say, "Look at his husky little biceps!" And they couldn't even say just plain "kitchy-coo." In fact, they all thought the Joneses were playing some kind of rude joke.

But, of course, the Joneses were not joking. "It's an X" was absolutely all they would say. And that made the friends and relatives very angry. The relatives all felt embarrassed about having an X in the family. "People will think there's something wrong with it!" some of them whispered. "There *is* something wrong with it!" others whispered back.

"Nonsense!" the Joneses told them all cheerfully. "What could possibly be wrong with this perfectly adorable X?"

. . .

Clearly, nothing at all was wrong. Nevertheless, none of the relatives felt comfortable about buying a present for a Baby X. The cousins who sent the baby a tiny football helmet would not come and visit any more. And the neighbors who sent a pink-flowered romper suit pulled their shades down when the Joneses passed their house.

. . .

Ms. and Mr. Jones had to be Xtra careful about how they played with little X. They knew that if they kept bouncing it up in the air and saying how *strong* and *active* it was, they'd be treating it more like a boy than an X. But if all they did was cuddle it and kiss it and tell it how *sweet* and *dainty* it was, they'd be treating it more like a girl than an X.

. . .

Meanwhile, the Joneses were worrying about other problems. Toys, for instance. And clothes. On his first shopping trip, Mr. Jones told the store clerk, "I need some clothes and toys for my new baby." The clerk smiled and said, "Well, now, is it a boy or a girl?" "It's an X," Mr. Jones said, smiling back. But the clerk got all red in the face and said huffily, "In *that* case, I'm afraid I can't help you, sir." So Mr. Jones wandered helplessly up and down the aisles trying to find what X needed But everything in the store was piled up in sections marked "Boys" or "girls." There were "Boys' Pajamas" and "Girls' Underwear" and "Boys' Fire Engines" and "Girls' Housekeeping Sets." Mr. Jones went home without buying anything for X. . . .

By the time X grew big enough to play with other children, the Joneses' troubles had grown bigger, too. Once a little girl grabbed X's shovel in the sandbox, and zonked X on the head with it. "Now, now, Tracy," the little girl's mother began to scold, "little girls mustn't hit little—" and she turned to ask X, "are you a little boy or a little girl, dear?"

Mr. Jones, who was sitting near the sandbox, held his breath and crossed his fingers.

X smiled politely at the lady, even though X's head had never been zonked so hard in its life. "I'm a little X," X replied.

"You're a *what*?" the lady exclaimed angrily. "You're a little b-r-a-t, you mean!

"But little girls mustn't hit little Xes, either!" said X, retrieving the shovel with another polite smile. "What good does hitting do, anyway?"

X's father, who was still holding his breath, finally let it out, uncrossed his fingers, and grinned back at X.

But then it was time for X to start school. The Joneses were really worried about this, because school was even more full of rules for boys and girls, and there were no rules for Xes. The teacher would tell boys to form one line, and girls to form another line. There would be boys' games and girls' games, and boys' secrets and girls' secrets. The school library would have a list of recommended books for girls, and a different list of recommended books for boys. There would even be a bathroom marked BOYS and another one marked GIRLS. Pretty soon boys and girls would hardly talk to each other. What would happen to poor little X?

. . .

Nobody in X's class had ever known an X before. What would they think? How would X make friends?

You couldn't tell what X was by studying its clothes—overalls don't even button right-to-left, like girls' clothes, or left-to-right, like boys' clothes. And you couldn't guess whether X had a girl's short haircut or a boy's long haircut. And it was very hard to tell by the games X liked to play. Either X played ball very well for a girl or played house very well for a boy.

Some of the children tried to find out by asking X tricky questions, like "Who's your favorite sports star?" That was easy. X had two favorite sports stars: a girl jockey named Robyn Smith and a boy archery champion named Robin Hood. Then they asked, "What's your favorite TV program?" And that was even easier. X's favorite TV program was "Lassie," which stars a girl dog played by a boy dog.

When X said that its favorite toy was a doll, everyone decided that X must be a girl. But then X said that the doll was really a robot, and that X had computerized it, and that it was pro-grammed to bake fudge brownies and then clean up the kitchen. After X told them that, the other children gave up guessing what X was. All they knew was they'd sure like to see X's doll.

After school, X wanted to play with the other children. "How about shooting some baskets in the gym?" X asked the girls, But all they did was make faces and giggle behind X's back.

"How about weaving some baskets in the arts and crafts room?" X asked the boys. But they all made faces and giggled behind X's back, too.

That night, Ms. and Mr. Jones asked X how things had gone at school. X told them sadly that the lessons were okay, but otherwise school was a horrible place for an X. It seemed as if the Other Children would never want an X for a friend.

. . .

X liked being itself. But X cried a lot that night, partly because it felt afraid. So X's father held X tight, and cuddled it, and couldn't help crying a little, too. And X's mother cheered them both up by reading an Xciting story about an enchanted prince called Sleeping Hand-some, who woke up when Princess Charming kissed him.

The next morning, they all felt much better, and little X went back to school with a brave smile and a clean pair of red-and-white checked overalls.

There was a seven-letter-word spelling bee in class that day. And a seven-lap boys' relay race in the gym. And a seven-layer-cake baking contest in the girls' kitchen corner. X won the spelling bee. X also won the relay race. And X almost won the baking contest, except it forgot to light the oven. Which only proves that no-body's perfect.

One of the Other Children noticed some-thing else, too. He said: "Winning or losing doesn't seem to count to X. X seems to have fun being good at boys' skills *and* girls' skills."

"Come to think of it," said another one of the Other Children, "maybe X is having twice as much fun as we are!"

So after school that day, the girl who beat X

at the baking contest gave X a big slice of her prizewinning cake. And the boy X beat in the relay race asked X to race him home.

From then on, some really funny things began to happen. Susie, who sat next to X in class, suddenly refused to wear pink dresses to school any more. She insisted on wearing red-and-white checked overalls—just like X's. Overalls, she told her parents, were much better for climbing monkey bars.

Then Jim, the class football nut, started wheeling his little sister's doll carriage around the football field. He'd put on his entire football uniform, except for the helmet. Then he'd put the helmet *in* the carriage, lovingly tucked under an old set of shoulder pads. Then he'd start jogging around the field, pushing the carriage and singing "Rockabye Baby" to his football helmet. He told his family that X did the same thing, so it must be okay. After all, X was now the team's star quarterback.

Susie's parents were horrified by her behavior, and Jim's parents were worried sick about him. But the worst came when the twins, Joe and Peggy, decided to share everything with each other. Peggy used Joe's hockey skates, and his microscope, and took half his newspaper route. Joe used peggy's needlepoint kit, and her cookbooks, and took two of her three baby-sitting jobs. Peggy started running the lawn mower, and Joe started running the vacuum cleaner.

Their parents weren't one bit pleased with Peggy's wonderful biology experiments, or with Joe's terrific needlepoint pillows. They didn't care that Peggy mowed the lawn better, and that Joe vacuumed the carpet better. In fact, they were furious. It's all that little X's fault, they agreed. Just because X doesn't know what it is, or what it's supposed to be, it wants to get everybody *else* mixed up, too!

Peggy and Joe were forbidden to play with X any more. So was Susie, and then Jim, and then *all* the Other Children. But it was too late; the Other Children stayed mixed up and happy and free, and refused to go back to the way they'd been before X.

. . .

READING 18

The Social Construction of Gender

Judith Lorber

Talking about gender for most people is the equivalent of fish talking about water. Gender is so much the routine ground of everyday activities that questioning its taken-for-granted assumptions and presuppositions is like thinking about whether the sun will come up.[1] Gender is so pervasive that in our society we assume it is bred into our genes. Most people find it hard to believe that gender is constantly created and re-created out of human interaction, out of social life, and is the texture and order of that social life. Yet gender, like culture, is a human production that depends on everyone constantly "doing gender" (West and Zimmerman 1987).

And everyone "does gender" without thinking about it. Today, on the subway, I saw a well-dressed man with a year-old child in a stroller. Yesterday, on a bus, I saw a man with a tiny baby in a carrier on his chest. Seeing men taking care of small children in public is increasingly common—at least in New York City. But both men were quite obviously stared at—and smiled at, approvingly. Everyone was doing gender—the men who were changing the role of fathers and the other passengers, who were applauding them silently. But there was more gendering going on that probably fewer people noticed. The baby was wearing a white crocheted cap and white clothes. You couldn't tell if it was a boy or a girl. The child in the stroller was wearing a dark blue T-shirt and dark print pants. As they started to leave the train, the father put a Yankee baseball cap on the child's head. Ah, a boy, I thought. Then I noticed the gleam of tiny earrings in the child's ears, and as they got off, I saw the little flowered sneakers and lace-trimmed socks. Not a boy after all. Gender done.

. . .

For the individual, gender construction starts with assignment to a sex category on the basis of what the genitalia look like at birth.[2] Then babies are dressed or adorned in a way that displays the category because parents don't want to be constantly asked whether their baby is a girl or a boy. A sex category becomes a gender status through naming, dress, and the use of other gender markers. Once a child's gender is evident, others treat those in one gender differently from those in the other, and the children respond to the different treatment by feeling different and behaving differently. As soon as they can talk, they start to refer to themselves as members of their gender. Sex doesn't come into play again until puberty, but by that time, sexual feelings and desires and practices have been shaped by gendered norms and expectations. Adolescent boys and girls approach and avoid each other in an elaborately scripted and gendered mating dance. Parenting is gendered, with different expectations for mothers and fathers, and people of different genders work at different kinds of jobs. The work adults do as mothers and fathers and as low-level workers and high-level bosses, shapes women's and men's life experiences, and these experiences produce different feelings, consciousness, relationships, skills—ways of being that we call feminine or masculine.[3] All of these processes constitute the social construction of gender.

. . .

To explain why gendering is done from birth, constantly and by everyone, we have to look not only at the way individuals experience gender but at gender as a social institution. As a social institution, gender is one of the major ways that human beings organize their lives. Human society depends on a predictable division of labor, a designated allocation of scarce goods, assigned responsibility for children and others who cannot care for themselves, common values and their systematic transmission to new members, legitimate leadership, music, art, stories, games, and other symbolic productions. One way of choosing people for the different tasks of society is on the basis of their talents, motivations, and competence—their demonstrated achievements. The other way is on the basis of gender, race, ethnicity—ascribed membership in a category of people. Although societies vary in the extent to which they use one or the other of these ways of allocating people to work and to carry out other responsibilities, every society uses gender and age grades. Every society classifies people as "girl and boy children," "girls and boys ready to be married," and "fully adult women and men," constructs similarities among them and differences between them, and assigns them to different roles and responsibilities. Personality characteristics, feelings, motivations, and ambitions flow from these different life experiences so that the members of these different groups become different kinds of people. The process of gendering and its outcome are legitimated by religion, law, science and the society's entire set of values.

GENDER AS PROCESS, STRATIFICATION, AND STRUCTURE

As a social institution, gender is a process of creating distinguishable social statuses for the assignment of rights and responsibilities. As part of a stratification system that ranks these statuses unequally, gender is a major building block in the social structures built on these un-equal statuses.

As a *process,* gender creates the social differences that define "woman" and "man." In social interaction throughout their lives, individuals learn what is expected, see what is expected, act and react in expected ways, and thus simultaneously construct and maintain the gender order. . . .

Gendered patterns of interaction acquire additional layers of gendered sexuality, parenting, and work behaviors in childhood, adolescence, and adulthood. Gendered norms and expectations are enforced through informal sanctions of gender-inappropriate behavior by peers and by formal punishment or threat of punishment by those in authority should behavior deviate too far from socially imposed standards for women and men.

. . .

As part of a *stratification* system, gender ranks men above women of the same race and class. Women and men could be different but equal. In practice, the process of creating difference depends to a great extent on differential evaluation. . . . The dominant categories are the hegemonic ideals, taken so for granted as the way things should be that white is not ordinarily thought of as a race, middle class as a class, or men as a gender. The characteristics of these categories define the Other as that which lacks the valuable qualities the dominants exhibit.

In a gender-stratified society, what men do is usually valued more highly than what women do because men do it, even when their activities are very similar or the same. In different regions of southern India, for example, harvesting rice is men's work, shared work, or women's work: "Wherever a task is done by women it is considered easy, and where it is done by [men] it is considered difficult" (Mencher 1988, 104). A gathering and hunting society's survival usually depends on the nuts, grubs, and small animals brought in by the women's foraging trips, but when the men's hunt is successful, it is the occasion for a cele-bration. Conversely, because they are the superior group, white men do not have to do the "dirty work," such as housework; the most inferior group does it, usually poor women of color (Palmer 1989).

. . .

When gender is a major component of structured inequality, the devalued genders have less power, prestige, and economic rewards than the valued genders. In countries that discourage gender discrimination, many major roles are still gendered; women still do most of the domestic labor and child rearing, even while doing full-time paid work; women and men are segregated on the job and each does work considered "appropriate"; women's work is usually paid less than men's work. Men dominate the positions of authority and leadership in government, the military, and the law; cultural productions, religions, and sports reflect men's interests.

In societies that create the greatest gender difference, such as Saudi Arabia, women are kept out of sight behind walls or veils, have no civil rights, and often create a cultural and emotional world of their own (Bernard 1981). But even in societies with less rigid gender boundaries, women and men spend much of their time with people of their own gender because of the way work and family are organized. This spatial separation of women and men reinforces gendered differences, identity, and ways of thinking and behaving (Coser 1986).

Gender inequality—the devaluation of "women" and the social domination of "men"—has social functions and social history. It is not the result of sex, procreation, physiology, anatomy, hormones, or genetic predispositions. It is produced and maintained by identifiable social processes and built into the general social structure and individual identities deliberately and purposefully. The social order as we know it in Western societies is organized around racial, ethnic, class, and gender inequality. I contend, therefore, that the continuing purpose of gender as a modern social institution is to construct women as a group to be the subordinates of men as a group.

THE PARADOX OF HUMAN NATURE

To say that sex, sexuality, and gender are all socially constructed is not to minimize their social power. These categorical imperatives govern our lives in the most profound and pervasive ways, through the social experiences and social practices of what Dorothy Smith calls the "everday/evernight world" (1990, 31–57). The paradox of human nature is that it is *always* a manifestation of cultural meanings, social relationships, and power politics; "not biology, but culture, becomes destiny" (J. Butler 1990, 8). Gendered people emerge not from physiology or sexual orientations but from the exigencies of the social order, mostly, from the need for a reliable division of the work of food production and the social (not physical) reproduction of new members. The moral imperatives of religion and cultural representations guard the boundary lines among genders and ensure that what is demanded, what is permitted, and what is tabooed for the people in each gender is well known and followed by most (C. Davies 1982). Political power, control of scarce resources, and, if necessary, violence uphold the gendered social order in the face of resistance and rebellion. Most people, however, voluntarily go along with their society's prescriptions for those of their gender status, because the norms and expectations get built into their sense of worth and identity as [the way we] think, the way we see and hear and speak, the way we fantasy, and the way we feel.

There is no core or bedrock in human nature below these endlessly looping processes of the social production of sex and gender, self and other, identity and psyche, each of which is a "complex cultural construction" (J. Butler 1990, 36). *For humans, the social is the natural. . . .*

NOTES

1. Gender is, in Erving Goffman's words, an aspect of *Felicity's Condition:* "any arrangement which leads us to judge an individual's . . . acts not to be a manifestation of strangeness. Behind Felicity's Condition is our sense of what it is to be sane" (1983:27). Also see Bem 1993; Frye 1983, 17–40; Goffman 1977.
2. In cases of ambiguity in countries with modern medicine, surgery is usually performed to make the genitalia more clearly male or female.
3. See J. Butler 1990 for an analysis of how doing gender is gender identity.

REFERENCES

Bem, Sandara Lipsitz. 1993. *The Lenses of Gender: Transforming the Debate on Sexual Inequality.* New Haven: Yale University Press.

Bernard, Jessie. 1981. *The Female World.* New York: Free Press.

Butler, Judith. 1990. *Gender Trouble: Feminism and the Subversion of Identity.* New York and London: Routledge.

Coser, Rose Laub. 1986. "Cognitive structure and the use of social space," *Sociological Forum* 1: 1–26.

Davies, Christie. 1982. "Sexual taboos and social boundaries," *American Journal of Sociology* 87: 1032–63.

Dwyer, Daisy, and Judith Bruce (eds.). 1988. *A Home Divided: Women and Income in the Third World.* Palo Alto, Calif.: Stanford University Press.

Frye, Marilyn. 1983. *The Politics of Reality: Essays in Feminist Theory.* Trumansburg, N.Y.: Crossing Press.

Goffman, Erving, 1977. "The arrangement between the sexes," *Theory and Society* 4:301–33.

Mencher, Joan. 1988. "Women's work and poverty: Women's contribution to household maintenance in South India," In *Dwyer and Bruce.*

Palmer, Phyllis. 1989. *Domesticity and Dirt: Housewives and Domestic Servants in the United States, 1920–1945.* Philadelphia: Temple University Press.

Smith, Dorothy. 1990. *The Conceptual Practices of Power: A Feminist Sociology of Knowledge.* Toronto: University of Toronto Press.

West, Candace, and Don Zimmerman. 1987. "Doing gender." *Gender & Society* 1: 125–51.

The Plurality of Gender-Based Realities

Virginia Sapiro

In complex societies marked by stratification and gender divisions of labor, the sex/gender system is composed of a *plurality of gender-based stereotypes* and expectations that depend on other aspects of social position and identity. . . . [T]here may be a central, widely unattainable ideal that can be met only by women with the highest status, but the dominant society also develops stereotypes and expectations aimed specifically at women in different social positions. Despite the great variety of American Indian communities and the many different roles women play in those communities, White American society historically imagined Native American women either as silent, oppressed, laboring squaws or as romantic and noble princesses, described in the popular stories of Pocahontas. African-American women came to be characterized as either promiscuous, earthy women who could be used as beasts of burden, or as Mammy, a loyal member of a White household with a special knowledge of nature and children. The late 20th century has added another African-American female figure: the welfare cheat, placing burdens on the system through having uncontrollable numbers of children for whom she cannot care or provide.

Esther Ngan-Ling Chow has offered further examples from the stereotyped views of Asian-American women, defined in a variety of closely related roles: Suzie Wong, geisha, picture bride, and sexpot. In each case, the definition of the Asian-American woman depends on both race and sex. These stereotypes often come together with colonialist myths, fostering male fantasies that serve as the basis of the frightening racialized sexual harassment that Asian-American women receive. As a result, Asian-American women find themselves victims of education and employment discrimination *despite* the popular image of being the model minority. Jewish women have their choice of stereotypes: the domineering, stifling "Jewish mother," or the bitchy, self-centered "Jewish princess."

Neither gender nor race nor ethnicity alone is sufficient to understand most women's situation. In each case, scholars have noted, the special characters of the stereotypes are not just accidents. These stereotypes serve the ideological needs of both an androcentric structure of power relations and the racial/ethnic structure of power by not just *describing* these power relations but *justifying* them. The cast of subculturally differentiated female characters could be extended indefinitely by turning to depictions based on other ethnic/racial groups or on socioeconomic class, sexuality, geographic region, or other aspects of sociocultural diversity. Lillian Faderman and Donna Penn, among others, have written about the historical development of stereotypes of lesbian women during the 20th century, including the pervasive view that lesbians can either be categorized as "butch," in which case they are hypermasculine predators of other women, or "femme," the feminized victim who might be rescued from homosexuality if the right man came along. The construction of female (and male) gender is also partly determined by region, as in the case of the Southern belle, the Boston "bluestocking," the "gentle tamer" of the West, the "madonna of the Plains," or the "tall woman" and the "mountain belle" of Appalachia. . . .

Evelyn Nakano Glenn's research on service work offers an excellent example of the institutionalization of specific racial–ethnic norms of womanhood. She has reminded us that woman's central role has been defined as both physical and social reproduction, or the "creation and re-creation of people as cultural and social, as well as physical beings." This role means having responsibility for the care of (but not the financial provision for) the household and the people within it.

Glenn has pointed out, however, an important contradiction in the expectations placed on women, which arose from the 19th-century cult of womanhood: Domestic labor is, in many respects, dirty, difficult, labor-intensive work, especially in a society without electricity. The image of the "domestic angel," therefore, is largely inconsistent with the actual domestic labor that is required to keep homes in the preferred domestic order. It should be no surprise, therefore, that in the era of industrial development, when labor was both plentiful and cheap, families of any means employed servants to do much of the domestic labor. First, the work was intensive enough that most women probably welcomed any help; only the most upper-class women tended to shift the entire burden of domestic labor to servants. Second, shifting the work to servants could reduce the contradiction within the gender role of the "lady" of the house.

This observation does not tell the whole story yet. This domestic labor was shifted from the hands of women to the hands of other women because it was gender-specified labor. Nonetheless, isn't there as much contradiction between the domestic-angel image and this dirty, laborious work for the women hired to do the labor as for the "lady" of the house? In the eyes of the employing class, there was not, because their gender norms depended not just on a woman's *gender*, but also on her *class* and *race/ethnicity*. Serving the domestic labor needs of strangers is entirely consistent with dominant culture definitions of appropriate womanhood for *some* types of women but not for others. As Glenn has pointed out, exactly which classification of women was supposed to perform these tasks changes historically and differs from geographic region to geographic region. In the northeastern United States at the

turn of the century, recent European immigrants, especially Irish-American women, were thought to be specially fitted to doing domestic labor. White women in the South turned to African-American women; in the Southwest, Mexican-American women filled the service roles, as did Japanese-American women on the Pacific coast and in Hawaii.

These groups of women engaged in paid domestic service because they needed the money and they lived in those areas in large numbers. In each of these regions, however, these women came to be culturally reinterpreted as a servant class *by nature*, marked out and determined by their gender and their race/ethnicity. Glenn has argued that in each case, the women, marked by their race/ethnicity, were understood to have inherent traits suiting them for service, and they were not perceived as mothers and wives in their own right, but rather as servants. Thus, Glenn has shown, in each region, young women were institutionally tracked into fulfilling their presumed natural destiny. She found examples of how Mexican girls in the Southwest and Japanese girls in Hawaii were blocked from school programs other than those that would lead to domestic service. Even in the job programs run by the federal World Progress Administration (WPA) in the New Deal response to the Great Depression of the 1930s, Chicanas and African-American and Asian-American women were funneled into domestic service jobs and out of others.

. . .

For another example, consider the story of Pocahontas. To Euro-American society, the story of Pocahontas is a romantic tale of a beautiful Indian princess who falls in love with an Englishman, who generously marries her and takes her off to England, where she is the talk of the town. The story can be seen as symbolizing to the Euro-American the unique "marriage" of the civilized European with the wildness of nature on the new continent, with all living happily ever after as Indians and the wilderness are "tamed." American Indians are more likely to hear the rest of the story and, presumably, to take a different message from it. Pocahontas was offered to John Smith as part of a policy of alliance, much as European aristocrats and royalty intermarried to solidify international agreements. When she went to London, although she was displayed in society, neither her husband nor the society in which she was now isolated ever accepted her, and while longing to return home to America, she died before her 25th birthday.

Each of these subcultures, defined by race/ethnicity, class, and geography (among other things), has distinctive ways of understanding gender and different norms about how women and men should do gender to some degree. For communities defined by race/ethnicity, religion, or geography, distinctive rituals and practices, cultural figures, myths and stories, and graphic representations offer a way of understanding the specific subcultural constructions of male and female. The Navajo Changing Woman, for example, responsible for the growth of crops and the birth of new life, presents a model of the woman warrior and defender of her home that is a cultural ideal for Navajo women. Young Jewish girls dress up at Purim as Queen Esther, a savior of her people, as often as they might, like many other American children, appear as fairy princesses and witches at Halloween. Many Appalachian authors incorporate the locally well-known image of the "tall women," so named because of the saying that "a tall woman casts a long shadow." This image of "strong women, who can manage the household and children as well as milk the cows and cultivate the fields" served as a positive cultural image of femininity for Appalachian women for whom the image of the Southern belle must have seemed foreign. From one part of the country to another, where the different flow of seasons and the different cultural traditions shape women's and men's lives differently, the understanding of women as women and men as men varies.

The more closely women's lives are scrutinized, the more clear it becomes that there is immense variation in the ways that gender is shaped and represented in a complex sex/gender system. Nevertheless, they are not completely independent. They are linked through the common social institutions that tie them all together into the larger society, including, for example, the government, the mass media, and the school and health-care systems. Thus, women (and men) do gender within sex/gender systems that often simultaneously demand different and sometimes conflicting things of them, in order to act in gender appropriate ways.

. . .

Rape would seem at first to offer a clear example of a form of oppression or violence based solely on gender. Slavery would seem at first to offer a clear example of a form of oppression or violence based solely on race. In fact, however, for a complete understanding of rape, it is necessary to look beyond gender, and for a complete understanding of slavery, it is necessary to look beyond race.

Gender is a crucial determinant of the degree to which women are regarded and treated as objects of sex and rape, but their race, ethnicity, class, and status as recent immigrants or native-born Americans are also important. The lower a woman's status is by almost any measure, the more likely she is to be a target of sexual violence. Some examples of how this works follow.

bell hooks offered a powerful analysis of the intertwined effects of race and gender on sexual oppression. Rape was an integral part of the female slave experience, beginning with the sea voyage, during which the slavers did what they could to break the Africans' spirits and make them passive and compliant. For the women, this process included rape. Neither race nor gender alone accounts for the experience of slavery because "while racism was clearly the evil that had decreed Black people would be enslaved, it was sexism that determined that the lot of the Black female would be harsher, more brutal than that of the Black male slave." Women were subjected to slavery because of their race, but they were also used as sexual objects and as breeders because of their sex. The same was true for the Native Americans held as slaves in the American Southwest. There are many other situations in which rape clearly depends not just on gender, but also on the race, ethnic, or class relations between perpetrator and victim. Susan Brownmiller's argument that rape has often been used as a tactic of war and imperialism depends on recognizing that rape does not occur just because of gender and sexual relations. A recent example in a long history may be found in the massive and systematic use of rape in Serbia against Muslim women in 1992–1993, during the civil war that followed the breakup of Yugoslavia.

Gender played other roles in differentiating the slave experience. For instance, bell hooks has pointed out that an important aspect of slavery in the United States was the requirement that women do labor regarded in America as men's work. Male slaves were less often subjected to the complementary treatment of being required to do women's work.

Race and gender also combined to affect the experience of slave owners in 19th-century America. White men could own slaves because of their race and gender. Their sex gave them the right to own property (married women could not own property), and their race gave them the right to own human beings (very few nonWhites owned slaves). In one sense, this gender difference among Whites is little more than a technical point. White women had great power over their husbands' slaves. Moreover, during the Civil War, about three quarters of White Southern men were in the military, so their wives had to take over the management of plantations, including the slaves. Drew Gilpin Faust's historical analysis shows that many of these women were especially uncomfortable with this role and were caught in a web of conflicting social norms. They lived in a society based on violence, in which White people could hold Black people in bondage and enforce their power with violence against them; on the other hand, gender norms defined women as nurturant and nonviolent.

Gender distinguished among White slaveholders in one important respect: White women knew about their husbands', brothers', and sons' sexual treatment of their slaves. They knew that the children of some of the enslaved women were progeny of their "loved ones" through rape. This knowledge motivated some White women, such as the Grimké sisters, to become abolitionists, but many others simply stored their resentment or even blamed the victimized Black women. In addition, hooks has suggested another dimension to this complex picture of gender and race by speculating, "Surely it must have occurred to White women that were enslaved Black women not available to bear the brunt of such intense anti-woman male aggression, they themselves might have been the victims." White society in general has tried to ignore the massive scale of the rapes that occurred.

Blaming the victim plays an important role in all forms of sexual- and gender-based violence. However, just as enslaved women were often held responsible for their own victimization, women of low-status groups, especially those perceived as alien, have often been regarded as excessively sexual (and even animal-like) and thus have become special targets for sexual violence and exploitation. As bell hooks has explained, by defining Black women as initiators of the sexual relationships that were in fact rapes, Whites reinforced a stereotype of Black women as sexual savages who, in effect, could not be raped. The same principle applied to Hispanic and Native American women. Likewise, in the late 19th and early 20th centuries, native-born Whites often claimed that immigrant women—Irish, Italian, Jewish, or whatever— were especially promiscuous and likely to ruin the morals of innocent American men. Young immigrant women, especially those helping to support their families, were constantly subjected to sexual harassment and exploitation and then labeled promiscuous.

These examples demonstrate that the forms of gender-based oppression and exploitation people experience depend in part on their other social characteristics, and that racial/ethnic- or class-based forms of oppression and exploitation depend in part on gender. In fact, the exploitation of gender relations may often be seen as a means of enforcing other types of oppression. Some examples from the legal control of sexuality and marriage follow.

The state's control over marriage and sexual relations gives it leverage to pursue many different goals. . . . Among these goals is the preservation of particular racial or ethnic hierarchies. In order to preserve a particular racial/ethnic social order, societies must ensure that different races or ethnic groups cannot intermarry or develop the mutual loyalty and commitment owed to intimates and family members. Thus, nations with an apartheid history, such as the United States and South Africa, declared *miscegenation,* racial intermarriage, illegal during those eras.

Laws against interracial sexual relations or marriage may seem to fall equally on the shoulders of women and men, and on those of different races or ethnic groups, but in fact, they do not. Higher status men, however defined, tend to have sexual rights over lower-status women, or at least, they are not punished as severely as their partners in interracial sexual contact. In the American past, sexual relations between White women and nonWhite men were punished more severely than relations between White men and nonWhite women. The first American antimiscegenation law, passed in 1664 in Maryland, declared that a White woman who had sexual relations with an enslaved Black male must herself become a slave. No such law applied to White men.

These dynamics appear not just through law, but also in the way societies have often treated mixed-race, -ethnicity, or even -class couples and their babies. If a low-status female becomes pregnant by a high-status male, it has little effect on their relative status. Patriarchal ideology keeps the male in control; if the woman makes too many claims, he can abandon and reject her with relatively little social cost, partly because he can accuse her of promiscuity. A situation involving a low-status male and a high-status female is very different. For example, a baby of mixed-race parentage born to a White woman has been regarded as a pollution of the White-race. Because women are regarded as the property of male protectors in a patriarchal society, a nonWhite male who has sexual relations with a White woman is ultimately seen as taking something from White men. The effects of this dual system of racial and sexual oppression lasted long after the end of slavery. The rape of a White woman by a nonWhite man has usually been treated by White society as the most serious type of heterosexual rape, whereas rape of a nonWhite woman by a White man has not often been regarded as rape at all. False charges that a Black man raped a White woman were often used as excuses for lynching Black men.

Almost a generation ago, women's studies researchers began to emphasize the need to take gender into account to understand important social issues. In recent years, they have been demanding yet more sophistication and argue that gender analysis is not complete without integrating it with an understanding of other structural bases of social life. Maxine Baca Zinn has offered a good example in her writing on the family and poverty. She has shown that efforts to understand and solve the problems of poverty are doomed to failure if researchers look only at culture or race and class structures or gender structures. Society and social relations are constructed of all of these elements.

When I Was Growing Up

Nellie Wong

I know now that once I longed to be white.
How? you ask.
Let me tell you the ways.

when I was growing up, people told me
I was dark and I believed my own darkness
in the mirror, in my soul, my own narrow vision

when I was growing up, my sisters
with fair skin got praised
for their beauty, and in the dark
I fell further, crushed between high walls

when I was growing up, I read magazines
and saw movies, blonde movie stars, white skin,
sensuous lips and to be elevated, to become
a woman, a desirable woman, I began to wear
imaginary pale skin

when I was growing up, I was proud
of my English, my grammar, my spelling
fitting into the group of small children
smart Chinese children, fitting in,
belonging, getting in line

when I was growing up and went to high school,
I discovered the rich white girls, a few yellow girls,
their imported cotton dresses, their cashmere sweaters,
their curly hair and I thought that I too should have
what these lucky girls had

when I was growing up, I hungered
for American food, American styles,
coded: white and even to me, a child
born of Chinese parents, being Chinese
was feeling foreign, as limiting,
was unAmerican

when I was growing up and a white man wanted
to take me out, I thought I was special,
an exotic gardenia, anxious to fit
the stereotype of an oriental chick

when I was growing up, I felt ashamed
of some yellow men, their small bones,
their frail bodies, their spitting
on the streets, their coughing,
their lying in sunless rooms,
shooting themselves in the arms

when I was growing up, people would ask
if I were Filipino, Polynesian, Portuguese.
They named all colors except white, the shell
of my soul, but not my dark, rough skin

when I was growing up, I felt
dirty. I thought that god
made white people clean
and no matter how much I bathed,
I could not change, I could not shed
my skin in the gray water

when I was growing up, I swore
I would run away to purple mountains,
houses by the sea with nothing over
my head, with space to breathe,
uncongested with yellow people in an area
called Chinatown, in an area I later learned
was a ghetto, one of many hearts
of Asian America

I know now that once I longed to be white.
How many more ways? you ask.
Haven't I told you enough?

Spiking the Punch
In Defense of Female Aggression

Natalie Angier

This study has been done many times. If you take a group of babies or young toddlers and dress them in nondescript, non-sex-specific clothes—yellow is always a good color—and make sure that their haircuts don't give them away, and if you put them in a room with a lot of adults watching, the adults will not be able to sex the children accurately. The adults will try, based on the behaviors of each child, but they will be right no more often than they would be if they flipped a coin. This has been shown again and again, but still we don't believe it. We think we can tell a boy or a girl by the child's behavior, specifically by its level of aggressiveness. If you show a person a video-tape of a crying baby and tell her the baby is a boy, the observer will describe the baby as looking angry; if you tell the person the baby is a girl, she will say the child is scared or miserable.

I am at a party with my daughter, who is sixteen months old. A boy who is almost eighteen months comes into the room and takes a toy away from my daughter. I say something humorous to her about how she's got to watch out for those older kids, they'll always try to push you around. And the boy's mother says, It's also because he's a boy. That's what happens at this age, she says. The boys become very boyish. A little while later, a girl who is almost eighteen months old takes my daughter's cup of milk away from her. The mother of the other girl doesn't say, It's because she's a girl, she's becoming girlish. Of course she doesn't say that; it would make no sense, would it? An older girl taking a cup away from a younger girl has nothing to do with the girlness of either party. But taking the toy away is viewed as inherent to the older boy's boyness.

I felt very aggressive about the whole thing; alas, not being a toddler, I couldn't go and kick anybody in the kneecap. Which is the sort of thing that toddlers do, whatever their sex. They kick, they hit, they scream, they throw objects around, they act like pills past their expiration date. And we adults put up with it, and we subscribe to the myth of the helpless, innocent child, and it's a good thing we do and that children are cute, because otherwise we might well see the truth: that our children are born with astonishing powers, and with brains that seem by default to counsel aggression.

"Young children are like animals," says Kaj Björkqvist, of Turku Akademi University in Finland. "Before they have language, they have their bodies. And through their bodies they can be aggressive, and so that is what they do, that is how they are. They are physically aggressive—boys, girls, all of them." Björkqvist studies female aggression. He has done cross-cultural comparisons of children in Europe, North America, the Middle East, and Asia. Everywhere he has found that young children are physically aggressive, and that before the age of three, there are no significant differences between girl aggression and boy aggression.

We grow into our sex-specific aggressions. We own the code of aggression from birth, and we perfect its idiom through experience and experimentation. Now I must do something artificial and divide aggression into two basic categories, "bad" aggression and "good" aggression. Earlier I said that context determines whether we see a behavior as good aggression or bad aggression and that even Lady Macbeth looks swell in Nordic gear. But for the sake of examining how female aggression evolves and what its multitudinous sources and expressions may be, it helps to do as researchers do and distinguish between the malign and the resolute. Henri Parens, a child psychiatrist at the Medical College of Pennsylvania, calls the two phyla of aggression "hostile aggression," which is "generated by excessive unpleasure and motivates fantasies and acts of anger, hostility and hate," and "nondestructive aggression," which is "inborn and fuels assertive and goal achieving behaviors." In the infant and toddler, the two aggressions are one, and they are of the reactive nervous system—anger, hate, assertiveness, whatever it takes, or whatever can be done, to maintain momentum and attract the attention of the parent, the intermediary between self and no self.

With the awakening of the mind, the child learns to channel aggressive impulses and to calculate and compare actions and responses. Children begin to learn the meaning of hurting another. A baby kicks you in the mouth and doesn't know she hurts you. By the age of two or three, a girl knows she can hurt other beings, and hurt them badly, and with that knowledge the distinctions between malign and resolute aggression become meaningful. The mainstream model posits that aggression is a public health crisis. Mainstream studies of female aggression focus on hostile aggression, the aggression aimed to hurt, with foreknowledge, with malice.

When the mind comes into its own and the child starts speaking fluently, purposefully, adults become less tolerant of physical aggression. Today, in most cultures, acceptance of physical aggression declines as the child gets older; by the time a person reaches puberty, the tendency to use physical force to wrest a desired object or behavior from another is considered frankly pathological. This is true for both sexes, but particularly for girls. Physical aggression is discouraged in girls in manifold and aggressive ways. Not only are they instructed against offensive fighting; they are rarely instructed in defensive fighting. Girls don't learn how to throw a punch. Humor is another form of aggression, and until recently humor has been used to squelch the very notion of a warrior female. Just the thought of a girl-fight, and people snicker and rub their hands with glee. Cat fight! Scratching, screeching, pulling hair, and falling on butt with skirt hiked in the air! Happily, the smirky parody of girl-fights has gotten a bit paunchy and dated of late, and instead we've been treated to images of GI Janes and bodiced Xenas wielding swords and Klingon women with brickbat fists, though whether the mass media's revisionist fighting female has been driven by attitudinal change or by the need to jolt a bored and distracted audience is unclear.

Whatever the media moment may be, girls still do not often engage in physical fights. The older children get, the less physically aggressive they become— though not always, and not everywhere—but the dropoff rate for the use of physical aggression in girls is much sharper than it is for boys. At least in the developed West, by the time girls and boys are in third grade, boys are about three times as likely as girls to kick or strike at somebody who makes them mad. What then do girls do with that aggressiveness, which in the bliss of preverbalism could speak through hands and feet? It does

not go away. It finds a new voice. It finds words. Girls learn to talk hornet talk. Mastering curse words and barbed insults is an essential task of childhood. Girls also learn to use their faces as weapons. Expressions like sticking out your tongue or rolling your eyes or curling your lip all seem funny to adults, but studies show that they aren't funny to children, and that they can be effective in conveying anger and dislike or in ostracizing an undesirable. Aggression researchers initially thought that girls had the edge over boys in verbal aggression and that they were more likely than boys to belittle their peers with words and facial flexions, but a series of Finnish studies of eight- and eleven-year-olds suggested otherwise. The researchers sought to determine how children responded when they were angry. They asked the children to describe themselves and their reactions to being roused to rage; they asked teachers and parents to describe how the children reacted in conflict; and they asked children to talk about each other, to rate each other's rileability and behaviors in a squall. The scientists found that boys and girls were equally likely to use verbal aggression against their cohorts, to call them nasty names to their faces, to yell, to mock, to try to make the despised ones look stupid And so boys kick and fight more than girls do, and the sexes argue and chide in equal amounts. We might then conclude, So boys *are* more aggressive, for they shout with their mouths and on occasion with their bodies, while the girls keep their fists to themselves.

There are other ways in which rage emerges among girls, though, ways that are roughly girl-specific. A girl who is angry often responds by stalking off, turning away, snubbing the offender, pretending she doesn't exist. She withdraws, visibly so, aggressively so. You can almost hear the thwapping of her sulk. Among eleven-year-olds, girls are three times more likely than boys to express their anger in the form of a flamboyant snub. In addition, girls at this age, more than boys, engage in a style of aggression called indirect aggression.

. . .

Indirect aggression is not pretty, nor is it much admired. To the contrary, it is universally condemned. When children and adults are asked to describe their feelings about the various methods of expressing anger, backstabbing behavior ranks at the bottom, below a good swift kick to the crotch. Yet there it is, with us, among us, not exclusively female by any means, but a recognizable hazard of girlhood. Part of the blame lies with the myth of the goo-girl, for the more girls are counseled against direct forms of aggression and the more geniality of temperament is prized, the greater is the likelihood that the tart girls will resort to hidden machinations to get what they want. In cultures where girls are allowed to be girls, to speak up and out, they are in fact more verbally, directly aggressive and less indirectly aggressive than in cultures where girls and women are expected to be demure. In Poland, for example, a good smart mouth is considered a female asset, and girls there rag each other and pull no punches and report feeling relatively little threat of intragroup skullduggery. Among female Zapotec Indians in Mexico, who are exceedingly subordinate to men, indirect aggression prevails. Among the Vanatinai of Papua New Guinea, one of the most egalitarian and least stratified societies known to anthropologists, women speak and move as freely as they please, and they sometimes use their fists and feet to demonstrate their wrath, and there is no evidence of a feminine edge in covert operations.

Another reason that girls may resort to indirect aggression is that they feel such extraordinary aggression toward their friends—lashing, tumbling, ever-replenishing aggression. Girl friendships are fierce and dangerous. The expression "I'll be your best friend" is not exclusively a girl phrase, but girls use it a lot. They know how powerful the words are, how significant the offer is. Girls who become good friends feel a compulsion to define the friendship, to stamp it and name it, and they are inclined to rank a close friend as a best friend, with the result that they often have many best friends. They think about their friends on a daily basis and try to figure out where a particular friend fits that day in their cosmology of friendships. Is the girl her best friend today, or a provisional best friend, pending the resolution of a minor technicality, a small bit of friction encountered the day before? The girl may want to view a particular girl as her best friend, but she worries how her previous best friend will take it—as a betrayal or as a potential benefit, a bringing in or a new source of strength to the pair. Girls fall in love with each other and feel an intimacy for each other that is hard for them to describe or understand.

When girls are in groups, they form coalitions of best friends, two against two, or two in edgy harmony with two. A girl in a group of girls who doesn't feel that she has a specific ally feels at risk, threatened, frightened. If a girl who is already incorporated into the group decides to take on a newcomer, to sponsor her, the resident girl takes on a weighty responsibility, for the newcomer will view her as (for the moment) her best friend, her only friend, the guardian of her oxygen mask.

When girls have a falling-out, they fall like Alice down the tunnel, convinced that it will never end, that they will never be friends again. The Finnish studies of aggression among girls found that girls hold grudges against each other much longer than boys do. "Girls tend to form dyadic relationships, with very deep psychological expectations from their best friends," Björkqvist said. "Because their expectations are high, they feel deeply betrayed when the friendship falls apart. They become as antagonistic afterwards as they had been bonded before." If a girl feels betrayed by a friend, she will try to think of ways to get revenge in kind, to truly hurt her friend, as she has been hurt. Fighting physically is an unsatisfactory form of punishing the terrible traitor. It is over too quickly. To express anger might work if the betrayer accepts the anger and responds to it with respect. But if she doesn't acknowledge her friend's anger or sense of betrayal, if she refuses to apologize or admit to any wrongdoing, or if she goes further, walking away or mocking or snubbing her friend, at that point a girl may aim to hurt with the most piercing and persistent tools for the job, the psychological tools of indirect, vengeful aggression, with the object of destroying the girl's position, her peace of mind, her right to be. Indirect aggression is akin to a voodoo hex, an anonymous but obsessive act in which the antagonist's soul, more than her body, must be got at, must be penetrated, must be nullified.

The intensities of childhood friendships, dyads, coalitions, and jihads subside with age, but sometimes just barely. Women remain, through much of their lives, unsettled about other women. We feel drawn and repelled, desirous of a connection and at the same time aggressive toward those who register on our radar screen. . . .

Women bond with other women, and yet our strongest aggressions and our most frightening hostilities may be directed against other women. We hear about the war between the sexes, but surprisingly few of our aggressive impulses are aimed against men, the putative adversaries in that war. We don't consider men our competitors, even now, in the market free-for-all, when they often are. It is so much easier to feel competitive with another woman, to feel our nerves twitch with anxiety and hyperattentiveness when another woman enters our visual field. We dress women in fairy white, we dress them in mafia black. We want them around us. We want to be alone among men.

Men say they envy women the depth of their friendships, their ability to emote with and engage each other. Men are also stunned when they see the ferocity of a failed friendship between women, the staggering thickness of the anger and bile. "Picking a fight can actually be a way for men to relate to one another, check each other out, and take a first step toward friendship," Frans de Waal wrote in *Good Natured*. "This bonding function is alien to most women, who see confrontation as causing rifts." It's not because we are nice and want to make nicer. Women know, from their experience and from their harrowing girlhood, that rifts often are hard to heal, and can last, and can consume them.

The fierceness of female friendships and the unease with which we regard other women are in my view related phenomena, and are the legacy of dissonance between our ancient primate and our neohominid selves and of our inherent strategic plasticity, the desire to keep all options open. Other females are a potential source of strength, and other females can destroy us. Or flip it around, as the English salonist Elizabeth Holland did, when she wrote at the turn of the nineteenth century, "as nobody can do more mischief to a woman than a woman, so perhaps one might reverse the maxim and say nobody can do more good."

READING 22

Boys Will Be Boys and Girls Will Not

Mariah Burton Nelson

> My aunts washed the dishes while the uncles
> squirted each other on the lawn with
>   garden hoses. Why are we in here,
> I said, and they are out there?
>   that's the way it is,
>   said Aunt Hetty, the shriveled-up one.
>   —Paulette Jiles, "Paper Matches"

Two scientists recently made this forecast: The fastest woman may eventually outrun the fastest man. Their prediction appeared only as a letter to the editor in *Nature* magazine, yet it generated a stampede of interest from the media. *Time*, the *Chicago Tribune*, *USA Today*, the *New York Times*, the *Washington Post*, and

Sports Illustrated printed stories. All quoted experts who ridiculed the conjecture as "ludicrous," "sheer ignorance," "a good laugh," "absurd," "asinine," "completely fallacious," and/or "laughable."

In one Associated Press report, the word ridiculous was used five times. *Science News* ran the headline "Women on the verge of an athletic showdown." *Runner's World* entitled its article "Battle of the Sexes." Unlike questionable projections that are dismissed without fanfare, this one seems to have struck a nerve.

The researchers, Brian Whipp and Susan Ward of the University of California, Los Angeles, calculated runners' average speeds during record-breaking races over the past seventy years, then compared the rates of increase. Nothing that women's average speeds are increasing at a faster rate than are men's, they projected that in the future, the best women may catch up to and even surpass the best men at various distances. For example: By 1998, the best woman and man would, if they continue to improve at current rates, complete the 26.2-mile marathon in two hours, two minutes. In subsequent years, the woman would sprint ahead.

Indisputably, neither women nor men will continue to improve at their current rates forever. Otherwise, humans would one day run the marathon in a matter of minutes But the very idea that women might someday beat men elicited passionate responses. *Runner's World* writers Amby Burfoot and Marty Post, as if verbally to stop women in their tracks, pointed out that in the past five years, women have made few improvements in world-record times. This is a sure sign, they said, that women "have already stopped" improving.

When I appear on radio and television shows to discuss women's sports or my first book, *Are We Winning Yet? How Women Are Changing Sports and Sports Are Changing Women,* I encounter a similar fury. Female callers are not the problem; they brag about their triceps or gripe about male egos or ask for advice about dis-

crimination. Some male callers tell stories about female martial artists or mountain climbers who taught them, in a way they could understand, about female strength. But at least half of the male callers act as if my views were heretical. Angry and antagonistic, they belittle me, my ideas, my book, and female athletes in general.

What seems to make them angriest is my observation that men are not better athletes than women are. In no sport are all men better than all women, I point out, and in many sports, women routinely defeat men. Although single-sex competitions are often appropriate, and men do have physical advantages in some sports, women should see themselves as men's peers, I suggest, rather than exclusively competing against women.

These men don't want to hear any of that. In voices I can only describe as high-pitched and hysterical, they say, "Yeah, but you're never going to see a woman play pro football!"

It is a taunt and, I think, a genuine fear. I'm not talking about football. I've never met a woman who aspires to play pro football. I'm talking about auto racing, horse racing, dog sled racing, equestrian events, rifle shooting, and marathon swimming, where women and men compete together at the elite levels. I'm talking about tennis, golf, racquetball, bowling, skiing, and other recreational sports, where a wife and husband or a female and male pair of friends are likely to find themselves evenly matched. In sports, as in the rest of life, women do compete with men on a daily basis, and often win.

So it intrigues me that in response to my discussion of women's athletic excellence, men change the subject to football. They try to assert football as the sine qua non of athleticism. Because "women could never play football," they imply, men are physically, naturally, biologically superior.

Most men can't play pro football themselves—but they can take vicarious comfort in the display of male physical competence and aggression.

They take comfort in professional baseball ("Women could never play pro baseball") and in professional basketball ("Women could never play pro basketball") and in boxing ("Women could never box") and in footraces ("Women could never win the marathon").

Here are a few more quotes from men on radio shows, on airplanes, at restaurants:

"Women can't dunk."

"OK, women can play golf, but they can't drive the ball as far as men can."

"OK, female jockeys win, but there's a horse involved."

"Women win at marathon swimming? Who cares? You call that a major sport? I'd like to see a 320-pound female linebacker. That's a laugh."

Most men are not 320-pound linebackers. But, identified with these hulks, average men take great pleasure in the linebackers' exploits (a revealing term). Football, baseball, basketball, boxing, and hockey are important to men in part *because* they seem to be all-male pursuits, because they seem to be activities that *only men can do.* When women demonstrate excellence in sports like running, tennis, and golf, men take great pains to describe that excellence as less important, less worthy, less of an achievement than male excellence.

Psychiatrist Arnold R. Beisser explains the phenomenon this way: "It is small wonder that the American male has a strong affinity for sports. He has learned that this is one area where there is no doubt about sexual differences and where his biology is not obsolete. Athletics help assure his difference from women in a world where his functions have come to resemble theirs."

Sports are about distinction. Who is better? One inch, one point, or one-hundredth of a second can differentiate winner from loser. One pound, one meal, one more set of two-hundred-meter sprints in practice can determine, or seem to determine, whether a person finishes first or last. Athletes may train for the sheer joy of moving their bodies through space, but eventually they grow curious to see how fast they can move, or how well they can perform, compared to others. They want to compare, to contrast, to differentiate. To know where they stand. To win.

It is in this comparative, competitive arena that we are repeatedly told that women and men are different. And men are better. Women may no longer be weak, granted, but they are still wea*ker.* Weaker than men. Still the weaker sex.

Still, as de Beauvoir said, the second sex.

Actually, in many ways, men are the weaker sex. Men die on average seven years earlier than women. Women have a better sense of smell, taste, hearing, and sight (colorblindness affects one woman for every sixteen men). Women are more susceptible to migraines, arthritis, and depression, but men commit suicide more and have higher rates of heart attack and stroke. "Women are sick, but men are dead," Edward Dolnick wrote in his *In Health* magazine article on the subject.

Yet men keep pointing to one physical advantage—upper-body strength— to maintain their illusion of supremacy. Sports that depend on such strength—that, indeed, were designed to showcase that strength—bolster the myth.

Those who claim male sports superiority are not thinking of male gymnasts, who lack the flexibility to use some of the apparatus women use. Or male swimmers, who can't keep up with women over long distances. Or male equestrians, who gallop side by side with—or in the dust of—their female peers.

They are not considering how much women and men have in common: the human experience of sport. These same people would never think of comparing Sugar Ray Leonard to Muhammad Ali. One weighed sixty pounds more than the other. Clearly, they deserved to box in different classes. Yet the top female tennis player is often compared to the top male tennis player ("Yeah but, she could never beat *him*"), who usually outweighs her by sixty pounds.

Those who claim male superiority are not remembering jockstraps. Because men's genitals dangle precariously outside the pelvis, they are vulnerable to speeding baseballs and to angry fists or feet. In addition, "bikes with dropped handlebars bring the rider's legs close to the stomach, and the testicles can get squashed or twisted against the saddle," notes sportswriter Adrianne Blue in *Faster, Higher, Further.* "This can lead to gangrene and amputation." Such cases have been noted in medical journals.

Blue also suggests that men's bigger bodies make more "dangerous missiles" that are more likely than women's bodies to cause injury when they collide. For this reason a case could be made, she says, for banning men from contact sports.

If women and men were to compete together in noncontact sports, a man would currently win at the elite levels of most existing events: running (as long as the race is under 100 miles); swimming (under about 22 miles); throwing shot, discus, or javelin. On average, men can carry and use more oxygen. They tend to be heavier—an advantage in football—and taller: handy in basketball and volleyball. Men have more lean muscle mass, convenient in sports requiring explosive power— which happens to include most of the sports men have invented.

Less muscle-bound, women generally have better flexibility, useful in gymnastics, diving, and skating. Our lower center of gravity can help in hockey, golf, tennis, baseball, and even basketball. We sweat better (less dripping, therefore better evaporation), which is critical since, like car engines, human bodies need to remain cool and well lubricated to function efficiently.

Physiologist Diane Wakat, associate professor of health education at the University of Virginia, tested athletes under various conditions of heat, humidity, exercise, and nutritional intake, and concluded that women are better able to adjust to the environmental changes. "In every case, females were better able to handle the stress," says Wakat.

The longer the race, the better women do. Women's superior insulation (fat) is, believe it or not, prized by some because it offers buoyancy, heat retention, and efficient use of fuel over long distances, whether by land or by sea.

Ann Trason, a California microbiology teacher, became in 1989 the first woman to win a coed national championship—the twenty-four-hour run—by completing 143 miles. The best male finisher completed four fewer miles. Of Ward and Whipp's prediction that women will one day hold the overall world record in the relatively short (26.2-mile) marathon, Trason says: "I'd be there and be really happy to see it, but it seems unlikely. I do think women will get closer."

Helen Klein's world-record distance in a twenty-four-hour race—109.5 miles— exceeds the best distance for an American man in her age group (65–69). She says of the possibility that a woman will one day set the overall marathon record, "I would not say no. There is hope. If I were younger, I might try it myself."

In marathon and long-distance cold-water swims, "women usually out-swim the men," says Bob Duenkel, curator of the International Swimming Hall of Fame. Penny Dean still holds the English Channel record she set in 1978. Diana Nyad is the only athlete to complete the swim from Bimini to Florida. Lynne Cox holds the records for swimming the Bering Strait and the Strait of Magellan. The first person to swim all five Great Lakes, and the first ever to cross Lake Superior (in 1988), was Vicki Keith.

Susan Butcher has been the overall winner of the 1,100-mile Iditarod dog sled race four times. A woman named Seana Hogan recently cycled the four hundred miles from San Francisco to Los Angeles in nineteen hours, forty-nine minutes, breaking the previous men's record by almost an hour.

But women's successes are rarely attributable to gender. In ultra-distance running, swimming, and cycling, as well as in equestrian events, horse racing, auto racing, and dog sled racing, success is determined primarily by physical and mental preparation, competitive spirit, self-discipline, or other non-gender-related factors. Because upper-body strength is not paramount in these sports, women and men become free to compete together as individuals, even at the highest levels of competition.

Men's strength advantage is actually marginal, meaning that there is more variation among individual men than between the average man and the average woman. It only becomes relevant when comparing trained, competitive athletes. On any recreational doubles tennis team, the female player might be stronger.

Age is also important. Men's strength advantage occurs primarily during the reproductive years. Before puberty, girls, who tend to mature faster, have a height and strength advantage which, if not nullified by institutional and cultural discrimination, would actually render the best of them superior to the best boys. In old age, there is little physical difference between female and male strength.

But we've so long been told that men are better athletes. I even catch myself thinking this way, despite daily evidence to the contrary. For instance, in my masters swimming program, the fastest athletes—including college competitors—swim in Lane 1, while the slowest—including fit, fast, white-haired folks in their seventies—swim in Lane 6. There are women and men in all the lanes.

I swim in Lane 3. In Lane 2 is Ken. Because he's about my age and height, I identify with him. We have the same stroke length, so we look at each other sometimes, his breathing to the left, my breathing to the right, as we windmill through the water. But eventually he pulls ahead. He's faster. At first, I attributed his greater speed to the fact that he is male. His shoulders are broader; his muscles are more prominent than mine.

But then I looked over at Lane 4. There swims Bruce. Also about my height and my age, Bruce is slower than I am. He's got those same broad shoulders and big muscles, but there he is anyway, poking along in Lane 4. I'm faster because I've trained longer, or I have better technique, or I'm in better shape, or I'm more competitive, or some combination of those factors—the same reasons Ken is faster than both Bruce and me, and the same reasons Susie, Karen, Diane, Denise, Lynn, and Martha are faster than Ken. It has nothing to do with gender.

. . .

Because "being masculine" has included access to diverse sporting opportunities and "being feminine" has not, it's shortsighted to postulate that current gaps between male and female athletic potential will not close, at least partially, in the future— or that, as Post and Burfoot asserted, women "have already stopped improving." Men prevented women from running marathons until 1967. The Olympics did not offer a women's marathon until 1984, and still doesn't offer a women's swimming event longer than eight hundred meters (the men swim fifteen hundred meters). For every college woman who gets a chance to play college sports, 2.24 men do. For every woman who received a college scholarship, 2.26 men do. The more women run, the greater the likelihood that some of them will run fast. Increased numbers of female runners—along with female-focused training, coaching, scholarships, equipment, and even clothing—account for the historical improvements in women's times, and greater numbers in the future are likely to improve times further.

If marathon swimming were our national sport, as it is in Egypt—if there were a nationally televised Super Bowl of marathon swimming, and spectators packed college swim meets like sardines—we might think differently about women's and men's athletic capabilities. If men competed against women on the balance beam, or in synchronized swimming or in rhythmic gymnastics, we might rephrase the question about who might catch up to whom.

. . .

One reason male–female athletic comparisons are tempting to make, and hard to argue with, is that they seem natural. What could be more natural than human bodies? Sports seem to offer measurable, inarguable proof of human physical potential. Especially when no machines or animals are involved, sports seem to represent a raw, quintessentially fair contest between individuals or teams. *Ready? Set? Go. May the best man win.*

In fact, few professional athletes have "natural" bodies; otherwise we'd bump into pro football–sized men in the supermarkets. The linebacker has been shaped by many behavioral (nutrition, weight lifting) and often chemical (steroids, growth hormones) factors. Women who play or do not play sports have also been shaped by various factors, including restricted access to training opportunities, restrictive shoes and clothing, ridicule by peers, and cultural pressure to limit food intake for the sake of creating a thin, rather than strong, body. There's nothing natural about any of that.

But because sports seem natural, and because in the sports media we so often see men who are bigger and stronger than the biggest, strongest women, these men make a convincing subliminal case: not only are men better athletes, men are superior physical specimens. And because the men engaged in sporting events are so often enacting some form of mock combat, we receive the message: Men are inherently, naturally aggressive and, as a gender, dominant.

. . .

As every first-grader knows, there are physical differences between women and men, but these differences would be largely irrelevant except in matters of sex, reproduction, urination, and toupee purchases if it weren't for our culture's insistence on categorizing people first and foremost as "male" or "female." It is from these cultural categories—not from biological realities—that most "masculine" and "feminine" behaviors emerge. Cynthia Fuchs Epstein, author of *Deceptive Distinctions*, writes, "The overwhelming evidence created by the

past decade of research on gender supports the theory that gender differentiation—as distinct of course from sexual differentiation—is best explained as a social construction rooted in hierarchy."

Here's where the hierarchy part comes in: we don't just say, boys shouldn't play with dolls and girls shouldn't play with pistols. Through our economic structure and through the media, we say that taking care of children—"women's work"—is less important than war—"men's work." We don't just say that football is for boys and cheerleading is for girls. We say that playing football is more valuable than cheerleading or field hockey or volleyball or Double Dutch jump rope or anything girls do—more important, more interesting, more newsworthy: better.

Thus boys have an incentive to cling religiously to "boy behaviors," and they do. Boys are more likely than girls to insist on sex-typed activities and toys, and with good reason— it cements their place in the dominant class. Boys also have an incentive to keep girls out of their tree forts and clubhouses and sports associations and military elite: like "undesirables" moving into a pricey neighborhood, females lower the property value. Women's participation challenges the entire concept of relevant differences between women and men. "To allow women into sport would be an ultimate threat to one of the last strongholds of male security and supremacy," write Mary A. Boutilier and Lucinda SanGiovanni in *The Sporting Woman*. To put it another way, if women can play sports then "men aren't really men."

Of course, it's too late to keep women out of sports. But they can be kept out of the public eye and kept out of key, visible, highly paid positions like a football or men's basketball coach. Their accomplishments can be ignored or trivialized or sexualized. They can be barred from "masculine" activities— a term having nothing, really, to do with who men are, and everything to do with what men want to claim as their own.

. . .

Female athletes, sweat soaking their muscled chests, aren't half-women, half-men. They aren't Lady Panthers or Lady Rams or Lady Cheetahs, trying in vain to catch up to Gentlemen Bulls. They're people in pursuit of perfection—a quest that human beings, in all their diversity, seem to enjoy.

What Are Little Boys Made Of?

Michael Kimmel

To hear some tell it, there's a virtual war against boys in America. Best-sellers' subtitles counsel us to "protect" boys, to "rescue" them. Inside, we hear how boys are failing at school, where their behavior is increasingly seen as a problem. Therapists advise anguished parents about boys' fragility, their hidden despair and despondence. Boys, we read, are depressed, suicidal, emotionally shut down.

And why? It depends on whom you ask. The backlash chorus—the cultural right as well as the authors of some of these books—chant "feminism." Because of feminism, they say, America has been so focused on girls that we've forgotten about the boys. Other writers blame patterns of male development, while still others find in feminism not the problem but its solution.

There's no question that there's a boy crisis. Virtually all the books cite the same statistics: boys are four to five times more likely to kill themselves than girls, four times more likely to be diagnosed as emotionally disturbed, three times more likely to be diagnosed with attention deficit disorder, and 15 times more likely to be victims of violent crime. The debate concerns the nature of the crisis, its causes, and, of course, its remedies. The startling number of advice manuals that have appeared in the past couple of years—almost all by male therapists—alternate between psychological diagnoses and practical advice about how to raise boys.

One group, epitomized by therapist Michael Gurian (*A Fine Young Man, The Wonder of Boys*), suggests that boys are both doing worse than ever and doing worse than girls—thanks to feminists' efforts. Gurian argues that as feminists have changed the rules, they've made boys the problem. By minimizing the importance of basic biological differences, and establishing girls' standards as the ones all children must follow, feminists have wrecked boyhood. Along with Australian men's movement guru Steve Biddulph (*Raising Boys*), Gurian argues that our educational system forces naturally rambunctious boys to conform to a regime of obedience. With testosterone surging through their little limbs, boys are commanded to sit still, raise their hands, and take naps.

To hear these critics tell it, we're no longer allowing boys to be boys. We've misunderstood boy biology, and cultural meddling—especially by misinformed women—won't change a thing. It's nature, not nurture, that propels boys toward obnoxious behavior, violence, and sadistic experiments on insects. What makes boys boys is, in a word, testosterone, that magical, catch-all hormone that drives them toward aggression and risk-taking, and challenging this fact gives them the message, Gurian says, that "boyhood is defective."

This facile biological determinism mars otherwise insightful observations. Gurian adroitly points out the nearly unbearable pressure on young boys to conform, to resort to violence to solve problems, to disrupt class-room decorum. But he thinks it's entirely due to biology—not peer culture, media violence, or parental influence. And Biddulph agrees: "Testosterone equals vitality," he writes. All we have to do is "honor it and steer it into healthy directions." This over-reliance on biology leads both writers to overstate the differences between the sexes and ignore the differences among boys and among girls. To argue that boys have a harder time in school ignores all reliable evidence from sources such as Myra and David Sadker's *Failing at Fairness: How America's Schools Cheat Girls.*

These misdiagnoses lead to some rather bizarre excuses for boys' behavior, and to the celebration of all things masculine as the simple product of that pubertal chemical elixir. In *The Wonder of Boys,* Gurian cites bewilderingly incongruous rites of passage, such as "military boot camp, fraternity hazings, graduation day, and bar mitzvah," as essential parts of every boy's life. Hazing and bar mitzvahs? Have you read any reports of boys dying at the hands of other boys at bar mitzvahs. Biddulph explains boys' refusal to listen to adult authority by reference to the "fact" that their ear canals develop in irregular spurts, "leading to a period of hearing loss." And did you know that baritone singers in Welsh choruses have more testosterone than tenors—and have more sex! Where do they get this stuff?

More chilling, though, are their strategies for intervention. Gurian suggests reviving corporal punishment both at home and at school—but only when administered privately with cool indifference and never in the heat of adult anger. (He calls it "spanking responsibly.") Biddulph, somewhat more moderately, proposes that boys start school a year later than girls, so they'll be on a par intellectually.

The problem is, there's plenty of evidence that boys are not "just boys" everywhere and in the same ways. If it's all biological, why is the slightest deviation from expected manly behavior so cruelly punished? Why aren't Norwegian or French or Swiss boys as violent, homophobic, and misogynist as many are in the U.S.? Boys are not doomed to be victims of what Alan Alda once facetiously called "testosterone poisoning." On the contrary, they can become men who express their emotions and treat their partners respectfully, who listen as well as act, and who love and nurture their children.

But how do we get there? Another group of therapists, including Dan Kindlon and Michael Thompson, and William Pollack, eschew testosterone-tinged testimonials and treat masculinity as an ideology to be challenged. For them, we need to understand the patterns of boys' development to more effectively intervene and set boys on the path to a manhood of integrity.

To do that, Kindlon and Thompson write in *Raising Cain,* we must contend with the "culture of cruelty" that forces a boy to deny emotional neediness, "routinely disguise his feelings," and end up emotionally isolated. In *Real Boys,* Pollack calls it the "Boy Code" and the "mask of masculinity"—a kind of swaggering attitude that boys embrace to hide their fears, suppress dependency and vulnerability, and present a stoic front.

. . .

The cause of all this posturing and posing is not testosterone, of course, but privilege. In adolescence, both boys and girls get their first real dose of gender inequality, and that is what explains their different paths. The interventions recommended by Kindlon and Thompson—allowing boys to have their emotions; accepting a high level of activity; speaking their language; treating them with respect; using discipline to guide and build; modeling manhood as emotionally attached (all of which are good suggestions and applicable to girls, also)—don't address male entitlement. Indeed, of the male therapists, only Pollack and James Gilligan (*Violence*) even seem to notice it. For the others, boys' troubles are all about fears suppressed, pain swallowed. Kindlon and Thompson write that the "culture of cruelty imposes a code of silence on boys requiring them to suffer without speaking of it and to be silent witnesses to acts of cruelty to others."

The books that are written with an understanding of male privilege—and the need to challenge it—are the ones that offer the most useful tools to improve boys' lives. Books by Myriam Miedzian and by Olga Silverstein and Beth Rashbaum, published several years ago, offer critiques of traditional boyhood and well-conceived plans for support and change. Eschewing biological determinism, these books see in feminism a blueprint for transforming both boyhood and manhood. Feminism encourages men—and their sons—to be more emotionally open and expressive, to develop empathic skills, and to channel emotional outbursts away from violence. And feminism demands the kinds of societal changes that make this growth possible.

That's all the more necessary, because there really is a boy crisis in America—not the crisis of inverted proportions that claims boys are the new victims of a feminist-inspired agenda run amok. The real boy crisis usually goes by another name. We call it "teen violence," "youth violence," "gang violence," "violence in the schools." Let's face facts: men and boys are responsible for 85 percent of all violent crimes in this country, and their victims are overwhelmingly male as well. From an early age, boys learn that violence is not only an acceptable form of conflict resolution, but one that is admired. Four times more teenage boys than teenage girls think fighting is appropriate when someone cuts into the front of a line. Half of all teenage boys get into a physical fight each year.

"Rescuing" or "protecting" isn't the answer, say British high school teachers Jonathan Salisbury and David Jackson. As their title, *Challenging Macho Values,* shouts, they want to take issue with traditional masculinity, to disrupt the facile "boys will be boys" model, and to erode boys' sense of entitlement. And for Paul Kivel (*Boys Will Be Men*), raising boys to manhood means confronting racism, sexism, and homophobia—both in our communities and in ourselves. These books are loaded with hands-on practical advice to help adolescents raise issues, confront fears, and overcome anxieties, and to help teachers dispel myths, encourage cooperation, and discourage violent solutions to perceived problems. Salisbury and Jackson's book will be most valuable to teachers seeking to transform disruptive behavior; Kivel's is geared more to parents, to initiate and continue those sensitive and difficult conversations. The most valuable material helps parents and teachers deconstruct sexuality myths and challenge sexual harassment and violence. "We believe that masculine violence is intentional, deliberate, and purposeful," write Salisbury and Jackson. "It comes from an attempt by men and boys to create and sustain a system of masculine power and control that benefits them every minute of the day." Forget testosterone; it's sexism! Even if these two books are less gracefully written and more relentlessly critical of traditional boyhood, they are not the only ones to recognize that not all boys are the same, and that one key to enabling boys to express a wider range of emotions is to challenge the power and privilege that is part of their cultural heritage.

Gilligan and Miedzian, along with James Garbarino (*Lost Boys*), understand that the real boy crisis is a crisis of violence—specifically the cultural proscriptions that equate masculinity with the capacity for violence. Garbarino's fortuitously timed study of youthful offenders locates the origins of men's violence in the way boys swallow anger and hurt. Among the boys he studied, "deadly petulance usually hides some deep emotional wounds, a way of compensating through an exaggerated sense of grandeur for an inner sense of violation, victimization, and injustice." In other words, as one prison inmate put it, "I'd rather be wanted for murder than not wanted at all."

Gilligan is even more specific. In his insightful study of violence, he places its origins in "the fear of shame and ridicule, and the overbearing need to prevent others from laughing at oneself by making them weep instead." The belief that violence is manly is not carried on any chromosome, not soldered into the wiring of the right or left hemisphere, not juiced by testosterone. (Half of all boys don't fight, most don't carry weapons, and almost all don't kill: are they not boys?) Boys learn it. Violence, Gilligan writes, "has far more to do with the cultural construction of manhood than it does with the hormonal substrates of biology."

That's where feminism comes in. Who, after all, has offered the most trenchant critique of that cultural construction but feminists? That's why the books written by women and men that use a feminist perspective (Gilligan, Kivel, Miedzian, Pollack, Salisbury and Jackson, and Silverstein and Rashbaum) are far more

convincing than those that either repudiate it (Gurian, Biddulph) or ignore it (Kindlon and Thompson).

Frankly, I think the antifeminists such as Gurian and Biddulph (and the right wing in general) are the real male bashers. When they say boys will be boys, they mean boys will be uncivilized animals. In their view, males are biologically propelled to be savage, predatory, sexually omnivorous creatures, hard-wired for violence. As a man, I find this view insulting.

Feminists imagine, and demand, that men (and boys) can do better. Feminism offers the possibility of a new boyhood and a new masculinity based on a passion for justice, a love of equality, and the expression of a full range of feelings.

DISCUSSION QUESTIONS FOR CHAPTER THREE

1. How do notions of sex and gender take shape within a cultural context? In what ways has your cultural context shaped your notions of sex and gender?

2. How would you describe the dominant notions of masculinity and femininity in U.S. society? How do these dominant notions help maintain systems of inequality?

3. How do people learn to "do" gender? Can you think of ways you've learned to do gender? From what sources did you learn to do gender?

4. How does gender ranking reinforce sexism?

5. How is the experience of sexism shaped by the confluences of other systems of oppression?

SUGGESTIONS FOR FURTHER READING

Bornstein, Kate. *My Gender Workbook*. New York: Routledge, 1998.

Fausto-Sterling, Anne. "The Five Sexes: Why Male and Female Are Not Enough." *The Sciences* 22 (1993).

Feinberg, Leslie. *Transgender Warriors*. Boston: Beacon, 1996.

Lorber, Judith. *Paradoxes of Gender*. New Haven, CT: Yale University Press, 1994.

Tavris, Carol. "The Mismeasure of Woman." *Feminism and Psychology* 3 (1993): 149–168.

West, Candace, and Don H. Zimmerman. "Doing Gender." *Gender and Society* 1 (1987): 125–151.

CHAPTER FOUR

Sex, Power, and Intimacy

Sexuality is a topic of great interest to most people. It entertains and intrigues and is a source of both personal happiness and frustration. Over the centuries men have struggled to control women's sexuality through a variety of physical and emotional means; controlling a woman's sexuality has often meant controlling her life. The flipside of this is that sexuality has the potential to be a liberating force in women's lives. To enjoy and be in control of one's sexuality and to be able to seek a mutually fulfilling sexual relationship can be an empowering experience. This chapter begins with a discussion of the social construction of sexuality and provides definitions for key terms. Following is a focus on two themes associated with sexuality: first, the politics of sexuality, and second, intimacy, romance, and communication.

THE SOCIAL CONSTRUCTION OF SEXUALITY

Human sexuality involves erotic attractions, identity, and practices, and it is constructed by and through societal sexual scripts. *Sexual scripts* reflect social norms, practices, and workings of power, and they provide frameworks and guidelines for sexual feelings and behaviors. There is often embarrassment, shame, and confusion associated with these sexual scripts, and they easily become fraught with potential misunderstandings. Misunderstandings associated with sexual scripts are humorously illustrated in the short excerpt by April Sinclair from *Coffee Will Make You Black.*

Sexual scripts vary across cultures and through time and are almost always heavily informed by societal understandings of gender. The article by Pepper Schwartz and Virginia Rutter, "Sexual Desire and Gender," emphasizes two key points: that sexuality is about society as much as it is about biological urges and that the most significant dimension of sexuality is gender. For example, as discussed in Chapter 3, feminine sexual scripts have often involved a double bind: to want sex is to risk being labeled promiscuous and to not want sex means potentially being labeled frigid and a prude. For many women, sexuality is shrouded in shame and fear, and, rather than seeing themselves as subjects in their own erotic lives, these women understand themselves as objects, seen through the eyes of

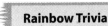

Rainbow Trivia

1. At what New York bar did the modern gay liberation movement begin?
   a. Studio 54
   b. Stonewall
   c. Club 57
   d. Scandals

2. What were homosexuals required to wear to identify them in concentration camps during World War II?
   a. a yellow star
   b. a lavender H
   c. a pink star
   d. a pink triangle

3. What Greek letter symbolizes queer activism?
   a. lambda
   b. alpha
   c. delta
   d. sigma

4. What is the name of the religious organization that supports queer Catholics?
   a. Spirit
   b. Celebration
   c. Dignity
   d. Affirmation

5. What is the country's largest political organization working specifically for queer rights?
   a. Human Rights Campaign
   b. ACT-UP
   c. NOW
   d. Christian Coalition

6. What famous athlete came out at the 1993 March on Washington?
   a. Greg Louganis
   b. Reggie White
   c. Tonya Harding
   d. Martina Navritalova

7. What show made television history by having the first gay lead character?
   a. *Soap*
   b. *Roseanne*
   c. *Ellen*
   d. *All in the Family*

8. Who of the following is not a famous lesbian performer?
   a. Sarah McLachlan
   b. Melissa Etheridge
   c. k.d. lang
   d. Indigo Girls

9. Which of the following is a must-read for any good lesbian?
   a. *The Well of Loneliness* by Radclyffe Hall
   b. *Rubyfruit Jungle* by Rita Mae Brown

c. anything by Dorothy Allison
d. all of the above

10. Which of the following movies did *not* have a lesbian character?
    a. *Boys on the Side*
    b. *Personal Best*
    c. *Desert Hearts*
    d. *none of the above*

Answers: 1. b 2. d 3. a 4. c 5. a 6. d 7. c 8. a 9. d 10. d

---

others. In terms of masculinity, sexual potency is a key aspect of doing gender for many men in contemporary Western societies.

Within the context of sexual scripts, individuals develop their own sexual self-schemas. *Sexual self-schemas* can be defined as identities or cognitive generalizations about sexual aspects of the self that are established from past and present experiences and that guide sexual feelings and behavior. What is desirable or acceptable to one person may be unacceptable or even disgusting to another. Note that sexual scripts are societal-level guidelines for human sexuality, whereas sexual self-schemas are individual-level understandings of the self.

Sexual scripts vary across such differences as race, class, and age. Different age cohorts often have different sexual values and indulge in different sexual practices. Likewise, there are class and race differences associated with interpersonal relationships that reflect the norms of specific communities. For example, Chicana lesbians have spoken out about intense homophobia that is related to the sexual scripts identifying women as wives and mothers in their communities. In "La Güera," Cherríe Moraga describes how coming out as a lesbian helped her connect with the inequities of race. She is a light-skinned Chicana who had learned to pass as White. She writes, "The joys of looking like a white girl haven't been so great since I realized I could be beaten on the street for being a dyke." Paula Gunn Allen's poem, "Some Like Indians Endure," also makes the connections between racism and heterosexism. Both Indians and lesbians have endured and survived oppression.

There have also been strong mandates in U.S. society (like anti-miscegenation laws) that have maintained racial superiority by outlawing interracial dating and marriage. Carolyn Reyes and Eric DeMeulenaere write about their love and friendship across ethnic and class barriers and the ways respect and trust have enriched their lives in their essay "Compañeros."

Sexual orientation is a person's attraction to, or preference for, people of a given sex. It is an individual's romantic and/or sexual (also called erotic) identity and behavior toward other people. Note that sexual orientation does not necessarily require sexual experience. *Heterosexuality* is a sexual orientation where romantic and/or sexual attachments and identification are between people of the opposite sex (popularly termed *straight*). *Homosexuality* is a sexual orientation where romantic and/or sexual attachments and identification are between people of the same sex. Because the term *homosexual* is stigmatized and because the term seems

Queer Youth

The following numbers are drawn from an Internet survey of queer and questioning youth done by OutProud, the national coalition for gay, lesbian, bisexual and transgender youth, and *Oasis* magazine.

- The average respondent realized she/he was queer at age 12.2 years but did not accept this fact until 15.6 years and did not tell anyone until 16.3 years.
- Seventy-five percent of the respondents have told at least one person that they're queer. Most (46 percent) told a best friend first. Only 9 percent told their parents first.
- The most commonly cited reasons for not coming out for those who haven't yet are fear of parents' and friends' reactions.
- Only 10 percent of respondents who attend school said their schools discuss homosexuality in a positive manner.
- Sixty-two percent of respondents in school have seen incidents of antiqueer harassment at their school. Sixty-four percent have been verbally assaulted, and 28 percent have been threatened with physical violence. Fourteen percent have been punched, kicked, or beaten, and 4 percent have been raped because they are queer.
- Twenty-three percent have tried to commit suicide. On average, they were 14 years old at their first attempt.
- Twenty-eight percent have not yet had a sexual experience with anyone. Those who have had a sexual experience with someone were, on average, 14 years old at the time of their first experience.

Source: www.outproud.org/survey.html.

to emphasize sexual behavior, homosexual communities have preferred the term *gay*. *Gay* and *homosexual* are terms inclusive of women, although they are used mainly to describe men. The term *lesbian* means the romantic and/or sexual attachment and identification between women, specifically.

To complicate matters, the term *queer* is also used by both gays and lesbians to describe gay sexual orientation. Originally an insult, gays and lesbians have claimed the term as a source of pride and positive identity. *Queer* is also inclusive of *bisexuality,* the sexual orientation where individuals have romantic and/or sexual attachments, identification, and orientation with both women and men. There are derogatory social connotations of bisexuality as hypersexualized: not only do these people have sex all the time, they are doing it with both women and with men, simultaneously. Of course, to be bisexual does not imply this at all; it just means the choice of lover can be either a woman or a man. Nonetheless, these connotations reflect the fact that there are many stigmas associated with bisexuality from both the straight and the lesbian and gay communities. Robyn Ochs shares her story about being a bisexual woman in "Bisexuality, Feminism, Men, and Me."

You might also hear the terms *dyke, butch,* and *femme. Dyke* is synonymous with *lesbian,* although it connotes a masculine or mannish lesbian. Like *queer, dyke* is a word that is used against lesbians as an insult and has been appropriated or reclaimed by lesbians with pride. This means that if you are not a member of the lesbian, gay, or queer communities, you should probably not use the terms *queer* and *dyke,* because they most likely will be taken as insults. *Butch* and *femme* are roles associated with gender that have been adopted by some lesbians, especially in the past. Butch means acting as the masculine partner, and femme means acting in a feminine role. Although today many lesbians avoid these role types because there is little incentive to mimic traditional heterosexual relationships, others enjoy these identities and appropriate them to suit themselves.

Finally, the term *coming out* refers to someone adopting a gay, lesbian, bisexual, or queer identity. Coming out is a psychological process that tends to involve two aspects: first, recognizing and identifying this to oneself, and second, declaring oneself in a public way. In terms of this second aspect, individuals usually come out to affirming members in their own community before they face a general public. Some never come out to families or coworkers for fear of rejection, reprisals, and retaliation. For some, coming out means becoming part of an identifiable political community; for others, it means functioning for the most part as something of an outsider in a straight world. The phrase *in the closet* means not being out at all. In the closet can imply that a person understands her/himself to be lesbian or gay but is not out to others. It can also imply that a person is in denial about her/his own sexual identity and is not comfortable claiming a homosexual orientation.

THE POLITICS OF SEXUALITY

The term *politics* used here implies issues associated with the distribution of power in sexual relationships. There are politics in sexual relationships because they occur in the context of a society that assigns power based upon gender and other systems of inequality and privilege. As discussed in Chapter 1, the personal is political: Issues and problems taken as personal or idiosyncratic within sexuality or relationships have broader social, political, and economic causes and consequences.

In terms of sexuality, when a woman and a man get together romantically, what results is more than the mingling of two idiosyncratic individuals. The politics of this relationship involves two issues: first, women and men bring the baggage of their gendered lives into relationships. They have negotiated gender and other systems of inequality and privilege, and these experiences have shaped who they are. Much of this baggage is so familiar that it's thoroughly normalized and seen as completely natural. Second, the baggage of differently gendered lives implies power in relationships. As many feminists have pointed out, heterosexuality is organized in such a way that the power men have in society gets carried into relationships and encourages women's subservience, sexually and emotionally. Practically, this might mean that a woman sees herself through the eyes of men, or a particular man, and strives to live up to his image of who she should be. It might mean that a woman feels that men, or again, a particular man, owns or has the right to control her body or sexuality, or that she should be the one to ease the emotional transitions of the household, or tend to a man's daily needs— preparing his meals, cleaning his home, washing his clothes, raising his children— while still working outside the home. Even though she might choose this life and enjoy the role she has, feminists would argue that this is still an example of male

Activist Profile: Emma Goldman

According to J. Edgar Hoover, she was one of the most dangerous women in America in the early twentieth century. Emma Goldman came to the United States from Russia as a teenager in 1885, but for a Jewish immigrant, America was not the land of opportunity she had envisioned. Rather, she found herself in slums and sweatshops, eking out a living. Goldman had witnessed the slaughter of idealist political anarchists in Russia, and in 1886 she saw the hangings of four Haymarket anarchists who had opposed Chicago's power elite. As a result of these experiences, Goldman was drawn to anarchism and became a revolutionary.

Goldman moved to New York, where she met anarchist Johann Most, who advocated the overthrow of capitalism. Most encouraged Goldman's public speaking, although she eventually began to distance herself from him, recognizing the need to work for practical and specific improvements such as higher wages and shorter working hours. In 1893, she was arrested and imprisoned for encouraging a crowd of unemployed men to take bread if they were starving.

In New York, Goldman also worked as a practical nurse in New York's ghettos where she witnessed the effects of lack of birth control and no access to abortion. She began a campaign to address this problem, and her views eventually influenced Margaret Sanger and Sanger's work to make contraception accessible. Goldman was even arrested for distributing birth control literature.

Goldman was particularly concerned about sexual politics within anarchism. She recognized that a political solution alone would not rectify the unequal relations between the sexes. Rather, she called for a transformation of values, particularly by women themselves— by asserting themselves as persons and not sex commodities, by refusing to give the right over her body to anyone, by refusing to have children unless she wants them.

Her involvement in no conscription leagues and rallies against World War I led to her imprisonment and subsequent deportation to Russia. There she witnessed the Russian Revolution and then saw the corruption of the Bolsheviks as they amassed power. Her experience led her to reassess her earlier approval of violence as a means to social justice. Instead, she argued that violence begets counterrevolution.

Goldman remained active in Europe and continued to exercise influence in the United States. In 1922 *Nation* magazine named her one of the twelve greatest living women. In 1934 she was allowed to lecture in the United States, and in 1936 she went to Spain to participate in the Spanish Revolution. Goldman died in 1940 and was buried in Chicago near the Haymarket martyrs.

domination in the private sphere. Men benefit from this. They have their emotional and domestic needs filled by women and are left free to work or play at what they want. Of course, their part of the bargain for these services is that they should provide for women economically. This is an arrangement that many women choose rationally.

We know that heterosexual relationships are a source of support and strength for many women; it is not heterosexuality that is faulted but the context in which heterosexual coupling takes place. When heterosexual intimacies are grounded in unequal power relationships, it becomes more and more difficult for women to love in healthy ways. This point is underscored in Naomi Wolf's article "Radical Heterosexuality." Wolf writes about ways that you can "hate sexism and love men."

The politics of sexuality also come into play in lesbian relationships. Women come together with the baggage of femininity to work out and often internalized homophobia as well. They also come together with few clear models for successful relationships. An example of this is the "Are we on a date?" syndrome that occurs as two women attempt to deal with the boundaries between being girlfriends and being romantically interested in each other. Often other sexual scripts complicate these encounters too. For example, in the short essay "Pleasures," Diane Hugs writes about disabled women learning to love each other and enjoy each other's bodies against the backdrop of a sexual script that assumes disabled people are asexual.

Lesbian relationships also occur in the context of *heteronormativity*, the way heterosexuality is constructed as the norm. A related concept is *compulsory heterosexuality*, as already discussed in previous chapters: that heterosexuality is the expected and desirable sexual orientation. For example, various institutions support and encourage heterosexual coupling and dating. Schools offer dances and proms, the entertainment industry generally assumes heterosexual dating, and there is a public holiday (Valentine's Day) that celebrates it. There are billboards, magazine covers, television shows and movies, public displays of heterosexual intimacy in the park, in the cinema, walking on the street, dancing close. And ultimately, there is marriage, an institution that does not legally (although there are increasingly challenges to this with various domestic partner legislation) recognize two committed people unless one is a woman and the other a man.

Learning Activity: As the World Turns

Tune into your favorite soap opera each day for a week. As you watch, record observations about the depictions, roles, and interactions of women and men. If all anyone knew about heterosexual relationships was what she or he saw on the soaps, what would this person believe?

Work with one or two other people in your class to devise an episode of a feminist soap opera. Who would be the characters? What dilemmas would they face? How would they resolve them? What would you call your soap opera? Is feminist soap opera possible? Would anyone watch?

Learning Activity: Heteronormativity: It's Everywhere

Heterosexism is maintained by the illusion that heterosexuality is the norm. This illusion is partly kept in place by the visibility of heterosexuality and the invisibility of other forms of sexuality. To begin to think about the pervasiveness of heterosexuality, grab a clipboard, pen, and paper and keep a tally.

- Go to a card store and peruse the cards in the "love" and "anniversary" sections. How many depict heterosexual couples? How many depict same-sex couples? What options are there for customers who wish to buy a card for a same-sex partner?
- Look at the advertisements in one of your favorite magazines. How many pictures of heterosexual couples do you find? How many pictures of same-sex couples? If a photo is of a man or woman alone, do you automatically assume the person is heterosexual? Or is that assumption so deep-seated that you don't even think about it at all?
- Watch the commercials during your favorite hour of television. How many images of heterosexual couples do you see? Of same-sex couples?
- Go to the mall or a park and people-watch for an hour. How many heterosexual couples holding hands do you see? How many same-sex couples?

Lesbian couples often encounter obstacles when adopting children, raising their biological children (products of previous heterosexual relationships, planned heterosexual encounters with the goal of conception, or artificial insemination), as well as gaining custody of these children. This is because being a lesbian is often constructed as an immoral and abnormal "choice" that could have negative consequences on children. It has generally been assumed that children of homosexual parents will grow up to be homosexual, although all the evidence shows that this is indeed not the case. Despite research that suggests that lesbians make fine mothers and lesbian couples fine parents, there are strong social imperatives against lesbian child rearing. A related prejudice is the notion that homosexuals abuse or recruit children. These negative and uninformed stereotypes reinforce homophobia and help maintain heterosexism. Research shows overwhelmingly that it is heterosexual males who are the major predators of children. Nonetheless, because of these societal stigmas, lesbians and gay men encounter many obstacles concerning voluntary parenting, and, in addition, are often not welcome in occupations involving children. In this way, sexual self-schemas develop in a social context and are framed by the various workings of power in society.

INTIMACIES

Courtship is that period when two people are attracted to each other, develop intimacy, enjoy each other's company, and identify as a couple. In our society this period usually involves dating. An essential aspect of courtship and dating is the development of romantic love: a mainstay of our culture and one of the most important mythologies of our time. *Romantic love* is about a couple coming together, sharing the excitement of an erotic relationship, and feeling united with the other in such a way that the other is unique and irreplaceable. The clichés of love

Learning Activity: It's in the Cards

Go to a local card shop and browse through the cards in the "love" or "romance" sections. What are their messages about heterosexual relationships? How do cards targeted toward women differ from cards targeted toward men?

Now get creative. Design a feminist romance greeting card. How does it differ from the ones you saw at the card shop? How do you think the recipient will feel about this card? Now, if you're really brave, mail it to the one you love.

abound: Love is blind; love is painful; love means never having to say you're sorry; love conquers all; and so forth.

Although cultural constructions of love would have us believe that romantic love as we know it has always been around, it is possible to trace the history of romantic love in U.S. society as a cultural phenomenon. There is a tight relationship between romantic love as an ideology and consumer culture as an industrial development. Prior to the twentieth century, dating as we know it did not exist. As dating developed after the turn of the century, it quickly became associated with consuming products and going places. The emerging movie industry glamorized romance and associated it with luxury products; the automobile industry provided those who could afford it with the allure of travel, get-aways, and private intimacy; and dancehalls allowed close contact between men and women in public. Romance became a commodity that could be purchased, and it made great promises. Women were (and still are) encouraged to purchase certain products with the promise of romantic love. Fashion and makeup industries began revolving around the prospect of romantic love, and the norms associated with feminine beauty became tied to glamorous, romantic images. Romantic love came to be seen as women's special domain; women were encouraged to spend enormous emotional energy, time, and money in the pursuit and maintenance of romantic love.

Romantic love is fun; it can be the spice of life and one of the most entertaining features of women's lives. In particular, it often contrasts starkly with our working lives because romance is associated with leisure, entertainment, and escape. At the same time, however, romantic love and its pursuit have become the means by which women are encouraged to form relationships and the justification for tolerating inequities in interpersonal relationships.

When it comes to sexuality, romantic love plays a large part in feminine sexual scripts. Research suggests that women make sense of sexual encounters in terms of the amount of intimacy experienced; love becomes a rationale for sex. If I am in love, women often reason, sex is okay. Men more easily accept sex for its own sake, with no emotional strings necessarily attached. In this way, sexual scripts for men have involved more of an *instrumental* (sex for its own sake) approach, whereas for women it tends to be more *expressive* (sex involving emotional attachments). There is evidence to suggest that women are moving in the direction of sex as an end in itself without the normative constraints of an emotional relationship, although, by and large, women are still more likely than men to engage in sex as an act of love. In this way, romantic love serves to bind women sexually to men.

As romantic relationships develop, individuals may become physically intimate and sexually active. These sexual practices can include kissing, hugging, petting, snuggling, caressing, oral sex (oral stimulation of genital area), penis in vagina sex, and anal sex (sexual stimulation of the anus with fingers, penis, or other object). Lesbians do many of the same things as straight couples, although there is no focus on penis-vagina sex. Some women, straight and lesbian, use dildos (penis-shaped objects that can be inserted into a bodily opening) when they are having sex or during masturbation (sexual self-stimulation).

In heterosexual relationships, sexual scripts tend to encourage men to be sexual initiators and sexually more dominant. Although this is not always the case, women who do initiate sex often run the risk of being labeled with terms that are synonymous with *slut*. Having one person in the relationship more sexually assertive and the other more passive is different from sado-masochistic sexual practices (S and M) where one person takes a domineering role and the other becomes dominated. There are both heterosexuals and homosexuals who enjoy sado-masochistic practices. Although usually consensual, S and M can also be coercive.

Emotional intimacy can be defined as sharing aspects of the self with others with the goal of mutual understanding. Intimacy can sometimes be a source of conflict in heterosexual relationships because women tend to be more skilled at intimacy than men, as the title of John Gray's popular book *Men Are from Mars, Women Are from Venus* suggests. Women have been socialized to be emotional and emotionally expressive, and men have been socialized to put their energy into shaping culture and society.

Although some scholars have suggested that women are inherently better at connecting with others and that this skill is rooted in early childhood psychosexual development, others have focused on the social context of childhood skill acquisition. They suggest that the interpersonal skills girls learn at an early age are a result of social learning. Certainly these skills are useful for women in terms of intimacy generally, and in terms of their role as keepers of heterosexual relationships in particular. For example, girls are more likely to play games that involve communication: talking and listening, as well as taking the role of the other through imaginary role-playing games. Boys, on the other hand, are more likely to play rule-bound games where the "rights" and "wrongs" of the game are predetermined rather than negotiated. As a result, girls learn to notice: They learn to be sensitive of others' feelings, and they are willing to do emotional work. Boys are often raised to repress and deny their inner thoughts and fears and learn not to notice them. Often they are taught that feelings are feminine or are for sissies. Girls become more comfortable with intimacy, and boys learn to shy away from it because intimacy is often seen as synonymous with weakness. Boys learn to camouflage feelings under a veneer of calm and rationality because fears are not manly. Importantly, as boys grow up they learn to rely on women to take care of their emotional needs, and girls learn that this request is part of being a woman.

Because emotional intimacy is about self-disclosure and revealing oneself to others, when people are intimate with each other, they open themselves to vulnerability. In the process of becoming intimate, one person shares feelings and information about her-/himself, and then the other person (if they want to maintain and develop intimacy) responds by sharing too. In turn each gives away little

Reprinted with permission from Nicole Hollander

pieces of oneself, and, in return, mutual trust, understanding, and friendship develop. Given the baggage of gender, however, what can happen is that one person does more of the giving away, and the other reveals less; one opens up to being vulnerable, and the other maintains personal power. The first person also takes on the role of helping the other share, drawing that person out, translating ordinary messages for their hidden emotional meanings, and investing greater amounts of energy into interpersonal communication. The first person has taken the role prescribed by femininity and the latter the role that masculinity endorses. The important point here is that intimacy is about power. Men tend to be less able to open themselves up because of anxiety associated with being vulnerable and potentially losing personal power.

Central in understanding masculine sexual scripts and issues around emotional intimacy is the mandate against homosexuality. Because boys and men may play rough and work closely together—touching each other physically in sports and other masculine pursuits—there are lots of opportunities for *homoeroticism* (arousal of sexual feelings through contact with people of the same sex). In response to this, strong norms against homosexuality regulate masculine behavior— norms fed by homophobia and enforced by such institutions as education, sports, media, family, the military, and the state. These norms discourage men from showing affection with each other and thus discourage intimacy between men. As an aside, they also encourage male bonding where women may function as objects in

Ideas for Activism

- Work with various women's groups on your campus to develop, publish, and distribute a "Check Up on Your Relationship" brochure. This brochure should contain a checklist of signs for emotional/physical/sexual abuse and resources to get help.
- Organize and present a forum on healthy dating practices.
- Organize a clothes drive for your local women's shelter.
- Research gay rights, such as protection against discrimination in employment or housing, domestic partner benefits, or hate crimes legislation in your city or state. If you find that gay, lesbian, bisexual, or transgender people in your area do not enjoy full civil rights, write your government officials to encourage them to enact policies providing civil rights for queer people.
- Organize a National Coming Out Day celebration on your campus.
- Organize an event on your campus in recognition of World AIDS Day, which is December 1.
- Become a member of the Human Rights Campaign. For more information see *www.hrc.org*.

order for men to assert sexual potency. Examples of this include women as entertainment for various kinds of stag parties, women as pinups in places where men live and/or work together, and, in the extreme, gang rape. Homophobia serves to keep women apart too, of course. In particular, women are encouraged to give up the love of other women in order to gain the approval of men.

A key aspect of intimacy, and thus sexuality, is interpersonal communication. Again, the ways we communicate in relationships have a lot to do with gender; these different styles help to maintain gender differences in status and power. Women and men tend to communicate differently in the following ways: First, in terms of speech patterns, women tend to use more polite speech, less profanity, and more standard forms. They use more fillers like "uhm," hedges like "sort of" and "I guess," and intensifiers like "really" and "very." They are more likely to tag questions on statements like "It's hot today, isn't it?" and to turn an imperative into a question: "Would you mind opening the door?" rather than "Open the door!" All these forms of speaking are less authoritative.

Second, women tend to use different intonations than men when they speak. Women have a higher pitch that is recognized as less assertive than a lower pitch. They tend to speak with more emotional affect than men and are more likely to end a sentence with a raised pitch. This sounds like a question and gives a more hesitant quality to women's speech.

Third, women and men use interruptions differently in speech. Although men and women interrupt at about the same rate in same-sex conversations, in mixed groups men interrupt more than women and are more likely to interrupt women than to interrupt men. Men are also more likely to change the subject in the process. Although there are cultural differences around interruptions, it is clear that who interrupts and who gets interrupted is about power.

Four, women tend to use more confirmations and reinforcements such as "Yes, go on" or "I hear you" or "uh-hums" during conversation. Examples of nonverbal confirmation of the speaker include leaning forward, eye contact, and nodding.

Finally, feminine and masculine speech fulfills different functions. Feminine speech tends to work toward maintaining relationships, developing rapport, avoiding conflict, and maintaining cooperation. Masculine speech, on the other hand, is more likely oriented toward attracting and maintaining an audience, asserting power and dominance, and giving information. Given these gendered differences in communication, it is easy to see how problems might arise in interpersonal interaction generally and in sexual relationships in particular, and how these issues are related to the give and take of interpersonal power.

In this way, sexual intimacy is as much about society as it is about physiology. Sexuality is wound up with our understandings of gender, and these norms channel our sense of ourselves as sexual persons. These social constructs encourage us to feel desire and enjoy certain sexual practices and relationships, and they guide the meanings we associate with our experiences.

Sexual Desire and Gender

Pepper Schwartz and Virginia Rutter

The gender of the person you desire is a serious matter seemingly fundamental to the whole business of romance. And it isn't simply a matter of whether someone is male or female; how well the person fulfills a lover's expectations of masculinity or femininity is of great consequence. . . .

. . . Although sex is experienced as one of the most basic and biological of activities, in human beings it is profoundly affected by things other than the body's urges. Who we're attracted to and what we find sexually satisfying is not just a matter of the genital equipment we're born with. . . .

Before we delve into the whys and wherefores of sex, we need to come to an understanding about what sex is. This is not as easy a task as it may seem, because sex has a number of dimensions.

On one level, sex can be regarded as having both a biological and a social context. The biological (and physiological) refers to how people use their genital equipment to reproduce. In addition, as simple as it seems, bodies make the experience of sexual pleasure available—whether the pleasure involves other bodies or just one's own body and mind. It should be obvious, however, that people engage in sex even when they do not intend to reproduce. They have sex for fun, as a way to communicate their feelings to each other, as a way to satisfy their ego, and for any number of other reasons relating to the way they see themselves and interact with others.

Another dimension of sex involves both what we do and how we think about it. *Sexual behavior* refers to the sexual acts that people engage in. These acts involve not only petting and intercourse but also seduction and courtship. Sexual behavior also involves the things people

do alone for pleasure and stimulation and the things they do with other people. *Sexual desire,* on the other hand, is the motivation to engage in sexual acts. It relates to what turns people on. A person's *sexuality* consists of both behavior and desire.

The most significant dimension of sexuality is *gender.* Gender relates both to the biological and social contexts of sexual behavior and desire. People tend to believe they know whether someone is a man or a woman not because we do a physical examination and determine that the person is biologically male or biologically female. Instead, we notice whether a person is masculine or feminine. Gender is a social characteristic of individuals in our society that is only sometimes consistent with biological sex. Thus, animals, like people, tend to be identified as male and female in accordance with the reproductive function, but only people are described by their gender, as a man or a woman.

When we say something is *gendered* we mean that social processes have determined what is appropriately masculine and feminine and that gender has thereby become integral to the definition of the phenomenon. For example, marriage is a gendered institution: The definition of marriage involves a masculine part (husband) and a feminine part (wife). Gendered phenomena, like marriage, tend to appear "naturally" so. But as recent debates about same-sex marriage underscore, the role of gender in marriage is the product of social processes and beliefs about men, women, and marriage. In examining how gender influences sexuality, moreover, you will see that gender rarely operates alone: Class, culture, race, and individual differences also combine to influence sexuality.

. . .

DESIRE: ATTRACTION AND AROUSAL

The most salient fact about sex is that nearly everybody is interested in it. Most people like to have sex, and they talk about it, hear about it, and think about it. But some people are obsessed with sex and willing to have sex with anyone or anything. Others are aroused only by particular conditions and hold exacting criteria. For example, some people will have sex only if they are positive that they are in love, that their partner loves them, and that the act is sanctified by marriage. Others view sex as not much different from eating a sandwich. They neither love nor hate the sandwich; they are merely hungry, and they want something to satisfy that hunger. What we are talking about here are differences of desire. As you have undoubtedly noticed, people differ in what they find attractive, and they are also physically aroused by different things.

Many people assume that differences in sexual desire have a lot to do with whether a person is female or male. In large representative surveys about sexual behavior, the men as a group inevitably report more frequent sex, with more partners, and in more diverse ways than the women as a group do . . . First, we should consider the approaches we might use to interpret it. Many observers argue that when it comes to sex, men and women have fundamentally different biological wiring. Others use the evidence to argue that culture has produced marked sexual differences among men and women. We believe, however, that it is hard to tease apart biological differences and social differences. As soon as a baby enters the world, it receives messages about gender and sexuality. In the United States, for example, disposable diapers come adorned in pink for girls and blue for boys. In case people aren't sure whether to treat the baby as masculine or feminine in its first years of life, the diaper signals them. The assumption is that girl babies really are different from boy babies and the difference ought to be displayed. This different treatment continues throughout life, and therefore a sex difference at birth becomes amplified into gender differences as people mature.

Gendered experiences have a great deal of influence on sexual desire. As a boy enters adolescence, he hears jokes about boys' uncontainable desire. Girls are told the same thing and told that their job is to resist. These gender messages have power not only over attitudes and behavior (such as whether a person grows up to prefer sex with a lover rather than a stranger) but also over physical and biological experience. For example, a girl may be discouraged from vigorous competitive activity, which will subsequently influence how she develops physically, how she feels about her body, and even how she relates to the adrenaline rush associated with physical competition. Hypothetically, a person who is accustomed to adrenaline responses experiences sexual attraction differently from one who is not.

What follows are three "competing" explanations of differences in sexual desire between men and women: a biological explanation, sociobiological and evolutionary psychological explanations, and an explanation that acknowledges the social construction of sexuality. We call these competing approaches because each tends to be presented as a complete explanation in itself, to the exclusion of other explanations. Our goal, however, is to provide a clearer picture of how "nature" and "nurture" are intertwined in the production of sexualities.

THE BIOLOGY OF DESIRE: NATURE'S EXPLANATION

Biology is admittedly a critical factor in sexuality. Few human beings fall in love with fish or sexualize trees. Humans are designed to respond to other humans. And human activity is, to some extent, organized by the physical equipment humans are born with. Imagine if people had fins instead of arms or laid eggs instead of fertilizing them during intercourse. Romance would look quite different.

Although biology seems to be a constant (i.e., a component of sex that is fixed and unchanging), the social world tends to mold biology as much as biology shapes humans' sexuality. Each society has its own rules for sex. Therefore, how people experience their biology varies widely. In some societies, women act intensely aroused and active during sex; in others, they have no concept of orgasm. In fact, women in some settings, when told about orgasm, do not even believe it exists, as anthropologists discovered in some parts of Nepal. Clearly, culture—not biology—is at work, because we know that orgasm is physically possible, barring damage to or destruction of the sex organs. Even ejaculation is culturally dictated. In some countries, it is considered healthy to ejaculate early and often; in others, men are told to conserve semen and ejaculate as rarely as possible. The biological capacity may not be so different, but the way bodies behave during sex varies according to social beliefs.

Sometimes the dictates of culture are so rigid and powerful that the so-called laws of nature can be overridden. Infertility treatment provides an example: For couples who cannot produce children "naturally," a several billion dollar industry has provided technology that can, in a small proportion of cases, overcome this biological problem. Recently, in California, a child was born to a 63-year-old woman who had been implanted with fertilized eggs. The cultural emphasis on reproduction and parenthood, in this case, overrode the biological incapacity to produce children. Nevertheless, some researchers have focused on the biological foundations of sexual desire. They have examined the endocrine system and hormones, brain structure, and genetics. Others have observed the mechanisms of arousal. What all biological research on sex has in common is the proposition that many so-called sexual choices are not choices at all but are dictated by the body. A prominent example comes from the study of the biological origins of homosexuality. However, contradictory and debatable findings make conclusions difficult.

The Influence of Hormones

Biological explanations of sexual desire concentrate on the role of hormones. *Testosterone,* sometimes called the male sex hormone, appears to be the most important hormone for sexual function. Numerous research studies identify testosterone as an enabler for male sexual arousal. But we cannot predict a man's sexual tastes, desires, or behavior by measuring his testosterone. Although a low level of testosterone in men is sometimes associated with lower sexual desire, this is not predictably the case. Furthermore, testosterone level does not always influence sexual performance. Indeed, testosterone is being experimented with as a male contraceptive, thus demonstrating that desire and the biological goal of reproduction need not be linked to sexual desire.

Testosterone has also been implicated in nonsexual behaviors, such as aggression. Furthermore, male aggression sometimes crosses into male sexuality, generating sexual violence. But recent research on testosterone and aggression in men has turned the testosterone-aggression connection on its head: Low levels of testosterone have been associated with aggression, and higher levels have been associated with calmness, happiness, and friendliness.

Testosterone is also found in women, although at levels as little as one-fifth those of men. This discrepancy in levels of testosterone has incorrectly been used as evidence for "natural" gender differences in sex drives. However, women's testosterone receptors are simply more sensitive than men's to smaller amounts of testosterone.

Estrogen, which is associated with the menstrual cycle, is known as the female hormone. Like testosterone, however, estrogen is found in both women and men. Furthermore, estrogen may be the more influential hormone in human aggression. In animal research, male mice whose ability to respond to estrogen had been bred out of them lost much of their natural aggressiveness. Researchers are currently investigating the association between adolescents' moodiness and their levels of estrogen. Of course, many social factors—such as changes in parental behavior toward their teenagers—help explain moodiness among adolescents.

Some biological evidence indicates that a woman's sexual desire may be linked to the impact of hormones as levels change during her reproductive cycle. (No evidence shows men's sexual desire to be cyclical.) Some scientists believe that women's sexual arousal is linked to the fertile portion of their cycle. They believe that sexual interest in women is best explained as the product of thousands of years of natural selection. Natural selection would favor for survival those women who are sexually aroused during ovulation (the time women are most likely to become pregnant). These women would be reproductively successful and therefore pass on to their children the propensity for arousal during ovulation. Neat though this theory is, it doesn't fit all the data. Other research finds no evidence of increased sexual interest among women who are ovulating. Instead, the evidence suggests that women's sexual interest actually tends to peak well before ovulation. Still other evidence finds no variation in sexual desire or sexual activity in connection to the menstrual cycle.

. . . [T]estosterone and estrogen are not clearly linked to either men's desire or women's. Research shows a complicated relationship between hormones and sexuality. Hormonal fluctuations may not be the central cause of sexual behavior or any social acts; instead, social circumstances may be the cause of hormonal fluctuation. A famous series of experiments makes the point. One animal experiment took a dominant rhesus monkey out of his environment and measured testosterone level. It was very high, suggesting that he had reached the top of the monkey heap by being hormonally superior. Then the monkey was placed among even bigger, more dominant monkeys than himself. When his testosterone was remeasured, it was much lower. One interpretation is that social hierarchy had influenced the monkey's biological barometer. His testosterone level had adjusted to his social status. In this case, the social environment shaped physiology.

. . .

SOCIOBIOLOGY AND EVOLUTIONARY PSYCHOLOGY

The past few decades of research on sexuality have produced a new school of human behavior—*sociobiology* and a related discipline, *evolutionary psychology*—that explains most gender differences as strategies of sexual reproduction. According to evolutionary psychologist David Buss, "evolutionary psychologists predict that the sexes will differ in precisely those domains in which women and men have faced different sorts of adaptive problems." By "those domains," Buss refers to reproduction, which is the only human function that depends on a biological difference between men and women.

The key assumption of sociobiological/evolutionary theory is that humans have an innate, genetically triggered impulse to pass on their genetic material through successful reproduction: This impulse is called *reproductive fitness*. The human species, like other species that sociobiologists study, achieves immortality by having children who live to the age of reproductive maturity and produce children themselves. Sociobiologists and evolutionary psychologists seek to demonstrate that almost all male and female behavior, and especially sexuality, is influenced by this one simple but powerful proposition.

Sociobiologists start at the species level. Species are divided into *r* and *K reproductive categories.* Those with *r* strategies obtain immortality by mass production of eggs and sperm. The *r* species is best illustrated by fish. The female manufactures thousands of eggs, the male squirts millions of sperm over them, and that is the extent of parenting. According to this theory, the male and female fish need not pair up to nurture their offspring. Although thousands of fertilized fish eggs are consumed by predators, only a small proportion of the massive quantity of fertilized eggs must survive for the species to continue. In the *r* species, parents need not stay together for the sake of the kids.

In contrast, humans are a *K*-strategy species, which has a greater investment in each fertilized egg. Human females and most female mammals have very few eggs, especially compared to fish. Moreover, offspring take a long time to mature in the mother's womb and are quite helpless when they are born, with no independent survival ability. Human babies need years of supervision before they are independent. Thus, if a woman wants to pass on her genes (or at least the half her child will inherit from her), she must take good care of her dependent child. The baby is a scarce resource. Even if a woman is pregnant from sexual maturation until menopause, the number of children she can produce is quite limited. This limitation was particularly true thousands of years ago. Before medical advances of the nineteenth and twentieth centuries, women were highly unlikely to live to the age of menopause. Complications from childbirth commonly caused women to die in their 20s or 30s. Where the food supply was scarce, women were less likely to be successful at conceiving, further reducing the possibility of generating offspring.

Sociobiologists and evolutionary psychologists say that men inseminate, women incubate. The human female's reproductive constraints (usually one child at a time, not so many children over a life cycle, and a helpless infant for a long period of time) shape most of women's sexual and emotional approaches to men and mating. According to their theory, women have good reason to be more selective than men

about potential mates. They want to find a man who will stick around and continue to provide resources and protection to this child at least until the child has a good chance of survival. Furthermore, because a woman needs to create an incentive for a man to remain with her, females have developed more sophisticated sexual and emotional skills specifically geared toward creating male loyalty and commitment to their mutual offspring.

Sociobiologists and evolutionary psychologists say that differences in reproductive capacity and strategy also shape sexual desire. Buss asserts that reproductive strategies form most of the categories of desire: Older men generally pick younger women because they are more fertile; younger women seek older men who have more status, power, and resources (a cultural practice known as *hypergamy*) because such men can provide for their children. Furthermore, health and reproductive capacity make youth generally sexier, and even certain shapes of women's bodies (such as an "ideal" hip-to-waist ratio epitomized by an hourglass figure, which correlate with ability to readily reproduce), are widely preferred—despite varying standards of beauty across cultures. Likewise, men who have demonstrated their fertility by producing children are more sought after than men who have not.

According to evolutionary psychologists, men's tastes for recreational sex, unambivalent lust, and a variety of partners are consistent with maximizing their production of children. Men's sexual interest is also more easily aroused because sex involves fewer costs to them than to women, and the ability for rapid ejaculation has a reproductive payoff. On the other hand, women's taste for relationship-based intimacy and greater investment in each sexual act is congruent with women's reproductive strategies.

In a field that tends to emphasize male's "natural" influence over reproductive strategies, evolutionary anthropologist Helen Fisher offers a feminist twist. Her study of hundreds of societies shows that divorce, or its informal equivalent, occurs most typically in the third or fourth year of a marriage and then peaks about every four years after that. Fisher hypothesizes that some of the breakups have to do with a woman's attempt to obtain the best genes and best survival chances for her offspring. In both agrarian and hunter-gatherer societies, Fisher explains, women breast-feed their child for three or four years—a practice that is economical and sometimes helps to prevent further pregnancy. At the end of this period, the woman is ready and able to have another child. She reenters the mating marketplace and assesses her options to see if she can improve on her previous mate. If she can get a better guy, she will leave the previous partner and team up with a new one. In Fisher's vision, unlike the traditional sociobiological view . . . , different male and female reproductive strategies do not necessarily imply female sexual passivity and preference for lifelong monogamy.

Sociobiologists and evolutionary psychologists tell a fascinating story of how male and female reproductive differences might shape sexuality. To accept sociobiological arguments, one must accept the premise that most animal and human behavior is driven by the instinct to reproduce and improve the gene pool. Furthermore, a flaw of sociobiology as a theory is that it does not provide a unique account of sexual behavior with the potential to be tested empirically. Furthermore, other social science explanations for the same phenomena are supported by more immediate, close-range evidence.

Consider hypergamy, the practice of women marrying men slightly older and "higher" on the social status ladder than they are. Sociobiologists would say women marry "up" to ensure the most fit provider for their offspring. But hypergamy makes little sense biologically. Younger men have more years of resources to provide, and they have somewhat more sexual resources. Empirically, however, hypergamy is fact. It is also a fact that men, overall and in nearly every subculture, have access to more rewards and status than women do. Furthermore, reams of imagery—in movies, advertising, novels—promote the appeal of older, more

resourceful men. Why not, when older, more resourceful men are generating the images? Social practice, in this case, overrides what sociobiologists consider the biological imperative.

THE SOCIAL ORIGINS OF DESIRE

Your own experience should indicate that biology and genetics alone do not shape human sexuality. From the moment you entered the world, cues from the environment were telling you which desires and behaviors were "normal" and which were not. The result is that people who grow up in different circumstances tend to have different sexualities. Who has not had their sexual behavior influenced by their parents' or guardians' explicit or implicit rules? You may break the rules or follow them, but you can't forget them. . . .

The Social Construction of Sexuality

Social constructionists believe that cues from the environment shape human beings from the moment they enter the world. The sexual customs, values, and expectations of a culture, passed on to the young through teaching and by example, exert a powerful influence over individuals. When Fletcher Christian sailed into Tahiti in Charles Nordhoff's 1932 account, *Mutiny on the Bounty,* he and the rest of his nineteenth-century English crew were surprised at how sexually available, playful, guilt free, and amorous the Tahitian women were. Free from the Judeo-Christian precepts and straightlaced customs that inhibited English society, the women and girls of Tahiti regarded their sexuality joyfully and without shame. The English men were delighted and, small wonder, refused to leave the island. Such women did not exist in their own society. The women back in England had been socialized within their Victorian culture to be modest, scared of sex, protective of their reputation, and threatened by physical pleasure. As a result, they were unavailable before marriage and did not feel free to indulge in a whole lot of fun after it. The source of the difference was not physiological differences between Tahitian and English women; it was sexual *socialization* or the upbringing that they received within their differing families and cultures.

If we look back at the Victorian, nineteenth-century England that Nordhoff refers to, we can identify *social structures* that influenced the norms of women's and men's sexuality. A burgeoning, new, urban middle class created separate spheres in the division of family labor. Instead of sharing home and farm or small business, the tasks of adults in families became specialized: Men went out to earn money, women stayed home to raise children and take care of the home. Although this division of labor was not the norm in all classes and ethnicities in England at the time, the image of middle-class femininity and masculinity became pervasive. The new division of labor increased women's economic dependence on men, which further curbed women's sexual license but not men's. When gender organizes one aspect of life—such as men's and women's position in the ecomony—it also organizes other aspects of life, including sex.

In a heterogeneous and individualistic culture like North America, sexual socialization is complex. A society creates an "ideal" sexuality, but different families and subcultures have their own values. For example, even though contemporary society at large may now accept premarital sexuality, a given family may lay down the law: Sex before marriage is against the family's religion and an offense against God's teaching. A teenager who grows up in such a household may suppress feelings of sexual arousal or channel them into outlets that are more acceptable to the family. Or the teenager may react against her or his background, reject parental and community opinion, and search for what she or he perceives to be a more "authentic" self. Variables like birth order or observations of a sibling's social and sexual expression can also influence a person's development.

As important as family and social background are, so are individual differences in response to that background. In the abstract, people raised to celebrate their sexuality must surely have a different approach to enjoying their bodies than those who are taught that their bodies will betray them and are a venal part of human nature. Yet whether or not a person is raised to be at ease with physicality does not always help predict adult sexual behavior. Sexual sybarites and libertines may have grown up in sexually repressive environments, as did pop culture icon and Catholic-raised Madonna. Sometimes individuals whose families promoted sex education and free personal expression are content with minimal sexual expression.

. . .

To summarize, social constructionists believe that a society influences sexual behavior through its norms. Some norms are explicit, such as laws against adult sexual activity with minors. Others are implicit, such as norms of fidelity and parental responsibility. In a stable, homogeneous society, it is relatively easy to understand such rules. But in a changing, complex society like the United States, the rules may be in flux or indistinct. Perhaps this ambiguity is what makes some issues of sexuality so controversial today.

AN INTEGRATIVE PERSPECTIVE ON GENDER AND SEXUALITY

Social constructionist explanations of contemporary sexual patterns are typically pitted against the biology of desire and the evolutionary understanding of biological adaptations. Some social constructionists believe there is no inflexible biological reality; everything we regard as either female or male sexuality is culturally imposed. In contrast, *essentialists*—those who take a biological, sociobiological, or evolutionary point of view—believe people's sexual desires and orientations are innate and hard-wired and that social impact is minimal.

Gender differences follow from reproductive differences. Men inseminate, women incubate. People are born with sexual drives, attractions, and natures that simply play themselves out at the appropriate developmental age. Even if social constraints conspire to make men and women more similar to each other (as in the 1990s, when the sensitive and nurturing new man is encouraged to get in touch with his so-called feminine, emotional side), people's essential nature is the same: Man is the hunter, warrior, and trailblazer, and woman is the gatherer, nurturer, and reproducer. To an essentialist, social differences, such as the different earning power of men and women, are the consequence of biological difference. In short, essentialists think the innate differences between women and men are the cause of gendered sexuality; social constructionists think the differences between men and women are the result of gendering sexuality through social processes.

Using either the social constructionist or essentialist approach to the exclusion of the other constrains understanding of sexuality. We believe the evidence shows that gender differences are more plausibly an outcome of social processes than the other way around. But a social constructionist view is most powerful when it takes the essentialist view into account. . . . [W]e describe this view of gender differences in sexual desire as *integrative*. Although people tend to think of sex as primarily a biological function—tab B goes into slot A— biology is only one part of the context of desire. Such sociological factors as family relationships and social structure also influence sex. A complex mix of anatomy, hormones, and the brain provides the basic outline for the range of acts and desires possible, but biology is neither where sexuality begins nor where it ends. Social and biological contexts link to define human sexual possibilities.

The integrative approach follows from a great deal that sexuality researchers have observed. Consider the following example: A research project, conducted over three decades ago, advertised for participants stating that its focus was how physical excitement influences a man's preference for one woman over another. The researchers connected college men to a monitor that allowed them to hear their heartbeats as they looked at photographs of women models. The men were told that they would be able to hear their heartbeat when it surged in response to each photograph. A greater surge would suggest greater physical attraction. The participants were then shown a photograph of a dark-haired woman, then a blonde, then a redhead. Afterward, each man was asked to choose the picture that he would prefer to take home. In each case, the man chose the photograph of the woman who, as he believed from listening to his own speeding heartbeat, had most aroused him. Or at least the man thought he was choosing the woman who had aroused him most. In reality, the men had been listening to a faked heartbeat that was speeded up at random. The men thus actually chose the women whom they believed had aroused them most. In this case, the men's invented attraction was more powerful than their gut response. Their mind (a powerful sexual organ) told them their body was responding to a specific picture. The participants' physiological experience of arousal was eclipsed by the social context. When social circumstances influence sexual tastes, are those tastes real or sincere? Absolutely. The social world is as much a fact in people's lives as the biological world.

Radical Heterosexuality

Naomi Wolf

All over the country, millions of feminists have a secret indulgence. By day they fight gender injustice; by night they sleep with men. Is this a dual life? A core contradiction? Is sleeping with a man "sleeping with the enemy"? And is razor burn from kissing inherently oppressive?

It's time to say you *can* hate sexism and love men. As the feminist movement grows more mature and our understanding of our enemies more nuanced, three terms assumed to be in contradiction—radical feminist heterosexuality—can and must be brought together.

RULES OF THE RELATIONSHIP

But how? Andrea Dworkin and Catharine MacKinnon have pointed out that sexism limits women to such a degree that it's questionable whether the decision to live with a man can ever truly be free. If you want to use their sound, if depressing, reasoning to a brighter end, turn the thesis around: radical heterosexuality demands substituting choice for dependency.

Radical heterosexuality requires that the woman be able to support herself. This is not to belittle women who must depend financially on men; it is to recognize that when our daughters are raised with the skills that would let them leave abusers, they need not call financial dependence love.

Radical heterosexuality needs alternative institutions. As the child of a good lifetime union, I believe in them. But when I think of pledging my heart and body to a man—even the best and kindest man—within the existing institution of marriage, I feel faint. The more you learn about its legal structure, the less likely you are to call the caterers.

In the nineteenth century, when a judge ruled that a husband could not imprison and rape his wife, the London *Times* bemoaned, "One fine morning last month, marriage in England was suddenly abolished." The phrase "rule of thumb" descends from English common law that said a man could legally beat his wife with a switch "no thicker than his thumb."

If these nightmarish echoes were confined to history, I might feel more nuptial; but look at our own time. Do I want the blessing of an institution that doesn't provide adequate protection from marital rape? That gives a woman less protection from assault by her husband than by a stranger? That assigns men 70 percent of contested child custodies?

Of course I do not fear any such brutality from the man I want to marry (no bride does). But marriage means that his respectful treatment of me and our children becomes, despite our intentions, a kindness rather than a legally grounded right.

We need a heterosexual version of the marriages that gay and lesbian activists are seeking: a commitment untainted by centuries of inequality; a ritual that invites the community to rejoice in the making of a new freely chosen family.

The radical heterosexual man must yield the automatic benefits conferred by gender. I had a lover once who did not want to give up playing sports in a club that had a separate door for women. It must be tempting to imagine you can have both—great squash courts *and* the bed of a liberated woman—but in the mess hall of gender relations, there is *no such thing as a free lunch.*

Radical heterosexual women too must give up gender benefits (such as they are). I know scores of women—independent, autonomous—who avoid assuming any of the risk for a romantic or sexual approach.

I have watched myself stand complacently by while my partner wrestles with a stuck window, an intractable computer printer, maps, or locks. Sisters, I am not proud of this, and I'm working on it. But people are lazy—or at least I am—and it's easy to rationalize that the person with the penis is the one who should get out of a warm bed to fix the snow on the TV screen. After all, it's the very least owed to me *personally* in compensation for centuries of virtual enslavement.

Radical heterosexuals must try to stay conscious—at all times, I'm afraid—of their gender imprinting, and how it plays out in their erotic melodramas. My own psyche is a flagrant *son et lumière* of political incorrectness. Three of my boyfriends had motorcycles; I am easy pickings for the silent and dysfunctional. My roving eye is so taken by the oil-stained persona of the labor organizer that myopic intellectuals have gained access to my favors merely by sporting a Trotsky button.

We feminists are hard on each other for admitting to weakness. Gloria Steinem caught flak from her left-wing sisters for acknowledging in *Revolution from Within* that she was drawn to a man because he could do the things with money and power that we are taught men must do. And some were appalled when Simone de Beauvoir's letters revealed how she coddled Sartre.

But the antifeminist erotic template is *in* us. We would not be citizens of this culture if swooning damsels and abandoned vixens had not been beamed at us from our first solid food to our first vote. We can't fight it until we admit it. And we can't identify it until we drag it, its taffeta billowing and its bosom heaving, into the light of day.

I have done embarrassing, reactionary, abject deeds out of love and sexual passion. So, no doubt, has Norman Schwarzkopf. Only when we reveal our conditioning can we tell how much of our self-abasement is neurotic femininity, and how much is the flawed but impressive human apparatus of love.

IN THE BEDROOM

Those are the conditions for the radical heterosexual couple. What might this new creation look like in bed? It will look like something we have no words or images for—the eroticization of consent, the equal primacy of female and male desire.

We will need to tell some secrets—to map our desire for the male body and admit to our fascination with the rhythms and forces of male arousal, its uncanny counterintuitive spell.

We will also need to face our creature qualities. Animality has for so long been used against us—bitch, fox, *Penthouse* pet—that we struggle for the merit badges of higher rationality, ambivalent about our animal nature.

The truth is that heterosexual women believe that men, on some level, are animals; as they believe that we are animals. But what does "animal" mean?

Racism and sexism have long used animal metaphors to distance and degrade the Other. Let us redefine "animal" to make room for that otherness between the genders, an otherness fierce and worthy of respect. Let us define animal as an inchoate kinship, a comradeship, that finds a language beyond our species.

I want the love of two unlikes: the look of astonishment a woman has at the sight of a male back bending. These manifestations of difference confirm in heterosexuals the beauty that similarity confirms in the lesbian or gay imagination. Difference and animality do not have to mean hierarchy.

MEN WE LOVE

What must the men be like? Obviously, they're not going to be just anyone. *Esquire* runs infantile disquisitions on "Women We Love" (suggesting, Lucky Girls!). Well, I think that the men who are loved by feminists are lucky. Here's how they qualify to join this fortunate club.

Men We Love understand that, no matter how similar our backgrounds, we are engaged in a cross-cultural (if not practically biracial) relationship. They know that we know much about their world and they but little of ours. They accept what White people must accept in relationships with people of other ethnicities: to know that they do not know.

Men We Love don't hold a baby as if it is a still-squirming, unidentifiable catch from the sea.

Men We Love don't tell women what to feel about sexism. (There's a postcard that shows a dashing young fellow, drawn Love-comix-style, saying to a women, "Let me explicate to you the nature of your oppression.") They do not presume that there is a line in the sand called "enlightened male," and that all they need is a paperback copy of Djuna Barnes and good digital technique. They understand that unlearning gender oppressiveness means untying the very core of how we become female and male. They know this pursuit takes a lifetime at the minimum.

Sadly, men in our lives sometimes come through on personal feminism but balk at it intellectually. A year ago, I had a bruising debate with my father and brother about the patriarchal nature of traditional religious and literary canons. I almost seized them by their collars, howling "Read Mary Daly! Read Toni Morrison! Take Feminism 101. *No, I can't* explain it to you between the entrée and dessert!"

By spring, my dad, bless his heart, had asked for a bibliography, and last week my brother sent me *Standing Again at Sinai*, a Jewish-feminist classic. Men We Love are willing, sooner or later, to read the Books We Love.

Men We Love accept that successful training in manhood makes them blind to phenomena that are fact to women. Recently, I walked down a New York City avenue with a woman friend, X, and a man friend, Y. I pointed out

to Y the leers, hisses, and invitations to sit on faces. Each woman saw clearly what the other woman saw, but Y was baffled. Sexual harassers have superb timing. A passerby makes kissy-noises with his tongue while Y is scrutinizing the menu of the nearest bistro. "There, there! Look! Listen!" we cried. "What? Where? Who?" wailed poor Y, valiantly, uselessly spinning.

What if, hard as they try to see, they cannot hear? Once I was at lunch with a renowned male crusader for the First Amendment. Another Alpha male was present, and the venue was the Supreme Court lunchroom—two power factors that automatically press the "mute" button on the male ability to detect a female voice on the audioscope. The two men began to rev their motors; soon they were off and racing in a policy-wonk grand prix. I tried, once or twice, to ask questions. But the free-speech champions couldn't hear me over the testosterone roar.

Men We Love undertake half the care and cost of contraception. They realize that it's not fair to wallow in the fun without sharing the responsibility. When stocking up for long weekends, they brave the amused glances when they ask, "Do you have this in unscented?"

Men We Love know that just because we can be irrational doesn't mean we're insane. When we burst into premenstrual tears—having just realized the cosmic fragility of creation—they comfort us. Not until we feel better do they dare remind us gently that we had this same revelation exactly 28 days ago.

Men We Love must make a leap of imagination to believe in the female experience. They do not call women nags or paranoid when we embark on the arduous, often boring, nonnegotiable daily chore of drawing attention to sexism. They treat it like adults taking driving lessons: if irked in the short term at being treated like babies, they're grateful in the long term that someone is willing to teach them patiently how to move through the world without harming the pedestrians. Men We Love don't drive without their gender glasses on.

A PLACE FOR THEM

It's not simple gender that pits Us against Them. In the fight against sexism, it's those who are for us versus those who are against us—of either gender.

When I was 16, my boyfriend came with me to hear Andrea Dworkin speak. While hearing great feminist oratory in a sea of furious women changed my life, it nearly ended my boyfriend's: he barely escaped being drawn and quartered.

It is time to direct our anger more acutely at the Men We Hate—like George Bush—and give the Men We Love something useful to do. Not to take over meetings, or to set agendas; not to whine, "Why can't feminists teach us how to be free?" but to add their bodies, their hearts, and their numbers, to support us.

I meet many young men who are brought to feminism by love for a woman who has been raped, or by watching their single mothers struggle against great odds, or by simple common sense. Their most frequent question is, "What can I do to help?"

Imagine a rear battalion of committed "Men Against Violence Against Women" (or Men for Choice, or what have you)—of all races, ages, and classes. Wouldn't that be a fine sight to fix in the eyes of a five-year-old boy?

Finally, the place to make room for radical feminist heterosexuality is within our heads. If the movement that I dearly love has a flaw, it is a tendency toward orthodoxies about other women's pleasures and needs. This impulse is historically understandable: in the past, we needed to define ourselves against men if we were to define ourselves at all. But today, the most revolutionary choice we can make is to affirm other women's choices, whether lesbian or straight, bisexual or celibate.

NOW President Patricia Ireland speaks for me even though our sexual lives are not identical. Simone de Beauvoir speaks for me even though our sexual lives are not identical. Audre Lorde speaks for me even though our sexual lives are not identical. Is it the chromosomes of your lovers that establish you as a feminist? Or is it the life you make out of the love you make?

Bisexuality, Feminism, Men, and Me

Robyn Ochs

. . .

My own route to feminism was long, convoluted and closely connected with my developing bisexual consciousness. In my early twenties I realized that my emotional and sexual attractions toward women as well as men were not going to go away, and I began to address those feelings. Forced off-balance by the turbulence of these emotions and their implications for my future, I began for the first time to consciously question the assumptions I had made

about my life. I began to understand that many of my choices had not been freely made, but rather had been made within the context of a system that Adrienne Rich calls "compulsory heterosexuality," a system that posits heterosexuality as the only way to be.[1] In this essay I describe my own journey: what I learned and what I unlearned, and how these changes in my thinking have fundamentally changed my relationships with men.

. . .

MY BODY AND ME

Like many women, I grew up hating my body. I remember wearing shorts over my bathing suit as a preteen to hide my "ugly" fat thighs. As a teenager, I spent a lot of time worrying whether I was attractive enough. Of course, I was never quite up to standard. I wanted very much to have the kind of exterior that would cause scouting agents from pinup magazines or from modeling agencies to approach me on the street to recruit me. Needless to say, this never happened, reinforcing my belief that physically I was a total failure as a woman. I fantasized about being a dancer but knew I did not have the requisite "dancer's body." I thought my size 7½ feet were enormous. For the record, I have always been more or less average in weight. But average was not good enough. As long as I didn't look like one of those women in *Playboy*, I wasn't pretty enough.

> Too big too short too stocky too busty too round too many zits blackheads disgusting pinch an inch fail the pencil test cellulite don't go out without makeup don't let them see what you *really* look like they'll run away in terror but if you are really lucky and have a few beers and do it in the dark he might not notice so make sure to turn off the light before . . .

I never questioned my standards of measurement, never realized that these standards are determined by a male-dominated culture and reinforced by a multibillion-dollar "femininity" industry that sells women cosmetics, diet aids, plastic surgery, fashion magazines, liposuction, creams and girdles. I took my inability to live up to these standards as personal failure and never drew any connections between my experience and that of other women.

MEN AND ME

Men, you can't live without 'em. Sooner or later I would end up with one. My grandfather used to tell me that it was good that I was short, as

that way I would have the option of marrying either a tall man or a short one. There aren't enough men to go around and it gets harder and harder to find one as you get older. Men aren't comfortable with women who are more educated/smarter/earn more than they. My fifty-year-old aunt never married. She waited *too long,* and by then it was *too late* because she was *too old, poor dear.* It's just as easy to fall in love with a rich man as a poor one. Men lead.

I always had a boyfriend. From age thirteen until after college, I don't remember going for more than a month without being in a relationship or at least having a crush. Having a boyfriend was a measure of my worth. I would select the boy and flirt with him until he asked me out. Most times, like the Mounties, I got my man. In dance, this is called backleading, directing the action from the follower's position. It allows the man to look like he is in control.

I learned that there's a man shortage. There are more women than men. And "good men" are extremely rare. Therefore, if you manage to get hold of a good one, you'd better hang on to him. This message got louder as I moved into my twenties. I saw older women in their thirties and beyond searching frantically for a suitable partner with whom to reproduce the human species and make their lives meaningful. I learned that you'd better pay attention to your "biological clock."

THE UNLEARNING

These messages had a powerful grip on me. How did I begin to unlearn them? The women's studies class I took in college helped a bit. However, I continued to consider feminism only in terms of situations outside myself. I looked at my environment and catalogued the injustices, but did not look inside.

It wasn't until I was considering a relationship with a woman that I began to see the relevance of the feminist theory I had read as a first-year college student to my own life. My perspective changed dramatically. For example, in my first relationship with a woman, it became quickly apparent that in many ways I fit quite neatly into the passive "femme" role of the butch/femme stereotype. I was behaving as I had always behaved in relationships, but for the first time, now that my lover was a woman, my "normal" behavior appeared to me (and probably to her as well) strange and unbalanced. Why were my lover and I behaving so differently? Suddenly our roles appeared constructed rather than natural. I won't pretend that I woke up one day and found myself suddenly freed of my conditioning. Rather, I spent several years unfolding and unraveling the layers of misinformation I had internalized, learning more with each subsequent relationship or incident.

My body image began to change. Through the firsthand experience of my own attractions, I learned that women, and their bodies, are beautiful, though I did not immediately apply this knowledge to my opinion of my own body. There was one woman friend on whom I had a crush for more than two years. I thought she was beautiful, with her solid, powerful angles and healthy fullness. One day, with a sense of shock, I realized that her body was not so very different from mine and that I had been holding myself to a different, unattainable standard than I had been holding her and other women to. It was this experience of seeing my image reflected in another woman that finally allowed me to begin developing a positive relationship with my own body.

I learned from firsthand experience about the privilege differential that results when the gender of your partner changes. Before I had experienced some of society's disapproval and disregard, I had no sense of the privileges I had experienced in heterosexual relationships. In subsequent years, each time I changed partners I was painfully aware of this absurd double standard and began to strategize ways to live in such a way that I could challenge rather than collaborate with these injustices. I have made a personal commitment to be "out" as bisexual at every possible opportunity and to avoid taking privileges with a male lover that I would not have with my female lover. For these reasons, I have chosen not to marry, though I hope someday to establish a "domestic partnership" and have a "commitment ceremony." If I feel someone would be unwilling to hear me talk about a same-sex lover, I disclose nothing about *any* of my relationships, even if my current partner is of the opposite sex. This is not very easy, and occasionally I backslide, but I am rewarded with the knowledge that I am not contributing to the oppression of lesbian, gay, and bisexual people when I am in an opposite-sex relationship.

It was empowering to realize that men as romantic partners were optional, not required. I no longer felt pressured to lower my relationship standards in light of the shortage of good men. Yes, I might get involved with and spend the rest of my life with one, but then again I might choose to spend my life with a woman. Or perhaps simply myself. This was to be my choice.

I realized how I had been performing my designated gender role. It's amazing how being in a same-sex relationship can make you realize just how much of most heterosexual relationships is scripted from the first date to the bedroom to the dishes. In relationships with women, I learned how to lead and learned that I like to lead sometimes. As sometimes I like to follow. And as sometimes I prefer to negotiate every step with my partner, or to dance alone.

Finally, I made a personal commitment to hold men and women to the same standards in relationships. I realized that in our society women are grateful when a man behaves in a sensitive manner, but expect sensitivity of a woman as a matter of course. I decided that I would not settle for less from men, realizing that it means that I may be categorically eliminating most men as potential partners. So be it.

My experience with being in relationships with women has been in a way like a trip abroad. I learned that many of the things I had accepted as natural truths were socially constructed, and the first time I returned to a heterosexual relationship things felt different. I hadn't yet learned how to construct a relationship on my own terms, but I was aware that things were not quite right. As time passed, my self-awareness and self-confidence increased. I gathered more experience in lesbian relationships and began to apply my knowledge to subsequent heterosexual relationships.

It is not possible to know who or where I would be today had I remained heterosexual in my attractions and in my self-identity. Perhaps other events in my life would have triggered a feminist consciousness. At any rate, it is entirely clear to me that it was loving a woman that made me realize I had fallen outside my "script," which in turn forced me to realize there *was* a script. From there, I moved toward a critical self-awareness and the realization that I could shape and write my own life.

NOTE

Thanks to Marti Hohmann, Rebecca Kaplan and Annie Senghas for their feedback and support while I was writing this essay.

1. Adrienne Rich, "Compulsory Heterosexuality and Lesbian Existence," *Signs: Journal of Women in Culture and Society* 5, no. 4, (1980), pp. 631–60.

READING 27

Coffee Will Make You Black

April Sinclair

"Mama, are you a virgin?"

I was practicing the question in my head as I set the plates with the faded roosters down on the shiny yellow table. When Mama came back into the kitchen to stir the rice or turn the fish sticks or check on the greens, I would ask her.

This afternoon at school a boy named Michael had passed a note with "Stevie" written on it; inside it had asked if I was a virgin.

My name is Jean Stevenson but the kids at school all call me Stevie counta there's been this other Jean in my class since the first grade. Now I am eleven and a half and in the sixth grade.

So, anyhow, I was really surprised to get this note from a boy like Michael Dunn, who's tall with muscles and has gray eyes, curly hair, skin the color of taffy apples, and wears Converse All-Stars even though they cost $10 a pair.

I'm not saying I look like homemade sin or anything. It's just that I'm taller than most of the other girls in my class and half of the boys. Mama says I'm at that awkward age, and that soon I won't just be arms and legs; I'll need a bra and a girdle. I can't picture myself needing a bra, as flat-chested as I am now. And to tell you the truth, I'm not too hot on having my behind all hitched up in a girdle. I have to help Mama into hers on Sunday mornings, and I feel sorry for her, all squeezed in so tight you wonder how she can even breathe.

I stirred the pitcher of cherry-flavored Kool-Aid. I loved Daylight Saving Time; it was after six o'clock and still light outside. The sunshine pouring in through the ruffled curtains made the flowers on the wallpaper look alive.

I studied my reflection in the pitcher of Kool-Aid. It wasn't like I wasn't cute. I had dimples and my features seemed right for my face. My straightened hair was long enough to make a ponytail. My skin was the color of Cracker Jacks. But most negroes didn't get excited over folks who were darker than a paper bag.

"Jean, turn off the oven!" Mama shouted from her bedroom.

"Okay."

I stared out the kitchen window at the row of gray back porches and dirt backyards. We had been in the middle of Social Studies when I had gotten Michael's note. I had lifted the lid of my wooden desk and felt behind the bag of old, wet sucked-on sunflower-seed shells and pulled out my hardcover dictionary. I'd snuck a peek inside and looked up the word "virgin." I'd seen the words "pure" and "spotless" and "like the Virgin Mary, mother of Jesus." I thought I was a good person for the most part. I didn't steal and I tried my best not to lie. I went to Sunday school, and when I stayed for church, I always put my dime in the collection plate. But I wasn't about to put myself up there with Jesus' mother. It seemed like Michael was asking me if I was a goody-two-shoes or something.

So I'd had no choice but to answer the note with the words "Not exactly" and pass it back to him. I wondered what Michael thought of my answer, I hadn't seen him after school. I hoped he would say something to me on Monday. I knew it wasn't my place as a girl to say anything to him. I would just have to wait and see what happened, I told myself.

Mama returned to the kitchen. She looked glad to be out of her girdle and work clothes. She was wearing her oldest print housedress, and the extra pounds showing around her waist didn't make her look fat, they just made her look like somebody's mother. Mama had tied a scarf around her hair so she wouldn't sweat it out, and she was wearing Daddy's old house slippers. It struck me how different Mama looked from June Cleaver or Donna Reed on TV, not just because of her pecan-colored skin but because they practically did their housework in pearls!

I turned facing Mama, and folded my arms across my chest. I watched her take the pan of fish sticks out of the oven and set them on a plate.

I cleared my throat. "Mama, are you a virgin?"

Mama lifted the top off the pot of collard greens and breathed in the steam. She glanced at me and turned off the gas. I could tell by the look on her face that she was trying to think up a good answer.

"Jean, where did you pick up that word, at church?" Mama asked, rearranging the pressing comb and the can of bacon grease on the stove.

I stared down at the yellowed gray linoleum.

"Well, no, not exactly . . . at school."

"Mrs. Butler brought it up?"

I pulled on the tie of my sailor blouse and twisted it around my fingers.

"No, Mama, Mrs. Butler ain't brought it up, this boy asked me if I was a virgin."

I had the nerve to glance at Mama. Her large dark eyes were arched up like she had seen a ghost.

"Don't say 'ain't'! Didn't I tell you to never say 'ain't'? I can run from 'ain't.'"

In my opinion, this was not time for an English lesson, so I just hunched my shoulders. "Mrs. Butler *didn't* bring it up, this boy asked me if I was a virgin." I repeated, correcting my English.

"Well, Jean Eloise, you should have told him he'll never get the chance to find out." Mama frowned as she stirred the rice. "Humph, you stay away from that boy; he's got his mind in the gutter." Mama pointed her finger in my face. "All men are dogs! Some are just more doggish than others. Do you hear me?"

"Mama, the dictionary said something about the word 'virgin' meaning pure and spotless, like the Virgin Mary. I don't understand why you say Michael's got his mind in the gutter then."

"'Cause he's a dog, that's why! I just got through telling you that."

I stuffed my hands into the pockets of my blue pedal pushers and looked Mama in the eye. "Mama, am I a virgin or not?"

"Lord, have mercy, I forgot about the cornbread." Mama opened the oven door and took out the pan of cornbread. It looked fine.

Mama let out a big breath. Maybe it was hard having a daughter at an awkward age, I thought. "Jean, all unmarried girls should be virgins."

"Mama, Michael knows I'm unmarried."

"You haven't even started your period yet, of course you're a virgin."

I stared down at my brown penny loafers. "Mama, what happens when you start your period?"

Mama patted her cornbread. "I don't think you're ready for this kind of discussion."

"Mama, I'll be twelve in four months."

"Jean Eloise, I'll tell you everything I want you to know when the time comes. Now, call your daddy and the boys for dinner, the fish sticks are gettin cold."

I groaned as I left the kitchen. Boy, I could've gotten more out of Beaver Cleaver's mother.

La Güera

Cherríe Moraga

It requires something more than personal experience to gain a philosophy or point of view from any specific event. It is the quality of our response to the event and our capacity to enter into the lives of others that help us to make their lives and experiences our own.

—*Emma Goldman*[1]

I am the very well-educated daughter of a woman who, by the standards in this country, would be considered largely illiterate. My mother was born in Santa Paula, Southern California, at a time when much of the central valley there was still farm land. Nearly thirty-five years later, in 1948, she was the only daughter of six to marry an Anglo, my father.

I remember all of my mother's stories, probably much better than she realizes. She is a fine story-teller, recalling every event of her life with the vividness of the present, noting each detail right down to the cut and color of her dress. I remember her stories of her being pulled out of school at the ages of five, seven, nine, and eleven to work in the fields, along with her brothers and sisters; stories of her father drinking away whatever small profit she was able to make for the family; of her going the long way home to avoid meeting him on the street, staggering toward the same destination. I remember stories of my mother lying about

her age in order to get a job as a hat-check girl at Agua Caliente Racetrack in Tijuana. At fourteen, she was the main support of the family. I can still see her walking home alone at 3 A.M., only to turn all of her salary and tips over to her mother, who was pregnant again.

The stories continue through the war years and on: walnut-cracking factories, the Voit Rubber factory, and then the computer boom. I remember my mother doing piecework for the electronics plant in our neighborhood. In the late evening, she would sit in front of the TV set, wrapping copper wires into the backs of circuit boards, talking about "keeping up with the younger girls." By that time, she was already in her mid-fifties.

Meanwhile, I was college-prep in school. After classes, I would go with my mother to fill out job applications for her, or write checks for her at the supermarket. We would have the scenario all worked out ahead of time. My mother would sign the check before we'd get to the store. Then, as we'd approach the checkstand, she would say—within earshot of the cashier—"Oh honey, you go 'head and make out the check," as if she couldn't be bothered with such an insignificant detail. No one asked any questions.

I was educated, and wore it with a keen sense of pride and satisfaction, my head propped up with the knowledge, from my mother, that my life would be easier than hers. I was educated; but more than this, I was *la güera:* 'fair-skinned.' Born with the features of my Chicana mother, but the skin of my Anglo father, I had it made.

No one ever quite told me this (that light was right), but I knew that being light was something valued in my family (who were all Chicano, with the exception of my father). In fact, everything about my upbringing (at least what occurred on a conscious level) attempted to bleach me of what color I did have. Although my mother was fluent in it, I was never taught much Spanish at home. I picked up what I did learn from school and from overheard snatches of conversation among my relatives and mother. She often called the other lower-income Mexicans *braceros,* or 'wet-backs,' referring to herself and her family as "a different class of people." And yet, the real story was that my family, too, had been poor (some still are) and farmworkers. My mother can remember this in her blood as if it were yesterday. But this is something she would like to forget (and rightfully), for to her, on a basic economic level, being Chicana meant being "less." It was through my mother's desire to protect her children from poverty and illiteracy that we became "Anglo-ized"; the more effectively we could pass in the white world, the better guaranteed our future.

From all of this, I experience daily a huge disparity between what I was born into and what I was to grow up to become. Because, as Goldman suggests, these stories my mother told me crept under my *güera* skin. I had no choice but to enter into the life of my mother. *I had no choice.* I took her life into my heart, but managed to keep a lid on it as long as I feigned being the happy, upwardly mobile heterosexual.

When I finally lifted the lid to my lesbianism, a profound connection with my mother was reawakened in me. It wasn't until I acknowledged and confronted my own lesbianism in the flesh, that my heartfelt identification with and empathy for my mother's oppression—due to being poor, uneducated, and Chicana—was realized. My lesbianism is the avenue through which I have learned the most about silence and oppression, and it continues to be the most tactile reminder to me that we are not free human beings.

You see, one follows the other. I had known for years that I was a lesbian, had felt it in my bones, had ached with the knowledge, gone crazed with the knowledge, wallowed in the silence of it. Silence *is* like starvation, Don't be fooled. It's nothing short of that, and felt most sharply when one has had a full belly most of her life. When we are not physically starving, we have the luxury to realize psychic and emotional starvation. It is from this starvation that other starvations can be recognized—if one is willing to take the risk of making the connection—if one is willing to be responsible to the result of the connection. For me, the connection is an inevitable one.

What I am saying is that the joys of looking like a white girl haven't been so great since I realized I could be beaten on the street for being a dyke. If my sister's being beaten because she's black, it's pretty much the same principle. We're both getting beaten any way you look at it. The connection is blatant; and in the case of my own family, the differences in the privileges attached to looking white instead of brown are merely a generation apart.

In this country, lesbianism is poverty—as is being brown, as is being a woman, as being just plain poor. The danger lies in ranking the oppressions. *The danger lies in failing to acknowledge the specificity of the oppression.* The danger lies in attempting to deal with oppression purely from a theoretical base. Without an emotional, heartfelt grappling with the source of our own oppression, without naming the enemy within ourselves and outside of us, no authentic, nonhierarchical connection among oppressed groups can take place.

When the going gets rough, will we abandon our so-called comrades in a flurry of racist / heterosexist / what-have-you panic? To whose camp, then, should the lesbian of color retreat?

Her very presence violates the ranking and abstraction of oppression. Do we merely live hand to mouth? Do we merely struggle with the "ism" that's sitting on top of our own heads?

The answer is: yes, I think first we do; and we must do so thoroughly and deeply. But to fail to move out from there will only isolate us in our own oppression—will only insulate, rather than radicalize us.

. . .

Within the women's movement, the connections among women of different backgrounds and sexual orientations have been fragile, at best. I think this phenomenon is indicative of our failure to seriously address ourselves to some very frightening questions: How have I internalized my own oppression? How have I oppressed? Instead, we have let rhetoric do the job of poetry. Even the word *oppression* has lost its power. We need new language, better words that can more closely describe women's fear of and resistance to one another; words that will not always come out sounding like dogma.

I don't really understand first-hand what it feels like being shit on for being brown. I understand much more about the joys of it— being Chicana and having family are synonymous for me. What I know about loving, singing, crying, telling stories, speaking with my heart and hands, even having a sense of my own soul comes from the love of my mother, aunts, cousins. . . .

But at the age of twenty-seven, it is frightening to acknowledge that I have internalized a racism and classism, where the object of oppression is not only someone outside of my skin, but the someone inside my skin. In fact, to a large degree, the real battle with such oppression, for all of us, begins under the skin. I have had to confront the fact that much of what I value about being Chicana, about my family, has been subverted by Anglo culture and my own cooperation with it. This realization did not occur to me overnight. For example, it wasn't until long after my graduation from the private college I'd attended in Los Angeles,

that I realized the major reason for my total alienation from and fear of my classmates was rooted in class and culture. *Click.*

Three years after graduation, in an apple-orchard in Sonoma, a friend of mine (who comes from an Italian working-class family), says to me, "Cherríe, no wonder you felt like such a nut in school. Most of the people there were white and rich." It was true. All along I had felt the difference, but not until I had put the words *class* and *culture* to the experience did my feelings make any sense. For years, I had berated myself for not being as "free" as my classmates. I completely bought that they simply had more guts than I did—to rebel against their parents and run around the country hitchhiking, reading books and studying "art." They had enough privilege to be atheists, for chrissake. There was no one around filling in the disparity for me between their parents, who were Hollywood filmmakers, and my parents, who wouldn't know the name of a filmmaker if their lives depended on it (and precisely because their lives didn't depend on it, they couldn't be bothered). But I knew nothing about "privilege" then. White was right. Period. I could pass. If I got educated enough, there would never be any telling.

Three years after that, another click. In a letter to a friend, I wrote:

I went to a concert where Ntozake Shange was reading. There, everything exploded for me. She was speaking a language that I knew—in the deepest parts of me—existed, and that I had ignored in my own feminist studies and even in my own writing. What Ntozake caught in me is the realization that in my development as a poet, I have, in many ways, denied the voices of my brown mother—the brown in me. I have acclimated to the sound of a white language which, as my father represents it, does not speak to the emotions in my poems—emotions which stem from the love of my mother.

The reading was agitating. Made me feel uncomfortable. Threw me into a week-long terror of how deeply I was affected. I felt that I had to start all over again. That I had turned only to the perceptions of white middle-class women to speak for me and all women. I am shocked by my own ignorance.

Sitting in that auditorium chair was the first time I had realized to the core of me that for years I had disowned the language I knew best—ignored the words and rhythms that were the closest to me. The sounds of my mother and aunts gossiping—half in English, half in Spanish—while drinking cerveza in the kitchen. And the hands—I had cut off the hands in my poems. But not in conversation; still the hands could not be kept down. Still they insisted on moving.

The reading had forced me to remember that I knew things from my roots. But to remember puts me up against what I don't know. Shange's reading agitated me because she spoke with power about a world that is both alien and common to me: "the capacity to enter into the lives of others." But you can't just take the goods and run. I knew that then, sitting in the Oakland auditorium (as I know in my poetry), that the only thing worth writing about is what seems to be unknown and therefore fearful.

The "unknown" is often depicted in racist literature as the "darkness" within a person. Similarly, sexist writers will refer to fear in the form of the vagina, calling it "the orifice of death." In contrast, it is a pleasure to read works such as Maxine Hong Kingston's *Woman Warrior,* where fear and alienation are described as "the white ghosts." And yet, the bulk of literature in this country reinforces the myth that what is dark and female is evil. Consequently, each of us—whether dark, female, or both—has in some way *internalized* this oppressive imagery. What the oppressor often succeeds in doing is simply *externalizing* his fears, projecting them into the bodies of women, Asians, gays, disabled folks, whoever seems most "other."

call me
roach and presumptuous
nightmare on your white pillow

your itch to destroy
the indestructible
part of yourself   —*Audre Lorde*[2]

But it is not really difference the oppressor fears so much as similarity. He fears he will discover in himself the same aches, the same longings as those of the people he has shit on. He fears the immobilization threatened by his own incipient guilt. He fears he will have to change his life once he has seen himself in the bodies of the people he has called different. He fears the hatred, anger, and vengeance of those he has hurt.

This is the oppressor's nightmare, but it is not exclusive to him. We women have a similar nightmare, for each of us in some way has been both the oppressed and the oppressor. We are afraid to see how we have taken the values of our oppressor into our hearts and turned them against ourselves and one another. We are afraid to admit how deeply "the man's" words have been ingrained in us.

To assess the damage is a dangerous act. I think of how, even as a feminist lesbian, I have so wanted to ignore my own homophobia, my own hatred of myself for being queer. I have not wanted to admit that my deepest personal sense of myself has not quite "caught up" with my "woman-identified" politics. I have been afraid to criticize lesbian writers who choose to "skip over" these issues in the name of feminism. In 1979, we talk of "old gay" and "butch and femme" roles as if they were ancient history. We toss them aside as merely patriarchal notions. And yet, the truth of the matter is that I have sometimes taken society's fear and hatred of lesbians to bed with me. I have sometimes hated my lover for loving me. I have sometimes felt "not woman enough" for her. I have sometimes felt "not man enough." For a lesbian trying to survive in a heterosexist society, there is no easy way around these emotions. Similarly, in a white-dominated world, there is little getting around racism and our own internalization of it. It's always there, embodied in some one we least expect to rub up against.

When we do rub up against this person, *there* then is the challenge. *There* then is the opportunity to look at the nightmare within us. But we usually shrink from such a challenge.

. . .

As Lorde suggests in the passage I cited earlier, it is in looking to the nightmare that the dream is found. There, the survivor emerges to insist on a future, a vision, yes, born out of what is dark and female. The feminist movement must be a movement of such survivors, a movement with a future.

Notes

1. Alix Kates Shulman, ed., "Was My Life Worth Living?" *Red Emma Speaks* (New York: Random House, 1972), p. 388.
2. From "The Brown Menace or Poem to the Survival of Roaches," *The New York Head Shop and Museum* (Detroit: Broadside, 1974), p. 48.

Pleasures

Diane Hugs

We both sat there, two disabled lesbians in our wheelchairs, each on opposite sides of the bed. Sudden feelings of fear and timidness came over us. But once we finished the transferring, lifting of legs, undressing and arranging of blankets, we finally touched. Softly and slowly we began to explore each other, our minds and bodies. Neither could make assumptions about the sensations or pleasures of the other. It was wonderful to sense that this woman felt that my body was worth the time it took to explore, that she was as interested in discovering my pleasure as I was in discovering hers.

From the first touch it was a stream of sensations; to listen to every breath, each sigh, and to feel every movement of our love intermingling. It was so intense, so mutual that I must say this beginning was one of the deepest and most fulfilling that I have ever experienced.

When I was an able-bodied lesbian, my approach to relating sexually had been to find out what moves turned someone on and go from there. Never before have I taken the time or had the opportunity to begin a relationship with such a beautiful feeling of pleasure, not only from the pot of gold at the end of the rainbow, but also from the exploration itself.

Compañeros

Carolyn Reyes and Eric DeMeulenaere

[E.D.] . . . I am known as someone who smiles a lot, but the truth is that it is Carolyn who keeps me smiling. We have always struggled with what to call each other not only for political reasons, but because wife, spouse and partner simply do not capture who we are to each other. The term I like best, both politically and emo-

tionally, is *compañera*. Its flavor is more soulful than its English counterpart: companion. Carolyn is *mi compañera*. And I cannot imagine life without her.

[C.R.] Eric had been smiling way before he met me. I could tell he was no novice. It was that smile that I first noticed about him and that lit my journey through my adulthood. Everything I love about Eric can be found in that smile. In his smile lies compassion—his immense capacity to enter into and share in the suffering of others and to be moved to action on their behalf. This is coupled by his deep love for justice—a commitment to a vision of the world as a safe place for all people and to participation in the realization of such a vision. . . . Eric is a most faithful friend and lover. I could ask for no better companion through life.

. . .

[E.D.] We met at what may be the most unlikely of places—a small religious liberal arts college in the suburbs of Chicago. I came from a white upper-middle class politically conservative and religious home. I began my youthful rebellion (which continues still) by registering as a Democrat and expressing my disbelief in God. Yet my background had enough momentum to propel me into the college my parents and church thought suitable. I never really felt like I belonged in the college environment in which I found myself, so I took pride in a relentless critique I waged against the school and all that I felt it stood for.

But if mentally I did not belong in that institution, at least my socio-economic class and race matched the unwritten standard. I looked like and spoke like the vast majority of the student body. Carolyn's story was much different. Coming from a low-income Latino family from Miami, she looked, spoke and thought very differently. Racism and sexism on campus slowly worked to push her to the social, political and spiritual edges of the campus. It was here that we found each other and our friendship developed as we vented our frustrations with the ultra-conservative, racist and sexist environment in which we existed.

[C.R.] Back then it didn't occur to me that we would have to negotiate racial or class differences or gender roles. I was aware of many of those differences but had given little thought to the idea that they could play a significant role in our relationship. I had no idea that the power dynamics that were at play at the wider societal level could have a bearing on our micro-level relationship. Neither had I given much thought to the possible social and political statements our relationship would make to the communities to which we belong and to society-at-large. It would be several years before we would hear my sister-in-law's father say to me in congratulatory fashion, *"Estás blanqueando la raza"* (You're whitening the race) when meeting Eric for the first time. It would be quite some time before I would face the disapproving looks from progressive people of color who count me as yet another traitor who is "sleeping with the enemy." It would take a lot less time for Eric to gain status among white liberals who believe his being in a relationship with a woman of color is an admirable and "down" reality.

[E.D.] Yet society affects even the most personal areas of our lives. We have clearly rejected societal expectations for our relationship in terms of gender roles, but in so doing we have often been just as controlled by those expectations when we try to live in opposition to them. It is fine for Carolyn to handle the finances and for me to do the laundry, for instance. But Carolyn's enjoyment of washing dishes and my greater knowledge about automotive mechanics often makes us feel uneasy. Whenever we notice ourselves or each other acting in traditional ways in terms of sex roles, we pause to critically examine why we're doing what we're doing. Are we sure we really want to be doing this or are we somehow giving in to societal pressures and expectations? The time and energy expended in this process reminds us that those forces continue to have some power in our lives—to some degree controlling us even though we are explicitly trying to break free from their constraints.

[C.R.] No place do we face societal constraints more directly than in our families. A pattern has evolved during our visits to Miami, and always in Eric's presence, in which both my sisters-in-law publicly bemoan being married to Latino men. During these visits when Eric cooks or washes the dishes, my sisters-in-law will often comment on my luck in finding such a helpful and supportive white man because they believe Latino men don't help much around the house. They praise Eric profusely for "helping" me and explain, "Eric, you just don't understand Latino men. They just don't do that," completely unaware of their internalized sexism and racism. They later go on to comment, "American [read "white"] men are the best!" Eric and I try to explain the dangers of generalizing from their experiences, but regardless of our words, these experiences fit their preconceived ideas and they continue to fail to see that sexism knows no ethnic boundaries and that there are men from all backgrounds who attempt to defy the stereotypical roles into which they have been socialized.

While my mother shares my sisters-in-law's perceptions, our relationship also makes her uncomfortable. She agrees that I am lucky to have such a helpful and caring man in my life but fears that I am too controlling and not supportive enough of him. When either of us goes out, whether to dance clubs or school events, unaccompanied by the other partner, my mother criticizes me for not supporting him. Eric is a high-school history teacher and I am finishing up my Masters degree in Social Work. There is something about our independence—and mine in particular—that does not sit well with her. In fact, it is my independence, in thought and action, that has caused her to label me *de carácter fuerte* ("of strong character— not a positive characteristic for a woman) and *dominante* (domineering). While my assertiveness is labeled domineering, Eric's more easygoing attitude makes him seem "wrapped-around my finger." *No hay nada mas feo que una mujer que domine a un hombre* (There's nothing uglier than a woman who dominates a man), I can hear her say. We're both quite certain that if the opposite were true it would go unchallenged.

[E.D.] In addition to our families expecting us to live out traditional gender roles, they also confront us with issues regarding race. Most of Carolyn's family's stereotypes about my whiteness, although unfair and restricting, are never-

theless intended to be positive. Such positive intentions are often lacking on the part of my family, however. My aunt's grimace at our bringing black beans for a Christmas dinner is just one of the many ways that Carolyn's culture is devalued in my family.

While my relatives seek to embrace Carolyn as part of the family, they fail to see why she might be reluctant to fully accept the welcome. My brother, in particular, believes that Carolyn and I are overly sensitive about issues of race and gender and feels frustrated that he has to be careful about everything he says. He has frequently argued that if Carolyn is offended by his words or actions it is because she is "hypersensitive." He accepts that he says things at times that we might find inappropriate, but he never intends to be hurtful. "Why can't you guys let anything slide?" he challenges when our frequent confrontations lead to tension and bitterness. While he has matured and changed in his level of consideration for Carolyn and people of color in general, problems still arise and both Carolyn and he continue to be hurt. This raises an important question for me. My brother wants very badly that we do not challenge him on everything he says that we find problematic. Carolyn and I want very badly that my brother stop saying—and more importantly, thinking—sexist and racist things. Given my relationship to Carolyn, what should my relationship to my brother be?

If Carolyn met someone like my brother in a different context, she would not choose to develop a relationship with him. But because he is my family it makes it very difficult. Holidays are very difficult times for us. Carolyn would prefer to avoid my family because even if nothing inappropriate is said, her ethnic and class background make her feel like an outsider. More importantly, she experiences a sense of otherness which no one understands nor even recognizes. And although she recognizes that my family is friendly and generous to her, this creates an incredible tension for her and makes her visits with my family miserable. I, however, am an insider and remain close to my family. I feel very comfortable with them, and I look forward to seeing them. How do I support and protect Carolyn while at the same time maintaining my relationship with my family? I see that Carolyn feels like an outsider in my family. Yet I also understand how her reluctance to accept my family's embrace hurts them. If both are my community, whose pain do I embrace? What does my stand against racism mean if the person closest to me has to struggle with her status in my own family?

These questions troubled me in an incident with my uncle. He and my aunt live in a small town, predominantly white, and align themselves with the religious Right. In the first interaction Carolyn had with my uncle, the subject of race came up. Speaking from his military experience, he boldly argued that "Blacks are okay one on one; it's when you get them in groups that they're a problem." Since then, Carolyn has understandably avoided virtually all contact with my uncle and his family. But my brother will be having a wedding in their town soon, and my parents are planning to move there after retirement. What are my responsibilities in dealing with these situations?

Such unanswered questions affect us because we are both isolated from each other's experiences. In these situations, I am an insider while Carolyn feels like an outsider. We are also isolated from each other in our individual struggles with identity. I cannot give Carolyn a sense of what it means to be Cuban. Her ethnic identity is best affirmed and supported, obviously, by people within her own ethnic community. More recently, I have also come to realize that Carolyn can be of limited assistance to me in my struggle to understand how I should live in the world as a white man who seeks to be anti-sexist and anti-racist. Developing an awareness of this reality was painful because we realized that we could not meet a very major need for each other. We came to understand the value of sharing our lives with people whose identities more closely resemble our own. Thus we have been forced to think seriously about what it means to share our lives together as people whose backgrounds and identities are very different. While there are insights to be gained from our differences, it is clear that our differences have their disadvantages as well.

[C.R.] Given the difficulties we have experienced in loving across the boundaries of race, class and gender, why do we bother? Why continue to struggle? My initial response to these questions is to explain that I have never been a stranger to struggle. I am reminded of my grandmother, who raised me, and who when asked how she was doing on any given day, would often respond, *"Aqui, en la lucha."* (Here, in the struggle.) Her statement was, to me, a declaration that life is, in essence, a struggle. It was less a statement of resignation than a recognition of her position in the world and a testament to her survival. Struggle, I learned early on, is not to be feared or avoided at any cost; rather it is to be embraced as a part of living.

. . .

READING 31

Some Like Indians Endure

Paula Gunn Allen

i have it in my mind that
dykes are indians

they're a lot like indians
they used to live as tribes
they owned tribal land
it was called the earth

they were massacred
lots of times
they always came back
like the grass
like the clouds
they got massacred again

they thought caringsharing
about the earth and each other
was a good thing
they rode horses
and sang to the moon

but i don't know
about what was so longago
and it's now that dykes
make me think i'm with indians
when i'm with dykes

because they bear
witness bitterly
because they reach
and hold
because they live every day
with despair laughing
in cities and country places
because earth hides them
because they know
the moon
because they gather together
enclosing
and spit in the eye of death

indian is an idea
some people have

of themselves
dyke is an idea some women
have of themselves
the place where we live now
is idea
because whiteman took
all the rest
because father
took all the rest
but the idea which
once you have it
you can't be taken
for somebody else
and have nowhere to go
like indians you can be
stubborn

the idea might move you on,
ponydrag behind
taking all your loves and
children maybe downstream

maybe beyond the cliffs
but it hangs in there
an idea
like indians
endures

it might even take your
whole village with it
stone by stone
or leave the stones
and find more
to build another village
someplace else

like indians
dykes have fewer and fewer
someplace elses to go
so it gets important
to know
about ideas and

to remember or uncover
the past
and how the people
traveled
all the while remembering
the idea they had
about who they were
indians, like dykes
do it all the time

dykes know all about dying
and that everything belongs
to the wind
like indians
they do terrible things
to each other
out of sheer cussedness
out of forgetting
out of despair
so dykes
are like indians
because everybody is related
to everybody
in pain
in terror
in guilt
in blood
in shame
in disappearance
that never quite manages
to be disappeared
we never go away

even if were're always
leaving

because the only home
is each other
they've occupied all
the rest
colonized it; an
idea about ourselves is all
we own

and dykes remind me of indians
like indians   dykes
are supposed to die out
or forget
or drink all the time
or shatter
go away
to nowhere
to remember what will happen
if they don't

they don't anyway—even
though the worst happens

they remember and they
stay
because the moon remembers
because so does the sun
because the stars
remember
and the persistent stubborn grass
of the earth

DISCUSSION QUESTIONS FOR CHAPTER FOUR

1. In what ways is the personal political for you in your relationships?

2. How is the personal political in heterosexual relationships generally?

3. How does socialization into gender affect intimacy in relationships?

4. How does homophobia discourage intimacy? Have there been instances in your life when homophobia has prevented you from developing intimacy with someone?

5. How would you describe women's and men's different ways of communicating? How do women's and men's different ways of communicating affect relationships?

6. How is romantic love related to consumerism? Give some examples.

SUGGESTIONS FOR FURTHER READING

Bright, Susie, ed. *Herotica: A Collection of Women's Erotic Fiction,* 2nd ed. San Francisco: Down There Press, 1998.

Collins, Patricia Hill. "Sexual Politics and Black Women's Relationships." *Black Feminist Thought.* New York: Routledge, 1991.

Penelope, Julia, and Susan J. Wolfe, eds. *The Original Coming Out Stories,* expanded ed. Freedom, CA: Crossing Press, 1989.

Snitow, Ann, Christine Stansell, and Sharon Thompson, eds. *Powers of Desire: The Politics of Sexuality.* New York: Monthly Review Press, 1983.

Stoltenberg, John. *Refusing to Be a Man: Essays on Sex and Justice.* New York: Meridian, 1989.

CHAPTER FIVE

Inscribing Gender on the Body

In contemporary U.S. society we are surrounded by images of beautiful, thin, young, White, smiling women. These images set standards for appearance and beauty that are internalized—standards that affect how we feel about our own bodies. As a result, most of us grow up disliking our bodies, or some parts of them. We are especially troubled by those parts of our bodies that we see as larger than societal ideals.

It is distressing that women often experience their bodies as sources of despair rather than joy and celebration. This is especially true as we age and measure our bodies against notions of youthful beauty. These images of perfect bodies are fabricated by a male-dominated culture and are reinforced by multibillion dollar industries that serve to maintain both corporate profits and patriarchal social relations. The images we are given are flawless and give the illusion of absolute perfection. In reality these images tend to be airbrushed and computer-enhanced; often even the models themselves do not look like their pictures. Fashion models today weigh more than 20 percent less than the average woman, with only about 5 percent of the female population in our society weighing in at the average fashion model's weight given her height. Obviously, real women come in all shapes and sizes. Our diversity is part of our beauty!

Although the body is an incredibly sophisticated jumble of physiological events, our understanding of the body cannot exist outside of the society that gives it meaning. Even though bodies are biophysical entities, what our bodies mean and how they are experienced is intimately connected to the meanings and practices of the society in which we reside. In this way, bodies are like cultural artifacts; culture becomes embodied and is literally inscribed or represented through the body at the same time that the *objectification* of women's bodies (seeing the body as an object and separate from its context) is supported by the media and entertainment industries. Note how these norms about the body rely on a notion of the healthy and/or abled body. As Susan Wendell in the reading "Feminism, Disability, and the Transcendence of the Body" suggests, the ability to transcend or disengage from the body, or, alternatively, the desire to live as an embodied person, is reduced when individuals experience chronic pain and suffering. This essay encourages us to develop a disability consciousness.

Bodies, however, are not only reflections of social norms and practices but also sites of *identity* and *self-expression*. It has been suggested that as our lives become

Activist Profile: Maggie Kuhn

Most people are getting ready to retire at 65. Maggie Kuhn began the most important work of her life at that age. In 1970, Kuhn was forced to retire from her career with the Presbyterian Church. In August of that year, she convened a group of five friends, all of whom were retiring, to talk about the problems faced by retirees—loss of income, loss of social role, pension rights, age discrimination. Finding new freedom and strength in their voices, they also concerned themselves with other social issues, such as the Vietnam War.

The group gathered in Philadelphia with college students opposed to the war at the Consultation of Older and Younger Adults for Social Change. A year later, more than 100 people joined the Consultation. As this new group began to meet, a New York television producer nicknamed the group the Gray Panthers, and the name stuck.

In 1972, Kuhn was asked at the last minute to fill in for someone unable to speak during the 181st General Assembly of the United Presbyterian Church. Her stirring speech launched the Gray Panthers into national prominence, and calls began to flood the organization's headquarters. Increased media attention came as the Gray Panthers became activists. They co-sponsored the Black House Conference on Aging to call attention to the lack of African Americans at the first White House Conference on Aging, and they performed street theater at the American Medical Association's 1974 conference, calling for health care as a human right. At the core of Panther activities was the belief that older people should seize control of their lives and actively campaign for causes in which they believe.

The Gray Panthers have been instrumental in bringing about nursing home reform, ending forced retirement provisions, and combating fraud against the elderly in health care. Kuhn, who was active with the Panthers until her death at age 89, offered this advice to other activists: "Leave safety behind. Put your body on the line. Stand before the people you fear and speak your mind—even if your voice shakes. When you least expect it, someone may actually listen to what you have to say. Well-aimed slingshots can topple giants."

more complex and we have less power over the way we live our lives, we are encouraged to focus more on the body as something we *can* control and as something we can use to express our identity. As a result, the body becomes something to be fashioned and controlled, at the same time, this control over body—and the ability to shape, clothe, and express it—becomes synonymous with personal freedom.

Perhaps the current trend for tattoos and piercing among young women is an example of this trend toward self-expression in the context of mass-market consumerism. Having a tattoo, or multiple tattoos—traditionally a masculine or an outlaw, rebellious act—is increasingly a form of self-expression for women. Similarly, the current fad of multiple piercing of many body parts, including erogenous and sexually charged areas of the body, can be seen as a form of rebellion against the constraints of gender. Both tattooing and piercing can also be interpreted as reactionary trends and as examples of the many ways women are encouraged to mutilate and change parts of their bodies. Note that these "rebellious" practices have now been appropriated as relatively ordinary fashion practices. You can buy nose and belly button rings, for example, that clip on without ever having to pierce anything, just as you can buy fake tattoos. In fact, the self-consciousness involved in the parody of the real thing is now a form of self-expression all its own.

Although men are taught to be concerned with their bodies and looks (and increasingly so given the advertising industry's desire to create a new market for beauty products), women are particularly vulnerable to the cultural preoccupation with the body. There is a *double standard* of beauty for women and men: Physical appearance is more important in terms of the way women are perceived and treated. This is especially true in terms of the aging body where there is a much stronger mandate for women to keep their bodies looking young.

We want to focus on two issues associated with the cultural preoccupation of women and the body: (1) the close relationship between women and nature and bodily functions, and (2) norms associated with appearance and beauty that help determine women's identity and worth. We examine these two issues next and then discuss eating disorders and methods for resisting the beauty ideal.

BODIES, NATURE, AND WOMEN

Although both women and men have bodies, an obvious aspect of the social construction of the body is that what female and male bodies stand for or signify implies different things in most cultures. Women have been associated with *nature*: the body, earth, and the domestic, whereas men, because of historical and mythological associations with the spirit and sky, have been associated with *culture*: the mind rather than the body and abstract reason rather than earthly mundane matters. Importantly, Western civilizations have not only incorporated a distinction between nature and culture but also a domination of culture and mind over nature and body. In particular, Western societies' notions of progress have involved the taming and conquering of nature in favor of civilization. As a result, the female/ nature side of this dichotomy is valued less and often denigrated.

Learning Activity: On the Rag

Collect a wide variety of women's magazines such as *Cosmopolitan, Glamour, Vogue, Elle, Mirabella,* and so on. Identify advertisements for "feminine hygiene products"—tampons, pads, douches, feminine hygiene sprays, yeast infection medicines. What do the visual images in the ads suggest? What do the words tell readers? What messages do these advertisements send about women's bodies? Now collect a variety of men's magazines such as *GQ, Maxim, Men's Journal.* Identify advertisements for "masculine hygiene products." What do you find? What does the difference imply about women's bodies in contrast to men's bodies? How does this implication reinforce structures of gender subordination?

A prime example of this is the way the normal processes of the female body have been seen as smelly, taboo, and distasteful. Menstruation is regarded negatively and described with a multitude of derogatory euphemisms like "the curse" and "on the rag," and girls are still taught to conceal menstrual practices from others (and men in particular). As Gloria Steinem suggests in the reading, "If Men Could Menstruate," the experience would be something entirely different if it was men who menstruated. Advertisements abound in magazines and on television about tampons, pads, douches, feminine hygiene sprays, and yeast infection medicines that give the message that women's bodies are constantly in need of hygienic attention. Notice we tend not to get ads for jock itch during prime-time television like we do ads for feminine "ailments." In this way, there is a strange, very public aspect to feminine bodily processes at the same time that they are coded as very private.

These notions about women and the body have helped shape gender ideologies and reinforce *biological determinism,* a tendency that sees women in terms of their reproductive and biological selves. Male bodies are not so marked by these earthly reminders, and men have been able to imagine their bodies free of such constraints. And, as feminist scholars have reminded us, men as a group have been able to project their fears and anxieties about frailty and mortality onto women's flesh. Although these notions affect all of us in Western societies, women and men, it is important to understand that the body and its expressions have stronger repercussions in women's lives.

THE BEAUTY IDEAL

In this section we discuss five points associated with the beauty ideal. First, contemporary images of female beauty are changeable. What was considered beautiful or feminine for an aristocratic Elizabethan woman in Tudor England involved whitening the face, plucking eyelashes, and shaving back the hairline to show a prominent forehead—hardly beauty practices that would help you get a date in contemporary U.S. society. Some societies consider large women especially attractive and see their fat as evidence of prosperity; again, in most contemporary Western societies, thin is closer to standards of ideal beauty, although there are differences within specific ethnic communities within the United States. In other words, what is considered beautiful is culturally produced and therefore changes across time and across cultures.

A look at standards of female beauty over time reveals that in the nineteenth century White, privileged women were encouraged to adopt a delicate, thin, and fragile appearance and wear bone-crushing (literally) corsets that not only gave them the hour-glass figure but also cramped and ruptured vital organs. These practices made women faint, appear frail, delicate, dependent, and passive—responses to nineteenth-century notions of middle-class femininity. Victorian furniture styles accommodated this ideal with special swooning chairs. Standards for weight and body shape changed again in the early twentieth century when a sleek, boyish look was adopted by the flappers of the 1920s. Women bound their breasts to hide their curves. Although more curvaceous and slightly heavier bodies were encouraged through the next decades, body maintenance came to dominate many women's lives. Fueled by an emerging multimillion-dollar fashion industry, the 1960s gave us a return to a more emaciated, long-legged look, but with very short skirts and long hair. At the beginning of this new century, we see a more eclectic look and a focus on health and fitness, but norms associated with ideal female beauty still construct the thin, White (tanned, but not too brown) body as the beautiful body.

A second point concerning the beauty ideal is that the ideal reflects various relations of power in society. Culture is constructed in complex ways, and groups with more power and influence tend to set the trends, create the options, and enforce the standards. There are two aspects to this. First, standards tend not to be created by the ordinary women whose lives these beauty ideals affect. In our culture, beauty standards are very much connected to the production and consumption of various products, and, indeed, the beauty product and fashion industries are multibillion dollar enterprises. As the reading excerpted from Joan Jacobs Brumberg's *The Body Project* explains, garment industries in the United States helped sexualize women's breasts through their development of the bra. Corporate powers, advertising, and the fashion, cosmetics, and entertainment industries all help create standards for us and help reinforce gender relations. Even the "natural look" is sold to us as something to be tried on, when obviously the real natural look is devoid of marketing illusions in the first place. Most of these industries are controlled by White males or by other individuals who have accepted what many scholars call ruling-class politics. The main point is that most of us get offered beauty and fashion options constructed by other people. Although we have choices and can reject them, lots of resources are involved in encouraging us to adopt the standards created by various industries.

Three, the beauty ideal offered to us reflects social power in that these standards tend to be White and middle class. White standards of beauty can humiliate fat or non-White women as well as the poor, the aged, and the disabled. In this way the norms help enforce racism, classism, ableism, ageism, and fat oppression, as well as sexism generally. Many ethnic communities, however, have alternative notions of feminine beauty and actively resist the normalizing standards of Anglo culture. Lisa Miya-Jervis understands the racial politics of appearance and explains in "Hold that Nose" why she avoided surgery to change the shape of her nose.

Body Image Quiz

INTRODUCTION

When was the last time you looked in the mirror and liked what you saw? Most women have to think long and hard before answering this question. Whether or not we admit it, women are active players in the beauty game, which requires us to think looks and body weight are the true sources of our happiness. The truth is women are their own worst critics when it comes to their bodies. Yet, experts tell us that self-esteem is closely tied to body image, even more so than our actual physical appearance. Take this quiz to learn more about body image and self-esteem.

1. In a national survey in which 200 women were asked, "If you could change one thing about your body, what would it be?" how many women said they would leave their bodies unchanged?
   a. 50
   b. 25
   c. 10
   d. 0

2. What percentage of American women overestimate their body size?
   a. 20 percent
   b. 35 percent
   c. 50 percent
   d. 95 percent

3. Which of the following do psychologists call "eating disorder breeding grounds" for women?
   a. sports teams
   b. dance troupes
   c. high schools and colleges
   d. commercial weight loss programs
   e. all of the above

4. In a national survey, women were asked what they thought was the "peak age" for attractiveness. Which was the most frequent age answer from the following choices?
   a. 16
   b. 22
   c. 33
   d. 45

5. How many women in the United States suffer from eating disorders?
   a. 200,000
   b. 2 million
   c. 4 million
   d. 5 million
   e. 12 million

ANSWERS

1. d. 0. In a body image survey, conducted by Rita Freeman, Ph.D., the author of *Bodylove: Learning to Like Our Looks — And Ourselves,* not a single woman out of 200 was willing to leave her body alone. Body areas and/or conditions that women seem most dissatisfied with run from head to toe. Some of the body changes women wish for include: wider eyes,

freckles, longer legs, smaller feet, better posture, firmer thighs, thinner ankles, longer nails, and bigger breasts. Above all else, American women want to lose weight. Two-thirds of the women surveyed wanted to drop weight, particularly in the area between their waist and knees. Why such an obsession with weight loss? Psychologists say the reasons abound. Obviously American society sets unrealistic, even ridiculous standards by glorifying models who are dangerously thin. Psychologists say there is also a social tendency to associate good looks and thinness with success. It's called "looksism," and it is a form of stereotyping.

2. d. 95 percent. The condition of not being satisfied with one's weight is far more prevalent in women than men, and it includes American women of all races, ethnic groups, religions, professions, and economic classes. Most women who weigh in the normal, healthy range for their age and height still tend to consider themselves overweight. Many remain in a life-long, futile diet mentality, thinking that life would be bliss if only they could lose 10 pounds. Two-thirds of all American women list fear of getting fat on their list of life's worst fears. Finally, women over age 60 report that gaining weight is their second most serious concern, with losing their memory as first.

Many health care experts believe that women have a poor notion of what a healthy weight should be for themselves. Health care providers say that a healthy weight is based on several factors, including weight history (your weight, age, and activity level over several years), genetic factors, age, activity level, as well as other factors such as hormonal changes, stress, and use of nicotine and/or alcohol.

3. c. high schools and colleges. It is during the teenage years that many women first begin their unhealthy preoccupation with their body and appearance. On the brink of puberty, many girls describe a tremendous pressure to be feminine, which, sadly, often equates to being beautiful like a movie star and having an emaciated look. For this reason, eating disorders, such as anorexia and bulimia, are detected more frequently in high school girls and college women than in any other group.

4. c. 33. The good news in the results of this survey is that most women didn't check off the earliest age. Still, 33 is less than half the age expectancy for most women, and psychologists say that women should strive to accept themselves at every age and to see themselves as continuously attractive in a different, more mature way.

A couple of myths exist on women and aging. Dispelling these myths may help women come to a better acceptance of themselves and their bodies.

Myth 1: As time passes, more women become increasingly unhappy with their bodies. In reality, a survey showed that women in their 20s, 30s, and 40s said they felt no different about their bodies than they had earlier in life.

Myth 2: With age women become even more self-conscious of their looks and minor imperfections. In reality, women become less self-conscious. Again, good news!

5. d. 5 million. Eating disorders are devastating mental illnesses that affect more than 5 million American women. Ninety percent of the people who suffer from anorexia nervosa and bulimia nervosa are women, according to the National Association of Anorexia Nervosa and Associated Disorders. Although they revolve around eating and body weight, eating disorders aren't about food, but about feelings and self-expression. Women with eating disorders use food and dieting as ways of coping with life's stresses. For some, food becomes a source of comfort and nurturing or a way to control or release stress. For others, losing weight is a way to gain the approval of friends and family. Eating disorders are not diets, signs of personal weakness, or problems that will go away without treatment. And although

(continued)

Body Image Quiz (*continued*)

the teenage years are considered a high-risk period for these eating disorders, women of all ages can experience the problem or have a relapse later in life.

Anorexia is a condition of self-induced starvation. The desire to lose weight becomes an obsession because the woman has a distorted body image and cannot see herself as anything but fat. Ten percent of women with anorexia die fom it.

Bulimia is an eating disorder that involves binging and purging. A bulimic woman will eat a large quantity of food and then take separate measures to purge herself of the food by vomiting, taking laxatives, or heavy exercising.

If you think you may have an eating disorder, you should consult a health care provider. Eating disorders are complex medical and psychological conditions, but with therapy and medical intervention, they can be treated.

Source: www.electra.com/electraquiz/admin/Body_Image_Quiz.html

The fourth point concerning beauty practices is that standards are enforced in complex ways. Of course, "enforcement" does not mean, as Sandra Bartky has said, that someone marches you off to electrolysis at gunpoint. Instead, we adopt various standards, integrate them as choices we make for ourselves, and police one another in a general sense. Norms are internalized, and we receive various positive and negative responses for complying with or resisting them. It is interesting to think about the everyday practices we engage in to maintain the body: the seemingly trivial routines, rules, and practices. Some scholars call these *disciplinary practices*. They are "practices" because they involve such taken-for-granted routinized behaviors as shaving legs, applying makeup, or curling/straightening/coloring hair; and they are "disciplinary" because they involve social control in the sense that we spend time, money, effort, and imbue meaning in these practices. Again, disciplinary practices are connected to the production and consumption of various products.

You can probably think of many disciplinary practices that you or your friends take part in. Men have their practices too, although these tend to be simpler and involve a narrower range of products. Alongside fashion and various forms of cosmetics and body sculpting, women are more likely to get face-lifts, eye tucks, nose jobs, collagen injections to plump up lips, liposuction, tummy tucks, stomach stapling, and, of course, breast implants as well as breast reductions. By the early 1990s, more than 150,000 women a year were paying for breast implants, with about 80 percent for nonmedical reasons. The FDA (Food and Drug Administration) now requires women receiving silicone-gel breast implants to sign a "known risks" (leaking and rupture, loss of sensation in the nipples) and "possible risks" (fibrositis or pain and stiffness of muscles, ligaments, and tendons) clause. In considering these practices—from following fashion and buying clothes and accessories to makeup application to breast enhancement and all the other practices in between—it is important to keep in mind how much they cost, how they channel women's energies away from other, perhaps more productive, pursuits, and how they may affect health and well-being.

The body and the various practices associated with maintaining the female body are probably the most salient aspects of what we understand as femininity and are crucial in social expressions of sexuality. Note how many of these bodily practices that are so wound up with contemporary femininity encourage women to stay small, not take up space, and stay young. Maturity in the form of body hair is unacceptable; we are encouraged to keep our bodies sleek, soft, and hairless—traits that some scholars identify with youth and powerlessness.

The final point regarding the beauty ideal is that, although there is a huge fashion, cosmetics, and entertainment industry associated with beauty ideals, there is also a huge weight-loss industry associated with it too. Millions of dollars are spent every year by people who seek to cram their bodies into smaller sizes. Of course, many individuals want to make their bodies smaller out of a concern for better health and mobility, and the weight and exercise industries help them attain these goals. But many have learned to despise flesh and fat and participate in these industries' profits out of a desire to more closely fit the cultural standard. Again, there is a double standard here whereby fat women have a harder time than fat men in our culture. This is not to say that fat men have an easy time; certainly prejudice against large-sized people is one of the last bulwarks of oppression in our society. Many people have no qualms about blatantly expressing their dislike and disgust for fat people even when they might keep sexist or racist attitudes hidden. However, fat women have an especially difficult time because of the interaction between sexism and fat phobia. In this way the beauty ideal supports the weight-loss industry and encourages looksism and fat oppression. Judith Joyce focuses on these issues in "My Fat Lover."

EATING DISORDERS

Contemporary eating disorders are compulsive behaviors that include *anorexia nervosa* (self-starvation) and *bulimia* (binge eating with self-induced vomiting and/or laxative use). They are serious problems with serious health consequences that can include death. Women with eating disorders tend to have a distorted body image and see themselves as fat and ugly irrespective of their weight and appearance. These problems are particularly rampant among young women aged 15 to 25 years and are especially prevalent on college campuses.

Many students who live in dorms and sororities report a high incidence of eating disorders; perhaps you have struggled with an eating disorder yourself or have had a close friend or sister similarly diagnosed. If the huge number of women who have various issues with food—always on a diet, overly concerned with weight issues, compulsive about what they do or do not eat—are also included in the figures on eating disorders, then the number of women with these problems increases exponentially. Indeed, one study has suggested that 80 percent of fifth-grade girls report being on a diet. Although this does not mean that 80 percent of these girls really *are* on a diet, it does highlight the way the discourses of dieting and bodily control are being internalized even by 10-year-old girls. Food and bodies are central preoccupations in so many women's lives. We need to ask, why women and why food?

Ideas for Activism

- Organize an eating disorders awareness event. Provide information about eating disorders and resources for help. Invite a therapist who specializes in treating eating disorders to speak. Create awareness posters to hang around your campus.
- Organize a letter-writing campaign to protest the representation of such a small range of women's shapes and sizes in a particular women's magazine.
- Organize a speak-out about beauty ideals.
- Organize a tattoo and piercing panel to discuss the politics of tattooing and piercing. Have a tattoo and piercing fashion show and discuss the meaning of the various tattoos/piercings.

Women have long been associated with food and domestic pursuits; food preparation and focus on food is a socially accepted part of female cultural training. Given that women have been relegated to the private sphere of the home more than the public world, food consumption is easily accessible and unquestioned. Second, food is something that nourishes and gives pleasure. In our culture food has been associated with comfort and celebration, and it is easy to see how eating can be a way of dealing with the anxieties and unhappiness of life. Put these two together, and we get food as the object of compulsion; when we add the third factor, the beauty ideal, with all the anxieties associated with closely monitoring the size and shape of women's bodies, the result can be eating disorders.

Scholars also emphasize that eating disorders might reflect the ways that women desire self-control in the context of little power and autonomy. In other words, young women turn to controlling their bodies and attempt to sculpt them to perfection because they are denied power and control in other areas of their lives. Central in understanding eating disorders, however, is the pressure in our society for women to measure up to cultural standards of beauty and attractiveness, what Becky Wangsgaard Thompson in the reading "A Way Outa No Way" calls the "culture of thinness." These standards infringe on all our lives whether we choose to comply with them or resist them. Messages abound telling women that they are not good enough or beautiful enough, encouraging us to constantly change ourselves, often through the use of various products. The result is that girls learn early on that they must aspire to some often-unattainable standard of physical perfection. Such a bombardment affects girls' self-esteem and constantly assaults women's psyches as we age. In this way, eating disorders can be read as cultural statements about gender.

RESISTING THE BEAUTY IDEAL

Although many women strive to attain the beauty ideal on an ongoing, daily basis, some actively resist such cultural norms. These women are choosing to not participate in the beauty rituals, not support the industries that produce both images and products, and create other definitions of beauty. Some women are actively appropriating these standards by highlighting and/or exaggerating the very norms

Learn to Love Your Body

Do you ever stand in front of the mirror dreaming about where you'd get a few nips and tucks? Or feeling like life would be better if only you had smaller thighs, a flatter tummy, or there was simply less of you? These are all signs of a not-so-hot body image.

It's important that you feel good about who you are. And until you like yourself as is, trying to change your body shape will be a losing proposition. High self-esteem is important for a healthy, balanced lifestyle — and it's a definite must if successful weight loss is one of your goals. So it's time to smile back at that image in the mirror and value all the wonderful characteristics about the person reflected there. Try these techniques:

1. *Recognize your special qualities.* Make a list of all your positive qualities — not including your physical traits. Are you kind? Artistic? Honest? Good in business? Do you make people laugh? Post your list near the mirror or another place where you'll see it every day.

2. *Put your body back together.* Most of us with negative body images have dissected our bodies into good and bad parts. "I hate my thighs and butt." "My butt's okay, but my stomach is fat and my arms are flabby." Reconnect with your body by appreciating how it all works to keep you going. Try stretching or yoga — the fluid movements are great for getting in touch with the wonders of the human body.

3. *Remember the kid inside you.* Give yourself permission not to be perfect. Inside all of us is the kid we used to be — the kid who didn't have to be perfect and worry about everything. Remember that kid, and give yourself a break. Place a photo of yourself as a child in your bedroom or at your desk at work, so you can see it each day and remember to nurture yourself and laugh a little.

4. *Enjoy your food.* Eating is pleasurable. So enjoy it! Food gives us energy and sustains life. Don't deprive yourself or consider eating an evil act. If you allow yourself to enjoy some of the foods you like, you'll be less likely to overeat. In turn, your body won't feel bloated and uncomfortable.

5. *Indulge in body pleasures.* One step toward being kind to your body, and inevitably yourself, is to indulge yourself. Get a massage, take a long, hot bath, use lotions that smell good, or treat yourself to a manicure or pedicure.

6. *Speak positively.* Pay attention to your self-talk. It's amazing how often we put ourselves down throughout the day. Each time you catch yourself making critical comments, fight back by immediately complimenting yourself.

7. *See the world realistically.* It's common to compare ourselves to people in magazines or movies, but this can make you feel self-conscious. If you want to compare yourself to others, look at the real people around you. They come in different shapes and sizes — and none of them are airbrushed or highlighted.

8. *Dress in clothes that fit.* When we feel badly about our bodies, we often dress in shabby clothes, waiting until we lose weight before we buy something we like. But why? Feel good now! Find attractive clothes that fit your current size. Treating yourself will make you feel renewed.

(continued)

9. *Be active.* Movement and exercise can make you and your body feel terrific. Not only does exercise help boost your mood, it stimulates your muscles, making you feel more alive and connected to your body.

10. *Thrive!* Living well will help you feel better about who you are and how you look. Strive to make your personal and professional lives fulfilling. You are a unique, amazing person. A healthy, happy life can be all yours!

Source: www.thriveonline.com/shape/countdown/countdown.feature2.week7.html

and standards themselves. They are carving out their own notions of beauty through their use of fashion and cosmetics. For them, empowerment involves playing with existing cultural standards. In "Dreadlocked," Veronica Chambers explores the social meanings associated with hair, and, in particular, how her dreadlocks came to help her form her own identity. Most women comply with some standards associated with the beauty ideal and resist others. We find a place that suits us, criticize some standards and practices and yet conform to others, usually learning to live with the various contradictions that this implies.

A question that might be raised in response to ideas about resisting beauty ideals and practices is, What's wrong with being beautiful? In response, feminists say that it is not beauty that is a problem, but rather the way that beauty has been constructed. This construction excludes many beautiful women and helps maintain particular (and very restricted) notions of femininity. Maya Angelou's poem "Phenomenal Woman" celebrates female beauty and encourages women to rejoice in themselves and their looks.

Another common question is, Can you wear makeup and enjoy the adornments associated with femininity and still call yourself a feminist? Most feminists answer with a resounding yes. In fact, you can claim back these trappings and go ultra-femme in celebration of your femininity and your right to self-expression. What is important from a feminist perspective is that these practices are *conscious*. In other words, when women take part in various reproductions of femininity, it is important to understand the bigger picture and be aware of the ways the beauty ideal works to limit women, encourages competitiveness (Is she better looking than me? Who is the cutest woman here? How do I measure up?), and ultimately tends to lower women's self-esteem. Understand also how many beauty products are tested on animals, how the packaging of cosmetics and other beauty products encourages the use of resources that end up polluting the environment, and how many fashion items are made by child and/or sweatshop global labor. The point is for us to make conscious and informed choices about our relationships to the beauty ideal and to love and take care of our bodies.

Breast Buds and the "Training" Bra

Joan Jacobs Brumberg

In every generation, small swellings around the nipples have announced the arrival of puberty. This development, known clinically as "breast buds," occurs before menarche and almost always provokes wonder and self-scrutiny. "I began to examine myself carefully, to search my armpits for hairs and my breasts for signs of swelling," wrote Kate Simon about coming of age in the Bronx at the time of World War I. Although Simon was "horrified" by the rapidity with which her chest developed, many girls, both in literature and real life, long for this important mark of maturity. In Jamaica Kincaid's fictional memoir of growing up in Antigua, *Annie John,* the main character regarded her breasts as "treasured shrubs, needing only the proper combination of water and sunlight to make them flourish." In order to get their breasts to grow, Annie and her best friend, Gwen, lay in a pasture exposing their small bosoms to the moonlight.

Breasts are particularly important to girls in cultures or time periods that give powerful meaning or visual significance to that part of the body. Throughout history, different body parts have been eroticized in art, literature, photography, and film. In some eras, the ankle or upper arm was the ultimate statement of female sexuality. But breasts were the particular preoccupation of Americans in the years after World War II, when voluptuous stars, such as Jayne Mansfield, Jane Russell, and Marilyn Monroe, were popular box-office attractions. The mammary fixation of the 1950s extended beyond movie stars and shaped the experience of adolescents of both genders. In that era, boys seemed to prefer girls who were "busty," and American girls began to worry about breast size as well as about weight. This elaboration of the ideal of beauty raised expectations about what adolescent girls should look like. It also required them to put even more energy and resources into their body projects, beginning at an earlier age.

The story of how this happened is intertwined with the history of the bra, an undergarment that came into its own, as separate from the corset, in the early twentieth century. In 1900, a girl of twelve or thirteen typically wore a one-piece "waist" or camisole that had no cups or darts in front. As her breasts developed, she moved into different styles of the same garment, but these had more construction, such as stitching, tucks, and bones, that would accentuate the smallness of her waist and shape the bosom. In those days, before the arrival of the brassiere, there were no "cups." The bosom was worn low; there was absolutely no interest in uplift, and not a hint of cleavage.

The French word *brassière*, which actually means an infant's undergarment or harness, was used in *Vogue* as early as 1907. In the United States, the first boneless bra to leave the midriff bare was developed in 1913 by Mary Phelps Jacobs, a New York City debutante. Under the name Caresse Crosby, Jacobs marketed a bra made of two French lace handkerchiefs suspended from the shoulders. Many young women in the 1920s, such as Yvonne Blue, bought their first bras in order to achieve the kind of slim, boyish figure that the characteristic chemise (or flapper) dress required. The first bras were designed simply to flatten, but they were superseded by others intended to shape and control the breasts. Our current cup sizes (A, B, C, and D), as well as the idea of circular stitching to enhance the roundness of the breast, emerged in the 1930s.

Adult women, not adolescents, were the first market for bras. Sexually maturing girls simply moved into adult-size bras when they were ready—and if their parents had the money. Many women and girls in the early twentieth century still made their own underwear at home, and some read the advertisements for bras with real longing. When she began to develop breasts in the 1930s, Malvis Helmi, a midwestern farm girl, remembered feeling embarrassed whenever she wore an old summer dimity that pulled and gaped across her expanding chest. As a result, she spoke to her mother, considered the brassieres in the Sears, Roebuck catalog, and decided to purchase two for twenty-five cents. However, when her hardworking father saw the order form, he vetoed the idea and declared, "Our kind of people can't afford to spend money on such nonsense." Although her mother made her a makeshift bra, Malvis vowed that someday she would have store-bought brassieres. Home economics teachers in the interwar years tried to get high school girls to make their own underwear because it saved money, but the idea never caught on once mass-produced bras became widely available.

The transition from homemade to mass-produced bras was critical in how adolescent girls thought about their breasts. In general, mass-produced clothing fostered autonomy in girls because it took matters of style and taste outside the dominion of the mother, who had traditionally made and supervised a girl's wardrobe. But in the case of brassieres, buying probably had another effect. So long as clothing was made at home, the dimensions of the garment could be adjusted to the particular body intended to wear it. But with store-bought clothes, the body had to fit instantaneously into standard sizes that were constructed from a pattern representing a norm. When clothing failed to fit the body, particularly a part as intimate as the breasts, young women were apt to perceive that there was something wrong with their bodies. In this way, mass-produced bras in standard cup sizes probably increased, rather than diminished, adolescent self-consciousness about the breasts.

Until the 1950s, the budding breasts of American girls received no special attention from either bra manufacturers, doctors, or parents. Girls generally wore undershirts until they were sufficiently developed to fill an adult-size bra. Mothers and daughters traditionally handled this transformation in private, at home. But in the gyms and locker rooms of postwar junior high schools, girls began to look around to see who did and did not wear a bra. Many of these girls had begun menstruating and developing earlier than their mothers had, and this visual information was very powerful. In some circles, the ability to wear and fill a bra was central to an adolescent girl's status and sense of self. "I have a figure problem," a fourteen-year-old wrote to *Seventeen* in 1952: "All of my friends are tall and shapely while my figure still remains up-and-down. Can you advise me?"

In an era distinguished by its worship of full-breasted women, interest in adolescent breasts came from all quarters: girls who wanted bras at an earlier age than ever before; mothers who believed that they should help a daughter acquire a "good" figure; doctors who valued maternity over all other female roles; and merchandisers who saw profits in convincing girls and their parents that adolescent breasts needed to be tended in special ways. All of this interest coalesced in the 1950s to make the brassiere as critical as the sanitary napkin in making a girl's transition into adulthood both modern and successful.

The old idea that brassieres were frivolous or unnecessary for young girls was replaced by a national discussion about their medical and psychological benefits. "My daughter who is well developed but not yet twelve wants to wear a bra," wrote a mother in Massachusetts to *Today's Health* in 1951. "I want her to wear an undervest instead because I think it is better not to have anything binding. What do you think about a preadolescent girl wearing a bra?" That same year a reader from Wilmington, Delaware, asked *Seventeen:* "Should a girl of fourteen wear a bra? There are some older women who insist we don't need them." The editor's answer was an unequivocal endorsement of early bras: "Just as soon as your breasts begin to show signs of development, you should start wearing a bra." By the early 1950s, "training" or "beginner" bras were available in AAA and AA sizes for girls whose chests were essentially flat but who wanted a bra nonetheless. Along with acne creams, advertisements for these brassieres were standard fare in magazines for girls.

Physicians provided a medical rationale for purchasing bras early. In 1952, in an article in *Parents' Magazine,* physician Frank H. Crowell endorsed bras for young girls and spelled out a theory and program of teenage breast management. "Unlike other organs such as the stomach and intestines which have ligaments that act as guywires or slings to hold them in place," Crowell claimed, the breast was simply "a growth developed from the skin and held up only by the skin." An adolescent girl needed a bra in order to prevent sagging breasts, stretched blood vessels, and poor circulation, all of which would create problems in nursing her future children. In addition, a "dropped" breast was "not so attractive," Crowell said, so it was important to get adolescents into bras early, before their breasts began to sag. The "training" that a training bra was supposed to accomplish was the first step toward motherhood and a sexually alluring figure, as it was defined in the 1950s.

In the interest of both beauty and health, mothers in the 1950s were encouraged to check their daughters' breasts regularly to see if they were developing properly. This was not just a matter of a quick look and a word of reassurance. Instead, Crowell and others suggested systematic scrutiny as often as every three months to see if the breasts were positioned correctly. One way to chart the geography of the adolescent bustline was to have the girl stand sideways in a darkened room against a wall covered with white paper. By shining a bright light on her and having her throw out her chest at a provocative angle, a mother could trace a silhouette that indicated the actual shape of her daughter's bosom. By placing a pencil under her armpit, and folding the arm that held it across the waist, mothers could also determine if their daughter's nipples were in the right place. On a healthy breast, the nipple was supposed to be at least halfway above the midway point between the location of the pencil and the hollow of the elbow.

Breasts were actually only one part of a larger body project encouraged by the foundation garment industry in postwar America. In this era, both physicians and entrepreneurs promoted a general philosophy of "junior figure control." Companies such as Warners, Maidenform, Formfit, Belle Mode, and Perfect Form (as well as popular magazines like *Good Housekeeping*) all encouraged the idea that young women needed both lightweight girdles and bras to "start the figure off to a beautiful future."

The concept of "support" was aided and abetted by new materials—such as nylon netting and two-way stretch fabrics—developed during the war but applied afterward to women's underwear. By the early 1950s, a reenergized corset and brassiere industry was poised for extraordinary profits. If "junior figure control" became the ideal among the nation's mothers and daughters, it would open up sales of bras and girdles to the largest generation of adolescents in American history, the so-called baby boomers. Once again, as in the case of menstruation and acne, the bodies of adolescent girls had the potential to deliver considerable profit.

There was virtually no resistance to the idea that American girls should wear bras and girdles in adolescence. Regardless of whether a girl was thin or heavy, "junior figure control" was in order, and that phrase became a pervasive sales mantra. "Even slim youthful figures will require foundation assistance," advised *Women's Wear Daily* in 1957. In both *Seventeen* and *Compact,* the two most popular magazines for the age group, high school girls were urged to purchase special foundation garments such as "Bobbie" bras and girdles by Formfit and

"Adagio" by Maidenform that were "teen-proportioned" and designed, allegedly, with the help of adolescent consultants. The bras were available in pastel colors in a variety of special sizes, starting with AAA, and they were decorated with lace and ribbon to make them especially feminine. In addition to holding up stockings, girdles were intended to flatten the tummy and also provide light, but firm, control for hips and buttocks. The advertisements for "Bobbie," in particular, suggested good things about girls who controlled their flesh in this way; they were pretty, had lots of friends, and drank Coca-Cola. As adults, they would have good figures and happy futures because they had chosen correct underwear in their youth.

By the mid-1950s, department stores and specialty shops had developed aggressive educational programs designed to spread the gospel of "junior figure control." In order to make young women "foundation conscious," Shillito's, a leading Cincinnati department store, tried to persuade girls and their mothers of the importance of having a professional fitting of the first bra. Through local newspaper advertisements, and also programs in home economics classes, Shillito's buyer, Edith Blincoe, promoted the idea that the purchase of bras and girdles required special expertise, which only department stores could provide. (*Seventeen* echoed her idea and advised a "trained fitter" for girls who wanted a "prettier" bosom and a "smoother" figure.) Blincoe acknowledged that teenage girls were already "100% bra conscious," and she hoped to develop the same level of attention to panty girdles. In order to attract junior customers and get them to try on both items, she had the corset department place advertising cards on the walls of dressing rooms in sections of the store where teenagers and their mothers shopped. Strapless bras were suggested on cards in the dress and formal wear departments; lightweight girdles were suggested in the sportswear and bathing suit sections.

In home economics classes, and also at the local women's club, thousands of American girls saw informational films such as *Figure Forum* and *Facts About Your Figure,* made by the Warner Brassiere Company in the 1950s. Films like these stressed the need for appropriate foundation garments in youth and provided girls with scientific principles for selecting them. They also taught young women how to bend over and lean into their bras, a maneuver that most of us learned early and still do automatically. Most middle-class girls and their mothers embraced the code of "junior figure control" and spent time and money in pursuit of the correct garments. Before a school dance in 1957, Gloria James, a sixteen-year-old African-American girl, wrote in her diary: "Mommy and I rushed to Perth Amboy [New Jersey] to get me some slacks, bras and a girdle. I don't even know how to get it [the girdle] on."

In the postwar world, the budding adolescent body was big business. Trade publications, such as *Women's Wear Daily,* gave special attention to sales strategies and trends in marketing to girls. In their reports from Cincinnati, Atlanta, and Houston, one thing was clear: wherever American girls purchased bras, they wanted to be treated as grown-ups, even if they wore only a AAA or AA cup. In Atlanta, at the Redwood Corset and Lingerie Shop, owner Sally Blye and her staff spoke persuasively to young customers about the importance of "uplift" in order "not to break muscle tissue." And at Houston's popular Teen Age Shop, specially trained salesgirls allowed young customers to look through the brassieres on their own, and then encouraged them to try on items in the dressing room without their mothers. Although many girls were shy at first, by the age of fourteen and fifteen most had lost their initial self-consciousness. "They take the merchandise and go right in [to the dressing room]," Blincoe said about her teenage clientele. Girls who could not be reached by store or school programs could send away to the Belle Mode Brassiere Company for free booklets about "junior figure control" with titles such as "The Modern Miss—Misfit or Miss Fit" and "How to Be Perfectly Charming." In the effort to help girls focus on their figures, Formfit, maker of the popular "Bobbies," offered a free purse-size booklet on calorie counting.

Given all this attention, it's not surprising that bras and breasts were a source of concern in adolescents' diaries written in the 1950s. Sandra Rubin got her first bra in 1951, when she was a twelve-year-old in Cleveland, but she did not try it on in a department store. Instead, her mother bought her a "braziere" while she was away on a trip and sent it home. "It's very fancy," Sandra wrote. "I almost died! I ran right upstairs to put it on." When she moved to New York City that September and entered Roosevelt Junior High School, Sandra got involved with a clique of seven girls who called themselves the "7Bs." Their name was not about their homeroom; it was about the cup size they wanted to be. "Flat, Flat! The air vibrates with that name as my friends and I walk by," Sandra wrote in a humorous but self-deprecating manner. By the time she was sixteen, Sandra had developed amply, so that her breasts became a source of pride. One night she had an intimate conversation with a male friend about the issue of chests: "We talked about flat-chested women (of which, he pointed out, I certainly am not [one])."

Breasts, not weight, were the primary point of comparison among high school girls in the 1950s. Although Sandra Rubin called herself a "fat hog" after eating too much candy, her diary reportage was principally about the bosoms, rather than the waistlines, she saw at school. Those who had ample bosoms seemed to travel through the hallways in a veritable state of grace, at least from the perspective of girls who considered themselves flat-chested. "Busty" girls made desirable friends because they seemed sophisticated, and they attracted boys. In December 1959, when she planned a Friday-night pajama party, thirteen-year-old Ruth Teischman made a courageous move by inviting the "gorgeous" Roslyn, a girl whom she wrote about frequently but usually only worshiped from afar. After a night of giggling and eating with her junior high school friends,

Ruth revealed in her diary the source of Roslyn's power and beauty: "Roslyn is very big. (Bust of course.) I am very flat. I wish I would get bigger fast." Many girls in the 1950s perused the ads, usually in the back of women's magazines, for exercise programs and creams guaranteed to make their breasts grow, allegedly in short order.

The lament of the flat-chested girl—"I must, I must, I must develop my bust"—was on many private hit parades in the 1950s. There was a special intensity about breasts because of the attitudes of doctors, mothers, and advertisers, all of whom considered breast development critical to adult female identity and success. Although "junior figure control" increased pressure on the entire body, and many girls wore waist cinches as well as girdles, it was anxiety about breasts, more than any other body part, that characterized adolescent experience in these years. As a result, thousands, if not millions, of girls in early adolescence jumped the gun and bought "training bras" at the first sight of breast buds, or they bought padded bras to disguise their perceived inadequacy. In the 1950s, the bra was validated as a rite of passage: regardless of whether a girl was voluptuous or flat, she was likely to purchase her first bra at an earlier age than had her mother. This precocity was due, in part, to biology, but it was also a result of entrepreneurial interests aided and abetted by medical concern. By the 1950s, American society was so consumer-oriented that there were hardly any families, even among the poor, who would expect to make bras for their daughters the way earlier generations had made their own sanitary napkins.

Training bras were a boon to the foundation garment industry, but they also meant that girls' bodies were sexualized earlier. In contemporary America, girls of nine or ten are shepherded from undershirts into little underwear sets that come with tops that are proto-brassieres. Although this may seem innocuous and natural, it is not the same as little girls "dressing up" in their mother's clothing. In our culture, traditional distinctions between adult clothing and juvenile clothing have narrowed considerably, so that mature women dress "down," in the garments of kids, just as often as little girls dress "up." While the age homogeneity of the contemporary wardrobe helps adult women feel less matronly, dressing little girls in adult clothing can have an insidious side effect. Because a bra shapes the breasts in accordance with fashion, it acts very much like an interpreter, translating functional anatomy into a sexual or erotic vocabulary. When we dress little girls in brassieres or bikinis, we imply adult behaviors and, unwittingly, we mark them as sexual objects. The training bras of the 1950s loom large in the history of adolescent girls because they foreshadowed the ways in which the nation's entrepreneurs would accommodate, and also encourage, precocious sexuality.

READING 33

If Men Could Menstruate

Gloria Steinem

A white minority of the world has spent centuries conning us into thinking that a white skin makes people superior—even though the only thing it really does is make them more subject to ultraviolet rays and to wrinkles. Male human beings have built whole cultures around the idea that penis-envy is "natural" to women—though having such an unprotected organ might be said to make men vulnerable, and the power to give birth makes womb-envy at least as logical.

In short, the characteristics of the powerful, whatever they may be, are thought to be better than the characteristics of the powerless—and logic has nothing to do with it.

What would happen, for instance, if suddenly, magically, men could menstruate and women could not?

The answer is clear—menstruation would become an enviable, boast-worthy, masculine event:

Men would brag about how long and how much.

Boys would mark the onset of menses, the longed-for proof of manhood, with religious ritual and stag parties.

Congress would fund a National Institute of Dysmenorrhea to help stamp out monthly discomforts.

Sanitary supplies would be federally funded and free. (Of course, some men would still pay for the prestige of commercial brands such as John Wayne Tampons, Muhammad Ali's Rope-a-dope Pads, Joe Namath Jock Shields—"For Those Light Bachelor Days," and Robert "Barretta" Blake Maxi-Pads.)

Military men, right-wing politicians, and religious fundamentalists would cite menstruation ("*men*struation") as proof that only men could serve in the Army ("you have to give blood to take blood"), occupy political office ("can women be aggressive without that steadfast cycle governed by the planet Mars?"), be priests and ministers ("how could a woman give her blood for our sins?"), or rabbis ("without the monthly loss of impurities, women remain unclean").

Male radicals, left-wing politicians, and mystics, however, would insist that women are equal, just different; and that any woman could enter their ranks if only she were willing to self-inflict a major wound every month ("you *must* give blood for the revolution"), recognize the preeminence of menstrual issues, or subordinate her selfness to all men in their Cycle of Enlightenment.

Street guys would brag ("I'm a three-pad man") or answer praise from a buddy ("Man, you lookin' *good!*") by giving fives and saying, "Yeah, man, I'm on the rag!"

TV shows would treat the subject at length. ("Happy Days": Richie and Potsie try to convince Fonzie that he is still "The Fonz," though he has missed two periods in a row.) So would newspapers. (SHARK SCARE THREATENS MENSTRUATING MEN. JUDGE CITES MONTHLY STRESS IN PARDONING RAPIST.) And movies. (Newman and Redford in "Blood Brothers"!)

Men would convince women that intercourse was *more* pleasurable at "that time of the month." Lesbians would be said to fear blood and therefore life itself—though probably only because they needed a good menstruating man.

Of course, male intellectuals would offer the most moral and logical arguments. How could a woman master any discipline that demanded a sense of time, space, mathematics, or measurement, for instance, without that in-built gift for measuring the cycles of the moon and planets—and thus for measuring anything at all? In the rarefied fields of philosophy and religion, could women compensate for missing the rhythm of the universe? Or for their lack of symbolic death-and-resurrection every month?

Liberal males in every field would try to be kind: the fact that "these people" have no gift for measuring life or connecting to the universe, the liberals would explain, should be punishment enough.

And how would women be trained to react? One can imagine traditional women agreeing to all these arguments with a staunch and smiling masochism. ("The ERA would force housewives to wound themselves every month": Phyllis Schlafly. "Your husband's blood is as sacred as that of Jesus—and so sexy, too!": Marabel Morgan.) Reformers and Queen Bees would try to imitate men, and *pretend* to have a monthly cycle. All feminists would explain endlessly that men, too, needed to be liberated from the false idea of Martian aggressiveness, just as women needed to escape the bonds of menses-envy. Radical feminists would add that the oppression of the nonmenstrual was the pattern for all other oppressions. ("Vampires were our first freedom fighters!") Cultural feminists would develop a bloodless imagery in art and literature. Socialist feminists would insist that only under capitalism would men be able to monopolize menstrual blood. . . . In fact, if men could menstruate, the power justifications could probably go on forever.

If we let them.

READING 34

My Fat Lover

Judith Joyce

My lover is fat.

It upsets some people to hear me state this so baldly. "Doesn't it hurt her feelings?" they ask, as if the polite thing were to act as if I hadn't noticed that she weighs nearly 300 pounds. Perhaps they think she hasn't noticed either.

"You are the only person in my life who hasn't discouraged me or made fun of me," she tells me one morning over breakfast, crying. She's listening to *musica de trios,* traditional Puerto Rican ballads, and it's making her nostalgic. She remembers how her mother used to dance to this music, spinning with the broom through their little house. She remembers island breakfasts with *cafe término medio*—half strong coffee, half warmed milk—French bread, and omelets filled with fried plantains. Then her face darkens as she also remembers how she was friendless throughout her childhood. "I weighed 180 pounds at age 12," she confesses, as if this were an explanation. She tried to kill herself at 16.

There are few things harder than growing up fat.

What about growing up with a disability? you might ask. What about growing up neglected, or on the streets? True, these conditions are enormously difficult, but they are not seen as the child's fault. Fatness is always the fat person's fault. As everyone knows, fat people eat like pigs. They smell bad. They don't bathe. They lack that revered American attribute: willpower. They are, quite simply, disgusting.

My lover showers every day. She has a closet full of stylish clothes in a wide range of sizes, reflecting her lifelong battle with the scale. But she grew up fat, and she is fat still. Not in a wheelchair, not on the streets, but the pariah of an entire culture.

I am not a "chubby-chaser"—someone erotically excited by fat—nor was I always, to use the politicized term, "fat-positive." I grew up in a family as red-bloodedly fat-phobic as most. My mother, who is five-foot-two and weighs just over 100 pounds, was perpetually on a diet. My father's and my grandmother's standard greeting to all family members they hadn't seen in a while was, "You look good—you've lost weight." At age 16, weighing barely 100 pounds myself, I, too, dieted. Some days I'd eat nothing but a single doughnut. When I got to college I made rules for myself: Each night I could have a salad and an entrée or a salad and dessert—but never all three.

Around the time our parents were splitting up, my younger sister, Jennifer, took to watching hours of TV each afternoon, her hand in a bag of snacks the whole time. By age 9 she'd grown chubby, a fact that did not go unnoticed

in our house, and by 12 she too had begun to diet. When she got down to 85 pounds, the family started noticing that this exercise of willpower had gone a little too far. Those were my mother's exact words: "I admire her willpower; she just takes it a little too far."

Jen went to a therapist and began eating again, but it was years before anyone realized what she did after she ate. Her anorexia had become bulimia, a far more insidious illness with its incessant vomiting and abuse of laxatives. In the meantime, I had discovered feminist theory. I took women's studies classes during my last year of college and read about the many kinds of oppression. I watched my sister; I made the connection. Furious, I resolved never to diet again.

"Jude, you're amazing," Jen would later tell me. "You're the only woman I know who can eat ice cream. . . . I mean, without throwing up afterward."

It was one thing to have a political stance against fat oppression. It is quite another, I found, to have a fat lover.

The problem didn't arise in bed. I wanted her, there was no question about that. The problem came when I looked at her naked body after we had made love. The body I saw was not one I knew how to call beautiful. My lover's belly was distended; her thighs were thick. Around her face, she had a double, perhaps a triple, chin. In the past, I'd had lovers who, like most people, disliked their bodies. It had been one of my talents as a lover to change those feelings. I'd praised their bodies, loving them with words as well as touch. Now I wanted to do the same thing for my fat lover. Yet I could not tell her she was beautiful. "I love your body," I told her instead as I kissed her, licking and stroking her flesh. "I love your body," I repeated like a mantra, to ward away the persistent, ugly remnants of my disgust.

Later, as she gained more weight, my lover began to worry that there was a limit to how much fat I could love, or perhaps how much fat I could overlook.

"It's your essence I'm attracted to," I assured her. "No amount of weight you could gain or lose would change my feelings for you."

And somewhere along the way, the judging portion of my brain grew thinner and thinner until, like a fingernail sliver of moon, it almost disappeared. "You're beautiful," I told my lover then, because it was true.

Later, as my lover's kidneys failed, I came to love her body in still other ways. Now that it had become a battleground, a locus of pain and discomfort rather than pleasure, I loved it in defiance, as if my passion could banish its ills. I loved it perhaps in the same way that some women love "unavailable" men, because I could not reach it, even as I lay naked beside it.

After the kidney transplant that saved her life, my lover gained another 50 pounds. She'd gone months with no appetite, weeks with nausea that forced her to live on just bread and applesauce, so it was a joy when food tasted good to her again. Besides, she was now taking prednisone, a steroid drug that made her constantly hungry and changed the way her body metabolized food.

It is also true that my lover is, in her own words, "addicted to food." She sometimes eats when she is not hungry. She has ignored her hunger so often—because she was dieting, or eating to fill other needs—she no longer knows what it is to feel full. These things are true of many thin women as well.

From time to time, my lover declares she wants to lose weight. I want to help her, I tell myself, so I start making her salads for lunch and cooking fat-free vegetable soups. And I catch myself beginning to watch what she eats. I feel the judgment growing in me again.

So I pay heed when my lover tells me that I am the first person who has ever loved her at her weight, not in spite of it. She tells me this over the breakfast I've made: a crustless quiche with potatoes, apples, red onion, and smoked mozzarella. Cooking has always been a way I nurture myself and the people I love.

I remember watching my sister refuse to eat. I think of the months when my brave and beautiful lover's failing kidneys made eating impossible. So tonight, I think, I'll cook us a meal to celebrate our appetites at their most joyous and untamable: maybe a garlicky Puerto Rican *asopao*, fresh-baked corn muffins, and a salad of greens, pecans, feta cheese, and pears.

READING 35

"A Way Outa No Way"
Eating Problems Among African-American, Latina, and White Women

Becky Wangsgaard Thompson

Bulimia, anorexia, binging, and extensive dieting are among the many health issues women have been confronting in the last 20 years. Until recently, however, there has been almost no research about eating problems among African-American, Latina, Asian-American, or Native American women, working-class women, or lesbians.[1] In fact, according to the normative epidemiological portrait, eating problems are largely a white, middle-, and upper-class heterosexual phenomenon. Further, while feminist research has documented how eating problems are fueled by sexism, there has been almost no attention to how other systems of oppression may also be implicated in the development of eating problems.

In this article, I reevaluate the portrayal of eating problems as issues of appearance based in the "culture of thinness." I propose that eating problems begin as ways women cope with various traumas including sexual abuse, racism, classism, sexism, heterosexism, and poverty. Showing the interface between these traumas and the onset of eating problems explains why women may use eating to numb pain and cope with violations to their bodies. This theoretical shift also permits an understanding of the economic, political, social, educational, and cultural resources that women need to change their relationship to food and their bodies.

. . .

METHODOLOGY

I conducted 18 life history interviews and administered lengthy questionnaires to explore eating problems among African-American, Latina, and White women. I employed a snowball sample, a method in which potential respondents often first learn about the study from people who have already participated. This method was well suited for the study since it enabled women to get information about me and the interview process from people they already knew. Typically, I had much contact with the respondents prior to the interview. This was particularly important given the secrecy associated with this topic (Russell 1986; Silberstein, Striegel-Moore, and Rodin 1987), the necessity of women of color and lesbians to be discriminating about how their lives are studied, and the fact that I was conducting across-race research.

. . .

Demographics of the Women in the Study

The women I interviewed included 5 African-American women, 5 Latinas, and 8 White women. Of these women, 12 are lesbian and 6 are heterosexual. Five women are Jewish, 8 are Catholic, and 5 are Protestant. Three women grew up outside of the United States. The women represented a range of class backgrounds (both in terms of origin and current class status) and ranged in age from 19 to 46 years old (with a median age of 33.5 years).

The majority of the women reported having had a combination of eating problems (at least two of the following: bulimia, compulsive eating, anorexia, and/or extensive dieting). In addition, the particular types of eating problems often changed during a woman's life span. (For example, a woman might have been bulimic during adolescence and anorexic as an adult.) Among the women, 28 percent had been bulimic, 17 percent had been bulimic and anorexic, and 5 percent had been anorexic. All of the women who had been anorexic or bulimic also had a history of compulsive eating and extensive dieting. Of the women, 50 percent were compulsive eaters and dieters (39 percent) or compulsive eaters (11 percent) but had not been bulimic or anorexic.

Two-thirds of the women have had eating problems for more than half of their lives, a finding that contradicts the stereotype of eating problems as transitory. The weight fluctuation among the women varied from 16 to 160 pounds, with an average fluctuation of 74 pounds. This drastic weight change illustrates the degree to which the women adjusted to major changes in body size at least once during their lives as they lost, gained, and lost weight again. The average age of onset was 11 years old, meaning that most of the women developed eating problems prior to puberty. Almost all of the women (88 percent) consider themselves as still having a problem with eating, although the majority believe they are well on the way to recovery.

THE INTERFACE OF TRAUMA AND EATING PROBLEMS

One of the most striking findings in this study was the range of traumas the women associated with the origins of their eating problems, including racism, sexual abuse, poverty, sexism, emotional or physical abuse, heterosexism, class injuries, and acculturation.[2] The particular constellation of eating problems among the women did not vary with race, class, sexuality, or nationality. Women from various race and class backgrounds attributed the origins of their eating problems to sexual abuse, sexism, and emotional and/or physical abuse.

Among some of the African-American and Latina women, eating problems were also associated with poverty, racism, and class injuries. Heterosexism was a key factor in the onset of bulimia, compulsive eating, and extensive dieting among some of the lesbians. These oppressions are not the same nor are the injuries caused by them. And certainly, there are a variety of potentially harmful ways that women respond to oppression (such as using drugs, becoming a workaholic, or committing suicide). However, for all these women, eating was a way of coping with trauma.

Sexual Abuse

Sexual abuse was the most common trauma that the women related to the origins of their eating problems. Until recently, there has been virtually no research exploring the possible relationship between these two phenomena. Since the mid-1980s, however, researchers have begun identifying connections between the two, a task that is part of a larger feminist critique of traditional psychoanalytical symptomatology (DeSalvo 1989; Herman 1981; Masson 1984). Results of a number of incidence studies indicate that between one-third and two-thirds of women who have eating problems have been abused (Oppenheimer et al. 1985; Root and Fallon 1988). . . .

Among the women I interviewed, 61 percent were survivors of sexual abuse (11 of the 18 women), most of whom made connections between sexual abuse and the beginning of their eating problems. Binging was the most common method of coping identified by the sur-

vivors. Binging helped women "numb out" or anesthetize their feelings. Eating sedated, alleviated anxiety, and combated loneliness. Food was something that they could trust and was accessible whenever they needed it. . . .

Extensive dieting and bulimia were also ways in which women responded to sexual abuse. Some women thought that the men had abused them because of their weight. They believed that if they were smaller, they might not have been abused. For example when Elsa, an Argentine woman, was sexually abused at the age of 11, she thought her chubby size was the reason the man was abusing her. Elsa said, "I had this notion that these old perverts liked these plump girls. You heard adults say this too. Sex and flesh being associated." Looking back on her childhood, Elsa believes she made fat the enemy partly due to the shame and guilt she felt about the incest. Her belief that fat was the source of her problems was supported by her socialization. Raised by strict German governesses in an upper-class family, Elsa was taught that a woman's weight was a primary criterion for judging her worth. Her mother "was socially conscious of walking into places with a fat daughter and maybe people staring at her." Her father often referred to Elsa's body as "shot to hell." When asked to describe how she felt about her body when growing up, Elsa described being completely alienated from her body. . . .

As is true for many women who have been abused, the split that Elsa described between her body and soul was an attempt to protect herself from the pain she believed her body caused her. In her mind her fat body was what had "bashed in her dreams." Dieting became her solution, but, as is true for many women in the study, this strategy soon led to cycles of binging and weight fluctuation. . . .

These women's experiences suggest many reasons why women develop eating problems as a consequence of sexual abuse. Most of the survivors "forgot" the sexual abuse after its onset and were unable to retrieve the abuse memories until many years later. With these gaps in memory, frequently they did not know why they felt ashamed, fearful, or depressed. When sexual abuse memories resurfaced in dreams, they often woke feeling upset but could not remember what they had dreamed. These free floating, unexplained feelings left the women feeling out of control and confused. Binging or focusing on maintaining a new diet were ways women distracted or appeased themselves, in turn, helping them regain a sense of control. As they grew older, they became more conscious of the consequences of these actions. Becoming angry at themselves for binging or promising themselves they would not purge again was a way to direct feelings of shame and self-hate that often accompanied the trauma.

Integral to this occurrence was a transference process in which the women displaced onto their bodies painful feelings and memories that actually derived from or were directed toward the persons who caused the abuse. Dieting became a method of trying to change the parts of their bodies they hated, a strategy that at least initially brought success as they lost weight. Purging was a way women tried to reject the body size they thought was responsible for the abuse. Throwing up in order to lose the weight they thought was making them vulnerable to the abuse was a way to try to find the body they had lost when the abuse began.

Poverty

Like sexual abuse, poverty is another injury that may make women vulnerable to eating problems. One woman I interviewed attributed her eating problems directly to the stress caused by poverty. Yolanda is a Black Cape Verdean mother who began eating compulsively when she was 27 years old. After leaving an abusive husband in her early 20s, Yolanda was forced to go on welfare. As a single mother with small children and few financial resources, she tried to support herself and her children on $539 a month. Yolanda began binging in the evenings after putting her children to bed.

Eating was something she could do alone. It would calm her, help her deal with loneliness, and make her feel safe. Food was an accessible commodity that was cheap. She ate three boxes of macaroni and cheese when nothing else was available. As a single mother with little money, Yolanda felt as if her body was the only thing she had left. . . . When she was eating, Yolanda felt a momentary reprieve from her worries. Binging not only became a logical solution because it was cheap and easy but also because she had grown up amid positive messages about eating. In her family, eating was a celebrated and joyful act. However, in adulthood, eating became a double-edged sword. While comforting her, binging also led to weight gain. During the three years Yolanda was on welfare, she gained seventy pounds.

Yolanda's story captures how poverty can be a precipitating factor in eating problems and highlights the value of understanding how class inequalities may shape women's eating problems. As a single mother, her financial constraints mirrored those of most female heads of households. The dual hazards of a race- and sex-stratified labor market further limited her options (Higginbotham 1986). . . .

The fact that many women use food to anesthetize themselves, rather than other drugs (even when they gained access to alcohol, marijuana, and other illegal drugs), is partly a function of gender socialization and the competing demands that women face. One of the physiological consequences of binge eating is a numbed state similar to that experienced by drinking. Troubles and tensions are covered over as a consequence of the body's defensive response to massive food intake. When food is eaten in that way, it effectively works like a drug with immediate and predictable effects. Yolanda said she binged late at night rather than getting drunk because she could still get up in the morning, get her children ready for school, and be clearheaded for the college classes she attended. By binging, she avoided the hangover or sickness that results from alcohol or illegal drugs. In this way, food was her drug of choice since it was possible for her to eat while she continued to care for her children, drive, cook, and study. Binging is also less expensive than drinking, a factor that is especially significant for poor women. Another woman I interviewed said that when her compulsive eating was at its height, she ate breakfast after rising in the morning, stopped for a snack on her way to work, ate lunch at three different cafeterias, and snacked at her desk throughout the afternoon. Yet even when her eating had become constant, she was still able to remain employed. While her patterns of eating no doubt slowed her productivity, being drunk may have slowed her to a dead stop.

Heterosexism

The life history interviews also uncovered new connections between heterosexism and eating problems. One of the most important recent feminist contributions has been identifying compulsory heterosexuality as an institution which truncates opportunities for heterosexual and lesbian women (Rich 1986). All of the women interviewed for this study, both lesbian and heterosexual, were taught that heterosexuality was compulsory, although the versions of this enforcement were shaped by race and class. Expectations about heterosexuality were partly taught through messages that girls learned about eating and their bodies. In some homes, boys were given more food than girls, especially as teenagers, based on the rationale that girls need to be thin to attract boys. As the girls approached puberty, many were told to stop being athletic, begin wearing dresses, and watch their weight. For the woman who weighed more than was considered acceptable, threats about their need to diet were laced with admonitions that being fat would ensure becoming an "old maid."

While compulsory heterosexuality influenced all of the women's emerging sense of their bodies and eating patterns, the women who linked heterosexism directly to the beginning of their eating problems were those who knew they were lesbians when very young and actively resisted heterosexual norms. One working-class Jewish woman, Martha, began compulsively eating when she was 11 years old, the same year she started getting clues of her lesbian identity. In junior high school, as many of her female peers began dating boys, Martha began fantasizing about girls, which made her feel utterly alone. Confused and ashamed about her fantasies, Martha came home every day from school and binged. Binging was a way she drugged herself so that being alone was tolerable. Describing binging, she said, "It was the only thing I knew. I was looking for a comfort." Like many women, Martha binged because it softened painful feelings. Binging sedated her, lessened her anxiety, and induced sleep.

Martha's story also reveals ways that trauma can influence women's experience of their bodies. Like many other women, Martha had no sense of herself as connected to her body. When I asked Martha whether she saw herself as fat when she was growing up she said, "I didn't see myself as fat. I didn't see myself. I wasn't there. I get so sad about that because I missed so much." In the literature on eating problems, *body image* is the term that is typically used to describe a woman's experience of her body. This term connotes the act of imagining one's physical appearance. Typically, women with eating problems are assumed to have difficulties with their body image. However, the term body image does not adequately capture the complexity and range of bodily responses to trauma experienced by the women. Exposure to trauma did much more than distort the women's visual image of themselves. These traumas often jeopardized their capacity to consider themselves as having bodies at all.

Given the limited connotations of the term body image, I use the term *body consciousness* as a more useful way to understand the range of bodily responses to trauma.[3] By body consciousness I mean the ability to reside comfortably in one's body (to see oneself as embodied) and to consider one's body as connected to one-self. The disruptions to their body consciousness that the women described included leaving their bodies, making a split between their body and mind, experiencing being "in" their bodies as painful, feeling unable to control what went in and out of their bodies, hiding in one part of their bodies, or simply not seeing themselves as having bodies. Binging, dieting, or purging were common ways women responded to disruptions to their body consciousness.

Racism and Class Injuries

For some of the Latinas and African-American women, racism coupled with the stress resulting from class mobility related to the onset of their eating problems. Joselyn, an African-American woman, remembered her White grandmother telling her she would never be as pretty as her cousins because they were lighter skinned. Her grandmother often humiliated Joselyn in front of others, as she made fun of Joselyn's body while she was naked and told her she was fat. As a young child, Joselyn began to think that although she could not change her skin color, she could at least try to be thin. When Joselyn was young, her grandmother was the only family member who objected to Joselyn's weight. However, her father also began encouraging his wife and daughter to be thin as the family's class standing began to change. When the family was working class, serving big meals, having chubby children, and keeping plenty of food in the house was a sign the family was doing well. But, as the family became mobile, Joselyn's father began insisting that Joselyn be thin. She remembered, "When my father's business began to bloom and my father was interacting more with White businessmen and seeing how they did business, suddenly thin became important. If you were a truly well-to-do family, then your family was slim and elegant."

As Joselyn's grandmother used Joselyn's body as territory for enforcing her own racism and prejudice about size, Joselyn's father used her body as the territory through which he channeled the demands he faced in the white-dominated business world. However, as Joselyn was pressured to diet, her father still served her large portions and bought treats for her and the neighborhood children. These contradictory messages made her feel confused about her body. As was true for many women in this study, Joselyn was told she was fat beginning when she was very young even though she was not overweight. And, like most of the women, Joselyn was put on diet pills and diets before even reaching puberty, beginning the cycles of dieting, compulsive eating, and bulimia.

. . .

The fact that some of the African-American and Latina women associated the ambivalent messages about food and eating to their family's class mobility and/or the demands of assimilation while none of the eight White women expressed this (including those whose class was stable and changing) suggests that the added dimension of racism was connected to the imperative to be thin. In fact, the class expectations that their parents experienced exacerbated standards about weight that they inflicted on their daughters.

EATING PROBLEMS AS SURVIVAL STRATEGIES

Feminist Theoretical Shifts

My research permits a reevaluation of many assumptions about eating problems. First, this work challenges the theoretical reliance on the culture-of-thinness model. . . .

Establishing links between eating problems and a range of oppressions invites a rethinking of both the groups of women who have been excluded from research and those whose lives have been the basis of theory formation. The construction of bulimia and anorexia as appearance-based disorders is rooted in a notion of femininity in which White middle- and upper-class women are portrayed as frivolous, obsessed with their bodies, and overly accepting of narrow gender roles. This portrayal fuels women's tremendous shame and guilt about eating problems—as signs of self-centered vanity. This construction of White middle- and upper-class women is intimately linked to the portrayal of working-class White women and women of color as their opposite: as somehow exempt from accepting the dominant standards of beauty or as one step away from being hungry and therefore not susceptible to eating problems. Identifying that women may binge to cope with poverty contrasts the notion that eating problems are class bound. Attending to the intricacies of race, class, sexuality, and gender pushes us to rethink the demeaning construction of middle-class femininity and establishes bulimia and anorexia as serious responses to injustices.

Understanding the link between eating problems and trauma also suggests much about treatment and prevention. Ultimately, their prevention depends not simply on individual healing but also on changing the social conditions that underlie their etiology. As Bernice Johnson Reagon sings in Sweet Honey in the Rock's song "Oughta Be a Woman," "A way outa no way is too much to ask/ too much of a task for any one woman" (Reagon 1980).[4] Making it possible for women to have healthy relationships with their bodies and eating is a comprehensive task. Beginning steps in this direction include insuring that (1) girls can grow up without being sexually abused, (2) parents have adequate resources to raise their children, (3) children of color grow up free of racism, and (4) young lesbians have the chance to see their reflection in their teachers and community leaders. Ultimately, the prevention of eating problems depends on women's access to economic, cultural, racial, political, social, and sexual justice.

NOTES

Author's Note The research for this study was partially supported by an American Association of University Women Fellowship in Women's Studies. An earlier version of this article was presented at the New England Women's Studies Association Meeting in 1990 in Kingston, Rhode Island. I am grateful to Margaret Andersen, Liz Bennett, Lynn Davidman, Mary Gilfus, Evelynn Hammonds, and two anonymous reviewers for their comprehensive and perceptive comments on earlier versions of this article.

1. I use the term *eating problems* as an umbrella term for one or more of the following: anorexia, bulimia, extensive dieting, or binging. I avoid using the term eating disorder because it categorizes the problems as individual pathologies, which deflects attention away from the social inequalities underlying them (Brown 1985). However, by using the term *problem* I do not wish to imply blame. In fact, throughout, I argue that the eating strategies that women develop begin as logical solutions to problems, not problems themselves.

2. By trauma I mean a violating experience that has long-term emotional, physical, and/or spiritual consequences that may have immediate or delayed effects. One reason the term *trauma* is useful conceptually is its association with the diagnostic label Post Traumatic Stress Disorder (PTSD) (American Psychological Association 1987). PTSD is one of the few clinical diagnostic categories that recognizes social problems (such as war or the Holocaust) as responsible for the symptoms identified (Trimble 1985). This concept adapts well to the feminist assertion that a woman's symptoms cannot be understood as solely individual, considered outside of her social context, or prevented without significant changes in social conditions.

3. One reason the term *consciousness* is applicable is its intellectual history as an entity that is shaped by social context and social structures (Delphy 1984; Marx 1964). This link aptly applies to how the women described their bodies because their perceptions of themselves as embodied (or not embodied) directly relate to their material conditions (living situations, financial resources, and access to social and political power).

4. Copyright © 1980. Used by permission of Songtalk Publishing.

REFERENCES

American Psychological Association. 1987. *Diagnostic and statistical manual of mental disorders*. 3rd ed. rev. Washington, DC: American Psychological Association.

Brown, Laura S. 1985. Women, weight and power: Feminist theoretical and therapeutic issues. *Women and Therapy* 4:61–71.

Delphy, Christine. 1984. *Close to home: A materialist analysis of women's oppression.* Amherst: University of Massachusetts Press.

DeSalvo, Louise. 1989. *Virginia Woolf: The impact of childhood sexual abuse on her life and work.* Boston, MA: Beacon.

Herman, Judith. 1981. *Father-daughter incest.* Cambridge, MA: Harvard University Press.

Higginbotham, Elizabeth. 1986. We were never on a pedestal: Women of color continue to struggle with poverty, racism and sexism. In *For crying out loud,* edited by Rochelle Lefkowitz and Ann Withorn, Boston, MA: Pilgrim Press.

Marx, Karl. 1964. *The economic and philosophic manuscripts of 1844.* New York: International.

Masson, Jeffrey. 1984. *The assault on the truth: Freud's suppression of the seduction theory.* New York: Farrar, Strauss & Giroux.

Oppenheimer, R., K. Howells, R. L. Palmer, and D. A. Chaloner. 1985. Adverse sexual experience in childhood and clinical eating disorders: A preliminary description. *Journal of Psychiatric Research* 19:357–61.

Reagon, Bernice Johnson. 1980. Oughta be a woman. On Sweet Honey in the Rock's album, *Good News.* Music by Bernice Johnson Reagon; lyrics by June Jordan. Washington, DC: Songtalk.

Rich, Adrienne. 1986. Compulsory heterosexuality and lesbian existence. In *Blood, bread and poetry.* New York: Norton.

Root, Maria P. P., and Patricia Fallon. 1988. The incidence of victimization experiences in a bulimic sample. *Journal of Interpersonal Violence* 3:161–73.

Russell, Diana E. 1986. *The secret trauma: Incest in the lives of girls and women.* New York: Basic Books.

Silberstein, Lisa, Ruth Striegel-Moore, and Judith Rodin. 1987. Feeling fat: A woman's shame. In *The role of shame in symptom formation,* edited by Helen Block Lewis. Hillsdale, NJ: Lawrence Erlbaum.

Trimble, Michael. 1985. Post-traumatic stress disorder: History of a concept. In *Trauma and its wake: The study and treatment of post-traumatic stress disorder,* edited by C. R. Figley. New York: Brunner/Mazel.

READING 36

Dreadlocked

Veronica Chambers

I have two relationships with the outside world: One is with my hair, and the other is with the rest of me. Sure, I have concerns and points of pride with my body. I like the curve of my butt but dislike my powerhouse thighs. My breasts, once considered too small, have been proclaimed perfect so often that not only am I starting to believe the hype, but also am booking my next vacation to a topless resort in Greece. But my hair. Oh my hair.

I have reddish brown dreadlocks that fall just below shoulder length. Eventually, they will cover my aforementioned breasts, at which time I will give serious thought to nude modeling at my local art school. I like my hair—a lot. But over the last eight years my dreadlocks

have conferred upon me the following roles: rebel child, Rasta mama, Nubian princess, drug dealer, unemployed artist, rock star, world-famous comedienne, and nature chick. None of which is true. It has occurred to me more than once that my hair is a whole lot more interesting than I am.

Because I am a black woman, I have always had a complicated relationship with my hair. Here's a quick primer on the politics of hair and beauty aesthetics in the black community vis-à-vis race and class in the late 20th century: "Good" hair is straight and, preferably, long. Think Naomi Campbell. Diana Ross. For that matter, think RuPaul. "Bad" hair is thick and coarse, aka "nappy," and, often, short. Think

Buckwheat in *The Little Rascals.* Not the more recent version, but the old one in which Buckwheat looked like Don King's grandson.

Understand that these are stereotypes: broad and imprecise. Some will say that the idea of "good" hair and "bad" hair is outdated. And it is less prevalent than in the '70s when I was growing up. Sometimes I see little girls with their hair in braids and Senegalese twists sporting cute little T-shirts that say HAPPY TO BE NAPPY and I get teary-eyed. I was born between the black power Afros of the '60s and the blue contact lenses and weaves of the '80s; in my childhood, no one seemed happy to be nappy at all.

I knew from the age of 4 that I had "bad" hair because my relatives and family friends discussed it as they might discuss a rare blood disease. "Something must be done," they would cluck sadly. "I think I know someone," an aunt would murmur, referring to a hairdresser as if she were a medical specialist. Some of my earliest memories are of Brooklyn apartments where women did hair for extra money. These makeshift beauty parlors were lively and loud, the air thick with the smell of lye from harsh relaxer, the smell of hair burning as the hot straightening comb did its job.

When did I first begin to desire hair that bounced? Was it because black Barbie wasn't, and still isn't, happy to be nappy? Was it Brenda, the redhead, my best friend in second grade? Every time she flicked her hair to the side, she seemed beyond sophistication. My hair bounced the first day back from the hairdresser's, but not much longer. "Don't sweat out that perm," my mother would call. But I found it impossible to sit still. Hairdressers despaired like cowardly lion tamers at the thought of training my kinky hair. "This is some hard hair," they would say. I knew that I was not beautiful and I blamed it on my hair.

The night I began to twist my hair into dreads, I was 19 and a junior in college. It was New Year's Eve and the boy I longed for had not called. A few months before, Alice Walker had appeared on the cover of *Essence,* her locks flowing with all the majesty of a Southern American Cleopatra. I was inspired. It was my family's superstition that the hours between New Year's Eve and New Year's Day were the time to cast spells. "However New Year's catches you is how you'll spend the year," my mother always reminded me.

I decided to use the hours that remained to transform myself into the vision I'd seen on the magazine. Unsure of how to begin, I washed my hair, carefully and lovingly. I dried it with a towel, then opened a jar of hair grease. Using a comb to part the sections, I began to twist each section into baby dreads. My hair, at the time, couldn't have been longer than an inch. I twisted for two hours, and in the end was far from smitten with what I saw: My full cheeks dominated my face now that my hair lay in flat twists around my head. My already short hair seemed shorter. I did not look like the African goddess I had imagined. I emerged from the bathroom and ran into my aunt Diana, whose luxuriously long, straight black hair always reminded me of Diahann Carroll on *Dynasty.* "Well, Vickie," she said, shaking her head. "Well, well." I knew that night my life would begin to change. I started my dreadlocks and began the process of seeing beauty where no one had ever seen beauty before.

There are, of course, those who see my hair and still consider it "bad." A family friend touched my hair recently, then said, "Don't you think it's a waste? All that lovely hair twisted in those things?" I have been asked by more than one potential suitor if I had any pictures of myself before "you did that to your hair." A failure at small talk and countless other social graces, I sometimes let my hair do the talking for me. At a cocktail party, I stroll though the room, silently, and watch my hair tell white lies. In literary circles, it brands me "interesting, adventurous." In black middle-class circles, I'm "rebellious" or, more charitably, "Afrocentric." In predominantly white circles, my hair doubles my level of exotica. My hair says, "Unlike the black woman who reads you the evening news, I'm not even trying to blend in."

For those ignorant enough to think that they can read hair follicles like tea leaves, my hair says a lot of things it doesn't mean. Taken to the extreme, it says that I am a pot-smoking Rasta-farian wannabe who in her off-hours strolls through her house in an African dashiki, light-ing incense and listening to Bob Marley. I don't smoke pot. In my house, I wear Calvin Klein nightshirts, and light tuberose candles that I buy from Diptyque in Paris. I play tennis in my off-hours and, while I love Bob Marley, I mostly listen to jazz vocalists like Ella Fitzgerald and Diana Krall.

Once after a dinner party in Beverly Hills, a white colleague of mine lit up a joint. Everyone at the table passed and when I passed too, the man cajoled me relentlessly. "Come on," he kept saying. "Of all people, I thought you'd in-dulge." I shrugged and said nothing. As we left the party that night, he kissed me good-bye. "Boy, were you a disappointment," he said, as if I had been a bad lay. But I guess I had denied him a certain sort of pleasure. It must have been his dream to smoke a big, fat spliff with a real live Rastafarian.

As much as I hate to admit it, I've been trained to turn my head to any number of names that aren't mine. I will answer to "Whoopi." I will turn when Jamaican men call out "Hey, Rasta" on the street. I am often asked if I am a singer, and I can only hope that I might be confused with the gorgeous Cassandra Wilson, whose dreadlocks inspired me to color my hair a jazzy shade of red. Walking through the streets of Marrakesh, I got used to trails of children who would follow me, trying to guess which coun-try I came from. "Jamaica!" they would shout. "Ghana! Nigeria!" I shook my head no to them all. They did not believe me when I said I was from America; instead, they called me "Mama Africa" all day long. It's one of my favorite memories of the trip.

Once, after the end of a great love affair, I watched a man cut all of his dreadlocks off and then burn them in the backyard. This, I suspect, is the reason that might tempt me to change my hair. After all, a broken heart is what started me down this path of twisting hair. Because I do not cut my hair, I carry eight years of history on my head. One day, I may tire of this history and start anew. But one thing is for sure, whatever style I wear my hair in, I will live happily—and nappily—ever after.

READING 37

Hold that Nose

Lisa Miya-Jervis

I'm a Jew. I'm not even slightly religious. Aside from attending friends' bat mitzvahs, I've been to temple maybe twice. I don't know Hebrew; my junior-high self, given the option of reli-gious education, easily chose to sleep in on Sunday mornings. My family skips around the Passover Haggadah to get to the food faster. Before I dated someone from an observant fam-ily, I wouldn't have known a mezuzah if it bit me on the butt. I was born assimilated.

But still, I'm a Jew, an ethnic Jew of a very specific variety: a godless, New York City–raised, neurotic middle-class girl from a solidly liberal-Democratic family, who at-tended largely Jewish, "progressive" schools. When I was growing up, almost everyone around me was Jewish; I was stunned when I found out that Jews make up only 2 percent of the American population. For me, being Jewish meant that on Christmas Day my family went out for Chinese food and took in the new Woody Allen movie. It also meant that I had a big honkin' nose.

And I still do. By virtue of my class and its sociopolitical trappings, I always knew I had the option to have my nose surgically altered. From adolescence on, I've had a standing offer from my mother to pay for a nose job.

"It's not such a big deal."

"Doctors do such individual-looking noses these days, it'll look really natural."

"It's not too late, you know," she would say to me for years after I flat-out refused to let someone break my nose, scrape part of it out, and reposition it into a smaller, less obtrusive shape. "I'll still pay." As if money were the reason I was resisting.

My mother thought a nose job was a good idea. See, she hadn't wanted one either. But when she was 16, her parents demanded that she get that honker "fixed," and they didn't take no for an answer. She insists that she's been glad ever since, although she usually rationalizes that it was good for her social life. (She even briefly dated a guy she met in the surgeon's waiting room, a boxer having his deviated septum corrected.)

Even my father is a believer. He says that without my mother's nose job, my sister and I wouldn't exist, because he never would have gone out with Mom. I take this with an entire salt lick. My father thinks that dressing up means wearing dark sneakers; that pants should be purchased every 20 years—and then only if the old ones are literally falling apart; and that haircuts should cost $10 and take as many minutes. The only thing he says about appearances is, "You have some crud . . ." as he picks a piece of lint off your sleeve. But he cared about the nose? Whatever.

Even though my mother is happy with her tidy little surgically altered nose, she wasn't going to put me through the same thing, and for that I am truly grateful. I'm also unspeakably glad that her comments stayed far from the "you'd be so pretty if you did" angle. I know a few people who weren't so lucky. Not that they were dragged kicking and screaming to the doctor's office; no, they were coerced and shamed into it. Seems it was their family's decision more than their own—usually older female relatives: mothers, grandmothers, aunts.

What's the motivation for that kind of pressure? Can it be that for all the strides made against racism and anti-Semitism, Americans still want to expunge their ethnicity from their looks? Were these mothers and grandmothers trying to fit their offspring into a more white, gentile mode? Possibly. Well, definitely. But on purpose? Probably not. Their lust for the button nose is probably more a desire for a typical femininity than for any specific de-ethnicizing. But given the society in which we live, the proximity of WASPy white features to the ideal of beauty is no coincidence. I think that anyone who opts for a nose job today (or who pressures her daughter to get one) would say that the reason for the surgery is to look "better" or "prettier." But when we scratch the surface of what "prettier" means, we find that we might as well be saying "whiter" or "more gentile" (I would add "bland," but that's my personal opinion).

Or perhaps the reason is to become unobtrusive. The stereotypical Jewish woman is loud and pushy—qualities girls really aren't supposed to have. So is it possible that the nose job is supposed to usher in not only physical femininity but a psychological, traditional femininity as well? Bob your nose, and become feminine in both mind and body. (This certainly seems to be the way it has worked with Courtney Love, although her issue is class more than ethnicity. But it's undeniable that her new nose comes with a Versace-shilling, tamed persona, in stark contrast to her old messy, outspoken self.)

Even though I know plenty of women with their genetically determined schnozzes still intact, sometimes I still feel like an oddity. From what my mother tells me, nose jobs were as compulsory a rite of passage for her peers as multiple ear-piercings were for mine. Once, when I was still in high school, I went with my mother to a Planned Parenthood fund-raiser, a cocktail party in a lovely apartment, with lovely food and drink, and a lovely short speech by Wendy Wasserstein. But I was confused: We were at a lefty charity event in Manhattan, and all the women had little WASP noses. (Most of them were blond, too, but that didn't really register. I guess hair dye is a more universal ritual.)

"Why are there no Jewish women here?" I whispered to my mother. She laughed, but I think she was genuinely shocked. "What do you mean?" she asked. "All of these women are Jewish." And then it hit me: It was wall-to-wall rhinoplasties. And worse, there was no reason to be surprised. These were women my mother's age or older who came of age in the late '50s or before, when anti-Semitism in this country was much more overt than it is today. Surface assimilation was practically the norm back then, and those honkers were way too, ahem, big a liability on the dating and social scenes. Nose jobs have declined since then. They're no longer among the top five plastic surgeries, edged out by liposuction and laser skin resurfacing.

I don't think it's a coincidence that, growing up in New York, I didn't consider my nose an "ethnic" feature. Almost everyone around me had that ethnicity, too. It wasn't until I graduated from college and moved to California that I realized how marked I was. I also realized how much I like being instantly recognizable to anyone who knows how to look. I once met another Jewish woman at a conference in California. In the middle of our conversation, she randomly asked, "You're Jewish, right?" I replied, "With this nose and this hair, you gotta ask?" We both laughed. The question was just a formality, and we both knew it.

Only once did I feel uneasy about being "identified." At my first job out of college, my boss asked, after I mentioned an upcoming trip to see my family, "So, are your parents just like people in Woody Allen movies?" I wondered if I had a sign on my forehead reading "Big Yid Here." His comment brought up all those insecurities American Jews have that, not coincidentally, Woody Allen loves to emphasize for comic effect: Am I *that* Jewish? I felt conspicuous, exposed. Still, I'm glad I have the sign on my face, even if it's located a tad lower than my forehead.

Judaism is the only identity in which culture and religion are supposedly bound closely: If you're Irish and not a practicing Catholic, you can still be fully Irish; being Buddhist doesn't specify race or ethnicity. To me, being a Jew is cultural, but it's tied only marginally—even hypothetically—to religion, and mostly to geography (New York Jews are different from California Jews, lemme tell ya). So what happens when identity becomes untied from religion? I don't know for sure. And that means I'll grab onto anything I need to keep that identity—including my nose.

Feminism, Disability, and Transcendence of the Body

Susan Wendell

Ideas of transcending the body have generally been rejected by feminists, including feminist theologians, because they are seen to originate from philosophies and/or religions that devalue the body (especially women's bodies) and bodily experience. For example, Naomi Goldenberg describes the notion of transcendence in traditional theology as "a wish for something beyond body, beyond time, and beyond specific relationships to life" and "a notion of perfect safety . . . probably motivated by a characteristically (but not exclusively) male fear of being merged with matter."

Feminist theorists have criticized the mind-body dichotomy and the intellectual derogation of the body, both of which make important contributions to motivations for transcending the body, and both of which are prevalent in the history of Western thought. We can see their philosophical roots in such ancient ideas as those of Plato and Aristotle, that abstract forms are superior to material things, and that reason is superior to the appetites that originate in the body. Feminists have also argued that the dominant forms of Christian theology strengthened these ancient views by representing the body as a major source of the desires and weaknesses that lead to sin, and overcoming the body as an essential ingredient in moral perfection.

Yet feminist theory has so far failed to appreciate the strength of another motive for wanting to transcend the body. We need to recognize that much of the appeal of philosophies of life that recommend some form of transcendence of the body lies, not in elevation of the mind and derogation of the body, but in the rational (as opposed to pathological) desire to make one's happiness, or at least one's sense of self, independent of illness, pain, weakness, exhaustion, and accident. We have not recognized this because feminist writing about the body has not fully confronted experience of the negative body. This is partly because feminism's primary concern has always been to identify and change social arrangements that cause preventable suffering, and we have applied this approach to the body. But it is also because we have focused the rest of our attention to the body on alienation from the body and on women's bodily differences from men, and these directions of focus have not been conducive to developing a feminist understanding of bodily suffering.

. . .

SOME STRATEGIES OF DISENGAGEMENT

Attempting to transcend or disengage oneself from the body by ignoring or discounting its needs and sensations is generally a luxury of the healthy and able-bodied. For people who are ill or disabled, a fairly high degree of attention to the body is necessary for survival, or at least for preventing significant (and sometimes irreversible) deterioration of their physical conditions. Yet illness and disability often render bodily experiences whose meanings we once took for granted difficult to interpret, and even deceptive. Barbara Rosenblum described how a "crisis of meaning" was created by the radical unpredictability of her body with cancer:

> In our culture it is very common to rely on the body as the ultimate arbiter of truth. . . . By noticing the body's responses to situations, we have an idea of how we "really feel about things." For example, if you get knots in your stomach every time a certain person walks into the room, you have an important body clue to investigate. . . . Interpretations of bodily signals are premised on the uninterrupted stability and continuity of the body. . . . When the body, like my body, is no longer consistent over time . . . when something that meant one thing in April may have an entirely different meaning in May, then it is hard to rely on the stability—and therefore the truth—of the body.

Chronic pain creates a similar (but more limited) crisis of meaning, since, to a healthy person, pain means that something is wrong that should be acted upon. With chronic pain, I must remind myself over and over again that the pain is meaningless, that there is nothing to fear or resist, that resistance only creates tension, which makes it worse. When I simply notice and accept the pain, my mind is often freed to pay attention to something else. This is not the same as ignoring my body, which would be dangerous, since not resting when I need to rest can cause extreme symptoms or a relapse into illness that would require several days' bed rest. I think of it as a reinterpretation of bodily sensations so as not to be overwhelmed or victimized by them. This process has affected profoundly my whole relationship to my body, since fatigue, nausea, dizziness, lack of appetite, and even depression are all caused by my disease from time to time, and thus all have changed their meanings. It is usually, though not always, inappropriate now to interpret them as indications of my relationship to the external world or of the need to take action. Unfortunately, it is often much easier to recognize that something is inappropriate than to refrain from doing it.

For this reason, I have found it important to cultivate an 'observer's' attitude to many bodily sensations and even depressive moods caused by my illness. With this attitude, I observe what is happening as a phenomenon, attend to it, tolerate the cognitive dissonance that results from, for example, feeling depressed or nauseated when there is nothing obviously depressing or disgusting going on, accommodate to it as best I can, and wait for it to pass. This is very different from the reactions that come most easily to me, which have to do with finding the causes of these feelings and acting on them. I find it hardest to adopt an observer's attitude toward depression, since although in the past I had brief illnesses that caused the other symptoms, I had never experienced severe depression without something to be depressed about. Thus, my first, easiest response to depression was to search my life for something that might be depressing me. Since my world (like virtually everyone's) is full of things that, if focussed upon, might cause depression, I increased and prolonged my depressions with this habitual response. Learning to regard severe depression (by this I mean, not the lows of everyday living, but the sorts of feelings that make you wish you were dead) as a physical phenomenon to be endured until it is over and not taken seriously has greatly reduced my suffering from it and may have saved my life. Register describes a similar strategy used by a man who suffers from recurring depressive illness.

In general, being able to say (usually to myself): "My body is painful (or nauseated, exhausted, etc.), but I'm happy," can be very encouraging and lift my spirits, because it asserts that the way my body feels is not the totality of my experience, that my mind and feelings can wander beyond the painful messages of my body, and that my state of mind is not completely dependent on the state of my body. Even being able to say, "My brain is badly affected right now, so I'm depressed, but I'm fine and my life is going well," is a way of asserting that the quality of my life is not completely dependent on the state of my body, that projects can still be imagined and accomplished, and that the present is not all there is. In short, I am learning not to identify myself with my body, and this helps me to live a good life with a debilitating chronic illness.

I know that many people will suspect this attitude of being psychologically or spiritually naive. They will insist that the sufferings of the body have psychological and/or spiritual meanings, and that I should be searching for them in order to heal myself. This is a widespread belief, not only in North America but in many parts of the world. . . . I do not reject it entirely. I too believe that, if my stomach tightens every time a particular person enters the room, it is an important sign of how I feel about her/him, and I may feel better physically if I avoid or change my relationship to that person. But, having experienced a crisis of meaning in my body, I can no longer assume that even powerful bodily experiences are psychologically or spiritually meaningful. To do so seems to me to give the body too little importance as a cause in psychological and spiritual life. It reduces the body to a mere reflector of other processes and implicitly rejects the idea that the body may have a complex life of its own, much of which we cannot interpret.

When I look back on the beginning of my illness, I still think of it, as I did then, as an involuntary violation of my body. But now I feel that such violations are sometimes the beginnings of a better life, in that they force the self to expand or be destroyed. Illness has forced me to change in ways that I am grateful for, and so, although I would joyfully accept a cure if it were offered me, I do not regret having become ill. Yet I do not believe that I became ill *because* I needed to learn what illness has taught me, nor that I will get well when I have learned everything I need to know from it. We learn from many things that do not happen to us because we need to learn from them (to regard the death of a loved one, for example, as primarily a lesson for oneself, is hideously narcissistic), and many people who could benefit from learning the same things never have the experiences that would teach them.

When I began to accept and give in to my symptoms, when I stopped searching for medical, psychological, or spiritual cures, when I began to develop the ability to observe my symptoms and reduced my identification with the transient miseries of my body, I was able to reconstruct my life. The state of my body limited the possibilities in new ways, but it also presented new kinds of understanding, new interests, new passions, and projects. In this sense, my experience of illness has been profoundly meaningful, but only because I accepted my body as a cause. If I had insisted on seeing it primarily as reflecting psychological or spiritual problems and devoted my energy to uncovering the 'meanings' of my symptoms, I would still be completely absorbed in being ill. As it is, my body has led me to a changed identity, to a very different sense of myself, even as I have come to identify myself less with what is occurring in my body.

People with disabilities often describe advantages of not identifying the self with the body. For those who are ill, the difficulty of living moment to moment with unpredictable, debilitating symptoms can be alleviated by having a strong sense of self that negotiates its ability to carry out its projects with the sick body. This sense of self and its projects provides continuity in lives that would be chaotic

if those who led them were highly identified with their bodies. The anthropologist Robert Murphy, who was quadriplegic and studied the lives of people with paralysis, described another motive for disembodying the self: "The paralytic becomes accustomed to being lifted, rolled, pushed, pulled, and twisted, and he survives this treatment by putting emotional distance between himself and his body."

In addition, people with disabilities often express a strong desire not to be identified with their bodily weaknesses, inabilities, or illnesses. This is why the phrase "people with disabilities" has come to be preferred over "disabled people." When the world sees a whole person as disabled, the person's abilities are overlooked or discounted. It is easy to slip into believing other people's perceptions of oneself, and this can take a great toll on the self-esteem of a person with a disability. Those people with disabilities who still have impressive and reliable physical abilities can counteract people's misperceptions by asserting those abilities. For those of us whose remaining physical abilities are unimpressive or unreliable, not to identify ourselves with our bodies may be the best defense. It is good psychological strategy to base our sense of ourselves, and therefore our self-esteem, on our intellectual and/or emotional experiences, activities, and connections to others.

Robert Murphy, whose paralysis increased steadily as a tumor in his spinal column grew, wrote eloquently about the consequences of losing the ability to move. He said of himself: "My thoughts and sense of being alive have been driven back into my brain, where I now reside," and: "Like all quadriplegics, I have a great fear of being left stranded and helpless, but my sense of self is otherwise shrunken to the confines of my head." Although Murphy did not shrink from recognizing what he had lost by this, he described vividly what he had gained:

> I have become a receptor in physical things, and I must continually fight the tendency for this

growing passivity to overcome my thoughts. But there is a certain security and comfort in returning to my little cocoon every night, enswathed in a warm electric blanket, settled into a microenvironment consisting of one's essentials. It is a breach of communication with the toils of social ties and obligations, a retreat into a private cerebral world. And it is at these times that my mind wanders furthest afield. In such deep quietude, one indeed finds a perverse freedom.

I do not want to give an exaggerated impression of the degree to which people with disabilities rely upon strategies of disembodiment. For all the advantages that some degree of disembodying the self may have in coping with illness or disability, the process of coming to identify with a sick or disabled body can play an important part in adjusting to it. For many of us who became ill or disabled as adults, reconstructing our lives depended upon forg-

ing a new identity. An important aspect of this process is what Register calls "acceptance: ability to regard the illness [*or, I would add, disability*] as your normal state of being." This could also be described as learning to identify with a new body, as well as, for most of us, a new social role. For me, this had many advantages: I stopped expecting to recover and postponing my life until I was well, I sought help and invented strategies for living with my sick body, I changed my projects and my working life to accommodate my physical limitations, and, perhaps most important, I began to identify with other people with disabilities and to learn from them. Thus, I do identify with my sick body to a significant degree, but I also believe that my thoughts and feelings are more independent from my experiences of it than they ever were from my experiences of my well body.

READING 39

Phenomenal Woman

Maya Angelou

Pretty women wonder where my secret lies.
I'm not cute or built to suit a fashion model's
   size
But when I start to tell them,
They think I'm telling lies.
I say,
It's in the reach of my arms,
The span of my hips,
The stride of my step,
The curl of my lips.
I'm a woman
Phenomenally.
Phenomenal woman,
That's me.

I walk into a room
Just as cool as you please,

And to a man,
The fellows stand or
Fall down on their knees.
Then they swarm around me,
A hive of honey bees.
I say,
It's the fire in my eyes,
And the flash of my teeth,
The swing in my waist,
And the joy in my feet.
I'm a woman
Phenomenally.
Phenomenal woman,
That's me.

Men themselves have wondered
What they see in me.

They try so much
But they can't touch
My inner mystery.
When I try to show them
They say they still can't see.
I say,
It's in the arch of my back,
The sun of my smile,
The ride of my breasts,
The grace of my style.
I'm a woman
Phenomenally.
Phenomenal woman,
That's me.

Now you understand
Just why my head's not bowed.

I don't shout or jump about
Or have to talk real loud.
When you see me passing
It ought to make you proud.
I say,
It's in the click of my heels,
The bend of my hair,
The palm of my hand,
The need for my care.
'Cause I'm a woman
Phenomenally.
Phenomenal woman,
That's me.

DISCUSSION QUESTIONS FOR CHAPTER FIVE

1. How are power relations reflected and reinforced in beauty norms?

2. How do beauty norms affect women and men differently? How have beauty norms affected you?

3. Two of your readings talk about women's connections with particular aspects of their bodies—dreadlocked hair and a big nose. What aspects of your body reflect key elements of your sense of self?

4. What are some of the connections between beauty standards and women's health?

5. How can women resist the beauty ideal?

SUGGESTIONS FOR FURTHER READING

Grogan, Sarah. *Body Image: Understanding Body Dissatisfaction in Men, Women, and Children*. New York: Routledge, 1999.

Hesse-Biber, Sharon. *Am I Thin Enough Yet?: The Cult of Thinness and the Commercialization of Identity*. New York: Oxford University Press, 1997.

Karp, Michelle. *The Bust Guide to the New Girl Order*. New York: Penguin, 1999.

Solovay, Sondra. *Tipping the Scales of Justice: Fighting Weight Based Discrimination*. Amherst, NY: Prometheus, 2000.

CHAPTER SIX

Health and Reproductive Rights

HEALTH AND WELLNESS

Health is a central issue in women's lives. Ask parents what they wish for their newborns and they speak first about hoping the baby is healthy; quiz people about their hopes for the new year and they speak about staying healthy; listen to politicians debate their positions before an election and health care is almost always a key issue. In contemporary U.S. society, good health is generally understood as a requirement for happy and productive living, at the same time that medical institutions provide different levels of service based upon health insurance status and general ability to pay. In other words, although health is a central aspect of everyday life, not all individuals are able to rely upon access to health and medical services.

Health is not just about medical services. Health conditions are related to such factors as poverty, diet, malnutrition and hunger, violence, stress, housing, and education. In essence, health is related to many aspects of our everyday lives as women. Heart disease, osteoporosis, migraine headaches, psychiatric disorders, substance abuse, and other health problems are closely related to gender. As suggested in "How Far We've Come," strides have been made in dealing with many health issues that affect women, but we still need activism to ensure optimal health care for women.

Two prominent health issues highlighted in the readings are breast cancer and AIDS. As the article "Breast Cancer: Is It the Environment?" suggests, breast cancer research has focused on finding a cure, when in reality a focus on environmental contributors could work more effectively to prevent breast cancer. Certainly the impact of the AIDS epidemic on women has concretely demonstrated the ways gender, race, and class intersect to affect women's lives in different ways. For example, women's manifestations of opportunistic infections were excluded from the definition of AIDS until 1993, most research is done on men and the findings are generalized to women, women are diagnosed later (often postmortem) than men, treated later, and die sooner after diagnosis. In addition, women of color are greatly overrepresented among AIDS patients, accounting for over 75 percent of AIDS cases among U.S. women. As Lisa Collier Cool argues in "Forgotten Women: How Minorities Are Underserved by Our Health Care System," racial discrimination complicates minority women's experiences in the health care system, resulting in inadequate care.

For Better or For Worse®   **by Lynn Johnston**

© Lynn Johnston Productions, Inc./Distributed by United Features Syndicate, Inc.

We've Come a Long Way? Women and Smoking

- Women make up nearly half of all smokers in the United States.
- Ninety percent of smokers take up the habit before age 20.
- The average teen smoker begins at age 13.
- The more formal education a woman receives, the less likely she is to be a smoker.
- In 1987, lung cancer surpassed breast cancer as the number one cause of cancer deaths among women. The American Cancer Society estimates that in 1998 lung cancer killed 67,000 women and breast cancer killed 43,500 women.
- In the last thirty years, the death rate from lung cancer among women has increased by more than 400 percent.
- Smoking kills more women than alcohol, illicit drugs, car accidents, suicide, and homicide combined.
- Smoking decreases fertility in women, increases the chances of premature menopause and osteoporosis, and disrupts pregnancy.
- Women smokers are more susceptible to reproductive tract infections and cervical cancer.
- Women smokers have more preterm stillbirths, and their children are more likely to suffer and die from a variety of birth defects.

Sources: Centers for Disease Control, Facts on Women and Tobacco, *www.cdc.gov;* Sharon Lerner. "If We've Come Such a Long Way, Why Are We Still Smoking?," *Ms.* (May/June 1995). National Women's Health Resource Center, Smoking, *www.healthywomen.org.*

Because women are prominent as both providers and consumers of health care, health issues and the health care system affect us on many levels. To make sense of the complexities of women's relationship to health care systems, we will discuss three concepts: androcentricism, medicalization, and gender stereotyping.

First, men's bodies have been seen as the norm, and much medical research has focused on men (mostly White men) and then been overgeneralized to women and people of color. This is an example of *androcentrism* (male-centeredness and the confusion of maleness with humanity) in the context of health care. More money has been spent on diseases that are more likely to afflict men. Related to this is the

Learning Activity: Test Your Knowledge of HIV/AIDS

True or false?

1. HIV stands for human immunodeficiency virus.
2. AIDS stands for acquired immunodeficiency syndrome.
3. HIV is airborne.
4. HIV can be transmitted through saliva.
5. HIV can be transmitted through blood, semen, and breast milk.
6. Women were not initially infected with HIV in the 1980s when the disease was primarily a problem for gay men.
7. Injection drug use is not a significant cause of HIV infection among women.
8. Poverty increases a woman's risk for contracting HIV.
9. HIV can be transmitted from a pregnant woman to her baby.
10. HIV is transmitted more easily from women to men than from men to women.
11. AIDS manifests through the same opportunistic infections in both women and men.
12. Heterosexual transmission is the most rapidly increasing transmission category among women with HIV.
13. Black and Latina women are disproportionately represented in AIDS cases.
14. A history of childhood sexual abuse is a risk factor for HIV infection.
15. Gender norms (for example, women are passive and submissive; nice women don't talk about sex) often make HIV prevention among women difficult.

Answers

1. T	6. F	11. F
2. T	7. F	12. T
3. F	8. T	13. T
4. F	9. T	14. T
5. T	10. F	15. T

notion of "anatomy is destiny" where female physiology, and especially reproductive anatomy, is seen as central in understanding behavior. Social norms about femininity have come to guide medical and scientific ideas about women's health, and female genital organs have long been seen as sources of special emotional and physical health problems. Furthermore, in "Man-Made Threats to Women's Health," Adrienne Germaine contends that men's political and social domination over women worldwide in itself constitutes a health threat for women.

In terms of women as health care providers, androcentrism has supported sexism and encouraged systems where men have more positions of power and influence in the health care system. Although nursing is still overwhelmingly a feminine occupation, increasingly more women are becoming physicians, even though most prestigious specialties are still dominated by men. It remains to be seen whether this increase in female physicians will change the face of medicine as we know it.

Medicalization is the process whereby normal functions of the body come to be seen as indicative of disease. This tends to be the model by which modern medicine works. This affects women in two ways. One, because women have more

Alcohol Abuse

Alcohol abuse and alcohol dependence are complicated illnesses that present unique threats to women's health. Women who abuse alcohol may develop addictions and substance abuse-related health problems faster than men. Ultimately medical research is showing that women are just more vulnerable. Recent surveys show that drinking is most common for:

- Women who are between the ages of 26 and 34
- Women who are divorced or separated

Binge drinking (consumption of five or more drinks) is most common among women who are ages 18 to 25. And drinking among women is more prevalent among Caucasians, although African American women are more likely to drink heavily.

All these statistics aside, the latest word from the National Institute on Alcohol Abuse and Alcoholism is that all women are more vulnerable to alcohol-related organ damage, trauma, and interpersonal difficulties:

- Liver damage: Women develop alcohol-induced liver disease in a shorter time period than men even if they consume less alcohol. And, women are more likely to develop alcohol hepatitis and die from cirrhosis (liver disease).
- Brain damage: Studies of brains (as seen via magnetic resonance imaging) show that women may be more vulnerable to brain damage due to alcohol consumption than men.
- Heart disease: Among heavy drinkers, women develop heart disease at the same rate as men, despite the fact that women use alcohol 60 percent less than men over their lifetimes.
- Breast cancer: Some studies have shown a link between moderate or heavy alcohol consumption and an increased risk for breast cancer.
- Violence: College women who drink are more likely to be the victims of sexual abuse. And high school girls who use alcohol are more likely to be the victims of dating violence.
- Traffic crashes: Although women are less likely than men to drive after drinking, they have a higher risk of dying.
- Women are more likely than men to use a combination of alcohol and prescription drugs.
- Women may begin to abuse alcohol and drugs following depression, to relax on dates, to feel more adequate, to lose weight, to decrease stress, or to help them sleep at night.

Poor self-esteem is a major issue for most women who develop problems with drugs and alcohol. The following conditions may also increase your risk for developing alcohol abuse problems:

- A history of physical or sexual abuse. Physical and sexual violence against women is common when one or both partners have been drinking or using drugs. Women also are more likely to drink or use drugs when their partners use.
- Depression, panic disorders, and posttraumatic stress disorders.

Researchers now know that there is a strong family component to addiction. If you have a family history of addiction, you should be aware of the risk for developing dependency, especially during stressful periods in your life.

Because very few women who abuse alcohol or drugs fit the addict stereotype, it is difficult for the addicted woman to see herself as an addict. It is also common for health care professionals to overlook substance abuse in women patients. If you suspect you may have an

(continued)

Alcohol (*continued*)

addiction problem, you might want to ask yourself the following questions, known as the CAGE Questionnaire:*

- Have you ever felt you should *c*ut down on your drinking or drug use?
- Have people *a*nnoyed you by criticizing your drinking or drug use?
- Have you ever felt bad or *g*uilty about your drinking or drug use?
- Have you ever had a drink or drug first thing in the morning to steady your nerves or to get rid of a hangover (*e*ye opener)?

Responses are scored 0 or 1, with a higher score an indication of alcohol problems. A total score of 2 or greater is considered clinically significant. If you scored greater than a 2 or if any of your answers bother you, it is time to talk to a health care professional about getting help.

*CAGE was developed by John Ewing, MD, founding Director of the Bowles Center for Alcohol Studies, University of North Carolina at Chapel Hill. CAGE is an internationally used assessment instrument for identifying alcoholics.

Source: National Women's Health Resource Center, *www.healthywomen.org.*

episodic changes in their bodies as a result of childbearing (for example, menstruation, pregnancy, childbirth, lactation, and menopause), they are more at risk for medical personnel interpreting these natural processes as problematic. Note how this tends to reinforce the argument that biology is destiny. Two, medicalization supports business and medical technologies. It tends to work against preventive medicine and encourages sophisticated medical technologies to "fix" problems after they occur. Medical services are dominated by drug treatments and surgery, and controlled by pharmaceutical companies, health maintenance organizations, and such professional organizations as the American Medical Association.

Third, *gender stereotyping* encompasses how notions about femininity and masculinity inform everyday understanding of health care occupations and influence how medical practitioners treat their patients. For example, patients often assume white-coated male orderlies to be doctors and call women doctors "nurse." Furthermore, as Patti Watkins and Diane Whaley suggest, women interact differently with the health care system and are treated differently, often to the detriment of women's health. For example, research suggests that physicians generally are more likely to consider emotional factors when diagnosing women's problems, and they are more likely to assume that the cause of illness is psychosomatic when the patient involved is female. It is well known that physicians also prescribe more mood-altering medication for women than they do for men. In addition, physicians attribute stereotypical notions of ethnicity, as well as gender, to patients, expecting Latinas/os, for example, to be more nervous and excitable.

REPRODUCTIVE CHOICE

Reproductive choice involves being able to have safe and affordable birthing and parenting options, reliable, safe, and affordable birth control technologies, freedom from forced sterilization, and the availability of abortion. In other words, a key aspect of reproductive rights is the extent to which women can control their reproduction and therefore shape the quality and character of their lives.

Sterilization Practices

Sterilization includes tubal ligation, a surgical procedure where the fallopian tubes are blocked, and hysterectomy, where the uterus is removed. Although hysterectomies are usually performed for medical reasons not associated with a desire for sterilization, this procedure results in sterilization. Countless women freely choose sterilization as a form of permanent birth control, and it is a useful method of family planning for many. "Freely choose," however, assumes a range of options not available to some women. In other words, "freely choose" is difficult in a racist, class-based, and sexist society that does not provide all women with the same options from which to choose. As a result, women on welfare are more likely to be sterilized than women who are not on welfare, and women of color and Third World women are disproportionately more likely to receive this procedure. Although Medicaid pays for sterilization, it does not pay for some other birth control options. Lingering here is the racist and classist idea that certain groups have more right to reproduce than others. Policies providing support for sterilization that make it free or very accessible obviously do not force women to be sterilized. Rather, policies like these make the option attractive at a time when other options are limited.

One of the unfortunate legacies of reproductive history has been that some women have been sterilized against their will, usually articulated as "against their full, informed consent." In the 1970s it was learned that many poor women—especially women of color, and Native American women in particular, as well as women who were mentally retarded or incarcerated—had undergone forced sterilization. Situations varied, but often they included women not giving consent at all, not knowing what was happening, believing they were having a different procedure, being strongly pressured to consent, or being unable to read or understand the options told to them. The latter was especially true for women who did not speak or read English. Forced sterilization is now against the law, although problems still remain.

Parenting Options

In considering reproductive choice, it is important to think about the motivations for having children as well as the motivations for limiting fertility. Most people, women and men, assume they will have children at some point in their lives, and, for some, reproduction and parenting are less of a choice than something that people just do. Although in many nonindustrial and developing societies children can be economic assets, in contemporary U.S. society, for the most part, children consume much more than they produce. Some women do see children as insurance in their old age, but generally today we have children for emotional reasons such as personal and marital fulfillment, and for social reasons like carrying on the family name and fulfilling religious mandates.

Childbirth is an experience that has been shared by millions of women the world over. Women have historically helped other women at this time, strengthening family and kinship bonds and the ties of friendship. As the medical profession gained power and status and developed various technologies (forceps, for example), women's traditional authority associated with birthing became eclipsed by an increasing medicalization of birthing. Again, the medicalization of childbirth regards birthing as an irregular episode that requires medical procedures, often including invasive forms of "treatment." Women who could afford it started going to hospitals to birth their children instead of being attended at home by relatives, friends, or midwives. Unfortunately, in these early days, hospitals were relatively dangerous places where sanitation was questionable and women in childbirth were attended by doctors who knew far less about birthing than did midwives. As the century progressed and birthing in hospitals became routine, women gave birth lying down in the pelvic exam position with their feet in stirrups, sometimes with their arms strapped down; they were given drugs, episiotomies (an incision from the vagina toward the anus to prevent tearing), and were routinely shaved in the pubic area. More recently, thanks to a strong consumer movement, women give birth under more humane conditions. Birthing centers now predominate in most hospitals, and doctors no longer perform the routine procedures and administer the drugs that they used to. Nonetheless, a large number of pregnant women do not receive any health care at all, and a larger number still receive inadequate health care. Women of color are especially underserved.

Why might women want to control their fertility? The first and obvious answer concerns health. Over a woman's reproductive life, she could potentially birth many children and be in a constant state of pregnancy and lactation. Such a regimen compromises maximum health. Second, birthing unlimited numbers of children might be seen as irresponsible in the context of a society and an earth with finite resources. Third, birthing is expensive and the raising of children even more expensive. Fourth, given that in contemporary Western societies women have primary responsibility for childcare and that the organization of mothering tends to isolate women in their homes, it is important to consider the emotional effects of constant child rearing. And, finally, if women had unlimited children, the constant care taking of these children would preempt women's ability to be involved in other productive work outside the home. This "work lost" concept involves the loss or limitation of financial autonomy, work-related or professional identity, and creative and ego development.

Although today women are as likely to have children as they ever were, three facts stand out. First, the average family size decreased as the twentieth century progressed. Second, women are having children later in life than they did in earlier times in our society. Both of these trends are related to changes in health care technologies that have raised health care standards and encouraged parenting at later ages, the availability of birth control and abortion, and the increase in women's education and participation in paid labor with subsequent postponement of marriage and child rearing. Third, there has been a large increase in the number of children born to single women, especially among non-White populations. This can be attributed to lack of knowledge about reproduction and contraception in the context of an increasingly sexually active population, poverty and lack of opportunities for work and employment, failure of family and school systems to keep young people in school, and increased use of alcohol and other drugs. Some girls see motherhood as a right of passage into adulthood, as a way to escape their families of origin, or as a way to connect with another human being who will love them unconditionally. The rise in the number of babies born to single women also reflects changing norms, at least among middle-class populations, that it is okay to raise a child alone rather than "having to get married."

Birth control technologies have been around for a long time. Many preindustrial societies used suppositories coated in various substances that blocked the cervix or functioned as spermicides; the condom was used originally to prevent the spread of syphilis, although it was discovered that it functioned as a contraceptive; and the concept of the intrauterine device was first used by bedouins who hoped to prevent camels from conceiving during long treks across the desert by inserting small pebbles into the uterus. Nineteenth-century couples in the United States used "coitus interruptus" (withdrawal before ejaculation), the rhythm method (sexual intercourse only during nonfertile times), condoms, and abstinence. Although technologies of one kind or another have been around for generations, the issue for women has been the control of and access to these technologies. Patriarchal societies have long understood that to control women's lives it is necessary to control women's reproductive options. In this way, information about, access to, and denial of birth control technologies are central aspects of women's role and status in society.

In the 1880s, the Comstock Law (statutes supposed to control pornography) limited contraception because these technologies were considered obscene. At the same time, however, women realized that the denial of contraception kept them in the domestic sphere, and, more importantly, exposed them to repetitive and often dangerous pregnancies. In response, a social movement emerged that was organized around reproductive choice. Called "voluntary motherhood," this movement not only involved giving women access to birth control, it also worked to facilitate reproduction and parenting under the most safe, humane, and dignified conditions. Margaret Sanger was a leader of this movement and writes about her decision to become involved in "My Fight for Birth Control."

One unfortunate aspect, however, was the early birth control movement's affiliation with an emerging eugenics movement. Following Charles Darwin's theory of the survival of the fittest, *eugenics* argued that only the "fit" should be encouraged to reproduce and that birth control was necessary to prevent the "unfit" from unlimited reproduction. The "unfit" included poor and immigrant populations, the "feeble-minded," and criminals. Using a rationale grounded in eugenics, birth control proponents were able to argue their case while receiving the support of those in power in society. Nonetheless, although contraceptive availability varied from state to state, it was not until a Supreme Court decision (*Griswold v. Connecticut*) in the mid-1960s that married couples were allowed rights to birth control. The Court's ruling said that the prohibition of contraceptive use by married people was unconstitutional in that it violated the constitutional

Activist Profile: Margaret Sanger

Margaret Sanger completed her nursing training in 1900 at the age of 21. Following her marriage and the birth of three children, Sanger returned to work as a visiting nurse in some of the worst slums in New York City. A great deal of her work involved assisting poor women in giving birth, and she began to see the impact of bearing too many children on the health and welfare of these women. She also saw the suffering and near fatality of many women who obtained unsafe, illegal abortions to avoid having even more children. Often these women would beg Sanger to tell them how to prevent pregnancy, but by law Sanger was forbidden to share this knowledge with them. When at last a young woman who had pleaded with Sanger for this information died from giving birth to yet another baby, Sanger decided to take action.

Convinced that women had a right to know how to prevent pregnancy and that the improvement of women's lives depended on family planning, Sanger began to educate herself about birth control. Armed with her newfound information, Sanger began her real life's work. Her plan was to educate the public about birth control, form a birth control organization to help raise awareness and money, seek to overturn the Comstock Law, which prevented sending birth control information through the U.S. mail, and lobby Congress to allow doctors to prescribe birth control devices, which were illegal even for married couples.

In 1914, Sanger started the *Woman Rebel,* a magazine encouraging women to think for themselves and promoting family planning. Under the Comstock Law, the magazine was banned by the U.S. Postal Service, and Sanger was charged with nine counts of obscenity. She fled to England for two years until the charges were dropped. Upon her return to New York, she founded the National Birth Control League, which later became Planned Parenthood. In 1916, she opened a birth control clinic in a poor section of Brooklyn. After only nine days in operation, the clinic was raided and shut down. Sanger was sentenced to thirty days in a workhouse. Upon her release, Sanger reopened the clinic out of her home.

In 1921, Sanger moved her battle to the national level and started *The Birth Control Review.* During the first five years of its publication, she received more than a million letters from women detailing the horrors of poverty and unwanted pregnancy. In 1928, Sanger organized 500 of the letters into a book, *Mothers in Bondage,* which became highly influential in the fight for birth control. Throughout the 1930s Sanger continued her fight, speaking and lobbying. At last, the Supreme Court overturned the Comstock Law in 1936, and the American Medical Association (AMA) reversed its position, giving doctors the right to distribute birth control devices. After her victory, Sanger persisted in her work for affordable and effective contraceptives. Her tireless efforts to secure research funding at last led to the development of the most significant contraceptive of the century—the birth control pill. Only a few months before Sanger died in 1966, the U.S. Supreme Court, in *Griswold v. Connecticut,* made birth control legal for married couples.

right to privacy. This right was extended to single people in 1972 and to minors in 1977.

Today there are a variety of contraceptive methods available. Their accessibility is limited by the availability of information about them, by cost, and by health care providers' sponsorship. As you read about these technologies, consider the following questions: Whose body is being affected? Who gets to deal with the side effects? Who is paying for these methods? Who will pay if these methods fail? Who will be hurt if these side effects become more serious?

Other than tubal ligation where women are surgically sterilized and vasectomy where men are surgically sterilized, birth control methods include, first, the intrauterine device (IUD), a small piece of plastic with copper inside it that is inserted into the uterus. It prevents the implantation of a fertilized egg. One trade name is the ParaGard; the Progestasert is another IUD that contains hormones. IUDs generally last up to ten years, can result in heavier periods, and may increase risk of pelvic inflammatory disease among women with multiple sexual partners. The Dalkon Shield was an IUD that caused infection, infertility, and death among women in the 1970s and was subsequently banned in the United States. (It was then exported for use by women overseas.)

Second, the pill is an oral contraceptive that contains two hormones: progestin and estrogen. It became widely available in the United States in the 1960s and quickly became the most popular means of contraception despite such side effects as nausea, weight gain, breast tenderness, and headaches. The minipill contains no estrogen and a small dose of progestin and has fewer side effects than the regular pill. Third is Norplant, a contraceptive device that lasts five years. Six flexible capsules are inserted beneath the skin on the upper arm where they release progestin to suppress ovulation. It can cause irregular bleeding and the possibility of pain and scarring upon removal. Fourth, depo-provera is an injection of synthetic hormones that suppresses ovulation for eleven to thirteen months. There are similar side effects as the pill, including depression and heavier, more frequent periods. In addition, the effects are not easily reversible, and it may take up to a year before a woman is fertile again. Some groups have questioned the safety of Norplant and depo-provera.

Next are the barrier methods. The diaphragm and cervical cap are barrier methods that are inserted into the vagina before sexual intercourse, fit over the cervix, and prevent sperm entering the uterus. They work in conjunction with spermicidal jelly that is placed along the rim of the device. Some women use them in conjunction with spermicidal foam that is inserted into the vagina with a small plunger. Unlike the other methods, spermicides are available at any drug store. Also available at drug stores are vaginal sponges that are coated with spermicide, inserted into the vagina, and work to block the cervix and absorb sperm. All these barrier methods work best when used in conjunction with a condom and are much less effective when used alone. The male condom is a latex rubber tube that comes rolled up and is unrolled on the penis. The female condom is a floppy polyurethane tube with an inner ring at the closed end that fits over the cervix and an outer ring at the open end that hangs outside the vagina. Condoms block sperm from entering the vagina and, when used properly in conjunction with other barrier methods, are highly effective in preventing pregnancy. Another very important aspect of

Sexually Transmitted Diseases

Every year more than 12 million cases of sexually transmitted diseases (STDs) are reported in the United States. These infections result in billions of dollars in preventable health care spending. In addition, the health impact of STDs is particularly severe for women. Because the infections often cause few or no symptoms and may go untreated, women are at risk for complications from STDs, including ectopic (tubal) pregnancy, infertility, chronic pelvic pain, and poor pregnancy outcomes.

CHLAMYDIA

Chlamydia is the most common bacterial sexually transmitted disease in the United States. It causes an estimated 4 million infections annually, primarily among adolescents and young adults. In women, untreated infections can progress to involve the upper reproductive tract and may result in serious complications. About 75 percent of women infected with chlamydia have few or no symptoms, and without testing and treatment the infection may persist for as long as fifteen months. Without treatment, 20–40 percent of women with chlamydia may develop pelvic inflammatory disease (PID). An estimated one in ten adolescent girls and one in twenty women of reproductive age are infected.

PELVIC INFLAMMATORY DISEASE

PID refers to upper reproductive tract infection in women, which often develops when STDs go untreated or are inadequately treated. Each year, PID and its complications affect more than 750,000 women. PID can cause chronic pelvic pain or harm to the reproductive organs. Permanent damage to the fallopian tubes can result from a single episode of PID and is even more common after a second or third episode. Damage to the fallopian tubes is the only preventable cause of infertility. As much as 30 percent of infertility in women may be related to preventable complications of past STDs.

One potentially fatal complication of PID is ectopic pregnancy, an abnormal condition that occurs when a fertilized egg implants in a location other than the uterus, often in a fallopian tube. It is estimated that ectopic pregnancy has increased about fivefold over a twenty-year period. Among African American women, ectopic pregnancy is the leading cause of pregnancy-related deaths. The economic cost of PID and its complications are estimated at $4 billion annually.

GONORRHEA

Gonorrhea is a common bacterial STD that can be treated with antibiotics. Although gonorrhea rates among adults have declined, rates among adolescents have risen or remained unchanged. Adolescent females aged 15–19 have the highest rates of gonorrhea. An estimated 50 percent of women with gonorrhea have no symptoms. Without early screening and treatment, 10–40 percent of women with gonorrhea will develop PID.

HUMAN IMMUNODEFICIENCY VIRUS

Human immunodeficiency virus (HIV) is the virus that causes AIDS. The risk of a woman acquiring or transmitting HIV is increased by the presence of other STDs. In particular, the presence of genital ulcers, such as those produced by syphilis and herpes, or the presence of an inflammatory STD, such as chlamydia or gonorrhea, may make HIV transmission easier.

HERPES SIMPLEX VIRUS (HSV)

Genital herpes is a disease caused by herpes simplex virus (HSV). The disease may recur periodically and has no cure. Scientists have estimated that about 30 million persons in the United States may have genital HSV infection. Most infected persons never recognize the symptoms of genital herpes; some will have symptoms shortly after infection and never again. A minority of those infected will have recurrent episodes of genital sores. Many cases of genital herpes are acquired from people who do not know they are infected or who had no symptoms at the time of the sexual contact. Acyclovir is a drug that can help to control the symptoms of HSV, but it is not a cure. HSV is frequently more severe in people with weakened immune systems, including people with HIV infection.

HUMAN PAPILLOMAVIRUS (HPV)

HPV is a virus that sometimes causes genital warts but in many cases infects people without causing noticeable symptoms. Concern about HPV has increased in recent years after several studies showed that HPV infection is associated with the development of cervical cancer. Approximately twenty-five types of HPV can infect the genital area. These types are divided into high-risk and low-risk groups based on whether they are associated with cancer. Infection with a high-risk type of HPV is one risk factor for cervical cancer, which causes 4,500 deaths among women each year. No cure for HPV infection exists.

SYPHILIS

Syphilis is a bacterial infection that can be cured with antibiotics. Syphilis cases increased dramatically from 1985 to 1990 among women of all ages. Data from 1993 show that female adolescents were twice as likely to have syphilis as male adolescents. African American women have syphilis rates that are seven times greater than the female population as a whole.

More than 3,000 cases of congenital syphilis were reported in 1993. Such infections among infants are largely preventable if women receive appropriate diagnosis and treatment during prenatal care. Death of the fetus or newborn infant occurs in up to 40 percent of pregnant women who have untreated syphilis.

CONDOM EFFECTIVENESS AND RELIABILITY

When used consistently and correctly, latex condoms are very effective in preventing a variety of STDs, including HIV infection. Multiple studies have demonstrated a strong protective effect of condom use. Because condoms are regulated as medical devices, they are subject to random testing by the Food and Drug Administration. Every latex condom manufactured in the United States is tested electronically for holes before packaging. Condom breakage rates are low in the United States — no higher than two per 100 condoms used. Most cases of condom failure result from incorrect or inconsistent use.

For further information, contact the Office of Women's Health, Centers for Disease Control and Prevention, 1600 Clifton Road, MS: D-51, Atlanta, GA 30033; phone: (404) 639-7230.

Source: www.cdc.gov/od/owh/whstd.htm

condoms is that they are the only form of contraception that offers prevention against sexually transmitted diseases (STDs) generally and HIV/AIDS in particular. All health care providers emphasize that individuals not in a mutually monogamous sexual relationship should always use condoms.

Abortion

Although induced abortion, the removal of the fertilized ovum or fetus from the uterus, is only one aspect of reproductive choice, it has dominated discussion of this topic. This is unfortunate because there is more to reproductive rights than abortion. Nonetheless, this is one topic that generates unease and often heated discussion. *Pro-choice* advocates believe abortion is women's choice, women should not be forced to have children against their will, a fertilized ovum should not have all the legal and moral rights of personhood, and all children should be wanted children. Some pro-choice advocates believe in a woman's right to have an abortion even though they might not make that decision for themselves. *Pro-life* advocates believe that human personhood begins at conception and a fertilized ovum or fetus has the right to full moral and legal rights of personhood. These rights about the sanctity of human life outweigh the rights of mothers. Some pro-life advocates see abortion as murder and doctors and other health care workers who assist in providing abortion services as accomplices to a crime.

Although there are exceptions, most people who consider themselves feminists are pro-choice. There are several issues raised by this perspective. The first issue is the moral responsibilities associated with requiring the birth of unwanted children, because the forces attempting to deny women safe and legal abortions are the very same ones that call for reductions in the social, medical, educational, and economic support of poor children. Does "pro-life" include being "for life" of these children once they are born? The second issue raised includes the moral responsibilities involved in requiring women to be mothers against their will. If you do grant full personhood rights to a fertilized ovum or fetus, then at what point do these rights take priority over the rights of another fully established full person, the mother? What of fathers' rights? Third, several studies have shown that between two-thirds and three-quarters of all women accessing abortions would have an illegal abortion if abortion were illegal. Illegal abortions have high mortality rates; issues do not go away just by making them illegal.

A 1996 poll reported over 50 percent of registered voters as "pro-choice" (defined as in favor of women's choice to access abortion services) and 36 percent as "pro-life" (defined as against abortion), with the rest uncertain. Here are some other statistics: Approximately 1.5 million abortions take place in the United States annually, with about 15,000 of these occurring after rape or incest. More than 50 percent of pregnancies among U.S. women are unintended, and about half of these pregnancies are terminated by abortion. At current rates, about 43 percent of women will have an abortion by the time they are 45 years old. Among women obtaining abortions, about half of these are younger than 25 years, and women aged 20 to 24 years obtain about a third of all abortions. African American and Latina women have higher rates of abortion than White women. Approximately

Learning Activity: Walk in Her Shoes

Go to the California Abortion Rights Action League (CARAL) homepage at *www.choice.org* and follow the links to "Walk in the Shoes" of a woman deciding about having an abortion in the time before choice was legal. Explore the barriers women faced in seeking an abortion before *Roe v. Wade*. Now go to the homepage of the International Planned Parenthood Federation (IPPF) at *www.ippf.org*. Follow the links to resources and then country profiles. Click on a country to find out the status of women's reproductive rights in that nation. Return to the IPPF homepage and follow the links to resources and then the IPPF Charter on Sexual and Reproductive Rights to learn what basic rights IPPF is demanding for women.

Facts About Abortion, Choice, and Women's Health

- Between 1973, when abortion was made legal in the United States, and 1990, the number of deaths per 100,000 legal abortion procedures declined tenfold. By 1990, the risk of death from legal abortion had declined to 0.3 deaths per 100,000. (This rate is half the risk of a tonsillectomy and one-hundredth the risk of an appendectomy.)
- The mortality rate associated with childbirth is ten times higher than for legal abortion.
- Worldwide, 125,000 to 200,000 women die each year from complications related to unsafe and illegal abortions.
- In 84 percent of the counties in the United States, no physicians are willing or able to provide abortions.
- Only 12 percent of ob-gyn residency programs in the United States offer routine training in abortion procedures.
- Eighty-eight percent of abortions are performed before the end of the first trimester of pregnancy.
- Sixty-four percent of states prohibit most government funding for abortion, making access to the procedure impossible for many poor women.
- Thirty-eight states have enacted parental consent or notice requirements for minors seeking abortions.
- Abortion has no overall effect on the risk of breast cancer.
- Abortion does not increase the risk of complications during future pregnancies or deliveries.
- Emergency contraceptives reduce a woman's chance of becoming pregnant by 75 percent when taken within 72 hours of unprotected sex with a second dose 12 hours after the first.
- Emergency contraceptives do not cause abortions; they inhibit ovulation, fertilization, or implantation before a pregnancy occurs.
- Use of emergency contraceptives could reduce the number of unintended pregnancies and abortions by half annually.
- Eighty-nine percent of women aged 18 to 44 have not heard of or do not know the key facts critical to the use of emergency contraceptives.

Sources: NARAL Publications: *www.naral.org*; Reproductive Health and Rights Center: *www.choice.org*.

two-thirds of all abortions are obtained by never-married women, and the same number (although not necessarily the same women), intend to have children in the future.

In the United States abortion was not limited by law or even opposed by the church until the nineteenth century. Generally, abortion was allowed before "quickening," understood as that time when the fetus's movements could be felt by the mother (usually between 3 and 4 months). In the 1820s, however, laws in New England declared abortion of an unquickened fetus a misdemeanor and a quickened fetus, second-degree manslaughter. As the century progressed, more restrictive laws were passed in various states, and in 1860 the Catholic Church officially ruled against abortion. Nonetheless, abortion rates continued. By the early twentieth century, abortion of any kind was illegal in the United States. In "Caught in the Crossfire," Cynthia Gorney describes the experiences of a group of people who provided illegal abortion services in the late 1960s.

The major abortion decision came in January 1973 with the Supreme Court ruling of *Roe v. Wade*. Although some states such as California and New York had reformed their abortion laws before this time, the Supreme Court ruling overturned all states' bans on abortion. The ruling used the *Griswold v. Connecticut* decision in arguing that abortion must be considered part of privacy rights in deciding whether to have children. It did not, however, attempt to decide the religious or philosophical decisions about when life begins. The Court did agree that, under the law, a fetus is not treated as a legal person with civil rights. The ruling went on to divide pregnancy into three equal stages or trimesters, and explained the differential interventions that the state could make during these different periods. During the first trimester, women have the right to an abortion upon demand and the state cannot interfere. During the second trimester, the state is allowed to regulate abortion in order to preserve maternal health and well-being, and in the third trimester, similarly, the state has full right to regulate abortion as well as ban it completely, unless the life of the mother is in jeopardy.

Although there has been a general chipping away of women's rights to abortion since *Roe v. Wade*, there has been no ruling that says life begins at conception and therefore no complete overturning of *Roe v. Wade*. In terms of the various nibblings at this legislation, they include, first the Hyde Amendment, sponsored by Henry Hyde, a Republican senator from Illinois. It was an amendment to the 1977 Health, Education, and Welfare Appropriations Act and gave states the right to prohibit the use of Medicaid funds for abortion, thus limiting abortion to those women who could afford to pay. Note that this was accompanied by Supreme Court rulings (*Beal v. Doe*, 1977) that said that states could refuse to use Medicaid funds to pay for abortions and that Congress could forbid states to use federal funds (including Medicaid) to pay for abortion services (*Harris v. McRae*, 1980). The latter ruling also allowed states to deny funds even for medically necessary abortions.

Second, the 1989 *Webster v. Reproductive Health Services*, sponsored by Missouri State Attorney William Webster, upheld a state's right to prevent public facilities or public employees from assisting with abortions, to prevent counseling concerning abortion if public funds were involved, and to allow parental notification rights. Third, *Planned Parenthood v. Casey*, although upholding *Roe v. Wade* in 1992,

Ideas for Activism: Ten Things You Can Do to Protect Choice

1. *Volunteer for a pro-choice organization.* Pro-choice organizations need volunteers. There are dozens of organizations working in various ways to help women get the services they need. For pro-choice organizations nationwide, check *www.choice.org.*
2. *Write a letter to a local clinic or abortion provider thanking them for putting themselves on the line for women.* Doctors and clinic workers hear vociferously from those opposed to abortion. Hearing a few words of thanks goes a long way.
3. *Monitor your local paper for articles about abortion.* Write a letter to the editor thanking them for accurate coverage or correcting them if coverage is biased.
4. *Find out how your elected representatives have voted on abortion.* Call and ask for their voting records, not just on bills relating to legality of abortion, but also on related issues such as funding for poor women, restrictions meant to impede a woman's access to services (such as waiting periods and informed consent), and contraceptives funding and/or insurance coverage. Whether or not you agree with the votes of your elected officials, write and let them know that this is an issue on which you make voting decisions. Anti-choice activists don't hesitate to do this; you should do it too.
5. *Talk to your children now about abortion. Explain why you believe it's a decision only a woman can make for herself.*
6. *If you have had an abortion, legal or illegal, consider discussing it with people in your life.* Over 40 percent of American women will have at least one abortion sometime during their lives. More openness about the subject might lead to less judgment, more understanding, and fewer attempts to make it illegal.
7. *Volunteer for a candidate whom you know to be pro-choice.*
8. *Be an escort at a clinic that provides abortions.*
9. *Vote!*
10. *Hold a house meeting to discuss choice with your friends.* You could show one or all of Dorothy Fadiman's excellent documentaries from the trilogy, *From the Back Alleys to the Supreme Court and Beyond. When Abortion Was Illegal* is a good conversation starter. For information on obtaining these videos, contact the CARAL Pro-Choice Education Fund or *Concentric Media.*

Source: *www.choice.org*

also upheld the state's right to restrict abortion in various ways: parental notification, mandatory counseling and waiting periods, and limitations on public spending for abortion services. As Rachel Roth notes in "How Women Pay for Fetal Rights," the more rights given a fetus, the more rights are stripped from women.

The situation at the turn of the century is that abortion is legal at the same time that its availability and accessibility has been limited. One piece of legislation, however, was passed in 1994 to safeguard women's right to access their legal rights. After the public outcry associated with the public harassment, wounding, and death of abortion services providers, and the vandalism and bombing of various clinics, the Supreme Court ruled in *Madsen et al. v. Women's Health Center, Inc.* to allow a buffer zone around clinics to allow patients and employees access and to control noise around the premises. The same year the Freedom of Access to Clinic Entrances (FACE) Act made it a federal crime to block access, harass, or incite violence in the context of abortion services.

How Far We've Come

Harvard Women's Health Watch

With the new millennium only weeks away, authorities in every field of science are marveling at the accomplishments in their fields over the last 1,000 years. When it comes to women's health, it isn't necessary to look back to 1000 to see how dramatically things have changed. The idea of providing medical care that is based on the assumption that women are different from men isn't much older than this decade.

In 1990, women were largely irrelevant to medical training. When the subject wasn't pregnancy, childbirth, or diseases of the reproductive organs, everything medical students learned was based on the male anatomy. Little wonder that doctors trained this way often miss heart disease and other disorders in women, whose symptoms are different from men's— and routinely dismiss as trivial premenstrual syndrome and conditions more prevalent in women, such as chronic fatigue syndrome.

Not only were women being ignored in medical training, but they were also excluded from clinical trials to test new drugs, including early trials of female hormones. Being banned from studies was said to be in premenopausal women's best interests. The birth defects that arose from thalidomide used by pregnant women in the 1960s were often cited as an example of the harm that could come from experimental treatments. Women were also deemed unreliable subjects because hormonal fluctuations might skew study results. When postmenopausal women participated in studies, their results were usually lumped together with those in men so it was impossible to determine whether men and women had different reactions to a particular procedure or drug.

Those days are over. One needs only to turn on the TV to see that women's health is now one of the most talked about subjects of our time. Newscasts bring the latest developments in breast-cancer treatments; magazine programs showcase infertility, PMS, and menopause; a commercial for a cholesterol-lowering drug depicts a woman at risk for heart disease; and announcements for screening opportunities, medical studies, and prevention programs abound. Middle-aged women, once deemed demographically undesirable, are aggressively sought by health plans, medical centers, and drug companies.

A BRIEF HISTORY OF WOMEN'S HEALTH

This turn-about was no overnight phenomenon; it had been in the making for more than 30 years. The availability of oral contraceptives in the 1960s and legalized abortion in the 1970s had given women a new sense of control over their reproductive lives. The 1973 publication of *Our Bodies, Ourselves* had demystified their physiology. The traditional, paternalistic model of medical care was overturned as women demanded partnerships in which they shared information and decision-making with their doctors.

Yet, at the same time, doctors who wanted to better serve their female patients found themselves without answers to many of their patients' questions. There just wasn't much data on women. In 1989, a coalition of female scientists and health professionals decided to go after the data. They founded the Society for the Advancement of Women's Health Research with the principal goal of effecting the changes that would deliver the information doctors needed and headed for Congress.

The activists were instrumental in initiating a 1990 General Accounting Office investigation, which verified that women had been overlooked with regard to health research. As a result, the Office of Research on Women's Health was established within the National Institutes of Health. The office launched the Women's Health Initiative, a study of 150,000 postmenopausal women—the largest to date. The Food and Drug Administration followed suit, abolishing a long-held policy that excluded fertile women from clinical trials and directing gender-specific investigations of subsequent study results.

By the mid-1990s the floodgates had opened.

By the end of the decade there were several major research efforts in the works, each with a government-issue acronym—PEPI, SWAN, HERS, WELL-HART, STAR, RUTH. All represent NIH-funded studies of measures to reduce health risks in older women. The fields of research that follow have been the beneficiaries.

MENOPAUSE

Silent no more, this passage is one of the most loudly heralded events of a woman's lifetime. The World Health Organization weighed in on menopause and has proclaimed that it is actually a construct—the point at which a year has passed since our last menstrual period. It's a marker between perimenopause—the stage when estrogen and progesterone levels fluctuate wildly and then drop—and postmenopause—when the ovaries have pretty much stopped producing either hormone.

As a result, perimenopause is not considered a transition that for some women is characterized by a host of symptoms, including hot flashes and insomnia. Postmenopause—the open-ended era that begins after menopause—is now known as the time when women become vulnerable to heart disease, osteoporosis, breast cancer, and other conditions. Drug companies, supplement manufacturers, and noncommercial interests are bending over backwards to provide new approaches to symptom relief and risk reduction.

The question for most women is: "Which among the burgeoning field of methods for relieving symptoms and reducing risk is best—or best for *me?*" It's a question fit for a multiple-choice test—with a long list of potential answers. The list would certainly begin with estrogen, in all its myriad forms and doses. While it reduces the risk of osteoporosis and lowers some of the risk factors for cardiovascular disease, it increases the risk of endometrial and breast cancers. Include a natural or synthetic progesterone, and the excess uterine cancer risk disappears, but the trade-off can be side effects that resemble PMS.

The dietary approach—relying on generous helpings of phytoestrogens from soy, flax, and herbs—would have a prominent place among potential answers. It may alleviate symptoms, but there are few data on its preventive effects.

Evista (raloxifene), a selective estrogen receptor modulator, or SERM, is one of the newest additions to the list. Like other SERMs being evaluated, Evista performs as an estrogen-mimic in some tissues and as an estrogen-block in others. It reduces fractures, lowers serum LDL (bad) cholesterol levels, and, according to early reports, may cut the risk of breast cancer.

Farther down on the list are other hormones under evaluation as supplements. These include testosterone, dehydroepiandrosterone (DHEA), human growth hormone, and melatonin.

The list terminates, of course, with "none of the above." Many still believe that if our grandmothers made it through this transition unaided, we can too.

The introduction of so many new approaches during the last decade has made postmenopause management a moving target. If your aim is to decide on an approach, the good news is that the Nurses' Health Study and others have indicated that the first five years of estrogen use are, in essence, a free trial period. You can take it to see how you like it without incurring an increased risk of breast cancer. You can see if it makes enough difference in your bone density to protect you from osteoporosis and whether it improves your cholesterol enough to protect you from heart disease. Meanwhile, you can await newer and potentially safer options.

Advances

- *An information explosion.* The last decade has seen the publication of hundreds of books, countless articles in periodicals and on the Internet, and immense coverage in scientific journals on research relating to menopause.
- *New interest in the psychosocial aspects of menopause.* Interest has grown exponentially. The government, nonprofit foundations, and pharmaceutical companies are sponsoring scores of new studies on midlife women. Among the most innovative is the Study of Women Across the Nation (SWAN), which is chronicling the midlife medical and social experiences of women in several ethnic groups.
- *New options for hormone replacement therapy.* These include natural progesterone in oral form (Prometrium), patch (CombiPatch), and vaginal gel (Crinone). New formulations and doses of estrogen continue to appear. Among the latest entrants are a vaginal ring (Estring) and conjugated estrogens from plants (Cenestin).

HEART DISEASE

Heart disease, the number one cause of death in women, is a paradigm of gender differences in health.

Epidemiologic studies have shown women do not develop heart disease until 10 years after their male counterparts do. Nonetheless, when women are stricken, they are more likely to die, and survivors are more likely to have another heart attack or go on to have a stroke than are men.

This outcome gap reflects a treatment gulf. Because women's symptoms aren't as likely to

be recognized, women may not be diagnosed as rapidly or treated as aggressively as men. Chest pain is less likely to signal coronary-artery disease in women, probably because women are more likely to have other conditions that can produce similar sensations, such as mitral-valve prolapse, vessel spasms, costochondritis (an inflamation of the ribs), or pleurisy. Women are more likely to experience nausea and vomiting, which are often interpreted as the flu, food poisoning, or indigestion. When heart disease is suspected, traditional nuclear imaging tests, such as gallium scintigraphy, are less informative in women because breast tissue can obstruct the signal from the radioactive agent.

Moreover, the track record for therapeutic procedures, such as angioplasty and bypass surgery, is worse in women than in men. Recent research indicates, however, that age, extent of disease, and physical condition—rather than gender—account for the difference. Women tend to be older and in poorer health than men when they undergo such procedures. When other factors are equal, women tend to fare as well as men do.

Because heart attacks tend to occur a decade later in women than in men, researchers assumed that the protective effect of estrogen was responsible. Observational studies added credence to that theory, but clinical trials have been less supportive. The Postmenopausal Estrogen/Progestin Intervention (PEPI) trial suggested that estrogen lessened many risk factors for heart disease, yet the Heart Attack and Estrogen Replacement Study (HERS) failed to show estrogen use protected against heart attacks in women with existing heart disease. The Women's Health Initiative, among other studies currently in progress, is expected to provide more definitive answers.

Advances

- *New studies.* The Women's Health Initiative and several other research projects will provide more information on the factors that increase a woman's risk of heart disease.

- *Better understanding.* In the last decade, researchers better defined the role of HDL cholesterol and suggested that women need higher levels of the good cholesterol for protection against heart disease. Research has also indicated that other blood markers, like serum triglycerides and homocysteine, may play more meaningful roles in defining women's heart disease risk.
- *Treatment.* Cholesterol-lowering drugs, such as Mevacor (lovastatin), are now suggested for women at a much earlier stage than previously and are being suggested as an alternative to estrogen for postmenopausal women at risk.

BREAST CANCER

We hear so much about the growing epidemic of breast cancer that the good news is often lost. In fact, the likelihood that a woman will die of breast cancer is decreasing steadily. For example, about a quarter of tumors are now spotted while they're still precancerous, that is, they haven't broken out of the mammary ducts or lobules. Ninety-five percent of women who undergo lumpectomy and radiation for these cancers are still alive five years later. This treatment, while still no picnic, is much more palatable than it once was. Biopsies employing stereotactic and ultrasound-guided techniques (in which a needle removes the required sample) produce less damage and scarring. Women who have small tumors can opt for lumpectomy and radiation rather than mastectomies. Those who choose to undergo mastectomy can now have reconstructive surgery at the same time. Sentinel-node biopsy and more precise surgical lymph-node sampling have emerged as promising new approaches that can improve the detection rate for metastases and reduce lymphedema in the affected arm.

Chemotherapy is easier to stomach thanks to new anti-nausea drugs. Women who have recurrences or metastatic disease also have more options for treatment. Herceptin—which employs an antibody that homes in on breast cancer cells—and Taxol have boosted survival rates in women with more advanced disease.

The treatment experience has also changed in other ways. In the past, it was routine to send patients from one medical facility to another to receive radiation, chemotherapy, and other tests. Comprehensive breast centers are springing up around the country. They provide all necessary forms of therapy and other services, such as support groups and nutritional counseling, under one roof.

Perhaps most importantly, breast cancer has come out of the closet; it is no longer kept a secret. Breast-cancer activist groups, such as the National Alliance of Breast Cancer Organizations, Y-Me, and the National Breast Cancer Coalition, have made the disease one that women can talk openly about and thus receive support. There is a much more active involvement of patients in decision-making and more emphasis on nutrition, exercise, and other lifestyle factors for women undergoing treatment.

However, the greatest advances in the last decade have come not in treatment, but in prevention. The introduction of tests for the BRCA1 and BRCA2 genes allows physicians to forecast with reasonable accuracy some women's risk of developing breast cancer, but it has also opened a Pandora's box of issues that require genetic counseling. Mathematical modeling has made risk estimation possible for women who aren't interested in genetic testing. Prophylactic mastectomy, albeit a drastic measure, has been demonstrated to reduce the expected rate of breast cancer by at least 90% in high-risk women. The pharmaceutical approach, tamoxifen, reduced the rate of breast cancer 40–50% in high-risk women in clinical trials, and raloxifene showed promise in reducing breast-cancer risk in women who were taking it to prevent osteoporosis. These two drugs will be tested head to head in the federally funded STAR trial, which plans to enroll 23,000 postmenopausal women in centers throughout the country.

Advances

- *Activism.* By bringing breast cancer to the forefront, activist groups have brought more research dollars to bear against the disease, established wide-reaching support networks for patients, and increased the flow of information.
- *Detection.* The Mammography Quality Standardization Act has ensured that all women have access to the same standard of mammography and that they are notified of the results within a week.
- *Treatment.* New surgery spares more tissue, both in the breast and under the arm. New chemotherapy procedures are more effective and have fewer side effects.
- *Prevention.* Drugs such as tamoxifen (and possibly raloxifene) can reduce risk over the short term. Prophylactic mastectomy has proven to be extremely effective for motivated women who are at high-risk.

OSTEOPOROSIS

Osteoporosis—which once went undetected until a fractured hip, forearm, or vertebra uncovered its presence—has been flushed out of hiding. Thanks to the widespread availability of bone density measurement, doctors can now identify women with osteoporosis well ahead of symptoms such as a broken bone. New drugs have allowed women to rebuild porous bone.

Dual-energy x-ray absorptiometry (DXA), the state-of-the-art technology for measuring bone density, is emerging as a reliable tool for pinpointing women who are at risk for osteoporotic bone fractures. The number of DXA machines in the nation has grown from 750 in 1994 to 4,000 today. The use of ultrasound to measure bone density at the heel is also increasing. These devices, which don't involve x-rays, are used in the doctor's office to flag women with very low bone density for further testing.

The availability of options for treatment has also expanded. At the beginning of the decade, the only approved choices were estrogen and calcitonin injections. Since then two new oral drugs—alendronate (Fosamax) and raloxifene (Evista)—and a nasal spray form of calcitonin have come on the market. Numerous studies over the decade have shown how valuable those drugs, taken with calcium and vitamin D, can be to increase or maintain bone density in patients with postmenopausal osteoporosis. Sodium fluoride, parathyroid hormone, and several new SERMs are being studied for approval.

A new treatment for painful vertebral compression fractures, a common consequence of osteoporosis, has been undertaken by interventional radiologists. The procedure, called vertebroplasty, involves injecting a surgical cement into the fractured bone to strengthen it and alleviate pain.

Advances

- *Diagnostics.* The growth of DXA testing and the availability of ultrasound for determining heel fractures has made it possible to identify women with low bone density long before fractures occur.
- *Treatment.* The approval of three new drugs, and several more in the pipeline, increases the options for women who have low bone density.

MENTAL HEALTH

The recognition of depression as one of the greatest health risks to women resulted in a number of new studies not only of major depression, but also of related disorders like dysthymia, premenstrual syndrome (PMS), and seasonal affective disorder (SAD). The National Institute of Mental Health produced a white paper, *Depression in Women,* noting the urgency and recommending increased screening programs and studies.

However, epidemiologic studies have indicated that depression is not as prevalent at certain life stages as once thought. For example, researchers have found no evidence that menopause is associated with an elevated rate of depression, which is a surprise to those who assumed women were prone to depression when their childbearing capacity—their perceived principal source of power in society—ceased.

If there is one factor that characterizes the change in treating depression, it may well be in the widespread use of a new generation of antidepressants, which, although not entirely free of side effects, are generally easier to tolerate than earlier classes were. The selective serotonin reuptake inhibitors (SSRIs) in particular have emerged as a class of drugs that is helpful in treating most of the depressive disorders, although some drugs are more effective than others for certain conditions. The mood-elevating effects of estrogen are also under study. There is some evidence that the hormone can enhance the work of SSRIs.

Treatment for depression is now successful in 80% of patients. Although the new antidepressants have contributed to this statistic, there's evidence that a combined treatment of drugs and psychotherapy provide the fastest relief.

Yet, there is also evidence that biology isn't exclusively responsible for depression in women. Studies have also pointed to the role of life experiences, particularly those of being in an abusive relationship, experiencing poverty, raising children without support, and having a lack of control over one's fate, as contributing to depression in women.

Anxiety disorders, which also affect women in greater numbers than men, became another focus during the 1990s. The recognition of the increasing incidence of eating disorders—anorexia, bulimia, and binge eating—spurred not only research into the causes, but also initiatives designed to prevent, detect, and develop effective treatments beginning in young girls.

Advances

- *New data.* Defining societal factors that increase the risk of depression in women.
- *Initiatives.* Awareness has led to initiatives, such as National Depression Screening Day and eating disorders awareness programs, that help identify these conditions in women.
- *New treatment approaches.* New medications and multidisciplinary approaches to eating disorders and depression have emerged.

READING 41

Gender Role Stressors and Women's Health

Patti Lou Watkins and Diane Whaley

WOMEN'S HEALTH PROBLEMS

Unarguably, significant gender differences exist in the experience of health problems. For instance, morbidity rates of musculoskeletal and connective tissue diseases such as osteoporosis are much greater for women. Women, more often than men, also experience neurologic disorders, including migraine headaches, as well as psychiatric disorders, particularly affective, anxiety, and eating disorders (Litt, 1993). In the keynote address at the Society of Behavioral

Medicine's annual meeting, Chesney (1997) implored those assembled to add domestic violence to the list of women's health problems. The Midcourse Review of the Healthy People 2000 goals (U.S. Department of Health & Human Services [USDHHS], 1995) acknowledged that, "Women are frequent targets of both physical and sexual assault often perpetrated by spouses, intimate partners, or others known to them" (p. 60). Unfortunately, this report also states that homicides, weapons-related violent deaths, and assault injuries have increased since 1990. As such, women account for nearly two thirds of the medical visits and are recipients of most medications prescribed (Hoffman, 1995).

Chronic disease risk factors, such as smoking, have increased dramatically among women in recent years (Litt, 1993). Furthermore, the USDHHS (1995) reported that although the general public has made progress toward smoking cessation goals, the inverse is true for pregnant women and women without a high school education. Obesity rates have also increased since health objectives were established in 1990, especially for women. The Surgeon General's Report on Physical Activity and Health (USDHHS, 1996) implicated women's relative lack of exercise in explanation of this trend. Gender differences in mortality rates are fast disappearing as cardiovascular disease (CVD) is now the leading cause of death among women as well as men. Cancer mortality rates are also roughly equivalent, with women's lung cancer death rate rising rapidly over the past 30 years. Finally, women are developing AIDS at a faster pace than men (Litt, 1993).

Given these patterns, it is little wonder that women consistently perceive themselves as having worse health than men (Verbrugge, 1989). Although women currently live approximately 7 years longer than men, the quality of their lives may be vastly diminished. Verbrugge (1989) contended that gender differences in health status transcend biological predispositions, resulting more from sociocultural forces such as well-documented employment inequities (Amott & Matthaie, 1996). Contributing to the problem, women are also less likely than men to have adequate health insurance coverage (Stanton & Gallant, 1995). Indeed, Anson, Paran, Neumann, and Chernichovsky (1993) found that gender differences in health perceptions disappeared when they controlled for risks embedded in the social construction of gender and gender roles, leading the authors to suggest that women's socialization results in less successful coping with the "inevitable stressors faced in human life" (p. 426). A feminist perspective, however, might argue that the stressors for women are not inevitable. Rather, many are socially constructed, and perpetuated through existing power structures.

In summary, contemporary women are suffering and dying from disorders that the lay public, along with the medical profession itself, have long considered diseases of men—and in the case of AIDS, gay men. Additionally, women experience debilitating, although not imminently life-threatening, medical problems more than men. In conjunction with relatively greater psychological distress, deteriorating health habits, and frequent victimization, women's quality of life may be severely compromised as they negotiate their life spans. The next section explores the influence of gender roles on these problems.

Gender Roles: Interpersonal Communication

Women interact with the health-care system differently than men do, with increased visits and different types of complaints. In turn, the health-care system responds to women and men in a different fashion, often to the detriment of women's health. Studies have shown that medical practitioners treat CVD less aggressively in women relative to men. In fact, across conditions, treatment protocols are based on a male model of medicine, with women's health problems viewed as deviations from a male-defined norm (Hoffman, 1995). Lee and Sasser-Cohen (1996) contended that the medical profession has, in fact, pathologized women's normal biological processes and body structure.

In a recent study, Chiaramonte and Friend (1997) asked medical students to review cases of women and men with either only symptoms of heart disease or heart disease symptoms accompanied by anxiety. When presented with unambiguous cases, students were able to detect heart disease in both genders. However, when presented with cases evidencing both cardiac and anxiety symptoms, they correctly detected heart disease among the male cases, referring them to cardiologists. Conversely, they more often misdiagnosed heart disease among the female cases, referring them instead to psychologists. Advanced medical students were more likely to make this error, suggesting that medical school training serves to increase gender biases in diagnostic and treatment decisions. Russo, Denious, Keita, and Koss (1997) asserted that battered women also escape detection when they are in medical settings. Like women with CVD symptoms, they are likely to receive psychiatric diagnoses along with tranquilizing medication.

Communication of diagnostic information and treatment recommendations by medical practitioners represents another area of concern for the female patient. Smith (1996) saw physicians' failure to interact with patients in a courteous, informative fashion as a breach of ethics, rather than a case of poor "bedside manner." In her view, most medical encounters constitute interviews in which patient-initiated questions are discouraged, thereby establishing the practitioner's position of power. Such interactions prevent patients from taking charge of their health. Smith contrasts this to a model in which practitioners might interact with patients as participants in a shared project, with mutual understanding as the goal. As

such, patients should have the right "to speak, to question, to challenge, and to express themselves" (p. 202). Smith contends that women, particularly women of color and those of lower socioeconomic status (SES), receive less information than male patients. In a survey of Black women who had been physically and sexually abused, Russo et al. (1997) found that lower income participants, indeed, perceived physicians as "patronizing and unhelpful" (p. 340). Although the FGRS construct suggests that women may be less inclined to assert themselves in such situations, Smith notes that practitioners dub women "difficult patients" when they ask questions during the medical interview. A female patient "may be taken as hostile, uncooperative, and confrontative, whereas a male patient might be viewed as rational and actively involved in his own treatment" (p. 194). Roter and Hall (1992) disagreed, noting that in some studies, female patients received relatively more information from practitioners. In fact, women's communication styles may make them "more savvy users of their time with doctors" (p. 44). These authors admit that exploration of gender differences in patient–practitioner communication is a relatively new endeavor, with many questions remaining unanswered at this point.

Indirect support for Smith's (1996) claims, however, may come from studies of individuals who present to medical settings with symptoms of anxiety and depression. A number of researchers (e.g., Agras, 1993) agree that these patients, predominantly women, leave the medical setting with a limited understanding of their complaints. Watkins, Nock, Champion, and Lidren (1996) found that practitioners typically spent less than 5 minutes explaining diagnostic information to individuals with panic disorder (PD). In only a few cases were patients actually provided with an accurate diagnosis. Rather, they received a variety of vague explanations such as "some strange flu" and "hidden problems" (p. 180). One participant remarked, "First few times he suggested it was 'just' stress, then, later, after a few months, he said it was depression, then later, without much concern, he suggested it was anxiety" (p. 184). This broad array of unclear explanations resulted in low levels of patient understanding and satisfaction, perhaps best summarized by one patient's experience of "resentment" toward the practitioner "for not being as sympathetic and respectful of this being a real and true experience for me" (p. 184). Watkins et al. (1996) found that participants rarely received referrals, although most received pharmacological treatment. Compared to cognitive-behavioral therapy (CBT) for PD, medications have a higher relapse rate (Gould, Otto, & Pollack, 1995). This difference may be due to the superior ability of CBT to enhance self-efficacy, the belief that one can successfully manage a situation, in this case panic attacks (PA) and the circumstances that surround them. Finally, the high cost of medications compared to various forms of CBT (Gould et al., 1995) may present a greater problem for women whose economic resources are generally less than those of their male peers.

Roter and Hall (1992) agreed that physicians often substitute medications for effective communication. In terms of gender differences, Travis (1988) observed that physicians prescribe psychotropic medications to women relatively more often and that these prescriptions extend for longer periods of time than those provided for men. She asserts that medicating women without attempting to impart coping skills, or more importantly, to resolve the inequities that women suffer at home and in the workplace, equates to oppression. This practice prompts women to nurture others at the expense of their own health. When physicians prescribe psychotropic medications, they may be abetting dysfunctional, possibly abusive, social arrangements as well as fostering women's self-blame.

Practitioner communication most assuredly warrants further research. Russo et al. (1997) suggested that such work address diversity issues within, as well as across, gender. Their findings also suggest that various presenting complaints may elicit specific types of problem behavior from practitioners. In their study, women who had been sexually abused reported that physicians had acted in sexually inappropriate ways toward them. Concurrent examination of practitioners' gender might enhance understanding of communication problems in the medical setting. Hall, Irish, Roter, Ehrlich, and Miller (1994) conducted a study in which they found female physicians to be more nurturant, expressive, and interpersonally oriented than males. This, along with Gross's (1992) finding that male physicians encounter more interpersonal difficulties with patients, aligns with the concepts of gender role stressors outlined here. Although organized efforts are underway to improve the communication skills of medical practitioners (e.g., Levinson & Roter, 1993), many Americans, especially women, are turning to treatment strategies that minimize practitioner contact. . . .

REFERENCES

Agras, W. S. (1993). The diagnosis and treatment of panic disorder. *Annual Review of Medicine, 4,* 39–51.

Ammott, T., & Matthaie, J. (1996). *Race, gender, and work: A multicultural economic history of women in the United States.* Boston: South End Press.

Anson, O., Paran, E., Neumann, L., & Chernichovsky, D. (1993). Gender differences in health perceptions and their predictors. *Social Science and Medicine, 36,* 419–427.

Chesney, M. A. (1997, March). *Unanswered challenges to behavioral medicine: Broadening the agenda.* Paper presented at the Society of Behavioral Medicine annual meeting, San Francisco.

Chiaramonte, G., & Friend, R. (1997, March). *Do medical schools reinforce gender bias in diagnosing CHD?* Paper presented at the annual meeting of the Society of Behavioral Medicine, San Francisco.

Fausto-Sterling, A. (1993). The five sexes: Why male and female are not enough. *The Sciences, 33,* 20–25.

Gould, R. A., Otto, M. W., & Pollack, M. H. (1995). A meta-analysis of treatment outcome for panic disorder. *Clinical Psychology Review, 15,* 819–844.

Gross, E. B. (1992). Gender differences in physician stress. *Journal of the American Medical Women's Association, 47,* 107–112.

Hall, J. A., Irish, J. T., Roter, D. L., Ehrlich, C. M., & Miller, L. (1994). Gender in medical encounters: An analysis of physician and patient communication in a primary care setting. *Health Psychology, 13,* 384–392.

Hoffman, E. (1995). *Our health, our lives: A revolutionary approach to health care for women.* New York: Simon & Schuster.

Lee, J., & Sasser-Cohen, J. (1996). *Blood stories: Menarche and the politics of the female body in contemporary U. S. society.* New York: Routledge.

Levinson, W., & Roter, D. (1993). The effects of two continuing medical education programs on communication skills of practicing primary care physicians. *Journal of General Internal Medicine, 8,* 318–324.

Litt, I. (1993). Health issues for women in the 1990s. In S. Matteo (Ed.), *American women in the nineties: Today's critical issues* (pp. 139–157). Boston: Northeastern University Press.

Roter, D. L., & Hall, J. A. (1992). *Doctors talking with patients/patients talking with doctors: Improving communication in medical visits.* Westport, CT: Auburn House.

Russo, N. F., Denious, J. E., Keita, G. P., & Koss, M. P. (1997). Intimate violence and Black women's health. *Women's Health: Research on Gender, Behavior, and Policy, 3,* 335–348.

Smith, J. F. (1996). Communicative ethics in medicine: The physician–patient relationship. In S. M. Wolf (Ed.), *Feminism and bioethics: Beyond reproduction* (pp. 184–215). New York: Oxford University Press.

Stanton, A. L., & Gallant, S. J. (1995). Psychology of women's health: Challenges for the future. In A. L. Stanton & S. J. Gallant (Eds.), *The psychology of women's health: Progress and challenges in research and application* (pp. 567–582). Washington, DC: American Psychological Association.

U.S. Department of Health and Human Services (1995). *Healthy people 2000: Midcourse review and 1995 revisions.* Washington, DC: Public Health Service.

U.S. Department of Health and Human Services (1996). *Physical activity and health: A report of the Surgeon General.* Atlanta, GA. USDHHS, Centers for Disease Prevention and Health Promotion.

Verbrugge, L. (1989). The twain meet: Empirical explanations of sex differences in health and mortality. *Journal of Health and Social Behavior, 30,* 282–304.

Watkins, P. L., & Lee, J. (1997). A feminist perspective on panic disorder and agoraphobia: Etiology and treatment. *Journal of Gender, Culture, & Health, 2,* 65–87.

Watkins, P. L., Nock, C., Champion, J., & Lidren, D. M. (1996). Practitioner–patient communication in the presentation of panic symptoms. *Mind/Body Medicine, 4,* 177–189.

READING 42

Forgotten Women
How Minorities Are Underserved by Our Health Care System

Lisa Collier Cool

Imagine living in a place where going to a doctor involves a difficult or even dangerous trek to a distant, overcrowded clinic where you wait hours for a few minutes of questionable medical care—a place where preventive treatment is so lacking that breast tumors sometimes protrude through the skin before they are diagnosed.

You might expect these conditions in a third world country, but actually they're faced every day by minority women in some parts of the U.S. Statistics show that "an African-American woman born in Harlem today has less chance of surviving to age 65 than a woman from Bangladesh, one of the poorest nations on earth," say Colin McCord, M.D., associate director of surgery at Harlem Hospital in New York City.

Although you might think that poverty is to blame, the truth is that even affluent minority women—whether black, Hispanic, Asian-American or Native American—fare poorly in our medical system. "An African-American woman who earns triple what a Euro-American female earns still has a greater chance of mortality from disease like breast cancer," says Faye Gary, Ed.D., distinguished service professor at the College of Nursing of the University of Florida in Gainesville.

What makes this all the more shocking is that even as progress has been made in women's health as a whole, the health disparities between black and white women have remained. Mortality from heart disease and cancer has fallen among white women, yet is unchanged in blacks. At every age, "African-American, Native American, Hispanic and Asian-American women suffer from poorer health and greater risk of premature death," says Dr. Gary.

DEADLY DISCRIMINATION

Socioeconomic factors explain only some of these inequities. While it's true that black women have triple the rate of poverty of white women and are slightly less likely to be insured, research reveals that they're also the victims of subtle but potentially fatal medical bias. A recent study at Boston University found that at every income level, black women over age 64 are only half as likely as whites to have a mammogram ordered for them by a doctor, even if they see a primary-care physician just as often. Mammography rates are even lower for Native American women. The result is that black and Native American women have 30% higher risk of dying of breast cancer, despite the fact that the disease is much less common in these groups than in whites.

The same pattern of prejudice prevails in hospital care: A study at Beth Israel Hospital in Boston found that doctors order 1½ times as much surgery and other high-tech treatment for whites as for equally ill blacks. It's not just costly procedures these patients are short-changed on, either: 20% of Latinas and 65% of Korean Americans have never had a pap smear, yet lab costs start at $16.

Even in the emergency room, your race or ethnicity can have more impact on your care than your condition, says Jane Delgado, Ph.D., president and CEO of the National Coalition of Hispanic Health and Human Services Organizations in Washington. "A study of people treated for a broken leg showed that the single greatest predictor of who got painkillers was whether they were Hispanic," she says. "The doctors often withheld painkillers from Hispanic patients even though Hispanic and non-Hispanic patients rated their pain as equally severe." This reminds Dr. Gary of the segregated care she received growing up in the south in the '50s. "My parents had to drive 100 miles to take me to the only white dentist who would see black people," she recalls. "I remember feeling grateful when he yanked out my teeth at his kitchen table, because I wasn't allowed into his office."

DEEP-ROOTED STEREOTYPES

Not only are minorities' medical needs dangerously neglected, but doctor prejudice can also result in substandard care for those who get treated, says Claudia R. Baquet, M.D., associate dean for policy and planning at University of Maryland School of Medicine in Baltimore. "In focus groups," she says, "minority women say that doctors assume they have multiple partners or start having sex at an early age. Racial and ethnic stereotyping is still rampant and a barrier to quality care."

Minority women are doubly disadvantaged because they may be subjected to sexism in addition to racial bias, notes Aida Giachello, Ph.D., director of the Midwest Latino Health Research, Training and Policy Center at the

University of Illinois in Chicago. Many Latinas report that doctors dismiss their complaints. "The stereotype is that Latinas overuse the health system," says Dr. Giachello. "But when we did a focus group with these women, the reality was that they had to go to the doctors over and over with the same symptoms, because the physicians would say it was stress while the real problem went undiagnosed, sometimes causing serious complications."

Equally damaging are the assumptions physicians may make if they judge a patient's ethnicity based on her skin color or surname. "If a Native American woman from the Southwest has a Latino last name, a doctor may misclassify her and not test for gallbladder disease, which is epidemic in that population," says Dr. Baquet. Others question the medical value of determining ethnicity at all. "Asking someone what race she considers herself to be doesn't tell you what her genetics are," points out Olivia Carter-Pokras, Ph.D., an epidemiologist and public health analyst at the Office of Minority Health in Washington. "Even sickle-cell anemia, thought of as a 'black' disorder, also appears in white people of Mediterranean origin."

RESEARCH BIAS

More serious still is the situation in clinical trials, where scientists develop the medicine of the future by testing new drugs, diagnostic techniques and other treatments. Despite laws mandating the inclusion of women and minorities in trials sponsored by the National Institutes of Health, many doctors don't seem to have gotten the message, reports Dr. Carter-Pokras, who says she constantly sees unconscious or even overt prejudice on the part of researchers. "A doctor may decide to recruit from her own clinic, never stopping to think that since her patients are 80% white, she needs to

be aggressive about finding minority cases," she says. Investigators often try to recruit Spanish speakers with no translators or bilingual materials. Not only do such attitudes reduce minority women's access to state-of-the-art care, but also underrepresentation in studies ensures that the second-class medical care will continue for decades to come.

Increasing the number of women of color participating in medical studies is important, but Dr. Gary feels it doesn't go far enough. "There also needs to be better representation of ethnic groups among the people who do the studies," she says. Despite doctors' best intentions, subtle biases and cultural differences can still interfere with good research.

CONSTRUCTIVE CHANGES

The outrage from women of color is finally starting to be heard on Capitol Hill. To determine how to end these inequities, 740 experts convened in Washington last January for the nation's first minority women's health conference, sponsored by the U.S. Public Health Service's Office on Women's Health. The agency is developing a culturally sensitive women's health curriculum for medical and nursing schools, and it has started programs to recruit more minority women into health careers and as participants in clinical trials.

Other federal agencies are creating their own initiatives. The Centers for Disease Control and Prevention is funding studies of chronic diseases that affect women of color disproportionately. But it's still up to women to help alert doctors to the potential for bias in diagnosis and treatment and to become more attuned to how our racial or ethnic background may affect our health. Each of these efforts shares the same crucial goal: to create a healthier tomorrow for *all* women.

Man-made Threats to Women's Health

Adrienne Germain

The expression "man-made threats" to women's health probably brings to mind environmental and occupational hazards that cause medical problems ranging from cancers to genetic defects. These are certainly important concerns for people everywhere, but the vast majority of the world's women face graver and more insidious dangers of man's making, dangers that lurk in their bedrooms, in the streets and in the corridors of power. What is the source of these perils? The age-old domestic, social and political dominion that men have over the lives—bodies and minds—of women.

A woman's well-being begins at home, yet home is hardly the healthy haven it is thought to be. Men routinely beat women for any number of reasons—for failing to have dinner on the table, for asking to use condoms during sex, or expressing their own opinions—and frequently for no reason at all. In the United States alone, as many as 4 million women each year are seriously battered by their male partners; in more than 20 countries where reliable, large-scale studies have been done, 16 to 52 per cent of women had been assaulted by an intimate partner. The vast majority of women beaten by their men almost never have a forum for redress or a place of refuge, not even the homes of their own parents. In South Asia, for example, women who are beaten by their husbands and seek shelter with their parents are told such violence is a part and parcel of marriage. More often than not, they are ordered to be "obedient" wives and return to their assailants.

Other dangers stemming from the power imbalance between the sexes have just as much potential to injure and kill. Men who refuse to use contraception or who prevent female partners from using it put women at risk for unwanted pregnancies. In too many cases, husbands also prevent their pregnant wives from seeking health care or skilled help to give birth, often with fatal consequences. Worldwide, botched abortions and unsafe childbirth claim the lives of some 600,000 women each year.

When men shirk their sexual responsibility by having sex with multiple partners and by refusing to use condoms, the women in their lives often end up with sexually transmitted diseases, including the human immunodeficiency virus (HIV). A recent study shows that young married women in India are being infected with HIV by their prostitute-visiting husbands at alarming rates. In Uganda, a country with a high prevalence of HIV, women are infected at far younger ages than men because men seek out virgins with whom to have safe sex, although their definition of safe does not mean they use condoms. Outside the home, in the community and the nation, the threat to women comes from man-made norms and social policies. Mass media, increasingly pervasive around the world, reduces women to sex objects and promotes male ownership and even violence against women's bodies.

Sexual harassment degrades and threatens girls and women in school and at work. Almost defying belief, rejected suitors in one country commonly throw acid in the faces of the women they desire so that no other men will want them. In some parts of another region, male "honour" is justification for murdering wives and sisters who commit adultery. Across a great part of the world, male privilege is reflected in the preference for sons in health care, in sex-selective abortion, and even in female infanticide. At least 2 million girls and young women each year are subjected to female genital mutilation to ensure their chastity and marriageability, with serious emotional and health consequences, including death. Trafficking in girls and women now crosses virtually all borders.

Women's relegation to second-class citizens in the name of religion seriously jeopardizes their health. A current—and extreme—example of this is the Taliban's system of medical apartheid in Afghanistan: women patients are to be seen only by female health professionals, of which there are very few, in segregated facilities with nothing like the medical equipment and supplies available for men. Around the world, other proscriptions on women's access to health care—opposition to contraception and safe induced abortion on the one hand; forced pregnancy, forced abortion and forced sterilization on the other—result in untold suffering and countless deaths. Some 12 Latin American countries exonerate rapists if they marry their victims.

The attitudes and beliefs that drive such practices on every continent also express themselves in social policies. In general, these man-made measures don't make women's health a priority; sometimes, it seems, their aim is quite the reverse. For one particular example, one need look no farther than the United States Congress. In recent months, a single American Congressman—one who relentlessly opposes a woman's right to protect her health and control her reproduction—has held hostage payment of United States dues to the United Nations and contributions to the International Monetary Fund in order to deny women access to safe, legal abortions and related information and services.

Bleak as it might appear, this picture is not one of utter darkness, and each day brings new hope. By organizing at the grassroots level, women all over the globe are now playing an increasingly vocal, visible and vital role in helping to shape the policies and programmes that determine their well-being. Significantly, these women are joined every day by more and more men who have begun to realize that they and their communities will benefit. Governments, too, are coming around: in Vienna in 1993, in Cairo in 1994, and in Beijing in 1995, the nations of the world committed themselves to action to promote the sexual and reproductive health of women. Major United Nations agencies and programmes have pledged to assist Governments to meet these commitments. While these are surely important steps, lasting improvements in women's well-being will come only when many more men change their ways—starting with how they behave at home.

READING 44

Breast Cancer
Is It the Environment?

Ms.

"For too long now breast cancer research has been dominated by the elusive search for the cure," says Andrea Martin, founder and executive director of the Breast Cancer Fund, a San Francisco–based group that has launched a major campaign to draw attention to the links between the environment and breast cancer. Citing the fact that only 5 to 10 percent of breast cancer cases are genetically caused and that the number of women with breast cancer nearly doubled between 1970 and 1990, the fund has teamed up with the Susan G. Komen Breast

Cancer Foundation to urge the public to agitate for more research into environmental causes of the disease. Last October the two groups rallied 70 individuals and organizations (including local breast cancer groups, the Coalition of Labor Union Women, and the YWCA) to sign a letter to President Clinton. The letter called for increased funding for research examining environmental links; monitoring by the Centers for Disease Control (CDC) of what chemicals are in our bodies and in what amounts; full funding for the Environmental Protection Agency's (EPA) program to screen for environmental toxins; and a cross-agency committee to oversee government funding for environmental health research.

The following is excerpted from the Breast Cancer Fund's publication *Examining the Environmental Links to Breast Cancer.*

Since 1971, the year President Richard Nixon declared a "war on cancer," more than $35 billion has been committed to research. Yet we still cannot pinpoint with certainty the causes behind the vast majority of breast cancer cases, nor have treatment options changed or improved much over the years. Women still must choose from surgery, radiation, and/or chemotherapy.

In addition, some in the medical establishment have misleadingly focused on mammography as a prevention measure, with the assumption that early detection can prevent serious illness. Mammography, however, is *not* prevention. It can only detect cancer that already exists and may have been present for eight to ten years. It fails to detect breast cancer 20 percent of the time in women over 50, and as much as 40 percent of the time in younger women.

WHAT WE KNOW

Hundreds of scientific studies of laboratory animals and wildlife have drawn links between exposure to toxic chemicals and cancer. Emerging science suggests that synthetic chemicals in the environment pose a risk to the human reproductive system, the endocrine system, and to human growth and development both *in utero* and after birth.

A rapidly evolving field of research involves the study of "endocrine disrupters" or "hormone mimickers"—synthetic chemicals found in pesticides like DDT, some fuels, plastics, detergents, and pharmaceutical drugs. We know that estrogen binds with receptors in mammary glands, signaling cells to grow. In 1993, scientists at Cornell University cautioned that growing evidence seemed to indicate that exposure to estrogen-mimicking chemicals, called xenoestrogens, can cause cells to rapidly grow out of control and form tumors. It has been postulated that xenoestrogens may be responsible for increasing a woman's chances of getting breast cancer. Researchers at Tufts University Medical School have demonstrated that xenoestrogens make human breast cancer cells grow in the laboratory, just as natural estrogen does.

There are also studies that show drastic changes in development, particularly in the reproductive system, when laboratory mice are exposed to estrogen mimickers during critical windows of vulnerability *in utero*. When cells are rapidly developing and proliferating, there can be a key period of vulnerability during which damaging or altering cell development can lead to cancer. Other windows of vulnerability include puberty and a woman's first pregnancy.

Studies tracking patterns of breast cancer development in humans also strongly suggest the influence of environmental factors. In Asia, women are four to seven times less likely to develop breast cancer than women in the U.S. Yet when Asian women migrate to the U.S., their risk of breast cancer rises over a two-generation span. Women who live in the U.S. for a decade or more have an 80 percent higher risk of developing breast cancer than more recent immigrants, and those whose grandparents were born in the U.S. have a 60 percent greater risk than women whose grandparents were born overseas.

Estrogen mimickers may be either beneficial or detrimental. Estrogen-mimicking compounds found in foods such as broccoli, soy products, and cauliflower may act as "good" estrogens, providing some protection against the effects of estradiol, the chief "bad" estrogen, made naturally by our bodies. Critics of the "xenoestrogen theory" argue that these beneficial compounds found in foods can balance possible hazards posed by human-made chemicals. Other scientists point out that the human body has been fine-tuned to handle plant estrogens through thousands of years of evolution, while human-made estrogen mimickers have been in the environment only since the 1940s. Since we do not yet understand how women's natural estrogen affects breast cancer, it is difficult to predict how estrogen mimickers might behave, even at low doses.

Studies have identified the presence of more than 200 foreign chemicals in women's breast milk, including significant levels of dioxin, a carcinogen that has been shown to disrupt children's hormone systems. Within six months of being breast-fed, a baby in the U.S. or Europe receives the maximum recommended lifetime dose of dioxin.

MORE RESEARCH NEEDED

Chemicals that are persistent in the environment accumulate in body fat and are carried by women in their breast tissue. Thus far, human data about the link between these chemicals and breast cancer are inconclusive. For example, some studies have shown that women with breast cancer have the same or lower levels of pesticide residue in their system than women without the disease.

However, other studies, by U.S. and Canadian scientists, have found that women with higher levels of organochlorines in their blood have four to ten times the risk of breast cancer than those with lower levels. [Organochlorines

are hydrocarbon-based chemicals containing chlorines like DDT. Many of these compounds break down very slowly in the environment and can be stored in the fat of animals, fish, and humans.] These seemingly inconsistent results point to the need for long-term prospective studies on this issue.

There are only two recognized causes of breast cancer: exposure to ionizing radiation and inherited genetic defects in breast cells. Other factors, though they have not been shown to *cause* the disease, are associated with higher risk: beginning menstruation before age 12, onset of menopause after 55, bearing children late in life or not at all, not breast-feeding, and prolonged use of estrogen after menopause.

More research is needed to examine why the established risk factors increase a woman's vulnerability. However, additional and different research is needed to determine which of the thousands of chemicals in the environment cause the disease, and how. Most important, we must conduct long-term prospective studies that measure exposures to chemicals during critical windows of breast development.

RESEARCH PRIORITIES

For many years the focus of the National Cancer Institute (NCI), the largest single government funding source for cancer investigations, has been on earlier detection with mammography, improved radiation and chemotherapy, and improved surgical techniques designed to help women survive the disease and live longer. Much research continues to be focused on the role of inherited gene defects. Currently, there is no breast cancer prevention research strategy at the NCI except for chemo-prevention through the use of raloxifene and tamoxifen in high-risk, healthy women.

The federal government has funded one multimillion-dollar, multiyear environment research study, the Long Island Breast Cancer Study Project, to determine whether environmental contaminants increase breast cancer risk. But overall, funding for environmental research represents only a tiny fraction of the government's budget for disease research. Of the National Institutes of Health's $15.7 billion budget last year, just $382 million, or 2.4 percent, went to the National Institute of Environmental Health Sciences, the primary agency conducting research on environmental health. Similarly, the CDC's National Center for Environmental Health received just $172 million for 1999.

A CALL FOR ACTION

Over the years, a growing movement has emerged calling for prevention-based research.

Breast cancer advocates and researchers have identified three important types of research currently underfunded by the federal government: testing and screening of industrial chemicals and pesticides for their toxicity and hormone-mimicking effects; measuring the levels of these chemicals in our bodies—a process known as "bio-monitoring"; and learning how girls and women are exposed to these chemicals, so we can study health effects and ultimately reduce health risks.

In 1996, an advisory committee of scientists and experts established by the EPA recommended the creation of a program to test the toxicity and hormonal effects of 9,000 chemicals, as required under the Food Quality Protection Act. However, this program has been grossly underfunded. Development of the tests alone will cost $50 million over a period of several years. The program's proposed 2000 budget is only $12 million. Further, as currently devised, the tests do not screen for toxicity during the prenatal and early development period when chemicals have been known to have different and often more harmful effects.

To fully understand the impact of environmental contaminants on humans, the EPA's data on the toxicity of these chemicals must be completed and complemented by an ongoing systematic program of bio-monitoring data to identify what chemicals exist in our bodies and at what levels.

Unfortunately, the CDC's National Environmental Health Laboratory, the agency that spearheads bio-monitoring research, is also severely underfunded. The Breast Cancer Fund is calling for more broad-based testing as well as testing on breast milk, a fluid that absorbs chemicals differently, and, in some cases, at higher and potentially more dangerous levels. Not only do women have the right to know what chemicals are in their breasts and breast milk, but investing in this kind of reseach is also a critical step to developing public policies and prevention strategies that will effectively address the breast cancer epidemic and other serious illnesses.

Yet research into the environmental causes of breast cancer remains a low priority among leading cancer organizations and government agencies. Advocates have attributed this lack of commitment, in part, to pressure from industry. Pharmaceutical companies, in particular, have a vested interest in keeping breast cancer research focused on drug therapies and away from environmental pollution. Breast Cancer Awareness Month was initiated by the pharmaceutical giant Zeneca, the maker of tamoxifen. [Activists often note Zeneca's link to Imperial Chemical Industries (ICI), the maker of pesticides, plastics, pharmacetical, and paper. Zeneca was a spin-off company of ICI, which was sued in 1990 by state and federal agencies for dumping DDT and PCBs in California harbors.] In 1999, Zeneca merged with the Swedish pharmaceutical company Astra to become the world's third-largest drug concern. AstraZeneca continues to be the primary sponsor of Breast Cancer Awareness Month.

A MATTER OF LIFE AND DEATH

If exposure to chemicals in the environment was shown to be associated with only 10 to

20 percent of breast cancer cases, and the U.S. acted to reduce or eliminate these hazardous chemicals, we would be able to prevent between 9,000 and 36,000 women from contracting the disease each year.

My Fight for Birth Control

Margaret Sanger

Mrs. Sacks was only twenty-eight years old; her husband, an unskilled worker, thirty-two. Three children, aged five, three and one, were none too strong nor sturdy, and it took all the earnings of the father and the ingenuity of the mother to keep them clean, provide them with air and proper food, and give them a chance to grow into decent manhood and womanhood.

Both parents were devoted to these children and to each other. The woman had become pregnant and had taken various drugs and purgatives, as advised by her neighbors. Then, in desperation, she had used some instrument lent to her by a friend. She was found prostrate on the floor amidst the crying children when her husband returned from work. Neighbors advised against the ambulance, and a friendly doctor was called. The husband would not hear of her going to a hospital, and as a little money had been saved in the bank a nurse was called and the battle for that precious life began.

It was in the middle of July. The three-room apartment was turned into a hospital for the dying patient. Never had I worked so fast, never so concentratedly as I did to keep alive that little mother. Neighbor women came and went during the day doing the odds and ends necessary for our comfort. The children were sent to friends and relatives and the doctor and I settled ourselves to outdo the force and power of an outraged nature.

Never had I known such conditions could exist. July's sultry days and nights were melted into a torpid inferno. Day after day, night after night, I slept only in brief snatches, ever too anxious about the condition of that feeble heart bravely carrying on, to stay long from the bedside of the patient. . . .

At the end of two weeks recovery was in sight, and at the end of three weeks I was preparing to leave the fragile patient to take up the ordinary duties of her life, including those of wifehood and motherhood. Everyone was congratulating her on her recovery. All the kindness of sympathetic and understanding neighbors poured in upon her in the shape of convalescent dishes, soups, custards, and drinks. Still she appeared to be despondent and worried. She seemed to sit apart in her thoughts as if she had no part in these congratulatory messages and endearing welcomes. I thought at first that she still retained some of her unconscious memories and dwelt upon them in her silences.

But as the hour of my departure came nearer, her anxiety increased, and finally with trembling voice she said: "Another baby will finish me, I suppose."

"It's too early to talk about that," I said, and resolved that I would turn the question over to the doctor for his advice. When he came I said: "Mrs. Sacks is worried about having another baby."

"She well might be," replied the doctor, and then he stood before her and said: "Any more such capers, young woman, and there will be no need to call me."

"Yes, yes—I know, Doctor," said the patient with trembling voice, "but," and she hesitated as if it took all of her courage to say it, "*what* can I do to prevent getting that way again?"

"Oh ho!" laughed the doctor good naturedly, "You want your cake while you eat it too, do you? Well, it can't be done." Then, familiarly slapping her on the back and picking up his hat and bag to depart, he said: "I'll tell you the only sure thing to do. Tell Jake to sleep on the roof!"

With those words he closed the door and went down the stairs, leaving us both petrified and stunned.

Tears sprang to my eyes, and a lump came in my throat as I looked at the face before me. It was stamped with sheer horror. I thought for a moment she might have gone insane, but she conquered her feelings, whatever they may have been, and turning to me in desperation said: "He can't understand, can he?—he's a man after all—but you do, don't you? You're a woman and you'll tell me the secret and I'll never tell it to a soul."

She clasped her hands as if in prayer, she leaned over and looked straight into my eyes and beseechingly implored me to tell her something—something *I really did not know*. It was like being on a rack and tortured for a crime one had not committed. To plead guilty would stop the agony; otherwise the rack kept turning.

I had to turn away from that imploring face. I could not answer her then. I quieted her as best I could. She saw that I was moved by the tears in my eyes. I promised that I would come back in a few days and tell her what she wanted to know. The few simple means of limiting the family like *coitus interruptus* or the condom were laughed at by the neighboring women when told these were the means used by men in the well-to-do families. That was not believed, and I knew such an answer would be swept aside as useless were I to tell her this at such a time.

A little later when she slept I left the house, and made up my mind that I'd keep away from

those cases in the future. I felt helpless to do anything at all, I seemed chained hand and foot, and longed for an earthquake or a volcano to shake the world out of its lethargy into facing these monstrous atrocities.

The intelligent reasoning of the young mother—how to *prevent* getting that way again—how sensible, how just she had been—yes, I promised myself I'd go back and have a long talk with her and tell her more, and perhaps she would not laugh but would believe that those methods were all that were really known.

But time flew past, and weeks rolled into months. That wistful, appealing face haunted me day and night. I could not banish from my mind memories of that trembling voice begging so humbly for knowledge she had a right to have. I was about to retire one night three months later when the telephone rang and an agitated man's voice begged me to come at once to help his wife who was sick again. It was the husband of Mrs. Sacks, and I intuitively knew before I left the telephone that it was almost useless to go.

I dreaded to face that woman. I was tempted to send someone else in my place. I longed for an accident on the subway, or on the street—anything to prevent my going into that home. But on I went just the same. I arrived a few minutes after the doctor, the same one who had given her such noble advice. The woman was dying. She was unconscious. She died within ten minutes after my arrival. It was the same result, the same story told a thousand times before—death from abortion. She had become pregnant, had used drugs, had then consulted a five-dollar professional abortionist, and death followed.

The doctor shook his head as he rose from listening for the heart beat. I knew she had already passed on; without a groan, a sigh or recognition of our belated presence she had gone into the Great Beyond as thousands of mothers go every year. I looked at that drawn face now stilled in death. I placed her thin hands across her breast and recalled how hard they had pleaded with me on that last memorable occasion of parting. The gentle woman, the devoted mother, the loving wife had passed on leaving behind her a frantic husband, helpless in his loneliness, bewildered in his helplessness as he paced up and down the room, hands clenching his head, moaning "My God! My God! My God!"

The Revolution came—but not as it has been pictured nor as history relates that revolutions have come. It came in my own life. It began in my very being as I walked home that night after I had closed the eyes and covered with a sheet the body of that little helpless mother whose life had been sacrificed to ignorance.

After I left that desolate house I walked and walked and walked; for hours and hours I kept on, bag in hand, thinking, regretting, dreading to stop; fearful of my conscience, dreading to face my own accusing soul. At three in the morning I arrived home still clutching a heavy load the weight of which I was quite unconscious.

I entered the house quietly, as was my custom, and looked out the window down upon the dimly lighted, sleeping city. As I stood at the window and looked out, the miseries and problems of that sleeping city arose before me in a clear vision like a panorama: crowded homes, too many children; babies dying in infancy; mothers overworked; baby nurseries; children neglected and hungry—mothers so nervously wrought they would not give the little things the comfort nor care they needed; mothers half sick most of their lives—"always ailing, never failing"; women made into drudges; children working in cellars; children aged six and seven pushed into the labor market to help earn a living; another baby on the way; still another; yet another; a baby born

dead—great relief; an older child dies—sorrow, but nevertheless relief—insurance helps; a mother's death—children scattered into institutions; the father, desperate, drunken; he slinks away to become an outcast in a society which has trapped him. . . .

. . . For hours I stood, motionless and tense, expecting something to happen. I watched the lights go out, I saw the darkness gradually give way to the first shimmer of dawn, and then a colorful sky heralded the rise of the sun. I knew a new day had come for me and a new world as well.

It was like an illumination. I could now see clearly the various social strata of our life; all its mass problems seemed to be centered around uncontrolled breeding. There was only one thing to be done: call out, start the alarm, set the heather on fire! Awaken the womanhood of America to free the motherhood of the world! I released from my almost paralyzed hand the nursing bag which unconsciously I had clutched, threw it across the room, tore the uniform from my body, flung it into a corner, and renounced all palliative work forever.

I would never go back again to nurse women's ailing bodies while their miseries were as vast as the stars. I was now finished with superficial cures, with doctors and nurses and social workers who were brought face to face with this overwhelming truth of women's needs and yet turned to pass on the other side. They must be made to see these facts. I resolved that women should have knowledge of contraception. They have every right to know about their own bodies. I would strike out—I would scream from the housetops. I would tell the world what was going on in the lives of these poor women. I *would* be heard. No matter what it should cost. *I would be heard.*

READING 46

Caught in the Crossfire

Cynthia Gorney

What happened in Sedalia was not a thing that Robert Duemler talked about: not the place, nor the smell, nor the low sick feeling that came to his stomach when he thought about it afterward. Doctors see things they wish they had not seen, he understood that, and Duemler was a quiet man who delivered babies for a living at a big Catholic hospital where they were cordial to him even though he belonged to the United Church of Christ. The hospital was outside St. Louis, which people liked to call a Catholic city, and when Duemler was at work, nurses in nuns' habits bustled down the corridors and nodded in their deferential nurses' way: Good morning, doctor.

Among the obstetrical nurses was a big, smart, opinionated woman named Judith Widdicombe, and sometimes after deliveries Duemler and Widdicombe would lean against a wall in their scrubs and talk. Duemler, in his 30s then, was older than she was, and it amused him to see her point out when and where she thought the senior physicians had bungled their work. She was not deferential. There was some undiplomatic clarity of vision to Judy Widdicombe that Duemler admired. They might be attending the birth of a patient's sixth or seventh child and know, without exactly saying it, that sometimes this felt like bringing forth the miracle of life and sometimes it felt like handing a small squalling package to a tired woman who was not interested in receiving it.

Widdicombe would say casually, "I bet she doesn't really want that kid." Maybe not, Duemler would say. And they would talk about something else. But he understood that Widdicombe, who was not a nun, was signaling him. There was a code at work, and Duemler knew that he was in on it somehow, and that

it had to do with ideas that might be dangerous to discuss in a public place.

After a while, he told her what had happened in Sedalia in 1962.

He was a young Air Force doctor, the first obstetrician on the base in central Missouri. Sometimes patients would call him in the middle of the night, and he would need to hurry to help them. That was when this call came, and when Duemler walked into the emergency room, what he saw, in more places than he would have thought possible, was blood. Blood on the walls. On the floor. On the gurney and on the towels and on the hands and arms of the emergency crew. Beneath them lay a woman whose skin had gone slack, and when Duemler lifted her legs into the stirrups, he saw that someone had pushed inside her vagina with a sharp instrument and aimed it toward the cervix and thrust straight up. The blood vessels to either side had emptied all over the emergency room and the car in which this woman's husband had driven her 20 miles, the distance between the abortionist and the hospital.

The husband told Duemler they had five children already.

Duemler remembered that for a long time afterward, when he was no longer able to summon up anything except the bewildered look on the husband's face as his wife was pronounced dead on the examining table.

Duemler had learned in medical school that you pull down the shade when you have to, that you cannot climb into the life of every patient; but after it was over he would think about Sedalia, and the words *stupid, stupid* would press up inside him. It was a stupid death. When he was a resident, an older doctor had asked him to assist at a dilation and curettage in the sterile operating room of a fine St. Louis hospital. The patient was a nice young woman whose boyfriend had come from a family of high social standing, and they had all invented a plausible diagnosis requiring termination of pregnancy to save her life. Duemler understood that his job was to hold the dilators and shut up, but when he thought about Sedalia he always thought about this other woman, the one with the fancy boyfriend. So he told Judy Widdicombe that story, too.

Then she knew she had been right about Bob Duemler, and she came to him one day and said: There is a group of us, and we are doing something illegal. We need your help.

In 1968, the year Judith McWhorter Widdicombe began recruiting medical doctors into a conspiracy to commit repeated felonies in the state of Missouri, she was 30 years old and lived in a modest house with her children and her husband, Arthur. At that time she had three occupations, each of which interested her deeply. From morning until early afternoon she cared for her two sons and other children who needed baby-sitting; from early afternoon until 11 at night she worked the hospital swing shift; and one evening each week she stayed home answering telephone calls from people threatening to commit suicide.

The phone work was a volunteer job, coordinated through a program called St. Louis Suicide Prevention, run by Gwyndolyn Harvey, a local psychologist. At first Widdicombe worked the phones in Suicide Prevention's office, but eventually the calls that came during her shift were routed to a telephone on the Widdicombes' back porch. She was very good at it. She liked sitting out there on the porch at night, leading her caller carefully away from harm, just as she might do up in the hospital wards.

As the service was publicized, pregnant women began to call, too. But they were not suicidal—not the way others were. They were direct. They would say: This is a telephone number for desperate people, right? I am desperate. I want an abortion.

Sometimes they would add, as though in deference to the name: If I don't get an abortion, I will kill myself.

Widdicombe didn't know what to say.

Call your doctor, she said at first, feeling foolish. If their doctors had been able to get these women abortions, the women would not have been calling Suicide Prevention. Widdicombe had never read the Missouri statute book, Section 559, where abortion was described as "felony manslaughter," but she knew it was illegal and, in the hospital where she worked, unspeakable. "In retrospect, I know that through the years there were women who'd come in for 'diagnostic D&Cs' who were really pregnant. But nobody talked about it," she recalls.

Gwyn Harvey told her that the other volunteers were reporting abortion callers too, even though nobody at Suicide Prevention had any useful information. When Harvey listened to the detailed accounts of these calls, it seemed to her that most of these women were not really looking for crisis intervention or a referral to a psychologist. What they wanted was an abortionist.

douches: Lysol, Hexol, bleach, green soap
    and glycerine, powdered kitchen mustard,
    hydrogen peroxide
potassium permanganate corrosive tablets
intrauterine installation of kerosene and
    vinegar
gauze packing
artist's paintbrush
curtain rod
slippery elm stick
garden hose
tubes: rubber or polyethylene
glass cocktail stirrer
ear syringe
wires: telephone, copper, coat hanger
nut pick
pencil
cotton swabs
clothespin

knitting needle
catheters: rubber, woven silk, or with stylette
chopsticks
bicycle pump and tube
football pump and plastic straw
plastic tube with soap solution
gramophone needle
bulb syringe
by mouth: castor oil, quinine, ergot,
    Humphries No. 11 tablets, turpentine

A roster of terrible specificity accumulated, before the late 1960s, in American medical journals. This was what she did it with, the examining physicians must have murmured. Sometimes a woman could be persuaded to describe the device that had been used; sometimes the doctors could look inside the vaginal area, or open an abdomen at autopsy, and recognize the markers left behind.

Air pumped into the uterus left the large blood vessels distended. Turpentine, ingested or introduced by douche, gave the urine an odor reminiscent of violets. Lower abdominal tenderness was a sign that soap or detergent might have been forced up the cervix. Potassium permanganate tablets, pushed into the vagina to stimulate bleeding that emergency-room doctors might misidentify as a miscarriage, left craters of corroded tissue along the vaginal walls; suturing them was like trying to put fine surgical stitches into softened butter.

There was no practical way to document the number of American women who ended their own pregnancies, or tried to. For some years the figure of 681,600 a year was used; this was a 1936 statistic from Frederick J. Taussig, a St. Louis professor whose book was for two decades the only serious reference work on abortion. He spent five pages explaining his calculations and extrapolations. Directly attributable to these abortions, Taussig asserted, were 8,179 deaths.

On a national scale, there was little else to go by. "The desire to avoid any public record of an event so often tied up with the moral life of the individual is bound to result in failure to get accurate information." Taussig wrote. "The same lack of honesty appears in our mortality records, where we find cases of abortion death registered as pneumonia, kidney disease, or heart failure."

By 1955, when the Planned Parenthood Federation of America medical director, Mary Steichen Calderone, convened a national conference, estimates of illegal abortions in this country ranged from 200,000 to 1.2 million a year. . . .

The very notion of a national conference was sufficiently alarming in 1955 that the participants were anxious that the press not get wind of it. It was a kind of declaration of intent, men and women with worthy institutions attached to their names, all discussing the problem of induced abortion. It was a problem because nobody could obtain respectable data. It was a problem because illegal abortion made a lot of women sick. It was a problem because there were urban public hospitals in which entire wards had been ceded to patients trying to recover from illegal abortions; at Los Angeles County, on any given afternoon, 50 to 100 women were separated off into what the doctors referred to as Infected OB.

. . .

By the mid-1960s, every state harbored at least a scattering of doctors . . . who had come to believe that something was wrong with American abortion law. Many of them traced their moment of conversion not to the battlefield of a hospital ward but instead to a single patient, a single detail, a single moment of helplessness or rage.

. . .

By 1968 a new form of civil disobedience had begun, its spiritual and organizational center lodged in a 19th-century brick Baptist church, called Judson Memorial, in Greenwich Village, in New York City. A lot of unusual activity went on there under the Reverend Howard Moody's supervision. Civil rights marchers, Vietnam War protesters, and local Democratic

Club organizers all mingled and argued at Moody's church, which was regarded less as a temple of God than as a stewpot for liberal politics.

In 1967 a young Jewish woman named Arlene Carmen was hired as a church administrator. Moody asked for her help with one project in particular: He had the idea that women looking for abortions should be able to receive detailed information from a minister who could counsel them first and help them find what they were looking for.

Such a minister would almost certainly be acting in violation of state abortion laws. Moody and Carmen both knew that. Publicly the stance was to be at once truculent and gravely ministerial. When in May 1967 Moody and others organized the first formal clergymen's counseling service, they used the word *abortion* in the name, declining euphemisms, and called *The New York Times*. The article appeared on the front page. "Twenty-one Protestant ministers and rabbis have announced the establishment of a Clergyman's Consultation Service on Abortion to assist women seeking abortions," began the story. "The clergymen cited 'higher laws and moral obligations transcending legal codes,' and said that it was their 'pastoral responsibility and religious duty to give aid and assistance to all women with problem pregnancies.'"

The telephone began to ring the day the story appeared. Within a week, distraught female voices had backed up on the answering-machine tape, and Moody was spending seven hours a day ushering women in and out of his office. The sheer volume astonished him, but more startling were the women who had telephoned Manhattan and then gotten on airplanes in places hundreds of miles away. There were so many of them that the clergymen's abbreviated lists of abortion doctors were inadequate. They had a doctor in Puerto Rico, a polite man whose patients came back with reports of scrubbed tile floors and attentive nurses; they had a doctor in Louisiana, a Tulane-educated gynecologist who worked alone out of a New Orleans hotel and put pot holders on the examining table stirrups to keep the metal from chilling the women's feet. But they needed more, and Carmen began visiting abortionists herself. She took notes. "Code: Nina." "Call & ask for Dr. SOS." "On probation for three years; slum area; filthy; bad procedure." "Butcher, avoid at all costs."

The list kept growing; Moody traveled to places like Cleveland and Chicago, working social webs laid out by the civil rights movement and Vietnam War protest. He would instruct the ministers he met that this was to be a counseling service, not a hand-over-the-address service; they should remain alert to ambivalence, should encourage women to keep their babies or give them up for adoption if the idea of abortion disturbed them. There was a famous story about a woman who called Judson Memorial in the early months, when Moody assumed their telephones were tapped.

"Is this where you can get an abortion?" she asked.

Moody explained that she had called a church, but could come in for abortion counseling.

"I don't need the Sermon on the Mount, Reverend," she said. "I need an abortion." And she hung up.

Within a year of its debut. Moody's office was ferrying information to and from the quiet regional abortion network headquartered on the Washington University campus in St. Louis. Compared to some of its more ambitious counterparts, this operation in 1967 was still modest in scope and discreet in its public presence. John Vavra, a medical professor, had enlisted medical students to examine and interview women before and after their abortions, but there was no letterhead or telephone listing. The service did not even have a name. It was simply known that Dr. Vavra and Reverend Ewing helped women find abortionists.

And when Gwyndolyn Harvey set out to learn about abortionists, she was directed to

Vavra, who received her in his office. He was soft-spoken, scholarly, and calm—"unflappable," Harvey recalls. "He looked as far from anybody doing anything radical as you could possibly imagine."

Vavra was careful about what he would and would not say; he offered up no names or telephone numbers, but when Harvey told him about the Suicide Prevention callers, he was interested at once. There was no conversation at all, that day or later, about why such a service might be justifiable, about what it was in their backgrounds or philosophies that might prompt two well-educated professionals to sit in a university office and make arrangements for the ongoing violation of state law. "We didn't have to discuss it," Harvey recalls. "There were people getting hurt."

Among her colleagues and from her volunteer roster, Harvey selected her initial recruits: a Washington University psychiatric social worker, and Judy Widdicombe. The model for her program already existed, Harvey explained: counselors, ministers, abortionists, and doctors, all linked together by a telephone network that would serve as each woman's initial point of contact. Vavra would lead them to the abortionists; Harvey and Widdicombe would assemble a medical and pastoral corps to attend to the women beforehand and afterward.

Widdicombe thought about what she was going to say to these doctors, and how best to say it, and approached Dr. Melvin Schwartz and Dr. Robert Duemler and Dr. George Wulff, who taught at the hospital where she had trained as a nurse and who had worked the Infected OB ward, and who had learned as an intern to recognize the caustic blackened stain of a self-administered potassium permanganate douche, and who answered her, like the others, without hesitation: Yes.

READING 47

How Women Pay for Fetal Rights

Rachel Roth

For months, David was a victim of torture. He was kept in a small darkened room. His food was poisoned and his brain severely damaged. And then one day he was born.

—*Minnesota fetal alcohol syndrome public awareness poster*

As government-sponsored materials depict fetuses as tortured prisoners, so do prosecutors hear fetal voices, psychologists dispense advice on behalf of fetal patients, factories exclude women lest they bring fetal visitors, legislators craft public policy for fetuses, and judges issue rulings based on fetuses' preferences, including one judge who denied a "surrogate mother" custody of a child she bore because there was "no evidence whatsoever" that the fetus had bonded with her. These are but a few developments in the expanding terrain of reproductive and gender politics that has come to be known as the politics of fetal rights.

People must commonly associate the term "fetal rights" with efforts to curtail legal abortion. Yet as the right-to-life movement's success in restricting women's access to abortion waxed and waned throughout the 1970s and 1980s, other targets of scrutiny and regulation in the name of fetal rights emerged: women who would be carrying their pregnancies to term and women who were not pregnant at all, but merely fertile.

The struggles over these women's lives are the ones explored here. . . .

. . . When institutions assert or accept rights claims on behalf of fetuses, their stated reasons usually involve protecting fetuses from potential harm and enhancing their chances of healthy birth and survival. As I show, however, the strategy of creating fetal rights is not necessary to achieve those goals, is often counterproductive to these goals, and always undermines women's equal standing as citizens.

Fetal rights do not come free. When courts, legislatures, or other political and social institutions decide to award rights to fetuses, the award translates into costs of others. Women currently bear a disproportionate share of the costs of ensuring fetal health, relative to the rest of society. This unequal distribution burdens women and fails to provide a clear pattern of benefit to fetuses or to society as a whole.

American ideology and social arrangements assign to women the primary responsibility for reproduction. When I speak of primary responsibility for reproduction, I refer to women's disproportionate responsibility for the entire reproductive process, which includes timing pregnancies and rearing children as well as gestating fetuses and giving birth. Because all women are perceived as potentially pregnant for much of their lives, they are susceptible to having restrictions imposed on them because of what others think about that potential. . . . This is most often done according to class, race, or culture. By culture, I mean a range of influences on someone's life, including religion, national origin, or first language. In addition, the ideological message of fetal rights politics—that women are not entitled to be as self-determining as men because they can become pregnant—exacts a high price from women as a class. Taken together, the many forms of fetal advocacy politics place a heavy burden on all women's opportunities and pursuit of equality.

Because rights claims resonate so deeply with American political and cultural values, fetal rights claims have been taken seriously in the political arena, and courts and legislatures have granted rights to fetuses. Although she does not address fetal advocacy politics in her book *Making All the Difference: Inclusion, Exclusion, and American Law,* Martha Minow offers some insights about the power of establishing rights for fetuses. When people make rights claims, they assert their identity as individuals entitled to equality and liberty, and emphasize their essential sameness to others as persons and as members of the polity. Rights analysis further "treats each individual as a separate unit, related only to the state rather than to a group or to social bonds." Fetal rights claims, then, present a rhetorically powerful strategy by giving the fetus an individual identity, asserting its equality with the woman, and establishing its independent relationship with the state that bypasses the pregnant women.

The logic of fetal rights depends on certain rhetorical constructions. First, proponents of fetal rights oppose them rhetorically to women's rights, constructing a contest of equal antagonists with only one possible winner. Consider these representative titles of journal and newspaper articles: "Fetal versus Maternal Rights: Medical and Legal Perspectives"; "When the Rights of Mother and Fetus Collide"; "Maternal versus Fetal Rights: A Clinical Dilemma"; and "Fetal Patients and Conflicts with Their Mothers." All set up a conflict between woman and fetus: a zero-sum choice.[1]

A second frequent formulation opposes fetal rights to women's responsibilities, as in this 1989 article in a medical journal: "Fetal Therapy and Surgery: Fetal Rights and Maternal Obligations." This title suggests that it is incumbent upon the pregnant woman to honor the right to surgery and medical treatment that doctors believe fetuses hold; in other words, women can be forcibly subjected to unwanted medical procedures. This kind of right is an entitlement enforceable against the pregnant woman. Its logic dictates that social institutions hold pregnant women accountable for the fulfillment of fetal rights. In this case, that means that pregnant women are responsible for ensuring the fetus's access to medical treatment, even though they themselves have no right to medical care.

These formulations have become so pervasive that supposedly objective news reporters use them freely. On National Public Radio's *All Things Considered,* news anchor Linda Wertheimer described a criminal charge of attempted murder against a woman who drank heavily during pregnancy as the latest chapter in the debate over how "to balance the rights of the woman against those of the fetus." This concept gains legitimacy through constant repetition in scholarly journals, popular media, and public discourse.

Creating individual fetal identities that are hostile to women's identities is not the only thing that rights rhetoric accomplishes. Rights rhetoric is also powerful because it obscures the question of costs. Both of the constructions I just described—maternal rights versus fetal rights and maternal responsibilities versus fetal rights—obscure the way that fetal rights function to distribute social costs. When a court or other institution decides to award rights, it has to assign the costs of those rights to some individual or group. That assignment—who should bear the costs of fetal rights—is a political question that has received very little direct public debate. It is the central concern of this study. The answer, explicit or implicit, has been to impose the costs of fetal rights on women.

These costs are tangible. They can't be measured solely in terms of money, although that is certainly at stake. Women also incur costs to their free, physical and mental security, identity, and privacy when they are denied jobs because they are fertile, when they are subjected to court-ordered medical operations against their will, and when they are given additional civil and criminal penalties for using drugs or alcohol during pregnancy that are never imposed on women who are not pregnant or on men. Women are assigned responsibility for taking care of fetuses without being given the resources they need to do so, and then penalized for falling short.

"There seems to be a qualitative difference between an invasion of privacy by your government and an invasion by a stranger," explain Ellen Alderman and Caroline Kennedy in their analysis of a class-action lawsuit women brought against the city of Chicago's policy to strip search every single woman brought to the jail, regardless of the circumstances of her arrest or the reason she was booked. "The women spoke of an abuse of a basic trust. They felt they had been violated by the very people who were supposed to be their protectors and expressed a sense of betrayal and vulnerability. All of them said they dreaded any future contact with the police." The feelings of abuse and subsequent loss of trust that characterized the Chicago women's experiences also characterize the experiences of women whose privacy and bodies are invaded in the name of fetal rights. When forced to submit to unwanted surgery such as a cesarean or sterilization, or when jailed without due process, women may come to mistrust the medical and legal institutions that they rely on for care and protection.[2] Their mistrust, and that of their families and friends, in turn creates costs for all of society.

Women inevitably bear some of the costs of reproducing the species. They bear the physical, emotional, and time costs associated with pregnancy and birth. The Centers for Disease Control (CDC) reports that the maternal death ratio has held steadily at 7 or 8 deaths per 100,000 births since 1982, and that half of these deaths are preventable. The United States lags behind 20 other countries and has made no progress toward its goal of cutting deaths to 3.3 per 100,000 by the year 2000. The causes of death include ectopic pregnancy, hemorrhage, infection, blood clots, and pregnancy-induced high blood pressure. The CDC also estimates that for every woman who dies as a result of pregnancy, 3,100 women are hospitalized for complications each year. In addition, there may be severe long-term consequences for some women. Women who have borne children appear much more likely than other women or men to get such autoimmune diseases as systemic sclerosis.

Women also *evitably* bear a disproportionate share of the physical, emotional, and time costs in rearing children. Although new trends in paternal involvement in child-rearing make headlines, studies overwhelmingly show that women continue to shoulder most of the child care, as well as homemaking, even when they work the same number of hours outside the home as men.

What is so troubling about fetal rights claims is that they make women bear almost all the costs, instead of distributing them more evenly across society. Consider, as an alternative model, how the demands of disabled people to participate fully in American life have led to newly articulated rights of access to education, housing, transportation, and work. In this case, when government actors and institutions decided that the rights claims of disabled Americans had merit, they distributed the attendant costs broadly to taxpayers, employers, and consumers. Rather than requiring disabled people to pay for their own access, Congress decided that society must share the burden, and enacted a series of laws culminating in the Americans with Disabilities Act (ADA) of 1990.[3]

Reproductive costs can also be distributed. . . . Moreover, the burdens that have been imposed on women in the name of fetal rights do not produce clear evidence of benefits to fetuses, calling into question the motives underlying fetal rights policy. By contrast, we can have more confidence that—if fully enforced—the ADA will improve the lives of its intended beneficiaries.

The notion of fetal rights is linked to another important rhetorical construct prevalent in public discourse—that of "maternal-fetal conflict." This notion is used to focus attention on women's behavior as the source of risk to fetal

health and away from other factors. This study critically examines this construct, which rests simultaneously on two assumptions: (1) that all pregnant women are already mothers and (2) that they are bad mothers, for if they were good mothers they wouldn't be having conflicts with their fetuses.

Maternal-fetal conflict erases all other aspects of a pregnant woman's identity. All pregnant women are *expectant* mothers (unless they plan to place their future children up for adoption), but only some pregnant women are already rearing children. Referring to pregnant women as "mothers" before they give birth evokes the qualities of selflessness and duty associated with motherhood and suggests that pregnant women have failed to demonstrate these important qualities. It also turns the fetus into a child. Cultural expectations and legal standards of parental duty then apply to pregnant women, and the fetus gains an independent identity that enables it to engage rhetorically in conflict with the pregnant woman ("mother"). Again, this serves to focus attention on the pregnant woman and away from her environment and the responsibilities that other individuals or institutions might have.

These rhetorical constructions are complemented by images that depict fetuses as independent. As Barbara Duden's book *Disembodying Women* aptly suggests, the politics of fetal rights has disembodied fetuses from pregnant women in visual culture and public discourse. From Lennart Nilsson's famous *Life* magazine photographs of "the drama of life before birth" to prime time ultrasound scans, images of disembodied fetuses abound. Rosalind Petchesky explains how ultrasound imaging of fetuses presents the fetus "as though removed from the pregnant woman's body, as though suspended in space." A 1991 Volvo ad does just this: A huge sonogramlike image of a fetus hovers above a tiny car at the bottom of the page; the text asks, "Is something inside telling you to buy a Volvo?" In the television version of the ad, a voice off-camera asks the same question. Janelle Taylor explains that fetal images "gain whatever power and meaning they may have precisely upon the strength of the ideological status of photographs as purely denotative, transparent representations of reality." Political movements can deploy these supposedly neutral, self-evident images in a variety of ways.[4]

Even a recent collection of feminist essays called *Expecting Trouble: Surrogacy, Fetal Abuse, and New Reproductive Technologies* recapitulates this problem on its cover. The cover design features the profile of a pregnant woman in front of the Supreme Court; she is merely a dark blue silhouette, while the fetus is rendered in intricate detail, its tiny features and fingers giving it the distinct human appearance the pregnant woman lacks. (Never mind that the term *fetal abuse* is not in quotation marks, implying it is an acceptable and unproblematic category.) As all of these examples show, the more the fetus is aggrandized, the more women tend to be diminished.

NOTES

1. All the titles also cast the pregnant woman in the role of mother. In our society, mothering connotes women's selfless devotion to children, a connotation that is at odds with any action that could potentially jeopardize the health of a fetus. I address this point later in this chapter.

2. The poor treatment many women receive when they bring rape charges to the criminal justice system is perhaps the paradigmatic experience of such institutional betrayal. Women who press charges often speak of being raped twice: once by the accused, and again by the state.

3. I would like to thank Eve Weinbaum for suggesting this contrast. Laura Rothstein's book *Disabilities and the Law* describes the requirements of the ADA, signed into law in 1990.

4. Echoing the idea that fetal rights politics and the construct of "maternal-fetal conflict" locate problems of fetal safety within pregnant women themselves, Taylor argues that the ad presents the pregnant woman "as potentially dangerous to the fetus, [whose] safety can be ensured only by enclosing it (and her) within a car. The Volvo ad implicitly suggests that the pregnant woman is herself a sort of transport vehicle, and a relatively unsafe one at that: the steel body of a Volvo is needed to encase her, if the fetus is to remain safe."

DISCUSSION QUESTIONS FOR CHAPTER SIX

1. How do patriarchal norms constitute a threat to women's health?

2. How are women treated differently in the health care system? What is the effect of this differential treatment? How does racism have an impact on the gendered experiences of women of color in the health care system? Have you ever had a negative experience based on gender in the health care system?

3. Why is reproductive choice important for women?

4. What have been the consequences of women's loss of control of their reproductive processes?

5. How does the chipping away of abortion rights threaten the achievements of *Roe v. Wade*?

SUGGESTIONS FOR FURTHER READING

Boston Women's Health Book Collective, *Our Bodies, Our Selves for the New Century.* New York: Simon & Schuster, 1998.

Farmer, Paul, Margaret Connors, and Janie Simmons, eds. *Women, Poverty, and AIDS: Sex, Drugs, and Structural Violence.* Monroe, ME: Common Courage, 1996.

Gorney, Cynthia. *Articles of Faith: A Frontline History of the Abortion Wars.* New York: Touchstone, 2000.

Solinger, Rickie, ed. *Abortion Wars: A Half Century of Struggle, 1950–2000.* Los Angeles: University of California Press, 1998.

Weddington, Sarah. *A Question of Choice.* New York: Penguin, 1993.

CHAPTER SEVEN

Family Systems, Family Lives

The title of this chapter, "Family Systems, Family Lives," reflects the reality of the family as both a major societal institution and as a place where individuals experience intimate relationships. At the institutional level, the family maintains patterns of privilege and inequity and is intimately connected to other institutions in society such as the economy, the political system, religion, and education. At the level of experience, the family fulfills basic human needs and provides most of us with our first experiences of love and relationship as well as power and conflict. A focus of recent scholarship on the family has demonstrated that family forms are historically and culturally constructed and that family is a place for the reproduction of power relations in society. In this way, the family is a primary social unit that maintains other institutions and reinforces existing patterns of domination. At the same time, however, family networks provide support systems that can reduce the indignities and/or challenge the inequities produced by various systems of inequality in society.

DEFINITIONS OF FAMILY

Families are part of what social scientists call kinship systems or patterns of relationships that define family forms. Kinship systems vary widely around the world, although they tend to pattern such features as the meaning of marriage, the number of marriage partners permitted at one time (monogamy involves one husband and one wife and polygamy is multiple spouses, the most common form being polygyny or multiple wives), norms about marriageability, determination of descent, and distribution of property. In the United States, there is no "normal" family even though it tends to be constructed as the nuclear family of the middle-class, White, married, heterosexual couple with children. Nuclear family implies a married couple residing together with their children, and it can be distinguished from an extended family in which a group of related kin, in addition to parents and children, live together in the same household. The nuclear family arose as a result of Western industrialization that separated the home from productive activities. In pre- and early-industrial America, the family was relatively self-sufficient in producing goods for family consumption and exchange with other families. As industrial capitalism developed, family members increasingly worked outside the home for wages that were spent on goods for family consumption.

Facts About U.S. Families

- There were 70.9 million family and 31.6 million nonfamily households in the United States in 1998.
- There were 110.6 million married adults living with their spouse.
- Average family size was 3.92 for Hispanics, 3.42 for Blacks, and 3.02 for Whites, not Hispanic.
- There were 19.4 million adults currently divorced.
- There were 2,244,000 marriages in 1998 and 1,163,000 divorces.
- About 19.8 million children under 18 lived with a single parent. Of these children 84.1 percent lived with their mother. About 40.3 percent of these children lived with mothers who had never been married.
- Seventy-six percent of White, non-Hispanic children lived with two parents, as compared to 36 percent of Black children and 64 percent of Hispanic children.
- In 1997, 65 percent of Native American, Eskimo, and Aleut families consisted of married couples; 25 percent were maintained by women with no husband present.
- About 4 million children lived in the household of their grandparents.
- Among adults aged 25–34 years old, 13.6 million had never been married.
- Nearly half of women 65 years old and over were widowed. Of the elderly widows, 70.1 percent lived alone.

Note: Statistics are for 1998 (except where noted) and are drawn from the U.S. Census Bureau and the Centers for Disease Control.

Traditional myths about the normative family are rampant in the United States, and they hide the reality of the wide diversity of family life: single parents, extended and multigenerational families, lesbian and gay families with and without children, people (single or not and with or without children) living in community with other adults, grandparents raising grandchildren or nieces and nephews, and so forth. And, of course, these families represent all social classes and all racial and ethnic groups. Even though some families are not legally recognized, they are still part of the diversity among America's families. In the reading "What We Call Each Other," Anndee Hochman writes about how the English language is devoid of words to adequately describe relationships and families outside of this norm.

The recent political debate concerning "family values" illustrates how supporters of the status quo (or existing power relations) in society have made the term *family values* synonymous with traditional definitions of the family and its role in society. This includes seeing women defined in terms of their domestic and reproductive roles and men as the rightful sources of power and authority in the family. Many people are offended by this narrow construction of family and its association with a repressive political agenda, and they reject these values as *their* family values. Determining what kinds of families get to be counted as "real" families and whose "family values" are used as standards for judging others have become heated debate topics in the United States.

The notion of family—with all its connotations of love, security, connectedness, and nurturing—is a prime target for nostalgia at the turn of the century. As economic forces have transformed the ways that families function, we yearn for a return to the traditional family, with its unconditional love and acceptance, to

Myths and Facts About Lesbian Families

Myth 1: Lesbians don't have lasting relationships.
Fact: Many lesbians are in long-term partnerships. Unfortunately, social supports and civil rights are not accorded to lesbian partnerships as they are to heterosexual marriages. No state in the country recognizes gay marriage, although in 1999 the Vermont Supreme Court ruled that denying lesbian and gay couples the benefits of marriage was unconstitutional and ordered the legislature to develop a form of civil union to allow lesbian and gay partnerships the same rights and responsibilities as married couples in Vermont.

Myth 2: Lesbians don't have children.
Fact: The American Bar Association estimates that at least 6 million American children have lesbian or gay parents. Many lesbians have children from previous heterosexual relationships before they came out. Others have children through artificial insemination, and others adopt children. Unfortunately, because the courts often believe stereotypes about lesbians, lesbian mothers often lose custody of their children in a divorce, despite research indicating the fitness of lesbian mothers. In many states, adoption is difficult for lesbians, and rarely can both partners in a lesbian relationship legally adopt a child together.

Myth 3: Children of lesbian parents develop psychological disorders.
Fact: Research indicates that there is no difference in the development or frequency of pathologies between children of heterosexual or homosexual parents. In fact, study after study suggests that children in lesbian families are more similar than different from children in heterosexual families. Studies of separation-individuation, behavior problems, self-concept, locus of control, moral judgment, and intelligence have revealed no major differences between children of lesbian mothers versus children of heterosexual mothers.

Myth 4: Children of lesbian parents become gay themselves.
Fact: Research indicates no difference between children raised in lesbian families and children raised in heterosexual families with respect to gender identity, gender role behavior, and sexual orientation. Studies suggest that children in lesbian families develop along the same lines as children in heterosexual families; they are as likely to be happy with their gender, exhibit gender role behaviors, and be heterosexual as children of heterosexual mothers.

Learning Activity: What Makes a Family?

Conduct an informal survey of the people on your dorm floor or in an organization to which you belong about the structure of their family of origin. Whom do they consider to be in their family? What relation do these people have to them? Did all of these people live in the same house? Who had primary responsibility for caring for them as children? Who was primarily responsible for the financial well-being of the family? For the emotional well-being of the family? Was the family closely connected to extended family? If so, which extended family members and in what ways?

Compare your findings with those of your classmates. What do your findings lead you to surmise about what makes a family? How closely do the families of your interviewees resemble the dominant notion of the nuclear family—a husband and wife (in their first marriage) and their two or three children? What do you think is the impact of our stereotype of the nuclear family on social policy? How do you think this stereotype affects real families dealing with the real problems of everyday family life?

escape from the complexities and harsh realities of society. Although many families do provide this respite, dominant ideologies about the family have idealized and sometimes glorified the family, and women's roles in the family, in ways that hide underlying conflict and violence. In addition, these ideologies present a false dichotomization between public (society) and private (family) spheres. Poor and non-White families have rarely enjoyed the security and privacy assumed in this split between family and society. For example, the state, in terms of both social welfare policies and criminal justice statutes, has stronger impact and more consequences on poor families than middle-class families. This is the topic of the next section: the connections between the family and other social institutions.

INSTITUTIONAL CONNECTIONS

The family interacts with other institutions in society and provides various experiences for family members. For example, economic forces shape women's family roles and help construct the balance between work and family responsibilities. As discussed in Chapter 8, women perform over two-thirds of household labor—labor that is constructed as family work and often not seen as work. In addition, the family work that women do in the home is used to justify the kinds of work women are expected to perform in the labor force. It is no coincidence that women are congregated in a small number of occupations known for their care taking, educating, and servicing responsibilities. In addition, the boundaries are more fluid between women's paid work and home life than men's. This is structured into the very kinds of jobs women tend to perform, as well as part of the expectations associated with hiring women. These assumptions can be used against women very easily as women attempt to advance in their careers. At the same time, the more rigid boundaries between work and home for male-dominated jobs means that men have a more difficult time with parenting responsibilities when they want to be more actively involved in their children's lives.

The economic system impacts families in many ways; in turn, families support and impact economic systems. Women care for and maintain male workers as well as socialize future generations of workers, thus supporting economic institutions that rely on workers to be fed, serviced, and able to fulfill certain work roles. Although in contemporary U.S. society some families are still productive units in that they produce goods directly for family consumption or for exchange on the market, most families are consumptive units in that they participate in the market economy through goods purchased for family consumption. As a result, advertisers target women as family shoppers. The family is a consumptive unit that provides the context for advertising, media, and other forms of entertainment. In these ways family systems are intimately connected to economic forces in society.

The impact of shifting economies and changing technologies on women and families varies considerably by class and race, such that a family's placement in the larger political economy directly influences diverse patterns of family organization. In this way families are shaped by their relationship to systems of inequality in society. This means, for example, that working class women's lack of flexible work scheduling affects how families are able to meet their needs, as does the

Families in Poverty*

CHARACTERISTIC	LIVING BELOW POVERTY	PERCENTAGE
Total People	34,476,000	12.7
Families†	7,186,000	10.0
White, not Hispanic	3,264,000	6.1
Black	1,981,000	23.4
Hispanic	1,648,000	22.7
Asian and Pacific Islander	270,000	11.0
Married couples	2,879,000	5.3
Female householder	3,831,000	29.9
White, not Hispanic	1,428,000	20.7
Black	1,557,000	40.8
Hispanic	756,000	43.7
Under 18 years of age	13,467,000	18.9

*Data are for 1998 and are from the U.S. Census Bureau.
†Data for Native American, Eskimo, and Aleuts are not shown separately because of the small sample size.

lower pay of working-class women, making them less able to afford quality day-care. Similarly, higher unemployment among men of color as compared to White men impacts families and pushes women in family relationships with unemployed men to work outside the home full time while also taking care of young children. As Betty Holcomb explains in the reading, "Friendly for Whose Family?" jobs with different incomes and levels of authority and seniority affect access to such family-friendly benefits as flextime, on-site childcare, and company-sponsored tax breaks for childcare. Parenting leave is a legal right of all U.S. employees, but many companies provide better family benefits for their higher level and better paid employees than they do for the lower level employees.

The family experience is also affected by the state and its legal and political systems. The government closely regulates the family and provides certain benefits to legally married couples. Couples need a license from the state to marry, and the government says they may file a joint tax return. Lesbian and gay couples who jointly own property and share income and expenses do not have the privileges of marriage (although this is now hotly contested), joint tax filing, and, in many situations, domestic partner benefits. Benefits accrue to certain family members but not to people who, even though they might see themselves as family, are not recognized as such by the state. In addition, although an advanced industrial society, the United States has no national funding of daycare centers, and this affects the social organization of the family and the experience of parenting. Federal and state policies also impact the family through legal statutes that regulate marriage and divorce legislation, reproductive choice, and violence in families.

Indeed, the family has connections to all societal institutions, and these connections help shape the kind and quality of experiences that we have as family members. Religion and the family are closely tied as social institutions. Religious socialization of children occurs in the family through religious and moral teachings,

Activist Profile: Hannah Solomon

Hannah Greenbaum Solomon believed that "woman's sphere is the whole wide world" and her first responsibility was to her family. Solomon worked tirelessly in turn-of-the-century Chicago for social reform. Laboring alongside Jane Addams at Hull House, Solomon worked to improve child welfare. She reformed the Illinois Industrial School for Girls, established penny lunch stations in the public schools, and led efforts for slum clearance, low-cost housing, child labor laws, mothers' pensions, and public health measures.

In 1876 Solomon became the first Jewish member of the Chicago Woman's Club, where she developed a sense of women's ability to work together for social good. In 1893, she organized the Jewish Women's Congress at the Chicago World's Fair, which led to her founding the National Council of Jewish Women (NCJW) to enhance social welfare and justice. Solomon saw her commitment to justice as a part of her responsibility as a Jew, a woman, and an American.

Under Solomon's leadership, the National Council of Jewish Women sponsored programs for the blind, formed the Port and Dock Department to assist immigrant women in finding housing and jobs, established a permanent immigrant aid station on Ellis Island, supported Margaret Sanger's National Birth Control League, raised relief dollars during World War I, and participated in the presidential effort to create jobs during the Depression.

Solomon's legacy has continued in the NCJW since her death in 1942. Following World War II, the NCJW provided assistance to Holocaust survivors in Europe and Israel. During the McCarthy era, NCJW organized the Freedom Campaign to protect civil liberties. Additionally, the organization was the first national group to sponsor Meals on Wheels, built the Hebrew University High School in Jerusalem, helped establish the Court Appointed Advocate Project (CASA) to protect the rights of children in court cases, and launched a national campaign to try to ensure that children were not harmed by changes in welfare law.

Currently, the National Council of Jewish Women has 90,000 members and continues the work of Hannah Solomon by bringing her vision of justice to bear in the world.

Learning Activity: Divorce Law: Who Benefits in My State?

Research your state's divorce laws. How is property divided in a divorce? How is custody determined? How are alimony and child support determined? How do these laws affect women and children in actuality in your state? What are the poverty rates for divorced women and their children in your state? How many fathers do not pay child support as ordered by the court? How does your state deal with nonpaying fathers? What can you do to challenge the legal system in your state to be more responsive to women and children's needs following divorce?

and religious institutions often shape societal understandings of families as well as provide rituals that help symbolize family and kin relations (such as baptisms, weddings, and funerals). Educational institutions rely on the family as a foundation for socialization and care and maintenance of children, and health systems rely on parents (and women in particular) to nurse and care for sick family members as well as provide adequate nutrition and cleanliness to prevent disease. Military institutions need the family as a foundation for ideologies of combat and for socialization and support of military personnel. Sports and athletics are tied to the family through gender socialization, the purchase of certain equipment and opportunities, and the consumption and viewing of professional sports in the home.

POWER AND FAMILY RELATIONSHIPS

At the direct level of experience, the family is the social unit where most people are raised, learn systems of belief, experience love, perhaps abuse and neglect, and generally grow to be a part of communities and society. It is in the family where most of us internalize messages about ourselves, about others, and our place in the world. In the reading "Justice: Childhood Love Lessons," bell hooks writes about the ways families teach about love and makes the point that there can be no love without justice. Some of us learn that love comes with an abuse of power as large people hit little people, all in the name of love. Others learn that love means getting our own way without responsibility—a lesson, hooks suggests, that detracts from the hopes of a civil society where individuals care about one another and the communities of which they are a part.

Family is where many of us first experience gender because societal understandings of the differences between girls and boys are transferred through early teachings by family members. Parents bring home baby girls and boys, dress them in gender "appropriate" colors, give them different toys, and decorate their bedrooms in different ways. As Chapter 3 emphasized, the family is a primary institution for teaching about gender. Experiences of gender are very much shaped by the gender composition of family members. A girl growing up in a family of brothers or a boy with only women and girls in his family have different experiences of gender. This is illustrated in the reading by Sandra Cisneros titled "Only Daughter."

Central in any discussion of family is a focus on power. Power in families is understood as access to resources (tangible or intangible) that allows certain family members to define the reality of others, have their needs met, and experience more resources. In most U.S. families today, power is distributed according to age and gender. Older family members (although not the aged, who often lose power in late life) tend to have more power than children and young people who are often defined as "dependents." Men have more power in the family than women do if this is measured in resource management and allocation and decision-making authority. Women, however, do have power if this is defined as day-to-day decisions about the running of the household and how certain household chores get done.

Ideas for Activism

- Become a Court Appointed Advocate (CASA) for children.
- Offer to babysit for free for a single mother one evening a month.
- Lobby your state lawmakers to enact legislation recognizing lesbian and gay unions.
- Organize an educational activity on your campus around alternative family models.

The United States has the highest marriage and the highest divorce rates of any industrialized country. Although a large number of people get divorced, this does not seem to indicate disillusionment with marriage because large numbers of people remarry. As Michael Kimmel emphasizes in the reading "The 'Constructed Problems' of Family Life" remarriage comprises about half of all marriages yearly. Marriage traditionally has been based upon gender relations that prescribe authority of husbands over wives and that entail certain norms and expectations that are sanctioned by the state. The traditional marriage contract assumes the husband will be the head of household with responsibilities to provide a family wage and the wife will take primary responsibility for the home and the raising of children and integrate her personal identity with that of her husband. As in "Mrs. John Smith" and "Dr. and Mrs. John Smith," Mrs. Smith easily can become someone who loses her identity to her husband. The declaration of "man and wife" in the traditional marriage ceremony illustrates how men continue to be men under this contract and women become wives. The rituals of marriage ceremonies also illustrate normative gender relations: the father "giving away" his daughter, representing the passage of the woman from one man's house to another; the wearing of white to symbolize purity and virginity; the engagement ring representing a woman already spoken for; and the throwing of rice to symbolize fertility and the woman's obligation to bear and raise children.

It is especially in the family where many girls and women experience gender oppression. Where women and girls are in close relationship with men, they often experience gender domination. In other words, in the home and family many girls and women feel the consequences of masculine power and privilege. Writing in 1910, socialist anarchist Emma Goldman saw marriage as an economic transaction that binds women into subservience to men (through love and personal and sexual services) and society (through unpaid housework). In the reading "Marriage and Love," she advocates "free love" that is unconstrained by marriage and relations with the state. Goldman believed love found in marriages occurred in spite of the institution of marriage and not because of it.

Sexism in interpersonal relationships among family members reduces female autonomy and lowers women's and girls' self-esteem. Consequences of masculine privilege in families can mean that men dominate women in relationships in subtle or not-so-subtle ways, expecting or taking for granted personal and sexual services, making and/or vetoing important family decisions, controlling money and expenditures, and so forth. In addition, power in family and marital relationships may lead to psychological, sexual, and/or physical abuse against women and children. Often the double standard of sexual conduct allows boys more freedom

*"Yes, this is a two career household.
Unfortunately I have both careers."*

Reprinted with permission from Carol Simpson Productions.

and autonomy compared to girls. Also, girls are very often expected to perform more household duties than boys, duties that often include cleaning up after their brothers or father.

In particular, the balance of power in marriage (or any domestic partnership) depends in part upon how couples negotiate paid labor and family work in their relationships. Marriages or domestic partnerships can be structured according to different models that promote various ways that couples live and work together. These models include: "head–complement," "junior partner/senior partner," and "equal partners"—relationships that each have different ways of negotiating paid work and family work, and, as a result, provide different balances of power within these relationships.

The "head–complement" model reflects the traditional marriage contract as discussed previously where the head/husband has responsibilities to provide a family wage and the complement/wife takes primary responsibility for the home and the raising of children. In addition the complement sees (usually her) role as complementing the head's role by being supportive and encouraging in both emotional and material ways. The balance of power in this family system is definitely tilted in the direction of the "head" of the head–complement couple. Power for the complement is to a large extent based upon the goodwill of the head as well as the resources (educational and financial in particular) that the complement brings into the relationship. Although the complement does tend to have control over the day-to-day running of the household, this power may disappear with divorce or other internal family disruption. It is estimated that heterosexual head–complement families make up only about 14 percent of all families in the United States.

The "junior partner/senior partner" model is where the traditional marriage contract has been modified. Both members of the couple work outside the home, although one member (usually wife or female domestic partner) considers her work to be secondary to the senior partner's job. She also takes primary responsibility for the home and childcare. This means that the junior partner has taken on some of the provider role while still maintaining responsibility for the domestic role. In practice this might mean that if the senior partner is transferred or relocated because of (usually his) work, the junior partner experiences a disruption in her work to follow. If someone is contacted when the children come home from school sick, it is the junior partner. She might enter and leave the labor force based upon the needs of the children and family. This model, the most frequently occurring structure for marriage or domestic partnerships today, encourages the double day of work for women where they work both inside and outside the home.

In terms of power, there is a more equitable sharing in this model because the junior partner is bringing resources into the family and has control over the day-to-day running of the household. Note in both models described here, the head and senior partner loses out to a greater or lesser degree on the joys associated with household work—especially the raising of children. Junior partners tend to fare better after divorce than the complements of the head–complement model. But junior partners do have the emotional stress and physical burdens of working two jobs. These stresses and burdens are affected by how much the senior partner helps out in the home.

The "equal partners" model is one where the traditional marriage contract is completely disrupted. Neither partner is more likely to perform provider or domestic roles. In practice this might mean both jobs or careers are valued equally such that one does not take priority over the other and domestic responsibilities are shared equally. Alternatively, it might mean an intentional sharing of responsibilities such that one partner agrees to be the economic provider for a period of time and the other agrees to take on domestic responsibilities, although neither is valued more than the other, and this is negotiated rather than implied. In this model financial power is shared, and the burdens and joys of domestic work and childcare are also shared. Although this arrangement gives women the most power in marriage or domestic partnerships, not surprisingly it is a relatively infrequent arrangement among contemporary couples. This is because most men in domestic relationships have been socialized to expect the privileges associated with having women service their everyday needs or raise their children, and most women expect to take on these responsibilities. Both men and women rarely question this taken-for-granted gendered division of labor. It is also because men's jobs are more likely to involve a separation of home and work, and it is more difficult for them to integrate these aspects of their lives. In addition, because men tend to earn more money than women do on the average, although it might be relatively easy to value women's paid work equally in theory, it is difficult to do so in practice if one job brings in a much higher salary than the other. For example, imagine an equal partner relationship between a dentist and a dental hygienist. These occupations are very gender segregated, with the majority of dentists being men and dental hygienists women. Although the couple may value each other's work equally, it might be difficult for a family to make decisions concerning relocation and so forth in favor of the one partner who works as the dental hygienist because she makes a small percentage of her partner's salary as a dentist.

It is important to emphasize that despite these various arrangements and the differential balance of power in marriage or domestic partnerships, for many women the family is where they feel most empowered. Many women find the responsibilities of maintaining a household or the challenges of child rearing fulfilling and come to see the family as a source of their competency and happiness. Sometimes this involves living in traditional family forms, and sometimes it means devising new ways of living in families. In this way the family is a positive source of connection, community, and/or productive labor. These diverse experiences associated with family life suggest how family relationships are a complex tangle of compliance to and resistance against various forms of inequities. Mothering, in particular, is one experience that often brings women great joy and shapes their experiences of family relations. This is the topic to which we now turn.

MOTHERING

Although the meaning and practice of motherhood is culturally constructed, it tends to be conflated with notions of innate, biologically programmed behavior and expectations of unconditional love and nurturance. In other words, even though the meanings associated with motherhood vary historically and culturally, women are expected to want to be mothers, and mothers are expected to take primary responsibility for the nurturing of children. Unlike the assumptions associated with "to father," "to mother" implies nurturing, comforting, and care taking. You might mother a kitten or a friend without the assumption of having given birth to them. To have fathered a kitten implies paternity: You are its parent; you did not cuddle and take care of it. Similarly, to father a friend makes no sense in this context.

This primary association between women and mothering has brought joys and opportunities for empowerment as well as problems and hardship. It has justified the enormous amount of work we do in the home and encouraged girls to set their sights on babies rather than on other forms of productive work. It has justified the type of labor women have traditionally done in the labor force as well as justified lower pay, has kept women out of specific positions such as in the military where they might be involved in taking life rather than giving life, and it has encouraged all kinds of explanations for why men are, and should be, in control in society. In addition, it has caused pain for women who are not able to have children as well as for those who have intentionally chosen to not have any.

Contemporary constructions of mothering, like the family, tend to be created around a mythical norm that reflects a White, abled, middle-class, heterosexual, and young adult experience. But, of course, mothers come in all types and reflect the wide diversity of women in the United States. Their understandings of their roles and their position within systems of inequality and privilege are such that mothering is a diverse experience. This is because society has different expectations of mothers depending upon class and culture and other differences at the

Children with Single Parents—How They Fare

Children living at home with both parents grow up with more financial and educational advantages than youngsters raised by one parent, as U.S. Census Bureau statistics have long shown. But even for those children living in single-parent homes, the marital status of the parent can affect the quality of life. More than a quarter of America's children now live with one parent.

Children living with a divorced parent typically have a big edge over those living with a parent who has never married—an even bigger edge if that parent is the father.

Never-married parents are significantly younger than divorced parents and on average tend to have fewer years of school completed and lower levels of income. Nonetheless, although age does have an effect, the differences remain.

DIVORCED PARENTS ARE MORE EDUCATED

About 85 percent of children living with either a divorced mother or father in 1995 were living with a parent who had finished high school. In contrast, among children living with a never-married parent, fewer than two-thirds had parents who had completed high school.

CHILDREN OF DIVORCED PARENTS ARE LESS LIKELY TO LIVE IN RENTAL HOMES

Of the 19 million children of single parents, two-thirds lived in rented homes. In 1995, about 78 percent of children living with never-married parents, and one-half (52 percent) of children living with divorced parents lived in rented homes.

CHILDREN OF DIVORCED PARENTS ARE LESS LIKELY TO BE POOR

Nearly six of ten children living with only their mother were near (or below) the poverty line. About 45 percent of children raised by divorced mothers and 69 percent of those raised by never-married mothers lived in or near poverty. Children living with their father (particularly if he was divorced) were more likely to be part of a family with a higher median income than those living with a single mom.

Employment was an important reason for this poverty. Although many single parents had jobs, there were 7.4 million children living with single moms who were unemployed or not in the labor force. Children of never-married mothers were twice as likely (59 percent) to have their moms unemployed or not in the labor force as children whose mothers were divorced (29 percent).

same time that these differences create different attitudes toward the experience of mothering. For example, although society often expects poor mothers to work outside the home rather than accept welfare, middle-class mothers might be made to feel guilty for "abandoning" their babies to daycare centers. Because of class, ethnicity, and/or religious orientation, some women experience more ambivalence than others when it comes to combining work and family roles. Differently-abled women often experience little support and encouragement when it comes to their decision to raise an abled child. A little over one-quarter of all births in the United States are to single mothers, and many more women become single in the process of raising children. Motherhood for single mothers is often constructed through societal notions of stigma, and, as Michael Kimmel explains in his article, because fatherlessness is often seen as a major cause of social problems, single mothers are blamed. He emphasizes that a correlation (relation between factors) does not imply causality and suggests that both social problems and fatherlessness are products of poverty.

Interracial or lesbian couples or people who adopt a child of another race are often accused of not taking into account the best interests of their children. Of course, it is society that has these problems and the families are doing their best to cope. Lesbian mothers in particular have to deal with two mutually exclusive categories that have been constructed as contradictory: mother and lesbian. This illustrates the narrow understandings of motherhood as well as the stereotypes associated with being a mother and with being a lesbian. In addition, lesbian mothers, although often mothering with a female partner who also parents, are legally understood as single mothers: women parenting with an absent father. As a result, they must deal with that stigma too.

In this way, American families are increasingly diverse forms of social organization that are intricately connected to other institutions in society. The family is a basic social unit around which much of society is built; it is fundamental to the processes of meeting individual and social needs. The centrality of the family in U.S. society encourages us to think about the way the family reproduces and resists gender relations and what it means to each of us in our everyday lives.

The "Constructed Problems" of Contemporary Family Life

Michael Kimmel

. . . Without a concerted national policy to assist working women and men to balance work and family obligations, we continue to put such enormous strains on two sets of bonds, between husbands and wives and between parents and children, and virtually guarantee that the "crisis" of the family will continue. And we will also continue to face a series of "constructed problems"—problems that stem from the strain felt by individual families as they negotiate the increased pressures of sustaining dual-career couples and dividing housework and child care in the absence of help from the outside.

In the 1950s, the government stepped in where once the community and extended kinship networks had sustained family life, and created an infrastructure (schools, hospitals, roads, and suburban homes) that supported and sustained family life. Today, we expect families to accomplish far more—expect them, for example, to support children often beyond high school and college and to provide for virtually all of an adult's emotional needs—on far less. It is from this widening chasm between what we expect from our families and what support we offer them that several "constructed problems" emerge. These problems are also the result of gender inequality—both its persistence and the efforts by women to remedy it. Only when we develop a sustained national effort—both individually and politically—to reduce the gender inequality in both the home and the workplace, will these constructed problems begin to ease.

THE "PROBLEM" OF DAY CARE

Take, for example, the "problem" of day care. Many Americans are reluctant to place their children in day care, and the government has no national funding for day-care centers. Yet the most common conclusion from the research on the impact of day care on children's development is that there are no negative psychological, intellectual, developmental, or emotional consequences to being in day care. And a 1996 National Institutes of Health study found that children's attachment to their mothers is not affected by whether or not they are in day care, what age they enter, or how many hours they spend there.

Despite these findings, we seem to be bombarded daily with headlines that remind us of such negative consequences, including child sexual abuse at day-care centers. The implication of such terrifying stories is that if these children were home with their mothers, where they "belong," such terrible things would not be happening to them. The "problem" of day care turns out to be a debate about whether or not women should be working outside the home. "Having a nanny read you a story isn't the same as having your mother do so," writes William R. Mattox, a senior writer for the conservative Family Research Council. "A mother's worth cannot be reduced to the cost of what a paid substitute might command. To suggest that it can is like saying that the value of a woman making love to her husband is equal to the going rate for prostitutes in the area."

To ask whether or not women should work outside the home is, of course, to ask the wrong question. For one thing, it poses a class-based contradiction, since we encourage poor women to leave the home and go to work, and middle-class women to leave the workplace and return home. The landmark Welfare Reform legislation of 1996 requires that welfare recipients start working within two years of going on welfare. "It is difficult to argue that poor mothers should find jobs but that middle-class mothers should stay home," writes family researcher Andrew Cherlin. And when they can find jobs, working-class and middle-class women are simply not going to stop working.

Nor is there any reason that they should, since there is no evidence whatsoever that mothers working outside the home adversely affects children. In fact, most of the evidence indicates that both direct and indirect benefits accrue to children of working mothers. Such children tend to have expanded role models, more egalitarian gender role attitudes, and more positive attitudes toward women and women's employment. Daughters of employed women are more likely to be employed, and in jobs similar to those of their mothers, than daughters of nonemployed women. Moreover, adolescent children of working mothers assume more responsibility around the home, which increases their self-esteem.

Working outside the home also increases women's self-esteem and sense of personal efficacy and well-being, so working mothers tend to be happier in their marriages—which makes divorce less likely. One study found that the happier wives were in their jobs, the happier they were in their marriages. In a four-year study sponsored by the National Institute for Mental Health, Rosalind Barnet observed three hundred dual-career families, and found that the women were neither depressed nor stressed out, but said they had good marriages and good relationships with their children. Another survey of more than eight hundred two-career couples found similar results.

Not only *will* women continue to work outside the home, but they *should* work outside the home, argues Joan Peters. "If they do not, they cannot preserve their identities or raise children" who are able to be both independent and family oriented. But, "women can do so successfully only if men take half the responsibility for child care." Again, the "solution" turns out to be social and political. Only one-third of all employees in large and midsize U.S. compa-

nies can even receive unpaid parental leave. Both nationally and in each family, the solution turns out to be greater gender equality—not women working less outside the home, but men working more inside it.

. . .

THE "PROBLEM" OF FATHERLESSNESS

The question of men's responsibility also surfaces in the debates about fatherlessness. In recent years, commentators have noticed that fathers are not around, having left their children either through divorce or cavalier indifference. Recent works such as David Blankenhorn's *Fatherless America* or David Popenoe's *Life without Father* have credited absent fathers with causing myriad social problems, ranging from juvenile delinquency, crime, and violence to unemployment. We read, for example, that 70 percent of all juveniles in state reform institutions come from fatherless homes. This bodes especially ill for young boys, because without a father, we are told, these young boys will grow up without secure foundation in their manhood. "In families where the father is absent, the mother faces an impossible task: She cannot raise a boy into a man. He must bond with a man as he grows up," writes psychologist Frank Pittman. It is a mistake to believe that "a mother is able to show a male child how to be a man." "Boys raised by traditionally masculine fathers generally do not commit crimes," adds David Blankenhorn. "Fatherless boys commit crimes." In a home without a father, Robert Bly writes somewhat more poetically, "the demons have full permission to rage." This has consequences for both the fathers and the boys, creating in one moment two sets of unattached and unconstrained males roaming around the streets. "Every society must be wary of the unattached male," family researcher David Popenoe reminds us, "for he is universally the cause of numerous social ills."

It is true that more children of both sexes are being raised in single-parent homes, and that the "single parent" doing that child raising is more often than not a woman. Whereas just over one in ten (11 percent) children were being raised by unmarried mothers in 1970, nearly one-fourth (24 percent) are being raised that way as of 1996. More than one in four (26 percent) of all births are to single women. And it is also true that the other side of the "feminization of poverty" coin is the "masculinization of irresponsibility"—the refusal of fathers to provide economically for their children. What is less certain, however, is the impact of fathers on the myriad social problems with which their absence seems to be correlated. Though father involvement may provide some benefits to children, family researchers Paul Amato and Alan Booth note that the effects are "far from overwhelming" and certainly are not decisive for the well-being of their children. Remember, also, that correlation is not causation, and though fatherlessness may be correlated with high crime rates, that does not mean that fatherlessness *caused* the criminality. In fact, it might just be the other way around. It turns out that high crime rates and fatherlessness are *both* products of a larger and more overwhelming problem: poverty.

The National Academy of Sciences reports that the single best predictor of violent crime is not fatherlessness but "personal and neighborhood income." And, it turns out, fatherlessness also varies with income; the higher the income bracket, the more likely the father is home—which suggests that the crisis of fatherlessness is actually a crisis of poverty. In his impressive ethnographic research on street gangs in Los Angeles, Martin Sanchez-Jankowski found "as many gang members from homes where the nuclear family was intact as there were from families where the father was absent" and "as many members who claimed close relationships with their families as those who denied them." Clearly something other than the mere presence or absence of a father is at work here.

The confusion of correlation and causation also reveals a deeper confusion of consequence and cause. Fatherlessness may be a conse-

quence of those larger, deeper, more structural forces that drive fathers from the home and keep them away—such as unemployment or increased workplace demands to maintain a standard of living. Pundits often attempt to transform the problem of fatherlessness into another excuse to blame feminism, and specifically women working outside the home. They yearn for a traditional nuclear family, with traditional gender inequality. For example, David Popenoe writes nostalgically about the family form of the 1950s—"heterosexual, monogamous, life-long marriage in which there is a sharp division of labor, with the female as the full-time housewife and the male as primary provider and ultimate authority"—without pausing to underscore that such a family form was also dramatically unequal when viewed from a gender perspective. Such a vision substitutes form for content, apparently under the impression that if only the family conformed to a specific form, then the content of family life would dramatically improve.

THE "PROBLEM" OF DIVORCE

It is hard to deny that divorce is a real problem. The divorce rate in the United States is astonishingly high, around half of all marriages. This is considerably higher than in other industrialized countries, more than double the rates in Germany and France, and nearly double the rate in Sweden and Britain, countries where individuals remain supported by national health care and children specifically benefit from adequate access to education and health care, while their custodial parents receive regular governmental stipends. (These, of course, ameliorate the harsh economic impact of divorce.) According to the Census Bureau, the number of divorced people had more than quadrupled from 4.3 million in 1970 to 19.3 million in 1997. This represents 10 percent of all adults aged eighteen or over, up from 3 percent in 1970.

Divorce may be a serious social problem, but not exactly for the reasons that many political commentators claim it is. First, these high divorce rates are not shattering the family. Rates of marital dissolution are roughly the same as they have been for a very long time. Looked at historically, high rates of divorce are merely accomplishing by conscious action what higher mortality rates had accomplished in an earlier period. As historian Lawrence Stone put it, "the median duration of marriage today is almost exactly the same as it was a hundred years ago. Divorce, in short, now acts as a functional substitute for death: Both are means of terminating marriage at a premature stage." (Of course, he adds that the psychological effects are not the same.) Nor does the number of divorces necessarily indicate a loss of faith in marriage. Ninety five percent of men and 94 percent of women between the ages of forty-five and fifty-four have been married. In fact, writes sociologist Constance Ahrons, author of *The Good Divorce*, "we like marriage so much that many of us will do it two, three, or more times." Remarriages now comprise about half of all marriages every year.

The problem with divorce is more accurately linked to the constructed problem of fatherlessness and the real problem of gender inequality. Divorce reform was promoted, after all, by feminist women at the turn of the century to provide some legal recourse to women who wanted to escape marriages that were desperately unhappy, and others brutally, even, violently oppressive. The option of divorce loosened the marital knot to keep it from choking women. Like birth control and abortion, both of which have also generated heated debates, divorce undermined men's power over women and reduced gender inequality in the family.

Although liberalizing divorce laws may have reduced gender inequality within marriage, they seem neither to have reduced it entirely nor reduced it after the marriage is dissolved. One recent study found that three of four women listed pathological behaviors by male partners (adultery, violence, substance abuse, abandonment) as their reason for divorce. Just

as there are "his" and "her" marriages, there are also "his" and "her" divorces because divorce affects wives and husbands differently. Divorce exaggerates gender differences in the marriage, exacerbating gender inequality. In the mid-1980s, family researcher Leonore Weitzman calculated that following divorce, the woman's income drops a precipitous 73 percent, while her ex-husband's income increases 42 percent. In recent years, these data have been revised as overly dramatic, but no research suggests that the economic and social statuses of women and men after divorce are equivalent, and researchers still agree that women's resources decline somewhat even as men's improve. As sociologist Paul Amato writes, "the greater the inequality between men and women in a given society, the more detrimental the impact of divorce on women."

. . .

THE "PROBLEM" OF CHILD CUSTODY

Whether or not divorce has simply accomplished by social policy what high mortality rates used to accomplish "naturally," there is one significant difference between the two methods to dissolve a marriage. With a divorce often comes the problem of child custody. Before the Industrial Revolution, children were seen as an economic "good," and courts used an economic means test to determine who would receive custody, and custody was regularly and routinely given to fathers. In the early years of the twentieth century, though, children came to be seen as a luxury, and so a new test, based on care and nurture, was used to determine custody arrangements, a policy that favored mothers. Today, the "best interest of the child" is the criterion employed to provide the foundation for custody decisions, although in practice, the best interests of the child are presumed to be better served by staying with the mother not the father, since the presumption is that mothers provide better child care, especially for young children, than do fathers.

Such a policy makes a certain amount of sense, since women perform most of the tasks that provide the care and nurture that children most need. And yet, in the late 1970s, 63 percent of fathers who requested custody received it, a significant increase from the 35 percent and 37 percent who requested and received it in 1968 and 1972 respectively. In a recent study of one thousand divorces in two California counties, psychologist Eleanor Maccoby and law professor Robert Mnookin found that a majority of mothers and fathers wanted joint legal custody, while those that didn't preferred that they, and not their spouses, be given custody. Nearly 82 percent of mothers and 56 percent of fathers requested the custody arrangement they wanted, while 6.7 percent of women and 9.8 percent of men requested more than they wanted and 11.5 percent of women and 34.1 percent of men requested less than they wanted. This suggests that "gender still matters" in what parents ask for and what they do to get it. That mothers were more likely to act on their desires by filing for a specific request also indicates that men need to ask for more up front to avoid feeling bitter later.

Maccoby and Mnookin's research is notable for another finding. Children living with mothers generally did as well as children living with fathers, that "the welfare of kids following a divorce did not depend a lot on who got custody," Maccoby told a journalist, "but rather on how the household was managed and how the parents cooperated." But one consequence of current custody arrangements is paternal withdrawal. Whether this is because the father is bereft at being kept from regular contact with his children or because once the marital bond is severed he experiences a euphoria of "freedom" and considers himself to have escaped from a conflict-ridden family situation, it appears that many men "see parenting and marriage as part of the same bargain—a package deal," write sociologists Frank Furstenberg and Andrew Cherlin. "It is as if they stop being fathers as soon as the marriage is over." In one nationally representative sample of 11- to 16-year-old children living with their mothers, almost half had not seen their fathers in the previous twelve months. Nearly half of all divorced fathers in the United States pay no child support; in Europe the comparable number is about one-fourth.

Paternal withdrawal, it turns out, actually affects the father-daughter relationship most significantly, even more than the much-touted father-son relationship, whereas the mother-daughter relationship seems to be the most resilient to divorce and custody disputes. This may surprise those who believe that the father-son bond is the most fragile and most hard-hit by postdivorce fatherlessness, but it illustrates how frequently daughters are ignored in that literature, and how both boys and girls benefit from paternal responsibility and continued presence in their children's lives.

In recent years, postdivorce fatherhood has become a political issue, as "father's rights" organizations have sprouted up, declaring men to be the victims of inequality in custody decisions. It is true, of course, that most court decisions grant custody to the mother, based on the "best interest of the child" standard. Father's rights groups challenge this assumption, and claim that, invariably, joint custody is preferable for children. Sometimes, it appears that their rhetoric substitutes these aggrieved fathers' vindictiveness against ex-wives, or their bewilderment at the entire divorce proceeding, for the "best interests" of children, but it also appears to be the case that all things being equal, joint physical and legal custody ought to be the norm in custody decisions. Here, of course, "all things being equal" means that there is no discernible danger to the child of sexual or physical abuse; that the parents can manage to contain their own postdivorce conflict and prevent the children from becoming pawns in a parental power struggle; and that the parents agree to equally support the children financially and emotionally. Such arrangements may be more difficult for parents than for children, who often report "a sense of being loved by both parents," as well as "feeling strongly attached to two psychological parents, in contrast to feeling close to just one primary parent." Contrary to some popular opinion, joint custody "does not create uncertainty or confusion," and seems to benefit children, who say they are more satisfied with the arrangement than those in single-custody homes and consider having two homes advantageous.

We know, too, that joint custody will benefit men, who will, by maintaining a legal connection to their children, be far more likely to continue to share financial responsibilities for their development. What's more, joint custody may relieve the deep sense of loss, disengagement, and depression often experienced by men who are cut loose from continued involvement with their families. On the other hand, mandated joint legal custody may not be so good for women. Feminist legal theorist Martha Fineman argues that mandated joint legal custody may appear to be gender neutral, but gender "neutrality" in one arena in an overall system of gender inequality may perpetuate gender discrimination, much the way the abandonment of affirmative action sounds race- or gender-neutral, but actually favors white males over others by withdrawal from explicit challenge to historical discrimination. As Fineman writes:

> What may have started out as a system which, focusing on the child's need for care, gave women a preference *solely* because they had usually been the child's primary caretaker, is evolving into a system which, by devaluing the content of necessity of such care, gives men more than an equal chance to gain the custody of their children after divorce if they choose to have it, because biologically equal parents are considered as equal in expressive regards. Nonnurturing factors assume importance which often favor men.

Perhaps the most judicious system of child custody will be one that recognizes the difference in "inputs" between fathers and mothers in the actual experiences of the children—time spent in child care, level of parental involvement in child development—while at the same time presuming that both parents are capable of and interested in (absent any evidence to the contrary) continued committed and involved relationships with their children. Men's increased involvement in predivorce child care ought to be reflected in custody arrangements, as should women's continuing to shoulder the overwhelming majority of such care, despite their commitments to work. Fathers' "rights" following divorce will come more readily if the fathers have recognized their responsibilities during the marriage.

THE "PROBLEM" OF GAY AND LESBIAN FAMILIES

Another recent constructed problem is that of gay and lesbian families. I often find it ironic that the same political commentators who fret about the decline of the family are the very people who would prevent gay men and lesbians from creating them. But the problems of gay families—marriage, child rearing—are actually less about families, and more about the legal status of homosexuals. As soon as the Hawaii state Supreme Court indicated the likelihood that it would recognize gay and lesbian marriages in 1997, for example, several states rescinded their adherence to the "full faith and credit" clause of the U.S. Constitution, the provision that requires one state to recognize contracts concluded in another state, such as marriage, voting, education, or driving. Soon thereafter, the U.S. Congress passed the Defense of Marriage Act, as if the institution of marriage were under attack by those who seek to enter it. It is expressly legal for gay men and lesbians to adopt children in only ten states and the District of Columbia (Alaska, California, Minnesota, Oregon, Washington, Massachusetts, New Jersey, New York, Pennsylvania, and Vermont).

One reason that many gay and lesbian couples want to marry is because so many benefits accrue to married couples—benefits that heterosexual couples often take for granted. These include the right to inherit from a spouse who dies without a will; the right to consult with doctors and make crucial medical decisions if the partner is incapacitated; the right of residency of a foreign spouse; the right to Social Security benefits; the right to include a spouse on one's health plan; the right to visit a spouse in a government institution like a prison or hospital; and the right to immunity from having to testify against one's spouse in a legal proceeding.

It is true that gay male relationships are more fragile than heterosexual relationships and that gay men are more "promiscuous" (have a greater number of different sexual partners) than heterosexuals, though neither of these statements is true of lesbians. Some of the reasons for this disparity can be found in masculine gender socialization, which discourages men from commitment to domestic life in the first place; exclusion from formal legal marriage, which cements heterosexual relationships and increases the couple's likelihood of staying together despite disagreement; lack of children, who are often the reason that heterosexual couples continue to work on their relationships; and social disapproval and institutionalized homophobia, which can destabilize any couple. "It is paradoxical that mainstream America perceives gays and lesbians as unable to maintain long-term relationships while at the same time denying them the very institutions that stabilize such relationships" argued Craig Dean, executive director of the Marriage Rights Fund.

Marriage is more than a legal right, more than a relationship. It is an institution, the bedrock institution of our ideal of the family. Without the right to marry, it is codified into law that gay relationships are less valuable, less important, than heterosexual ones. Such a devaluation leads to the very promiscuity that is used

as the rationale for denying the right to marry in the first place.

In many cases, gay and lesbian couples provide a model of family life. For one thing, gay and lesbian couples are "less likely to fall into patterns of inequality" that define heterosexual marriages. By bringing together two people of the same gender, gender inequality is neutralized and gender difference eliminated. Compared with heterosexual couples, gay and lesbian couples are more likely to share housework; lesbian couples are the most egalitarian of all couple arrangements. And, it turns out, gay men and lesbians often make excellent parents. In the late 1960s, one woman lamented her position, not as a lesbian, but as a nonparent:

> One of my mother's big disappointments was the fact that there would be no grandchildren. I love both of my parents a great deal, and I would do almost anything for their happiness, but I couldn't do that. I think I was saddened too, when, . . . I knew that I wasn't ever going to have children. And I would like to have some . . . for myself.

Just as heterosexual women once felt they were forced to choose between having a career and having a family, many gay men and lesbians felt forced to choose between acknowledging their sexuality and having a family. And just as women today are unwilling to make that choice, wanting to "have it all," so too are gays and lesbians, who have decided that their homosexuality ought not to disqualify them as good parents. In 1976, there were between 300,000 and 500,000 gay and lesbian parents; today there are an estimated 1.5 million to 5 million lesbian mothers, and between 1 million and 3 million gay fathers. Currently, between 6 million and 14 million children (about 5 percent of all children in the United States) are being raised by at least one gay parent.

None of the feared consequences of gay parenting has materialized. There is no evidence that gay fathers or lesbian mothers exert any special negative influence on child development or that they sexually abuse their children. In fact, the few studies that have been conducted show that "the outcomes for children in these families tend to be better than average." For example, when fathers come out to their children, even if they are not raising the children themselves, it tends to relieve family stress and strengthen the bond between father and child. The research on lesbian mothers suggests that their children, both boys and girls, have similar patterns of gender identity development to children of heterosexual parents at comparable ages, and display no differences in intelligence or adjustment. "Quality of mothering" rather than sexual orientation is the crucial determinant of children's development. . . .

THE REAL PROBLEM OF FAMILY VIOLENCE

For too many Americans, children and parents alike, the family bears only a passing resemblance to the "haven in a heartless world" of nostalgic myth. Far from shielding their members from the cold and violent world outside its doors, the family *is* that cold and violent world. Violence tears at the fabric of the family. . . . Family violence is remarkably gendered, reproducing and reinforcing gender inequality. The overwhelming amount of family violence is perpetrated by males: husbands beating wives, fathers hitting children, or sons hitting their parents, boys hitting their brothers or their sisters. "The actual or implicit threat of physical coercion is one of many factors underlying male dominance in the family," writes sociologist Murray Straus.

Violence against children by parents is among the most controversial types of family violence. Although widespread support exists for corporal punishment—over three-fourths of Americans believe that it is all right for a parent to spank a child—that support disappears when such violent behaviors by parents against children become systematic or extreme. Although most Americans have hit their children,

and most children have been hit by their parents, we nightly gasp at news reports of parental violence against children. The most common forms of parental violence against children are spanking or slapping, though one in five parents have hit their child with an object, almost 10 percent have kicked, bit, or hit their children with their fist, and almost one in twenty families have experienced a parent beating up a child. Though mothers as well as fathers commit this violence, they are not equivalent. In one study, Bergman and his colleagues found that men are more than ten times more likely to inflict serious harm on their children, and that every perpetrator of the death of a child in this limited sample was either a father or a father surrogate.

The most evident consequence of parental violence against children is observed in the behaviors of children. Children see that violence is a legitimate way to resolve disputes, and learn to use it themselves. Violence against siblings is ubiquitous in American families. As Straus writes:

> Violence between siblings often reflects what children see their parents doing to each other, as well as what the child experiences in the form of discipline. Children of non-violent parents also tend to use non-violent methods to deal with their siblings and later with their spouses and children. If violence, like charity, begins at home, so does non-violence.

(Parents wondering how to discourage violence among their children might begin by resisting the temptation to hit them, and settling marital problems without resorting to violence.)

The long-term consequences of parental violence against children are also evident. The greater the corporal punishment experienced by the child, the greater the probability that the child will hit a spouse as an adult. And the likelihood is also higher that children hit by their parents will strike back. Child-to-parent violence is also serious; nearly one in ten (9 percent) of all parents of children aged ten to seventeen are victims of violence perpetrated by their own children. Mothers are more likely to be victims of such violence, especially in the more severe cases.

The antecedent causes of children hitting their parents, and especially their mothers, are directly related to the severity of the violence experienced by the child and the severity of the spousal violence the child observes. Children see their mothers hit by their fathers, and they "learn that mothers are an appropriate and acceptable target for intrafamily violence," writes sociologist Richard Gelles. Nowhere is the gender inequality of the family more evident than when a young boy hit his mother because he has learned by watching his father that violence against women is acceptable behavior for a boy coming into manhood.

Marriage and Love

Emma Goldman

The popular notion about marriage and love is that they are synonymous, that they spring from the same motives, and cover the same human needs. Like most popular notions this also rests not on actual facts, but on superstition.

Marriage and love have nothing in common; they are as far apart as the poles; are, in fact, antagonistic to each other. No doubt some marriages have been the result of love. Not, however, because love could assert itself only in marriage; much rather is it because few people can completely outgrow a convention. There are today large numbers of men and women to whom marriage is naught but a farce, but who submit to it for the sake of public opinion. At any rate, while it is true that some marriages are based on love, and while it is equally true that in some cases love continues in married life, I maintain that it does so regardless of marriage, and not because of it.

On the other hand, it is utterly false that love results from marriage. On rare occasions one does hear of a miraculous case of a married couple falling in love after marriage, but on close examination it will be found that it is a mere adjustment to the inevitable. Certainly the growing-used to each other is far away from the spontaneity, the intensity, and beauty of love, without which the intimacy of marriage must prove degrading to both the woman and the man.

Marriage is primarily an economic arrangement, an insurance pact. It differs from the ordinary life insurance agreement only in that it is more binding, more exacting. Its returns are insignificantly small compared with the investments. In taking out an insurance policy one pays for it in dollars and cents, always at liberty to discontinue payments. If, however, woman's premium is a husband, she pays for it with her name, her privacy, her self-respect, her very life, "until death doth part." Moreover, the marriage insurance condemns her to life-long dependency, to parasitism, to complete uselessness, individual as well as social. Man, too, pays his toll, but as his sphere is wider, marriage does not limit him as much as woman. He feels his chains more in an economic sense.

Thus Dante's motto over Inferno applies with equal force to marriage. "Ye who enter here leave all hope behind."

. . .

From infancy, almost, the average girl is told that marriage is her ultimate goal; therefore her training and education must be directed towards that end. Like the mute beast fattened for slaughter, she is prepared for that. Yet, strange to say, she is allowed to know much less about her function as wife and mother than the ordinary artisan of his trade. It is indecent and filthy for a respectable girl to know anything of the marital relation. Oh, for the inconsistency of respectability, that needs the marriage vow to turn something which is filthy into the purest and most sacred arrangement that none dare question or criticize. Yet that is exactly the attitude of the average upholder of marriage. The prospective wife and mother is kept in complete ignorance of her only asset in the competitive field—sex. Thus she enters into lifelong relations with a man only to find herself shocked, repelled, outraged beyond measure by the most natural and healthy instinct, sex. It is safe to say that a large percentage of the unhappiness, misery, distress, and physical suffering of matrimony is due to the criminal ignorance in sex matters that is being extolled as a great virtue. Nor is it at all an exaggeration when I say that more than one home has been broken up because of this deplorable fact.

If, however, woman is free and big enough to learn the mystery of sex without the sanction of State or Church, she will stand condemned as utterly unfit to become the wife of a "good" man, his goodness consisting of an empty brain and plenty of money. Can there be anything more outrageous than the idea that a healthy, grown woman, full of life and passion, must deny nature's demand, must subdue her most intense craving, undermine her health and break her spirit, must stunt her vision, abstain from the depth and glory of sex experience until a "good" man comes along to take her unto himself as a wife? That is precisely what marriage means. How can such an arrangement end except in failure? This is one, though not the least important, factor of marriage, which differentiates it from love.

Ours is a practical age. The time when Romeo and Juliet risked the wrath of their fathers for love, when Gretchen exposed herself to the gossip of her neighbors for love, is no more. If, on rare occasions, young people allow themselves the luxury of romance, they are taken in care by the elders, drilled and pounded until they become "sensible."

The moral lesson instilled in the girl is not whether the man has aroused her love, but rather is it, "How much?" The important and only God of practical American life: Can the man make a living? Can he support a wife? That is the only thing that justifies marriage. Gradually this saturates every thought of the girl; her dreams are not of moonlight and kisses, of laughter and tears; she dreams of shopping tours and bargain counters. This soul poverty and sordidness are the elements inherent in the marriage institution. The State and the Church approve of no other ideal, simply because it is the one that necessitates the State and Church control of men and women.

Doubtless there are people who continue to consider love above dollars and cents. Particularly is this true of that class whom economic necessity has forced to become self-supporting. The tremendous change in woman's position, wrought by that mighty factor, is indeed phenomenal when we reflect that it is but a short time since she has entered the industrial arena. Six million women wage workers; six million women, who have the equal right with men to be exploited, to be robbed, to go on strike; aye, to starve even. Anything more, my lord? Yes, six million wage workers in every walk of life, from the highest brain work to the mines and railroad tracks; yes, even detectives and policemen. Surely the emancipation is complete.

Yet with all that, but a very small number of the vast army of women wage workers look upon work as a permanent issue, in the same light as does man. No matter how decrepit the latter, he has been taught to be independent, self-supporting. Oh, I know that no one is really independent in our economic treadmill; still, the poorest specimen of a man hates to be a parasite; to be known as such, at any rate.

The woman considers her position as worker transitory, to be thrown aside for the first bidder. That is why it is infinitely harder to organize women than men. "Why should I join a union? I am going to get married, to have a home." Has she not been taught from infancy to look upon that as her ultimate calling? She learns soon enough that the home, though not so large a prison as the factory, has more solid doors and bars. It has a keeper so faithful that naught can escape him. The most tragic part, however, is that the home no longer frees her from wage slavery; it only increases her task.

According to the latest statistics submitted before a Committee "on labor and wages, and congestion of population," ten per cent of the wage workers in New York City alone are married, yet they must continue to work at the most poorly paid labor in the world. Add to this horrible aspect the drudgery of housework, and what remains of the protection and glory of the home? As a matter of fact, even the middle-class girl in marriage can not speak of her home, since it is the man who creates her sphere. It is not important whether the husband is a brute or a darling. What I wish to prove is that marriage guarantees woman a home only by the grace of her husband. There she moves about in *his* home, year after year, until her aspect of life and human affairs becomes as flat, narrow, and drab as her surroundings. Small wonder if she becomes a nag, petty, quarrelsome, gossipy, unbearable, thus driving the man from the house. She could not go, if she wanted to; there is no place to go. Besides, a short period of married life, of complete surrender of all faculties, absolutely incapacitates the average woman for the outside world. She becomes reckless in appearance, clumsy in her movements, dependent in her decisions, cowardly in her judgment, a weight and a bore, which most men grow to hate and despise. . . .

The institution of marriage makes a parasite of woman, an absolute dependent. It incapacitates her for life's struggle, annihilates her social consciousness, paralyzes her imagination, and then imposes its gracious protection, which is in reality a snare, a travesty on human character.

Justice
Childhood Love Lessons

bell hooks

Severe separations in early life leave emotional scars on the brain because they assault the essential human connection: The [parent-child] bond which teaches us that we are lovable. The [parent-child] bond which teaches us how to love. We cannot be whole human beings—indeed, we may find it hard to be human—without the sustenance of this first attachment.

—*Judith Viorst*

We learn about love in childhood. Whether our homes are happy or troubled, our families functional or dysfunctional, it's the original school of love. I cannot remember ever wanting to ask my parents to define love. To my child's mind love was the good feeling you got when family treated you like you mattered and you treated them like they mattered. Love was always and only about good feeling. In early adolescence when we were whipped and told that these punishments were "for our own good" or "I'm doing this because I love you," my siblings and I were confused. Why was harsh punishment a gesture of love? As children do, we pretended to accept this grown-up logic; but we knew in our hearts it was not right. We knew it was a lie. Just like the lie the grown-ups told when they explained after harsh punishment, "It hurts me more than it hurts you." There is nothing that creates more confusion about love in the minds and hearts of children than unkind and/or cruel punishment meted out by the grown-ups they have been taught they should love and respect. Such children learn early on to question the meaning of love, to yearn for love even as they doubt it exists.

On the flip side there are masses of children who grow up confident love is a good feeling who are never punished, who are allowed to believe that love is only about getting your needs met, your desires satisfied. In their child's minds love is not about what they have to give, love is mostly something given to them. When children like these are overindulged either materially or by being allowed to act out, this is a form of neglect. These children, though not in any way abused or uncared for, are usually as unclear about love's meaning as their neglected and emotionally abandoned counterparts. Both groups have learned to think about love primarily in relation to good feelings, in the context of reward and punishment. From early childhood on, most of us remember being told we were loved when we did things pleasing to our parents. And we learned to give them affirmations of love when they pleased us. As children grow they associate love more with acts of attention, affection, and caring. They still see parents who attempt to satisfy their desires as giving love.

Children from all classes tell me that they love their parents and are loved by them, even those who are being hurt or abused. When asked to define love, small children pretty much agree that it's a good feeling, "like when you have something to eat that you really like" especially if it's your f-a-v-o-r-i-t-e. They will say, "My mommy loves me 'cause she takes care of me and helps me do everything right." When asked how to love someone, they talk about giving hugs and kisses, being sweet and cuddly. The notion that love is about getting what one wants, whether it's a hug or a new sweater or a trip to Disneyland, is a way of thinking about love that makes it difficult for children to acquire a deeper emotional understanding.

We like to imagine that most children will be born into homes where they will be loved. But love will not be present if the grown-ups who parent do not [know] how to love. Although lots of children are raised in homes where they are given some degree of care, love may not be sustained or even present. Adults across lines of class, race, and gender indict the family. Their testimony conveys worlds of childhood where love was lacking—where chaos, neglect, abuse, and coercion reigned supreme. In her recent book *Raised in Captivity: Why Does America Fail Its Children?*, Lucia Hodgson documents the reality of lovelessness in the lives of a huge majority of children in the United States. Every day thousands of children in our culture are verbally and physically abused, starved, tortured, and murdered. They are the true victims of intimate terrorism in that they have no collective voice and no rights. They remain the property of parenting adults to do with as they will.

There can be no love without justice. Until we live in a culture that not only respects but also upholds basic civil rights for children, most children will not know love. In our culture the private family dwelling is the one institutionalized sphere of power that can easily be autocratic and fascistic. As absolute rulers, parents can usually decide without any intervention what is best for their children. If children's rights are taken away in any domestic household, they have no legal recourse. Unlike women who can organize to protest sexist domination, demanding both equal rights and justice, children can only rely on well-meaning adults to assist them if they are being exploited and oppressed in the home.

We all know that, irrespective of class or race, other adults rarely intervene to question or challenge what their peers are doing with "their" children.

. . .

One of the most important social myths we must debunk if we are to become a more loving culture is the one that teaches parents that abuse and neglect can coexist with love. Abuse and neglect negate love. Care and affirmation, the opposite of abuse and humiliation, are the foundation of love. No one can rightfully claim to be loving when behaving abusively. Yet parents do this all the time in our culture. Children are told that they are loved even though they are being abused.

It is a testimony to the failure of loving practice that abuse is happening in the first place.

Many of the men who offer their personal testimony in *Boyhood, Growing Up Male* tell stories of random violent abuse by parents that inflicted trauma. In his essay "When My Father Hit Me," Bob Shelby describes the pain of repeated beatings by his dad, stating: "From these experiences with my father, I learned about the abuse of power. By physically hitting my mother and me, he effectively stopped us from reacting to his humiliation of us. We ceased to protest his violations of our boundaries and his ignoring our sense of being individuals with needs, demands and rights of our own." Throughout his essay Shelby expresses contradictory understandings about the meaning of love. On the one hand, he says: "I have no doubt that my father loved me, but his love became misdirected. He said he wanted to give me what he didn't have as a child." On the other hand, Shelby confesses: "What he most showed me, however, was his difficulty in being loved. All his life he had struggled with feelings of being unloved." When Shelby describes his childhood it is clear that his dad had affection for him and also gave him care some of the time. However, his dad did not know how to give and receive love. The affection he gave was undermined by the abuse.

Writing from the space of adult recollection, Shelby talks about the impact of physical abuse on his boyhood psyche: "As the intensity of the pain of his hits increased, I felt the hurt in my heart. I realized what hurt me the most were my feelings of love for this man who was hitting me. I covered my love with a dark cloth of hate." A similar story is told by other men in autobiographical narrative—men of all classes and races. One of the myths about lovelessness

is that it exists only among the poor and deprived. Yet lovelessness is not a function of poverty or material lack. In homes where material privileges abound, children suffer emotional neglect and abuse. In order to cope with the pain of wounds inflicted in childhood, most of the men in *Boyhood* sought some form of therapeutic care. To find their way back to love they had to heal.

Many men in our culture never recover from childhood unkindnesses. Studies show that males and females who are violently humiliated and abused repeatedly, with no caring intervention, are likely to be dysfunctional and will be predisposed to abuse others violently. In Jarvis Jay Masters's book *Finding Freedom: Writings from Death Row*, a chapter called "Scars" recounts his recognition that a vast majority of the scars covering the bodies of fellow inmates (not all of whom were on death row) were not, as one might think, the result of violent adult interactions. These men were covered with scars from childhood beatings inflicted by parenting adults. Yet, he reports, none of them saw themselves as the victims of abuse: "Throughout my many years of institutionalization, I, like so many of these men, unconsciously took refuge behind prison walls. Not until I read a series of books for adults who had been abused as children did I become committed to the process of examining my own childhood." Organizing the men for group discussion, Masters writes: "I spoke to them of the pain I had carried through more than a dozen institutions. And I explained how all these events ultimately trapped me in a pattern of lashing out against everything." Like many abused children, male and female, these men were beaten by mothers, fathers, and other parental caregivers.

When Master's mother dies he feels grief that he cannot be with her. The other inmates do not understand this longing, since she neglected and abused him. He responds: "She had neglected me, but am I to neglect myself as well by denying that I wished I'd been with her when she died, that I still love her?" Even on death row, Masters's heart remains open. And he can honestly confess to longing to give and receive love. Being hurt by parenting adults rarely alters a child's desire to love and be loved by them. Among grown-ups who were wounded in childhood, the desire to be loved by uncaring parents persists, even when there is a clear acceptance of the reality that this love will never be forthcoming.

Often, children will want to remain with parental caregivers who have hurt them because of their cathected feelings for those adults. They will cling to the misguided assumption that their parents love them even in the face of remembered abuse, usually by denying the abuse and focusing on random acts of care.

In the prologue to *Creating Love,* John Bradshaw calls this confusion about love "mystification." He shares: "I was brought up to believe that love is rooted in blood relationships. You naturally loved anyone in your family. Love was not a choice. The love I learned about was bound by duty and obligation. . . . My family taught me our culture's rules and beliefs about love . . . even with the best intentions our parents often confused love with what we would now call abuse." To demystify the meaning of love, the art and practice of loving, we need to use sound definitions of love when talking with children, and we also need to ensure that loving action is never tainted with abuse.

In a society like ours, where children are denied full civil rights, it is absolutely crucial that parenting adults learn how to offer loving discipline. Setting boundaries and teaching children how to set boundaries for themselves prior to misbehavior is an essential part of loving parenting. When parents start out disciplining children by using punishment, this becomes the pattern children respond to. Loving parents work hard to discipline without pun-

ishment. This does not mean that they never punish, only that when they do punish, they choose punishments like time-outs or the taking away of privileges. They focus on teaching children how to be self-disciplining and how to take responsibility for their actions. Since the vast majority of us were raised in households where punishment was deemed the primary, if not the only, way to teach discipline, the fact that discipline can be taught without punishment surprises many people. One of the simplest ways children learn discipline is by learning how to be orderly in daily life, to clean up any messes they make. Just teaching a child to take responsibility for placing toys in the appropriate place after playtime is one way to teach responsibility and self-discipline. Learning to clean up the mess made during playtime helps a child learn to be responsible. And they can learn from this practical act how to cope with emotional mess.

. . .

Until we begin to see loving parenting in all walks of life in our culture, many people will continue to believe we can only teach discipline through punishment, and that harsh punishment is an acceptable way to relate to children. Because children can innately offer affection or respond to affectionate care by returning it, it is often assumed that they know how to love and therefore do not need to learn the art of loving. While the will to love is present in very young children, they still need guidance in the ways of love. Grown-ups provide that guidance.

Love is as love does, and it is our responsibility to give children love. When we love children we acknowledge by our every action that they are not property, that they have rights—that we respect and uphold their rights.

Without justice there can be no love.

Friendly for Whose Family?

Betty Holcomb

One might assume that Lynnell Minkins, a single mother of three, would be thrilled to work for Marriott International. Last year, Marriott made *Working Mother* magazine's list of the 100 best companies for working mothers, largely because it offers flexible work schedules, hot lines to help employees deal with child-care emergencies, and three on-site child-care centers. Minkins, a food server at the San Francisco Marriott, could use that sort of help. But it's not available to her. Instead, she never knows from week to week what her hours will be, making it hard to find and hold on to decent child care, let alone make plans. "How can I get doctor appointments if I don't know when I'll be working?" she asks. "A month ahead, the clinic says there are only these days. I take them, and then I have to work."

When her kids were younger, she relied on a neighbor, paying a flat rate to send them over whenever she had to work. But now that they're in school, she has to figure out how to get them there on days she has to be at work early. A simple schedule change could solve everything, but she hasn't asked for one. "I don't dare bring it up. I'm afraid I'll get written up." A write-up means getting disciplined, and too many write-ups can lead to losing her job.

The irony is that, at least officially, Marriott offers flextime to its approximately 135,000 U.S. employees. Yet the one time Minkins tried it, her supervisors constantly pressed her to fix the "problem," and in her annual performance review that year she was described as being "challenged" by time management. "I should have called them on it, but I let it go," she says. "People who work in these jobs, they need the money. So you don't tell anybody what's going on." Senior managers, says Minkins, don't seem to suffer the same scrutiny. "It doesn't

look like their job is being challenged. The lower people, the people in the back of the house, they're having the problems."

So it goes for hundreds of thousands of lower-level workers at companies widely recognized for their "family-friendly" policies. In fact, the research conducted by the Families and Work Institute exclusively for this article shows that the workers who most need benefits such as child care and flexible hours are the least likely to get them.

Consider these facts from the study. Workers in low-wage jobs are

- half as likely as managers and professionals to have flextime;
- less likely to have on-site child care;
- more likely to lose a day's pay when they must stay home to care for a sick child;
- three times less likely to get company-sponsored tax breaks to help pay for child care.

In addition, other studies show that workers in entry-level, low-paying, or low-status jobs are much less likely to be offered a paid maternity leave than managers are, and in the case of unpaid leave, they are less likely to get as much time off after having a baby.

"It's clear that more advantaged workers have more access to certain benefits," says Ellen Galinsky, president of the Families and Work Institute. Put another way, some families seem to count more than others. "You ask yourself if people really care about the family benefits of people who clean the toilets, who clean the office buildings after everyone else leaves," says Netsy Firestein, director of the Labor Project for Working Families in Berkeley, California. "Who's taking care of their kids? Often it's older children putting younger ones to bed, while the parents struggle to make wages and get health insurance paid."

The types of benefits currently offered are also skewed toward higher-paid workers. Child-care help, for example, comes most often in the form of company-sponsored tax breaks or "resource and referral" hot lines. Both are useless to workers like Minkins, who don't make enough to pay much in taxes and can't afford the licensed child care the hot line refers them to. "Most of it is as much as $100 a week just to watch my kids before and after school. Maybe I could afford $50, but not $100!" Minkins says. Her problem is far from unique. According to the *Wall Street Journal*, a huge 85 percent of Marriott's U.S. employees are hourly workers—meaning low-wage. Its "core hourly employees simply couldn't afford paid care, the cost of which can easily exceed 50 percent of gross income," reports the *Journal*.

The rare companies that offer on-site child care—about 5,000 of the nation's millions of employers—often do so only at headquarters, where managers and executives work, and the fees may still be too high for the clerical and office support staff. Just as much of a problem is that many benefits are offered only at the discretion of supervisors—who expect lower-level workers to stick to unbending schedules.

. . .

Perhaps the biggest irony behind family-friendly benefits is that the workers most likely to get them don't need the help. Last year, the Hyatt Regency San Diego touted the success of a job-sharing initiative. Six women out of a workforce of 800 were sharing three jobs, and each of the women said they could afford to stop working if they had to.

. . .

It's not that corporate leaders haven't confronted the issue of equity. Most trumpet their efforts to make benefits universally available. In presentations, Marriott officials stress that family-friendly benefits are meant for everyone, from the most senior manager to the busboy in the company's restaurants. "We have a firm stake in the sand in seeing to it that our hourly employees are served well," says Donna Klein, vice president for diversity and workforce effectiveness, and chief architect of many of Marriott's family-friendly benefits. "We have master's-level social workers dedicated to Marriott callers 24 hours a day. We help with everything from finding child care, child-care subsidies, even immigration and housing issues."

But for Minkins, that's just a lot of talk if she can't afford the benefits. Meanwhile, Marriott has refused to contribute to a fund created by hotel workers' unions to help pay for care, saying they won't contribute to something that involves employees from other companies. If Marriott participated in the union/management effort, Minkins could receive a child-care subsidy based on need—just the opposite of the way most companies dole out benefits.

The central question is whether management thinks of lower-wage workers as important to their companies, and therefore deserving of benefits. This was the issue that a group of human resource executives from the nation's leading corporations found themselves asking at a conference on the family-friendly workplace in New York City back in April of 1995. Wining and dining at the luxurious Waldorf-Astoria, they began to talk about a problem emerging in the field. They'd broken ground by introducing flextime, part-time work with benefits, job-sharing, and on-site child care at their companies. And they were getting plenty of attention for their efforts. But now, in an attack of conscience, they turned their attention to the workers who made their beds, served their food, and cleared their tables while they set workplace policies. "What about the chambermaids?" asked Arlene Johnson, a leading researcher on work-family conflict who was chairing the plenary session. "How are we meeting their needs?"

J. Thomas Bouchard, a senior vice president of IBM, who had championed the growing visibility of family-friendly benefits a few minutes earlier, now sounded a more somber note. "I don't see how we can or will. Who's going to pay for it if we try to make these things universal?" In fact, he insisted, it was probably best to not even suggest that all workers might someday have access to child care and flexible schedules via their employers. "There's nothing worse than false hope," he insisted. Better to simply acknowledge that most companies don't want to add costly new benefits or change the way people work.

. . .

Finding solutions isn't easy. Many advocates of family-friendly benefits say we have to challenge the notion that work and family are separate spheres; the workplace has to bend to the demands of the home. But those are long-range goals. In the short term, advocates are trying to win over executives by making a business case for these benefits. They are trying to disprove the ideas of people like IBM's J. Thomas Bouchard that companies can't afford benefits for all. The data is most assuredly there. Studies have shown again and again that family-friendly policies help the bottom line. Xerox, for example, improved productivity in its call centers simply by letting workers devise their own schedules.

In the end, the question is really one of power and privilege. Who has the power to change things, on what terms, and for whom? For the moment, the most progressive innovations arise out of the goodwill and good vision of a few corporate leaders. But even they are hesitant to challenge the notion that family-benefit funds could be better spent. If you ask them, "If there isn't enough money to provide benefits for everyone, why not spend what is available on the people who need it most?" they look at you as though you were speaking a foreign language. The truth is that professional, skilled workers are the ones corporations are trying to keep, and they do it with expensive benefits packages, among other things. Nonprofessional staff is more easily replaced, they believe, and thus not worth the financial investment. At the moment most employers see

no need for dramatic change. "The companies sure do like getting on the lists and getting publicity," says Paul Ruppert of WFD, one of the leading consulting firms on work-family conflict in the U.S. "But you have to wonder how much change they really want to make."

The most lasting victories have come through collective action. The 40-hour work week, paid vacations, antidiscrimination laws, and, recently, the Family and Medical Leave Act were won by feminists, organized labor, and progressives working together. At long last, the labor movement has begun to take up the mantle of family-friendliness.

"The unions are finally getting religion on this," says Donna Dolan, director of work-family issues for the Communications Workers of America. Dolan has worked since the early 1980s to win pacts that include paid leave for childbirth, time off to care for sick family members, and subsidies for child care. She and other union activists helped create the first big family-friendly pact in 1989, when NYNEX agreed to create a $6 million fund to help develop and pay for child care.

In recent years, Dolan has been heartened to see the AFL-CIO take up the cause in earnest. "When you hear John Sweeney [president of the AFL-CIO] on the stump on these issues, you know we're getting somewhere," she says. Indeed, a growing number of unions have bargained for and won funds to help pay for family-friendly benefits. And there is a move afoot to help push for a paid family leave, one that replicates the sort of parental leave that workers in all other industrialized countries already have.

It is this sort of victory that gives Lynnell Minkins hope. Minkins has worked for Marriott for three years, and the stress has worn her down. "I have stomach problems, and I'm sure it's the tension of all this," she says. But she's not about to go elsewhere. "We've been fighting for three long years to get Marriott to give us regular schedules and to do what's right for people's families, to do the things that the other hotels are doing," she says. "I'm not going to quit until we win that fight for everybody."

What We Call Each Other

Anndee Hochman

My eighty-nine-year-old grandfather and I had covered all the routine subjects—the weather in Portland, the weather on the New Jersey shore (it was summer in both places). I'd thanked him for sending me a paperback copy of *The Joys of Yiddish*. Then he asked, "So, how's your lady friend?"

I gulped. It was possible he meant my roommate, Rachael, and "lady friend" was a quaint attempt to cover up the fact that he'd forgotten her name. But I'd never heard him use that phrase, with its tinge of old-fashioned, coy romance, to describe an acquaintance of mine.

Finally, I mumbled that she was just fine, thanks. There was no response. Later, I told my "lady friend" about the comment, and we both laughed. But I still don't know if my grandfather knew what he asked, if he grasped what he heard. Words are like that. They can swab the air clean of illusion, or they can fog the truth in a comfy, opaque veil.

So many of the words for romantic or sexual partners make women mere appendages of men, extend a long-standing power imbalance. What is the term to describe a relationship of equals, two adults trying to make a life together? I like "partner," with its hints of adventure and readiness, the idea of moving together through a love affair or a life. Most of my friends, gay or straight, use it to describe their romantic associates.

But even "partner" isn't perfect. For one thing, it conveys a sense of stability that doesn't apply to all relationships, especially brand new ones. Heterosexual couples have a whole vocabulary that hints at changing degrees of intimacy and intention. First "lovers" or "boyfriend/girlfriend"; then "fiancée"; finally "spouse." But unmarried or gay partners have no language to describe those shifts.

The words commonly used in such cases are designed to mask the truth rather than tell it. The euphemisms for gay and lesbian lovers—"constant companion" or "very special friend"—hide the true nature of the relationship under a cloak of decorum. But it's a cloak made to be seen through; everyone knows it's a cover for something else. It indicates that the real thing is too scandalous even for discourse; the word itself can't go out of doors unclad.

One lesbian couple I know dislikes "partner" for the same reasons I'm drawn to it—because it is democratic, gender-neutral. These women refer to each other as "girlfriends," refusing, even in casual conversation, to pass.

Slowly, slowly, names gather a new history; the weight of a word can shift. When lesbians and gay men appropriate the language of the mainstream, filling in their partners' names where government forms say "spouse," insisting that they deserve a "family" membership to the YMCA, they force others to reorder their mental maps. Those maps would change even faster if heterosexual couples boycotted marriage and its honorifics, if they, too combed the language for words that more precisely describe their bonds.

Girlfriend. Boyfriend. Mistress. Beau. Old man. Lady friend. Steady. Helpmate. Fiancé/e. Lover. Paramour. Spouse. Domestic partner. Soul mate. Significant other. Homeslice. Sweetie. Co-habitant. Ally. Longtime companion. Live-in. Partner. Collaborator. Consort. Intimate. Confidant/e. Familiar. Alter ego. Mainstay. Second self. Complement. Mate.

Even words that don't carry a gender bias can be suspect, quiet enforcers of the status quo. I used the word "single" to describe women without intimate partners until the irony of the term struck me. I was writing about these women precisely because they'd built networks of support through work, friends, housemates, yet my easy description of them conveyed someone alone and unconnected, with no important social ties.

"Are you in a relationship?" people inquire euphemistically, when what they mean is "Are you sexually involved with someone?" The notion of *a* relationship—primary, intimate, more weighty than the rest— doesn't fit the lives of people who choose celibacy, or who are in nonmonogamous relationships involving two or more significant "others."

Then there's "friend," which doesn't begin to cover enough ground. It describes everyone from the colleague I chat with once a month at a writers' meeting to the woman I've known since infancy but haven't seen for a decade, to Rachael, whom I lived with for more than five years. The word, forced to stand for such a range of connections, erases distinction, implies all friendships are the same.

Names wake us to the particulars of a thing. If I call Diana my mainstay, Pattie my soul mate, and Rachael my sister, I remember that these women have different qualities, that my friendship with each is unique.

I say Rachael is my "sister," and then pause. Why is that the only term that seems to fit? I struggle to describe closeness and am left holding a simile, a stand-in phrase that only gropes at description. "He's like a brother to me," we say, revealing not only the assumed potency of sibling bonds but the dearth of words to describe intense, nonsexual attachments.

There's a level of intimacy that "friend" seems too small to contain. Then we make it even smaller, often denigrating it with the qualifier "just." They're "just friends," we concede, as if friendship were automatic and uninteresting, less full of potential than any romantic pairing. In fact, the vast majority of people in our lives fall into that maligned category; friendship deserves a vocabulary of its own.

Acquaintance. Colleague. Buddy. Bosom-buddy. Sidekick. Chum. Amiga. Compadre. Homegirl.

Mate. Pal. Sister. Fellow. Right-hand man. Companion. Compañera. Associate. Cohort. Crony. Aficionado. Compeer. Confrere. Ally. Comrade. Familiar. Accomplice. Mainstay. Primary. Neighbor. Friend.

I've wrestled, too, with "childless." It's a gender-weighted word—we don't refer, with quite the same sense of anomaly and pity, to "childless" men. And it assumes childbearing is the norm and *not* childbearing a lesser version of life; it defines an existence by what it lacks. "Nonparent" makes the same mistake.

I've seen women use "child-free," which seems tipped in the other direction—as though children were a burden and only people without them have liberty. Besides, many women who choose not to be parents include children in their lives as nieces and nephews, neighbors, clients, friends. I thought about words like "adult-based" or "adult-centered" for women who don't have much to do with children. But I've yet to find a term that expresses, without judgment, the facets of this complicated choice.

And there are relationships, existences we scarcely have language to describe. The words for an unmarried woman—maiden aunt, spinster—are all pejorative. "Old maid," in particular, holds layers of judgment—a woman who contradicts her own nature, at once old and young, a perpetual servant. Thanks to Mary Daly and others, feminists are reclaiming "spinster" as a source of creative pride; one woman I know named her sewing business "Spinster Textiles."

Few terms exist to describe former lovers who now are good friends, or nonbiological parents, or relationships between the childhood families of a gay couple. I've heard a woman explain to her child, conceived through alternative (as opposed to "artificial") insemination, that there are "seed daddies" as well as the kind of daddies who live at home, and a lesbian friend coined "sister-outlaws" to describe her lover's siblings.

The contemporary women's movement and gay and lesbian liberation helped prompt people to create new honorifics, such as "Ms.," and reclaim old names, taking them back from the domain of those who hate. Queer. Dyke. Crone. Cripple. Faggot. Fat person. Fairy. When we use these words for ourselves, we become powerful, filled with the awesome responsibility that is naming. We print the words on buttons, shout them in parades. We repossess the names and, in the process, repossess ourselves.

Language changes from the edges; new terms ripple back to the center. Gradually, I have seen "partner" replace "longtime companion" in news stories about gay men and lesbians. Several papers even have begun listing gay commitment ceremonies. As such events become more popular and public, terms unimagined as yet may enter the lexicon.

Coupling. Espousals. Union. Match. Bond. Pairing. Knot. Joining. Dovetailing. Commitment ceremony. Intentional. Dedication. Webbing. Mingling. Intertwining. Weaving. Blending. Braiding. Concord. Alignment. Alchemy. Convergence. Handfasting. Tryst.

What we call each other—how we refer to lovers and friends, partnerships and families— is more than a matter of etiquette. The words tell us who is owned and who is free, who really counts and who is merely secondary.

The language of the nuclear family continues to sway our speech, crowd out equally valid models of living. Homeless teenagers I worked with took the words of the families that failed them and applied them to each other. I heard them use "sister" and "brother" for their friends, but also "mother" and "kid," outlining large and intricate networks of street kin.

The actual people represented by those terms may have abused or abandoned these teenagers, but the words themselves seem to carry an infinitely renewable potency, a hope that someday someone will grow into the legend that is "mother," "sister," or "son."

"Blood family" itself carries that mythic power—"blood," with its symbolism of oath and source, a magical connection that cannot be undone. "Biological family" is less poetic but equally weighted. Married couples aren't related genetically, nor are adopted children. In families formed through remarriage, in foster families and extended families, "blood" connections have little to do with linkage.

I've toyed with "first family," "original family," and "childhood family" to describe the groups we grow up with, and "present family," "chosen family," or "adult family" for those we have now.

But the word "family" itself is loaded. The term can help justify secrecy ("let's keep it in the family") or serve as an argument for public hands-off ("that's a family matter"). And it is used disingenuously, as in "We're all one big happy family here" by businesses that want to promote childlike docility from employees and avuncular rule from bosses.

No mere noun, it's a way of categorizing society, even allocating resources, with "family" memberships and "family" fares on airlines and trains. "Family values" is political shorthand, evoking marriage, patriotism, and obedient children, a code aimed to halt a changing world.

Imagination is larger than language. The names claim who we already are and who we wish to become. We don't require them in order to live, but they make our living known, translatable, turn it into something we can talk about. There is room for more words, for the finest of distinctions, for as many possibilities as our minds can shape.

Someday, [my parents'] white house in New Jersey will be mine. I cannot imagine selling it. I want it to remain in the family. Families. Meaning me, my cousins, our parents, our children, if we have them. And more than that. The partners and compatriots, lovers and allies, cronies and intimates, all those who share the everyday acts of our lives.

I can see it. Someone will tap on the glass between the front stairs and the kitchen. I will look up, out the window, through the house and the window beyond it, straight out to the ocean we all come from. I will recognize the face, and I will wave.

Welcome, I might say, to my tribe. My group. Cabal. Circle. Club. Nucleus. Team. Neighborhood.

Community. Affinity group. Kin. Karass. People. Coalition. League. Assemblage. Confederation. Gang. Clique. Coterie. Set. Crew. Crowd. Cadre. We-group. Affiliates. Relations. Folk. Household. Brood. Collection. Cronies. Network.

Welcome to my company, my clan.

Only Daughter

Sandra Cisneros

Once, several years ago, when I was just starting out my writing career, I was asked to write my own contributor's note for an anthology I was part of. I wrote: "I am the only daughter in a family of six sons. *That* explains everything."

Well, I've thought about that ever since, and yes, it explains a lot to me, but for the reader's sake I should have written: "I am the only daughter in a *Mexican* family of six sons." Or even: "I am the only daughter of a Mexican father and a Mexican-American mother." Or: "I am the only daughter of a working-class family of nine." All of these had everything to do with who I am today.

I was/am the only daughter and *only* a daughter. Being an only daughter in a family of six sons forced me by circumstance to spend a lot of time by myself because my brothers felt it beneath them to play with a *girl* in public. But that aloneness, that loneliness, was good for a would-be writer—it allowed me time to think and think, to imagine, to read and prepare myself.

Being only a daughter for my father meant my destiny would lead me to become someone's wife. That's what he believed. But when I was in the fifth grade and shared my plans for college with him, I was sure he understood. I remember my father saying, "*Que bueno, mi'ja, that's good.*" That meant a lot to me, especially since my brothers thought the idea hilarious.

What I didn't realize was that my father thought college was good for girls—good for finding a husband. After four years in college and two more in graduate school, and still no husband, my father shakes his head even now and says I wasted all that education.

In retrospect, I'm lucky my father believed daughters were meant for husbands. It meant it didn't matter if I majored in something silly like English. After all, I'd find a nice professional eventually, right? This allowed me the liberty to putter about embroidering my little poems and stories without my father interrupting with so much as a "What's that you're writing?"

But the truth is, I wanted him to interrupt. I wanted my father to understand what it was I was scribbling, to introduce me as "My only daughter, the writer." Not as "This is only my daughter. She teaches." *Es maestra*—teacher. Not even *profesora*.

In a sense, everything I have ever written has been for him, to win his approval even though I know my father can't read English words, even though my father's only reading includes the brown-ink *Esto* sports magazines from Mexico City and the bloody *¡Alarma!* magazines that feature yet another sighting of *La Virgen de Guadalupe* on a tortilla or a wife's revenge on her philandering husband by bashing his skull in with a *molcajete* (a kitchen mortar made of volcanic rock). Or the *fotonovelas,* the little picture paperbacks with tragedy and trauma erupting from the characters' mouths in bubbles.

My father represents, then, the public majority. A public who is disinterested in reading, and yet one whom I am writing about and for, and privately trying to woo.

When we were growing up in Chicago, we moved a lot because of my father. He suffered bouts of nostalgia. Then we'd have to let go of our flat, store the furniture with mother's relatives, load the station wagon with baggage and bologna sandwiches and head south. To Mexico City.

We came back, of course. To yet another Chicago flat, another Chicago neighborhood, another Catholic school. Each time, my father would seek out the parish priest in order to get a tuition break, and complain or boast: "I have seven sons."

He meant *siete hijos,* seven children, but he translated it as "sons." "I have seven sons." To anyone who would listen. The Sears Roebuck employee who sold us the washing machine. The short-order cook where my father ate his ham-and-eggs breakfasts. "I have seven sons." As if he deserved a medal from the state.

My papa. He didn't mean anything by that mistranslation, I'm sure. But somehow I could feel myself being erased. I'd tug my father's sleeve and whisper: "Not seven sons. Six! and *one daughter.*"

When my oldest brother graduated from medical school, he fulfilled my father's dream that we study hard and use this—our heads, instead of this—our hands. Even now my father's hands are thick and yellow, stubbed by a history of hammer and nails and twine and coils and springs. "Use this," my father said, tapping his head, "and not this," showing us those hands. He always looked tired when he said it.

Wasn't college an investment? And hadn't I spent all those years in college? And if I didn't marry, what was it all for? Why would anyone go to college and then choose to be poor? Especially someone who had always been poor?

Last year, after ten years of writing professionally, the financial rewards started to trickle in. My second National Endowment for the Arts Fellowship. A guest professorship at the University of California, Berkeley. My book, which sold to a major New York publishing house.

At Christmas, I few home to Chicago. The house was throbbing, same as always: hot tamales and sweet tamales hissing in my mother's pressure cooker, and everybody—my mother, six brothers, wives, babies, aunts, cousins—talking too loud and at the same time. Like in a Fellini film, because that's just how we are.

I went upstairs to my father's room. One of my stories had just been translated into Spanish and published in an anthology of Chicano writing and I wanted to show it to him. Ever since he recovered from a stroke two years ago, my father likes to spend his leisure hours horizontally. And that's how I found him, watching a Pedro Infante movie on Galavisión and eating rice pudding.

There was a glass filled with milk on the bedside table. There were several vials of pills and balled Kleenex. And on the floor, one black sock and a plastic urinal that I didn't want to look at but looked at anyway. Pedro Infante was about to burst into song, and my father was laughing.

I'm not sure if it was because my story was translated into Spanish, or because it was published in Mexico, or perhaps because the story dealt with Tepeyac, the *colonia* my father was raised in and the house he grew up in, but at any rate, my father punched the mute button on his remote control and read my story.

I sat on the bed next to my father and waited. He read it very slowly. As if he were reading each line over and over. He laughed at the right places and read lines he liked out loud. He pointed and asked questions: "Is this So-and-so?" "Yes," I said. He kept reading.

When he was finally finished, after what seemed like hours, my father looked up and asked: "Where can we get more copies of this for the relatives?"

Of all the wonderful things that happened to me last year, that was the most wonderful.

DISCUSSION QUESTIONS FOR CHAPTER SEVEN

1. What are some myths about the normative U.S. family? To what degree does your family reflect this norm? Has your family experienced discrimination in any ways based on deviation from this norm? What are some of the realities of the diversity of U.S. families?

2. How are families both places of comfort, security, and nurture and at the same time places of domination, conflict, and violence?

3. How do social institutions reinforce power relations in the family? How does the family often reflect power relations of the dominant social order? How do power relations operate in your family?

4. How does the difference between mothering and fathering reflect dominant social norms for women and men?

5. What tasks do various members of your family do within the home? Do these tasks reflect typical social norms?

SUGGESTIONS FOR FURTHER READING

Coontz, Stephanie. *The Way We Never Were: American Families and the Nostalgia Trap,* reprint. Austin, TX: Basic, 2000.

————.*The Way We Really Are: Coming to Terms with America's Changing Families.* Austin, TX: Basic, 1998.

Lehr, Valerie. *Queer Family Values: Debunking the Myth of the Nuclear Family (Queer Politics, Queer Theories).* Philadelphia: Temple University Press, 1999.

Stacey, Judith. *In the Name of the Family: Rethinking Family Values in the Postmodern Age.* Boston: Beacon, 1997.

CHAPTER EIGHT

Women's Work Inside and Outside the Home

There is an important truth in the saying "women's work is never done." In the United States and around the world, women work longer hours than men because work for women often involves unpaid domestic labor and care of dependent family members as well as paid labor. In addition, when they do get paid for their work, women tend to earn lower wages compared to men and are less likely to have control over the things they produce and the wages they receive. When the United Nations World Conference on Women met in Beijing, China, in 1995, the Platform for Action prioritized strategies to promote economic autonomy for women, ensure their access to productive resources, and encourage equitable sharing of family responsibilities. In this chapter we examine both women's domestic unpaid labor and their employment in the labor force. In the latter the focus is on the global economy and the changing nature and patterns of women's labor force participation and remuneration. We close the chapter with a discussion of comparable worth.

UNPAID LABOR IN THE HOME

The work women do in the home is often not considered work at all: It is something women do for love, or because they are women, and it is the natural thing for women to do. On the *Roseanne* situation comedy, Roseanne Barr was asked by a family member whether she knew the location of a lost item. "How should I know," she responded. "What do you think a uterus is, a tracking device?" Her point was that there is nothing natural about the fact that women on the average do over two-thirds of all household work. The fact that they may be better at it is only because of years of practice. Gender norms that associate women, the home, and domesticity reinforce the assumption that housework and childcare is women's work.

The reading by Barbara Ehrenreich, "Maid to Order," explains the politics of housework in contemporary U.S. society. She emphasizes that housework is not degrading because it involves manual labor, but instead because it is embedded in degrading relationships that have the potential to reproduce male domination from one generation to the next. She suggests that a contemporary solution to the housework problem among those who can afford it is to hire someone else to do the work. That "someone" is most likely a woman and very often a woman of color. Domestic work is one occupation traditionally held by women of color; it is also an occupation that is usually nonunionized, has low pay, little power, and few or no benefits. In addition, individuals who used to contract services directly with employers are now being replaced by corporate cleaning services that control a good portion of the housecleaning business. Because this new relationship between cleaners and those who can afford to employ them abolishes the traditional "mistress-maid" relationship, it allows middle-class people who are sensitive to the political issues involved with hiring servants to avoid confronting these issues.

Most researchers who study household labor define it as all tasks involved in household maintenance, purchasing and preparing food, taking care of children, garden and yard work, and routine care and maintenance of vehicles. Three major findings emerge in this area, summarized as follows. First, women perform more household work than men do, with the figure averaging out at around two-thirds. The other third tends to be shared by men and children, with female children performing a greater amount of housework than male children. In addition, men tend to overestimate the work they do in the home and women underestimate it.

The second major finding is that women and men do different kinds of work in the home. Women tend to do the repetitive, ongoing, daily kinds of tasks, and men are more likely to perform the less repetitive or seasonal tasks. This is called the gender division of household work. Some tasks are seen as more masculine and some as more feminine. Note that if household labor were defined solely as housework, the amount of male participation would decrease. Because the definition generally includes fixing things and yard and garage work, men's contributions tend to increase. These tasks are often (though not always) more interesting, require more skills, and have a higher status than the repetitive household cleaning tasks that women are more likely to perform. Also, in terms of the gender division of labor, it is important not to forget the emotional and behind the scenes kind of work that women do that is so crucial to family functioning. These include such activities as calling the baby-sitter, remembering somebody needs his or her math book or school lunch, corresponding with family and friends, and organizing holidays and vacations. These activities are difficult to measure in a quantitative sense.

Third, it seems that when women and men perform various tasks they tend to do so in different ways. Women are much more likely to "multitask" or perform a series of tasks simultaneously. This means, for example, that they might be folding laundry at the same time that they are feeding the baby, or are cooking dinner at the same time that they are vacuuming. Men are less likely to do this; they tend to focus on one task at a time.

Many readers are probably remembering their father doing the housework or have a partner who shares equally in domestic labor. Although there have been changes over the past decades with some men taking on greater household responsibilities and some assuming an equal share, unfortunately this averages out across men generally as a matter of an increase in minutes per day. For every ten men who do little to no housework, there is a large group who "help" to a greater or lesser extent, and less than one who takes equal responsibility. Note how the term *helping* assumes that it is someone else's responsibility. Nonetheless, it is

Learning Activity: Who Does the Work at Your School and in Your Home?

Use the following charts to discover who does various kinds of work at your school and in your home. Discuss your findings with your classmates. What patterns do you notice? What do your findings suggest about how systems of inequality function in the institution of work, both inside and outside the home?

Who Does the Work at Your School?

JOB DESCRIPTION	WHITE MEN	WHITE WOMEN	MEN OF COLOR	WOMEN OF COLOR
Top administration				
Teaching				
Secretarial				
Groundskeeping				
Electrical/Carpentry				
Janitorial				
Food preparation				
Security				
Intercollegiate coaching				

Who Does the Work in Your Home?

JOB DESCRIPTION	PERSON IN THE FAMILY WHO GENERALLY DOES THIS JOB	SEX OF PERSON WHO GENERALLY DOES THIS JOB	HOURS PER WEEK SPENT IN DOING THIS JOB
Laundry			
Mowing the lawn			
Maintaining the car			
Buying the groceries			
Cooking			
Vacuuming			
Washing dishes			
Making beds			
Cleaning bathroom			

important to state that housework, although often dreary and repetitive, can also be creative and more interesting than some paid labor. And, although raising children is among the hardest work of all, it is also full of rewards. Men who do not participate in household work and childcare miss the joys associated with this work even while they have the privilege of being free to do other things.

PAID LABOR

Trends and Legalities

The reading "A Brief History of Working Women" by Sharlene Hesse-Biber and Gregg Lee Carter overviews the changes in women's labor force participation over the past centuries for different groups of women. Briefly, as U.S. society became industrialized in the nineteenth century, the traditional subsistence economies of producing what families needed to survive from the home, taking in work (like spinning or washing), or working in others' homes or on their land was changed in favor of a more distinct separation between work and home. Factories were established, employees were congregated under one roof (and thus more easily controlled), and emerging technologies started producing mass-produced goods. Instead of making products in the home for family consumption, people were working outside the home and spending their earnings on these mass-produced goods. Urban centers grew up around these sites of production, and ordinary people tended to work long hours in often very poor conditions. In *Women and Economics,* written in 1898, Charlotte Perkins Gilman explains that the harsh conditions associated with women's wage labor coincided with continuing domestic servitude in the home. This double day of work was recognized by scholars such as Gilman over a hundred years ago and is still a central aspect of women's lives today.

At the same time that working-class women and children were working in factories, mines, and sweatshops, the middle-class home came to be seen as a haven from the cruel world, and middle-class women were increasingly associated with this sphere. From this developed the "cult of true womanhood"—prescriptions for femininity that included piety, purity, and domesticity. Although these notions of femininity could barely be achieved by other than privileged White women, these norms came to influence women generally. At the same time, some women were starting to enter higher education. With the founding of Oberlin Collegial Institute in 1833, other women's colleges like Mount Holyoke, Bryn Mawr, and Wellesley were established as the century progressed. In addition, state universities (beginning with Utah in 1850) started admitting women. By the turn of the century, there were cohorts of (mostly privileged White) women who were educated to be full political persons and who helped shape the Progressive Era with a focus on reform and civic leadership. These women entered the labor force in large numbers, and many chose a career over marriage and the family.

As the twentieth century progressed, more women entered the public sphere. The years of the Great Depression slowed women's advancement, and it was not until World War II that women were seen working in traditionally male roles in unprecedented numbers. The government encouraged this transition, and many women were, for the first time, enjoying decent wages. All this would end after the war as women were encouraged or forced to return to the home so that men could claim their jobs in the labor force. Childcare centers were dismantled, and the conservative messages of the 1950s encouraged women to stay home and partake in the rapidly emerging consumer society. The social and cultural upheavals of the 1960s and the civil rights and women's movements fought for legislation to help women gain more power in the workplace.

The most important legislative gains included, first, the Equal Pay Act of 1963 that made it illegal to pay women and men different salaries for the same job. Next came Title VII of the 1964 Civil Rights Act (which went into effect in 1965) banning discrimination in employment. It made it illegal to discriminate in hiring, firing, compensation, terms, conditions, or privileges of employment. Title VII said gender could not be used as a criterion in employment except where there is a "bona fide occupational qualification," meaning it is illegal unless an employer can prove that gender is crucial to job performance. For the most part, the law had little influence until the establishment of the Equal Employment Opportunity Commission in the early 1970s to enforce the law. The courts have fine-tuned Title VII over the years, and it remains the most important legislation that protects working women and people of color.

In 1976 the Supreme Court expanded the interpretation of Title VII to include discrimination on the basis of pregnancy as sex discrimination, and ten years later it declared that sexual harassment is also a form of sex discrimination. In 1993 the Supreme Court then broadened this ruling by stating that women suing on the basis of sexual harassment did not have to prove that they had suffered "concrete psychological harm." Sexual harassment legislation made a distinction between "quid pro quo" (sexual favors are required in return for various conditions of employment) and "hostile work environment" (no explicit demand for an exchange of sexual acts for work-related conditions but being subjected to a pattern of harassment as part of the work environment).

Affirmative action policies that encouraged employers to take gender and race into account in terms of hiring were first initiated by President Kennedy in the 1960s. Since that time, affirmative action has helped diversify the workplace and encouraged the hiring of women and people of color. However, there is a lot of misunderstanding as well as serious hostility associated with affirmative action, as evidenced by the dismantling of affirmative action guidelines in many states. Basically, affirmative action requests that employers take gender and race into account to correct the historical discrimination against these groups. Affirmative action encourages the diversification of the job pool, but it does not encourage the hiring of unqualified women or people of color. It is a misunderstanding of these policies to think that White males now have a hard time getting jobs because they are being undercut by unqualified women or people of color.

At the turn of the twenty-first century, it is important to understand the changing nature of the workplace in the United States and the connection between U.S. corporate capitalism and the global economy. Electronic communications have revolutionized the marketplace; they have also made it increasingly possible for corporations to cross national boundaries. Multinational corporations have

What Is Sexual Harassment?

Sexual harassment is legally defined as unwelcome sexual advances or requests for sexual favors. It also includes any verbal or physical conduct of a sexual nature when the following criteria are met:

- Submission is made explicitly or implicitly a term or condition of an individual's employment.
- Submission to or rejection of such conduct by an individual is used as the basis for employment decisions affecting such individual.
- Such conduct has the purpose or effect of substantially interfering with an individual's work performance or creating an intimidating, hostile, or offensive working environment.

Sexual harassment may include physical conduct, verbal conduct, or nonverbal conduct such as sexual gestures or pornographic pictures.

TWO TYPES OF SEXUAL HARASSMENT

Quid Pro Quo. Unwelcome sexual advances, requests for sexual favors, and other verbal or physical conduct of a sexual nature constitute quid pro quo sexual harassment when:

Submission to such conduct is made either explicitly or implicitly a term or condition of an individual's employment or submission to or rejection of such conduct by an individual is used as the basis for employment decisions affecting such individual.

Hostile Work Environment. In determining whether or not an environment is hostile, it must be determined whether or not the conduct unreasonably interfered with an individual's work performance or created an intimidating, hostile, or offensive work environment.

The EEOC (Equal Employment Opportunity Commission) suggests that the courts look at the following criteria:

- Whether the conduct was verbal, physical, or both
- How frequently the conduct was repeated
- Whether the conduct was hostile or patently offensive
- Whether the alleged harasser was a coworker or a supervisor
- Whether others joined in perpetrating the harassment
- Whether the harassment was directed at more than one individual
- Whether the remarks were hostile and derogatory
- Whether the harasser singled out the charging party
- Whether the charging party participated in the exchange
- The relationship between the charging party and alleged harasser

The Supreme Court established a two-pronged test for determining a hostile environment:

1. The conduct must "be severe or pervasive enough to create an objectively hostile or abusive environment that a reasonable person would find hostile or abusive."
2. The victim must "subjectively perceive the environment to be abusive."

Bernice Sandler of the National Association of Women in Education reports that surveys indicate that up to 30 percent of female college students and 70 percent of women in the workplace have been sexually harassed.

Ideas for Activism

- Advocate with your elected representatives for an increase in the minimum wage.
- Encourage your school to analyze pay equity and to make corrections where needed.
- Write your elected representatives to encourage legislation and funding for childcare.
- Investigate exploitative employment practices of major national and multinational corporations and launch boycotts to demand improved conditions for workers.
- Encourage your elected representatives to support affirmative action.

grown in size and influence, and various mergers have resulted in a smaller number of corporations controlling a larger part of the market. Because many U.S.-based corporations rely on the cheaper, nonunionized labor force and looser environmental restrictions outside the United States, much manufacturing is done overseas. In addition, the military has close ties to the economy, creating what some scholars call the military-industrial complex. The presence of various international military forces in developing countries serves in part to "stabilize" these nations and protect foreign business interests. These issues are discussed in the reading, "The Globetrotting Sneaker" by Cynthia Enloe.

The effects of the global economy often include profound inequalities between rich and poor nations as well as between rich and poor citizens within individual countries. Often these inequalities are based upon older inequities resulting from nineteenth- and early twentieth-century colonization and imperialism. For individual women, although multinational corporations do give women a wage, they often upset subsistence economies, cause increasing consumerism, encourage sex trading and cultural dislocation, and pollute fragile environments. Women often work in poor and unhealthy conditions for little pay. In addition, many thousands of U.S. workers have lost their jobs as corporations have moved productive processes overseas. These events are not random but part of a broader pattern of capitalist expansion.

Horizontal and Vertical Segregation

The major change in terms of trends in women's workforce participation has been the increase in the number of women who are in paid employment as the last century progressed. The U.S. Bureau of Labor Statistics reports that this number has grown from 5.3 million in 1900 to 18.4 million in 1950 and 65 million in 1999. About three-quarters of all working women work full-time. Women made up 18 percent of the labor force in 1900, almost 30 percent in 1950, 46 percent in 1999, and are expected to comprise 48 percent of the labor force by 2005. The Women's Bureau of the U.S. Department of Labor reports that 60 percent of women aged 16 years and over were labor force participants in 1999, with African American women having the highest participation rates at 65 percent.

Another major change is the number of women with preschool-aged children in the labor force. In 1999, 61 percent of women with children under 3 years old were employed in the labor force. Historically, although mothers have always

Activist Profile: Dolores Huerta

Dolores Huerta is one of the most powerful and influential labor leaders in the United States. Born in Dawson, New Mexico, in 1930, Huerta grew up in Stockton, California, and eventually earned a teaching certificate from Stockton College. After one year of teaching, however, she quit to work with Community Service Organization (CSO) because she thought she could do more to help the hungry children she saw at school by helping organize their farmworker parents.

While with CSO, she met César Chavez, and in 1962 they founded the United Farm Workers of America. Although Chavez was more comfortable in the fields organizing workers, Huerta became the voice of the union, becoming the first woman and first Chicana negotiator in labor history. The UFW met with great success in the 1965 Delano Grape Strike, which won the first collective bargaining agreement for farmworkers, and Huerta was instrumental in the negotiations. She also became consciously involved with the feminist movement when she met Gloria Steinem in 1968, although she had always focused on issues specific to women farmworkers.

In 1972 she co-chaired the California delegation to the Democratic Convention, and she led the struggle for unemployment insurance, collective bargaining rights, and immigration rights for farmworkers under the 1985 amnesty legalization program. She was the first Latina inducted into the National Women's Hall of Fame, and she received the National Organization for Women's Woman of Courage award and the American Civil Liberties Union's Bill of Rights Award. She continues to struggle for farmworkers through the UFW and serve as a role model for Chicanas in their fight against discrimination.

worked outside the home, they have been less likely to work when they had babies and small children. The increase in paid labor participation among this group of women can be explained by several factors: One, there is a strong need among families for the money married women earn; two, the increase in single, female-headed households has meant that women have had no choice but to work outside the home; three, societal norms about gender have changed as well as the expectations for how individual women should live their lives; four, there has been an increase in women's education; and, finally, legislative changes to protect working women have resulted in the increased labor force participation of these women.

Given the large number of women working in the labor force, what kinds of work are they doing? The answer is everything. Women are doing all kinds of work and can be found in all segments of the labor force. At the same time, however, women are much more likely to be found in some sectors than others and are crowded into a small number of fields. The Women's Bureau reports that the largest share of employed women is in technical, sales, and clerical and administrative support positions. In addition, more women work as teachers (excluding postsecondary), secretaries, and cashiers than any other line of work, with one out of every five employed women working in these occupations. This phenomenon

Selected Nontraditional Occupations for Women in 1999*

OCCUPATION	EMPLOYED, BOTH SEXES	EMPLOYED, FEMALE	PERCENT FEMALE
Physicians	720,000	176,000	24.5
Farm managers (except horticultural)	146,000	30,000	20.7
Police and detectives (supervisors)	96,000	17,000	17.3
Dentists	173,000	28,000	16.5
Architects	194,000	30,000	15.7
Clergy	352,000	50,000	14.2
Engineers	2,081,000	221,000	10.6
Forestry and logging	107,000	7,000	7.0
Machinists	515,000	29,000	5.6
Truck drivers	3,116,000	153,000	4.9
Construction laborers	920,000	38,000	4.1
Airplane pilots and navigators	143,000	4,000	3.1
Firefighters	223,000	4,000	1.9
Automobile mechanics	837,000	12,000	1.4

*Nontraditional occupations are any that women comprise 25 percent or less of the total employed.
Source: U.S. Department of Labor.

of segregating women and men into different jobs is termed *occupational segregation by gender* or *horizontal segregation* (meaning segregation *across* jobs). In the reading "Go Figure," Ellen Bravo calls this sex segregation. Not only are women crowded into certain fields, but these types of horizontal segregation have been relatively continuous throughout the twentieth century. These jobs are often called pink-collar jobs and can be understood as an extension of women's work in the home. One of the most female-segregated jobs is sex work such as prostitution, where women workers have often struggled to control the conditions of their work against the demoralization and abuse by customers, pimps, and police. Priscilla Alexander's article, "Prostitution: A Difficult Issue for Feminists," discusses prostitution, the legalities surrounding it, and the necessity for prostitutes to have some say in deciding the future of their profession.

The term *blue collar* implies working class or involved with industrial, production, and factory work and can be contrasted with *white collar,* which means office or professional work and is often characterized as middle-class occupations. Note the slippage between industrial work and male-segregated work such that blue collar means working class but also implies male-segregated work with its use of the word *blue* as opposed to *pink.* The Bureau of Labor Statistics reports the following occupations as the most male segregated: engineers, mechanics and drivers, carpenters and construction trades, firefighters, airline pilots and navigators, and forestry and logging work. You will note the obvious ways feminine jobs involve working with people, children, cleaning, and administrative support, whereas masculine employment tends to involve working with machines and inanimate objects. There are other differences too, such as the wages for the heavily

Learning Activity: Working Women and Unions

Visit the web page of the AFL-CIO at *www.aflcio.org* to learn more about women in the workforce. What are some of the key issues for working women identified by the AFL-CIO? What legislative issues does the AFL-CIO identify that would be beneficial to working women? What is a union? What benefits do unions provide? Why are unions important for working women? What steps would people take to form a union at their workplace?

male-segregated jobs tend to be higher than wages for the female-segregated, pink-collar work. That is because these jobs are valued more, and they are more likely to be unionized, which tends to pay more. Indeed, if you compare the median weekly earnings of unionized versus nonunionized women in 1997, the union members earned on the average almost $150 a week more than nonunion women and also received better health and pension benefits.

An important aspect of occupational segregation by gender is that there is gender segregation even within the same job classification. This is termed *vertical segregation* (segregation *within* jobs), and, like horizontal segregation, it functions as a result of sexism in society. For example, although the number of women physicians is increasing, women are still overwhelmingly found in such specialties as pediatrics, dermatology, and public health work, and less likely to be found in surgical specialties, orthopedics, and more entrepreneurial positions. Female physicians on the average make only 77 percent of what male physicians make. Similarly, female lawyers are less likely to be in criminal law and are more likely to practice family law and make about 70 percent of male lawyers' salaries. Male teachers are more likely to teach sciences and are more likely to be with older children; female professors are more typically in the humanities and the social sciences and found in smaller number in the physical and applied sciences and technical fields. Usually the specialties and fields that men occupy are more prestigious and the salaries are higher. In this way, women and men do not just tend to perform different jobs, but the jobs that they do are valued differently and have different levels of status and power. This differential is related to sexism in society generally.

Barriers to advancement in the labor force (what is often called the glass ceiling) have been challenged by women, by the courts, and by the women's movement. And, although these barriers are beginning to come down, they are still holding strong in many areas. Women tend not to be promoted at the same rate as men, and they continue to face obstacles when trying to enter the most prestigious and best-paid occupations. A 1996 study found that women hold only 2 percent of powerful positions in the corporate world, and almost 20 percent of the Fortune 500 have no top women directors. These figures get worse if you focus on the advancement of women of color. The reading by Ann Morrison and others titled "Breaking the Glass Ceiling and Hitting the Wall" focuses on the barriers to female executives' advancement in the corporate world.

Finally, it is interesting to look at how the development of certain occupations as female segregated has affected the status and conditions of work. For example,

Take Our Daughters to Work Day

Research in the 1990s demonstrated that girls have a strong sense of self-confidence until about age 11. With the beginning of adolescence, most girls experience a significant drop in self-esteem and begin to feel self-doubt and insecurity. They often begin to focus on appearance and fear competing with or in front of boys.

Responding to this phenomenon, the Ms. Foundation for Women gathered research, experimented with programs, and eventually launched Take Our Daughters to Work Day in 1993. The goals of the program are to involve adults with pre- and early adolescent girls in visible and positive ways, to provide girls with the opportunity to see their value in the workplace, to provide girls with a space and time to be visible and heard, and to call adults' attention to the transition girls go through in adolescence. Take Our Daughters to Work Day focuses on girls' abilities rather than appearance and helps to heighten girls' aspirations by providing them an opportunity to see women and men at work. A poll in 1999 reported that young adults believed that girls perceived a wider range of career options available to them than they did ten years earlier.

Some people have complained that such a day neglects boys. Although boys, too, have developmental needs as they enter adolescence, boys and girls do not face the same constraints. An effective program for girls should not be perceived as a loss for boys. In fact, the Ms. Foundation has developed a curriculum to use with boys on Take Our Daughters to Work Day.

For more information on Take Our Daughters to Work Day, visit the website at *www.takeour daughterstowork.org.*

clerical work, although low prestige, was definitely a man's job until the turn of the twentieth century when women quickly became associated with this work due to the following factors: There was a large pool of women with few other opportunities; clerical work's low status made it easier for women to be accepted; typewriter manufacturers began promoting the typewriter as something women used; and the personal service aspect of the work fit gender norms about the feminine aspect of secretarial work. As more women entered this profession, the gap between clerical wages and blue-collar wages generally increased, and the status of the clerical profession fell. A more recent example is the field of pharmacy. Two trends—the increasing number of pharmacies attached to chain drugstores and the increasing number of female pharmacists—have been seen as the reasons why the status of pharmacy has fallen as a profession.

Wages and Comparable Worth

Currently, women earn about 77 percent of the earnings of men: a difference of $144 a week between the median earnings of women and men. For women of color, this figure drops to 64 percent. Men of color also earn less than White men. The U.S. Bureau of Labor Statistics reports that although in 1999 the median weekly earnings of men and women generally were $612 and $468, respectively, White men's median weekly earnings were $629. Black men's median weekly earn-

STUDIES SHOW THAT WOMEN WITH "SEXY" NAMES LIKE DAWN AND CHERYL ARE...

LESS LIKELY TO BE PROMOTED TO MANAGERIAL JOBS THAN WOMEN WITH NAMES LIKE...

BILL OR ROGER.

Reprinted with permission from Nicole Hollander.

ings were $483, and White women's were $477, Black women's were $408, Latino/Hispanic men's were $407, and Latina/Hispanic women's were the lowest at $348. Overall, these figures have risen significantly in the last couple of decades. In 1982, on average, women earned 59 cents for every dollar a man earned. Despite the increase to 77 cents in recent years, the Institute for Policy Research reports that over a lifetime of work, the average 25-year-old woman who works full-time, year-round until she retires at age 65 will earn on the average $523,000 less than the average working man. As Ellen Bravo explains in "Go Figure," the wage gap still exists despite arguments to suggest that these disparities are a result of the choices women make.

These statistics on the wage gap do not include part-time or seasonal workers and only compare year-round, full-time male and female workers. Because a larger number of women work part-time jobs, the inclusion of part-time workers in this statistic would most likely result in a lowering of the above figures because part-time work is often lower status, less stable, and has fewer job-related benefits like health insurance.

So why do women earn less money than men on the average? Because of both horizontal and vertical segregation. In terms of horizontal segregation, women tend to be crowded into different jobs than men, and these jobs are more likely to be paid less. Recall that although the Equal Pay Act of 1963 said that men and women working in the *same* job could not receive different compensation, this does not help women who are in *different*, less valued jobs. In terms of vertical segregation, even within the same fields there are forces to keep women in positions that are less prestigious and poorer paid. The equal pay legislation tends not to apply to distinctions within the same field where women and men are in different subspecialties. Traditional norms about gender, race, social class, and age work to create patterns of institutionalized inequalities that reinforce ideas concerning women's and men's worth and the kind of work various people can do. These forces maintain both horizontal and vertical segregation.

Comparable worth, also known as pay equity, is one means to pay women and men in different occupations comparably. Basically, comparable worth works to compare different jobs on experience, skill, training, and job conditions and assigns relative points on these indices in order to determine their worth. There is no

Working Women Say . . .

In 1997, the AFL-CIO conducted a national study of working women. According to these women, the following benefits are important to them, although very often these women do not receive these benefits from their places of employment:

BENEFIT	VERY IMPORTANT	SOMEWHAT IMPORTANT	LESS IMPORTANT	CURRENTLY PROVIDED BY THEIR JOB	GAP*
Protection from layoffs and downsizing	72%	20%	6%	34%	54%
Elder care	25%	22%	48%	8%	39%
Child care	33%	13%	49%	8%	38%
Paid leave to care for family members who are sick	70%	20%	8%	52%	35%
Equal pay for equal work	94%	5%	1%	62%	32%
Flexible hours or control	61%	25%	13%	61%	30%
Continuing education and training	59%	30%	11%	61%	31%
Pension and retirement benefits	79%	13%	7%	65%	27%
Paid sick leave for yourself	82%	13%	5%	68%	25%
Secure, affordable health insurance	87%	7%	5%	68%	25%
Paid vacation time	76%	17%	7%	77%	17%
Punishment for sexual harassment	78%	13%	6%	65%	14%
A safe and healthy workplace	93%	5%	0%	89%	9%

*The percent who say each item is at least somewhat important, minus the percent who actually have it.
Note: Percentages may not total 100 due to rounding and "don't know" responses.

federal-level comparable worth legislation, although many states have enacted laws demanding comparable worth comparisons in determining pay for state workers. In addition, the courts have ruled both for and against workers who have brought comparable worth suits against various corporations. When the courts have ruled in favor of plaintiffs, it has often meant a considerable amount of money in back pay to compensate female workers for years of financial inequities.

In this way gender inequality in women's work lives has important consequences for gender inequality in other spheres of life. Because most women work both inside and outside the home and spend a considerable part of their lives working, it is of central importance to understand the conditions under which women work as well as to strive for equality in the workplace.

Women and Economics

Charlotte Perkins Gilman

. . . Because of her maternal duties, the human female is said to be unable to get her own living. As the maternal duties of other females do not unfit them for getting their own living and also the livings of their young, it would seem that the human maternal duties require the segregation of the entire energies of the mother to the service of the child during her entire adult life, or so large a proportion of them that not enough remains to devote to the individual interests of the mother. . . .

Is this the condition of human motherhood? Does the human mother, by her motherhood, thereby lose control of brain and body, lose power and skill and desire for any other work? Do we see before us the human race, with all its females segregated entirely to the uses of motherhood, consecrated, set apart, specially developed, spending every power of their nature on the service of their children?

We do not. We see the human mother worked far harder than a mare, laboring her life long in the service, not of her children only, but of men; husbands, brothers, fathers, whatever male relatives she has; for mother and sister also; for the church a little, if she is allowed; for society, if she is able; for charity and education and reform,—working in many ways that are not the ways of motherhood.

It is not motherhood that keeps the housewife on her feet from dawn till dark; it is house service, not child service. Women work longer and harder than most men, and not solely in maternal duties. . . . Many mothers, even now, are wage-earners for the family, as well as bearers and rearers of it. And the women who are not so occupied, the women who belong to rich men,—here perhaps is the exhaustive devotion to maternity which is supposed to justify an admitted economic dependence. But we do not find it even among these. Women of ease and wealth provide for their children better care than the poor woman can; but they do not spend more time upon it themselves, nor more care and effort. They have other occupation.

In spite of her supposed segregation to maternal duties, the human female, the world over, works at extra-maternal duties for hours enough to provide her with an independent living, and then is denied independence on the ground that motherhood prevents her working!

A Brief History of Working Women

Sharlene Hesse-Biber and Gregg Lee Carter

WOMEN WORKERS IN PRE-INDUSTRIAL AMERICA

Seven hundred and fifty thousand Europeans came to America between 1600 and 1700. The bulk of them were from Britain, but the colonies also saw significant numbers from Holland, France, and Germany. Many came as indentured servants, exchanging their labor for the cost of passage to the American colonies. Indentured servants often worked from five to ten years to pay back their creditors. As early as the 1600s, prior to the slave trade, some Africans also came to the colonies as indentured servants; they often worked side by side with white indentured servants. Women's lives in this country differed drastically, depending on their race, class, and marital status.

White Women

European women usually arrived in the New World with their families, as daughters and wives, under the auspices of fathers or husbands. In the pre-industrial economy of the American colonial period (from the seventeenth century to the early eighteenth century), work was closely identified with home and family life. The family was the primary economic unit, and family members were dependent on one another for basic sustenance. Men performed the agricultural work, while women's work was done chiefly in the home, which was a center of production in colonial America. In addition to cooking, cleaning, and caring for children, women did spinning and weaving, and made lace, soap, candles, and shoes. Indeed, they manufactured nearly all articles used in daily life. This work was highly valued, and the colonies relied on the production of these "cottage industries."

Single women remained within the domestic sphere, living with relatives, often as "assistant homemakers." For married women, the nature of their work depended on the economic circumstances of their husbands:

> In cash-poor homes and among frontier families, women bore the burden of filling most of the family's basic needs. They worked to reduce cash expenditures by growing vegetables in the kitchen garden and making the family's clothes, candles, soap and household furnishings. If a husband were a craftsman or the proprietor of a shop or tavern, his wife and children might also work in the business, in addition to all the other tasks. In contrast, the wife of a successful farmer, plantation owner, or merchant did little actual

work; instead, she supervised household servants and slaves who purchased or made the goods the family needed, cooked the meals, and maintained the house.

The social codes of colonial America did not exclude a woman from working outside the home, and many did so. Colonial women engaged in a great range of occupations, and as old documents are discovered and new histories of women's work are written, that range appears greater still. Women were innkeepers, shopkeepers, crafts workers, nurses, printers, teachers, and landholders. In the city of Boston during 1690, for example, women ran approximately 40 percent of all taverns. During that year, city officials also granted more than thirty women the right to saw lumber and manufacture potash. Women acted as physicians and midwives in all the early settlements, producing medicines, salves, and ointments. Many of the women who worked outside their homes were widows with dependent children, who took their husbands' places in family enterprises. It seems that at one time or another, colonial women engaged in many of the occupations practiced by men. Indeed, most models of the "patriarchal family economy" ill fit the historical evidence; for example, eighteenth-century diaries describe "a world in which wives as well as husbands traded with their neighbors" and "young women felt themselves responsible for their own support." Not surprisingly, however, women's wages in this period were significantly lower than those of men.

For poor women, there were special incentives to work outside the home. Local poor laws encouraged single poor women to work rather than become recipients of relief. The choice of jobs was much more limited, and many poor women became laundresses, house servants, or cooks. Again, however, female laborers were paid approximately 30 percent less than the lowest-paid unskilled, free, white male workers and 20 percent less than hired-out male slaves.

The fact that some women worked in so-called "masculine fields"—that they were merchants, tavern owners, shopkeepers, and so on—has sometimes been interpreted to mean that the colonial period was a "golden age of equality" for women. Contemporary historians argue instead, however, that these jobs were exceptions to the rule, and that in fact "colonial times were characterized by a strict and simple division of labor between men and women, which assigned them to fields and house, or to the public and private spheres, respectively." The dominant ideology was still that a woman's place was at home, raising children. . . .

Women of Color

Historically, the experiences of women of color have differed dramatically from those of white women. If we consider only the present time period, it may appear that women of color and white women have certain experiences in common—relatively low economic position, being the target of discriminatory practices in education and in work, and overall marginality in the power structure. But women of color and white women have reached their present circumstances through very different histories. Although white women's status was clearly inferior to that of white men, they were treated with deference, and they shared in the status privileges of their husbands. African American women almost never had the option of choosing between work and leisure, as did some white women. They were not included in the image of the "colonial housewife." African American women were not considered "weak" females, but were treated more like beasts of burden. Thus these women of color suffered a double oppression of sexism and racism.

Nowhere is this double oppression more clearly demonstrated than within the institution of slavery, which became established in late seventeenth- and early eighteenth-century colonial society—largely as a result of the demand for cheap agricultural labor, especially within the Southern plantation economy. Historians estimate the slave population in the United States, Caribbean, and Brazil consisted of 9.5 million blacks. More than double that number are estimated to have died in transit to the New World. Slave women in the Southern colonies were without doubt the most exploited of all women. They were exploited not only as workers but as breeders of slaves. The following advertisement was typical of the time:

> **Negroes for Sale:** A girl about twenty years of age (raised in Virginia) and her two female children, four and the other two years old—remarkably strong and healthy. Never having had a day's sickness with the exception of the smallpox in her life. She is prolific in her generating qualities and affords a rare opportunity to any person who wishes to raise a family of strong and healthy servants for their own use.

Slave women were also sometimes exploited as sex objects for white men. Like male slaves, they were considered intrinsically inferior. Slaves were property, not people. They faced severe cultural and legal restrictions: their family lives were controlled by their owners, their children were not their own, and their educational opportunities were almost nonexistent.

Sojourner Truth, formerly a slave and an activist in the abolitionist and women's rights movements, eloquently expressed the differences in treatment, under slavery, of black and white women: "That man over there says that women need to be helped into carriages and lifted over ditches, and to have the best place everywhere. Nobody ever helped me into carriages, or over mud puddles, or gives me any best place . . . and ain't I a woman?"

Before the Civil War, a black woman in one of the "cotton states," working on one of the larger plantations, would have been either a house servant or one of several million field hands who produced major cash crops. In the Southern plantation economy, we thus find a "bifurcated" concept of woman. The European woman became "the guardian of civilization," while the African American woman was "spared neither harsh labor nor harsh punishment," though the experience of slaves differed depending on the economic status and individual personality of the slave owner. Even pregnancy did not deter some slavemasters from cruel treatment: "One particular method of whipping pregnant slaves was used throughout the South; they were made to lie face down in a specially dug depression in the ground, a practice that provided simultaneously for the protection of the fetus and the abuse of its mother."

Some white women benefited from such slave labor and shared with their husbands the role of oppressor, although the slave-mistress relationship was psychologically complex: "In their role as labor managers, mistresses lashed out at slave women not only to punish them, but also to vent their anger on victims even more wronged than themselves. We may speculate that, in the female slave, the white woman saw the source of her own misery, but she also saw herself—a woman without rights or recourse, subject to the whims of an egotistical man." Conflict between white and African American women often resulted in violence, in which "mistresses were likely to attack with any weapon available—knitting needles, tongs, a fork, butcher knife, ironing board, or pan of boiling water." Yet, while the relationship was often filled with strife, white and African American women " also shared a world of physical and emotional intimacy that is uncommon among women of antagonistic classes and different races."

Slavery was justified by notions of race involving the "biological superiority" of the colonists. It was assumed that Europeans in the colonies made up an easily identifiable and discrete biological and social entity; a "natural" community of class interests, racial attributes, political and social affinities, and superior culture. This was of course not exactly true, but given that the differences between white skin and black skin were more noticeable than many of the differences among Europeans

themselves, and given that whites were in dominant positions politically and socially, it could easily *seem* to be true.

Slave families often resisted the oppressive workloads by banding together to help one another in the fields and to lessen the workloads of older, weaker, or sicker workers. The extended family was of vital importance under the slave system. African American mothers labored most of the day, some of then caring for white women's families, while their own children were left under the care of grandmothers and old or disabled slaves. While the two-parent, nuclear family may have been the most typical form of slave cohabitation, close relatives were often very much involved in family life. Stevenson's study suggests that in colonial and antebellum Virginia, the slave family was a "malleable extended family that, when possible, provided its members with nurture, education, socialization, material support, and recreation in the face of the potential social chaos that the slaveholder imposed."

Even though African American men were unable to own property, to provide protection and support for their children, or to work within the public sphere, there was a sexual division within the slave household. Men collected the firewood and made furniture—beds, tables, chairs—and other articles of wood, such as animal traps, butter paddles, and ax handles. They also wove baskets and made shoes. African American women grew, prepared, and preserved foods; spun thread, wove and dyed cloth, and sewed clothes; and made soap and candles.

In the North, while slavery was an accepted practice, it was not nearly as widespread. Many African American women worked as free laborers as domestic servants; others worked as spinners, weavers, and printers.

Native American Women

The work and family life experience of Native American women prior to European colonization differed depending on the region of the country and the type of tribal society. But in every Native American nation, women played very important roles in the economic life of their communities:

> They had to be resourceful in utilizing every aspect of the environment to sustain life and engaging in cultural exchanges to incorporate new productive techniques. They gathered wild plants for food, herbs for medicines and dyes, clay for pottery, bark and reeds for weaving cloth. In many nations, they also tilled the soil and sowed the seeds, cultivated and harvested, made cloth and clothing, dried vegetables, and ground grains for breads. In hunting societies, they cured the meats and dried the skins. They also assisted in the hunt in some cultures.

As a general rule, men hunted and women engaged in agricultural work. The more important hunting was to a community's survival, the more extensive the male power within the community; the greater the dependence on agriculture, the greater the power and independence of women. Women had the responsibility for raising children and maintaining hearth and home. Men engaged in hunting, fishing, and warfare.

In the East especially, many Indian communities were predominantly agricultural. Women constituted the agricultural labor force within these communities. An English woman who was held captive by a Seneca tribe observed that

> Household duties were simple and Seneca women, unlike English wives and daughters, were not slaves to the spinning wheel or the needle. In the summer, the women went out each morning to the fields, accompanied by their children, to work cooperatively and in the company of friends and relatives, planting and tending the corn, beans, and squash at a pace to their individual rhythms and skills rather than to the demands of an overseer. They moved from field to field, completing the same tasks in each before returning to the first.

Women within agricultural communities would often maintain control over tools and land—as well as any surplus foods they gathered from the land. This often enabled them (especially elderly women who were heads of households) to garner some political clout within their tribal communities. For instance, if Iroquois women opposed war on certain occasions, they might refuse to let the men have the cornmeal they would have needed to feed their raiding parties or armies. These communities often had a matrilineal family structure (inheritance and family name were through the female line, with family connections through the mother) and matrilocal residence (upon marriage a man lived with his mother-in-law's relatives).

Through the lens of the white colonist, the work roles and family structure of Native American society appeared deviant and, in some cases, perverse. After all, English society was characterized by a patriarchal family structure with patrilocal residence:

> To Europeans, Indian family patterns raised the specter of promiscuous women, freed from accountability to their fathers and husbands for the offspring they produced. . . . Equally incomprehensible—and thus perverse—to many Europeans were the work roles accepted by Indian men and women. In the world the English knew, farming was labor and farmers were male. Masculinity was linked, inexorably, to agriculture: household production and family reproduction defined femininity. That Indian men hunted was not a sufficient counterpoise for, in the England of the seventeenth century, hunting was a sport, not an occupation. Many concluded that Indian men were effeminate, lazy; Indian women were beasts of burden, slaves to unmanly men.

European colonization and conquest pushed Native Americans off their land, depriving them of food and livelihood, culture and traditions. Disease or warfare demolished whole societies. Others were radically transformed, especially with regard to the traditional gender and work roles. Having used military force to remove Native Americans from their lands onto reservations, the U.S. government "began a systematic effort to destroy their cultures and replace them with the values and practices of middle-class whites."

Confined to relatively small reservations, Native American men could no longer hunt as extensively as before (nor, defeated by U.S. forces, could they any longer carry on warfare). They therefore needed to redefine their social roles and to find new economic activities. In many a Native American tribe, the men took over agriculture, traditionally the women's work. Family structure also changed, at the prompting of missionaries and others including government officials, to become more like that of the Europeans, with less emphasis on the matrilineal extended family and more on the nuclear family and the husband-wife relationship.

THE ARRIVAL OF INDUSTRIALIZATION

The transformation from an agrarian rural economy to an urban industrial society ushered in a new era in women's work. With the advent of industrialization, many of the products women made at home—clothes, shoes, candles—gradually came to be made instead in factories. For a while, women still performed the work at home, using the new machines. Merchants would contract for work to be done, supplying women with the machines and the raw materials to be made into finished articles. The most common of these manufacturing trades for women was sewing for the newly emerging clothing industry. Since women had always sewn for their families, this work was considered an extension of women's traditional role, and therefore a respectable activity. As the demand for goods increased, however, home production declined and gave way to the factory system, which was more efficient in meeting emerging needs.

The rise of factory production truly separated the home from the workplace. With the decline of the household unit as the center of industrial and economy activity, the importance of women's economic role also declined. Male and female spheres of activity became more separated, as did the definitions of men's and women's roles. Man's role continued to be primarily that of worker and provider; woman's role became primarily supportive. She was to maintain a smooth and orderly household, to be cheerful and warm, and thus to provide the husband with the support and services he needed to continue his work life. The industrial revolution created a set of social and economic conditions in which the basic lifestyle of white middle-class women more nearly approached society's expectations concerning woman's role. More and more middle-class women could now aspire to the status formerly reserved for the upper classes—that of "lady." The nineteenth-century concept of a lady was that of a fragile, idle, pure creature, submissive and subservient to her husband and to domestic needs. Her worth was based on her decorative value, a quality that embraced her beauty, her virtuous character, and her temperament. She was certainly not a paid employee. This ideal was later referred to as the "cult of true womanhood" because of its rigid, almost religious standards.

Biological and social arguments were also often used to justify women's exclusion from the labor force. Women were seen as too weak and delicate to participate in the rough work world of men. It was believed they lacked strength and stamina, that their brains were small, that the feminine perspective and sensitivity were liabilities in the marketplace. Such arguments rationalized women's accepting the roles of homemaker and mother almost exclusively, as the industrial revolution spread across the country.

During the early years of industrialization, however, because many men were still primarily occupied with agricultural work and were unavailable or unwilling to enter the early factories, male laborers were in short supply. American industry depended, then, on a steady supply of women workers. Yet how could society tolerate women's working in the factories, given the dominant ideology of the times, which dictated that a woman's place was at home? Single white women provided one answer. Their employment was viewed as a fulfillment of their family responsibilities, during an interlude before marriage.

The employment of young, single women in the early Lowell (Massachusetts) mills is a prime example of the reconciliation of ideology with the needs of industry. Francis Cabot Lowell devised a respectable route into employment for such women. Recruiting the daughters of farm families to work in his mill, which opened in 1821 in Lowell, he provided supervised boardinghouses, salaries sufficient to allow the young women to offer financial aid to their families or to save for their own trousseaux, and assurances to their families that the hard work and discipline of the mill would help prepare them for marriage and motherhood.

In the early industrial era, working conditions were arduous and hours were long. By the late 1830s, immigration began to supply a strongly competitive, permanent workforce willing to be employed for low wages in the factories, under increasingly mechanized and hazardous conditions. By the late 1850s, most of the better-educated, single, native-born women had left the mills, leaving newly immigrated women (both single and married) and men to fill these positions.

While women thus played a crucial role in the development of the textile industry, the first important manufacturing industry in America, women also found employment in many other occupations during the process of industrialization. As railroads and other business enterprises expanded and consolidated, women went to work in these areas as well. In fact, the U.S. Labor Commissioner reported that by 1890 only 9 out of 360 general groups to which the country's industries had been assigned did not employ women.

By 1900, more than five million women or girls, or about one in every five of those 10 years old and over, had become a paid employee. The largest proportion (40%) remained close to home in domestic and personal service, but domestic service was on the decline for white working-class women at the turn of the century. About 25 percent (1.3 million) of employed women worked in the manufacturing industries: in cotton mills, in the manufacture of woolen and worsted goods, silk goods, hosiery, and knit wear. The third largest group of employed women (over 18%) were working on farms. Women in the trade and transportation industries (about 10%) worked as saleswomen, telegraph and telephone operators, stenographers, clerks, copyists, accountants, and bookkeepers. Women in the professions (about 9 percent, and typically young, educated, and single, of native-born parentage) were employed primarily in elementary and secondary teaching or nursing. Other professions—law, medicine, business, college teaching—tended to exclude women. The fastest growing of these occupational groups were manufacturing, trade, and transportation. In the last thirty years of the nineteenth century, the number of women working in trade and transportation rose from 19,000 to over half a million. These women also tended to be young, single, native-born Americans; immigrants and minority women were excluded from these white-collar positions.

. . .

By the turn of the century, the labor market had become clearly divided according to gender, race, and class. Fewer manufacturing jobs were being defined as suitable for white women, especially with the rising dominance of heavy industry employment for which female workers were considered too delicate. Working-class women were increasingly devalued by their continued participation in activities men had primarily taken over (such as factory work), because these activities were regarded as lacking in the Victorian virtue and purity called for by the "cult of true womanhood." As the economy expanded and prosperity came to more and more white middle-class families, middle-class women could "become ladies." A "woman's place" was still defined as at home. If these women did work outside the home, the appropriate occupation was a white-collar job (sales, clerical, and professional occupations). White women's occupations shifted from primarily domestic service—which became increasingly identified as "black women's work"—and from light manufacturing to the rapidly growing opportunities in office and sales work. These jobs were also considered more appropriate for feminine roles as defined by the cult of true womanhood. Women of color did not share in this occupational transformation. In 1910, for example, 90.5 percent of African American women worked as agricultural laborers or domestics, compared with 29.3 percent of white women.

The Legacy of Slavery

African American women were not part of the "cult of true womanhood." They were not sheltered or protected from the harsh realities, and "while many white daughters were raised in genteel refined circumstances, most black daughters were forced to deal with poverty, violence and a hostile outside world from childhood on." After emancipation, their employment and economic opportunities were limited, in part because the skills they had learned on the plantation transferred to relatively few jobs, and those only of low pay and status.

African American women's concentration in service work—especially domestic work—was largely a result of limited opportunities available to them following the Civil War. The only factory employment open to them was in the Southern tobacco and textile industries, and until World War I most African American working women were farm laborers, domestics, or laundresses. . . .

Despite the limited range of job opportunities, a relatively large proportion of African American women were employed. The legacy of slavery may partly account for the relatively high labor-force participation rate of African American women. Although women's labor-force participation rate is generally lower than men's, African American women's participation rate was historically much higher than that of white women. Thus, for example, white women's labor-force participation in 1890 was 16.3 percent, while African American women's rate was 39.7 percent.

WORLD WAR I AND THE DEPRESSION

World War I accelerated the entry of white women into new fields of industry. The pressure of war production and the shortage of male industrial workers necessitated the hiring of women for what had been male-dominated occupations. Women replaced men at jobs in factories and business offices, and, in general, they kept the nation going, fed, and clothed. The mechanization and routinization of industry during this period enabled women to quickly master the various new skills. For the most part, this wartime pattern involved a reshuffling of the existing female workforce, rather than an increase in the numbers of women employed. Although the popular myth is that homemakers abandoned their kitchens for machine shops or airplane hangars, only about 5 percent of women workers were new to the labor force during the war years. . . .

Thus the wartime labor shortage temporarily created new job opportunities for women workers, and at higher wages than they had previously earned. This was not necessarily the case for African American women, however. Although World War I opened up some factory jobs to them, these were typically limited to the most menial, least desirable, and often the most dangerous jobs—jobs already rejected by white women. These jobs included some of the most dangerous tasks in industry, such as carrying glass to hot ovens in glass factories and dyeing furs in the furrier industry.

World War I produced no substantial or lasting change in women's participation in the labor force. The employment rate of women in 1920 was actually a bit lower (20.4%) than in 1910 (20.9%). The labor unions, the government, and the society at large were not ready to accept a permanent shift in women's economic role. Instead, women filled an urgent need during the wartime years and were relegated to their former positions as soon as peace returned. As the reformer Mary Von Kleeck wrote, "When the immediate dangers . . . were passed, the prejudices came to life once more."

When the men returned from the war, they were given priority in hiring, and although a number of women left the labor force voluntarily, many were forced out by layoffs. Those remaining were employed in the low-paying, low-prestige positions women had always occupied and in those occupations that had become accepted as women's domain. . . .

The Great Depression of the 1930s threw millions out of work. The severe employment problems during this period intensified the general attitude that a woman with a job was taking that job away from a male breadwinner. Yet during the 1930s, an increasing number of women went to work for the first time. The increase was most marked among younger, married women, who worked at least until the first child, and among older, married women, who re-entered the marketplace because of dire economic need or in response to changing patterns of consumer demand. Most jobs held by women were part-time, seasonal, and marginal. Women's labor-force participation increased slowly throughout this period and into the early 1940s . . . , except in the professions (including feminized professions such as elementary teaching, nursing, librarianship,

and social work). The proportion of women in all professions declined from 14.2 percent to 12.3 percent during the Depression decade.

WORLD WAR II

The ordeal of World War II brought about tremendous change in the numbers and occupational distribution of working women. As during World War I, the shortage of male workers, who had gone off to fight, coupled with the mounting pressures of war production brought women into the workforce. A corresponding shift in attitudes about women's aptitudes and proper roles resulted. Women entered the munitions factories and other heavy industries to support the war effort. The War Manpower Commission instituted a massive advertising campaign to attract women to the war industries. Patriotic appeals were common.

. . .

Equal work did not mean equal pay for the women in these varied wartime occupations. Although the National War Labor Board issued a directive to industries that stipulated equal pay for equal work, most employers continued to pay women at a lower rate. Furthermore, women had little opportunity to advance in their new occupations.

World War II marked an important turning point in women's participation in the paid labor force. The social prohibition concerning married women working gave way under wartime pressure, and women wartime workers demonstrated that it was possible for women to maintain their households while also assuming the role of breadwinner with outside employment. More women than ever before learned to accommodate the simultaneous demands of family and work. The experience "pointed the way to a greater degree of choice for American women."

However, at the war's end, with the return of men to civilian life, there was a tremendous pressure on women to return to their former positions in the home. During this time, a new social ideology began to emerge; Betty Friedan later called it "the feminine mystique." This ideology drew in social workers, educators, journalists, and psychologists, all of whom tried to convince women that their place was again in the home. It was not until the "cult of true womanhood" advanced in the late 1800s to differentiate middle-class women from working-class women. As Friedan notes, in the fifteen years following World War II, the image of "women at home" rather than "at work" became a cherished and self-perpetuating core of contemporary American culture. A generation of young people were brought up to extol the values of home and family, and woman's role was defined as the domestic center around which all else revolved. Women were supposed to live like those in Norman Rockwell *Saturday Evening Post* illustrations. The idealized image was of smiling mothers baking cookies for their wholesome children, driving their station wagons loaded with freckled youngsters to an endless round of lessons and activities, returning with groceries and other consumer goods to the ranch houses they cared for with such pride. Women were supposed to revel in these roles and gladly leave the running of the world to men.

. . .

Yet, unlike the post-World War I period, after World War II women did not go back to the kitchens. Instead, women's labor-force participation continued to increase throughout the post-World War II decades, so that by the late 1960s, 40 percent of American women were in the labor force, and by the late 1990s, 60 percent were. Who were the women most likely to be part of this "new majority" of women at work?

AFTER WORLD WAR II: THE RISE OF THE MARRIED WOMAN WORKER

Between 1890 and the beginning of World War II, single women comprised at least half the female labor force. The others were mostly married African American, immigrant, or working-class women.

The decade of the 1940s saw a change in the type of woman worker, as increasing numbers of married women left their homes to enter the world of paid work. . . . Although single women continued to have the highest labor-force participation rates among women, during the 1940s the percentage of married women in the workforce grew more rapidly than any other category. Between 1940 and 1950, single women workers were in short supply because of low birthrates in the 1930s. Furthermore, those single women available for work were marrying at younger ages and leaving the labor market to raise their families. On the other hand, ample numbers of older, married women were available, and these women (who had married younger, had had fewer children, and were living longer) were eager for paid employment.

In 1940, about 15 percent of married women were employed; by 1950, 24 percent. This increase has continued: by 1960, 32 percent of married women; in 1970, over 41 percent; in 1980, 50 percent; and by 1995, 61 percent. Indeed, as the twentieth century comes to a close, we can see that labor-force participation rates of single and married women have become almost identical. . . .

During the 1940s, 1950s, and 1960s, it was mainly older, married women entering the workforce. In 1957, for example, the labor-force participation rate among women aged forty-five to forty-nine years exceeded the rate for twenty- to twenty-four-year-old women. During the 1960s, young married mothers with preschool- or school-age children began to enter the workforce. This trend continued for the next three decades; by 1995, more than three-quarters of married women with children between six and seventeen years of age were employed, and, most significantly, almost two-thirds of those women with children under the age of six were in the labor force. . . . In short, whereas before 1970 the overwhelming majority of married women stopped working after they had children, today the overwhelming majority of married women do not.

WOMEN OF COLOR

Denied entrance to the factories during the rise of industrialization and, for much of the twentieth century, facing discriminatory hiring practices that closed off opportunities in the newly expanded office and sales jobs, many women of color entered domestic service. From 1910 to 1940, the proportion of white women employed in clerical and sales positions almost doubled, and there was a decline in the numbers of white women in domestic work. Private household work then became the province of African American women: the percentage of African American household workers increased from 38.5 percent in 1910 to 59.9 percent in 1940. . . . For the next three decades, African American women remained the single largest group in domestic service.

African American women's economic status improved dramatically from 1940 through the 1960s, as a result of an increase in light manufacturing jobs, as well as changes in technology. African American women moved from private household work into manufacturing and clerical work, and made significant gains in the professions. Whereas in 1940, 60 percent of employed African American females worked in private households, by the late 1960s only 20 percent did. Their job prospects continued to improve, and by the 1980s, almost half of all working African American women were doing so in "white collar" jobs—clerical and sales positions, as well as professional jobs in business, health-care, and education. Through the 1990s, the historic, job-prestige gap between African American and white working women continued to close. Almost two-thirds of working African American women had jobs in the white-collar world by 1996, compared with nearly three-quarters of working white women. . . .

Other Women of Color at Work

Each minority group has had a different experience in American society and has faced different opportunities and obstacles. Women in each group share with African American women the concerns of all minority women; they share with the men of their ethnic groups the problems of discrimination against that particular ethnic minority.

Native American Women. As we noted earlier, gender roles in Native American communities were disrupted during the conquest and oppression by whites. For example, Navajo society was traditionally matrilineal, with extended families the norm; Navajo women owned property and played an important role in family decisions. But beginning in the 1930s, government policy disrupted this system by giving land only to males. As they could no longer make a sufficient living off the land, more and more Navajo men had to seek employment off the reservations. Nuclear families became the norm. Navajo women became dependent on male providers. With the men away much of the time, these women are often isolated and powerless. They often face divorce or desertion and thus economic difficulties, because the community frowns on women seeking work off the reservation.

Such disruption of the traditional Native American society left Native American women in very grim economic circumstances. But in recent decades, more and more of them have gotten jobs. Native American women's labor-force participation rate in 1970 was 35 percent (compared to 43% for all women). This rate rose sharply to 55 percent by the early 1990s and is now within a few percentage points of the rate for all women.

Like their African American counterparts over the past half century, Native American women have gradually moved out of low-skill farm and nonfarm work and domestic jobs into clerical, sales, professional, technical, and other "white-collar" jobs. In 1960, one in six working Native American women was employed as domestic household worker; by the early 1990s only one in a hundred was. During the same period, the proportion of Native American women involved in agricultural work also went from ten to one in a hundred. Manufacturing work was increasingly replaced by white-collar work, reflecting the overall trends in the occupational structure; more specifically, while the percentage involved in factory work (much of it in textiles and traditional crafts) fell from 18.1 to 14.2, the percentage doing white-collar work soared from 28.9 to 61.3. Although many of these white-collar jobs are classified as "professional" (15.7% of all working Native American women) or "managerial" (9.4%), two-thirds of Native American women are still concentrated in the "secondary" sector of the labor market—which is characterized by low wages, few or no benefits, low mobility, and high instability. They are kept there because of the "stagnation of the reservation economy," discrimination, and their relatively low level of educational attainment. A significant number do not have a high school diploma (in 1990, more than one-third of all those over the age of 25, compared to one-fifth of white women).

Latina [Chicana] Women. . . . Large numbers of Chicanas migrated, usually with husband and children, from Mexico to the United States during the 1916–1920 labor shortage created by World War I. They found work in the sprawling "factory farms" of the Southwest, harvesting fruits, vegetables, and cotton in the Imperial and San Joaquin valleys of California, the Salt River valley of Arizona, and the Rio Grande valley of Texas. They also went to the Midwest, for instance to Michigan and Minnesota, to harvest sugar beets. Such migrant workers typically were exploited, spending long, tedious, and physically demanding hours in the fields for very low pay. Some became tenant farmers, which might seem a step up, except too often this system "created debt peonage; unable to

pay the rent, tenants were unable to leave the land and remained virtually permanently indebted to their landlords."

During the 1920s, with a shortage of European immigration, new job opportunities opened up for Mexican Americans, and they began to migrate from rural, farm country to the urban, industrial centers, where they found work as domestics and factory workers. By 1930, one-third of working Chicanas were domestics and a quarter worked in manufacturing; at the time, the share employed in agriculture, forestry, and mining had fallen to 21 percent. Wage scales varied according to ethnicity, however. It was not uncommon to pay Chicana workers lower wages than "Anglo" (whites of European descent) women for doing the same job, whether as domestics, laundresses, or workers in the food-processing industries of the West and Southwest. Then the Depression years of the 1930s, with the general shortage of jobs, brought a backlash against Mexican American labor, and thousands of Mexicans were deported or pressured to leave.

World War II once again opened up the American labor market for Mexican migrants, as their labor was needed to offset wartime labor shortages. However, their treatment was deplorable by modern standards. In short, Mexican workers comprised a "reserve army" of exploited labor. Through the government-sponsored Bracero or "Manual Workers" program, Mexican workers were granted temporary work visas so that they could be employed on large corporate farms and elsewhere, but too often they were treated like slaves or prisoners.

World War II and the years following saw a massive shift in the occupational and geographical distribution of Chicana workers:

> Many left Texas for California, and the population became increasingly more urban. Women continued their move from the fields into garment factories throughout the Southwest. . . . [A] comparison of the 1930 and 1950 [census] data shows the magnitude of these shifts. For

instance, the share of employed southwestern Chicanas working on farms dropped from 21 percent in 1930 to 6 percent in 1950, while the percentage in white-collar work doubled.

By the 1960s, the largest occupational category for Chicana workers was operatives, followed by clerical and service work. Chicanas became concentrated in particular industries—food processing, electronics (including telecommunications), and garments. Like their Native American counterparts, Chicana women have made some progress in entering professional and managerial occupations (primarily noncollege teaching, nursing, librarianship, and social work). In 1960, 8.6 percent were in these occupations; by 1980, 12.6 percent, and by the early 1990s 17.5 percent. However, like the Native Americans, Chicana women are still overwhelmingly found in the secondary labor market (75%); much more so than women (60%) and men (32%) of white European heritage.

The dominant reasons behind the low occupational prestige of all minority groups are the same: discrimination and low educational attainment. In the case of Chicana women, over 15 percent "are illiterate by the standard measure (completion of less than five years of schooling)," but studies of functional illiteracy during the 1970s and 1980s suggest "much higher rates—perhaps as high as 56 percent." At the other end of the educational attainment spectrum, only 8.4 percent of Latina women have completed four or more years of college— compared with 21.0 percent of white women and 12.9 percent of blacks. However, education is only part of the formula for success in the U.S. occupational system: for when education is held constant, Latina women only make between 84 and 90 percent of what white women do.

Beyond lack of education, Chicana women face other important obstacles in the labor market. They have high rates of unemployment and underemployment. Many of the jobs they hold are seasonal and often nonunionized. This lack of advancement translates into higher poverty rates (23% for Chicana/os in the early 1990s). The median income for full-time Chicana workers is lower than that of any other U.S. racial-ethnic group. For Latina women (in general) with children and no husband present, the poverty rate is even worse: 49.4 percent compared with 26.6 percent of white women in this situation.

Increasingly, Chicana women, like many female workers of color around the globe, are doing service or assembly work for multi-national corporations, especially in the apparel, food-processing, and electronics industries. These women have often displaced men in assembly work because they can be paid less and many do not receive job benefits. The work hours are long, and women are often assigned monotonous tasks that are dangerous to their health.

. . .

Asian-American Women. . . . Asian Americans are considered to be the "model minority," . . . However, this is as much myth as fact. While many among both the native-born and the recent arrivals have high levels of education and professional skills and can readily fit into the labor market, others lack such advantages, often finding work only as undocumented laborers in low-paying jobs with long work days, little or no job mobility, and no benefits.

> We are told we have overcome our oppression, and that therefore we are the model minority. Model refers to the cherished dictum of capitalism that "pulling hard on your bootstraps" brings due rewards. . . . Asian American success stories . . . do little to illuminate the actual conditions of the majority of Asian Americans. Such examples conceal the more typical Asian American experience of unemployment, underemployment and struggle to survive. The model minority myth thus classically scapegoats Asian Americans. It labels us in a way that dismisses the real problems that many do face, while at the

same time pitting Asians against other oppressed people of color.

In 1996, 37.3 percent of Asian women who were 25 years and over had at least a bachelor's degree, compared with 23.2 percent of non-Latina whites. Filipina American women secured the highest college graduation rate of all women, a rate 50 percent greater than that of white males. Following closely behind are Chinese American and Japanese American women, who exceed both the white male and female college graduation rates. Yet, these educational achievements bring lower returns for Asian women than for whites. Census data reveal a gap between achievement and economic reward for Asian American women, who suffer from both race and sex discrimination within the labor market. . . .

And it would be wrong to equate "Asian" with "well educated," because the majority of Asian women immigrating to the United States since 1980 have low levels of education. Though, as just noted, Asian women are much more likely to be college-educated than non-Latina white women, they are also much more likely—two and a half times more likely—to be grade-school drop outs: in 1996, 12.5 percent of Asian women had not gone beyond the eighth grade, compared to only 5.2 percent of their non-Latina white counterparts. This fact is linked to the other most obvious difference between Asian and white women . . . — the proportions working as "operators, fabricators, and laborers," where we find significantly more Asian women.

These women are most commonly employed as sewing machine operators at home or in small sweatshops in the Chinatowns of New York and San Francisco. Asian immigrant women are also heavily employed in the microelectronics industry. Women in general comprise 80 to 90 percent of assembly workers in this industry, and approximately "half of these assembly workers are recent immigrants from the Philippines, Vietnam, Korea, and South Asia." Within the microelectronics industry

jobs are often "structured along racial and gender lines, with men and white workers earning higher wages and being much more likely to be promoted than women and workers of color." Karen Hossfeld's research on relationships between Third World immigrant women production workers and their white male managers in the high-tech Silicon Valley of California relates how immigrant women of color negotiate and often employ resistance to primarily white, middle-class management demands. One Filipina circuit board assembler in Silicon Valley puts it this way:

> The bosses here have this type of reasoning like a seesaw. One day it's "you're paid less because women are different than men," or "immigrants need less to get by." The next day it's "you're all just workers here—no special treatment just because you're female or foreigners."
>
> Well, they think they're pretty clever with their doubletalk, and that we're just a bunch of dumb aliens. But it takes two to use a seesaw. What we are gradually figuring out here is how to use their own logic against them.

As clerical or administrative support workers, Asian American women are disproportionately represented as cashiers, file clerks, office machine operators, and typists. They are less likely to obtain employment as secretaries or receptionists. Noting that there is an "overrepresentation of college-educated women in clerical work," Woo suggests that education functions less as a path toward mobility into higher occupational categories, and more as "a hedge against jobs as service workers and as machine operatives or assembly workers."

Asian American women with a college education who obtain professional employment are often restricted to the less prestigious jobs within this category. Asian American women "are more likely to remain marginalized in their work organization, to encounter a 'glass ceiling', and to earn less than white men, Asian American men, and white women with comparable educational backgrounds." They are least represented in those male-dominated positions of physician, lawyer, and judge, and are heavily concentrated in the more female-dominated occupations of nursing and teaching.

Asian women have been subjected to a range of stereotypes. The "Lotus Blossom" stereotype depicts them as submissive and demure sex objects: "good, faithful, uncomplaining, totally compliant, self-effacing, gracious servants who will do anything and everything to please, entertain, and make them feel comfortable and carefree." At the opposite extreme, the Dragon Lady stereotype portrays Asian women as "promiscuous and untrustworthy,"

> as the castrating Dragon Lady who, while puffing on her foot-long cigarette holder, could poison a man as easily as she could seduce him. "With her talon-like six-inch fingernails, her skin-tight satin dress slit to the thigh," the Dragon Lady is desirable, deceitful and dangerous.

Asian American feminist Germaine Wong notes how stereotypes concerning Asian women operate in the workplace, serving to deter their advancement into leadership roles and to increase their vulnerability to sexual harassment. Additionally, these stereotypes have fostered a demand for "X-rated films and pornographic materials featuring Asian women in bondage, for 'Oriental' bathhouse workers in U.S. cities, and for Asian mail-order brides."

In sum, the notion of Asian Americans as the "model minority" deviates considerably from sociological reality. While Asian American women as a group have achieved some "success" in terms of high educational attainment, they receive lower returns on this investment compared to the white population. They have not "escaped the stigmatization of being minority and recent immigrants in a discriminatory job market."

READING 56

Go Figure

Ellen Bravo

Oh, the thorny problem of the wage gap—what's the right wing to do? They used to say that women didn't deserve as much money as men. But hey, it's the dawn of the twenty-first century; you can't stand by that outdated notion anymore. So in the name of progress, the right has decided to prove that the gap simply doesn't exist. Select a few statistics here, throw in some rosy predictions there, pin any disparity on the choices women themselves have made, and voilà—the wage gap disappears.

The arguments against the gap are all set out in *Women's Figures: An Illustrated Guide to the Economic Progress of Women in America,* by Diane Furchtgott-Roth and Christine Stolba, published by the conservative American Enterprise Institute. The authors maintain that young women without children make almost the same amount as men in their fields. Therefore, wherever women earn less than men, factors other than discrimination are at play. Women "choose" lower-paying jobs because these positions offer "much-needed flexibility." Women earn less because they work fewer hours and take more breaks from work to spend time with their children. And women just haven't been in the workforce long enough to gain the experience necessary to rise to the top. Given the growing array of flexible options at work, the greater number of women in jobs previously dominated by men, and the simple passage of time, those women who want to reach the top will be able to do so. Or so say the wage-gap vaporizers.

First off, let's admit it: there's a tiny bit of truth in their argument. Young women who don't have any children and who are just entering the workforce do earn roughly the same salaries as men in their fields. *Women's Figures* would have you believe that those equal paychecks will last. If only it were so. Wait five or ten years. Even if she doesn't take time off to have a family, and puts in the same amount of "face time," the woman who started out on a par with the guy next to her will have gotten fewer raises, smaller bonuses, and less frequent promotions. It's certainly not because she's less competent. This truth was brought home to professors and administrators at the Massachusetts Institute of Technology recently. The university conducted a pay-equity study that confirmed women professors' gut feeling that they weren't faring as well as their male colleagues. It wasn't that the university offered unequal pay—at least not at first. But over the years, men were offered research grants more often than women, given better teaching assignments, nominated for awards more often. And all of that led to higher salaries. MIT is doing something about the problem, thanks to the establishment of a committee on women faculty. Yet Furchtgott-Roth and Stolba want us to think there's no problem, so why remedy the situation?

And what about jobs that aren't quite equal, although the work is at least comparable by anyone's standards? Why do maintenance workers make more than cleaning women? The authors of *Women's Figures* don't have an answer to that, since it's a fact that in *any* job or profession where women concentrate, the salaries are lower than in those where men predominate—even when they're doing virtually the same work.

Despite the figures in Women's Figures, *it's hard to find jobs in which women make what men do.*

- The Web is one of the newest industries around. But female Internet technology professionals pull in only 88 percent of what

men in the field make. Same job, equal seniority, but the paychecks don't match.
- Women in executive, administrative, and managerial positions earn 68 percent of what their male counterparts bring home.
- Female general surgeons take home 77 percent of the average male general surgeon's salary.
- Overall, women still earn only 76 cents for every dollar a man earns. Part of the reason is the poverty wages many women earn. Twelve percent of women in year-round, full-time jobs earned less than $12,500 in 1998. The figures for women of color are even worse—16 percent of African American women and 24 percent of Latinas had such low earnings. Nevertheless, the wage gap between men and women in the U.S. has decreased—it was 59 cents to a dollar in 1961, when the Census Bureau first began looking at pay equity. But the improvement isn't just because women's wages have gone up; it's also because of a drop in men's earnings. Downsizing and the closing of manufacturing plants have forced men to take lower-paying jobs. Men of color have been particularly hard hit by declining pay.

What about Furchtgott-Roth and Stolba's other arguments?

- Women choose lower-paying jobs because they offer more flexibility. That's really playing fast and loose with statistics and with logic. Women may cheerfully choose to be child care workers, but they hardly choose to live in poverty as a result. And forget about flexibility. Most women can't get time off to care for their families. Half of the workforce—mostly the low-paid half—isn't covered by the Family and Medical Leave Act. And many of those who are covered can't afford time off because it's unpaid. Meanwhile, 80 percent of working-poor mothers have less than one week of sick leave, which they have to use to care for family members as well as themselves.

- Women work fewer hours and take more time off than men. Furchtgott-Roth and Stolba are right about women making sacrifices to care for their families. The question is, should there be a penalty for that? And if so, how long should it last? One study of professional women showed that years after they had taken an average of only 8.8 months of family leave, they still earned 17 percent less than women who had not taken leave. For lower-wage women, taking time off can have even worse repercussions. It may mean losing a job altogether.
- Women haven't been in the workforce long enough to earn what men do. Forget it. We've already seen that women make less compared to men as time goes on, not more.

There are other ways *Women's Figures* flouts both statistics and logic. It argues that the reason women are so underrepresented in many occupations is that those jobs require physical strength and involve great hazards. Yet this hardly explains why women make up a scant 3.4 percent of airline pilots or navigators, 10 percent of engineers, and 27 percent of physicians. Nor does it explain the discrepancy between the wage and the inherent worth of work traditionally done by women. Why do accountants make more than kindergarten teachers when both jobs require equal levels of training?

The truth is, women's earnings are still much lower than men's—and so low period—for complex reasons, most of which come down to the persistence of sex segregation and the legacy of discrimination.

- *Sex Segregation* While there has been growing opportunity in jobs formerly closed to women, most women do the same jobs they've always done, and those jobs pay less than comparable jobs done by men. Even within certain occupations, such as sales, women are clustered in the lower-paying jobs. For instance, women constitute 82 percent of employees in gift and novelty shops but only 19 percent of those in higher-paying car dealerships. Women of color are concentrated in the lowest-paying jobs, including domestic workers, nurse's aides, and sewing machine operators.
- *Discrimination* The continuation of discrimination holds women back—whether it is the traditional "We don't want a woman doing that job" or something more subtle, such as when women are left out of informal gatherings where people pass on skills, connections, and workplace savvy. Because of the expense and often the humiliation involved, women who experience this type of discrimination tend to leave jobs in higher numbers than those who don't. This affects their earnings as well as their opportunities for advancement.

We know how to end both the wage gap and poverty wages. We need to lobby for comparable pay standards that guarantee that the jobs done by women are valued as much as those done by men. We need to continue to push for women to enter traditionally male fields, like construction and engineering. We need to expand equal-pay protection to part-time workers. And certainly not least, we need to organize—to join unions and to become activists.

By masking the wage gap, the right hopes to eliminate the fight for these solutions: you don't need better pay, honey, you just need to embrace the choices you've made, or make different ones.

Why do they think women will buy this lie? Go figure.

READING 57

Breaking the Glass Ceiling and Hitting the Wall

Ann M. Morrison, Randall P. White, Ellen Van Velsor,
and the Center for Creative Leadership

We began this research prepared to accept the notion that there might be a glass ceiling, a transparent barrier, that kept women from rising above a certain level in corporations. That's why we retained our criteria for the exceptional women we did interview. In conducting the research, we began to perceive more than one barrier that keeps women out of powerful executive positions. Women who manage to break through the glass ceiling often find that they are walled out of more senior management.

Many women have paid their dues, even a premium, for a chance at a top position, only to find a glass ceiling between them and their goal. The glass ceiling is not simply a barrier for an individual, based on the person's inability to handle a higher-level job. Rather, the glass ceiling applies to women as a group who are kept from advancing higher *because they are women*.

The glass ceiling may exist at different levels in different companies or industries. For the purposes of this book, we have placed it just short of the general manager position. Even in more progressive companies, it is rare to find women at the general management level. The general management level can mean having to deal with the development, manufacture, sales, and marketing of a product. The product can range from a new type of toilet tissue to a new type of credit card. Or a general manager might be in charge of a portfolio of products, each with its specific market and use. General managers in this situation might be responsible for coordinating product development, manufacture, sales, marketing, and overall business strategy for tens or hundreds of products. A position at this level represents a major and difficult transition in responsibility, according to both the female and the male executives we

interviewed. In large corporations, these jobs represent less than 1 percent of the entire work force. In a corporation with fifty thousand employees, fewer than five hundred people are at this level.

It is difficult to break through the glass ceiling, but an increasing number of women are doing so. Most of this book is devoted to describing how these women accomplished this feat (or are shortly expected to) and offers advice for others who want to do the same. Once women break this first barrier, however, they unexpectedly encounter another barrier—a wall of tradition and stereotype that separates them from the top executive level. This wall keeps women out of the inner sanctum of senior management, the core of business leaders who wield the greatest power. This barrier has been broken by very few women, and, as explained by one executive interviewed for Hilary Cosell's book *Woman on a Seesaw*, it discourages those who are so near and yet so far:

I think we're being terribly misled about how much success women as a group have achieved and about how real that success actually is. I think there may be a bitter day of reckoning for many of us that's not too far off. A day where women will say, "I gave up my personal life, I destroyed my marriage, I didn't have children, I gave up this and I gave up that and what was it for? I still haven't been able to achieve the way men do, in the same arena they do, the way I was told I could." Let's face it: women are no longer disenfranchised, but we don't have anything like the power of the white male corporate establishment. I don't know if we'll ever acquire that kind of power, but if we do, it's not going to be anytime in the near future.[1]

THREE LEVELS OF PRESSURE

All of the female executives we interviewed differed from their male counterparts in one fundamental way. Throughout their careers, they had to operate with three levels of pressure constantly pushing on them. These pressures—of the job itself, of their pioneer role in the job, and of the strain of their family obligations—made their advancement that much harder and that much more remarkable. Let's examine the pressures and how they impact the lives of female executives.

The first kind of pressure that women face is the pressure of the job itself. For women and men, general management is frequently an overwhelming burden that taxes and frustrates even the most overachieving soul. They frequently face no-win decisions, confront angry customers and disgruntled employees, and make endless phone calls—and they escape home late each night only to feel, often, that they haven't accomplished anything. The demands on executives to handle enormous responsibilities are unrelenting. The work could continue twenty-four hours a day for many executives, so each time they stop to do something else, including sleep, they feel they are falling farther behind.

Executives work at a hectic, frantic pace. They have to obtain vital information in short bursts—brief phone calls or hasty chats in the corridors are not unusual. They are responsible for the strategy and tactics of a business unit, such as deciding which parts of the business to grow and which, if any, need pruning. They must continually grapple with problems that have no "right" answers and often are only symptomatic of some larger, but not yet understood, problem. Meanwhile, they motivate work teams to carry out the business plan, heading forward until new information dictates otherwise.

They must use their extensive contact network—including peers, subordinates, superiors, customers, and interested outsiders—to

gather information to guide day-to-day as well as long-range thought and action. And as executives in large, sometimes multinational enterprises, they are on call twenty-four hours a day, since events thousands of miles away may have an immediate and powerful impact on their business. As one executive put it:

> For me to be marginally competent, ten hours a day are required, and three to four hours a day on weekends. . . . You gotta love it!

Many things must be accomplished, and the need to do them well constitutes the first level of pressure. Taking new challenges and business risks is built into management, and the higher you go, the more overwhelming the demands. One ad agency chairman who was recently interviewed for the *Wall Street Journal* said: "A chief executive doesn't take time off if he wants to remain chief executive."[2] Achievement-driven people are attracted to executive jobs, thriving on the satisfaction of taking control and moving the organization in the right direction. They typically expect a lot of themselves, sometimes even more than others expect of them. So they endure the pressure to do an enormous job, driving as close to perfection as they can get.

A second level of pressure is that of being a *female* executive. As two senior executives we interviewed said:

> There is an element of derailment built into the system for women—the pressure created by having to be a role model and a "first" along with personal competency. Men don't have to deal with this added pressure.
>
> Women are a minority in this business. A woman coming into a high-level meeting will see few other women. They have difficulty finding a supportive ear or shoulder. So they feel distinctly different.

Being a woman where few, if any, women have been before is a liability that creates stress. Harvard professor Rosabeth Moss Kanter elaborated on the dilemmas and pressures that confront the "token" women at high levels in her landmark 1977 book, *Men and Women of the Corporation*.[3] Female executives are "public creatures" who attract attention with anything they do. They are "stand-ins for all women . . . symbols of how-women-can-do" who must find a way to conform without being self-estranged. In our study, we found that female executives performing in a "glass house" dreaded even the thought that they might fail on the job because it would not only affect their own progress but also limit the opportunities given to the women who come after them. Our article in the October 1986 *Working Woman* magazine describes the pressure to *always* succeed:

> "I feel that if I fail, it will be a long time before they hire another woman for the job," one executive confided. Carrying that burden can lead women to play it safe, to be ultraconservative, to opt out if a situation looks chancy.[4]

The pressure is in being a minority, set apart by gender before anything is said or done, and in being responsible for representing women as a group because there is no one, or few others, to share that responsibility. In addition to being scrutinized, a number of executive women are also unwelcome. "There is still the good ole boy feeling in senior management here," remarked a higher-level executive at one of the companies.

The third level of pressure has to do with managing the demands in life outside of work, a dilemma that now dominates what is written about executive women. Women are still expected to take major responsibility for maintaining a household, raising children, even nurturing an intimate relationship. The time demands alone are ominous. But there is also the strain of switching from the role required at the office—tough, no-nonsense, efficient, and so on—to the personal sphere, which includes being tender, undemanding, even playful or sexy.

Their career success can be a stigma for women who want personal relationships with men. "I bet she gives instructions in bed" was one male executive's comment about a woman who performed well in a management role. On ABC-TV's show "After the Sexual Revolution" aired on July 30, 1986, one man interviewed said he would support a woman who wanted to be a corporate CEO. "Whether I'm going to continue to date her or not is another question," he added, insinuating that he would not find such a successful woman acceptable for a personal relationship.[5] The lack of male companions in their personal life troubles some executive women. Others who have a family are baffled by how to surmount the variety of problems they face. The host of issues present in trying to juggle work and personal relationships (let alone time to oneself!) are complex and emotionally draining. The choices and frustrations that face many women who want a "full" life that includes executive status add up to a burden that often exceeds the pressure of the most difficult business decisions. With such pressures on them, it is no wonder that female executives in one 1984 survey ranked self-discipline as the most important quality they had to develop to perform their job.[6]

Two researchers from Wellesley College, Anne Harlan and Carol Weiss, reported in 1981 on a study they had done comparing 25 male and 25 female managers on a variety of factors. They described the "successful male myth," which "assumes that men are highly successful, have well-planned careers, receive excellent training and development, have good working relationships with other company employees, have all their skills utilized in their work setting, and encounter no problems on the road to top management—the position to which all men aspire."[7] This is, of course, a myth. Men as well as women derail, and for many of the same reasons. The same pressures that have such a strong impact on executive women are not foreign to men. It's not a piece of cake for anyone.

Although Harlan and Weiss were impressed with the similar hurdles that men and women confront in management, they also noticed that sex bias creates some different experiences and additional hurdles for women on the job. And the pressure of managing the demands in life outside of work generally affects women far more than men. At higher levels, these pressures can become debilitating. The support systems available to help men are not there for many women. Susan Borman (wife of former astronaut and Eastern Airlines President Frank Borman) says that *no* CEO makes it to the top without a lot of sacrifice from dedicated family members. "Families pay the price. They [CEOs] have had mothers, fathers, wives, and children supporting them all the way."[8]

It can be very discouraging to try to manage all the demands and expectations, especially when the standards are high. In *Woman on a Seesaw*, Hilary Cosell remarked:

I am not really sure that it is possible for most of us to fuse the personal and professional into one smooth, charming, comfortable, and competent whole—doing everything our mothers did, and everything our fathers did as well.[9]

We face a critical time for female executives in corporate America. Women have struggled to get into management, and some companies have struggled also to get them there. They have made significant headway in moving up the corporate ladder, only to be stopped dead near the top. At a time when American industry is restructuring itself to face more effective worldwide competition, companies need all of the talent they can get—men and women. We hope our research will help everyone to take a clear-eyed look at the complex problems women face in corporations and point toward some possible solutions. The three levels of pressure that executive women struggle with are not likely to disappear; however, it is possible to ease at least part of the pressure by gaining a richer understanding of what women have accomplished in the past and what they can expect to achieve in the future.

We are at a crossroads in corporate America. Women are stuck below the level of challenge

that will satisfy them and fully use the resource they represent to companies. These women, and the executives who want to solve the problem, don't know what to do. They once thought that the increased number of women in middle management would push some into senior management, but that isn't happening; something else is needed if we are to make everyone's investment pay off. People are getting restless, according to Jane Evans, a managing partner of Montgomery Securities, in a June 1986 speech to the New York Financial Women's Association:

Although I thoroughly enjoy the success I have achieved, I am dismayed that so few other women can claim to be making it in the business world. For years, I have felt that it would be my generation that would bring true equality for men and women to the workplace. Contrarily, I find the eighties to be a dangerous and precarious period because corporate and government leaders are beginning to perceive that an investment in the training and leadership development of women is unlikely to yield the same return as an equivalent investment in men.[10]

NOTES

1. Hilary Cosell, *Women on a Seesaw: The Ups and Downs of Making It* (New York: Putnam, 1985), p. 135.
2. "Even Bosses Unwind; At Least Some Do, Some of the Time," *Wall Street Journal*, 5 August 1986, p. 1.
3. Rosabeth Moss Kanter, *Men and Women of the Corporation* (New York: Basic Books, 1977), p. 239.
4. Ann Morrison, Randall P. White, and Ellen Van Velsor, "The Glass House Dilemma: Why Women Executives Dare Not Fail," *Working Woman* (October 1986), 146.
5. "After the Sexual Revolution," *ABC News Close-up*, 30 July 1986.
6. Charles Margerison and Andrew Kakabadse, *How American Chief Executives Succeed: Implications for Developing High-Potential Employees*, An AMA Survey Report (New York: American Management Association, 1984), p. 25.

7. Anne Harlan and Carol Weiss, *Moving Up: Women in Managerial Careers,* Working Paper no. 86 (Wellesley, Mass.: Wellesley College, Center for Research on Women, September 1981), p. 99.

8. Norman N. Mlachak, "Life with the CEO," *Industry Week,* 1 October 1984, p. 75.

9. Cosell, *Woman on a Seesaw,* p. 188.

10. Jane Evans, "Leadership—A New Role for Women" (Speech given to the New York Financial Women's Association, 3 June 1986).

READING 58

Maid to Order
The Politics of Other Women's Work

Barbara Ehrenreich

In line with growing class polarization, the classic posture of submission is making a stealthy comeback. "We scrub your floors the old-fashioned way," boasts the brochure from Merry Maids, the largest of the residential-cleaning services that have sprung up in the last two decades, "on our hands and knees." This is not a posture that independent "cleaning ladies" willingly assume—preferring, like most people who clean their own homes, the sponge mop wielded from a standing position. In her comprehensive 1999 guide to homemaking, *Home Comforts,* Cheryl Mendelson warns: "Never ask hired housecleaners to clean your floors on their hands and knees; the request is likely to be regarded as degrading." But in a society in which 40 percent of the wealth is owned by 1 percent of households while the bottom 20 percent reports negative assets, the degradation of others is readily purchased. Kneepads entered American political discourse as a tool of the sexually subservient, but employees of Merry Maids, The Maids International, and other corporate cleaning services spend hours every day on these kinky devices, wiping up the drippings of the affluent.

I spent three weeks in September 1999 as an employee of The Maids International in Portland, Maine, cleaning, along with my fellow team members, approximately sixty houses containing a total of about 250 scrubbable floors—bathrooms, kitchens, and entryways requiring the hands-and-knees treatment. It's a different world down there below knee level, one that few adults voluntarily enter. Here you find elaborate dust structures held together by a scaffolding of dog hair; dried bits of pasta glued to the floor by their sauce; the congealed remains of gravies, jellies, contraceptive creams, vomit, and urine. Sometimes, too, you encounter some fragment of a human being: a child's legs, stamping by in disgust because the maids are still present when he gets home from school; more commonly, the Joan & David–clad feet and electrolyzed calves of the female homeowner. Look up and you may find this person staring at you, arms folded, in anticipation of an overlooked stain. In rare instances she may try to help in some vague, symbolic way, by moving the cockatoo's cage, for example, or apologizing for the leaves shed by a miniature indoor tree. Mostly, though, she will not see you at all and may even sit down with her mail at a table in the very room you are cleaning, where she would remain completely unaware of your existence unless you were to crawl under that table and start gnawing away at her ankles.

Housework, as you may recall from the feminist theories of the Sixties and Seventies, was supposed to be the great equalizer of women. Whatever else women did—jobs, school, child care—we also did housework, and if there were some women who hired others to do it for them, they seemed too privileged and rare to include in the theoretical calculus. All women were workers, and the home was their workplace—unpaid and unsupervised, to be sure, but a workplace no less than the offices and factories men repaired to every morning. If men thought of the home as a site of leisure and recreation—a "haven in a heartless world"—this was to ignore the invisible female proletariat that kept it cozy and humming. We were on the march now, or so we imagined, united against a society that devalued our labor even as it waxed mawkish over "the family" and "the home." Shoulder to shoulder and arm in arm, women were finally getting up off the floor.

In the most eye-catching elaboration of the home-as-workplace theme, Marxist feminists Maria Rosa Dallacosta and Selma James proposed in 1972 that the home was in fact an economically productive and significant workplace, an extension of the actual factory, since housework served to "reproduce the labor power" of others, particularly men. The male worker would hardly be in shape to punch in for his shift, after all, if some woman had not fed him, laundered his clothes, and cared for the children who were his contribution to the next generation of workers. If the home was a quasi-industrial workplace staffed by women for the ultimate benefit of the capitalists, then it followed that "wages for housework" was the obvious demand.

But when most American feminists, Marxist or otherwise, asked the Marxist question *cui bono?* they tended to come up with a far simpler answer—men. If women were the domestic proletariat, then men made up the class of domestic exploiters, free to lounge while their mates scrubbed. In consciousness-raising groups, we railed against husbands and boyfriends who refused to pick up after themselves, who were unaware of housework at all, unless of course it hadn't been done. The "dropped socks," left by a man for a woman to gather up and launder, joined lipstick and spike heels as emblems of gender oppression. And if, somewhere, a man had actually dropped a sock in the calm expectation that his wife would retrieve it, it was a sock heard round the world. Wherever second-wave feminism took root, battles broke out between lovers and spouses over sticky countertops, piled-up laundry, and whose turn it was to do the dishes.

The radical new idea was that housework was not only a relationship between a woman and a dust bunny or an unmade bed; it also defined a relationship between human beings, typically husbands and wives. This represented a marked departure from the more conservative Betty Friedan, who, in *The Feminine Mystique*, had never thought to enter the male sex into the equation, as either part of the housework problem or part of an eventual solution. She raged against a society that consigned its educated women to what she saw as essentially janitorial chores, beneath "the abilities of a woman of average or normal human intelligence," and, according to unidentified studies she cited, "peculiarly suited to the capacities of feeble-minded girls." But men are virtually exempt from housework in *The Feminine Mystique*—why drag them down too? At one point she even disparages a "Mrs. G.," who "somehow couldn't get her housework done before her husband came home at night and was so tired then that he had to do it." Educated women would just have to become more efficient so that housework could no longer "expand to fill the time available."

Or they could hire other women to do it—an option approved by Friedan in *The Feminine Mystique* as well as by the National Organization for Women, which she had helped launch. At the 1973 congressional hearings on whether to extend the Fair Labor Standards Act to household workers, NOW testified on the affirmative side, arguing that improved wages and working conditions would attract more women to the field, and offering the seemingly self-contradictory prediction that "the demand for household help inside the home will continue to increase as more women seek occupations outside the home." One NOW member added, on a personal note: "Like many young women today, I am in school in order to develop a rewarding career for myself. I also have a home to run and can fully conceive of the need for household help as my free time at home becomes more and more restricted. Women know [that] housework is dirty, tedious work, and they are willing to pay to have it done. . . ." On the aspirations of the women paid to do it, assuming that at least some of them were bright enough to entertain a few, neither Friedan nor these members of NOW had, at the time, a word to say.

So the insight that distinguished the more radical, post-Friedan cohort of feminists was that when we talk about housework, we are really talking, yet again, about power. Housework was not degrading because it was manual labor, as Friedan thought, but because it was embedded in degrading relationships and inevitably served to reinforce them. To make a mess that another person will have to deal with—the dropped socks, the toothpaste sprayed on the bathroom mirror, the dirty dishes left from a late-night snack—is to exert domination in one of its more silent and intimate forms. One person's arrogance—or indifference, or hurry—becomes another person's occasion for toil. And when the person who is cleaned up after is consistently male, while the person who cleans up is consistently female, you have a formula for reproducing male domination from one generation to the next.

Hence the feminist perception of housework as one more way by which men exploit women or, more neutrally stated, as "a symbolic enactment of gender relations." An early German women's liberation cartoon depicted a woman scrubbing on her hands and knees while her husband, apparently excited by this pose, approaches from behind, unzipping his fly. Hence, too, the second-wave feminists' revulsion at the hiring of maids, especially when they were women of color: At a feminist conference I attended in 1980, poet Audre Lorde

chose to insult the all-too-white audience by accusing them of being present only because they had black housekeepers to look after their children at home. She had the wrong crowd; most of the assembled radical feminists would no sooner have employed a black maid than they would have attached Confederate flag stickers to the rear windows of their cars. But accusations like hers, repeated in countless conferences and meetings, reinforced our rejection of the servant option. There already were at least two able-bodied adults in the average home— a man and a woman— and the hope was that, after a few initial skirmishes, they would learn to share the housework graciously.

A couple of decades later, however, the average household still falls far short of that goal. True, women do less housework than they did before the feminist revolution and the rise of the two-income family: down from an average of 30 hours per week in 1965 to 17.5 hours in 1995, according to a July 1999 study by the University of Maryland. Some of that decline reflects a relaxation of standards rather than a redistribution of chores; women still do two thirds of whatever housework—including bill paying, pet care, tidying, and lawn care—gets done. The inequity is sharpest for the most despised of household chores, cleaning: in the thirty years between 1965 and 1995, men increased the time they spent scrubbing, vacuuming, and sweeping by 240 percent—all the way up to 1.7 hours per week—while women decreased their cleaning time by only 7 percent, to 6.7 hours per week. The averages conceal a variety of arrangements, of course, from minutely negotiated sharing to the most clichéd division of labor, as described by one woman to the *Washington Post:* "I take care of the inside, he takes care of the outside." But perhaps the most disturbing finding is that almost the entire increase in male participation took place between the 1970s and the mid-1980s. Fifteen years after the apparent cessation of hostilities, it is probably not too soon to announce the score: in the "chore wars" of the Seventies and Eighties, women gained a little ground, but overall, and after a few strategic concessions, men won.

Enter then, the cleaning lady as *dea ex machina,* restoring tranquillity as well as order to the home. Marriage counselors recommend her as an alternative to squabbling, as do many within the cleaning industry itself. A Chicago cleaning woman quotes one of her clients as saying that if she gives up the service, "my husband and I will be divorced in six months." When the trend toward hiring out was just beginning to take off, in 1988, the owner of a Merry Maids franchise in Arlington, Massachusetts, told the *Christian Science Monitor,* "I kid some women. I say, 'We even save marriages. In this new eighties period you expect more from the male partner, but very often you don't get the cooperation you would like to have. The alternative is to pay somebody to come in. . . .'" Another Merry Maids franchise owner has learned to capitalize more directly on housework-related spats; he closes between 30 and 35 percent of his sales by making follow-up calls Saturday mornings, which is "prime time for arguing over the fact that the house is a mess." The micro-defeat of feminism in the household opened a new door for women, only this time it was the servants' entrance.

In 1999, somewhere between 14 and 18 percent of households employed an outsider to do the cleaning, and the numbers have been rising dramatically. Mediamark Research reports a 53 percent increase, between 1995 and 1999, in the number of households using a hired cleaner or service once a month or more, and Maritz Marketing finds that 30 percent of the people who hired help in 1999 did so for the first time that year. Among my middle-class, professional women friends and acquaintances, including some who made important contributions to the early feminist analysis of housework, the employment of a maid is now nearly universal. This sudden emergence of a servant class is consistent with what some economists have called the "Brazilianization" of the American economy: We are dividing along the lines of traditional Latin American societies—into a tiny overclass and a huge underclass, with the latter available to perform intimate household services for the former. Or, to put it another way, the home, or at least the affluent home, is finally becoming what radical feminists in the Seventies only imagined it was—a true "workplace" for women and a tiny, though increasingly visible, part of the capitalist economy. And the question is: As the home becomes a workplace for someone else, is it still a place where you would want to live?

. . .

The trend toward outsourcing the work of the home seems, at the moment, unstoppable. Two hundred years ago women often manufactured soap, candles, cloth, and clothing in their own homes, and the complaints of some women at the turn of the twentieth century that they had been "robbed by the removal of creative work" from the home sound pointlessly reactionary today. Not only have the skilled crafts, like sewing and cooking from scratch, left the home but many of the "white collar" tasks are on their way out, too. For a fee, new firms such as the San Francisco–based Les Concierges and Cross It Off Your List in Manhattan will pick up dry cleaning, baby-sit pets, buy groceries, deliver dinner, even do the Christmas shopping. With other firms and individuals offering to buy your clothes, organize your financial files, straighten out your closets, and wait around in your home for the plumber to show up, why would anyone want to hold on to the toilet cleaning?

Absent a major souring of the economy, there is every reason to think that Americans will become increasingly reliant on paid housekeepers and that this reliance will extend ever further down into the middle class. For one thing, the "time bind" on working parents shows no sign of loosening; people are willing to work longer hours at the office to pay for the people—house-cleaners and baby-sitters—who are filling in for them at home. Children, once a handy source of household help, are now off at soccer practice or SAT prep classes; grandmother has relocated to a warmer climate or taken up a second career. Furthermore, despite the fact that people spend less time at home than ever, the square footage of new homes swelled by 33 percent between 1975 and 1998, to include "family rooms," home entertainment rooms, home offices, bedrooms, and often bathrooms for each family member. By the third quarter of 1999, 17 percent of new homes were larger than 3,000 square feet, which is usually considered the size threshold for household help, or the point at which a house becomes unmanageable to the people who live in it.

One more trend impels people to hire outside help, according to cleaning experts such as Aslett and Mendelson: fewer Americans know how to clean or even to "straighten up." I hear this from professional women defending their decision to hire a maid: "I'm just not very good at it myself" or "I wouldn't really know where to begin." Since most of us learn to clean from our parents (usually our mothers), any diminution of cleaning skills is transmitted from one generation to another, like a gene that can, in the appropriate environment, turn out to be disabling or lethal. Upper-middle-class children raised in the servant economy of the Nineties are bound to grow up as domestically incompetent as their parents and no less dependent on people to clean up after them. Mendelson sees this as a metaphysical loss, a "matter of no longer being physically centered in your environment." Having cleaned the rooms of many overly privileged teenagers in my stint with The Maids, I think the problem is a little more urgent than that. The American overclass is raising a generation of young people who will, without constant assistance, suffocate in their own detritus.

If there are moral losses, too, as Americans increasingly rely on paid household help, no one has been tactless enough to raise them. Almost everything we buy, after all, is the prod-uct of some other person's suffering and miserably underpaid labor. I clean my own house (though—full disclosure—I recently hired someone else to ready it for a short-term tenant), but I can hardly claim purity in any other area of consumption. I buy my jeans at The Gap, which is reputed to subcontract to sweatshops. I tend to favor decorative objects no doubt ripped off, by their purveyors, from scantily paid Third World craftspersons. Like everyone else, I eat salad greens just picked by migrant farm workers, some of them possibly children. And so on. We can try to minimize the pain that goes into feeding, clothing, and otherwise provisioning ourselves—by observing boycotts, checking for a union label, etc.—but there is no way to avoid it altogether without living in the wilderness on berries. Why should housework, among all the goods and services we consume, arouse any special angst?

And it does, as I have found in conversations with liberal-minded employers of maids, perhaps because we all sense that there are ways in which housework is different from other products and services. First, in its inevitable proximity to the activities that compose "private" life. The home that becomes a workplace for other people remains a home, even when that workplace has been minutely regulated by the corporate cleaning chains. Someone who has no qualms about purchasing rugs woven by child slaves in India or coffee picked by impoverished peasants in Guatemala might still hesitate to tell dinner guests that, surprisingly enough, his or her lovely home doubles as a sweatshop during the day. You can eschew the chain cleaning services of course, hire an independent cleaner at a generous hourly wage, and even encourage, at least in spirit, the unionization of the housecleaning industry. But this does not change the fact that someone is working in your home at a job she would almost certainly never have chosen for herself—if she'd had a college education, for example, or a little better luck along the way—and the place where she works, however enthusiastically or resentfully, is the same as the place where you sleep.

It is also the place where your children are raised, and what they learn pretty quickly is that some people are less worthy than others. Even better wages and working conditions won't erase the hierarchy between an employer and his or her domestic help, because the help is usually there only because the employer has "something better" to do with her time, as one report on the growth of cleaning services puts it, not noticing the obvious implication that the cleaning person herself has nothing better to do with her time. In a merely middle-class home, the message may be reinforced by a warning to the children that that's what they'll end up doing if they don't try harder in school. Housework, as radical feminists once proposed, defines a human relationship and, when unequally divided among social groups, reinforces preexisting inequalities. Dirt, in other words, tends to attach to the people who remove it—"garbagemen" and "cleaning ladies." Or, as cleaning entrepreneur Don Aslett told me with some bitterness—and this is a successful man, chairman of the board of an industrial cleaning service and frequent television guest—"The whole mentality out there is that if you clean, you're a scumball."

One of the "better" things employers of maids often want to do with their time is, of course, spend it with their children. But an underlying problem with post-nineteenth-century child-raising, as Deirdre English and I argued in our book *For Her Own Good* years ago, is precisely that it is unmoored in any kind of purposeful pursuit. Once "parenting" meant instructing the children in necessary chores; today it's more likely to center on one-sided conversations beginning with "So how was school today?" No one wants to put the kids to work again weeding and stitching; but in the void that is the modern home, relationships with children are often strained. A little "low-quality time" spent washing dishes or folding clothes together can provide a comfortable space for confidences—and give a child the dignity of knowing that he or she is a participant in, and not just the product of, the work of the home.

There is another lesson the servant economy teaches its beneficiaries and, most troubling, the children among them. To be cleaned up after is to achieve a certain magical weightlessness and immateriality. Almost everyone complains about violent video games, but paid housecleaning has the same consequence-abolishing effect: you blast the villain into a mist of blood droplets and move right along; you drop the socks knowing they will eventually levitate, laundered and folded, back to their normal dwelling place. The result is a kind of virtual existence, in which the trail of litter that follows you seems to evaporate all by itself. Spill syrup on the floor and the cleaning person will scrub it off when she comes on Wednesday. Leave *The Wall Street Journal* scattered around your airplane seat and the flight attendants will deal with it after you've deplaned. Spray toxins into the atmosphere from your factory's smokestacks and they will be filtered out eventually by the lungs of the breathing public. A servant economy breeds callousness and solipsism in the served, and it does so all the more effectively when the service is performed close up and routinely in the place where they live and reproduce.

Individual situations vary, of course, in ways that elude blanket judgment. Some people—the elderly and disabled, parents of new babies, asthmatics who require an allergen-free environment—may well need help performing what nursing-home staff call the "ADLs," or activities of daily living, and no shame should be attached to their dependency. In a more generous social order, housekeeping services would be subsidized for those who have health-related reasons to need them—a measure that would generate a surfeit of new jobs for the low-skilled people who now clean the homes of the affluent. And in a less gender-divided social order, husbands and boyfriends would more readily do their share of the chores.

However we resolve the issue in our individual homes, the moral challenge is, put simply, to make work visible again: not only the scrubbing and vacuuming but all the hoeing, stacking, hammering, drilling, bending, and lifting that goes into creating and maintaining a livable habitat. In an ever more economically unequal culture, where so many of the affluent devote their lives to such ghostly pursuits as stock-trading, image-making, and opinion-polling, real work—in the old-fashioned sense of labor that engages hand as well as eye, that tires the body and directly alters the physical world—tends to vanish from sight. The feminists of my generation tried to bring some of it into the light of day, but, like busy professional women fleeing the house in the morning, they left the project unfinished, the debate broken off in midsentence, the noble intentions unfulfilled. Sooner or later, someone else will have to finish the job.

READING 59

Prostitution
A Difficult Issue for Feminists

Priscilla Alexander

WHY PROSTITUTION?

Prostitution exists, at least in part, because of the subordination of women in most societies. This subordination is reflected in the double standard of sexual behavior for men and women, and is carried out in the discrepancy between women's and men's earning power.

. . .

The specific reasons that prostitutes have given for choosing their work, as revealed in the studies of Dr Jennifer James in Seattle, have included money, excitement, independence, and flexibility, in roughly that order. First person accounts by women in the sex industry often mention economics as a major factor, coupled with rebellion at the restricted and tedious jobs available to them.[1] Dr James and others have also revealed a high incidence of child sexual abuse in the life histories of prostitutes: around fifty percent for adult prostitutes; seventy-five to eighty percent for juvenile prostitutes.[2] The traditional psychoanalytic explanation for the relationship between childhood sexual abuse and later involvement in prostitution is that the child has come to view sex as a commodity, and that she is masochistic. The connection many prostitutes report, however, is that the involvement in prostitution is a way of taking back control of a situation in which, as children, they had none. Specifically, many have reported that the first time they ever felt powerful was the first time they 'turned a trick.'[3] . . . It is important to remember that many women with no history of sexual assault become prostitutes (and many survivors of child sexual abuse never work as prostitutes), so the relationship between prostitution and early sexual trauma is far from clear.

A number of authors have also looked at the fact that men and women do not appear to view sex in the same way and that men as a class seem to view sex as power, with rape being the most extreme form of the use of sex as power. Women as a class tend to see sex as nurture, and this generalization is subject to great individual differences. Prostitution also involves an equation of sex with power: for the man/customer, the power consists of his ability to 'buy' access to any number of women; for the woman/prostitute, the power consists of her ability to set the terms of her sexuality, and to demand substantial payment for her time and skills. Thus, prostitution is one area in which women have traditionally and openly viewed sex as power.

. . .

THE LAW

. . . In 1949, the United Nations passed a convention paper that called for the decriminalization of prostitution and the enforcement of laws against those who exploit women and children in prostitution. The paper, which was read to the United Nations General Assembly by Eleanor Roosevelt, has been ratified by more than fifty countries, but not the United States. Most European countries have 'decriminalized' prostitution by removing laws which prohibit 'engaging' in an act of prostitution; although most have retained the laws against 'soliciting' 'pimping' 'pandering' 'running a disorderly house' and 'transporting a woman across national boundaries for the purposes of prostitution.' The United States, on the other hand, has retained the laws prohibiting the act of prostitution as well (except in rural counties in the state of Nevada with populations less than 250,000, which have the option of allowing legal, regulated brothels). Prostitution is also prohibited outright in Japan, and in many Asian countries, including those in which 'sex tourism' is a major industry. It is decriminalized in the [former] Soviet Union, but women who work as prostitutes there are arrested for violating the law against being a parasite (i.e., not having a legally-recognized job).

In addition to laws prohibiting soliciting or engaging in an act of prostitution, and the related issues of pimping and pandering, or procuring, the United States has laws that bar anyone who has ever been a prostitute from entering this country, remaining in this country as a resident, or becoming a citizen. Deportation proceedings on those grounds were instituted in the early 1980s against a French woman who managed a brothel in Nevada, even though the business was perfectly legal.

[Former] West Germany, in addition to decriminalizing the act itself, has developed a variety of approaches ranging from a tightly controlled, single-zone brothel system in Hamburg, to a laissez-faire, open-zone system in [former] West Berlin. Denmark has repealed most of the laws restricting the right of prostitutes to work, and has passed laws designed to help women who want to get out of prostitution.

In Holland, after a prostitute was murdered a few years ago, the government decided it might be a good idea to examine the laws and to see if there weren't ways to reduce the isolation of prostitutes. The government has been working closely with the feminist prostitutes' rights movement—the Red Thread, an organization of prostitutes and ex-prostitutes, and the Pink Thread, a feminist solidarity group. In late 1986, the Dutch government allocated funds to provide the Red Thread with three employees and an office.

The countries with the most restrictive legal systems, including the United States and many countries in Southeast Asia, have the most problems with violence against prostitutes (and women perceived to be *like* prostitutes), thefts associated with prostitution, pimping (especially brutal pimping), and the involvement of juveniles. Conversely, the countries with the least restrictive measures, including the Netherlands, [former] West Germany, Sweden and Denmark, have the least problems. No country, however, is totally safe for prostitutes. The stigma still isolates the women, and the remaining laws still serve to perpetuate that stigma, rather than to dispel it and truly legitimize the women who work as prostitutes.

. . .

WHO BENEFITS FROM THE SYSTEM

It is difficult to see how anyone benefits from the present system. At the time the United States prohibition was enacted, it was at least partly in response to feminist concerns about the abuse of women and children involved in prostitution. After an extensive muckraking campaign in the press, exposing the 'horrors' of brothel prostitution, there was much pressure to close brothels.

. . .

While the enactment of laws before World War I prohibiting prostitution, pimping, running brothels, transporting women across state lines for 'immoral' purposes, etc., did nothing to reduce prostitution, it did have other effects. Before prohibition, most brothels were owned and managed by women, most of whom had been prostitutes themselves. After the legal brothels were closed, the brothel business went underground and was headed by a male, criminal hierarchy that continues. Most massage parlors and escort services today are owned by men. Closing the brothels also forced many women to work on the streets, subjecting them to greater risks of violence. The basic conditions of women's lives, which caused some of them to choose to work as prostitutes, did not change.

For most of recorded history, prostitution has been set up for the benefit of the customer, no matter what system was in place. The stigma enforced by the prohibition in America is also enforced by systems of regulation that require prostitutes to dress differently or to live and work in special districts, or deny them the right to relationships. The health schemes that require prostitutes to have weekly checks for sexually transmitted diseases are similarly designed to benefit the customer, since there is no equivalent requirement that customers be checked to protect the prostitute, or regulation requiring brothels to provide condoms, disability insurance, workers' compensation, or health insurance. What constantly amazes me is that there is so little variation in the way nations deal with prostitution, under the law, even where there is enormous variation in just about every other aspect of society.

. . .

OPTIONS FOR CHANGE

. . .

There are two main alternatives to prohibition, generally termed decriminalization and legalization. In Europe, decriminalization is sometimes referred to as abolition, and refers to the abolition or repeal of the prostitution laws. However, the term abolition is also used by some activists, including Kathleen Barry in the United States, and The Abolitionist Society in Europe, to refer to the long-term goal of eliminating all prostitution.

Ideally, decriminalization would mean the repeal of all existing criminal codes regarding voluntary prostitution, per se, between consenting adults, including mutually voluntary relationships between prostitutes and agents or managers (pimp/prostitute relationships), and non-coercive pandering (serving as a go-between). It could involve no new legislation to deal specifically with prostitution, but merely leave the businesses which surround prostitution subject to general civil, business, and professional codes that exist to cover all businesses. Such problems as fraud, theft, negligence, collusion, and force would be covered by existing penal code provisions. Alternatively, existing sections of the penal code could be modified to specifically address the issue of coercion, and business codes could be enacted to require management to provide sick leave and vacation, as well as disability, workers' compensation, and health insurance. Decriminalization of prostitution and the regulation of pimping and pandering, it seems to me, offers the best chance for women who are involved in prostitution to gain some measure of control over their work. It would make it easier to prosecute those who abuse prostitutes, either physically or economically, because the voluntary, non-abusive situations would be left alone.

Decriminalization allows for the possibility that the lives of prostitutes can become less dangerous. For one thing, under a comprehensive decriminalization scheme, it would be possible for prostitutes to join unions and engage in collective bargaining in order to improve their working conditions. It would also be possible for prostitutes to form professional associations, and develop codes of ethics and behavior designed to reduce the problems involved in prostitution as it now exists. Finally, it would be possible for experienced prostitutes to train new prostitutes, so that their first experiences would be less dangerous.

Legalization, on the other hand, has generally meant a system of control of the *prostitute*, with the state regulating, taxing, and/or licensing whatever form of prostitution is legalized, leaving all other forms illegal, without any concern for the prostitute herself. Traditional regulation has often involved the establishment of special government agencies to deal with prostitution.

The brothels in Nevada, for example, are licensed and regulated by the government, and the women who work in them are registered as prostitutes with the sheriff. As discussed earlier, they are severely restricted in their movements outside of the brothel. Independent prostitution is illegal, as is prostitution in massage parlors, for escort services, and of course, street prostitution. The women generally work fourteen-hour shifts, on three-week (seven days a week) tours of duty, during which they may see ten or fifteen customers a day, or more. They have little or no right to refuse a customer (although the management tries to keep out potentially dangerous customers), and they have not been allowed to protect themselves from sexually transmitted diseases by using condoms (although at least two houses in Nevada are now all-condom houses, to prevent AIDS). Because of the grueling aspects of the long work shifts, many of the women use drugs (to help them stay awake and alert or to help them sleep) supplied by the same doctor who performs regular health checks.

Before much can be done to help prostitutes, the laws must be changed. The transaction between prostitute and client must be removed from the purview of the law, and the other laws dealing with prostitution must be reevaluated, and repealed or changed as necessary. Since street prostitution is singled out as 'the problem' it is important for residents, business people, and prostitutes to get together to iron out compromises that take into consideration the right of prostitutes to work without harassment, and the right of other residents and businesses to go about their lives and work without harassment.

In the meantime, until prostitution has been decriminalized, the non-coercive managers regulated, and those who use fraud and force prosecuted, pressure must be put on police and sheriff's departments, district attorneys, public defenders, bail bondspeople, judges, and pretrial diversion and probation programs to improve the treatment of persons arrested under these archaic and oppressive laws.

Should the laws in this country be changed as a result of pressure from men, including well-intentioned civil liberties attorneys, or pornographers with their own motives, there is a good chance that a brothel system will be imposed or that high-class prostitution will be decriminalized and working class prostitution (i.e., street prostitution) will remain a crime, as was proposed by the New York Bar Association in 1985. Unless there is a strong voice pointing out the oppressiveness of brothel systems, both to the women in such a system and to their sisters outside, most people in this country will assume that such a system works to the benefit of all concerned. In a brothel system, prostitution will be kept off the street, and out of the sight of children, they assume, and all in all, it would just be better, safer, and cleaner. The problem is that none of those assumptions are correct, and in exchange for a false sense of security, we would get a punitive system.

Whatever you or I think of prostitution, women have the right to make up their own minds about whether or not to work as prostitutes, and under what terms. They have the right to work as freelance workers, as do nurses, typists, writers, doctors, and so on. They also have the right to work for an employer, a third party who can take care of administration and management problems. They have the right to relationships outside of work, including relationships in which they are the sole support of the other person, so long as the arrangement is acceptable to both parties. They have the right to raise children. They have the right to a full, human existence. As feminists, we have to make that clear. We have to end separation of women into whores and madonnas.

Our experience with the Equal Rights Amendment and with abortion—not to mention sexual assault, domestic violence, sexual harassment, sex discrimination, lesbian/gay rights, and the rest of the issues on our agenda—should tell us that if we leave the issues up to male legislators and pressure groups, the resulting legislation will not be in our interests. The same is true with prostitution.

Finally, the onus for the abuses that co-exist with illegal prostitution must be put on the system that perpetuates those abuses, and no longer on the prostitutes who are abused. If we ensure that prostitution remains under the control of the prostitutes—and not in the hands of pimps, customers, and police—then we will have given the prostitutes the power, and the support, to change that institution. We will all benefit.[4]

NOTES

1. See Jaget, *Prostitutes,* Roberts, *The Front Line.*
2. See Jennifer James, 'Prostitutes and prostitution', in Edward Sagarin and Fred Montanino (eds), *Deviants: Voluntary Actors in a Hostile World,* General Learning Press, Scott, Foresman & Co., 1977; Mimi H., Silbert, PhD, principal investigator, *Sexual Assault of Prostitutes,* San Francisco: Delancey Street Foundation, 1981.
3. See Millet, *The Prostitution Papers,* Jaget, *Prostitutes.*
4. In 1984, the total number of arrests declined, for the first time since COYOTE began keeping track in 1973, to 112,200. There are many possible explanations: unemployment reached its peak in 1982, and has been declining ever since; heavy crackdowns in most cities have encouraged those who could move their business off the street or, retire; fear of AIDS may be discouraging new women from beginning to work as prostitutes. Gloria Lockett, Co-Director of COYOTE, who worked on the street for many of the seventeen years she was a prostitute, says that the percentage of street prostitutes in San Francisco who use IV drugs has increased sharply, which may mean that it is women who don't use drugs who have been able to leave the street or change their occupation.

The Globetrotting Sneaker

Cynthia Enloe

Four years after the fall of the Berlin Wall marked the end of the Cold War, Reebok, one of the fastest growing companies in United States history, decided that the time had come to make its mark in Russia. Thus it was with considerable fanfare that Reebok's executives opened their first store in downtown Moscow in July 1993. A week after the grand opening, store managers described sales as well above expectations.

Reebok's opening in Moscow was the perfect post-Cold War scenario: commercial rivalry replacing military posturing; consumerist tastes homogenizing heretofore hostile peoples; capital and managerial expertise flowing freely across newly porous state borders. Russians suddenly had the "freedom" to spend money on U.S. cultural icons like athletic footwear, items priced above and beyond daily subsistence: at the end of 1993, the average Russian earned the equivalent of $40 a month. Shoes on display were in the $100 range. Almost 60 percent of single parents, most of whom were women, were living in poverty. Yet in Moscow and Kiev, shoe promoters had begun targeting children, persuading them to pressure their mothers to spend money on stylish, Western sneakers. And as far as strategy goes, athletic shoe giants have, you might say, a good track record. In the U.S. many inner-city boys who see basketball as a "ticket out of the ghetto" have become convinced that certain brand-name shoes will give them an edge.

But no matter where sneakers are bought or sold, the potency of their advertising imagery has made it easy to ignore this mundane fact: Shaquille O'Neal's Reeboks are stitched by someone; Michael Jordan's Nikes are stitched by someone; so are your roommate's, so are your grandmother's. Those someones are women, mostly Asian women who are supposed to believe that their "opportunity" to make sneakers for U.S. companies is a sign of their country's progress—just as a Russian woman's chance to spend two month's salary on a pair of shoes for her child allegedly symbolizes the new Russia.

As the global economy expands, sneaker executives are looking to pay women workers less and less, even though the shoes that they produce are capturing an ever-growing share of the footwear market. By the end of 1993, sales in the U.S. alone had reached $11.6 billion. Nike, the largest supplier of athletic footwear in the world, posted a record $298 million profit for 1993—earnings that had nearly tripled in five years. And sneaker companies continue to refine their strategies for "global competitiveness"—hiring supposedly docile women to make their shoes, changing designs as quickly as we fickle customers change our tastes, and shifting factories from country to country as trade barriers rise and fall.

The logic of it all is really quite simple; yet trade agreements such as the North American Free Trade Agreement (NAFTA) and the General Agreement of Tariffs and Trade (GATT) are, of course, talked about in a jargon that alienates us, as if they were technical matters fit only for economists and diplomats. The bottom line is that all companies operating overseas depend on trade agreements made between their own governments and the regimes ruling the countries in which they want to make or sell their products. Korean, Indonesian, and other women workers around the world know this better than anyone. They are tackling trade politics because they have learned from hard experience that the trade deals their governments sign do little to improve the lives of workers.

Hourly Wages in Athletic Footwear Factories

$7.38–7.94

$2.02–2.27

$.65–.74
Thailand

$.10–.14
China

$.16–.20
Indonesia

South Korea

U.S.

Guarantees of fair, healthy labor practices, of the rights to speak freely and to organize independently, will usually be left out of trade pacts—and women will suffer. The recent passage of both NAFTA and GATT ensures that a growing number of private companies will now be competing across borders without restriction. The result? Big business will step up efforts to pit working women in industrialized countries against much lower-paid working women in "developing" countries, perpetuating the misleading notion that they are inevitable rivals in the global job market.

All the "New World Order" really means to corporate giants like athletic shoemakers is that they now have the green light to accelerate long-standing industry practices. In the early 1980s, the field marshals commanding Reebok and Nike, which are both U.S.-based, decided to manufacture most of their sneakers in South Korea and Taiwan, hiring local women. L.A. Gear, Adidas, Fila, and Asics quickly followed their lead. In short time, the coastal city of Pusan, South Korea, became the "sneaker

capital of the world." Between 1982 and 1989 the U.S. lost 58,500 footwear jobs to cities like Pusan, which attracted sneaker executives because its location facilitated international transport. More to the point, South Korea's military government had an interest in suppressing labor organizing, and it had a comfortable military alliance with the U.S. Korean women also seemed accepting of Confucian philosophy, which measured a woman's morality by her willingness to work hard for her family's well-being and to acquiesce to her father's and husband's dictates. With their sense of patriotic duty, Korean women seemed the ideal labor force for export-oriented factories.

U.S. and European sneaker company executives were also attracted by the ready supply of eager Korean male entrepreneurs with whom they could make profitable arrangements. This fact was central to Nike's strategy in particular. When they moved their production sites to Asia to lower labor costs, the executives of the Oregon-based company decided to reduce their corporate responsibilities further. Instead of owning factories outright, a more efficient strategy would be to subcontract the manufacturing to wholly foreign-owned—in this case, South Korean—companies. Let them be responsible for workers' health and safety. Let them negotiate with newly emergent unions. Nike would retain control over those parts of sneaker production that gave its officials the greatest professional satisfaction and the ultimate word on the product: design and marketing. Although Nike was following in the footsteps of garment and textile manufacturers, it set the trend for the rest of the athletic footwear industry.

But at the same time, women workers were developing their own strategies. As the South Korean pro-democracy movement grew throughout the 1980s, increasing numbers of women rejected traditional notions of feminine duty. Women began organizing in response to the dangerous working conditions, daily humiliations, and low pay built into their work.

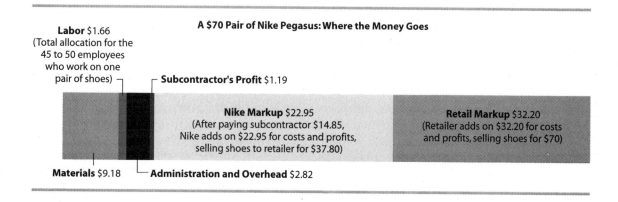

A $70 Pair of Nike Pegasus: Where the Money Goes

Labor $1.66
(Total allocation for the
45 to 50 employees
who work on one
pair of shoes)

Subcontractor's Profit $1.19

Nike Markup $22.95
(After paying subcontractor $14.85,
Nike adds on $22.95 for costs and profits,
selling shoes to retailer for $37.80)

Retail Markup $32.20
(Retailer adds on $32.20 for costs
and profits, selling shoes for $70)

Materials $9.18

Administration and Overhead $2.82

Such resistance was profoundly threatening to the government, given the fact that South Korea's emergence as an industrialized "tiger" had depended on women accepting their "role" in growing industries like sneaker manufacture. If women reimagined their lives as daughters, as wives, as workers, as citizens, it wouldn't just rattle their employers; it would shake the very foundations of the whole political system.

At the first sign of trouble, factory managers called in government riot police to break up employees' meetings. Troops sexually assaulted women workers, stripping, fondling, and raping them "as a control mechanism for suppressing women's engagement in the labor movement," reported Jeong-Lim Nam of Hyosung Women's University in Taegu. It didn't work. It didn't work because the feminist activists in groups like the Korean Women Workers Association (KWWA) helped women understand and deal with the assaults. The KWWA held consciousness-raising sessions in which notions of feminine duty and respectability were tackled along with wages and benefits. They organized independently of the male-led labor unions to ensure that their issues would be taken seriously, in labor negotiations and in the pro-democracy movement as a whole.

The result was that women were at meetings with management, making sure that in addition to issues like long hours and low pay, sexual assault at the hands of managers and health care were on the table. Their activism paid off: in addition to winning the right to organize women's unions, their earnings grew. In 1980, South Korean women in manufacturing jobs earned 45 percent of the wages of their male counterparts; by 1990, they were earning more than 50 percent. Modest though it was, the pay increase was concrete progress, given that the gap between women's and men's manufacturing wages in Japan, Singapore, and Sri Lanka actually *widened* during the 1980s. Last but certainly not least, women's organizing was credited with playing a major role in toppling the country's military regime and forcing open elections in 1987.

Without that special kind of workplace control that only an authoritarian government could offer, sneaker executives knew that it was time to move. In Nike's case, its famous advertising slogan—"Just Do It"—proved truer to its corporate philosophy than its women's "empowerment" ad campaign, designed to rally women's athletic (and consumer) spirit. In response to South Korean women workers' newfound activist self-confidence, the sneaker company and its subcontractors began shutting down a number of their South Korean factories in the late 1980s and early 1990s. After bargaining with government officials in nearby China and Indonesia, many Nike subcontractors set up shop in those countries, while some went to Thailand. China's government remains nominally Communist; Indonesia's ruling generals are staunchly anti-Communist. But both are governed by authoritarian regimes who share the belief that if women can be kept hard at work, low paid, and unorganized, they can serve as a magnet for foreign investors.

Where does all this leave South Korean women—or any woman who is threatened with a factory closure if she demands decent working conditions and a fair wage? They face the dilemma confronted by thousands of women from dozens of countries. The risk of job loss is especially acute in relatively mobile industries; it's easier for a sneaker, garment, or electronics manufacturer to pick up and move than it is for an automaker or a steel producer. In the case of South Korea, poor women had moved from rural villages into the cities searching for jobs to support not only themselves, but parents and siblings. The exodus of manufacturing jobs has forced more women into the growing "entertainment" industry. The kinds of bars and massage parlors offering sexual services that had mushroomed around U.S. military bases during the Cold War have been opening up across the country.

But the reality is that women throughout Asia are organizing, knowing full well the risks involved. Theirs is a long-term view; they are taking direct aim at companies' nomadic advantage, by building links among workers in countries targeted for "development" by multinational corporations. Through sustained grassroots efforts, women are developing the skills and confidence that will make it increasingly difficult to keep their labor cheap. . . .

Indonesian workers' efforts to create unions independent of governmental control were a surprise to shoe companies. Although their moves from South Korea have been immensely profitable [see chart], they do not have the sort of immunity from activism that they had expected. In May 1993, the murder of a female labor activist outside Surabaya set off a storm of local and international protest. Even the U.S. State Department was forced to take note in its 1993 worldwide human rights report, describing a system similar to that which generated South Korea's boom 20 years earlier: severely restricted union organizing, security forces used to break up strikes, low wages for men, lower wages for women—complete with government rhetoric celebrating women's contribution to national development.

Yet when President Clinton visited Indonesia last November, he made only a token effort to address the country's human rights problem. Instead, he touted the benefits of free trade, sounding indeed more enlightened, more in tune with the spirit of the post-Cold War era than do those defenders of protectionist trading policies who coat their rhetoric with "America first" chauvinism. But "free trade" as actually being practiced today is hardly *free* for any workers—in the U.S. or abroad—who have to accept the Indonesian, Chinese, or Korean workplace model as the price of keeping their jobs.

The not-so-new plot of the international trade story has been "divide and rule." If women workers and their government in one country can see that a sneaker company will pick up and leave if their labor demands prove more costly than those in a neighbor country, then women workers will tend to see their neighbors not as regional sisters, but as competitors who can steal their precarious livelihoods. Playing women off against each other is, of course, old hat. Yet it is as essential to international trade politics as is the fine print in GATT.

But women workers allied through networks like the Hong Kong-based Committee for Asian Women are developing their own post-Cold War foreign policy, which means addressing women's needs: how to convince fathers and husbands that a woman going out to organizing meetings at night is not sexually promiscuous; how to develop workplace agendas that respond to family needs; how to work with male unionists who push women's demands to the bottom of their lists; how to build a global movement.

These women refuse to stand in awe of the corporate power of the Nike or Reebok or Adidas executive. Growing numbers of Asian women today have concluded that trade politics have to be understood by women on their own terms. . . . If women in Russia and Eastern Europe can challenge Americanized consumerism, if Asian activists can solidify their alliances, and if U.S. women can join with them by taking on trade politics—the post-Cold War sneaker may be a less comfortable fit in the 1990s.

NOTE

This article draws from the work of South Korean scholars Hyun Sook Kim, Seung-kyung Kim, Katherine Moon, Seungsook Moon, and Jeong-Lim Nam.

DISCUSSION QUESTIONS FOR CHAPTER EIGHT

1. How are systems of inequality evident in women's work inside the home?

2. How do women experience sexism in the paid labor force? How does racism shape the ways women experience sexism in the paid labor force? Have you had experiences of discrimination in the workplace?

3. Why has legislation requiring equal pay and prohibiting discrimination failed to bring about equality for women in the workforce?

4. How has the perception of certain work as feminine affected women's work, both inside and outside the home?

5. What changes do you think need to occur to create equitable systems of work for all women?

SUGGESTIONS FOR FURTHER READING

Fletcher, Joyce K. *Disappearing Acts: Gender, Power, and Relational Practice at Work.* Cambridge, MA: MIT Press, 1999.

Meyer, Madonna Harrington. *Care Work: Gender, Labor, and the Welfare State.* New York: Routledge, 2000.

Neville, Kathleen. *Internal Affairs: The Abuse of Power, Sexual Harassment, and Hypocrisy in the Workplace.* New York: McGraw-Hill, 1999.

Williams, Joan. *Unbending Gender: Why Family and Work Conflict and What to Do About It.* New York: Oxford University Press, 1999.

CHAPTER NINE

Women Confronting
and Creating Culture

Although literature and the arts remain important cultural forms in the twenty-first century, various forms of popular culture—television, movies, rock music, magazines, the Internet—also play a significant role in reflecting, reinforcing, and sometimes subverting the dominant systems and ideologies that help shape gender. Popular cultural forms in particular are very seductive; they reflect and create societal needs, desires, anxieties, and hopes through consumption and participation. As emphasized in Chapter 5, popular culture plays a huge role in setting standards of beauty and encouraging certain bodily disciplinary practices. Popular culture *is* culture for many people; the various forms pop culture takes help shape identity and guide people's understandings of themselves and one another.

Popular culture provides stories and narratives that shape our lives and identities. They give us pleasure at the end of a long day and enable us to take our minds off work or other anxieties. In this regard, some scholars have suggested that popular culture regulates society by "soothing the masses," meaning that energy and opposition to the status quo is redirected in pursuit of the latest in athletic shoes or tickets to an award-winning movie. Of course, popular culture creates huge multimillion dollar industries that themselves regulate society by providing markets for consumption that consolidate power and status among certain groups and individuals. For example, in 1999, the world's largest media company, Time Warner, was acquired by the largest online company, America Online (AOL), for $162 billion in stock. Time Warner owns CNN, HBO, *Time, People,* and *Sports Illustrated* magazines, and the Warner Bros. movie, television, and music properties. This came after another merger of CBS Corporation and Viacom Inc. These mergers consolidate resources across various technologies and help form powerful conglomerates that control the flow of information to the public.

The Internet is also transforming society, making personal computers a necessity for communication and entertainment. Although providing new opportunities for making money and helping people connect across wide geographical expanses, the Internet has also encouraged a further widening of the gap between the "haves" (those with the wealth to acquire the necessary computer, modem, Internet service provider, high speed connection, DVD player, rewritable CD-ROM, and the list goes on) and the "have-nots" (those who, due to lack of access to the technology, are further disadvantaged). When it comes to new electronic technologies, we find that, again, it is a field overwhelmingly dominated by men, illustrating how the tangle of various privileges works to encourage and maintain power in society. Although there are exceptions, women generally have been less interested in those technologies and fields of expertise that have been coded as masculine. With the increased number of computers in the school and in the home, however, many girls are growing up expecting to use computers and these technologies in their environments. There will most likely be very interesting developments in this area as the century progresses.

TELEVISION

Television is one of the most influential forms of media because it is so pervasive and its presence is taken for granted in most households in the United States. Television has changed family life because it encourages passive interaction, replacing alternative family interaction. In addition, television is a visual medium that broadcasts multiple images on a continual basis. These images come to be seen as representing the real world and influence people's understanding of others and the world around them. This is especially significant for children because it is estimated that most children, on the average, watch far more television than is good for them. Of course, the range and quality of television shows vary, and a case can be made for the benefits of educational television. Unfortunately, educational programming is only a small percentage of television viewing. It is estimated, for example, that by the time children reach their mid-teens, they might have watched more than 13,000 violent deaths on television. They learn messages about gender, about race, about class, and certainly about looks. Television is one of the major ways that children learn social norms, roles, and values.

Advertising sponsors control the content of most commercial television. During male sporting events, for example, there are commercials for beer, cars, electronic products, Internet commerce, and other products targeted at a male audience. During daytime soap operas or evening family sitcoms, on the other hand, commercials are aimed at women and focus on beauty and household products. As a result, commercial sponsors have enormous influence over the content of television programming. If they want to sell a certain product, they are unlikely to air the commercial during a feature that could be interpreted as criticizing such products or consumerism generally. In this way, commercial sponsors shape television content.

Television messages about gender tend to be very traditional. In fact, the assumed differences between the genders very often drive the plot of television programming. The format of shows is also gendered. For example, daytime soap operas focus on relationships and family and employ rather fragmented narratives with plots weaving around without closure or resolution, enabling women to tune in and out as they go about multiple tasks. Scholars have pointed out that these shows reconcile women to the fragmented nature of their everyday lives and to male-dominated interpersonal relationships generally. In other words, soap operas, produced with a female viewing audience in mind, help enforce gendered

Learning Activity: Talking About Talk Shows

Watch several television talk shows. Keep a journal describing the topic of the show, the guests, and the commercial sponsors. How would you characterize the host? What do you notice about the interactions among host, guests, and audience? In what ways does gender operate in the shows? Do you think the shows are in any way empowering for the guests, audience members, or television viewers? How do you think these shows reflect either dominant or subordinate American cultures? How do you think these shows contribute to public discourse?

social relations. Other scholars argue that these shows enable women viewers to actively critique blatant male-dominated situations in ways that help them reflect on their own lives. Jane M. Shattuc makes this point in "The Oprahification of America" by claiming that daytime television talk shows are both sensational commercialism and a new forum for political debate, especially for women.

A similar analysis can be made of evening family sitcoms. These shows are funny and entertaining because they are relatively predictable. The family or work group is made up of characters with distinct personalities and recognizable habits; each week this family is thrown into some kind of crisis, and the plot of the show is to resolve that crisis back to situation as usual. For the most part, the messages are typical in terms of gender, race, class, and other differences, and they often involve humor that denigrates certain groups of people and ultimately maintains the status quo. Some sitcoms, however, do revolve around conflict between groups. These include social classes in the *Beverly Hillbillies* or *Frasier,* between women and men in *I Love Lucy, Home Improvement,* or *Seinfeld,* and between children and adults in *Family Ties* or *Growing Pains.* Although these shows model the status quo, they also offer opportunities for modeling critique and resistance. When Ellen DeGeneres's lesbianism became an issue for viewers and sponsors of her show *Ellen,* people began addressing the issue, and many criticized the homophobic reactions of some sponsors.

Increasingly, we are seeing shows and advertisements that resist the usual gendered representations, or at least show them with a new twist. Changes in society's views of gender have made sponsors realize that they have a new marketing niche. Often, unfortunately, these new representations involve the same old package tied up in new ways; typically they involve women and men resisting some of the old norms while keeping most intact. For example, although women are starting to be shown as competent, strong, athletic, and in control of their lives rather than ditsy housewives or sex symbols, they still are very physically attractive and preoccupied with men and relationships. Jane Feuer writes about this "double-edgedness" in her discussion of the increased visibility of fat women in the media in the reading "Averting the Male Gaze: Visual Pleasure and Images of Fat Women." This increased visibility results from both the capitalist-driven need to create a new marketing niche and sell clothing to large women as well as from pressures from fat women and the women's movement.

THE MOVIES

In her groundbreaking work on cinema, Laura Mulvey identifies the "male gaze" as a primary motif for understanding gender in filmmaking. Mulvey argues that movies are essentially made through and for the male gaze and fulfill a voyeuristic desire for men to look at women as objects. She notes that the gaze functions in multiple and related ways. First, in most movies, men are present to act and carry the plot forward; women, on the other hand, are more likely present to be looked at and are rarely the heroes. Second, filmmakers tend to be men, and they anticipate male audiences and female audiences who also have been taught to gaze at women's bodies. Third, in the showing of the film, female characters represented on the screen are also seen by the audience through the eyes of the male protagonist in the movie. Some feminist scholars have suggested the possibility for "subversive gazing" by viewers who refuse to gaze the way filmmakers expect.

Probably the best genre of film in which to observe gender is the romantic comedy or romantic drama. These films are packed with subtle and not too subtle notions of gender, and they are very seductive in the way that they offer fun entertainment. For example, *Pretty Woman* is a contemporary retelling of the Cinderella story, in which a young woman waits for her Prince Charming to rescue her from her undesirable situation. In this case, the prostitute-with-a-heart-of-gold is swept away in a white limousine by the older rich man who procured her services and then fell in love with her. Other types of films are also revealing in terms of norms about gender. Slasher films and horror movies are often spectacular in terms of their victimization of women. The killers in these movies, such as Noman Bates in the classic *Psycho,* are often sexually disturbed and hound and kill women who arouse them. In Norman Bates's case, it was his dysfunctional, demanding mother who pushed him into such psychosis. This is also the subtext of other films like *The Texas Chainsaw Massacre* movies and *Motel Hell.* Often it is sexually active couples who are killed, either after sex or in anticipation of it. The killer usually watches, as in *Halloween II,* as he impersonates the male lover before he then kills the female partner. Although both women and men claim to be entertained by these films, it is important to talk about the messages they portray about men, about women, and about the normalization of violence.

Pornography is an extreme example of the male gaze and the normalization of violence against women (discussed in Chapter 10). With its print media counterpart, pornography extends the sexualization and objectification of women's bodies for entertainment. In pornographic representations, women are often reduced to body parts and are shown deriving pleasure from being violated and dominated. Additionally, racism intersects with sexism in pornography, and African American women in particular are often portrayed in especially demeaning and animalistic ways. Although many feminists, ourselves included, oppose pornography, others, especially those described as "sex radicals," feel that pornography can be a form of sexual self-expression for women. They argue that women who participate in the production of pornography are taking control of their own sexuality and are profiting from control of their own bodies. In "Confessions of a Feminist Porno Star," Nina Hartley argues that as a porn star she is challenging dominant social norms that restrict women's sexuality.

Janet and Susan's Chick Flick Picks

One of the results of the feminist movement has been the growing number of films about women that do not follow the same old scripts about women either falling in love or being killed. These films explore women's lives and relationships more realistically, or at least posit resourceful women who do not need to be rescued by a man. Very often these films are made by independent producers, and rarely do they achieve the commercial success of standard-script movies. Here we've listed some of our favorite "chick flicks" that you may not have seen. Watch at least one of these movies and compare its representation of women to the representation of women in the recent blockbusters you've seen.

- *Thelma & Louise* The first of the "feminist-buddy" films, *Thelma & Louise* follows the journey of two friends who start out for a fun weekend vacation and end up dealing with the ugly consequences of unexpected violence.

- *Strangers in Good Company* A busload of elderly women get stranded in the Canadian wilderness. As they work out their own rescue, they get to know one another as complex, fascinating individuals.

- *I've Heard the Mermaids Singing* A klutzy "person-Friday" gets a part-time job as a clerical worker in an art gallery run by a lesbian, on whom she develops a crush. Through her misadventures, she and the gallery director gain entry into each other's worlds.

- *Bagdad Café* A German businesswoman finds herself stranded in the Mojave Desert after her husband leaves her beside the road. She stumbles upon a run-down café, where she becomes involved with its offbeat patrons.

- *Shirley Valentine* A middle-aged English housewife travels to Greece without her husband and finds a new lease on life and on her relationship.

- *The Incredibly True Adventures of Two Girls in Love* Two high school girls come together across social classes to experience first love. This funny, gentle movie very effectively normalizes relationships between women.

- *Antonia's Line* On the day she decides to die, 90-year-old Antonia recalls her unconventional life and the wide variety of relationships between women that have characterized it.

- *Bhaji on the Beach* A group of ethnic Indian women living in England take a bus outing to the seaside resort of Blackpool. Their differences and their bonding are focal as they spend their day at the beach.

- *Women on the Verge of a Nervous Breakdown* This comedy of errors follows the intersecting lives of a film dubber, her ex-lover, his crazed ex-mistress, his new lover, his son, and his son's girlfriend, who find the importance of love in the midst of misadventure.

Some of the more pervasive and lasting gender images in American culture derive from Walt Disney feature films such as *Cinderella, Sleeping Beauty,* and *The Little Mermaid.* Disney heroines live, however, not only on the big screen but also as dolls in little girls' rooms, on their sheets and curtains, on their lunchboxes, and even on their t-shirts. In "Construction of the Female Self: Feminist Readings of the Disney Heroine," Jill Henke, Diane Umble, and Nancy Smith argue that, on the whole, Disney characters reflect White, heterosexual, middle-class, patriarchal norms. Later representations, such as Pocahontas, still rely on these norms, even as they attempt to be more inclusive of diversity.

As women have made societal gains, Hollywood filmmaking has also changed and become more inclusive of new norms about gender. In some instances, as in *Terminator 2: Judgment Day* and *Aliens,* women are shown to be powerful, although in both movies the heroines are beautiful, fit, and often scantily clad. In other instances, especially when women have more control over the film as in a number of independent movies, films become more reflective of women's actual lives and concerns.

CONTEMPORARY MUSIC AND MUSIC VIDEOS

Popular music like rock, grunge, punk, heavy metal, techno, and rap are contemporary cultural forms targeted at youth. Often this music offers resistance to traditional cultural forms and contains a lot of teenage angst attractive to young people who are figuring out who they are in relation to their parents and other adults in positions of authority in their lives. In this way, such music serves as contemporary resistance and can work to mobilize people politically. Certainly music functions to help youth shape notions of identity. The various musical forms offer different kinds of identities from which young people can pick and choose to sculpt their own sense of self. In this way, music has, and continues to play, a key role in the consolidation of youth cultures in society. There is a huge music industry in the United States, and it works in tandem with television, film, video, and radio.

Just as rock music was an essential part of mobilizing the youth of the 1960s to rebel against traditional norms, oppose the war, and work for civil rights, rap music (and hip-hop culture generally) has been influential in recent decades as a critique of racial cultural politics. Originating in African American urban street culture of the late 1970s, rap was influenced by rhythm and blues and rock and quickly spread beyond its roots into television (like the sitcom *Living Single*), fashion, film, and, in particular, music videos. At the same time that the rap music industry has been able to raise the issue of racism, poverty, and social violence in the context of its endorsement of Black nationalism, rap has also perpetuated misogyny and violence against women in its orientation and musical lyrics. Although there are Black women performers in hip-hop and new female rappers are receiving much more attention, their status in the industry is far below the male bands. In "From Fly-Girls to Bitches and Hos," Joan Morgan argues that although feminists rightly critique the misogyny of much rap music, they must also address the racist contexts that give rise to the music and create such anger in young Black men.

About thirty years after the advent of rock music, the combination of music with visual images gave rise to the music video genre, which gained immense popularity with the prominence of MTV, a 24-hour music video station. Music videos are unique in blending television programming with commercials such that while the viewer is actually watching a commercial, the illusion is of programmatic

Test Your Knowledge of Women and Rock 'n' Roll

1. Who first recorded "Hound Dog?"
   a. Elvis Presley b. Big Mama Thornton c. Billie Holiday d. Hank Williams

2. Who made the first blues recording ("Crazy Blues" and "That Thing Called Love") in 1920?
   a. B. B. King b. Bo Diddley c. Ma Rainey d. Mamie Smith

3. Who was given the title "The Matriarch of Rock"?
   a. Bonnie Raitt b. Ma Rainey c. Bessie Smith d. Memphis Minnie

4. Who was the original "bad girl" of rock?
   a. Etta James b. Madonna c. Cher d. Mary Wells

5. Who performed at the inauguration of Franklin Delano Roosevelt?
   a. Georgia Tom Dorsey b. Mahalia Jackson c. Sister Rosetta Tharpe d. Elvis Presley

6. By the mid-1940s who was one of the highest paid Black entertainers in the United States?
   a. B. B. King b. Billie Holiday c. Koko Taylor d. Nina Simone

7. Who wrote "Ball and Chain," a song made famous by Janis Joplin in the 1960s?
   a. Big Mama Thornton b. Joan Baez c. Janis Joplin d. Ira Gershwin

8. Who pioneered an innovative guitar technique in which the melody is played on the bass string with the thumb, while rhythmically strumming with the other fingers? This technique influenced the guitar's shift from a rhythm to a lead instrument.
   a. B. B. King b. Bo Diddley c. Bonnie Raitt d. Maybelle Carter

9. What was the first Country-Western number one by a woman?
   a. Kitty Wells's "It Wasn't God Who Made Honky Tonk Angels" b. Loretta Lynn's "Coal Miner's Daughter" c. Tammy Wynette's "Stand by Your Man" d. Dolly Parton's "I Will Always Love You"

10. Who was the only female band to tour with the Beatles?
    a. The Supremes b. The Chiffons c. The Ronettes d. The Shangri-Las

11. Who was the first woman inducted into the Rock and Roll Hall of Fame (1987)?
    a. Diana Ross b. Janis Joplin c. Martha Reeves d. Aretha Franklin

12. Who is Aretha Franklin's favorite singer?
    a. Little Richard b. Mahalia Jackson c. Janet Jackson d. Michael Jackson

13. What Los Angeles band created the reproductive rights organization Rock for Choice?
    a. X b. The Bangles c. The Go-Gos d. L7

14. Who was the first pop singer who did not base her work in the realm of the love song, preferring to write and sing about masturbation, incest, and infant sexuality?
    a. Amy Ray b. Patti Smith c. Donna Summer d. Kate Bush

15. Who heads Elektra Entertainment Record Company?
    a. David Geffen b. Sylvia Rhone c. Ted Turner d. Barbra Streisand

16. Who had eight songs banned from various radio stations?
    a. Madonna b. Cher c. Loretta Lynn d. Tina Turner

(continued)

Test Your Knowledge of Women and Rock 'n' Roll (*continued*)

17. Who started Righteous Babe Records?
   a. Ani DiFranco b. Natalie Merchant c. Joni Mitchell d. Liz Phair

18. Who was the highest paid woman in rock in 1978?
   a. Cher b. Stevie Nicks c. Linda Ronstadt d. Chrissie Hynde

19. Who wrote or co-wrote "Will You Love Me Tomorrow?" "The Loco Motion," "Up on the Roof," "One Fine Day," "I'm into Something Good," and "A Natural Woman"?
   a. Diana Ross b. Carole King c. Aretha Franklin d. Laura Nyro

20. Who won best rhythm and blues solo vocal performance, female (a category created especially for her) eight years in a row?
   a. Aretha Franklin b. Whitney Houston c. Diana Ross d. Mariah Carey

21. Who had their own brand of white bread?
   a. The Chiffons b. The Shirelles c. The Supremes d. The Shangri-Las

22. Who was the first artist to place seven top-five singles from one album on *Billboard*'s pop singles chart?
   a. Madonna b. Janet Jackson c. Michael Jackson d. Prince

23. How many times has Jewel's CD "Pieces of You" gone platinum?
   a. twice b. three times c. four times d. five times

24. Who cofounded RAIN (Rape, Abuse, and Incest National Network), a hotline for victims of abuse or violence?
   a. Emily Saliers b. Tori Amos c. Sarah McLachlan d. Bjork

25. Who were the first hip-hop artists to set rhymes to a go-go beat?
   a. Run DMC b. N.W.A c. Salt-N-Pepa d. BWP

26. Who simultaneously promoted pro-woman activism and pro-Black consciousness in hip-hop?
   a. Queen Latifah b. M.C. Lyte c. Yo Yo d. Salt-N-Pepa

27. Who earned her first Grammy in a Country-Western category and then followed with a Grammy in pop vocals?
   a. Patsy Cline b. Whitney Houston c. k.d. lang d. Tracy Chapman

28. Who is the biggest-selling female group of all time?
   a. The Supremes b. TLC c. En Vogue d. The Runaways

29. Which Latino/a artist has reached the greatest level of mass-market success?
   a. Selena b. Gloria Estefan c. Tito Puente d. Julio Iglesias

30. Which group set up female-only areas at stage front and sent boys to the back of the mosh pit?
   a. Frightwig b. Bikini Kill c. Hole d. Babes in Toyland

Answers: 1. b 2. d 3. b 4. a 5. c 6. b 7. a 8. d 9. a 10. c 11. d 12. b 13. d 14. d 15. b 16. c 17. a 18. c 19. b 20. a 21. c 22. b 23. d 24. b 25. c 26. a 27. c 28. b 29. a 30. b entertainment. Music videos are essentially advertisements for record company products and focus on standard rock music, although different musical genres like Country-Western also have their 24-hour video formatting. Most music videos are fairly predictable in the ways they sexualize women, sometimes in violent ways. As in movies, women are generally present in music videos to be looked at. In fact, music videos featuring male musicians are aired in greater numbers than those featuring female musicians.

Nonetheless, we could also argue that the music video industry has allowed women performers to find their voice (literally) and to script music videos from their perspective. This opportunity has given women audience recognition and industry backing. Music videos have also helped produce a feminine voice that has the potential to disrupt the traditional gendered perspective. At its peak in the mid-1980s, MTV helped such women as Tina Turner, Cyndi Lauper, and Madonna find success. Madonna is especially interesting because she has been cast simultaneously as both a feminist nightmare perpetuating gendered stereotypes about sexualized women and an important role model for women who want to be active agents in their lives. On the latter, she has been regarded as someone who returns the male gaze by staring right back at the patriarchy.

PRINT MEDIA

No discussion of popular culture is complete without a discussion of the print media. These mass media forms include magazines, newspapers, comic books, and other periodicals. Like other media, they are a mix of entertainment, education, and advertising. Fashion magazines are heavy on advertising, whereas comic books tend to be geared toward entertainment and rely more on product sales of the comic books themselves. Newspapers fall somewhere in between.

Women's magazines are an especially fruitful subject of study for examining how gender works in contemporary U.S. society. As discussed in Chapter 5, women's magazines are a central part of the multibillion dollar industries that produce cosmetics and fashion and help shape the social construction of beauty. Alongside these advertising campaigns are bodily standards against which women are encouraged to measure themselves. Because almost no one measures up to these artificially created and often computer-generated standards, the message is to buy these products and your life will improve.

Ideas for Activism

- Write letters to encourage networks to air television shows that depict the broad diversity of women.
- Write letters to sponsors to complain about programs that degrade or stereotype women.
- Form a reading group to study novels by female authors.
- Sponsor a media awareness event on campus to encourage other students to be aware of media portrayals of women.

Learning Activity: Looking Good, Feeling Sexy, Getting a Man

Collect a number of women's magazines, such as *Cosmopolitan, Vogue, Elle, Mirabella, Redbook,* and *Woman's Day.* Read through the magazines and fill in the chart listing the number of articles you find about each topic. What do you observe from your analysis? What messages about gender are these magazines presenting?

MAGAZINE TITLE	MAKEUP	CLOTHES	HAIR	SEX/DATING	DIETING	FOOD/RECIPES	HOME DECORATION	WORK	POLITICS

Generally, women's magazines can be divided into three distinct types. First are the fashion magazines that focus on beauty, attracting and satisfying men, self-improvement, and (occasionally) work and politics. Examples of these are *Vogue* (emphasizing fashion and makeup), *Cosmopolitan* (emphasizing sexuality and relationships with men), and *Self* (emphasizing self-improvement and employment), although the latter two are also heavy on beauty and fashion and the former is also preoccupied with sex. Most of these magazines have a White audience in mind; *Ebony* is one similar kind of magazine aimed at African American women. Note that there are a whole series of junior magazines in this genre, such as *Seventeen,* aimed at teenage women. However, although its title suggests the magazine might be oriented toward 17-year-olds, it is mostly read by younger teenagers and even preadolescent girls. Given the focus of teen magazines on dating, fashion, and makeup, the effects of such copy and advertisements on young girls are significant.

The second genre of women's magazines includes those oriented toward the family, cooking, household maintenance and decoration, and keeping the man you already have. Examples include *Good Housekeeping, Redbook,* and *Better Homes and Gardens.* These magazines (especially those like *Good Housekeeping*) also include articles and advertising on fashion and cosmetics, although the representations of these products are different. Instead of the seductive model dressed in a shiny, revealing garment (as is usually featured on the cover of *Cosmo*), *Redbook,* for example, features a more natural-looking woman (although still very beautiful) in more conservative clothes, surrounded by other graphics or captions featuring various deserts, crafts, and so forth. The focus is off sex and onto the home.

The third genre of women's magazines is the issue periodical that focuses on some issue or hobby that appeals to many women. *Parents* magazine is an example of an issue periodical aimed at women (although not exclusively). *Ms.* magazine is one aimed at feminists. Examples of hobby-type periodicals include craft magazines on needlework or crochet, fitness magazines, and so forth. There are many specialized issue periodicals aimed at men (such as hunting and fishing and out-door activities periodicals, computer and other electronic-focused magazines, car and motorcycle magazines, and various sports periodicals). The best known of the latter is *Sports Illustrated,* famous also for its swimsuit edition that always produces record sales. This magazine has been described as ultra-soft pornography because of its sexualization of female athletes' bodies. That there are more issue periodicals for men reflects the fact that men are assumed to work and have specialized interests, and women are assumed to be preoccupied with looking beautiful, working on relationships, and keeping a beautiful home.

LITERATURE AND THE ARTS

In "Thinking About Shakespeare's Sister," Virginia Woolf responds to the question, Why has there been no female Shakespeare? Similarly, in the early 1970s, Linda Nochlin wrote a feminist critique of art history that sought to answer the question, Why have there been no great women artists? Woolf and Nochlin reached very similar conclusions. According to Nochlin, the reason there had been no great women artists was not because no woman had been capable of producing great art but because the social conditions of women's lives prevented such artistic endeavors.

Woolf wrote her essay in the late 1920s, but still today many critics and professors of literature raise the same questions about women's abilities to create great

Activist Profile: Maxine Hong Kingston

As a young girl, Maxine Hong Kingston could not find herself in the images in the books she read. The public library in her hometown of Stockton, California had no stories of Chinese Americans and very few that featured girls. For Kingston, this meant a significant need and open space for the telling of her stories.

Kingston was born in Stockton in 1940 to Chinese immigrant parents. Her mother was trained as a midwife in China, and her father was a scholar and teacher. Arriving in the United States, Tom Hong could not find work and eventually ended up working in a gambling business. Maxine was named after a successful blonde gambler who frequented her father's establishment.

Growing up in a Chinese American community, Kingston heard the stories of her culture that would later influence her own storytelling. By earning eleven scholarships, she was able to attend the University of California at Berkeley, where she earned a B.A. in literature. She married in 1962, and she and her new husband moved to Hawaii, where they both taught for the next ten years.

In 1976, Kingston published her first book, *The Woman Warrior: Memoirs of a Girlhood Among Ghosts*. This story of a young Chinese American girl who finds her own voice won the National Book Critic's Circle Award. Kingston's portrayal of the girl's struggle with silence was met with a great deal of criticism from many Chinese men who attacked Kingston's exploration of critical gender and race issues among Chinese Americans.

Kingston followed *Woman Warrior* with *China Men* in 1980, which also won the National Book Critic's Circle Award. This book explored the lives of the men in Kingston's family who came to the United States, celebrating their achievements and documenting the prejudices and exploitation they faced. Her 1989 novel, *Tripmaster Monkey: His Fake Book*, continued her explorations of racism and oppression of Chinese Americans. Although some critics have accused Kingston of selling out because her stories have not reflected traditional notions of Chinese culture, she has maintained her right to tell her story in her own words with her own voice.

literature. Rarely, for example, does a seventeenth- or eighteenth-century British literature course give more than a passing nod to women authors of the periods. Quite often, literature majors graduate having read perhaps only Virginia Woolf, George Eliot, Jane Austen, or Emily Dickinson. The usual justification is that women simply have not written the great literature that men have or that to include women would mean leaving out the truly important works of the literary canon (those written by White men).

In her essay, Woolf argues that it would have been impossible due to social constraints for a woman to write the works of Shakespeare in the age of Shakespeare. Although women did write, even in the time of Shakespeare, their works were often neglected by the arbiters of the literary canon because they fell outside the narrowly constructed definitions of great literature. For example, women's novels often dealt with the subjects of women's lives—family, home,

Janet and Susan's Must-Read Novels

A lot of great literature has been produced by women, especially in the last thirty years. Here are some of our favorites. We recommend that you add these to your summer reading list! You may also want to consider subscribing to the *Women's Review of Books*.

- Isabel Allende, *House of the Spirits* and *Eva Luna*
- Dorothy Allison, *Bastard Out of Carolina*
- Maya Angelou, *I Know Why the Caged Bird Sings*
- Margaret Atwood, *The Handmaid's Tale*
- Rita Mae Brown, *Rubyfruit Jungle*
- Sandra Cisneros, *The House on Mango Street*
- Annie Dillard, *Pilgrim at Tinker Creek*
- Marilyn French, *The Women's Room*
- Mary Gordon, *The Company of Women*
- Kaye Gibbons, *Ellen Foster*
- Ursula Hegi, *Stones from the River* and *Floating in My Mother's Palm*
- Zora Neale Hurston, *Their Eyes Were Watching God*
- Barbara Kingsolver, *The Bean Trees*
- Toni Morrison, *Sula* and *The Bluest Eye*
- Gloria Naylor, *The Women of Brewster Place*
- Marge Piercy, *The Longings of Women* and *Gone to Soldiers*
- May Sarton, *The Education of Harriet Hatfield*
- Amy Tan, *The Joy Luck Club* and *The Hundred Secret Senses*
- Alice Walker, *The Color Purple* and *The Temple of My Familiar*

love—subjects not deemed lofty enough for the canon of literature. Additionally, women often did not follow accepted forms, writing in fragments rather than unified texts. As the canon was defined according to White male norms, women's writing and much of the writing of both women and men of color were omitted.

Yet, toward the end of the twentieth century, more women began to publish novels and poetry, and these have been slowly introduced into the canon. These works have dealt with the realities of women's lives and have received wide acclaim. For example, writers such as Toni Morrison (who received the Nobel Prize for literature), Alice Walker, and Maya Angelou have written about the dilemmas and triumphs faced by Black women in a White, male-dominated culture. Annie Dillard won a Pulitzer Prize at the age of 29 for her nature essays about a year spent living by Tinker Creek. Rita Mae Brown, May Sarton, Gloria Anzaldúa, Dorothy Allison, and Audre Lorde write about lesbian lives and the confluences of sexism, heterosexism, racism, and classism. These writers have been joined by feminist playwrights such as Wendy Wasserstein, feminist performance artists such as Lily Tomlin and Lori Anderson, and feminist comedians such as Suzanne Westenhoffer, Tracey Ullman, and Margaret Cho. In the readings, Audre Lorde and Gloria Anzaldúa write about the importance of literature for women.

Just as female writers have been ignored, misrepresented, and trivialized, so too female artists and musicians have faced similar struggles. Women's art has often been labeled "crafts" rather than art. This is because women, who were often barred from entering the artistic establishment, have tended to create works of art that were useful and were excluded from the category of art. Often, female artists, like their sisters who were writing novels and poetry, used a male pen name and disguised their identity in order to have their work published or shown. With the influence of the women's movement, women's art is being reclaimed and introduced into the art history curriculum, although it is often taught in the context of "women's art." This emphasizes the ways the academy remains androcentric with the contributions of "others" in separate courses. Female artists such as Georgia O'Keeffe and Judy Chicago have revitalized the art world by creating women-centered art and feminist critiques of masculine art forms.

The works of female composers and musicians have also been ignored, and very few women have been given the opportunity to conduct orchestras until recently. In fact, through the nineteenth century, only certain instruments such as the keyboard and harp were considered appropriate for women to play, and, even today, women are still directed away from some instruments and toward others. Women continue to produce literature and art and to redefine the canon. As in other male-dominated arenas, women have had to struggle to create a place for themselves. But, as a keen observer once quipped, "Ginger Rogers did everything Fred Astaire did, only backwards and in heels."

Thinking About Shakespeare's Sister

Virginia Woolf

. . . [I]t is a perennial puzzle why no woman wrote a word of extraordinary literature when every other man, it seemed, was capable of song or sonnet. What were the conditions in which women lived, I asked myself; for fiction, imaginative work that is, is not dropped like a pebble upon the ground, as science may be; fiction is like a spider's web, attached ever so lightly perhaps, but still attached to life at all four corners. Often the attachment is scarcely perceptible; Shakespeare's plays, for instance, seem to hang there complete by themselves. But when the web is pulled askew, hooked up at the edge, torn in the middle, one remembers that these webs are not spun in midair by incorporeal creatures, but are the work of suffering human beings, and are attached to grossly material things, like health and money and the houses we live in.

I went therefore, to the shelf where the stories stand and took down one of the latest, Professor Trevelyan's *History of England.* Once more I looked up Women, found "position of," and turned to the pages indicated. "Wifebeating," I read "was a recognized right of man, and was practiced without shame by high as well as low. . . . Similarly," this historian goes on, "the daughter who refused to marry the gentleman of her parents' choice was liable to be locked up, beaten and flung about the room, without any shock being inflicted on public opinion. Marriage was not an affair of personal affection, but of family avarice, particularly in the 'chivalrous' upper classes. . . . Betrothal often took place while one or both of the parties was in the cradle, and marriage when they were scarcely out of the nurses' charge." That was about 1470, soon after Chaucer's time. The next reference to the position of women is some two hundred years later, in the time of the Stu-

arts. "It was still the exception for women of the upper and middle class to choose their own husbands, and when the husband had been assigned, he was lord and master, so far at least as law and custom could make him. Yet even so," Professor Trevelyan concludes, "neither Shakespeare's women nor those of authentic seventeenth-century memoirs, like the Vemeys and the Hutchinsons, seem wanting in personality and character." Certainly, if we consider it, Cleopatra must have had a way with her; Lady Macbeth, one would suppose, had a will of her own; Rosalind, one might conclude, was an attractive girl. Professor Trevelyan is speaking no more than the truth when he remarks that Shakespeare's women do not seem wanting in personality and character. Not being a historian, one might go even further and say that women have burnt like beacons in all the works of all the poets from the beginning of time—Clytemnestra, Antigone, Cleopatra, Lady Macbeth, Phèdre, Cressida, Rosalind, Desdemona, the Duchess of Malfi, among the dramatists; then among the prose writers: Millamant, Clarissa, Becky Sharp, Anna Karenine, Emma Bovary, Madame de Guermantes—the names flock to mind, nor do they recall women "lacking in personality and character." Indeed, if woman had no existence save in fiction written by men, one would imagine her a person of the utmost importance, very various; heroic and mean; splendid and sordid; infinitely beautiful and hideous in the extreme; as great as a man, some think even greater. But this is woman in fiction. In fact, as Professor Trevelyan points out, she was locked up, beaten and flung about the room.

A very queer, composite being thus emerges. Imaginatively she is of the highest importance; practically she is completely insignificant. She pervades poetry from cover to cover; she is all but absent from history. She dominates the lives of kings and conquerors in fiction; in fact she was the slave of any boy whose parents forced a ring upon her finger. Some of the most inspired words, some of the most profound thoughts in literature fall from her lips; in real life she could hardly read, could scarcely spell, and was the property of her husband.

. . .

Be that as it may, I could not help thinking, as I looked at the works of Shakespeare on the shelf . . . it would have been impossible, completely and entirely, for any woman to have written the plays of Shakespeare in the age of Shakespeare. Let me imagine, since facts are so hard to come by, what would have happened had Shakespeare had a wonderfully gifted sister, called Judith, let us say. Shakespeare himself went, very probably—his mother was an heiress—to the grammar school, where he may have learnt Latin—Ovid, Virgil and Horace—and the elements of grammar and logic. He was, it is well known, a wild boy who poached rabbits, perhaps shot a deer, and had, rather sooner than he should have done, to marry a woman in the neighbourhood, who bore him a child rather quicker than was right. That escapade sent him to seek his fortune in London. He had, it seemed, a taste for the theatre; he began by holding horses at the stage door. Very soon he got work in the theatre, became a successful actor, and lived at the hub of the universe, meeting everybody, knowing everybody, practising his art on the boards, exercising his wits in the streets, and even getting access to the palace of the queen. Meanwhile his extraordinarily gifted sister, let us suppose, remained at home. She was as adventurous, as imaginative, as agog to see the world as he was. But she was not sent to school. She had no chance of learning grammar and logic, let alone of reading Horace and Virgil. She picked up a book now and then, one of her brother's perhaps, and read a few pages. But then her parents came in and told her to mend the stockings or mind the stew and not moon about with books and papers. They would have spoken sharply but kindly, for they were substantial people who knew the conditions of life for a woman and loved their daughter—indeed, more likely than not she was the apple of her father's eye. Perhaps she scribbled some pages up in an apple loft on the sly, but was careful to hide them or set fire to them. Soon, however, before she was out of her teens, she was to be betrothed to the son of a neighbouring wool-stapler. She cried out that marriage was hateful to her, and for that she was severely beaten by her father. Then he ceased to scold her. He begged her instead not to hurt him, not to shame him in this matter of her marriage. He would give her a chain of beads or a fine petticoat, he said; and there were tears in his eyes. How could she disobey him? How could she break his heart? The force of her own gift alone drove her to it. She made up a small parcel of her belongings, let herself down by a rope one summer's night and took the road to London. She was not seventeen. The birds that sang in the hedge were not more musical than she was. She had the quickest fancy, a gift like her brother's, for the tune of words. Like him, she had a taste for the theatre. She stood at the stage door; she wanted to act, she said. Men laughed in her face. The manager—a fat, loose-lipped man—guffawed. He bellowed something about poodles dancing and women acting—no woman, he said, could possibly be an actress. He hinted—you can imagine what. She could get no training in her craft. Could she even seek her dinner in a tavern or roam the streets at midnight? Yet her genius was for fiction and lusted to feed abundantly upon the lives of men and women and the study of their ways. At last—for she was very young, oddly like Shakespeare the poet in her face, with the same grey eyes and rounded brows—at last Nick Greene the actor-manager took pity on her; she found herself with child by that gentleman and so—who shall measure the heat and violence of the poet's heart when caught and tangled in a woman's body?—killed herself one winter's night and lies buried at some crossroads where the omnibuses now stop outside the Elephant and Castle.

That, more or less, is how the story would run, I think, if a woman in Shakespeare's day had had Shakespeare's genius. . . .

This may be true or it may be false—who can say?—but what is true in it, so it seemed to me, reviewing the story of Shakespeare's sister as I had made it, is that any woman born with a great gift in the sixteenth century would certainly have gone crazed, shot herself, or ended her days in some lonely cottage outside the village, half witch, half wizard, feared and mocked at. For it needs little skill in psychology to be sure that a highly gifted girl who had tried to use her gift for poetry would have been so thwarted and hindered by other people, so tortured and pulled asunder by her own contrary instincts, that she must have lost her health and sanity to a certainty. No girl could have walked to London and stood at a stage door and forced her way into the presence of actor-managers without doing herself a violence and suffering an anguish which may have been irrational—for chastity may be a fetish invented by certain societies for unknown reasons—but were none the less inevitable. . . .

But for women, I thought, looking at the empty shelves, these difficulties were infinitely more formidable. In the first place, to have a room of her own, let alone a quiet room or a sound-proof room, was out of the question, unless her parents were exceptionally rich or very noble, even up to the beginning of the nineteenth century. Since her pin money, which depended on the good will of her father, was only enough to keep her clothed, she was debarred from such alleviations as came even to Keats or Tennyson or Carlyle, all poor men, from a walking tour, a little journey to France, from the separate lodging which, even if it were miserable enough, sheltered them from the claims and tyrannies of their families. Such material difficulties were formidable; but much worse were the immaterial. The indifference of the world which Keats and Flaubert and other men of genius have found so hard to bear was in her case not indifference but hostility. The world did not say to her as it said to them, Write if you choose; it makes no difference to me. The world said with a guffaw, Write? What's the good of your writing? . . .

READING 62

Poetry Is Not a Luxury

Audre Lorde

The quality of light by which we scrutinize our lives has direct bearing upon the product which we live, and upon the changes which we hope to bring about through those lives. It is within this light that we form those ideas by which we pursue our magic and make it realized. This is poetry as illumination, for it is through poetry that we give name to those ideas which are—until the poem—nameless and formless, about to be birthed, but already felt. That distillation of experience from which true poetry springs births thought as dream births concept, as feeling births idea, as knowledge births (precedes) understanding.

As we learn to bear the intimacy of scrutiny and to flourish within it, as we learn to use the products of that scrutiny for power within our living, those fears which rule our lives and form our silences begin to lose their control over us.

For each of us as women, there is a dark place within, where hidden and growing our true spirit rises, "beautiful /and tough as chestnut /stanchions against (y)our nightmare of weakness/"[1] and of impotence.

These places of possiblity within ourselves are dark because they are ancient and hidden; they have survived and grown strong through that darkness. Within these deep places, each one of us holds an incredible reserve of creativity and power, of unexamined and unrecorded emotion and feeling. The woman's place of power within each of us is neither white nor surface; it is dark, it is ancient, and it is deep.

When we view living in the european mode only as a problem to be solved, we rely solely upon our ideas to make us free, for these were what the white fathers told us were precious.

But as we come more into touch with our own ancient, noneuropean consciousness of living as a situation to be experienced and interacted with, we learn more and more to cherish our feelings, and to respect those hidden sources of our power from where true knowledge and, therefore, lasting action comes.

At this point in time, I believe that women carry within ourselves the possibility for fusion of these two approaches so necessary for survival, and we come closest to this combination in our poetry. I speak here of poetry as a revelatory distillation of experience, not the sterile word play that, too often, the white fathers distorted the word *poetry* to mean—in order to cover a desperate wish for imagination without insight.

For women, then, poetry is not a luxury. It is a vital necessity of our existence. It forms the quality of the light within which we predicate our hopes and dreams toward survival and change, first made into language, then into idea, then into more tangible action. Poetry is the way we help give name to the nameless so it can be thought. The farthest horizons of our hopes and fears are cobbled by our poems, carved from the rock experiences of our daily lives.

As they become known to and accepted by us, our feelings and the honest exploration of them become sanctuaries and spawning grounds for the most radical and daring of ideas. They become a safe-house for that difference so necessary to change and the conceptualization of any meaningful action. Right now, I could name at least ten ideas I would have found intolerable or incomprehensible and frightening, except as they came after dreams and poems. This is not idle fantasy, but a disciplined attention to the true meaning of "it feels right to me." We can train ourselves to respect our feelings and to transpose them into a language so they can be shared. And where that language does not yet exist, it is our poetry which helps to fashion it. Poetry is not only dream and vision; it is the skeleton architecture of our lives. It lays the foundations for a future of change, a bridge across our fears of what has never been before.

Possibility is neither forever nor instant. It is not easy to sustain belief in its efficacy. We can sometimes work long and hard to establish one beachhead of real resistance to the deaths we are expected to live, only to have that beachhead assaulted or threatened by those canards we have been socialized to fear, or by the withdrawal of those approvals that we have been warned to seek for safety. Women see ourselves diminished or softened by the falsely benign accusations of childishness, of nonuniversality, of changeability, of sensuality. And who asks the question: Am I altering your aura, your ideas, your dreams, or am I merely moving you to temporary and reactive action? And even though the latter is no mean task, it is one that must be seen within the context of a need for true alteration of the very foundations or our lives.

The white fathers told us: I think, therefore I am. The Black mother within each of us—the poet—whispers in our dreams: I feel, therefore I can be free. Poetry coins the language to express and charter this revolutionary demand, the implementation of that freedom.

However, experience has taught us that action in the now is also necessary, always. Our children cannot dream unless they live, they cannot live unless they are nourished, and who else will feed them the real food without which their dreams will be no different from ours? "If you want us to change the world someday, we at least have to live long enough to grow up!" shouts the child.

Sometimes we drug ourselves with dreams of new ideas. The head will save us. The brain alone will set us free. But there are no new ideas still waiting in the wings to save us as women, as human. There are only old and forgotten ones, new combinations, extrapolations and recognitions from within ourselves— along with the renewed courage to try them out. And we must constantly encourage ourselves and each other to attempt the heretical actions that our dreams imply, and so many of our old ideas disparage. In the forefront of our move toward change, there is only poetry to hint at possibility made real. Our poems formulate the implications of ourselves, what we feel within and dare make real (or bring action into accordance with), our fears, our hopes, our most cherished terrors.

For within living structures defined by profit, by linear power, by institutional dehumanization, our feelings were not meant to survive. Kept around as unavoidable adjuncts or pleasant pastimes, feelings were expected to kneel to thought as women were expected to kneel to men. But women have survived. As poets. And there are no new pains. We have felt them all already. We have hidden that fact in the same place where we have hidden our power. They surface in our dreams, and it is our dreams that point the way to freedom. Those dreams are made realizable through our poems that give us the strength and courage to see, to feel, to speak, and to dare.

If what we need to dream, to move our spirits most deeply and directly toward and through promise, is discounted as a luxury, then we give up the core—the fountain—of our power, our womanness; we give up the future of our worlds.

For there are no new ideas. There are only new ways of making them felt—of examining what those ideas feel like being lived on Sunday morning at 7 A.M., after brunch, during wild love, making war, giving birth, mourning our dead—while we suffer the old longings, battle the old warnings and fears of being silent and impotent and alone, while we taste new possibilities and strengths.

Note

1. From "Black Mother Woman," first published in *From A Land Where Other People Live* (Broadside Press, Detroit, 1973), and collected in *Chosen Poems: Old and New* (W.W. Norton and Company, New York, 1982) p. 53.

READING 63

The Path of the Red and Black Ink

Gloria Anzaldúa

"Out of poverty, poetry;
out of suffering, song."

— *a Mexican saying*

When I was seven, eight, nine, fifteen, sixteen years old, I would read in bed with a flashlight under the covers, hiding my self-imposed insomnia from my mother. I preferred the world of the imagination to the death of sleep. My sister, Hilda, who slept in the same bed with me, would threaten to tell my mother unless I told her a story.

I was familiar with *cuentos*—my grandmother told stories like the one about her getting on top of the roof while down below rabid coyotes were ravaging the place and wanting to get at her. My father told stories about a phantom giant dog that appeared out of nowhere and sped along the side of the pickup no matter how fast he was driving.

Nudge a Mexican and she or he will break out with a story. So, huddling under the covers, I made up stories for my sister night after night. After a while she wanted two stories per night. I learned to give her installments, building up the suspense with convoluted complications until the story climaxed several nights later. It must have been then that I decided to put stories on paper. It must have been then that working with images and writing became connected to night.

INVOKING ART

In the ethno-poetics and performance of the shaman, my people, the Indians, did not split the artistic from the functional, the sacred from the secular, art from everyday life. The religious, social and aesthetic purposes of art were all intertwined. Before the Conquest, poets gathered to play music, dance, sing and read poetry in open-air places around the *Xochicuahuitl, el Árbol Florido,* Tree-in-Flower. (The *Coaxihuitl* or morning glory is called the snake plant and its seeds, known as *ololiuhqui,* are hallucinogenic.) The ability of story (prose and poetry) to transform the storyteller and the listener into something or someone else is shamanistic. The writer, as shape-changer, is a *nahual,* a shaman.

In looking at this book that I'm almost finished writing, I see a mosaic pattern (Aztec-like) emerging, a weaving pattern, thin here, thick there. I see a preoccupation with the deep structure, the underlying structure, with the gesso underpainting that is red earth, black earth. I can see the deep structure, the scaffolding. If I can get the bone structure right, then putting flesh on it proceeds without too many hitches. The problem is that the bones often do not exist prior to the flesh, but are shaped after a vague and broad shadow of its form is discerned or uncovered during beginning, middle and final stages of the writing. Numerous overlays of paint, rough surfaces, smooth surfaces make me realize I am preoccupied with texture as well. Too, I see the barely contained color threatening to spill over the boundaries of the object it represents and into other "objects" and over the borders of the frame. I see a hybridization of metaphor, different species of ideas popping up here, popping up there, full of variations and seeming contradictions, though I believe in an ordered structured universe where all phenomena are interrelated and imbued with spirit. This almost finished product seems an assemblage, a montage, a beaded work with several leitmotifs and with a central core, now appearing, now disappearing in a crazy dance. The whole thing has had a mind of its own, escaping me and insisting on putting together the pieces of its own puzzle with minimal direction from my will. It is a rebellious, willful entity, a precocious girl-child forced to grow up too quickly, rough, unyielding, with pieces of feather sticking out here and there, fur, twigs, clay. My child, but not for much longer. This female being is angry, sad, joyful, is *Coatlicue,* dove, horse, serpent, cactus. Though it is a flawed thing—a clumsy, complex, groping blind thing—for me it is alive, infused with spirit. I talk to it; it talks to me.

I make my offerings of incense and cracked corn, light my candle. In my head I sometimes will say a prayer—an affirmation and a voicing of intent. Then I run water, wash the dishes or my underthings, take a bath, or mop the kitchen floor. This "induction" period sometimes takes a few minutes, sometimes hours. But always I go against a resistance. Something in me does not want to do this writing. Yet once I'm immersed in it, I can go fifteen to seventeen hours in one sitting and I don't want to leave it.

My "stories" are acts encapsulated in time, "enacted" every time they are spoken aloud or read silently. I like to think of them as performances and not as inert and "dead" objects (as the aesthetics of Western culture think of art works). Instead, the work has an identity; it is a "who" or a "what" and contains the presences of persons, that is, incarnations of gods or ancestors or natural and cosmic powers. The work manifests the same needs as a person, it needs to be "fed," *la tengo que bañar y vestir.*

When invoked in rite, the object/event is "present;" that is, "enacted," it is both a physical thing and the power that infuses it. It is metaphysical in that it "spins its energies between gods and humans" and its task is to move the gods. This type of work dedicates itself to managing the universe and its energies. I'm not sure what it is when it is at rest (not in performance). It may or may not be a "work" then. A mask may only have the power of presence during a ritual dance and the rest of the time it may merely be a "thing." Some works exist forever invoked, always in performance. I'm thinking of totem poles, cave paintings. Invoked art is communal and speaks of everyday life. It is dedicated to the validation of humans; that is, it makes people hopeful, happy, secure, and it can have negative effects as well, which propel one towards a search for validation.

The aesthetic of virtuosity, art typical of Western European cultures, attempts to manage the energies of its own internal system such as conflicts, harmonies, resolutions and balances. It bears the presences of qualities and internal meanings. It is dedicated to the validation of itself. Its task is to move humans by means of achieving mastery in content, technique, feeling. Western art is always whole and always "in power." It is individual (not communal). It is "psychological" in that it spins its energies between itself and its witness.

Western cultures behave differently toward works of art than do tribal cultures. The "sacrifices" Western cultures make are in housing their art works in the best structures designed by the best architects; and in servicing them with insurance, guards to protect them, conservators to maintain them, specialists to mount and display them, and the educated and upper classes to "view" them. Tribal cultures keep art works in honored and sacred places in the home and elsewhere. They attend them by making sacrifices of blood (goat or chicken), libations of wine. They bathe, feed, and clothe them. The works are treated not just as objects, but also as persons. The "witness" is a participant in the enactment of the work in a ritual, and not a member of the privileged classes.

Ethnocentrism is the tyranny of Western aesthetics. An Indian mask in an American museum is transposed into an alien aesthetic system where what is missing is the presence of power invoked through performance ritual. It has become a conquered thing, a dead "thing" separated from nature and, therefore, its power.

Modern Western painters have "borrowed," copied, or otherwise extrapolated the art of tribal cultures and called it cubism, surrealism, symbolism. The music, the beat of the drum, the Blacks' jive talk. All taken over. Whites, along with a good number of our own people, have cut themselves off from their spiritual roots, and they take our spiritual art objects in an unconscious attempt to get them back. If they're going to do it, I'd like them to be aware of what they are doing and to go about doing it the right way. Let's all stop importing Greek myths and the Western Cartesian split point of view and root ourselves in the mythological soil and soul of this continent. White America has only attended to the body of the earth in order to exploit it, never to succor it or to be nurtured in it. Instead of surreptitiously ripping off the vital energy of people of color and putting it to commercial use, whites could allow themselves to share and exchange and learn from us in a respectful way. By taking up *curanderismo*, Santeria, shamanism, Taoism, Zen and otherwise delving into the spiritual life and ceremonies of multi-colored people, Anglos would perhaps lose the white sterility they have in their kitchens, bathrooms, hospitals, mortuaries and missile bases. Though in the conscious mind, black and dark may be associated with death, evil and destruction, in the subconsious mind and in our dreams, white is associated with disease, death and hopelessness. Let us hope that the left hand, that of darkness, of femaleness, of "primitiveness," can divert the indifferent, right-handed, "rational" suicidal drive that, unchecked, could blow us into acid rain in a fraction of a millisecond.

Construction of the Female Self
Feminist Readings of the Disney Heroine

Jill Birnie Henke, Diane Zimmerman Umble, and Nancy J. Smith

Disney's early heroines, Cinderella and Aurora, are portrayed as helpless, passive victims who need protection. Indeed, Cinderella is the quintessential "perfect girl," always gentle, kind, and lovely. Their weaknesses are contrasted with the awesome and awful power of the evil women with whom they struggle. However, later Disney films shift from simple stories of passive, young virgins in conflict with evil, mature women to more complex narratives about rebellion, exploration, and danger. Heroines Ariel, Belle, and Pocahontas display an increasingly stronger sense of self, of choice, and of voice.

This growing empowerment of Disney heroines is reflected in shifting depictions of their intimate relationships. While early heroines fall in love at first sight and easily marry to live happily ever after, love relationships for the later heroines come at a cost. Ariel temporarily gives up her voice and ultimately relinquishes her cultural identity. Belle discovers love only through trials, sacrifice, and learning to look beneath the surface. Ultimately, though, her love releases the Beast from the bonds of his own selfishness so they, too, are "empowered" to live happily ever after together.

Of all of Disney's characters, Pocahontas seems to break new ground. The narrative begins with her as a young woman in possession of a strong, well-developed sense of self, and a conviction that her destiny only remains to be discovered. Unlike other Disney heroines, she resists losing her identity to another for the sake of a marriage relationship. Her position and value in her community, her relationships with other females, and her understanding of her interdependence with the earth provide the most holistic picture yet of a co-actively empowered character in Disney animated films.

. . .

The five films we examine situate the central female character—who is portrayed as gentle, kind, beautiful, and virginal—in an oppressive social milieu where mothers or other sources of female guidance and wisdom are largely absent. Until *Pocahontas,* in fact, these young heroines faced the challenges of their lives without the benefit of other women's support, nurturance, or guidance.

Cinderella, Aurora, Ariel, Belle, and Pocahontas also share another quality: they all have dreams. Each differs, however, in her power to make that dream come true. The conventional Disney tale introduces the heroine near the film's beginning through a song in which she expresses these dreams. For example, viewers first meet Cinderella when she awakens from a dream and sings, "No matter how your heart is grieving, if you keep on believing, the dream that you wish will come true." Minutes later, viewers discover that her daily reality is anything but dreamy. Supported by an army of mice and barnyard animals who come to her aid, Cinderella is continuously reminded by humans in the household that she is unworthy of their "refined" company. Cinderella's stepmother and stepsisters control Cinderella, keeping her locked away from both society and opportunity. Cinderella is portrayed as powerless to act on her own behalf. Hence, she can only dream.

Perhaps Cinderella best illustrates the Disney pattern of subjugating and stifling heroines' voices and selfhood. Her gentleness and goodness are defined by her lack of resistance to abuse by her stepfamily in the film's world. She never disobeys an order, never defends her rights, and never challenges their authority over her. She rarely eats, seldom sleeps, and receives not even the simplest of courtesies, except from her animal friends. Her father's fortune is squandered for the benefit of her stepsisters. She is powerless to control her own fate in her own home. Unable to control her own time, she also is unable to control her own destiny. Cinderella does not act, she only reacts to those around her, a sure sign of both external and internalized oppression. In the face of all this abuse, she somehow remains gentle, kind and beautiful—the perfect girl.

Similarly, *Sleeping Beauty*'s Aurora is a playful teenager whose friends are forest animals, and whose dream is expressed in the song "Some day my prince will come." Aurora is on the verge of celebrating her sixteenth birthday—the day her identity will be revealed to her. At this point she has no knowledge that she really is a princess who was betrothed at birth. Her parents' choices for her define Aurora's destiny; and she has no voice in shaping that destiny.

Like Cinderella, Aurora is obedient, beautiful, acquiescent to authority, and essentially powerless in matters regarding her own fate. Furthermore, there is no one Aurora can trust. Although the fairies "protect" her from the truth about her identity and the curse on her future "for her own good," Aurora can take no ac-

tion on her own behalf. Passively, she is brought back to the castle where she falls under the spell of Maleficent, touches the spinning wheel, and sleeps through most of the film while others battle to decide her future. When she awakens, she finds her "dream come true," a tall, handsome prince who rescues her from an evil female's curse.

Beginning with *The Little Mermaid*, however, the female protagonist shows signs of selfhood. Near the beginning of the film, Ariel sings of her dream to explore and her feelings of being misunderstood. She also expresses frustration and resistance: "Betcha on land they understand. Bet they don't reprimand their daughters. Bright young women, sick of swimmin', ready to stand." She asks, "When's it my turn?"

In contrast to the two previous demure female protagonists, Ariel is characterized as willful and disobedient. She follows her dreams even though she knows her actions run counter to the wishes of her father, King Triton. As a result, Triton charges the crab, Sebastian, with chaperoning his daughter "to protect her from herself." One might also read his actions as patriarchy's efforts to prevent her from achieving an independent identity. However, despite Triton's efforts to control Ariel, she explores, she asks questions, she makes choices, and she acts. For example, she rescues the human, Prince Eric, from the sea. She strikes a bargain with the sea witch, Ursula, to trade her voice for legs. Additionally, she prevents Eric's marriage to Ursula and protects him from Ursula's attack in the film's final battle. Nevertheless, it is Eric who finally kills the sea witch and it is Triton whose power enables Ariel to return to the human world by transforming her permanently into a human. Thus, while Ariel chooses to leave her own people for a life with Eric, it is still not her power but her father's power which enables her dreams to come to fruition.

Articulating one's own dreams and wishes—possessing an autonomous voice—is a strong indicator of the development of selfhood. Little wonder, then, that alarms sound for feminists concerned with the psychological development of girls and women's sense of self when Ariel literally sacrifices her voice and mermaid body to win Eric's love. What is gained by females who silence themselves in a masculinist society? What are the costs to their psychic selves for not doing so? Scholars in feminist psychological development describe the seductiveness of external rewards by denying one's selfhood. Having a voice, a sense of selfhood, is risky because it is inconsistent with images of the "perfect girl" or the true woman. When one's loyalty is not to the "masculinist system," one can end up on the margins at best and at worst socially "dead." Ultimately, Ariel's voice is silenced and she sacrifices her curiosity to gain the love of a man.

Reality for Belle in *Beauty and the Beast* means being female and wanting to experience adventure in the "great wide somewhere." Like the earlier Disney heroines, Belle dreams of having "so much more than they've got planned." Belle is the first of the Disney heroines to read, but her reading also alienates her from others in the community. She experiences herself as an "other." Townspeople call her peculiar and say that "she don't quite fit in." While Belle is aware of their opinions of her, and understands that she is supposed to marry a villager, raise a family, and conform, she also knows that she *is* different and *wants* something different—something "grand." Although Belle is unsure about how to attain her dreams, she does refuse to marry Gaston, the community "hunk" and its most eligible bachelor. She reads rather than socialize with the villagers, and she accepts that she can be nothing other than different from them. Belle likes herself and trusts her own judgment. Nevertheless, Belle is marginalized by the community for her uniqueness, for her sense of self.

Unlike her counterparts in *Cinderella* and *Sleeping Beauty,* Belle is no damsel in distress. Neither is she a helpless witness to the film's action nor removed from it. Belle occupies double the screen time of any other character in the film, and Belle acts for herself. She dreams of more than a "provincial life"; she wants adven-

ture and, as she sings, "for once it might be grand, to have someone understand, I want so much more than they've got planned." The line might have continued, "for a girl!"

Gaston, the village brute, is attracted to Belle because of her appearance not her brain. He sings that she's "the most beautiful, so that makes her the best." He offers her a place in the community with his marriage proposal. While other women swoon for his attention, Belle rejects him: "His little wife. No, sir. Not me!" Belle's sense of self is strong enough that she refuses to settle for less than a relationship which acknowledges and values her mind, in essence, her self. However, when her father is captured by the Beast, Belle comes to his rescue and offers herself in his place. By trading her life for her father's, she seems to have relinquished her selfhood. Once a prisoner in the Beast's castle, she laments to Mrs. Potts, a kind teapot, that she has lost her father, her dreams, "everything." However, this lament suggests that she still has dreams of her own and a sense of identity apart from that of a dutiful daughter.

Belle's dilemma occurs in part because she has a caring, co-active power relationship with her father. Decision making undertaken by women who attempt to maintain selfhood but also exist in a power-with relation to others becomes much more complex, as Gilligan notes. This complexity is further illustrated by the choices that Belle subsequently makes in her relationship with the Beast. Belle negotiates the conflict she feels between freedom from the Beast and her growing affection for him. She decides not to leave him in the woods after he rescues her from wolves. Although she could escape, she chooses to help him instead. Later in the film, she again chooses to return to the Beast's castle to warn him of the impending mob, even though the Beast has released her from her promise to stay in his castle.

Like Ariel, Belle has freedom to make choices and to act on her own behalf as well as on the behalf of others; and she exercises that freedom. However, whereas Ariel at least initially seems to act out of a sense of rebellion,

Belle's motivation appears to come from a craving for intellectual engagement. A simple masculinist interpretation might be that Belle acts out of a sense of personal honor or duty (to sacrifice her freedom first to help her father and later to keep the Beast). A more feminist interpretation based on Gilligan's psychoanalytic development work and standpoint theory might be that Belle acts as a result of the tension from seeking selfhood and relationships with others simultaneously. Thus, Belle's actions can be read as a series of complex decisions about when to act, and when to care for someone, how to administer comfort, when to take matters into her own hands, when to risk her personal safety. She is concerned not only with others but with herself as well, and her actions speak to both needs.

No victim, Belle sets the terms for the bargains she makes. In this sense, she exercises more power on her own behalf than previous Disney heroines. For Cinderella, Aurora, and Ariel, someone in power established the conditions within which their dreams could be realized. For example, Cinderella's fairy godmother gave her only until midnight to make her dream come true. At Aurora's christening, the good fairy Merryweather saved Aurora from Maleficent's death curse by decreeing that Aurora would sleep until awakened by a prince's kiss. And when Ariel gave her voice to Ursula in return for the sea witch's magical ability to transform Ariel into a human, Ursula placed a three day time limit on Ariel's pursuit to win Eric's love. Unlike Belle, these females have limited and tenuous opportunities to achieve their dreams. In contrast, Belle exercises substantial control over setting the terms of her own fate. She preserves her own options—by refusing Gaston's overtures and brushing off the villagers' criticisms, and she gives others options—by freeing her father from the Beast's prison, becoming a prisoner herself, and saving the Beast from the wolves. *She* holds *their* futures in her hands. Yet, ironically, one reading of the narrative conclusion is that Belle's liberation of the Beast from his spell ends with her becoming yet another "perfect girl" who marries the prince and lives happily ever after.

Another theme introduced in *Beauty and the Beast*—heroine as teacher—is expanded in *Pocahontas*. Just as Belle teaches the Beast how to be civil, gentle, and caring, Pocahontas teaches John Smith, her tribe, and the Englishmen about nature, power, and peace. Like Belle, Pocahontas exercises power over her future. Viewers first are introduced to Pocahontas going where the wind (the spirit of her mother) leads her; as the chief's daughter, however, she knows that she must take "her place" among her people. Her father tells her, "Even the wild mountain stream must someday join the big river." She sings, "We must all pay a price. To be safe, we lose our chance of ever knowing what's around the river bend. . . . Why do all my dreams stand just around the river bend. . . . Is all my dreaming at an end?"

Like Ariel, Pocahontas defies her father in exploring the world. Like Belle, she is an active doer, not a passive victim. She also has a savage to tame in the form of an Englishman. Pocahontas introduces John Smith to the colors of the wind and to the mysteries of the world of nature. She takes political stances such as advocating alternatives to violence, and she makes choices about her life. For example, Pocahontas' decision to reject both her father's wish that she marry Kocoum, the Powhatan warrior, and John Smith's plea to go with him back to England signify that the power to control her actions is in her hands. Pocahontas' choices reflect a sense of selfhood that is a bold stroke for a Disney heroine. A feminist psychological reading might see in her decision to embrace her cultural roots an alternative to Disney's typical heterosexual narratives in which the "perfect girl's" destiny is a monogamous relationship with a (white) man. Indeed, far more than Belle, Pocahontas finds power within to express a self which is separate from that defined through relationships to a father or love interest.

Our reading of Pocahontas implies that she is clearly the most elaborate and complex character in this group of heroines. Her dreams direct her choices. She weighs the risks of choosing a smooth course versus seeking the unknown course to see what awaits her just around the river bend. With counsel from female mentors, Grandmother Willow and the spirit of the wind that symbolizes her mother, Pocahontas finds the strength to listen to her own inner voice, and to choose the less safe, uncharted course of autonomous womanhood. When confronted with the option of leaving her community in order to accompany her love interest, John Smith, she rejects his offer and instead takes her place as an unattached female leader of her people.

Pocahontas brings to the forefront the absence of diversity among Disney's previous female characters. From Cinderella through Belle, Disney's female protagonists easily could be the same characters with only slight varia-tions in hair color. Pocahontas, too, varies only slightly in skin color, but she is the first non-Anglo heroine who is the subject of a Disney animated film. Furthermore, although some of the women may not have difficult family circumstances, (e.g., Cinderella), as Caucasians, they all belong to the privileged class in their societies, as daughters of kings, Indian chiefs, and educated inventors.

As this examination of Cinderella, Aurora, Ariel, Belle, and Pocahontas demonstrates, over time Disney's female protagonists have begun to look beyond home, to practice resistance to coercion, and to find their own unique female voices. Indeed, in Pocahontas Disney offers an adventurous female who develops a sense of self in a culture other than the dominant Anglo culture, and who chooses a destiny other than that of heterosexual romantic fulfillment.

From Fly-Girls to Bitches and Hos

Joan Morgan

Any feminism that fails to acknowledge that black folks in nineties America are living and trying to love in a war zone is useless to our struggle against sexism. Though it's often portrayed as part of the problem, rap music is essential to that struggle because it takes us straight to the battlefield.

My decision to expose myself to the sexism of Dr. Dre, Ice Cube, Snoop Dogg, or the Notorious B.I.G. is really my plea to my brothers to tell me who they are. I need to know why they are so angry at me. Why is disrespecting me one of the few things that make them feel like men? What's the haps, what are you going through on the daily that's got you acting so foul?

As a black woman and a feminist I listen to the music with a willingness to see past the machismo in order to be clear about what I'm *really* dealing with. What I hear frightens me. On booming track after booming track, I hear brothers talking about spending each day high as hell on malt liquor and Chronic. Don't sleep. What passes for "40 and a blunt" good times in most of hip-hop is really alcoholism, substance abuse, and chemical dependency. When brothers can talk so cavalierly about killing each other and then reveal that they have no expectation to see their twenty-first birthday, that is straight-up depression *masquerading* as machismo.

Anyone curious about the process and pathologies that form the psyche of the young, black, and criminal-minded needs to revisit our dearly departed Notorious B.I.G.'s first album, *Ready to Die*. Chronicling the life and times of the urban "soldier," the album is a blues-laden soul train that took us on a hustler's life journey. We boarded with the story of his birth, strategically stopped to view his dysfunctional, warring family, his first robbery, his first stint in jail, murder, drug-dealing, getting paid, partying, sexin', rappin', mayhem, and death. Biggie's player persona might have momentarily convinced the listener that he was livin' phat without a care in the world but other moments divulged his inner hell. The chorus of "Everyday Struggle": *I don't wanna live no more / Sometimes I see death knockin' at my front door* revealed that "Big Poppa" was also plagued with guilt, regret, and depression. The album ultimately ended with his suicide.

The seemingly impenetrable wall of sexism in rap music is really the complex mask African-Americans often wear both to hide and express the pain. At the close of this millennium, hip-hop is still one of the few forums in which young black men, even surreptitiously, are allowed to express their pain.

When it comes to the struggle against sexism and our intimate relationships with black men, some of the most on-point feminist advice I've received comes from sistas like my mother, who wouldn't dream of using the term. During our battle to resolve our complicated relationships with my equally wonderful and errant father, my mother presented me with the following gems of wisdom, "One of the most important lessons you will ever learn in life and love, is that you've got to love people for what they are—not for who you would like them to be."

This is crystal clear to me when I'm listening to hip-hop. Yeah, sistas are hurt when we hear brothers calling us bitches and hos. But the real crime isn't the name-calling, it's their failure to love us—to be our brothers in the way that we commit ourselves to being their sistas. But recognize: Any man who doesn't truly love himself is incapable of loving us in the healthy way we need to be loved. It's extremely telling that men who can only see us as "bitches" and "hos" refer to themselves only as "niggas."

In the interest of our emotional health and overall sanity, black women have got to learn to love brothers realistically, and that means differentiating between who they are and who we'd like them to be. Black men are engaged in a war where the real enemies—racism and the white power structure—are masters of camouflage. They've conditioned our men to believe the enemy is brown. The effects of this have been as wicked as they've been debilitating. Being in battle with an enemy that looks just like you makes it hard to believe in the basics every human being needs. For too many black men there is no trust, no community, no family. Just self.

Since hip-hop is the mirror in which so many brothers see themselves, it's significant that one of the music's most prevalent mythologies is that black boys rarely grow into men. Instead, they remain perpetually post-adolescent or die. For all the machismo and testosterone in the music, it's frighteningly clear that many brothers see themselves as powerless when it comes to facing the evils of the larger society, accepting responsibility for their lives, or the lives of their children.

So, sista friends, we gotta do what any rational, survivalist-minded person would do after finding herself in a relationship with someone whose pain makes him abusive. We've gotta continue to give up the love but *from a distance that's safe*. Emotional distance is a great enabler of unconditional love and support because it allows us to recognize that the attack, the "bitch, ho" bullshit—isn't personal but part of the illness.

And the focus of black feminists has got to change. We can't afford to keep expending energy on banal discussions of sexism in rap when sexism is only part of a huge set of problems. Continuing on our previous path is akin to demanding that a fiending, broke crackhead not rob you blind because it's *wrong* to do so.

If feminism intends to have any relevance in the lives of the majority of black women, if it intends to move past theory and become functional it has to rescue itself from the ivory towers of academia. Like it or not, hip-hop is not only the dominion of the young, black, and male, it is also the world in which young black women live and survive. A functional game plan for us, one that is going to be as helpful to Shequanna on 142nd as it is to Samantha at Sarah Lawrence, has to recognize hip-hop's ability to articulate the pain our *community* is in and use that knowledge to create a redemptive, healing space.

Notice the emphasis on "community." Hip-hop isn't only instrumental in exposing black men's pain, it brings the healing sistas need right to the surface. Sad as it may be, it's time to stop ignoring the fact that rappers meet "bitches" and "hos" daily—women who re-affirm their depiction of us on vinyl. Backstage, the road, and the 'hood are populated with women who would do anything to be with a rapper sexually for an hour if not a night. It's time to stop fronting like we don't know who rapper Jeru the Damaja was talking about when he said:

> Now a queen's a queen but a stunt's a stunt
> You can tell whose who by the things they want

Sex has long been the bartering chip that women use to gain protection, material wealth, and the vicarious benefits of power. In the black community, where women are given less access to all of the above, "trickin'" becomes a means of leveling the playing field. Denying the jus-tifiable anger of rappers—men who couldn't get the time of day from these women before a few dollars and a record deal—isn't empower-ing or strategic. Turning a blind eye and scam-pering for moral high ground diverts our at-tention away from the young women who are being denied access to power and are suf-fering for it.

It might've been more convenient to direct our sista-fied rage attention to "the sexist rep-resentation of women" in those now infamous Sir Mix-A-Lot videos, to fuss over *one* sexist rapper, but wouldn't it have been more pro-ductive to address the failing self-esteem of the 150 or so half-naked young women who were willing, unpaid participants? And what about how flip we are when it comes to using the b-word to describe each other? At some point we've all been the recipients of competitive, unsisterly, "bitchiness," particularly when vy-ing for male attention.

Since being black and a woman makes me fluent in both isms, I sometimes use racism as an illuminating analogy. Black folks have finally gotten to the point where we recognize that we sometimes engage in oppressive be-haviors that white folks have little to do with. Complexion prejudices and classism are ill-nesses which have their *roots* in white racism but the perpetrators are certainly black.

Similarly, sistas have to confront the ways we're complicit in our own oppression. Sad to say it, but many of the ways in which men ex-ploit our images and sexuality in hip-hop is done with our permission and cooperation. We need to be as accountable to each other as we believe "race traitors" (i.e., 100 or so brothers in blackface cooning in a skinhead's music video) should be to our community. To acknowledge this doesn't deny our victimization but it does raise the critical issue of whose responsibility it is to end our oppression. As a feminist, I believe it is too great a responsibility to leave to men.

A few years ago, on an airplane making its way to Montego Bay, I received another gem of girlfriend wisdom from a sixty-year-old self-declared non-feminist. She was meeting her husband to celebrate her thirty-fifth wedding anniversary. After telling her I was twenty-seven and very much single, she looked at me and shook her head sadly. "I feel sorry for your generation. You don't know how to have rela-tionships, especially the women." Curious, I asked her why she thought this was. "The women of your generation, you want to be right. The women of my generation, we didn't care about being right. We just wanted to win."

Too much of the discussion regarding sex-ism and the music focuses on being right. We feel we're *right* and the rappers are wrong. The rappers feel it's their *right* to describe their "reality" in any way they see fit. The store owners feel it's their *right* to sell whatever the consumer wants to buy. The consumer feels it's his *right* to be able to decide what he wants to listen to. We may be the "rightest" of the bunch but we sure as hell ain't doing the winning.

I believe hip-hop can help us win. Let's start by recognizing that its illuminating, informative narration and its incredible ability to articulate our collective pain is an invaluable tool when examining gender relations. The information we amass can help create a redemptive, healing space for brothers and sistas.

We're all winners when a space exists for brothers to honestly state and explore the roots of their pain and subsequently their misogyny, sans judgment. It is criminal that the only space our society provided for the late Tupac Shakur to examine the pain, confusion, drug addiction, and fear that led to his arrest and his eventual assassination was in a prison cell. How can we win if a prison cell is the only space an immensely talented but troubled young black man could dare utter these words: "Even though I'm not guilty of the charges they gave me, I'm not innocent in terms of the way I was acting. I'm just as guilty for not doing things. Not with this case but with my life. I had a job to do and I never showed up. I was so scared of this responsibility that I was running away from it." We have to do better than this for our men.

And we have to do better for ourselves. We desperately need a space to lovingly address the uncomfortable issues of our failing self-esteem, the ways we sexualize and objectify ourselves, our confusion about sex and love and the unhealthy, unloving, unsisterly ways we treat each other. Commitment to developing these spaces gives our community the potential for remedies based on honest, clear diagnoses.

As I'm a black woman, I am aware that this doubles my workload—that I am definitely going to have to listen to a lot of shit I won't like—but without these candid discussions, there is little to no hope of exorcising the illness that hurts and sometimes kills us.

READING 66

Averting the Male Gaze
Visual Pleasure and Images of Fat Women

Jane Feuer

It follows from all this, however, that there is such a process as coming out as a fat woman. Like the other, more materially dangerous kind of coming out, it involves the risk—here, a certainty—of uttering bathetically as a brave declaration that truth which can scarcely in this instance ever have been less than self-evident. Also like the other kind of coming out, however, denomination of oneself as a fat woman is a way in the first place of making clear to the people around one that their cultural meanings will be, and will be heard as, assaultive and diminishing to the de-gree that they are not fat-affirmative. In the second place and far more importantly, it is a way of staking one's claim to insist on, and participate actively in, a renegotiation of the representational contract between one's body and one's world.

—Eve Sedgwick, "Divinity," in Tendencies (1993)

Two things happened in the 1980s that led to the increasing visibility of fat women in the mass media: the clothing industry discovered fat women as a market; and the size acceptance movement grew to the point where there existed enough fat women with sufficient self-esteem to fill that market. Thus the impetus for the increased media representation of the fat female body in the 1990s came both from mainstream capitalist market-driven needs and from the more organic needs of fat women to achieve self-respect. This essay analyzes the emergence of the fat woman to a position of visibility in contemporary media representations. My approach to this topic attempts to unite two perspectives central to cultural studies today—the idea of a social movement and the idea of the "male gaze." As a social movement—or rather a bundle of social movements ranging from demands for civil rights to a radical rethinking of body politics—fat liberation resembles but is not identical to black, gay, and women's liberation movements. The parallels between fat acceptance/fat liberation and these other social movements are, however, striking. In fact, fat activism sprang from the women's movement as early as the early 1970s; civil rights activism for fat Americans began even earlier. Both, however, thrived in the 1980s, the supposed era of political inactivity (unless you were gay or fat or both). Resembling other social movements, the "fat movement" has always possessed both a "radical" and a "mainstream" branch: the former questioning the fat phobia of even the most radical lesbian feminists; the latter organizing for civil rights and fat acceptance. (NAAFA was originally called "National Association to Aid Fat Americans." It was later changed to "advance fat *acceptance*," a term long associated with quests for equal rights under the law.) Like gay rights and other civil rights battles, fat politics based on an end to discrimination against fat Americans has anchored itself philosophically in recent "scientific" research showing that fat people are born that way and do not eat more than thin people. In other words, like homosexuality as it is now conceptualized on TV talk shows, fat is nature, not nurture; therefore, it is wrong to discriminate against fat people, since they are *not* merely thin people who eat too much.

On the other hand, the seemingly more radical politics of fat liberation stems from lesbian feminist politics and the failure of these women's movements to critique their own fat phobia. According to Vivian F. Mayer, "So far, feminist fat liberation is the only fat voice that offers a cogent and radical analysis of fat oppression, and that suggests ways to end the oppression that are linked with other human liberation struggles." It was a supposedly radical feminist branch of the fat movement that has been most influenced by psychoanalytical interpretations of why women are fat; Susie Orbach's *Fat Is a Feminist Issue* promised that the resolution of psychic conflicts would lead to the reduction of compulsive eating and hence weight loss. It should be noted that many lesbian feminist fat activists do not subscribe to Orbach's Freudian disease model of fat; in fact, they prefer not to psychoanalyze at all. That's why the brief history I am giving here is already too binary: one could equally argue that the very rejection of psychological models for fat is the most radical position of all. But that is not the subject of this essay.

The antidieting/fat acceptance movement is a grassroots political movement that was rapidly taken up by capitalist industries. It was the commodification/objectification of the fat body made possible by the fashion industry's constructing the fat consumer as a *market* that enabled this movement to achieve media representation. That is to say, in order for fat women to achieve visual representation in the 1980s, we had to enter into beauty culture. This was accomplished by an expansion of beauty culture and fashion to include women who wore sizes 16 to 26. The plus-size clothing industry expanded at all levels: the older lower-priced chains (such as Lane Bryant) became more trendy; up-scale boutiques for fat women sprang up in various cities (for example, The Forgotten Woman in New York, Chicago, and other cities); and a more politicized, feminist branch of the clothing industry provided natural fibers for the very fattest women as well (notably, Making it Big in California) while maintaining a cottage-industry relationship to its mail-order public. Thus it's difficult to say whether the growth of the plus-size fashion industry during the eighties was the cause or the effect of fat-affirmative politics insofar as these politics enabled media representation. In other words, how can you be on TV with nothing to wear? But how can you create a market for beautiful clothing for fat women to wear without having first imaged them in an affirmative way? Therefore the fat acceptance movement challenges certain Marxist social movement theories that equate commodification with alienation. It also challenges those feminist theories of representation based on the idea that the objectification and commodification of the female body is necessarily the property of a male gaze that is productive of visual pleasure.

The generally acknowledged mother and father of the theory of the male gaze are Laura Mulvey and John Berger. In spite of the fact that she was writing about classical Hollywood film language and he was writing about a much older tradition of European oil painting, the theories are remarkably similar in their emphasis on the fact of the gaze and the fascination posed by its object. For Berger, a male spectator-owner gazes at the woman in the oil painting; she is aware of being seen and responds with calculated charm. For Mulvey, to put it in Berger's terms, men in classical Hollywood cinema act and women appear. Men forward the narrative; women stop it for the gaze. The Hollywood goddess thus objectified in the gaze becomes the object of a presumed male spectator/subject's scopophilia.

Although I do not deny the value of these views from the 1970s or even their explanatory power for many, many images in today's popular culture, I wonder that neither author ever mentioned that the women portrayed in the oil paintings and in the movies (e.g., Jane Russell) are, by today's standards, decidedly fat. Hollywood pinups of the 1940s are at least zaftig by comparison to the early 1990s "waif look" of model Kate Moss; the women in oil paintings are, by any contemporary standard of measurement, obese.

The theory of the male gaze should always be historicized according to the beauty norms of its period. An exemplary text in this regard is Susan Bordo's essay "Reading the Slender Body," in which she "reads" a cultural shift occurring throughout the eighties and early 1990s from a preference for bodies that are merely thin to ones with "firm bodily margins." As Bordo argues, "Until the 1980s, excess weight was the target of most ads for diet products; today, one is much more likely to find the enemy constructed as bulge, fat, or flab." She refers to a *20/20* show in which ten-year-old boys responded to a slight bulge about the hips of emaciated fashion models by calling them fat.

I seriously doubt that the images cited by Berger and Mulvey would evoke a lustful look in my young male students today, and I know for a fact that the women students (whose body-image standards tend to be thinner than the boys') find them repulsive. So where is the much-touted pleasure in looking that is supposed to evoke the male gaze? Does the male gaze of 1994 look away or make little pig noises when it realizes these Renaissance babes are porkers? That is to say, the Berger / Mulvey theory of the male gaze tends to be used in a manner that is both ahistorical and formalist. It analyzes the fact and direction and subjectivity of the gaze without always considering the simple vulgar content of the image.

To refuse the male gaze is not necessarily to refuse the norms of beauty culture. We need to distinguish among issues involving the male gaze, those involving norms of beauty culture at a given time, and those involving body size per se. In fact, I argue that it is only by approximating other norms of beauty culture and thus evoking a male gaze that fat women today can gain access to representation in a form that does not code them as repellent. . . .

On a 1992 *Maury Povich Show*, a proud, fat Latina appeared on stage with three formerly fat women now dressed up as parodies of seventeen-year-old skinny girls. The fat woman was dressed in a short silk nightie with see-through negligee and dyed-to-match high heels. Her purpose was to proudly display to the world evidence that at 200-plus pounds, a woman could still be sexy. Both the other women on the panel and some men in the audience were not buying it, although the women protested far more vehemently. In fact, a man in the audience wasn't even hostile; he simply could not understand why this woman liked herself. Finally, an aging blonde in a go-go dress summed it up from the podium, "Let's face it. Men do not find fat sexy." Almost any talk show on the subject of fat will arrive at the same contradictions, despite variations (for instance, Oprah tends more toward probing group-therapy discourse and self-display). That is to say, women who are not ashamed to be fat will be placed on the hot seat, using other women guests and audience members as custodians of the male gaze. In almost every case, a contradiction arises between the talk show ethos that in America everyone has the *right* to be themselves and the intuitive knowledge of social power relations that tells us heterosexual women had better be thin if they wish to attract the male gaze that will assure their position in the world. It is still difficult to find an example of a self-loving fat woman whose position is not set up as a *debate* with thin or formerly fat women.

. . .

Several years of random taping (1990–94) have brought me to the following conclusions as to the conditions under which fat women may appear on TV and not be subject to ridicule. Although it has long been acceptable for fat women to serve as objects of pity on TV talk shows (especially when they are holding Richard Simmons's hand), talk show guests may now be fat even if that is not the "issue" discussed on the program, so long as they are coded as "white trash." Oprah Winfrey may be fat, but she cannot at the same time be "svelte" or glamorous or self-fulfilled. Sexy Hispanic fat women may appear in see-through negligees on *Maury Povich*. The faceless heroic rescuers

(usually 911 phone operators) of reality TV may be quite fat, as may the mothers of children being rescued (although the actresses playing them in the re-creations are usually thinner). Roseanne, in the role of the blue-collar Roseanne Connor, was welcomed into homes everywhere (*Roseanne*, ABC, 1988–97). In short, fat women may appear "invisibly" on TV shows when they are also coded as lower class, asexual, and/or nonwhite.

The fat sister in the singing group Wilson Phillips (Carnie Wilson) can appear in the group's music videos but always fully clothed or in a headshot. If the other two appear in bathing suits on the beach, she must appear in a cover-up. When they appear on stage in skimpy dresses, she must be fully jacketed. While the camera eye gazes at the thin singers, it tends to avert its gaze from the fat one. Yet outside MTV, more avant-garde images are possible. There is an interesting centerfold of Wilson Phillips in the June 1992 *Vanity Fair*. The fat sister, Carnie Wilson, occupies the center of the photo and lays claim to not one but two male gazes. She is posed in décolletage, with cleavage, fingers lingering on her own breasts and eyes gazing outward in a sultry glance as two shirtless young men plant kisses on either cheek. To the other side of each man is one of the thinner members of the group, more fully clothed and in the effaced childlike poses of fashion photography. In many respects, however, this photo is a reversal of their more mainstream videos.

Ricki Lake may be fat in the movie *Hairspray* (John Waters, 1988), in *Babycakes* (1989; a made for TV remake of the 1985 German film *Sugarbaby* [Perdy Adlon]), and on *China Beach* (for the 1989–90 season), but not as the hostess of her own TV talk show. That is to say, fat women achieve media representation when they are already viewed as nonglamorous on the basis of other exclusions, or when they appear in media already otherwise marginalized. In the case of Ricki Lake, an emergence out of the John Waters/Divine tradition of the grotesque permitted her early screen career. In the case of

Jessye Norman, a large woman became a television diva by virtue of her status as an opera singer and the correspondence between her extraordinary body and her extraordinary voice. In her appearances on PBS and even riding in the Macy's Thanksgiving Day Parade, she is thus coded as exotic and "other" for TV viewers.

In the wake of the fat liberation movement, however, a few fat women have attempted to gain entry to mass media representation as an alternative model of beauty. The new Roseanne, still fat by conventional standards, but otherwise substantially altered, occupies an ambiguous position on the cover of the February 1994 *Vanity Fair,* as opposed to the infamous mud-wrestling issue *Vanity Fair* cover of herself and Tom Arnold in December 1990 (both photographed by Annie Leibovitz). In the 1990 incarnation, entitled "Roseanne on Top," Roseanne occupies the grotesque representational space of Divine, a parody of a woman. Her pendulous breasts weigh down on Tom Arnold's chest as she laughs wickedly from under a blonde wig. But the 1994 post-transformation cover is more ambiguous. She

poses in a semi-pornographic manner in a black bustier with high heels, stockings, and garter belt. Still a dominatrix, is she still also a parody of a woman? I would argue that the cover photo and the ones inside are readable as "parodies of woman" more in the manner of Madonna than of Divine. That is to say, they are meant to be taken half-seriously as glamour photos. Like Madonna in a similar pose, they may be interpreted as parodic but also erotic. The 1994 cover at least invites a male gaze; the 1990 cover crushes an actual man underneath Roseanne's fat body. Drawing on imagery from fat pornographic videos and magazines for "fat admirers," these eroticized images of fat women have met with mixed reactions from feminists. Yet as Laura Kipnis argues, "pornography's celebration of fat, even its "objectification" of fat women, is in defiance of all societal norms and social controls. . . . Pornography's insistence on visibility for fat forces the spectacle of fat as fat, rather than as an array of connotations. Fat is what our culture, for all of the reasons suggested, doesn't want to look at. Pornography, in response, puts it on view."

READING 67

The Oprahification of America
Talk Shows and the Public Sphere

Jane M. Shattuc

Today I am sitting between two people who have never been this close face to face since one very unforgettable night two years ago. Debbie says that the man sitting across from her locked her in a closed room, held a gun to her, and violently raped her. Jawah says Debbie is lying.

—Oprah Winfrey, The Oprah Winfrey Show, *May 3, 1994*

Are daytime TV talk shows simply sensational commercialism, or could they be a new form of political debate? Oprah Winfrey's visceral de-

scription from her May 3, 1994, show seemingly relegates the social issues involved in rape to the realm of cheap thrills. But on another level, the program's dramatic and individualized account allows ordinary citizens—in the studio and at home—to enter into a debate about sexual power in their everyday lives, a rare moment on network television.

Traditionally, democratic thought assumes that there must be an independent public arena where political opinion can be formed freely.

The arena should be entirely free of the taint of government control as well as that of corporation capitalism. For many Americans, the town meeting is the ideal of participatory democracy: the citizen takes part in the politics of the local community by standing up and speaking up. But such direct communication is becoming less tenable in the age of information technology and global communication.

If TV has become the central communicator of information in late capitalist America, no other public forum replicates the town meeting's democratic sensibility better than the first generation of daytime TV talk shows born in the 1970s and 1980s: *The Oprah Winfrey Show, Sally Jessy Raphael, Donahue,* and even *Geraldo.*[1] Here, "average" Americans debate important, albeit sensationalized, issues that are central to their political lives: racism, sexuality, welfare rights, and religious freedom. Would Jürgen Habermas have included the American talk show as part of the public sphere when he defined the latter as "the realm of our social life in which something approaching public opinion can be formed. . . . A portion of the public sphere comes into being in every conversation in which private individuals assemble to form a public body"?[2] The answer depends on whose definition of politics one invokes.

The concept of the public sphere—the place where public opinion can be formed—looms over all analyses of talk shows. From "The Talk Show Report" in *Ladies Home Journal* to think pieces about tabloid culture in the *New York Times* to a Marxist collective analysis of the genre in *Sociotext* to an article on talk and female empowerment in *Genders,* our culture is hyperconscious that daytime TV talk shows are involved in the political arena.[3] They are a rare breed: highly popular programs that depend on social topics and participation from average citizens. However, there is a fear that the programs may be trivializing "real" politics by promoting irrational, victimized, and anomalous individuals as representative of the citizenry. The print press often has pejoratively

alluded to the "Oprahification" of America. Yet the popularity of the shows continually highlights two questions: Can the content of talk shows be defined as "political"? And, more important, can the shows—the children of corporate media interests—be considered public arenas where the "people" form opinion freely?

Even though the women's movement has shown that politics in the late twentieth century includes the personal, American culture still is uncomfortable with describing the content of daytime talk shows as political. The term *political* is derived from the Latin *politicus,* which means relating to a citizen.[4] A citizen is defined by her or his allegiance to a state, which in return offers protection to the citizen. Obviously, the shows, with their dependence on spectacle, individualism, and sensation, deviate radically from the traditional political discussions about social policy that define citizenship—such as Oxford debates, congressional deliberations, union hall meetings, and even network news, which all emphasize established political institutions. Although the practice of debate has shifted from the Aristotelian model of speaker and listener to the coordinated discussion, the shows are more personal and emotional in content and vertiginous in structure, breaking with traditional structures in political discussion. Here, American politics moves from the "analytical is political" tradition to "the personal as political" in the latter half of the century.[5]

No other TV genre—not news, prime-time drama, or soap opera—generates more ongoing social controversy than daytime talk shows. Beyond the headline-grabbing *Jenny Jones* murder or Winfrey's cocaine confession, the shows provoke endless debates about everyday experience.[6] Not only does viewer give-and-take occur as part of the shows, but discussions continue on the news, in the workplace, and at home: the popularization of current political, social, and theoretical topics. The shows raise questions about fact versus fiction as the audience tests the credibility of the stories presented. (In the common vernacular: "Are those people for real?") They test the demarcation between entertainment and news, as they mix political issues and personal drama. Finally, the programs use ordinary people to stage social issues that are infrequently discussed elsewhere on television: homosexuality, familial conflict, sexual relations, and racial divisions. As the events of the 1990s bring into the political arena an angry African American underclass, gay activists, and working women, might the *Oprah* audience be the newest incarnation of the public sphere?

Even though Habermas concedes that, historically, the public sphere has been more an ideal than a fact, the concept still influences the assumptions of capitalist democracy. Hopes of a public sphere are evoked whenever a writer bemoans the passing of considered discussion of current events where the commercial pressures for "entertainment" have destroyed objectivity and truth. The *New York Times* represents this stance as the principal defender of "real" news when John J. O'Connor, the paper's TV critic, warns against "trash TV" and talk show sensation:

> There's a battle being waged in television these days and broadly speaking, it's taking place along "us versus them" cultural lines. Depending on your vantage point, the results so far could be interpreted as either democracy taking the offensive or the barbarians . . . are in the business of inventing emotional "wallops," and are openly contemptuous of what they like to refer to as "pointy-headed" journalists, meaning for the most part the college-educated kind that works in non-tabloid print.[7]

Here a newspaperman who writes about television for a traditional news medium suppresses questions about the objectivity in news reporting in favor of charges that tabloid or talk shows are manipulative or promote what another *New York Times* reporter calls "the new kind of dumbness."[8] This nostalgia for the loss

for the bourgeois public sphere is deeply intertwined with a kind of politics in which clear categories of power are maintained: a class, culture, and gender hierarchy based on the centrality of the educated white bourgeois male.[9] Not surprisingly, Phil Donahue is often nominated by the written press as the most "responsible" or "trusted" of hosts.[10]

The talk show industry self-consciously trades on the concept of "the people speaking." But when cultural studies critics speak of it as "an active audience," other critics have decried the concept as a "naive, unattainable ideal."[11] Within this pessimistic perspective, the problem of active viewers is twofold. Under a veneer of participation the talk show audience is a passive mass led by commercial interests and self-promoting hosts. The active audience of the shows can also be a forum for social control when the audience taunts, shouts down, and demands conformity of the "guest deviants."

Nevertheless, the feminist movement has launched a thoroughgoing critique of the public sphere and the dichotomy of a serious/trivial split that underpins the discussion about daytime talk shows.[12] From a feminist point of view, the problem lies in the fact that the public sphere is contrasted to the private sphere and therefore produces a not-so-subtle division between masculine and feminine realms: men participate in the serious realm of politics and rational debate; women govern the realm of the domestic arena and emotionalism.[13]

As a result, many feminists have come to champion talk shows as a new public sphere or counter-public sphere. Talk shows not only promote conversation and debate, they break down the distance between the audience and the stage. They do not depend on the power of expertise or bourgeois education. They elicit common sense and everyday experience as the mark of truth. They confound the distinction between the public and the private. Talk shows are about average women as citizens talking about and debating issues and experience.

. . .

. . . *Oprah* does challenge the supposed objectivity of traditional patriarchal power. The host—a big, black woman—undercuts the authority of the talk show debate format with her self-confessional style; she routinely admits her early sexual and drug abuse and a chronic struggle with weight loss. Her program also represents a potentially radical public sphere that privileges process over a single truth or closure.

Yet the structure of an *Oprah* program is typical of most daytime talk shows: problem/solution. Most often, the problem is introduced as a personal problem (for example, obesity, HIV positive, a bisexual spouse), but then is generalized to a larger social issue. For instance, an April 15, 1994, program on mothers who want to give up their violent children was generalized by Winfrey as "what really makes a child act this way." Either by taking the opposite side or by teasing out the other view, Winfrey questions the guest to flesh out the problem. The ubiquitous guest labels or "I.D.s" (in production parlance) underline the social representativeness of the guests; for example, one is a "mother who wants to give away a violent child," another is a "convicted woman who plotted her husband's death." The labeling offers a popularized version of the logic of identity politics, which attempts to break down the hegemonic notion of homogeneity or that "we all are one." Yet not all social divisions are represented; talk shows favor gender, sexual preference, familial, and criminal labels. Race and class remain structuring absences. The audience intuits these categories through the guest's appearance, words, and actions.

After establishing the guest's problem and social representativeness. Winfrey directs the debate through her selection of questioners and specifically through the rhetorical use of the pronouns *you, I,* and *we.* She invokes the audience as a larger social collectivity: "I am sure what mothers out there are thinking"; or "When I first heard about this, like everybody, I wondered what the big deal is"; or (my favorite, because it's Winfrey at her most self-aggrandizing) "The question we all have, I am speaking for the audience here and the audience around the world listening to you." As these quotations reveal, Winfrey engages an audience that actively thinks and adjudicates. It is also important that she positions herself with the audience as one of many outside observers/judges who have a social/personal stake in the issue.

Even though the host changes alignment from being sole authority to being a member of the audience, her/his authority is never relinquished. What many observers celebrate as Winfrey's debunking of her authority—she will even sit in the audience—also can be seen as a subtle move that allows her to orchestrate a collective response from the audience. When Wendy Kaminer in *I'm Dysfunctional, You're Dysfunctional* laments about her experience on *Oprah:* "If all issues are personalized, we lose our capacity to entertain ideas, to generalize from our own or someone else's experiences, to think abstractly," she has missed the point.[14] Such shows continually move from personal identification to larger group identification in order to be popular as a broad commercial medium. The host generalizes the particular experience into a larger social frame to capture the interest of a large audience. For all their individualized narratives, the shows speak in social generalities. They just do not speak about or advocate changing specific social and political institutions.

. . .

In general, talk shows do not offer traditional political topics. Rather, they translate politics into the everyday experience of the political. So the shows are rarely overtly "political." They are ultimately feminist not because they say they are but because they are populated by women and they discuss domestic and everyday experience as social problems. They do not follow the classical tradition of the bourgeois public sphere, where, J. B. Thompson maintains, "the authority of the state could be criticized by an informed and reasoning public or 'publicness.'"[15] The audience may or may not connect the discussion of abuse, sexual partners, and interracial conflict to legislation, elections, and news stories.

However, talk shows do offer proof that social experience is not a matter of ideology or false consciousness but, rather, has demonstrable consequences that can be proven through the physical and emotional evidence of its victims. Although the program and the experts establish and resolve the debate, the distant evidence of expert knowledge alone is no longer valid. Nor are the synthetic spectacles of commercial television programming acceptable. Rather, the talk show relies on the tangible or physical signs of the society: testimonials, emotions, and the body as well as laughter, facial expression, and tears. These are forms of argument and evidence available to the nonexperts or underclasses. And they are gaining acceptance as talk shows test the centrality of the educated bourgeoisie to define politics and debate.

Oddly enough, in this age of postmodern simulation, talk shows demand a belief in the authenticity of lived experience as a social truth. Perhaps, this belief is what the "Oprahification" of America really is. As one *Oprah* audience member stated on April 14, 1994: "Don't tell me how to feel. I am my experience."

Notes

1. I want to separate this first generation of talk shows of the 1970s and 1980s from the second generation of the 1990s hosted by Ricki Lake, Richard Bev, Gordon Elliot, Jenny Jones, and Jerry Springer. The phenomenal financial success of *The Oprah Winfrey Show* by 1990 spawned numerous new talk shows. Under the competition, the new programs changed the format considerably by removing the expert and social issues, emphasizing the implicit excess and sensation, and adding a campy or more tongue-in-cheek style. For further discussion of this generic shift, see my book, *The Talking Cure: Women and Talk Shows* (New York: Routledge, 1996).

2. "The Public Sphere: An Encyclopedia Article," *New German Critique* (autumn 1984): 49. For a more thorough discussion of the relation of talk shows to Habermas's public sphere, see Sonia Livingston and Peter Lunt, *Talk on Television: Audience Participation and Public Debate* (London: Routledge, 1994).

3. Barbara Lippert, "The Talk Show Report," *Ladies' Home Journal,* April 1994, 154–56, 210; John Corry, "A New Age of Television Tastelessness?" *New York Times,* 29 May 1988, 1; John J. Connor, "Defining What's Civilized and What's Not," *New York Times,* 25 April 1989, C18; Paolo Carpignano, Robin Andersen, Stanley Aronowitz, and William Difazio, "Chatter in the Age of Electronic Reproduction: Talk Television and the 'Public Mind,'" *Sociotext* 25–26 (1990): 33–55; Gloria-Jean Masciarotte, "C'mon Girl: Oprah Winfrey and the Discourse of Feminine Talk," *Genders* 11 (fall 1991): 81–110.

4. *Webster's New World Unabridged Dictionary,* 2d ed. (New York: Simon and Schuster, 1983), 1392.

5. Masciarotte, "C'mon Girl: Oprah and the Discourse of Feminine Talk," 89.

6. On March 6, 1995, during a taping of a Jenny Jones show on secret admirers, a Michigan man Scott Amedure surprised a male friend, Jon Schmitz, by admitting that he had a crush on him. The next day, Schmitz murdered Amedure, alleging that he had been "humiliated" by the exposure on national television. Jenny Jones and talk shows in general were blamed in the press for being irresponsible for misleading guests. See the cover story, Michelle Green, "Fatal Attraction," *People,* 27 March 1995, 40–44.

   Oprah Winfrey, host of *The Oprah Winfrey Show,* "confessed" her use of cocaine in front of a live audience during the taping of a program in late January 1995. The statement was reported on the evening news as well as the printed press. For the tabloid coverage, see cover stories, Jim Nelson, "Oprah and Cocaine: The Shocking Story She Didn't Tell You on TV," *National Inquirer,* 31 January 1995, 5; and Ken Harrell, "Oprah: 'How a Man Made Me Slave to Cocaine,'" *Globe,* 31 January 1995, 37.

7. O'Connor, "Defining What's Civilized and What's Not," C18.

8. Corry, "A New Age of Television Tastelessness?" sec. 2, 1.

9. Consider how a series of binary oppositions surface in these discussions of the liberal news tradition and the exploitative talk show genre: democratic versus biased, independent versus profit-oriented, serious versus trivial, educated versus uneducated, and masculine versus feminine.

10. For an example, see Eric Sherman, "Who's the Best? Donahue? Oprah? Someone Else?" *TV Guide*, 26 March 1986, 26. *Newsweek* describes Phil Donahue as "America's most trusted tour guide across today's constantly shifting social and cultural terrain" (*Newsweek*, 29 October 1979, 78).

11. Michael Schudsen, "Was There Ever a Public Sphere? If So, When? Reflections on the American Case," in *Habermas and the Public Sphere*, ed. Craig Calhoun (Cambridge, Mass.: MIT Press, 1992), 143–63.

12. See Nancy Fraser, *Unruly Practices: Power, Discourse, and Gender in Contemporary Social Theory* (Minneapolis: University of Minnesota Press, 1989), 113–43; Masciarotte, "C'mon Girl: Oprah and the Discourse of Feminine Talk," 81–110; and Patricia Mellencamp, *High Anxiety: Catastrophe, Scandal, Age, and Comedy* (Bloomington: Indiana University Press, 1990), 194–229.

13. In *Unruly Practices*, Nancy Fraser outlines this debate: "Consider, first, the relations between (official) private economy and private family as mediated by the roles of worker and consumer.

These roles, I submit, are gendered roles. And the links they forge between family and (official) economy are effected as much in the medium of gender identity as in the medium of money" (Fraser, *Unruly Practices*, 124). According to Fraser, one should also consider how the concept of the "citizen" is one associated with men: "as Habermas understands it, the citizen is centrally a participant in political debate and public opinion formation. This means that citizenship, in his view, depends crucially on the capacities for consent and speech, the ability to participate on a par with others in dialogue. But these are capacities connected with masculinity in a male-dominated, classical capitalism; they are in ways denied women and deemed at odds with femininity" (ibid.). As further evidence, Fraser cites studies on the inequalities in male/female dialogues and the lack of respect women have over consent in marital rape. She concludes by quoting Carole Pateman: "If women's words about consent are consistently reinterpreted, how can they participate in the debate among citizens?" (ibid.).

14. Wendy Kaminer, *I'm Dysfunctional. You're Dysfunctional: The Recovery Movement and Other Self-Help Fashions* (New York: Vintage, 1993), 38.

15. J. B. Thompson, *Ideology and Modern Culture: Critical Social Theory* (Cambridge: Polity Press, 1990), 112.

READING 68

Confessions of a Feminist Porno Star

Nina Hartley

"A feminist porno star?" Right, tell me another one, I can hear some feminists saying. I hear a chorus of disbelief, a lot like the two crows in the Disney movie "Dumbo"—"I thought I'd seen everything till I saw an elephant fly." On the surface, contradictions seem to abound. But one of the most basic tenets of feminism, a tenet with which I was inculcated by the age of ten, was the *right* to sexual free expression, without

being told by society (or men) what was right, wrong, good, or bad. But why porno? Simple— I'm an exhibitionist with a cause: to make sexually graphic (hard core) erotica, and today's porno is the only game in town. But it's a game where there is a possibility of the players, over time, getting some of the rules changed.

As I examine my life, I uncover the myriad influences that led me to conclude that it was perfectly natural for me to choose a career in adult films. I find performing in sexually explicit material satisfying on a number of levels. First, it provides a physically and psychically safe environment for me to live out my exhibitionistic fantasies. Secondly, it provides a surprisingly flexible and supportive arena for me to grow in as a *performer*, both sexually and non-sexually. Thirdly, it provides me with erotic material that I like to watch for my own pleasure. Finally, the medium allows me to explore the theme of celebrating a positive female sexuality—a sexuality that has heretofore been denied us. In choosing my roles and characterizations carefully, I strive to show, always, women who thoroughly enjoy sex and are forceful, self-satisfying and guilt-free without also being neurotic, unhappy or somehow unfulfilled.

. . .

Once I passed puberty, two books in particular were very influential in the continuing development of my personal sexual philosophy: *Our Bodies, Ourselves* and *The Happy Hooker.* The former taught me that women deserved to be happy sexually, that their bodies were wonderful and strong, and that all sexual fantasies were natural and okay as long as coercion was not involved. The latter book taught me that an intelligent, sexual woman could choose a job in the sex industry and not be a victim, but instead emerge even stronger and more self-confident, with a feeling, even, of self-actualization.

High school was uneventful—I became deeply involved in the excellent drama department at Berkeley High, exploring a long-standing interest in the theater arts. Contrary to a lot of adolescents' experiences with peer pressure in the realm of sex and drugs, I was lucky to have no pressure placed on me one way or another. . . . Consequently, I had a more active fantasy life than sex life, and was very ripe when I lost my virginity at eighteen to a man with whom I had my first long term relationship. This, unfortunately, had more forgettable moments than memorable ones. The sex and in-

timacy were mediocre at best, and I realized that my libido was not to have a good future with this man. My present husband is just the opposite. He gave full support for my long-dormant lesbian side; for the past four years I have lived with him and his long term woman lover in a close-knit, loving, supportive and intellectually stimulating *menage-a-trois.*

I stripped once a week while getting my bachelor's degree in nursing, magna cum laude, enjoying it to the fullest and using the performance opportunity to develop the public side of my sexuality. I went into full time movie work immediately following graduation, having done a few movies while still in school.

I know there are people who wonder, "Is she naive or something? What kind of a cause is porno?" But let's face it, folks: while the sex drive may be innate, modes of sexual behavior are learned, and I don't see Nancy Reagan setting up any "Happy, Healthy, Sex Life" institutes in the near future. If the media can have an effect on people's behavior, and I believe it does, why is it assumed that sex movies must always reinforce the most negative imagery of women? That certainly isn't what I'm about. From my very first movie I have always refused to portray rape, coercion, pain-as-pleasure, woman-as-victim, domination, humiliation and other forms of nonconsensual sex.

I can look back on all of my performances and see that I have not contributed to any negative images or depictions of women; and the feedback I get from men and women of all ages supports my contention. I get a lot of satisfaction from my job—for me it is a job of choice. As feminists, we must all fight to change our society so that women who don't want to do gender-stereotyped jobs can be free to work, support their families decently, and fulfill their potential in whatever job they choose. This includes not feeling compelled to do sex work because other well-paying options are severely limited.

Each of us has some idea or action that we hate but that is still protected by the First Amendment. I consider myself a reformer, and as a reformer I need a broad interpretation of the First Amendment to make my point. As a feminist I have principles that won't allow me to take license with that precious right to free speech. There have always been, and to some degree will always be, extremists who see the First Amendment as their license to do or say whatever, and not as a right which has implied responsibilities. Of course the sexual entertainment medium is no exception to this. I say censure them, but do not censor me.

DISCUSSION QUESTIONS FOR CHAPTER NINE

1. How do you think cultural forms shape gender? How might cultural forms function subversively to challenge traditional gender norms?

2. How do some television shows reflect changing gender norms while at the same time keeping most other norms intact? Can you name some examples?

3. What are some recent movies you've seen? How are women depicted in these movies? How is the gaze constructed in these movies?

4. How does pornography as a cultural form influence gender norms in U.S. society?

5. Why do you think some critics suggest there has never been a female Shakespeare or a female da Vinci? Do you agree with this assessment? Why or why not?

SUGGESTIONS FOR FURTHER READING

Brunsdon, Charlotte. *The Feminist, the Housewife, and the Soap Opera.* New York: Oxford University Press, 2000.

Hollows, Joanne. *Feminism, Femininity, and Popular Culture.* Manchester, England: Manchester University Press, 2000.

Meyers, Marian, ed. *Mediated Women: Representations in Popular Culture.* Bridgehampton, NY: Hampton Press, 1999.

Pollock, Griselda. *Differencing the Canon: Feminist Desire and the Writing of Art's Histories.* New York: Routledge, 1999.

Roberts, Robin. *Sexual Generations: 'Star Trek, the Next Generation' and Gender.* Champaign: University of Illinois Press, 1999.

Whiteley, Sheila. *Women and Popular Music: Sexuality, Identity, and Subjectivity.* New York: Routledge, 2000.

CHAPTER TEN

Resisting Violence against Women

Sexual, verbal, and physical abuse of women in the United States occurs at an alarming rate. About 2,000 rapes are committed daily at the rate of about one every 5 minutes. One out of every four women on college campuses has experienced sexual violence, and about one in three women will experience such violence in their lifetime. A woman is battered every 15 seconds, more than 4 million U.S. women are physically assaulted by their partners each year, and about 1,500 women are murdered every year by their partners. In 90 percent of cases where children are raped, it is by someone they know, and almost 30 percent of all rape victims are under the age of 11.

Violence against girls and women is a persistent problem all over the world, with some countries condoning or legalizing such crimes. The reading "Violence Against Women: An Issue of Human Rights" explains how violence against girls and women is the most pervasive form of human rights abuse in the world today. When the United Nations World Conference on Women met in Beijing, China, in 1995, the Platform for Action gave priority to addressing global violence against women as a human rights issue. Historically violence against women has also been a central aspect of wars and military occupation. Fiona Lee's article, "Militarism and Sexual Violence" explores the ways various military forces have encouraged the sexual exploitation of women.

What do you think would be the societal response if men and boys routinely were victimized in these ways by women and girls? As discussed in Chapter 2, because these crimes are against a whole group of people whose only connection is that they are female, it is appropriate to consider these abuses crimes of hate and misogyny. Although violence against women is not generally understood as a hate crime, there are various laws that have helped in this struggle. These include rape shield laws, which prevented a victim's sexual history from being used by defense attorneys, and various state rape reform laws. Mandatory arrest procedures in cases of domestic violence and the creation of protective or temporary restraining orders have helped survivors of domestic abuse. In addition, the 1994 Violence Against Women Act provides some legal protections for women, although currently this act is under review.

Any discussion attempting to address the issue of violence against women must involve several key points. First, violence against women must be understood in the context of socially constructed notions of gender. If boys are raised

Race, Class, Sexual Orientation, and Violence Against Women

- Among Asian/Pacific Islander women, 6.8 percent reported being raped at some point in their lifetime; 17.7 percent of White women, 18.8 percent of African American women, 24.4 percent of mixed race women, and 34.1 percent of Native American/Native Alaskan women reported being raped. Among Hispanic women, 19.6 percent reported being raped.*
- Among Asian/Pacific Islander women, 49.6 percent reported being physically assaulted at some point in their lifetime; 51.3 percent of White women, 52.1 percent of African American women, 57.5 percent of mixed race women, and 61.4 percent of Native American/Native Alaskan women reported physical assault. Among Hispanic women, 53.2 percent reported physical assault.*
- Native American/Native Alaskan women were most likely to report rape and physical assault. Asian/Pacific Islander women were least likely to report victimization, although many did talk about violence as a significant concern.*
- Women of all races and Hispanic and non-Hispanic women were about equally vulnerable to violence by an intimate.†
- Rape/sexual assault rates increased as household income decreased.†
- Battering occurs in lesbian relationships at the same rate as in heterosexual relationships.

*Statistics are from the National Violence Against Women Survey.
†Statistics are from the National Crime Victimization Survey.

to hide emotion, see sensitivity as a weakness, and view sexual potency as wound up with interpersonal power, and girls are raised to be dependent and support masculine entitlement, then interpersonal violence should be no surprise. Second, violence by men must be seen as related to masculine dominance in society generally. Indeed, entitlements associated with masculinity produce a range that some scholars term the *rape spectrum*. This means that all sexist behaviors are arranged along a continuum from perhaps unexamined feelings of superiority over women on one end to rape on the other. In this sense, all these behaviors, even though they are so very different in degree, are connected at some level. Male domination of the political systems that address these crimes is also an issue. In "Supremacy Crimes," Gloria Steinem explains this relationship between privilege and violence against others.

Third, male sexual violence is related to the ways violence is eroticized and sexuality is connected to violence. Although pornography is the best example of this problem, women's magazines and advertising generally are rampant with these themes. Finally, we must understand violence against women in terms of the normalization of violence in society. We live in a society where violence is used to solve problems every day.

Consider the following story told to us several weeks ago. The woman, a White professional in her early 30s, had been having a drink with her colleagues one early evening after work. A well-dressed man struck up a conversation with her, and they chatted a while. When she was leaving with her colleagues, the man asked if he could call her sometime, and she gave him her business card that listed only work information. He called her at work within the next week and asked her

Activist Profile: Del Martin

In the 1950s, few lesbians were able to be out about their sexual identity. In fact, in most places homosexual sex was illegal, and lesbians and gay men were easy targets for violence, even by police. Nonetheless, in 1955 Del Martin (left), her partner Phyllis Lyon, and six other women co-founded the Daughters of Bilitis. The group started as a social club for lesbians seeking to meet and socialize with other lesbians, but before long it expanded its mission to include social reform, and chapters of the organization were launched around the country. Martin was president of the national organization from 1957 to 1960.

Martin became involved in the feminist movement in the early 1970s, and in 1976 wrote *Battered Wives*, a revolutionary examination of the experiences of victims of domestic violence. One of the most significant contributions of the book was identifying the origins of domestic violence in the patriarchal structure of the nuclear family. She wrote, "The nuclear family is the building block of American society, and the social, religious, educational and economic institutions of society are designed to maintain, support and strengthen family ties even if the people involved can't stand the sight of one another." Martin advocated collective thinking among members of government, social agencies, religious institutions, and political action groups. Her vision led to the creation of a movement addressing the problem of battered women.

In 1975, she helped found the Coalition for Justice for Battered Women. She also co-founded *La Casa de las Madres*, a refuge for battered women in San Francisco. She helped write the protocol for the San Francisco criminal justice system and served three years on the California Commission on Crime Control and Violence Prevention.

Partners since 1953, in the late 1990s, Martin and Lyons continued to work for issues of justice, particularly those related to aging. In 1995, they were appointed delegates to the White House Conference on Aging. For nearly fifty years they have worked tirelessly on behalf of marginalized people in order to bring about a more just world.

to have dinner with him, and, seeing no reason not to, she agreed to meet him at such-and-such a restaurant after work. She was careful to explain to us that both times she saw this man she was dressed in her professional work clothes and it was early evening in a public space. There was nothing provocative, she emphasized, about her clothes or her demeanor. At some point during the meal she started feeling uncomfortable. The man was very pushy; he chose and ordered her food for her and started telling her that if she wanted to date him, he had certain requirements about how his girlfriends dressed and acted. She panicked and felt a strong need to get away from him, so, at some point she quietly excused herself saying she needed to visit the ladies' room. She then did a quick exit and did not return to the table. Unfortunately, this was not the end of the story. The man found out where her home was and started to stalk her. One evening he forced his way into her apartment and beat her very badly. Fortunately, he did not rape her. Although she took out a restraining order on him, he managed to gain entrance into her apartment building again and beat her senseless one more time in the hallway outside her apartment.

This story is a tragic illustration of misogyny and masculine entitlement. The man felt he had the right to define the reality of women in his life and expected them to be subordinate. He believed it was his entitlement. He was so full of rage that when a woman snubbed him, he would have to subdue her. In addition, the woman's telling of the story is illustrative of societal norms that blame women for their own victimization. When tearfully sharing her story, she had felt the shame and humiliation that comes with such an experience; she wanted it to be known that she had not been "asking for it": He had given no indication that he was anything but clean-cut and upstanding, she was dressed appropriately, she took no risks other than accepting a date, she gave him only her work numbers, and she agreed to meet him in a public place. What more could she have done except be wary of all men she might meet?

Men are also survivors of sexual abuse, especially childhood sexual abuse. They are most likely to have been hurt by an older boy or man, although sometimes by women or older female family members. Given the norms in our society about masculine invulnerability, it is often hard for men to talk about such abuse and to seek help. As a result, men are more likely than women to be in denial about such experiences. Sometimes men who have been abused react by trying to master the abuse, identifying with the source of their abuse to avoid the weakness associated with being a victim.

Sexual harassment at school, in the street, in public places, and in the workplace is also a form of sexual violence. Sexual violence can also occur online or in an Internet chat room. In this chapter we discuss sexual assault and rape, physical abuse, and incest and end with a discussion of pornography as a form of violence against women. Because many forms of pornography are legal, some object to thinking about pornography in the context of sexual violence and claim instead that it is a legitimate type of entertainment. Despite these concerns, we have decided to discuss it in the context of sexual violence because pornography eroticizes unequal power relations between women and men and often involves representations of coercive sex. Men are the major consumers of pornography, and women's bodies tend to be the ones on display. Pornography thus represents a particular aspect of gender relations that reflects the issue of male sexual violence against women.

RAPE

Although rape can be defined as sex without consent, it is best understood as a crime of aggression rather than sex because the focus is on hurting and dominating rather than on sexual desire. More specifically, it is the penetration of any bodily orifice by a penis or object without consent. Someone who is asleep, passed out, or incapacitated by alcohol or drugs cannot give consent. Silence, or lack of continued resistance, does not mean consent. Likewise, consent is not the same as giving in to pressure and intimidation. Consent is a freely made choice that is clearly communicated. Consensual sex is negotiated through communication where individuals express their feelings and desires and are able to listen to and respect others' feelings and desires. Rape can happen to anyone—babies who are months old to women in their 90s, people of all races, ethnicities, and socioeconomic status. Both women and men are raped, and, as already discussed, overwhelmingly it is a problem of men raping women and other men. Rape occurs relatively frequently in prisons where dominant men rape men they perceive as inferior. Often dominant inmates refer to these men as "women." In this way, rape is about power, domination, and humiliation and must be understood in the context of male dominance and power in gender relations.

Individuals may be sexually assaulted without being raped. Sexual assault can be defined as any sexual contact without consent and/or that involves the use of force. Like rape, sexual assault is an act of power, control, and domination. The terms can get confusing because sexual assault, sexual abuse, and rape are often used interchangeably. Basically, rape is a form of sexual assault or sexual abuse, but sexual assault or abuse do not necessarily imply rape. The sexual abuse of children is often termed *molestation,* which may or may not involve rape. When children are molested or raped by family members, it is termed *incest.* Although the rates of rape are very high, sexual assault rates generally (which include but are not limited to rape) are even higher.

In addition to the rape figures given at the beginning of the chapter, only about one in every ten rapes is ever reported and less than 5 percent of perpetrators or fewer than five in 100 are ever convicted. Acquaintance rape, often termed *date rape,* where each person is known to the other, is the most frequent form of rape, and it is the most underreported. Among college women, more than 80 percent report that the assault involved someone the survivor knew. Women are more likely to report a rape if the perpetrator is someone they did not know. Seventy to 80 percent of campus rapes involve drugs and alcohol. The highest rates of rape on college campuses (especially gang rapes) occur by fraternity members, often as part of male bonding rituals. The differences between high- and low-risk fraternities as potentially dangerous places for women are discussed in the reading "Fraternities and Collegiate Rape Culture" by A. Ayres Boswell and Joan Z. Spade.

Learning Activity: How Safe Is Your Campus?

Investigate the safety and security of your campus by asking these questions:

- How many acts of violence were reported on your campus last year?
- Does your campus have a security escort service?
- What resources does your campus provide to ensure safety?
- What training and educational opportunities about safety does your college provide?
- What specialized training about violence is offered to fraternities and sports teams on your campus?
- How does your school encourage the reporting of violence?
- What support services does your school offer to victims of violence?
- What is your school administration's official protocol for dealing with complaints of violence?
- How does your school's code of conduct address violence?
- Are there dark areas of your campus that need additional lighting?
- Are emergency phones available around your campus?

Very often women realize that a past sexual encounter was actually a rape, and, as a result, they begin to think about the experience differently. They may have left the encounter hurt, confused, or angry but without being able to articulate what happened. Survivors need to talk about what occurred and get support. It is never too late to get support from people who care. Feeling ashamed, dirty, or stupid is a typical reaction for those who have experienced sexual assault.

Societal myths about rape include the following:

- *Rapes happen less frequently in our society than women believe. Feminists in particular blow this out of proportion by focusing on women's victimization.* This is false; rape happens at an alarming rate. We do not know the actual rate because so much rape goes unreported. Although feminists care about the victimization of women, we focus on surviving, empowerment, and making changes to stop rapes from happening.
- *Women are at least partly responsible for their victimization in terms of their appearance and behavior (encouraging women to feel guilty when they are raped).* This is false; rape is the only violent crime when the victim is not de facto perceived as innocent. Consider the suggestion that a man who has just been robbed was asking to have his wallet stolen.
- *Men are not totally responsible for their actions. If a woman comes on to a man sexually, it is impossible for him to stop.* This is false; men are not driven by uncontrollable biological urges, and it is insulting to men to assume that this is how men behave. Note how this myth is related to the previous one that blames the victim.

These myths not only support masculine privilege concerning sexuality and access to women and therefore support some men's tendency to sexually abuse women, but they also are important means for controlling women's lives. Recall again the discussion of sexual terrorism in Chapter 2. Such terrorism limits women's activities and keeps us in line by the threat of potential sexual assault. Research on rapists in the early 1980s revealed that, although there are few psychological differences between men who have raped and those who have not, the former group were more likely to believe in the rape myths, were more tolerant of interpersonal domination of women generally, and showed higher levels of sexual arousal around depictions of rape.

As discussed in the next chapter, political institutions have historically supported men's access to women as sexual property and therefore have been slow to respond to women's rights in this arena. For example, there are still some states with marital exemption policies that do not characterize the rape of wives as crimes because wives are characterized as the sexual property of husbands. The history of racism in the South and the lynching of Black men for fabricated rapes of White women have influenced how society and the courts deal with the interaction of race and sexual violence. Men of color get longer sentences when they are convicted of rape than do White men, just as women of color have less credibility in the courtroom than White women.

BATTERING AND PHYSICAL ABUSE

There are several terms for the physical abuse of women in relationships and in the home: domestic abuse, spouse abuse, dating abuse or violence, wife battering, or wife abuse. The first three terms have been rejected by some scholars and activists in this area because these terms imply that women and men perpetrate violence at the same rate. The objection to this is similar to the one against "school violence" or "teen shootings" to which Steinem refers in the reading "Supremacy Crimes." Popular understanding of school and street violence avoids the fact that primarily males are the perpetrators of violence. Although there are some women who physically abuse men and some girls who bring handguns to school, overwhelmingly this is a problem of men hitting women and boys shooting other children in schools. Similarly, in the home most violent crimes are committed by men against women. Again, consider the response if it were girls and women who were the major perpetrators of violence. We believe that society would make note of the gendered nature of these acts if the situation were reversed.

Women who are physically abused are also always emotionally abused because they experience emotional abuse by virtue of being physically terrorized. Emotional abuse, however, does not always involve physical abuse. A man, for example, who constantly tells his partner that she is worthless, stupid, or ugly can emotionally abuse without being physically abusive. Sometimes the scars of emotional abuse take longer to heal than physical abuse.

Why do some men physically abuse women or abuse other men? They abuse because they have internalized sexism and the right to dominate women (or others they perceive as subordinate) in their lives, have learned to use violence as a way to deal with conflict, and have repressed anger. Given this, how is it possible to explain why some women abuse men or abuse other women? Abusive behavior is an act of domination. Women too can internalize domination and can see men in their interpersonal relationships as subordinate to them, even though there is little support for that in society generally. Women in romantic relationships with other

Ideas for Activism

- Volunteer at a local domestic violence shelter.
- Organize a food, clothing, and toiletries drive to benefit your local domestic violence shelter.
- Interrupt jokes about violence against women.
- Organize Domestic Violence Awareness Month (October) activities on your campus.
- Create and distribute materials about violence against women on your campus.

Check Up on Your Relationship

DOES YOUR PARTNER

Constantly put you down?

Call you several times a night or show up to make sure you are where you said you would be?

Embarrass or make fun of you in front of your friends or family?

Make you feel like you are nothing without him/her?

Intimidate or threaten you? "If you do that again, I'll ..."

Always say that it's your fault?

Pressure you to have sex when you don't want to?

Glare at you, give you the silent treatment, grab, shove, kick, or hit you?

DO YOU

Always do what your partner wants instead of what you want?

Fear how your partner will act in public?

Constantly make excuses to other people for your partner's behavior?

Feel like you walk on eggshells to avoid your partner's anger?

Believe if you just tried harder, submitted more, that everything would be okay?

Stay with your partner because you fear what your partner would do if you broke up?

These indicators suggest potential abuse in your relationship. If you've answered yes to any of these questions, talk to a counselor about your relationship. Remember, when one person scares, hurts, or continually puts down the other person, it's abuse.

Created by the President's Commission on the Status of Women, Oregon State University.

women can likewise negotiate dominance and subordination in their relationships and act this out. Battering is a problem in the lesbian community.

Another question is why do women so often stay in abusive relationships? The research on this suggests that when women leave abusive relationships they return about five to seven times before actually leaving for good. The testimonial essay by Scherryl Jefferson Harrison, "Her Toughest Case," illustrates the interpersonal dynamics between abusers and their partners. There are several complicated and interconnected reasons that women stay. First, emotional abuse often involves feelings of shame, guilt, and low self-esteem. Women in these situations (like rape survivors generally) often believe that the abuse is their fault. They may see themselves as worthless and have a difficult time believing that they deserve better. Low self-esteem encourages women to stay and to return to abusive men. Second, some women who are repeatedly abused become desensitized to the violence; they may see it as a relatively normal aspect of gender relationships and therefore something to tolerate.

A third reason women stay in abusive relationships is that men who abuse women tend to physically isolate them from others. This often involves a pattern where women are prevented from visiting or talking to family and friends, are left without transportation, and/or have no access to the telephone. Notice how, when women are abused, the shame associated with this situation can encourage women to isolate themselves. An outcome of this isolation is that women do not get the reality check they need about their situation. Isolation thus helps keep self-esteem low, prevents support, and minimizes women's options in terms of leaving the abusive situation.

A fourth reason women stay is that they worry about what people will think, and this worry keeps them in abusive situations as a consequence of the shame they feel. Most women in abusive relationships worry about this to some extent, although middle-class women probably feel it the most. The myth that this is a lower-class problem and that it does not happen to "nice" families who appear to have everything going for them is part of the problem. And, indeed, the question about what people will think is a relevant one: Some churches tell abused women to submit to their husbands and hide the abuse, neighbors often look the other way, mothers worry about their children being stigmatized at school, and certainly there is embarrassment associated with admitting your husband or boyfriend hits you. For men this issue is even more pertinent, and the shame and embarrassment may be even greater for abused men.

A fifth reason women stay is that they cannot afford to leave. Women in this situation fear for the economic welfare of themselves and their children should they leave the abusive situation. These women tend to have less education and to have dependent children. They understand that the kind of paid work they could get would not be enough to support the family. Reason six is that some survivors believe that children need a father—and even a bad father might be better than no father. Although this belief is erroneous in our view, it does keep women in abusive situations "for the sake of the children." Interestingly, the primary reason women do permanently leave an abusive relationship is also the children: When women see that their children are being hurt, this is the moment when they are most likely to leave for good.

Another reason women stay is that there is often nowhere to go. Although the increase in the numbers of crisis lines and emergency housing shelters is staggering given their absence only a few decades ago, some women still have a difficult time imagining an alternative to the abusive situation. This is especially true of women who live in rural areas and who are isolated from friends and family. Reason eight is that battered women often believe their partner will change. Part of the cycle of violence noted by scholars in this area is the "honeymoon phase" after the violent episode. First comes the buildup of tension when violence is brewing, second is the violent episode, and third is the honeymoon phase when men tend to be

The Cycle of Violence

Domestic violence may seem unpredictable, but it actually follows a typical pattern no matter when it occurs or who is involved. Understanding the cycle of violence and the thinking of the abuser helps survivors recognize they are not to blame for the violence they have suffered—and that *the abuser is the one responsible.*

1. *Tension building* The abuser might set up the victim so she is bound to anger him. The victim, knowing her abuser is likely to erupt, is apologetic. She may even defend his actions.

2. *The abuse* The batterer behaves violently, inflicting pain and abuse on the victim.

3. *Guilt and fear of reprisal* After the violence, the abuser may have feelings of "guilt"— not normal guilt, in which he'd feel sorry for hurting another person, but actually a fear of getting caught. He might blame alcohol for his outburst.

4. *Blaming the victim* The abuser can't stand any kind of guilt feeling for long, so he quickly rationalizes his actions and blames the victim for causing him to hurt her. He might tell her that her behavior "asked for it."

5. *"Normalcy"* At this point, the batterer exhibits kind and loving behavior. Welcomed by both parties, an unusual calm will surround the relationship. He may bring gifts and promise the violence will never happen again.

6. *Fantasy/set-up* Batterers and abusers fantasize about their past and future abuses. These fantasies feed the abuser's anger. He begins to plan another attack by placing his victim in situations that he knows will anger him.

Reprinted from *Take Care: A Guide for Violence-Free Living,* a publication of Raphael House of Portland.

especially remorseful—even horrified that they could have done such a thing— and ask for forgiveness. Given that the profile of many batterers is charm and manipulation, such behavior during this phase can be especially persuasive. Women are not making it up when they think their partner will change.

Finally, women stay because they believe their partner might kill them—or hurt or kill the children—should they leave. Again, his past violence is often enough to make her realize this is no idle threat. Men do kill in these situations and often after wives and girlfriends have fled and brought restraining orders against them.

INCEST

This topic is especially poignant as the poem by Grace Caroline Bridges "Lisa's Ritual, Age 10" demonstrates. Incest is the sexual abuse (molestation, inappropriate touching, rape, being forced to watch or perform sexual acts on others) of children by someone significant to the child. "Significant" might include such people as, for example, a baby-sitter, Boy Scout leader, boyfriend of an older sister, as well as immediate family members, friends, and relatives. We started this chapter with the statistic that in 90 percent of cases where children are raped it is by someone they know. Studies suggest that one in every three to five girls have experienced some kind of childhood sexual abuse by the time they are 16 years old. For boys this number is one in eight to ten, although this may be underestimated because boys are less likely to admit that they are survivors. Again, like other forms of abuse, this crosses all ethnic, class, and religious lines. Power is always involved in incest, and, because children are the least powerful group in society, the effects upon them can be devastating. Children who are abused often have low self-esteem and may find it difficult to trust.

Incest can be both direct and indirect. Direct forms include vaginal, oral, and rectal penetration, sexual rubbing, excessive, inappropriate hugging; body and mouth kissing, bouncing a child on a lap against an erection; and sexual bathing. Direct incest also includes forcing children to watch or perform these acts on others. Indirect incest includes sexualizing statements or joking, speaking to the child as a surrogate spouse, inappropriate references to a child's body, or staring at the child's body. Other examples involve intentionally invading children's privacy in the bathroom or acting inappropriately jealous when adolescents start dating. These indirect forms of incest involve sexualizing children and violating their boundaries.

Often siblings indulge in relatively normal uncoerced sexual play with each other that disappears over time. When this involves a child who is several years older or one who uses threats or intimidation, however, then the behavior can be characterized as incestuous. Indicators of abuse in childhood include excessive crying, anxiety, night fears and sleep disturbances, depression and withdrawal, clinging behaviors, and physical problems like urinary tract infections and trauma to the perineal area. Adolescent symptoms often include eating disorders, psychosomatic complaints, suicidal thoughts, and depression. Survivors of childhood sexual violence may get involved in self-destructive behaviors like alcohol and drug abuse or cutting on their bodies as they turn their anger inward, or they may express their anger through acting out or promiscuous behavior. In particular, girls internalize their worthlessness and their role as sexual objects used by others; boys often have more anger because they were dominated, an anger that is sometimes projected onto their future sexual partners as well as onto themselves. Although it takes time, we can heal from being sexually violated.

PORNOGRAPHY

Pornography involves the sexualization and objectification of women's bodies and parts of bodies for entertainment value. According to Catherine MacKinnon, who has written on and debated the issue of pornography at length, pornography can be defined as the graphic, sexually explicit subordination of women through pictures and/or words. She says pornography includes one or more of the following: women presented as dehumanized sexual objects, things, or commodities; shown as enjoying humiliation, pain, or sexual assault; tied up, mutilated, or physically hurt; depicted in postures or positions of sexual submission or servility; shown with body parts—including though not limited to vagina, breasts, or buttocks—exhibited such that women are reduced to those parts; women penetrated by animals or objects; and women presented in scenarios of degradation, humiliation, torture, shown as filthy or inferior, bleeding, bruised, or hurt in a context that makes these conditions sexual. MacKinnon adds that the use of men, children, or transsexuals in the place of women is also pornography. Note the definition includes the caveat that because a person has consented to being harmed, abused, or subjected to coercion does not alter the degrading character of the behavior.

Just as there are degrees of objectification and normalization of violence in pop culture forms, so too in pornography there is a continuum from the soft porn of *Playboy* to the hard-core *Hustler* and along to illegal forms of representation like child pornography and snuff films. Snuff films are illegal because women are actually murdered in the making of these films. The Internet is one of the largest sites for pornography. It is calculated that there are about 40,000 pornography sites on the Web, and *sex* is still the top search word. In addition to Internet pornography there is the problem of Internet prostitution, as this technology is utilized for the global trafficking and sexual exploitation of women and children. The reading by Donna Hughes, "The Internet and the Global Prostitution Industry," explains this important social problem.

Many people do not oppose pornography because they feel that it represents free speech, or because they feel that the women have chosen to be part of it, or because they like the articles in these magazines. This is especially true of soft porn like *Playboy*. Some see pornography as a mark of sexual freedom and characterize those who would like to limit pornography as prudish. In the reading "Pornography and Freedom," John Stoltenberg explains how sexual freedom requires sexual justice and suggests that pornography is a violation of this justice rather than an expression of it. He writes about pornography in the context of gender and male domination in society.

Some make a distinction between hard core and soft porn and feel that the former is harmful and the latter relatively harmless. Others oppose pornography entirely as a violation of women's rights against objectification and sexualization for male pleasure and believe that people's rights to consume such materials are no longer rights when they violate the rights of others. This is an important debate that has brought together some interesting coalitions that normally do not work together, such as feminists and conservative religious groups.

In this way acts of violence and the threat of violence have profound and lasting effects on all women's lives. We tend to refer to those who have survived violence as "survivors" rather than "victims" to emphasize that it is possible to go on with our lives after such experiences, difficult though that might be. Understanding and preventing violence against women has become a worldwide effort, bringing women and men together to make this a safer place for everyone.

Violence Against Women
An Issue of Human Rights

Women in Action

Violence against women is the most pervasive form of human rights abuse in the world today. It includes assault, battery, rape, sexual slavery, mutilation, and murder. It is not a new phenomenon. It is not tied to poverty or economic upheaval. It is not related to the social displacement of peoples. Instead, it cuts across social and economic situations and is deeply embedded in cultures around the world—so much so that millions of women consider it a way of life.

Over the past decade, national and international groups have turned a spotlight on the hidden brutality of violence against women. They have called on the international community to value a woman's right to be free from violence as a human right. This focus on violence against women has spurred the development of strategies and programs to address the problem. Still, efforts to eradicate violence remain in their infancy and most societies continue to consider violence against women a private, so-called "family" matter.

ABUSED AT HOME

The highest percentage of violence against women occurs at home. A recent World Bank analysis indicates that one-quarter to one-half of all the world's women have been battered by an intimate partner. Regional studies confirm the level of violence. Statistics from Latin America show that between 26 and 60 percent of adult women have been beaten at least once in their lives. In Asia, 60 percent of all women have been assaulted. In sub-Saharan Africa, approximately 42 percent of women report being battered regularly by an intimate partner.

VICTIMS OF RAPE

Data on rape provides another chilling picture: One out of five women worldwide is a victim of rape. Most of them know their attackers. Young girls are the most frequent targets. Forty to 60 percent of all known sexual assaults are committed against girls aged 15 years and younger.

And although rape as a weapon of war has been internationally condemned since the Nuremberg trials following World War II, armies continue to use it in conflicts around the world. In 1992, as many as 20,000 women were raped in the first months of the war in Bosnia-Herzegovina. In Rwanda, between 2,000 and 5,000 rape-related pregnancies were reported in 1994. Over the past 10 years, mass rape has been documented in Peru, Myanmar, Liberia, Cambodia, Somalia, and Uganda.

OTHER FORMS OF VIOLENCE

Female infanticide and sex-selective abortions are also forms of violence against women. Demographers estimate that 60 million women are "missing" from the populations of South and West Asia, China, and North Africa, as a result. In India, particularly the northern regions, and in China and the Republic of Korea, genetic testing for sex has grown into a booming business. A recent study of amniocentesis procedures in a Bombay hospital found that 95.5 percent of aborted fetuses are female. UNICEF reports anecdotal evidence of the practice of female infanticide in some Asian communities.

Another fatal practice, "dowry killing," occurs in India. There, women are killed because they cannot meet the dowry demands of husbands' families. More than a dozen women are reported killed each day in dowry-related incidents—higher than 5,000 per year.

Female genital mutilation, practiced in at least 28 countries, mainly in Africa, is another form of violence against women. Considered a rite of passage for young girls, an estimated 130 million women and girls alive today have undergone a procedure in which all or part of the outer genitalia is removed. Two million girls each year undergo the operation, which is not only painful but also often results in a lifetime of health-related problems.

RESPONDING TO THE VIOLENCE: THE ROLE OF THE INTERNATIONAL COMMUNITY

The international community has a role to play in reducing the violence against women. The 1979 approval by the United Nations of the Convention on the Elimination of Forms of Violence Against Women (CEDAW) marked a significant beginning in addressing the problem. Today, 160 countries have ratified the convention. Although it is a milestone in international efforts to reduce violence against women, nearly one-third of the signatory countries have declared that they will not be subject to several CEDAW provisions. These include equal rights to nationality and citizenship, equal ownership of family property, and an equal role in marriage and family life.

NATIONAL CONSTITUTIONS AND CRIMINAL CODES

At the national level, many countries have constitutions and laws intended to protect women against violence. Constitutions include bans on violence against human beings and the right to the integrity of the body and the right of life. Most prohibit discrimination against citizens.

Brazil's new constitution requires the state to combat violence against women. Colombia declares violence in the family destructive and provides for penalties by law. Equality under the law is written into most constitutions. Some refer specifically to women, like the constitutions of China, Greece, and Poland. These types of provisions are important because, in the absence of other laws or regulations, they can be used to protect women from violence.

National laws that protect against violence are usually part of the penal code. However, only 44 countries worldwide have laws that specifically protect women against domestic violence. Of these, some have expanded the law to cover cultural practices. For example, 12 countries have now criminalized the practice of female genital mutilation.

Most countries have laws against sexual assault and rape. The problem lies, however, in the level of protection guaranteed by the law. Efforts to reform rape law have been ongoing for decades and have centered on determining what constitutes rape. Only 17 countries now consider marital rape to be a criminal offense. Twelve Latin American countries still allow a rapist to escape prosecution if he marries his victim.

Supremacy Crimes

Gloria Steinem

You've seen the ocean of television coverage; you've read the headlines: "How to Spot a Troubled Kid," "Twisted Teens," "When Teens Fall Apart."

After the slaughter in Colorado that inspired those phrases, dozens of copycat threats were reported in the same generalized way: "Junior high students charged with conspiracy to kill students and teachers" (in Texas); "Five honor students overheard planning a June graduation bombing" (in New York); "More than 100 minor threats reported statewide" (in Pennsylvania). In response, the White House held an emergency strategy session titled "Children, Violence, and Responsibility." Nonetheless, another attack was soon reported: "Youth With 2 Guns Shoots 6 at Georgia School."

I don't know about you, but I've been talking back to the television set, waiting for someone to tell us the obvious: it's not "youth," "our children" or "our teens." It's our sons—and "our" can usually be read as "white," "middle class," and "heterosexual."

We know that hate crimes, violent and otherwise, are overwhelmingly committed by white men who are apparently straight. The same is true for an even higher percentage of impersonal, resentment-driven, mass killings like those in Colorado; the sort committed for no economic or rational gain except the need to say, "I'm superior because I can kill." Think of Charles Starkweather, who reported feeling powerful and serene after murdering ten women and men in the 1950s; or the shooter who climbed the University of Texas Tower in 1966, raining down death to gain celebrity. Think of the engineering student at the University of Montreal who resented females' ability to study that subject, and so shot to death 14 women students in 1989, while saying, "I'm against feminism." Think of nearly all those who have killed impersonally in the workplace, the post office, McDonald's.

White males—usually intelligent, middle class, and heterosexual, or trying desperately to appear so—also account for virtually all the serial, sexually motivated, sadistic killings, those characterized by stalking, imprisoning, torturing, and "owning" victims in death. Think of Edmund Kemper, who began by killing animals, then murdered his grandparents, yet was released to sexually torture and dismember college students and other young women until he himself decided he "didn't want to kill *all* the coeds in the world." Or David Berkowitz, the Son of Sam, who murdered *some* women in order to feel in control of *all* women. Or consider Ted Bundy, the charming, snobbish, young would-be lawyer who tortured and murdered as many as 40 women, usually beautiful students who were symbols of the economic class he longed to join. As for John Wayne Gacy, he was obsessed with maintaining the public mask of masculinity, and so hid his homosexuality by killing and burying men and boys with whom he had had sex.

These "senseless" killings begin to seem less mysterious when you consider that they were committed disproportionately by white, nonpoor males, the group most likely to become hooked on the drug of superiority. It's a drug pushed by a male-dominant culture that presents dominance as a natural right; a racist hierarchy that falsely elevates whiteness; a materialist society that equates superiority with possessions, and a homophobic one that empowers only one form of sexuality.

As Elliott Leyton reports in *Hunting Humans: The Rise of the Modern Multiple Murderer*, these killers see their behavior as "an appropriate— even 'manly'—response to the frustrations and disappointments that are a normal part of life."

In other words, it's not their life experiences that are the problem, it's the impossible expectation of dominance to which they've become addicted.

This is not about blame. This is about causation. If anything, ending the massive cultural cover-up of supremacy crimes should make heroes out of boys and men who reject violence, especially those who reject the notion of superiority altogether. Even if one believes in a biogenetic component of male aggression, the very existence of gentle men proves that socialization can override it.

Nor is this about attributing such crimes to a single cause. Addiction to the drug of supremacy is not their only root, just the deepest and most ignored one. Additional reasons why this country has such a high rate of violence include the plentiful guns that make killing seem as unreal as a video game; male violence in the media that desensitizes viewers in much the same way that combat killers are desensitized in training; affluence that allows maximum access to violence-as-entertainment; a national history of genocide and slavery; the romanticizing of frontier violence and organized crime; not to mention extremes of wealth and poverty and the illusion that both are deserved.

But it is truly remarkable, given the relative reasons for anger at injustice in this country, that white, non-poor men have a near-monopoly on multiple killings of strangers, whether serial and sadistic or mass and random. How can we ignore this obvious fact? Others may kill to improve their own condition—in self-defense, or for money or drugs; to eliminate enemies; to declare turf in drive-by shootings; even for a jacket or a pair of sneakers—but white males addicted to supremacy kill even when it worsens their condition or ends in suicide.

Men of color and females are capable of serial and mass killing, and commit just enough to prove it. Think of Colin Ferguson, the crazed black man on the Long Island Railroad, or Wayne Williams, the young black man in At-

lanta who kidnapped and killed black boys, apparently to conceal his homosexuality. Think of the Aileen Carol Wuornos, the white prostitute in Florida, who killed abusive johns "in self-defense," or Waneta Hoyt, the upstate New York woman who strangled her five infant children between 1965 and 1971, disguising their cause of death as sudden infant death syndrome. Such crimes are rare enough to leave a haunting refrain of disbelief as evoked in Pat Parker's poem "jonestown": "Black folks do not / Black folks do not / Black folks do not commit suicide." And yet they did.

Nonetheless, the proportion of serial killings that are not committed by white males is about the same as the proportion of anorexics who are not female. Yet we discuss the gender, race, and class components of anorexia, but not the role of the same factors in producing epidemics among the powerful.

The reasons are buried deep in the culture, so invisible that only by reversing our assumptions can we reveal them.

Suppose, for instance, that young black males—or any other men of color—had carried out the slaughter in Colorado. Would the media reports be so willing to describe the murderers as "our children"? Would there be so little discussion about the boys' race? Would experts be calling the motive a mystery, or condemning the high school cliques for making those young men feel like "outsiders"? Would there be the same empathy for parents who gave the murderers luxurious homes, expensive cars, even rescued them from brushes with the law? Would there be as much attention to generalized causes, such as the dangers of violent video games and recipes for bombs on the Internet?

As for the victims, if racial identities had been reversed, would racism remain so little discussed? In fact, the killers themselves said they were targeting blacks and athletes. They used a racial epithet, shot a black male student in the head, and then laughed over the fact that they could see his brain. What if *that* had been reversed?

What if these two young murderers, who were called "fags" by some of the jocks at Columbine High School, actually had been gay? Would they have got the same sympathy for being gay-baited? What if they had been lovers? Would we hear as little about their sexuality as we now do, even though only their own homophobia could have given the word "fag" such power to humiliate them?

Take one more leap of the imagination: suppose these killings had been planned and executed by young women—of any race, sexuality, or class. Would the media still be so disinterested in the role played by gender-conditioning? Would journalists assume that female murderers had suffered from being shut out of access to power in high school, so much so that they were pushed beyond their limits? What if dozens, even hundreds of young women around the country had made imitative threats—as young men have done—expressing admiration for a well-planned massacre and promising to do the same? Would we be discussing their youth more than their gender, as is the case so far with these male killers?

I think we begin to see that our national self-examination is ignoring something fundamental, precisely because it's like the air we breathe:

the white male factor, the middle-class and heterosexual one, and the promise of superiority it carries. Yet this denial is self-defeating—to say the least. We will never reduce the number of violent Americans, from bullies to killers, without challenging the assumptions on which masculinity is based: that males are superior to females, that they must find a place in a male hierarchy, and that the ability to dominate *someone* is so important that even a mere insult can justify lethal revenge. There are plenty of studies to support this view. As Dr. James Gilligan concluded in *Violence: Reflections on a National Epidemic*, "If humanity is to evolve beyond the propensity toward violence . . . then it can only do so by recognizing the extent to which the patriarchal code of honor and shame generates and obligates male violence."

I think the way out can only be found through a deeper reversal: just as we as a society have begun to raise our daughters more like our sons—more like whole people—we must begin to raise our sons more like our daughters— that is, to value empathy as well as hierarchy; to measure success by other people's welfare as well as their own.

But first, we have to admit and name the truth about supremacy crimes.

Fraternities and Collegiate Rape Culture
Why Are Some Fraternities More Dangerous Places for Women?

A. Ayres Boswell and Joan Z. Spade

Date rape and acquaintance rape on college campuses are topics of concern to both researchers and college administrators. Some estimate that 60 to 80 percent of rapes are date or acquaintance rape (Koss et al. 1988). Further, 1 out of 4 college women say they were raped or experienced an attempted rape, and 1 out of 12 college men say they forced a woman to

have sexual intercourse against her will (Koss, Gidycz, and Wisniewski 1985).

Although considerable attention focuses on the incidence of rape, we know relatively little about the context or the *rape culture* surrounding date and acquaintance rape. Rape culture is a set of values and beliefs that provide an environment conducive to rape (Buchwald,

Fletcher, and Roth 1993; Herman 1984). The term applies to a generic culture surrounding and promoting rape, not the specific settings in which rape is likely to occur. We believe that the specific settings also are important in defining relationships between men and women.

Some have argued that fraternities are places where rape is likely to occur on college campuses (Martin and Hummer 1989; O'Sullivan 1993; Sanday 1990) and that the students most likely to accept rape myths and be more sexually aggressive are more likely to live in fraternities and sororities, consume higher doses of alcohol and drugs, and place a higher value on social life at college (Gwartney-Gibbs and Stockard 1989; Kalof and Cargill 1991). Others suggest that sexual aggression is learned in settings such as fraternities and is not part of predispositions or preexisting attitudes (Boeringer, Shehan, and Akers 1991). To prevent further incidences of rape on college campuses, we need to understand what it is about fraternities in particular and college life in general that may contribute to the maintenance of a rape culture on college campuses.

Our approach is to identify the social contexts that link fraternities to campus rape and promote a rape culture. Instead of assuming that all fraternities provide an environment conducive to rape, we compare the interactions of men and women at fraternities identified on campus as being especially *dangerous* places for women, where the likelihood of rape is high, to those seen as *safer* places, where the perceived probability of rape occurring is lower. Prior to collecting data for our study, we found that most women students identified some fraternities as having more sexually aggressive members and a higher probability of rape. These women also considered other fraternities as relatively safe houses, where a woman could go and get drunk if she wanted to and feel secure that the fraternity men would not take advantage of her. We compared parties at houses identified as high-risk and low-risk houses as well as at two local bars frequented by college students. Our analysis provides an opportunity to examine situations and contexts that hinder or facilitate positive social relations between undergraduate men and women.

The abusive attitudes toward women that some fraternities perpetuate exist within a general culture where rape is intertwined in traditional gender scripts. Men are viewed as initiators of sex and women as either passive partners or active resisters, preventing men from touching their bodies (LaPlante, McCormick, and Brannigan 1980). Rape culture is based on the assumptions that men are aggressive and dominant whereas women are passive and acquiescent (Buchwald et al. 1993; Herman 1984). What occurs on college campuses is an extension of the portrayal of domination and aggression of men over women that exemplifies the double standard of sexual behavior in U.S. society (Barthel 1988; Kimmel 1993).

Sexually active men are positively reinforced by being referred to as "studs," whereas women who are sexually active or report enjoying sex are derogatorily labeled as "sluts" (Herman 1984; O'Sullivan 1993). These gender scripts are embodied in rape myths and stereotypes such as "She really wanted it; she just said no because she didn't want me to think she was a bad girl" (Burke, Sets, and Pirog-Good 1989; Jenkins and Dambrot 1987; Lisak and Roth 1988; Malamuth 1986; Muehlenhard and Linton 1987; Peterson and Franzese 1987). Because men's sexuality is seen as more natural, acceptable, and uncontrollable than women's sexuality, many men and women excuse acquaintance rape by affirming that men cannot control their natural urges (Miller and Marshall 1987).

Whereas some researchers explain these attitudes toward sexuality and rape using an individual or a psychological interpretation, we argue that rape has a social basis, one in which both men and women create and recreate masculine and feminine identities and relations. Based on the assumption that rape is part of the social construction of gender, we examine how men and women "do gender" on a college campus (West and Zimmerman 1987). We focus on fraternities because they have been identified as settings that encourage rape (Sanday 1990). . . .

Gender Relations

Relations between women and men are shaped by the contexts in which they meet and interact. As is the case on other college campuses, *hooking up* has replaced dating on this campus, and fraternities are places where many students hook up. Hooking up is a loosely applied term on college campuses that had different meaning for men and women on this campus.

Most men defined hooking up similarly. One man said it was something that happens

> when you are really drunk and meet up with a woman you sort of know, or possibly don't know at all and don't care about. You go home with her with the intention of getting as much sexual, physical pleasure as she'll give you, which can range anywhere from kissing to intercourse, without any strings attached.

The exception to this rule is when men hook up with women they admire. Men said they are less likely to press for sexual activity with someone they know and like because they want the relationship to continue and be based on respect.

Women's version of hooking up differed. Women said they hook up only with men they cared about and described hooking up as kissing and petting but not sexual intercourse. Many women said that hooking up was disappointing because they wanted longer-term relationships. First-year women students realized quickly that hook-ups were usually one-night stands with no strings attached, but many continued to hook up because they had few opportunities to develop relationships with men on campus. One first-year woman said that "70 percent of hook-ups never talk again and try to avoid one another; 26 percent may actually hear from them or talk to them again, and 4 percent may actually go on a date, which

can lead to a relationship." Another first-year woman said, "It was fun in the beginning. You get a lot of attention and kiss a lot of boys and think this is what college is about, but it gets tiresome fast."

Whereas first-year women get tired of the hook-up scene early on, many men do not become bored with it until their junior or senior year. As one upperclassman said, "The whole game of hooking up became really meaningless and tiresome for me during my second semester of my sophomore year, but most of my friends didn't get bored with it until the following year."

In contrast to hooking up, students also described monogamous relationships with steady partners. Some type of commitment was expected, but most people did not anticipate marriage. The term *seeing each other* was applied when people were sexually involved but free to date other people. This type of relationship involved less commitment than did one of boyfriend/girlfriend but was not considered to be a hook-up.

The general consensus of women and men interviewed on this campus was that the Greek system, called "the hill," set the scene for gender relations. The predominance of Greek membership and subsequent living arrangements segregated men and women. During the week, little interaction occurred between women and men after their first year in college because students in fraternities or sororities live and dine in separate quarters. In addition, many non-Greek upper-class students move off campus into apartments. Therefore, students see each other in classes or in the library, but there is no place where students can just hang out together.

Both men and women said that fraternities dominate campus social life, a situation that everyone felt limited opportunities for meaningful interactions. One senior Greek man said,

> This environment is horrible and so unhealthy for good male and female relationships and interactions to occur. It is so segregated and male

dominated. . . . It is our party, with our rules and our beer. We are allowing these women and other men to come to our party. Men can feel superior in their domain.

. . .

Treatment of Women

Not all men held negative attitudes toward women that are typical of a rape culture, and not all social contexts promoted the negative treatment of women. When men were asked whether they treated the women on campus with respect, the most common response was "On an individual basis, yes, but when you have a group of men together, no." Men said that, when together in groups with other men, they sensed a pressure to be disrespectful toward women. A first-year man's perception of the treatment of women was that "they are treated with more respect to their faces, but behind closed doors, with a group of men present, respect for women is not an issue." One senior man stated, "In general, college-aged men don't treat women their age with respect because 90 percent of them think of women as merely a means to sex." Women reinforced this perception. A first-year woman stated, "Men here are more interested in hooking up and drinking beer than they are in getting to know women as real people." Another woman said, "Men here use and abuse women."

Characteristic of rape culture, a double standard of sexual behavior for men versus women was prevalent on this campus. As one Greek senior man stated, "Women who sleep around are sluts and get bad reputations; men who do are champions and get a pat on the back from their brothers." Women also supported a double standard for sexual behavior by criticizing sexually active women. A first-year woman spoke out against women who are sexually active: "I think some girls here make it difficult for the men to respect women as a whole."

. . .

Fraternity men most often mistreated women they did not know personally. Men and women alike reported incidents in which brothers observed other brothers having sex with unknown women or women they knew only casually. A sophomore woman's experience exemplifies this anonymous state: "I don't mind if 10 guys were watching or it was videotaped. That's expected on this campus. It's the fact that he didn't apologize or even offer to drive me home that really upset me." . . .

Attitudes Toward Rape

The sexually charged environment of college campuses raises many questions about cultures that facilitate the rape of women. How women and men define their sexual behavior is important legally as well as interpersonally. We asked students how they defined rape and had them compare it to the following legal definition: the penetration of an act of sexual intercourse with a female against her will and consent, whether her will is overcome by force or fear resulting from the threat of force, or by drugs or intoxicants; or when, because of mental deficiency, she is incapable of exercising rational judgment. (Brownmiller 1975, 368)

When presented with this legal definition, most women interviewed recognized it as well as the complexities involved in applying it. A first-year woman said, "If a girl is drunk and the guy knows it and the girl says, 'Yes, I want to have sex,' and they do, that is still rape because the girl can't make a conscious, rational decision under the influence of alcohol." Some women disagreed. Another first-year woman stated, "I don't think it is fair that the guy gets blamed when both people involved are drunk."

The typical definition men gave for rape was "when a guy jumps out of the bushes and forces himself sexually onto a girl." When asked what date rape was, the most common answer was "when one person has sex with another person who did not consent." Many men said, however, that "date rape is when a woman wakes up the next morning and regrets having sex." Some men said that date rape was too gray an area to define. "Consent is a fine line," said a Greek senior man student. For the most part, the men we spoke with argued that rape did not occur on this campus. One Greek sophomore man said, "I think it is ridiculous that someone here would rape someone." A first-year man stated, "I have a problem with the word rape. It sounds so criminal, and we are not criminals; we are sane people."

Whether aware of the legal definitions of rape, most men resisted the idea that a woman who is intoxicated is unable to consent to sex. A Greek junior man said, "Men should not be responsible for women's drunkenness." One first-year man said, "If that is the legal definition of rape, then it happens all the time on this campus." A senior man said, "I don't care whether alcohol is involved or not; that is not rape. Rapists are people that have something seriously wrong with them." A first-year man even claimed that when women get drunk, they invite sex. He said, "Girls get so drunk here and then come on to us. What are we supposed to do? We are only human."

DISCUSSION AND CONCLUSION

These findings describe the physical and normative aspects of one college campus as they relate to attitudes about and relations between men and women. Our findings suggest that an explanation emphasizing rape culture also must focus on those characteristics of the social setting that play a role in defining heterosexual relationships on college campuses (Kalof and Cargill 1991). The degradation of women as portrayed in rape culture was not found in all fraternities on this campus. Both group norms and individual behavior changed as students went from one place to another. Although individual men are the ones who rape, we found that some settings are more likely places for

rape than are others. Our findings suggest that rape cannot be seen only as an isolated act and blamed on individual behavior and proclivities, whether it be alcohol consumption or attitudes. We also must consider characteristics of the settings that promote the behaviors that reinforce a rape culture.

Relations between women and men at parties in low-risk fraternities varied considerably from those in high-risk houses. Peer pressure and situational norms influenced women as well as men. Although many men in high- and low-risk houses shared similar views and attitudes about the Greek system, women on this campus, and date rape, their behaviors at fraternity parties were quite different.

Women who are at highest risk of rape are women whom fraternity brothers did not know. These women are faceless victims, nameless acquaintances—not friends. Men said their responsibility to such persons and the level of guilt they feel later if the hook-ups end in sexual intercourse are much lower if they hook up with women they do not know. In high-risk houses, brothers treated women as subordinates and kept them at a distance. Men in high-risk houses actively discouraged ongoing heterosexual relationships, routinely degraded women, and participated more fully in the hook-up scene; thus, the probability that women would become faceless victims was higher in these houses. The flirtatious nature of the parties indicated that women go to these parties looking for available men, but finding boyfriends or relationships was difficult at parties in high-risk houses. However, in the low-risk houses, where more men had long-term relationships, the women were not strangers and were less likely to become faceless victims.

. . .

Alcohol consumption was a major focus of social events here and intensified attitudes and orientations of a rape culture. Although pressure to drink was evident at all fraternity parties and at both bars, drinking dominated high-risk fraternity parties, at which non-alcoholic beverages usually were not available and people chugged beers and became visibly drunk. A rape culture is strengthened by rules that permit alcohol only at fraternity parties. Under this system, men control the parties and dominate the men as well as the women who attend. As college administrators crack down on fraternities and alcohol on campus, however, the same behaviors and norms may transfer to other places such as parties in apartments or private homes where administrators have much less control. At commercial bars, interaction and socialization with others were as important as drinking, with the exception of the nights when the bar frequented by under-class students became crowded. Although one solution is to offer nonalcoholic social activities, such events receive little support on this campus. Either these alternative events lacked the prestige of the fraternity parties or the alcohol was seen as necessary to unwind, or both.

. . .

Students on this campus were aware of the contexts in which they operated and the choices available to them. They recognized that, in their interactions, they created differences between men and women that are not natural, essential, or biological (West and Zimmerman 1987). Not all men and women accepted the demeaning treatment of women, but they continued to participate in behaviors that supported aspects of a rape culture. Many women participated in the hook-up scene even after they had been humiliated and hurt because they had few other means of initiating contact with men on campus. Men and women alike played out this scene, recognizing its injustices in many cases but being unable to change the course of their behaviors.

. . .

Our findings indicate that a rape culture exists in some fraternities, especially those we identified as high-risk houses. College administrators are responding to this situation by providing counseling and educational programs that increase awareness of date rape including campaigns such as "No means no." These strategies are important in changing attitudes,

values, and behaviors; however, changing individuals is not enough. The structure of campus life and the impact of that structure on gender relations on campus are highly determinative. To eliminate campus rape culture, student leaders and administrators must examine the situations in which women and men meet and restructure these settings to provide opportunities for respectful interaction. Change may not require abolishing fraternities; rather, it may require promoting settings that facilitate positive gender relations.

REFERENCES

Barthel, D. 1988. *Putting on Appearances: Gender and Advertising*. Philadelphia: Temple University Press.

Boeringer, S. B., C. L. Shehan, and R. L. Akers. 1991. "Social Contexts and Social Learning in Sexual Coercion and Aggression: Assessing the Contribution of Fraternity Membership." *Family Relations* 40: 58–64.

Brownmiller, S. 1975. *Against Our Will: Men, Women and Rape*. New York: Simon & Schuster.

Buchwald. E., P. R. Fletcher, and M. Roth (eds.). 1993. *Transforming a Rape Culture*. Minneapolis, MN: Milkweed Editions.

Burke, P., J. E. Stets, and M. A. Pirog-Good. 1989. "Gender Identity, Self-Esteem, Physical Abuse and Sexual Abuse in Dating Relationships." In M. A. Pirog-Good and J. E. Stets (eds.), *Violence in Dating Relationships: Emerging Social Issues*. New York: Praeger.

Gwartney-Gibbs, P., and J. Stockard. 1989. "Courtship Aggression and Mixed-Sex Peer Groups." In M. A. Pirog-Good and J. E. Stets (eds.), *Violence in Dating Relationships: Emerging Social Issues*. New York: Praeger.

Herman, D. 1984. "The rape culture." In J. Freeman (ed.), *Women: A Feminist Perspective*. Mountain View, CA: Mayfield.

Jenkins, M. J., and F. H. Dambrot. 1987. "The Attribution of Date Rape: Observer's Attitudes and Sexual Experiences and the Dating Situation." *Journal of Applied Social Psychology* 17: 875–895.

Kalof, L., and T. Cargill. 1991. "Fraternity and Sorority Membership and Gender Dominance Attitudes." *Sex Roles* 25: 417–423.

Kimmel, M. S. 1993. "Clarence, William, Iron Mike, Tailhook, Senator Packwood, Spur Posse, Magic

. . . and Us." In E. Buchwald, P. R. Fletcher, and M. Roth (eds.), *Transforming a Rape Culture*. Minneapolis, MN: Milkweed Editions.

Koss, M. P., T. E. Dinero, C. A. Seibel, and S. L. Cox. 1988. "Stranger and Acquaintance Rape: Are There Differences in the Victim's Experience?" *Psychology of Women Quarterly* 12: 1–24.

Koss, M. P., C. A. Gidycz, and N. Wisniewski. 1985. "The Scope of Rape: Incidence and Prevalence of Sexual Aggression and Victimization in a National Sample of Higher Education Students." *Journal of Consulting and Clinical Psychology* 55: 162–170.

LaPlante, M. N., N. McCormick, and G. G. Brannigan. 1980. "Living the Sexual Script: College Students' Views of Influence in Sexual Encounters." *Journal of Sex Research* 16: 338–355.

Lisak, D., and S. Roth. 1988. "Motivational Factors in Nonincarcerated Sexually Aggressive Men." *Journal of Personality and Social Psychology* 55: 795–802.

Malamuth, N. 1986. "Predictors of Naturalistic Sexual Aggression." *Journal of Personality and Social Psychology* 50: 953–962.

Martin, P. Y., and R. Hummer. 1989. "Fraternities and Rape on Campus." *Gender and Society* 3: 457–473.

Miller, B., and J. C. Marshall. 1987. "Coercive Sex on the University Campus." *Journal of College Student Personnel* 28: 38–47.

Muehlenhard, C. L., and M. A. Linton. 1987. "Date Rape and Sexual Aggression in Dating Situations: Incidence and Risk Factors." *Journal of Counseling Psychology* 34: 186–196.

O'Sullivan, C. 1993. "Fraternities and the Rape Culture." In E. Buchwald, P. R. Fletcher, and M. Roth (eds.), *Transforming a Rape Culture*. Minneapolis, MN: Milkweed Editions.

Peterson, S. A., and B. Franzese. 1987. "Correlates of College Men's Sexual Abuse of Women." *Journal of College Student Personnel* 28: 223–228.

Sanday, P. R. 1990. *Fraternity Gang Rape: Sex, Brotherhood, and Privilege on Campus.* New York: New York University Press.

West, C., and D. Zimmerman. 1987 "Doing Gender." *Gender and Society* 1: 125–151.

READING 72

Her Toughest Case

Constance Johnson

You could call it the Black woman's first commandment. We don't take stuff from our men. You know the mantra we've heard sisters with hands on hips recite: "Girl, if a man ever touches me, I'm out." If I heard about a sister being slapped around by her man, I would even say these words myself. Yet four years ago I almost lost my life to a man who had beaten me for nearly 30 years, who threatened to kill me—and once even held a gun to my head.

I am the last person anyone would've thought of as a battered wife. I am a domestic-violence prosecutor who, after battling for my life the night before, would march into court and indict *other* women's abusers. To everyone around me, my life seemed picturesque: I had a beautiful house on nine acres of Alabama land, two well-mannered sons and a charming, handsome husband who seemed to adore me. But behind the pretty portrait, my life was spiraling into disaster.

When I tell sisters that my husband beat me, they often ask, "Why did you stay?" The simple answer is that I wanted my dream of a happy family to be real, and when I discovered it wasn't, I chose to overlook that reality. But the deeper reason has to do with who I was before meeting my husband: a 19-year-old girl who longed to be in love and to be loved. I subconsciously longed for someone, *anyone,* to fill a void in my heart. In 1965, the year I entered college, I gave my heart to the man I thought could do that.

THE BEN I ADORED

I loved Ben before I met him. He was a tall, handsome, popular 21-year-old senior at Morehouse, and I was a barely-19 freshman at Spelman. I admired Ben as he strolled across campus, flashing his bright smile at the other sisters who eyed him. Secretly I longed for him to notice me. So when he walked toward me at a party one night, I nearly fainted. With Smoky Robinson and the Miracles cooing in the background, Ben escorted me, queenlike, onto the floor. I can't remember ever feeling more cherished and important.

Our romance blossomed quickly as he and I exchanged stories. He grew up in a wealthy family in Troy, Alabama, and his parents, who owned a funeral home, had a loving marriage. I grew up as an army brat, but spent my teenage years in Macon, Georgia. My alcoholic father's verbal tirades left me feeling worthless, but they made me determined to succeed. Ben and I talked of our shared passion for civil rights and how we both wanted to become attorneys.

I immediately fell in love with his attentiveness. When I talked with him, he listened as if nothing was more important than what I was saying. When I told him how worthless my father had made me feel as a child, he always said the right words to comfort me. He was polished, articulate and well-read, and sometimes as I watched him I thought about how lucky I was to have a man like him.

The only thing that bothered me was his possessiveness. If he saw me chatting with another guy, he'd ask, "Why were you talking with *him* so long?" Other times he'd suggest that an outfit I wore—one that he himself had purchased—was too revealing. I resisted his control, but secretly I enjoyed it. *If a man like Ben wants to keep me to himself,* I thought, *then I must be important.*

We married after I finished college in 1969, and a year later we had our first son. I took on a part-time job in Atlanta as a substitute teacher so I could stay home with the baby;

Ben, saving toward law school, worked as a counselor in an alcohol-abuse program. Even amid tight finances and Ben's hectic schedule, our marriage flourished. After a stressful day or an argument, we'd often joke with each other or kiss and embrace; at nights as the baby slept, we talked for hours about our dream of one day starting a law practice. Our friends saw us as a model couple: always loving and laughing and lifting up each other.

Not until the third year in our marriage did I see signs of trouble. I noticed that when we discussed anything—politics, law, parenting— he always had to be right. And if anything went wrong in our marriage, it was my fault. Then came the slights: He often hinted that I was too fat—I weighed around 110 pounds—or he complained about my cooking. But because on most days Ben was charming and responsible—he often surprised me with fine jewelry, kissed and cooed at the baby for hours and almost never missed work—I excused his behavior. I craved Ben's love and approval so much that I did whatever I could to keep him happy.

Yet even with our moments of tension, I had never felt more fulfilled. I knew that I had what many of my Spelman sisters could only envy: an intelligent, responsible, good-looking brother who seemed to adore me. What I didn't know was that my world would soon crumble beneath my feet.

DID HE REALLY HIT ME?

When I was about six months pregnant with our second child, we moved to Troy, Alabama, to be near Ben's aging parents and to help with his family's funeral business. Though it was Ben's choice to move, he seemed unhappy. When I questioned him about this, he waved me off. But one morning, after I set out his grits and sausage, it became clear that my husband was far unhappier than I'd known.

"I don't want this," he snapped.

"Then fix your own breakfast," I shot back.

Slap. I stared at Ben in disbelief, my mind racing for answers: *Did he really hit me?* Seconds later the reality of what Ben had done jolted me from my shock, and I waddled from the kitchen into our bedroom. Ben, a step behind me, shoved me onto my back on the bed. "Don't make me hit you again!" he ordered. Then he grabbed my wrists and pinned my body down. Through screams, I struggled free, and he darted out the door to work.

The attack left me dazed. As I moved zombie-like about the house that day, my mind replayed the incident in slow motion: *Did Ben really hit me?* For a moment I considered packing up my things and driving off with the baby. But somehow I couldn't bring myself to walk away from the only man who had ever made me feel loved. The thought of leaving the security of our lives together—of facing the world alone—was too overwhelming.

That evening Ben begged my forgiveness. "I don't know what came over me, Scherryl," he pleaded. "I'm so sorry." Still stunned and angry, I at first dismissed his apologies. But my heart softened because he seemed so sincere. As he apologized repeatedly, I blamed his behavior on the stress of the move. *It'll never happen again,* I told myself. And for more than a year it didn't.

In 1973 Ben finally went to law school in Miami. Our family moved to Florida together, but we couldn't find affordable housing, so I moved back to Alabama, stayed with his parents and took on another part-time teaching position. But when Ben was in his third year of law school, his father died, among other personal catastrophes. He dropped out of school and returned to Troy to run his family's business.

Amid Ben's grief over his dad's death and the stress of running the funeral home, the abuse started again. If it wasn't physical, it was verbal. Ben would hurl insults like "You're too stupid to live," or he'd accuse me of having affairs and call me a slut. If I disagreed with something he said, he'd punch me in the stomach until I was doubled over, yank my head back by my hair or hit me in the chest. He never broke any of my bones, but he often shoved me hard enough to leave my body aching for days.

When I tried to discuss the abuse with Ben or encouraged him to get counseling, he'd say, "You made me do that to you" or "You know I love you."

I didn't think any of my relatives, most of whom lived in Georgia, knew that Ben was attacking me. I explained away the bruises by saying I had run into something or fallen. Or to avoid answering questions about puffy eyes from crying or redness that my makeup didn't hide, I isolated myself. I even tried to hide the abuse from my children: When Ben became agitated, I would move the argument into our bedroom. And I put on a false face with my girlfriends, assuring them that everything was perfect. All the pretending left me feeling desperate and alone.

Each time Ben hit me I threatened to leave him. *But to do what and go where?* I'd ask myself. I had a solid education when I first married Ben, but I had never lived on my own—and I feared that I couldn't. I no longer felt like the smart, strong woman who'd graduated from Spelman. Whenever I mustered the courage to walk away, Ben's voice became my father's: "You won't make it out there alone!" I was sure that if I left, I would prove that both Ben and my father were right. When I did finally leave for the first time, in 1976, I walked away not for myself but for my children.

I had begun taking out my shame and rage on our kids, then 6 and 2. Neither I nor Ben had ever physically abused them, but I could hear my father's angry voice in my own as I yelled at them for minor things like leaving the milk out or not putting their toys away. I hated the mother I was becoming, angry, impatient and physically drained from all the screaming. And I feared that if my boys ever saw their father hit me, one of them would snap, or, worse, that they would grow up and imitate his behavior. One day I sobbed as I thought of the pit I'd let myself fall into. *You've got to change all this, girl,* I told myself. *You've got to do better for your kids.*

That day, with Ben still at work and his parents away, I walked out on my marriage. I sat my children between suitcases in the backseat of our Pontiac and fled to my parents' home in Macon, Georgia. During the entire four-hour drive, I sobbed as I remembered the violence, the put-downs, the shame. Instead of feeling as if I had escaped, I thought that my life was over. It was as if I could hear Ben saying, "You will never make it without me—you'll fall flat on your face."

When he finally tracked me down a few days later, pleading for me to come back, I told him, "I want a divorce." The irony was that I really didn't want a divorce—I just thought I could shock him into changing his behavior.

THE SCHERRYL I HID

After leaving Ben, I set my sights on becoming a defense attorney. When my teenage cousin was wrongfully convicted of a crime, I became passionate about helping others like him. Mom watched the kids as I attended Mercer University Law School in Macon.

While I was in school, Ben visited the children every other weekend. With each visit he was more endearing—he brought the kids treats and played with them for hours. And no matter how aloof I was, he begged me to reconcile with him.

After his visits, the children talked adoringly of their dad, and part of me felt guilty for taking my boys away from him. Then, as the months passed, I began thinking about how much I missed my husband—the way he soothed me when I felt down, his charm, his attentiveness. So inch by inch I let him back into my life. Deep down I knew he hadn't really changed, but I ignored the warning voice in my head. I *wanted* to believe Ben was a new man, so I chose to forget the beatings, the insults, and to remember only the good times.

By the time I finished school in 1981, I had decided not to finalize the divorce. The kids and I returned to Troy to restart our life with Ben in our own house. As my husband managed the funeral home, I opened a private law practice. To the community we were a model family—two great careers, two wonderful kids

and a rebuilt marriage. But at home the put-downs, slapping and shoving resumed. Now the kids were old enough to see what was happening. But when they noticed my bruises or seemed worried after one of our late-night fights, I reassured them with, "Mom and Dad just have to work out a few things, but I'll be okay." I thought I was fooling them, but years later when they were grown, I learned they had known the truth all along.

Most of the time I avoided Ben, never sure what might cause him to snap. My self-respect was shot. I hated myself for allowing him to control me, for not sticking to my resolve to leave him. The only time I felt good about myself was when I stepped into the courtroom. To anesthetize my pain I threw myself into my work. When I walked out my door, I became Scherryl, the self-assured attorney, not Scherryl, Ben's weak and abused wife.

In the late 1980's I heard about a woman who, fleeing her violent husband, had filed for divorce. But after the separation, the man broke into the woman's house and beat her with a champagne bottle; left for dead, she crawled to the neighbors. Disgusted that he was sentenced to only three years in prison, I promised myself I would help such women—those who, like me, were mired in abusive relationships. In 1987 I was asked to join the district attorney's office, and I began requesting domestic-violence cases. Ironically, my anger over such cases didn't drive me to leave my husband; instead it fueled my passion to protect other women in these relationships. I often prosecuted abusers for inflicting less violence than what I was enduring.

Ben denied that he was jealous of my career achievements, but his outbursts seemed to intensify in proportion to my success in the courtroom. A backhand if dinner didn't taste right. Threats to blow my face off if I disagreed about the kids or protested his behavior. Over time I stopped fighting back and simply tried to stay out of his way. Or, to keep him happy, I tried to anticipate his needs—whether he wanted sex, whether he wanted to talk, whether he wanted to sleep. I would often lie awake all night, wondering how my life had deteriorated to this.

My work and home lives were in sharp contrast: As I defended battered women in the courtroom, who could have known that *I* feared for my life? Almost daily I shifted between anger, denial and depression. After prosecuting in a capital case in which the victim left her abusive husband and was later murdered by him in her bed, I thought, *That dead sister could have been me.* But just when I was angry enough to leave Ben, I'd reason, *My life is not that bad. Yes, Ben hits me sometimes—but he really does love me.* Time and again I justified his behavior and made myself believe I should stay.

One morning after a beating I dragged myself in to work because I had to be in court. My whole body ached. The night before, Ben had shoved me, thrown me into furniture and made me stand in a corner of our bedroom as he ranted and raved until the early-morning hours. He'd even punched me in the abdomen and choked me into unconsciousness. I was in so much pain that for the first time I drove myself to the hospital after work. Though I explained away my bruises as accidental, an ER doctor suspected abuse and reported my case to the police. But I begged the police officer, a friend of mine, not to reveal my secret. As a domestic-violence prosecutor, I knew I had to keep Ben's abuse quiet. If people knew I let Ben mistreat me, I would lose one of the few things that now made me feel worthwhile—the respect I'd earned in my career. And what abused woman would trust a prosecutor who herself was being abused?

Yet I knew I needed help. In shame I had isolated myself from all my nearby girlfriends, my church and my family. So when I confided in a doctor outside of town, he sent me to a professional counselor. I felt uncomfortable with that counselor, so I turned instead to my minister, who told me I didn't deserve to be treated so poorly. He wanted to help me, but he knew that if he talked to Ben, my husband would take out his wrath on me.

When an old college friend visited me, I spilled my guts. "It's time for you to do for yourself what you do for other women, Scherryl," she insisted. "You must stop allowing this." I knew she was right, but I still wanted to believe that Ben would change. And for six months or even a year at a time, he would.

But the violence would always begin again, and I would find myself back in the same position—excusing Ben's behavior and even blaming myself. I vacillated between loving him, fearing him and wanting to kill him. At one point the attacks became so frequent that I sneaked his pistol into my purse and carried it around. I knew I wouldn't use it, but just carrying it made me feel less defenseless. Not until the summer of 1996, my sons grown and gone, did I finally find the courage to end my hell.

"THIS MAN WILL KILL ME"

One sweltering summer evening, Ben stormed through our front door. I was about to fry some shrimp.

"Where's dinner?" he barked.

"I wanted your food to be hot, so—"

Slap!

The more I explained why I hadn't finished dinner, the more enraged Ben became. "You stupid bitch!" he yelled, throwing me into the bedroom and against a dresser. "You don't deserve to live!" He had screamed these words at me many times, but this time a fury I hadn't seen in him shot through his eyes. He wrapped his long fingers around my throat, cutting off my oxygen. For the first time I thought, *This man is going to kill me.*

Then Ben walked away, and I thought his tirade was over. But before I could get up from the floor, he leaned over me, his hot breath hitting my ear. *Click.* The sound of a cocking revolver at my temple made me shudder. "Bitch, I'll blow your goddamn face off!" he yelled. *I'm gonna die,* I thought. *This is it.* As I looked up over his shoulder I saw a baby picture of my boys, which gave me courage. In desperation, I whispered, "If you let me out of here, you won't ever see me again." Seconds later Ben lifted the gun away.

Without a word I flew out of the house and locked myself in our car. As tears flooded my face, all the attacks of the last 23 years whirled through my head—the bloody noses, the bruised cheeks, the aching ribs. How could my marriage have unraveled into this? Ben would never change, and I knew that— I always had. But it took having this man hold a gun to my head to shock me into walking away. I had long ago tired of his terrorism, of his promises to change. Yet not until I saw my death in Ben's eyes did I realize what I'd always known deep inside—that staying with him had *already* cost me my life.

I finally started the car, and without even gathering my possessions I drove to a friend's house. That night I promised myself I would never look back.

For the rest of the summer Ben pleaded with me to come home, but I refused to see him. After all he had done to me, I was still tempted to see him, sometimes dreaming that we could work things out. Yet when these thoughts came, I reminded myself that loving this man—and loving *myself*—meant staying away from him.

A year after I left, I heard that he was in a car accident and had broken five ribs, and I went to see him. As he lay in intensive care, doctors feared he wouldn't make it. For the time first since the evening he tried to kill me, he and I were alone, face-to-face.

"Well," I said over the hum of hospital machines, a mix of anger and sarcasm in my voice, "do you hurt as badly as I did when you kicked me in the ribs?"

"Why you bringin' up something like that?" he whispered, struggling to breathe. "You know I love you. I've always loved you."

Somehow, as I watched Ben lie in pain, I wanted to forgive him— for myself, for him and for our children. Seeing him brought up all the emotions I'd struggled with since fleeing for my life—I wavered between feelings of rage and love for him. But I knew that all I could do was let go of my bitterness and move on. The week after I visited Ben in the hospital, he died.

As I shared my story with relatives and friends after Ben's death, many said they had suspected he was beating me. But most were surprised. The irony is that while I fooled many of them for years, I had also fooled myself into thinking things were fine.

Even now I'm baffled that I allowed the abuse to continue for so long—and all while I prosecuted other abusers. Yet I am trying to heal myself. I keep a journal, and every morning I reread passages from Iyanla Vanzant's book *Faith in the Valley*. The words help me understand that I allowed Ben to beat me because I loved him more than I loved myself. Now I understand that *no* man, no matter how smart or charming, can make me whole. I am whole and lovable simply because God created me that way, and no one can devalue me unless I allow it. I now listen to the advice I have so often given to other women: No one can steal my dignity and self-worth unless I give them up.

Sometimes I pray and meditate with my children, who have also looked to spirituality to overcome the pain from years of living in an abusive environment. My sons have become my best friends. When we talk about how they can heal, I often tell them, "Abuse is not hereditary. Learn from your dad's mistakes, and then decide not to pass the hurt on to your children." As I watch how they handle themselves, I know they will not.

On days when the memories of my failed marriage and the abuse are tough to handle, I remind myself of the saying, "The past cannot be changed, but the future is whatever you want it to be." I hold on to that. Now I don't see myself as a victim but as a survivor. Instead of regretting that I chose to stay for so long, I use my pain to grow strong and to begin nurturing myself. And by openly telling my story to other women, I'm helping them see that they don't have to wait as long as I did to reclaim their lives.

Lisa's Ritual, Age 10

Grace Caroline Bridges

Afterwards when he has finished
lots of mouthwash helps
to get rid of her father's cigarette taste.
She runs a hot bath
    to soak away the pain
        like red dye leading from her
            school dress in the washtub.

She doesn't cry.
When the bathwater cools she adds more hot.
She brushes her teeth for a long time.

Then she finds the corner of her room,
curls against it. There the wall is
hard and smooth
as teacher's new chalk, white
as a clean bedsheet. Smells
fresh. Isn't sweaty, hairy, doesn't stick
to skin. Doesn't hurt much
when she presses her small backbone
into it. The wall is steady
while she falls   away:
    first the hands   lost

arms dissolving   feet gone
    the legs   dis-   jointed
        body cracking down
          the center like a fault
          she falls inside
            slides down like
dust   like kitchen dirt
           slips off
the dustpan into
              noplace
a place where
nothing happens,
nothing ever happened.

When she feels the cool
wall against her cheek
she doesn't want to
come back. Doesn't want to
think about it.
The wall is quiet, waiting.
It is tall like a promise
only better.

Pornography and Freedom

John Stoltenberg

There is a widespread belief that sexual freedom is an idea whose time has come. Many people believe that in the last few decades we have gotten more and more of it—that sexual freedom is something you can carve out against the forces of sexual repressiveness, and that significant gains have been won, gains we dare not give up lest we backslide into the sexual dark ages, when there wasn't sexual freedom, there was only repression.

Indeed many things seem to have changed. But if you look closely at what is supposed to be sexual freedom, you can become very confused. Let's say, for instance, you understand that a basic principle of sexual freedom is that people should be free to be sexual and that one way to guarantee that freedom is to make sure that sex be free from imposed restraint. That's not a bad idea, but if you happen to look at a magazine photograph in which a woman is bound and gagged and lashed down on a plank with her genital area open to the camera, you might well wonder: Where is the freedom from restraint? where's the sexual freedom?

Let's say you understand that people should be free to be sexual and that one way to guarantee that freedom is to make sure people can feel good about themselves and each other sexually. That's not a bad idea. But if you happen to read random passages from books such as the following, you could be quite perplexed:

> "Baby, you're gonna get fucked tonight like you ain't never been fucked before," he hissed evilly down at her as she struggled fruitlessly against her bonds. The man wanted only to abuse and ravish her till she was totally broken and subservient to him. He knelt between her widespread legs and gloated over the cringing little pussy he was about to ram his cock into.

. . .

After reading that, you might well ask: Where's the freedom from hatred? where's the freedom from degradation? where's the sexual freedom?

Let's say you understand people should be free to be sexual and that one way to guarantee that freedom is to make sure people are not punished for the individuality of their sexuality. And then you find a magazine showing page after page of bodies with their genitals garroted in baling wire and leather thongs, with their genitals tied up and tortured, with heavy weights suspended from rings that pierce their genitals, and the surrounding text makes clear that this mutilation and punishment are experienced as sex acts. And you might wonder in your mind: Why must this person suffer punishment in order to experience sexual feelings? why must this person be humiliated and disciplined and whipped and beaten until he bleeds in order to have access to his homoerotic passion? why have the Grand Inquisitor's most repressive and sadistic torture techniques become what people do to each other and call sex? where's the sexual freedom?

If you look back at the books and magazines and movies that have been produced in this country in the name of sexual freedom over the past decade, you've got to wonder: *Why has sexual freedom come to look so much like sexual repression? why has sexual freedom come to look so much like unfreedom?* The answer, I believe, has to do with the relationship between freedom and justice, and specifically the relationship between *sexual* freedom and *sexual* justice. When we think of freedom in any other sense, we think of freedom as *the result* of justice. We know that there can't truly *be* any freedom until justice has happened, until justice exists. For any people in history who have struggled for freedom, those people have understood that their freedom exists on the future side of justice. The notion of freedom *prior to* justice is understood to be meaningless. Whenever people do not have freedom, they have understood freedom to be that which you arrive at by achieving justice. If you told them they should try to have their freedom without there being justice, they would laugh in your face. Freedom *always* exists on the far side of justice. That's perfectly understood—except when it comes to sex.

The popular concept of sexual freedom in this country has never meant sexual justice. Sexual-freedom advocates have cast the issue only in terms of having sex that is free from suppression and restraint. Practically speaking, that has meant advocacy of sex that is free from institutional interference; sex that is free from being constrained by legal, religious, and medical ideologies; sex that is free from any outside intervention. Sexual freedom on a more personal level has meant sex that is free from fear, guilt, and shame—which in practical terms has meant advocacy of sex that is free from value judgments, sex that is free from responsibility, sex that is free from consequences, sex that is free from ethical distinctions, sex that is essentially free from any obligation to take into account in one's consciousness that the other person is a *person*. In order to free sex from fear, guilt, and shame, it was thought that institutional restrictions on sex needed to be overthrown, but in fact what needed to be over-thrown was any vestige of an interpersonal ethic in which people would be real to one another; for once people are real to one another, the consequences of one's acts matter deeply and personally; and particularly in the case of sex, one risks perceiving the consequences of one's acts in ways that feel *bad* because they do not feel *right*. This entire moral-feeling level of sexuality, therefore, needed to be undone. And it was undone, in the guise of an assault on institutional suppression.

Sexual freedom has never really meant that individuals should have sexual self-determination, that individuals should be free to experience the integrity of their own bodies and be free to act out of that integrity in a way that is totally within their own right to choose. Sexual freedom has never really meant that people should have absolute sovereignty over their own erotic being. And the reason for this is simple: Sexual freedom has never really been about *sexual justice between men and women*. It has been about maintaining men's superior status, men's power over women; and it has been about sexualizing women's inferior status, men's subordination of women. Essentially, sexual freedom has been about preserving a sexuality that preserves male supremacy.

. . .

PORNOGRAPHY AND MALE SUPREMACY

Male-supremacist sexuality is important to pornography, and pornography is important to male supremacy. Pornography *institutionalizes* the sexuality that both embodies and enacts male supremacy. Pornography says about that sexuality, "Here's how": Here's how to act out male supremacy in sex. Here's how the action should go. Here are the acts that impose power over and against another body. And pornography says about that sexuality, "Here's who": Here's who you should do it to and here's who she is: your whore, your piece of ass, yours. Your penis is a weapon, her body is your target.

And pornography says about that sexuality, "Here's why": Because men are masters, women are slaves; men are superior, women are subordinate; men are real, women are objects; men are sex machines, women are sluts.

Pornography institutionalizes male supremacy the way segregation institutionalizes white supremacy. It is a practice embodying an ideology of biological superiority; it is an institution that both expresses that ideology and enacts that ideology—makes it the reality that people believe is true, keeps it that way, keeps people from knowing any other possibility, keeps certain people powerful by keeping certain people *down*.

Pornography also *eroticizes* male supremacy. It makes dominance and subordination feel like sex; it makes hierarchy feel like sex; it makes force and violence feel like sex; it makes hate and terrorism feel like sex; it makes inequality feel like sex. Pornography keeps sexism sexy. It keeps sexism *necessary* for some people to have sexual feelings. It makes reciprocity make you go limp. It makes mutuality leave you cold. It makes tenderness and intimacy and caring make you feel like you're going to disappear into a void. It makes justice the opposite of erotic; it makes injustice a sexual thrill.

Pornography exploits every experience in people's lives that *imprisons* sexual feelings—pain, terrorism, punishment, dread, shame, powerlessness, self-hate—and would have you believe that it *frees* sexual feelings. In fact the sexual freedom represented by pornography is the freedom of men to act sexually in ways that keep sex a basis for inequality.

You can't have authentic sexual freedom without sexual justice. It is only freedom for those in power; the powerless cannot be free. Their experience of sexual freedom becomes but a delusion borne of complying with the demands of the powerful. Increased sexual freedom under male supremacy has had to mean an increased tolerance for sexual practices that are predicated on eroticized injustice between men and women: treating women's bodies or body parts as merely sexual objects or things;

treating women as utterly submissive maso-
chists who enjoy pain and humiliation and
who, if they are raped, enjoy it; treating
women's bodies to sexualized beating, mutilation, bondage, dismemberment. . . . Once you
have sexualized inequality, once it is a learned
and internalized prerequisite for sexual arousal
and sexual gratification, then anything goes.
And that's what sexual freedom means on this
side of sexual justice.

PORNOGRAPHY AND HOMOPHOBIA

Homophobia is absolutely integral to the system of sexualized male supremacy. Cultural
homophobia expresses a whole range of antife-
male revulsion: It expresses contempt for men
who are sexual with men because they are believed to be "treated like a woman" in sex. It expresses contempt for women who are sexual
with women just *because* they are women and
also because they are perceived to be a rebuke
to the primacy of the penis.

But cultural homophobia is not merely an
expression of woman hating; it also works to
protect men from the sexual aggression of other
men. Homophobia keeps men doing to women
what they would not want done to themselves.
There's not the same sexual harassment of men
that there is of women on the street or in the
workplace or in the university; there's not
nearly the same extent of rape; there's not the
same demeaned social caste that is sexualized,
as it is for women. And that's thanks to homophobia: Cultural homophobia keeps men's sexual aggression directed toward women. Homophobia keeps men acting in concert as male
supremacists so that they won't be perceived as
an appropriate target for male-supremacist
sexual treatment. Male supremacy *requires* homophobia in order to keep men safe from the
sexual aggression of men. Imagine this country
without homophobia: A woman raped every
three minutes *and a man* raped every three
minutes. Homophobia keeps that statistic at
a "manageable" level. The system is not fool-

proof, of course. There are boys who have been
sexually molested by men. There are men who
have been brutalized in sexual relationships
with their male lovers, and they too have a
memory of men's sexual violence. And there
are many men in prison who are subject to the
same sexual terrorism that women live with almost all the time. But for the most part—happily—homophobia serves male supremacy by
protecting "real men" from sexual assault by
other real men.

Pornography is one of the major enforcers
of cultural homophobia. Pornography is rife
with gay-baiting and effemiphobia. Portrayals
of allegedly lesbian "scenes" are a staple of
heterosexual pornography: The women with
each other are there for the male viewer, the
male voyeur; there is not the scantest evidence
that they are there for each other. Through
so-called men's-sophisticate magazines—the
"skin" magazines—pornographers outdo one
another in their attacks against feminists, who
are typically derided as lesbians—"sapphic" at
best, "bulldykes" at worst. The innuendo that a
man is a "fairy" or a "faggot" is, in pornography, a kind of dare or a challenge to prove his
cocksmanship. And throughout pornography,
the male who is perceived to be the passive
orifice in sex is tainted with the disdain that
"normally" belongs to women.

. . .

PORNOGRAPHY AND MEN

Now this is the situation of men within male
supremacy: Whether we are straight or gay, we
have been looking for a sexual freedom that is
utterly specious, and we have been looking for
it through pornography, which perpetuates the
very domination and subordination that stand
in the way of sexual justice. Whether we are
straight or gay, we have been looking for a notion of freedom that leaves out women; we
have been looking for a sexuality that preserves
men's power over women. So long as that is
what we strive for, we cannot possibly feel

freely, and no one can be free. Whatever sexual freedom might be, it must be after justice.

I want to speak directly to those of us who live in male supremacy as men, and I want to speak specifically to those of us who have come to understand that pornography does make sexism sexy; that pornography does make male supremacy sexy; and that pornography does define what is sexy in terms of domination and subordination, in terms that serve *us as men*—whether we buy it or not, whether we buy into it or not—because it serves male supremacy, which is exactly what it is for.

I want to speak to those of us who live in this setup as men and who recognize—in the world and in our very own selves—the power pornography can have over our lives: It can make men believe that our penises are like weapons. It can make men believe—for some moments of orgasm—that we are just like the men in pornography: virile, strong, tough,

maybe cruel. It can make men believe that if you take it away from us, we won't have sexual feelings.

. . .

We've got to be telling our sons that if a man gets off by putting women down, *it's not okay.*

We've got to be telling merchants that if they peddle women's bodies and lives for men's consumption and entertainment, *it's not okay.*

We've got to be telling other men that if you let the pornographers lead you by the nose (or any other body part) into believing that women exist to be tied up and hung up and beaten and raped, *it's not okay.*

We've got to be telling the pornographers—Larry Flynt and Bob Guccione and Hugh Hefner and Al Goldstein and all the rest—that whatever they think they're doing in our names as men, as entertainment for men, for the sake of some delusion of so-called manhood . . . well, it's not okay. It's not okay with *us.*

READING 75

The Internet and the Global Prostitution Industry

Donna M. Hughes

The Internet has become the latest place for promoting the global trafficking and sexual exploitation of women and children. This global communication network is being used to promote and engage in the buying and selling of women and children. Agents offer catalogues of mail order brides, with girls as young as 13. Commercial prostitution tours are advertised. Men exchange information on where to find prostitutes and describe how they can be used. After their trips men write reports on how much they paid for women and children and give pornographic descriptions of what they did to them. New technology has enabled an online merger of pornography and prostitution, with videoconferencing bringing live sex shows to the Internet.

SEXUAL EXPLOITATION ON THE INTERNET

Global sexual exploitation is on the rise. The profits are high, and there are few effective barriers at the moment. Because there is little regulation of the Internet, the traffickers and promoters of sexual exploitation have rapidly utilised the Internet for their purposes.

Traffickers and pornographers are the leading developers of the Internet industry. *PC Computing* magasine urges entrepreneurs to visit pornography Web sites. "It will show you the future of on-line commerce. Web pornographers are the most innovative entrepreneurs in the Internet." The pornographers and other promoters of sexual exploitation are the Internet leaders in the developing privacy services, secure payment schemes and online data base management.

The development and expansion of the Internet is an integral part of globalisation. The Internet sex industry has made local, community and even, national standards obsolete. Nichols Negroponte, Director of the Media Laboratory at the Massachusetts Institute of Technology, and founder of *Wired* magazine said, "As we interconnect ourselves, many of the values of a nation-state will give way to those of both larger and smaller electronic communities." The standards and values on the Internet are being set by the sex industry and its supporters and users. This has meant that women are increasingly "commodities" to be bought, sold, traded and consumed.

NEWSGROUPS AND WEB SITES FOR MEN WHO BUY WOMEN AND CHILDREN

The oldest forum on the Internet for promoting the sexual exploitation of women is the alt.sex.prostitution. Its "aim is to create market transparency for sex-related services." Postings from this newsgroup are archived into a site called The World Sex Guidem which provides "comprehensive, sex-related information about every country in the world."

The guide includes information and advice from men who have bought women and children in prostitution. They tell others where and how to find and buy prostituted women and children in 110 countries. . . .

The men buying women and posting the information see and perceive the events only from their self-interested perspective. Their awareness of racism, colonisation, global economic inequalities, and of course, sexism, is limited to how these forces benefit them. A country's economic or political crisis and the accompanying poverty are advantages, which produce cheap readily available women for the men. Often men describe how desperate the women are and how little the men have to pay.

The postings also reveal that men are using the Internet as a source of information in selecting where to go and how to find women and children to buy prostitution. Men describe taking a computer print out of hotels, bar addresses and phone numbers with them on their trips, or describe how they used the Internet search engines to locate sex tours. . . .

This rapid publishing electronic medium has enabled men to pimp and exploit individual women. Now, men can go out at night, buy a woman, go home, and post the details on the newsgroup. By morning anyone in the world with an Internet connection can read about it and often have enough information to find the same woman. For example, in Nevada, one man bought a woman called "Honey" and named the brothel where she could be found. Within a couple of weeks other men went and bought "Honey" themselves and posted their experiences to the newsgroup. Within a short period of time men were having an orgy of male bonding by describing what each of them did to this woman. The men are keeping a special Web site on the Internet for men to post their experiences of buying this one woman. Additional sites have been created for other identifiable women. To my knowledge this is completely unprecedented. The implications for this type of public exchange in a fast-publishing easily accessible medium like the Internet are very serious for the sexual exploitation of women in the future.

. . .

PROSTITUTION TOURS

Centers for prostitution tourism are also the sources of women trafficked for purposes of sexual exploitation to other countries. For centers of prostitution in European countries, women from poor countries are imported legally and illegally to fill the brothels. Among the largest sources of trafficked women today are the countries of the former Soviet Union.

Advertisements for prostitution tours to these sites appear on the Internet, usually described as "romance tours" or "introduction tours."

Prostitution tours enable men to travel to "exotic" places and step outside whatever community bounds may constrain them at home. In foreign cities they can abuse women and girls in ways that are more risky or difficult for them in their hometowns.

As prostitution has become a form of tourism for men, it has become a form of economic development for poor countries. Tourism was recommended by the United States advisory boards as a way to generate income and repay debts. Nation-states set their own tourist policies and could, if they chose to do so, prevent or suppress the development of prostitution as a form of tourism. Instead, communities and countries have to rely on the sale of women and children's bodies as their cash crop. As the prostitution industry grows, more girls and women are turned into sexual commodities for sale to tourists. In the bars of Bangkok, women and girls don't have names—they have numbers pinned to their skimpy clothes. The men pick them by numbers. They are literally interchangeable sexual objects.

Prostitution tourism centers in industrialised countries are receiving sites for trafficked women from poor countries. The Netherlands is the strongest international proponent for legalised prostitution. Its capital, Amsterdam, is the leading prostitution tourism center in Europe. In 1997 the Netherlands legalized brothels. The result has been increased trafficking to Amsterdam from all over the world.

. . .

BRIDE TRAFFICKING

Mail order bride agents have moved to the Internet as their preferred marketing location. The Internet reaches a prime group of potential buyers—men from Western countries with higher than average incomes. The new technology enables Web pages to be quickly and easily updated; some services claim they are updating their selection of women weekly. The Internet reaches a global audience faster and less expensively than any other media.

The agents offer men assistance in finding a "loving and devoted" woman whose "views on relationships have not been ruined by unreasonable expectations." The agencies describe themselves as "introduction services," but a quick examination of many of the Web sites reveals their commercial interests in bride trafficking, sex tours and prostitution.

The catalogues offer women mostly from Asia, Eastern Europe and Latin America, although in mid-1998 special catalogues of women from Africa appeared. They are called "African Queens," and "Brides of Nubia." Pictures of the women are shown with their names, height, weight, education and hobbies. Some catalogues include the women's bust, waist and hip measurements. The women range in age from 13 to 50. One of the commonly promoted characteristics of women from Eastern Europe is that they "traditionally expect to marry gentlemen that are 10 to 20 years older." The women are marketed as "pleasers," who will make very few demands on the men, and will not threaten them with expectations in their relationships, as women from the U.S. and Western Europe do.

In 1990 the Philippine government banned the operation of prostitution tour and mail order bride agencies in the Philippines. One trafficker lamented this new law, and told his customers that now he was operating out of the United States with his computer. He sent his own Filipina wife back to the Philippines to make contact and recruit women and adolescent girls for his Web site. Another complained that with the ban, the Philippine government is "definitely working against the interests of their own people. These girls want and need to leave that country." The same agent also complained that the U.S. government will not allow his youngest "brides" on offer into the country. "The service itself is not restricted by the American government, although they are real picky about getting your bride into the United States—they won't give a visa to a bride under sixteen." In his catalog of potential brides 19 girls are aged 17 or younger.

The bride traffickers sell addresses to men. Later they offer to arrange tours for the men to go to meet the woman with whom they have been corresponding, or to meet as many women as possible. Men pay for these services over the Internet with their credit cards.

. . .

LIVE VIDEO CONFERENCING

The most advanced technology on the Internet is live video conferencing, in which live audio and video are transmitted over the Internet from video recorder to computer. This advanced technology is being used to sell live sex shows over the Internet. Real time communication is possible, so the man can personally direct the live sex show as he is viewing it on his computer.

The only limitation on this type of global sex show is the need for high-speed transmission, processing and multimedia capabilities. The software required is free, but the most recent versions of Web browsers have these capabilities built into them. As more men have access to high-speed multimedia computer and transmission equipment, this type of private sex show will grow. There are no legal restrictions on live sex shows that can be transmitted over the Internet. As with all Internet transmissions, there are no nation-state border restrictions. With Internet technology a man may be on one continent, while directing and watching a live strip show, a live sex show, or the sexual abuse of a child on another continent. There have been several documented cases of live transmission of the sexual abuse of children through live video conferencing.

. . .

Who buys women over the Internet? According to the Internet Entertainment Group (EIG), the largest pimp on the Web, the buyers for live strip shows are 90 percent male, 70 percent are between the ages of 18 and 40. The buyers are young men in college, and businessmen and professionals who log on from work. This information was obtained from analysis of credit card usage.

GROWTH OF THE COMMERCIAL PROSTITUTION INDUSTRY ON THE INTERNET

. . .

The estimated number of pornographic Web sites varies widely. In late 1997, according to Naughty Linx, an online index, there were 28,000 "sex sites" on the Web with about half of them trying to make money selling pornography, videos, or live sex shows. Another study estimated that there were 72,000 pornographic Web sites on the Internet. At the end of 1997, Leo Preiser, the Director of the Center for Technology at National University estimated that 60 percent of the electronic commerce on the Web was pornography.

At the end of 1997, the online sex industry was estimated to be making US$1 billion a year, just in the United States. In findings from a 1997 survey, *Inter@ctive Week* magazine reported that 10,000 sex industry sites were bringing in approximately US$1 billion per year. A midsize site that was accessed 50,000 times per day made approximately US$20,000 each month. Established sex industry sites could expect to make 50 to 80 percent profits. Forrester Research, an Internet analyst firm, estimated that the Internet sex industry would make close to US$1 billion in 1998. "We know of at least three sites doing more than US$100 million a year. And there are hundreds of sites out there."

REGULATION

The new technologies of the Internet have leapt over national borders and have left lawmakers scrambling to catch up. Internet users have adopted and defend an unbridled libertarianism. Any kind of regulation or restriction is met with hysterics and predictions of a totalitarian society. Even the most conservative restrictions on the transmission of child pornography are greeted with cries of censorship. The December 1996 issue of *Wired,* the leading professional publication on the Internet, stated that a new law in the United States, which made it illegal to transmit indecent materials to minors, was censorship. Internet libertarianism coupled with United States free speech absolutism is setting the standard for Internet communications.

Expressions of concern or condemnation of forms of sexual exploitation of women and children on the Internet are minimized by claims that pornographers have always been the first to take advantage of new technology— first photography, then movies, then VCRs, now the Internet. Those concerned about the use of the Internet for sexual exploitation are chastened with history lectures on new technology and pornography.

The solution that is being promoted is software programs that will screen out sexually explicit material. U.S. President Bill Clinton just announced that he supported a rating system on the Internet, so pornography would be rated and software programs will screen it out. This is seen as a way to protect children. Most adults are only concerned that their children may see pornography on the Internet. They aren't concerned about the women who are being exploited in the making of the pornography. In any search for a solution to pornography and prostitution it is crucial to remember, that sexual exploitation starts with real people and the harm is to real people.

We need international judicial and police co-operation in regulating the Internet and ending the trafficking and prostitution of women and the girls. If it is illegal to run a prostitution tour agency or mail order bride agency in the Philippines, then it should be illegal to advertise these services on a computer in the USA. The countries that send the men on tours and receive the mail order brides should also ban the operation of such agencies and prohibit the advertisement of these services from computer servers in their country.

The European Union defines trafficking as a form of organised crime. It should be treated the same way on the Internet. All forms of sexual exploitation should be recognised as forms of violence against women and human rights violations, and governments should act accordingly. Although the Internet offers open communication to people throughout the world, it should not be permitted to be dominated and controlled by men's interests or the interests of the prostitution industry, at the expense of women and children.

Militarism and Sexual Violence

Fiona Lee

Throughout history women have been fundamental to the military's ability to operate successfully. While women have worked as soldiers, nurses, and support staff, they have also played other roles. In particular, women have been used as a form of recreation at the same time that the torture and rape of enemy women has functioned to humiliate and demonstrate power over the enemy.

The military uses a social construction of masculinity that relies on the objectification of women in order to sustain soldiers' morale and discipline. Military personnel are trained to dehumanize as a part of preparation for war. Often the easiest way to achieve this is to teach men to exercise their power over women. Ordinary training ditties often compare guns to penises and war to sex; men are called pussies and sissies and quickly learn that the definition of masculine is "not feminine." During the Vietnam War, "rest and recreation," or "R and R," was frequently re-labeled "I and I" for "intercourse and intoxication," clearly establishing the fact that military leave was analogous to the sexual violation of women (Enloe 1990).

Prostitution and various forms of sexual slavery have been among the spoils of military conquest for as long as war has existed (Elshtain 1989; Leuchtag 1995). Military prostitution has been justified by the theory that soldiers need an outlet for sexual energy. It is argued that if prostitution is not provided, soldiers will inevitably go out and rape civilian women due to the fact that they are men, and men need sex. Thus, the atrocities of military prostitution are hidden under the guise of protecting "innocent" women: daughters, sisters and wives. Yet, despite the guise of protection, military prostitution has resulted in a huge increase in local violence directed towards women. Incidents of domestic violence, sexual harassment and rape increase in communities of military occupation (Enloe 1990). In this way, prostitution is used by militaries as a tool, a tactic, and a strategy for the domination of whole communities.

The close relationship between militarism and the commodification of women's bodies and militarism as a masculinized concept encourages international prostitution. Such prostitution, in effect, depends on a concept of global patriarchy that encourages male sexual prerogatives (Watanabe 1995). Current levels of local prostitution in Saigon, Thailand, Vietnam and the Philippines are a direct result of U.S. military bases in these areas (Sturdevant and Stoltzfus 1992). It is difficult to argue that these women are making conscious choices to sell sex; economic situations drive them to support themselves and their families in this way. Most come from poor families and have little education. A prostitute in Nepal was quoted as commenting, "If I were a man, maybe I would have committed murder to fill my stomach. But as a woman, I became a prostitute" (Hornblower and Morris 1993: 44). This illustrates the dire circumstances in which many of these women find themselves. A similar situation has occurred in more recent times in Bosnia. When a merchant was asked how the people of Kapsovar would greet the Americans, he replied that the building of brothels was underway (Raymond 1999).

The rape of enemy women has also been recorded as a by-product of military action throughout history. It is a well-known fact that rape is one of the most effective strategies to "drive a wedge through a community, to shatter a society, and to destroy a people" (MacKinnon 1994: 190). In effect, rape of this kind results in the "castration" or de-masculinization of enemy men. This tactic has been used in conjunction with other forms of "ethnic cleansing" in Bosnia (Rejali 1998). Thousands of Croatian women have been raped and forced to bear children of Serbian descent.

While prostitution and rape were tactics used by both sides of the conflict during World War II, it is especially the plight of the "comfort women" that illustrates the complex relationship between prostitution and rape in wartime. During this war the Japanese government sanctioned a system of sexual slavery and enslaved thousands of comfort women as prostitutes for the Japanese Imperial army. These were young Chinese, Korean, and Philippino women who were deceived or abducted and forced into prostitution (Dolgopol 1995; Lord 1999). The first woman to break the comfort women's fifty year silence of shame that followed the sexual atrocities in World War II was Kim Haku in 1990: "When I was seventeen years old, the Japanese soldiers came along in a truck, beat us and dragged us into the back. . . . I was told that if I were drafted, I would earn lots of money at the textile company. . . . The first day I was raped and the rapes never stopped" (Watanabe 1995: 505). Her story is not unusual. It is estimated that approximately 150,000 to 200,000 women were forced into sexual slavery between 1928 and 1945. Often just 1,000 women would be forced to serve approximately 50,000 soldiers. The young women, sometimes as young as 14 and 15 years old, were made to perform sexually up to 20 and 30 times a day; one source says 80 times a day (anon. 1992: 32). These "prostitutes" were, in effect, raped over and over again.

The aftermath of the war was equally painful for these women. Fewer than 30% survived to the end of the war. Many died during the course of service, felled by disease or abuse, slain by fleeing troops, left to starve in the jungle, or killed by the Japanese to prevent them from telling their stories. Those who did survive suffered an acute sense of shame and worthlessness, and were often faced with sexually transmitted diseases or sterility (Watanabe 1995; anon. 1992).

In this way, since militaries are built on the solid foundation of patriarchal cultures that encourage the subordination and dehumanization of women, sexual violence has established itself as an inevitable accompaniment to war. Indeed, it could be maintained that it is essential to war: a concern for all those who seek equality, peace, and freedom.

REFERENCES

Anonymous. 1992. "Comfort Without Joy." *Economist* 322: 32.

Chenoy, Anuadha M. 1998. "Militarization, Conflict, and Women in South Asia." Pp. 101–110 in *The Women and War Reader*, edited by Lois Ann Lorentzen and Jennifer Turpin (New York: New York University Press).

Dolgopol, Ustina. 1995. "Women's Voices, Women's Pain." *Human Rights Quarterly* 17, 1: 127–154.

Elshtain, Jean Bethke. 1989. *Women and War*. (New York: Basic Books).

Enloe, Cynthia. 1990. *Bananas, Beaches and Bases: Making Feminist Sense of International Politics.* (Berkeley: University of California Press).

Hornblower, Margot and Morris, Nomi. 1993. "The Skin Trade." *Time* June 21: 44.

Leuchtag, Alice. 1995. "Merchants of Flesh." *Humanist* 55: 11.

Lord, Mary. 1999. "The Comfort Woman's Cry." *US News and World Report* December 16: 26.

MacKinnon, Catharine. 1994. "Rape, Genocide, and Women's Human Rights" in *Mass Rape: The War Against Women in Bosnia-Herzegovi,* edited by Alexandra Stiglmayer (Lincoln: University of Nebraska Press).

Raymond, Janice G. "Prostitution Is Rape that Is Paid For" *http://www.uvi.edu/artsci/wms/hughes/catw/kinrap.html*. Viewed 2/11/99.

Rejali, Darius M. 1998. "After Feminist Analyses of Bosnian Violence." Pp. 26–32 in *The Women and War Reader*, edited by Lois Ann Lorentzen and Jennifer Turpin (New York: New York University Press).

Sturdevant, Saundra Pollock and Stoltzfus, Brenda. 1992. *Let the Good Times Roll: Prostitution and the U.S. Military in Asia* (New York: New York Press).

Watanabe, Kazuko. 1995. "Trafficking in Women's Bodies: Then and Now." *Peace and Change* 20: 501–151.

DISCUSSION QUESTIONS FOR CHAPTER TEN

1. How do violence and the threat of violence exert social control on women? Do you ever fear gender-based violence? How do you think your gender affects your answer to this question?

2. Why do you think many feminists suggest that acts of violence against women are actually hate crimes? Do you think these acts should be classified as hate crimes?

3. Why do you think violence against women is so prevalent in society? Why do you think violence against women is primarily perpetrated by men?

4. How do myths about violence against women silence women and perpetuate sexist systems of oppression?

5. What steps do you believe need to be taken in order to address the problem of violence against women?

SUGGESTIONS FOR FURTHER READING

Bass, Ellen, and Laura Davis. *The Courage to Heal: A Guide for Women Survivors of Child Sexual Abuse,* rev. ed. New York: Harperperennial, 1994.

Evans, Patricia. *The Verbally Abusive Relationship: How to Recognize It and How to Respond.* Holbrook, MA: Adams Media Corp., 1996.

Jones, Ann. *Next Time, She'll Be Dead: Battering & How to Stop It,* rev. ed. Boston: Beacon, 2000.

Raine, Nancy Venable. *After Silence: Rape and My Journey Back.* New York: Three Rivers Press, 1999.

Warshaw, Robin. *I Never Called It Rape: The Ms. Report on Recognizing, Fighting, and Surviving Date and Acquaintance Rape.* New York: Harperperennial, 1994.

CHAPTER ELEVEN

State, Law, and Social Policy

As we have noted in earlier chapters, societal institutions are established patterns of social behavior organized around particular needs and purposes. Gender, race, class, and other systems of inequality structure social institutions, creating different effects on different people. The state, the institution explored in this chapter, is a major social institution organized to maintain systems of legitimized power and authority in society. The state plays an important role in both teaching and enforcing social values. It is a very powerful institution that has profound implications for women's everyday lives.

The *state* is an abstract concept that refers to all forms of social organization representing official power in society: the government, law and social policy, the courts and the criminal system, the military, and the police. The state determines how people are selected to govern others and controls the systems of governance they must use. With considerable authority in maintaining social order, the state influences how power is exercised within society. The definition of *state* here is different from state as a geographic region, such as California or Ohio.

Because the state is a conduit for various patterns of social inequity, it does not always fairly regulate and control social order. Historically, women and people of color have been treated very poorly by the state, and there are still many problems and challenges at all levels of the political system. However, the state has also been a tool for addressing historical forms of social, political, and economic inequalities (as evidenced by civil rights and affirmative action legislation). Many people are involved in the struggle to effect change through laws and social policies. A key focus of this chapter is the interaction between the state and gender relations in society.

The state provides basic institutional structure in the sense that it regulates other institutions—for instance, the family (such as the Family Leave Act or considering some families to be illegitimate and thus ineligible for state benefits), education (such as Title IX), the economic system (such as antitrust laws that prevent monopolies), and religion (such as state rules for the separation of church and state). In this way, the state is a very powerful regulator of society.

GOVERNMENT AND REPRESENTATION

Although the terms *government* and *state* tend to be used interchangeably, the government is actually one of the institutions that make up the state. The government creates laws and procedures that govern society and is often referred to as the political system. Although the U.S. government or political system is purported to be a democracy based on the principle of equal representation, the government is not representative of all people, and those who participate as elected officials do not necessarily represent all interests equitably.

The U.S. Constitution was formed at a time when White men were regarded as the only legal entity, women or people of color were not considered equal before the law. As a result, these individuals have had a complicated relationship with the Constitution. In the early formation of the republic, women were excluded because it was assumed that politics and citizenship were purely masculine domains. The founding fathers believed that women's political identity should be restricted because their presence in politics was immoral, corruptive, and potentially disruptive. Instead it was believed that women should be confined to the private sphere of the home where they would be dependent upon men (fathers, husbands, brothers) to represent them. Therefore, because women had no separate legal identity and were legal beings only through their relationship to a man, they had no claims to citizenship rights as women.

As you know from Chapter 1, the Seneca Falls convention in 1848 produced the Declaration of Sentiments and Resolutions that aimed to ensure citizenship rights for women. Women would have to wait until 1920 with the passage of the Nineteenth Amendment to the U.S. Constitution to receive the vote. In 1868, however, the Fourteenth Amendment was ratified, asserting that no state shall "make or enforce any law which will abridge the privileges or immunities of citizens of the United States, nor . . . deprive any person of life, liberty, or property without due process of law, nor deny to any person within its jurisdiction the equal protection of laws." This "person" was assumed to be male, and, as a result, women could still not vote, and the government did not (and, many would argue, still does not) extend the same protection of the law to women as it does to men. Susan B. Anthony, one of the first feminists who helped write the Declaration of Sentiments

Reprinted with permission from Nicole Hollander.

Learning Activity: The League of Women Voters

The League of Women Voters was founded by Carrie Chapman Catt in 1920 during the convention of the National American Woman Suffrage Association, just six months before the Nineteenth Amendment was ratified. In its early years, the league advocated for collective bargaining, child labor laws, minimum wage, compulsory education, and equal opportunity for women in government and industry. Today the league is still involved in advocacy for justice, working on such issues as Medicare reform, campaign finance reform, and environmental preservation, as well as continuing the work begun over eighty years ago to encourage women to use their political voices. To learn more about the League of Women Voters or to join the league, visit their website at *www.lwv.org*.

and Resolutions, wanted to test her belief that the Fourteenth Amendment should give women, as citizens, the right to vote. She voted in an election in Rochester, New York, and was fined. Hoping to push the case to the Supreme Court, Anthony refused to pay the fine. The case, however, was dropped in order to avoid this test of law. In the Anthony reading "Constitutional Argument," she argues her right to vote as a citizen under the terms guaranteed by the Fourteenth Amendment. This excerpt is from a speech Anthony gave in 1873.

In 1923 the Equal Rights Amendment was introduced into Congress to counter the inadequacies of the Fourteenth Amendment concerning women and citizenship. It was rewritten in the 1940s to read: "Equality of rights under the law shall not be denied or abridged by the United States or by any state on account of sex" and it eventually passed Congress (almost fifty years later) in 1972. Unfortunately, it failed to be ratified by the states and suffered a serious defeat in the early 1980s.

An illustration of how the government has handled women and citizenship concerns the treatment of women who have married non-U.S. citizens. Prior to the mid-1920s, nonnative-born women who married U.S. citizens automatically became American, and native-born women who married non-U.S. citizens automatically lost their citizenship and were expected to reside in their husband's country. They also lost their right to vote, once women had been given the vote in 1920. When laws were passed to retain women's citizenship in the mid-1920s, still only men were able to pass on citizenship to their children. Laws equalizing citizenship on these issues were eventually passed in the mid-1930s.

In addition to rights, citizenship also entails such obligations as taxation, jury duty, and military service. Although women have shared taxation with men, in the past they have been prevented from service and/or exempted from jury duty because of their role as mothers and housewives. It was not until the 1970s that the Supreme Court declared that juries had to be representative of the community. Even then juries were often racially biased such that it was not unusual for an African American to face a White jury. A 1986 Supreme Court ruling stated that juries could not be constituted on the basis of race, and a 1994 ruling declared that gender too could not be used as a basis for jury competence. The obligation for military service, which many women have wanted to share with men, is outlined in more detail later in the chapter. Of course, women have served in auxiliary roles

Activist Profile: Wilma Mankiller

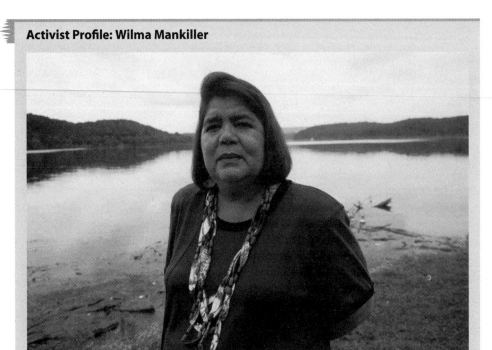

With her election as chief of the Cherokee Nation, Wilma Mankiller took both a step forward and a step backward. Although Mankiller was the first woman to serve as chief of a major Native American tribe in modern times, her election recalled the importance women had among the Cherokee before colonization by Europeans. Precontact Cherokee society was matrifocal and matrilineal. Women owned the property and maintained the home and were intimately involved in tribal governance.

Mankiller first became committed to involvement in Native American rights in 1969 when Native activists, including some of her own siblings, occupied Alcatraz island in San Francisco Bay. The nineteen-month occupation became a turning point in Mankiller's life. She became director of the Native American Youth Center in Oakland, California, and in 1973 she watched as her brother joined other Native American activists as they held off FBI agents for seventy-two days at Wounded Knee, South Dakota.

Following a divorce, Mankiller returned to her family's land in Oklahoma and began to work for the Cherokee Nation; as an economic stimulus coordinator, she had the task of encouraging Cherokee people to train in environmental health and science and then return to their communities to put their knowledge to use. In 1981, she became director of the Cherokee Nation Community Development Department, and her work was so successful that she attracted the attention of Chief Ross Swimmer, who asked her to run as his deputy chief in 1983.

Despite sexist rhetoric and verbal threats from opponents, Swimmer and Mankiller won. In 1985, Swimmer was named head of the Bureau of Indian Affairs by President Ronald Reagan, and Mankiller became chief of the Cherokee Nation. In 1987, Mankiller ran on her own and was elected chief in her own right. That year, *Ms.* magazine named her Woman of the Year. She was re-elected in 1991, winning by 83 percent of the vote. During her tenure as chief, Mankiller focused on addressing high unemployment and low education rates among Cherokee people, improving community health care, implementing housing initiatives and child and youth projects, and developing the economy of northeastern Oklahoma. She created the Institute for Cherokee Literacy, emphasizing the need for Cherokee people to retain their traditions. She did not run for re-election in 1995. In 1998 President Bill Clinton awarded her the Presidential Medal of Freedom.

as nurses, transport drivers, and dispatchers for many years and are now able to participate in combat positions within some divisions of the armed services.

Although women tend to be as involved as men in electoral politics (and sometimes even more involved) in terms of voting, showing support, and volunteering for campaigns, there are markedly fewer women involved in official political positions associated with campaigns. Women still constitute a relatively small number of candidates for local, state, and national offices, and their presence is greater at the local rather than national levels. As political offices get more visible, higher level, better paid, and more authoritative or powerful, there are fewer women in these positions. Several explanations may explain this gap. Although some suggest that women are just not interested and that they lack the credentials, the main reasons are conflict between family and work roles, lack of political financing, and discrimination and sexist attitudes toward women in politics.

The 106th Congress of the year 2000 includes fifty-six women or 13 percent in the House of Representatives, nine women or 9 percent in the Senate, and 12 percent overall in Congress. In terms of politicians who are non-White (both women and men), the 106th Congress includes seven Asian Americans, thirty-nine African Americans and twenty-one Latinos/as, again making up 12 percent of the total overall. These figures, although much improved compared to pre-1990s statistics, are still alarming; they illustrate male and White domination in society and challenge the extent to which women and people of color are represented. However, remember that females do not necessarily represent women's interests, just as people of color do not necessarily support issues that improve the status of non-White groups. Many feminists vote for men in political office over opposing women candidates because they understand that being a female does not necessarily mean that her politics, or those of the party she represents, are pro-women. In terms of the gender gap in voting, on the average women tend to lean toward the Democratic Party more than men do and are more likely to be concerned about such issues as education, welfare, health care, and the environment. These differences vary, however, with different electoral campaigns.

WOMEN AND THE LAW

The United States inherited British common law that utilized the doctrine of *femme couverte* or covered women: Husband and wife were one person under law, and she was his sexual property. As a result, married women could not seek employment without the husband's consent, keep their own wages, own property, sue, exercise control over their children, and control their reproductive lives. The

Women in Elective Office 2000

In 2000, sixty-five women served in the U.S. Congress. A record nine women served in the Senate, and fifty-six women served in the House, also an all-time high. The number of women in statewide elective executive posts is ninety-two, an all-time high, although the proportion of women in state legislatures is 22.5 percent.

CONGRESS   In 2000, women hold 65, or 12.1%, of the 535 seats in the 106th U.S. Congress — 9, or 9.0%, of the 100 seats in the Senate and 56, or 12.9%, of the 435 seats in the House of Representatives. In addition, two women serve as Delegates to the House from the Virgin Islands and Washington, DC.

Nine women serve in the Senate: Barbara Boxer (D-CA); Susan Collins (R-ME); Dianne Feinstein (D-CA); Kay Bailey Hutchison (R-TX); Mary Landrieu (D-LA); Blanche Lincoln (D-AR); Barbara Mikulski (D-MD); Patty Murray (D-WA); and Olympia Snowe (R-ME).

Fifty-six women from 24 states serve in the House of Representatives; 39 are Democrats and 17 are Republicans. In addition, two Democratic women serve as the Delegates to the House from the Virgin Islands and Washington, DC.

STATEWIDE
ELECTIVE
EXECUTIVE
OFFICES

In 2000, 92 women hold statewide elective executive offices across the country; women hold 28.5% of the 323 available positions. Among these women, 47 are Democrats, 42 are Republicans, 1 is a member of Independence Party, and 2 were elected in non-partisan races.

GOVERNORS — 3 (1D, 2R)
Jane Dee Hull (R-AZ)
Jeanne Shaheen (D-NH)
Christine Todd Whitman (R-NJ)

LIEUTENANT GOVERNORS — 19
   (7D, 11R, 1IP*)
Fran Ulmer (D-AK)
M. Jodi Rell (R-CT)
Ruth Ann Minner (D-DE)
Mazie K. Hirono (D-HI)
Sally Pederson (D-IA)
Corrine Wood (R-IL)
Kathleen Blanco (D-LA)
Kathleen Kennedy Townsend (D-MD)
Jane Swift (R-MA)
Mae Schunk (IP*-MN)
Amy Tuck (D-MS)
Judy Martz (R-MT)
Lorraine Hunt (R-NV)
Mary O. Donohue (R-NY)
Rosemarie Myrdal (R-ND)
Maureen O'Connor (R-OH)
Mary Fallin (R-OK)
Carole Hillard (R-SD)
Olene S. Walker (R-UT)

Attorney General — 11 (8D, 3R)

Secretary of State — 14 (7D, 7R)

State Treasurer — 10 (6D, 4R)

State Comptroller — 4 (2D, 2R)

State Auditor — 5 (3D, 2R)

Chief Agricultural Official — 2 (1D, 1R)
   (title varies from state to state)

Chief State Education Official — 10
   (4D, 4R, 2NP†)
   (title varies from state to state)

Commissioner of Elections — 1R

Commissioner of Insurance — 3 (2D, 1R)

Commissioner of Labor — 1R

Commissioner of Public Lands — 1D

Corporation Commissioner — 1D

Public Regulatory Commissioner — 1D

Public Service Commissioner — 4 (3D, 1R)

Public Utilities Commissioner — 2 (1D, 1R)

*IP = Independence Party.
†NP = election was nonpartisan.

STATE LEGISLATURES

In 2000, 1,670, or 22.5%, of the 7,424 state legislators in the United States are women. Women hold 396, or 20.0%, of the 1,984 state senate seats and 1,274, or 23.5%, of the 5,440 state house seats. The number of women serving in state legislatures has increased more than five-fold since 1969 when 301, or 4.0%, of all state legislators were women.

The ten states with the highest percentages of women state legislators are:

State	% Women	State	% Women
Washington	40.8	New Hampshire	31.8
Nevada	36.5	Vermont	31.7
Arizona	35.6	Oregon	30.0
Colorado	34.0	Connecticut	29.4
Kansas	33.3	Maryland	29.3

MUNICIPAL OFFICIALS

As of May 1999, among the 100 largest cities in the U.S., 16 had women mayors. One is African American (Sharon Sayles Belton, Minneapolis) and one is Latina (Judith Valles, San Bernardino). In order of city population,* the mayors were:

City	Mayor	Rank
San Diego, CA	Susan Golding	7th
Portland, OR	Vera Katz	28th
Kansas City, MO	Kay Barnes	33rd
Virginia Beach, VA	Meyera E. Oberndorf	34th
Long Beach, CA	Beverly O'Neill	36th
Tulsa, OK	Susan Savage	40th
Minneapolis, MN	Sharon Sayles Belton	47th
Cincinnati, OH	Roxanne Qualls	50th
Colorado Springs, CO	Mary Lou Makepeace	51st
Lexington, KY	Pam Miller	67th
Greensboro, NC	Carolyn Allen	80th
Lubbock, TX	Windy Sitton	81st
Glendale, CA	Ginger Bremberg	92nd
San Bernardino, CA	Judith Valles	93rd
Orlando, FL	Glenda Hood	94th
Huntsville, AL	Loretta Spencer	95th

As of May 1999, of the 228 mayors of U.S. cities with populations over 100,000, 45 or 19.7% were women, including one African American and four Latinas. Of the 978 mayors of U.S. cities with populations over 30,000, 192, or 19.6%, were women.[†]

Percentages of Women in Elective Offices

Level of Office	1979	1981	1983	1985	1987	1989	1991	1993	1995	1997	1999	2000
U.S. Congress	3%	4%	4%	5%	5%	5%	6%	10%	10%	11%	12%	12%
Statewide Elective	11%	11%	11%	14%	14%	14%	18%	22%	26%	26%	28%	29%
State Legislatures	10%	12%	13%	15%	16%	17%	18%	21%	21%	22%	23%	23%

*According to data from the U.S. Bureau of the Census.
[†] *Source:* CAWP. Information was compiled using the United States Conference of Mayors' January 1999 directory, "The Mayors of America's Principal Cities," as the primary reference.

Ideas for Activism

- Visit the homepage for Women Leaders Online at *www.wlo.org*. Women Leaders Online is the first and largest women's activist group on the Internet. WLO provides action alerts to make people aware of issues that need activism. The organization also promotes voter education and facilitates email access to your U.S. senators and representatives.
- For more information about political issues of concern to women, visit the homepage of the Feminist Majority Foundation at *www.feminist.org*. Follow the link to Take Action for ideas about what you can do to make a difference.

reading by Margaret Conway and others, "Women and Family Law: Marriage and Divorce," explains laws and public policies governing marriage under British common law. Because husbands and wives were "one" in marriage, wives were sexual property of husbands, and rape within marriage was legally condoned. It was legally impossible to charge a husband with raping his wife because it would imply that the husband was raping himself. The phrase "rule of thumb" meant that it was okay to beat a woman so long as an implement no wider than the thumb was used. Although the Married Women's Property Act of 1848 allowed women to own and inherit property, the other constraints on their lives remained intact through the twentieth century. Even with the passage of these property acts, however, the law allowed the husband to control community property (jointly owned legally by husband and wife) until the 1970s.

Prior to the 1960s most states decriminalized violence in the family and operated marital rape exemption laws. It was not until the 1980s and 1990s that women had legal protections against violence; these protections include legislation such as the rape shield laws, mandatory arrest procedures in cases of domestic violence, public notification programs about convicted sex offenders in communities, the creation of protective or temporary restraining orders, state rape reform laws, and the 1994 Violence Against Women Act. As the reading by Conway explains, although most states have abolished marital rape exemptions, there are states that retain these laws in some fashion today. And, certainly, as the readings in Chapter 10 suggest, violence against women is increasing rather than decreasing in contemporary society.

Also prior to the 1960s, women's reproductive lives were a function of state control because the state had criminalized access to contraceptive information and procedures. As discussed in Chapter 6, before the passage of *Griswold v. Connecticut* in 1965, women had no legal right to contraceptives, and before the early 1970s with the passage of state abortion rulings and *Roe v. Wade,* they had no legal right to an abortion. The issue of reproductive rights is still controversial, and the legal arena is the site for many of these battles today.

In terms of work and employment, *Muller v. Oregon* in 1908 reaffirmed the state's justification for limiting women's employment. This legislation approved Oregon's right to prevent women from working in factories or similar facilities for more than 10 hours a day based upon the state's interest in protecting the reproductive functions of women. It was considered important for the "well-being of the

Affirmative Action: Myth Versus Reality

Myth: Women don't need affirmative action any more.

Reality: Though women have made gains in the last thirty years, they remain severely under-represented in most nontraditional professional occupations as well as blue-collar trades. The U.S. Department of Labor's Glass Ceiling Commission Report (1995) states that although White men are only 43 percent of the Fortune 2000 workforce, they hold 95 percent of the senior management jobs.

Myth: Under affirmative action, minorities and women receive preferences.

Reality: Affirmative action does not require preferences, nor do women and minorities assume that they will be given preference. Race, gender, and national origin are factors that can be considered when hiring or accepting qualified applicants, which is similar to the preferences given to veterans in hiring and to children of alumni in college admissions.

Myth: Affirmative action is really quotas.

Reality: Affirmative action provides women and minorities with full educational and work-place opportunities. Race, national origin, and gender are among several factors to be considered, but relevant and valid job or educational qualifications are not to be compromised. Further, the Supreme Court has made clear that affirmative action or programs that claim to be affirmative action are illegal if: (1) an unqualified person receives benefits over a qualified one; (2) numerical goals are so strict that the plan lacks reasonable flexibility; (3) the numerical goals bear no relationship to the available pool of qualified candidates and could therefore become quotas; (4) the plan is not fixed in length; or (5) innocent bystanders are impermissibly harmed.

Myth: Affirmative action leads to reverse discrimination.

Reality: Evidence demonstrates that reverse discrimination is rare. For example, of the 91,000 employment discrimination cases before the Equal Employment Opportunities Commission, approximately 3 percent are reverse discrimination cases. Further, a study conducted by Rutgers University and commissioned by the U.S. Department of Labor (1995) found that reverse discrimination is not a significant problem in employment and that a "high proportion" of claims brought by White men are "without merit."

Myth: Affirmative action programs that aid the economically disadvantaged—needs-based programs—are enough to address discrimination.

Reality: Women and minorities face discrimination as they climb the corporate ladder and bump up against the glass ceiling.

Myth: Unqualified individuals are being hired and promoted for the sake of diversity/affirmative action.

Reality: Only affirmative action plans that do not compromise valid job or educational qualifications are lawful. Plans must be flexible, realistic, reviewable, and fair. The Supreme Court has found that there are at least two permissible bases for voluntary affirmative action by employers under Title VII: (1) to remedy a clear and convincing history of past discrimination by the employer or union, and (2) to cure a manifest imbalance in the employer's workforce.

Myth: Affirmative action does not have a place in government contracts.

Reality: Congress has created federal procurement programs to counter the effects of discrimination that have raised artificial barriers to the formation, development, and utilization of businesses owned by disadvantaged individuals, including women and minorities.

(continued)

Affirmative Action: Myth Versus Reality (*continued*)

Only qualified businesses can participate in these procurement programs. These programs are still needed because although minorities own almost 9 percent of all businesses and women own 34 percent of all businesses, together minorities and women receive only about 8.8 percent of the over $200 billion in federal contract awards.

Myth: Title VII alone is sufficient to address discrimination.

Reality: Affirmative action means taking positive, proactive, and preemptive steps to root out discrimination, rather than waiting for after-the-fact litigation. Title VII addresses discrimination, but it does so only after an instance of discrimination has been claimed. Affirmative action policies are a means to end discrimination in a far less costly and disruptive way than protracted litigation.

Myth: Underrepresentation of minorities and women in the corporate world (or other high-paying jobs) is not due to discrimination.

Reality: Although discrimination is not the sole reason for the lack of women and minorities in the corporate world, we must still deal with past and present discrimination. A study of the 1982 Stanford MBA graduating class found that in 1992, 16 percent of the men held CEO titles compared to 2 percent of the women. Twenty-three percent of men become corporate vice presidents, but only 10 percent of the women, whereas 15 percent of men served as directors, compared to 8 percent of the women.

Myth: The so-called earnings gap between men and women has closed significantly in recent years; therefore, affirmative action is no longer needed to achieve pay equity.

Reality: In 1993, the total amount of wages women lost due to pay inequity was nearly $100 billion. The average woman loses approximately $420,000 over a lifetime due to unequal pay practices. Working women still earn just 76 cents for every dollar men earn. Much of this wage gap is due to the fact that women are still segregated into traditionally female-dominated jobs where wages are low. Further, the pay gap exists even within the same occupation. In eighty-six occupations tracked by the Bureau of Labor Statistics, women earn 20 to 35 percent less than men.

Myth: Most analyses that point to wage differentials between men and women do not take into account differences in hours worked and years of uninterrupted work experience between the sexes. Female earnings are depressed because women work, on average, fewer hours per week than men and have more interruptions over their working lives than do men.

Reality: The wage inequities most often cited are based on Department of Labor and Census Bureau data on year-round, full-time workers who have a permanent attachment to the workforce. These data do not compare full-time male workers to part-time female workers, nor do they compare permanent workers to part-time and contingent workers.

Source: www.civilrights.org/aa/mythreal.html.

race" that women's ability to contract freely be limited. As discussed in Chapter 8, by the 1960s various civil rights legislation was passed including the Equal Pay Act and Title VII, preventing employers from discriminating against women and people of color in employment. Affirmative action legislation of the 1970s and sexual harassment legislation of the 1980s further attempted to dismantle gender- and race-based inequities in the labor force. Challenges remain in this area, however, as systems of inequality still shape labor force experiences.

The state also affects women through the institution of marriage. Women had access to divorce in the nineteenth century, although divorce was much more difficult to obtain. In addition, divorce carried a considerable stigma, especially to the divorced wife. Prior to the advent of no-fault divorce in the 1970s (divorce on demand by either or both parties), partners had to sue for divorce. Grounds to sue were based on a spouse's violation of the marriage contract such as by cruelty, abandonment, or adultery, and the courts needed to prove that someone had committed a crime. This procedure was difficult and expensive for women; it also tended to involve a double standard of behavior based upon gender. Nonetheless, because this procedure allowed wives to show that husbands were "guilty," wives might receive relatively generous compensation. With the advent of no-fault divorce, this has changed because no one is charged with blame.

Likewise *alimony*, the payment that women have traditionally received as compensation for their unpaid roles as wives and mothers, has been reduced or eliminated through various legislation since 1970. Although eliminating alimony indicates a more gender-neutral situation where women are not simply viewed as dependent wives and mothers and may even have higher earnings than the husband, it has caused problems. This is because despite the gender-neutral language and intentions, society is stratified along gender, and women still tend to be financially subordinate to men. For example, the reading by Conway reports a California study that showed the living standard of wives and children decreased by 73 percent whereas that of men increased by 42 percent after divorce. This financial hardship is often exacerbated by court-mandated child support that does not get paid to women. Some states have enforced legislation to track errant child support monies and enforce payment.

PUBLIC POLICY

State policies determine people's rights and privileges, and, as a result, the state has the power to exclude groups, discriminate against groups, and create policies in favor of groups. By maintaining inequality, the state reflects the interests of the dominant groups in society and supports policies that work in their interests and reinforce their power. Native Americans, for example, have suffered because of state policies that required relocation, and African Americans have been harmed by Jim Crow laws that helped enforce segregation in the South and prevented African Americans from voting. There were miscegenation laws in the United States that prevented interracial marriage and aimed to maintain racial purity and superiority, and many states instigated laws that prevented African Americans from residing in certain communities and/or being in a town after sundown. Some of these laws were still on the books into the late twentieth century.

An example of how policy reinforces systems of inequality is seen in lesbian and gay plaintiffs who are in the court system for child custody, contract, or property disputes. It is also evident in current discussions concerning gay marriage. Homophobia in the system tends to work against gays and lesbians. The Defense of Marriage Act (DOMA), which allows states not to recognize gay unions performed in other states, is a current piece of legislation that attempts to prevent lesbians and gay men from enjoying the privilege of state recognition of marriage. In "The Crime that Had No Name," Mary Frances Berry reports that "new stories" are infiltrating the justice system in ways that offer hope for lesbians and gay men.

Welfare policy is especially illustrative of the ways the state is a conduit for the perpetuation of systems of inequality. Ideologies (recall from Chapter 2 that these are sets of beliefs that support institutions in society) about who is deserving of wealth rely on the individualistic notion that success is a result of hard work and ambition; thus, anyone who works hard and pushes him- or herself will succeed economically. The corollary of this, of course, is that the fault associated with lack of economic success rests with the individual. This was referred to in Chapter 2 as the bootstrap myth. This myth avoids looking at structural aspects of the labor force and social systems that perpetuate classism and instead focuses on the individual. It helps explain the stigma associated with welfare in the United States and the many stereotypes associated with women on welfare—that they are lazy, cheat the system, and have babies to increase their welfare check. The testimonial reading by Cindy Ballard titled "I Was a Welfare Mom" demonstrates the difficulties associated with being on welfare, and the reading by Randy Albelda and Chris Tilly explains the myths associated with welfare recipients. The latter also presents information about the triple whammy single mothers experience: They are women facing lower paid work, they are mothers and have domestic responsibilities and childcare expenses, and they are single with only one pay check. Indeed, if women earned as much as comparable men, then single women generally would see a rise in their incomes and a substantial drop in poverty rates. If we applied this comparable situation to single mothers, poverty rates would be cut almost in half, from 25 percent to 13 percent.

A most obvious example of policies working to favor dominant groups is the practice often called "wealthfare" or "welfare for the rich." These policies reflect the ties political leaders have to the economic system and the ways the government subsidizes corporations and reduces taxes and other payments to the state for some corporations and businesses. Wealthfare involves five major types: direct grants; allowing publicly funded research and development to be used free by private for-profit corporations; discounted fees for public resources (such as grazing fees on public land); tax breaks for the wealthy; and corporate tax reductions and loopholes. In 1995 it was estimated that more than $200 billion in corporate welfare could be saved over the next five years if policies reining in these favors were instigated. Neither Republican nor Democratic lawmakers want to do this because they fear losing donations to their respective parties.

THE CRIMINAL JUSTICE SYSTEM

The law can be defined as formal aspects of social control that determine what is permissible and what is forbidden in a society. The courts are created to maintain the law through adjudicating conflicts that may be unlawful and deciding punishments for people who have broken the law. The role of the police is to enforce these laws and keep public order. Prisons are responsible for punishing those who have broken the law and protecting society from people who have committed crimes. All these fit together to maintain the control of the state.

Although women are especially likely to be victims of certain crimes, such as rape and battering, they constitute a small proportion of people arrested for crimes (about 20 percent) and a smaller number of those who are sent to prison. Women of color are more likely to be incarcerated than White women; the group with the highest levels of incarceration is young African American males. These figures are related to gendered forms of behavior that encourage more males into violence and risk-related activities as well as the perception by criminal justice officials that women (especially White women) are less dangerous than men. Among men, poor men and men of color are more likely to be considered a danger to society and tend to receive the longest sentences.

Nonetheless, the rate of crime committed by women has increased in recent years with the largest increase being drug-related criminal behavior. Most of the homicides enacted by women involve male victims, and they are most likely to have taken place in the home. Women are more likely to be first-time offenders than men, are less likely to use firearms, and are more likely to use kitchen knives and other household implements. This evidence suggests that much female homicide is done in self-defense. Although prior to the 1980s women who killed in self-defense almost always lost their plea, today juries are more understanding of the

Women in Policing

- Women comprise 14.3 percent of all sworn law enforcement positions among municipal, county, and state law enforcement agencies in the United States, with 100 or more sworn officers. Women of color hold 6.8 percent of these positions.
- Women are 14.2 percent of all federal officers.
- From 1990 to 1999, the representation of women in sworn law enforcement increased by only 5.3 percent.
- Women hold 5.6 percent of sworn Top Command law enforcement positions. Women of color hold only 1.1 percent of Top Command positions.
- In state agencies, women comprise only 6.2 percent of officers, compared with 16.6 percent in municipal agencies and 11.1 percent in county agencies.
- Women hold 66.1 percent of lower-paid civilian law enforcement positions. Women of color hold 25.7 percent of civilian positions.

Source: National Center for Women & Policing, "Equality Denied: The Status of Women in Policing: 1999," www.feminist.org.

Women in Prison

- In 1998, 3.2 million women were arrested, accounting for 22 percent of all arrests.
- The per capita rate of arrest among juvenile women was nearly twice the adult rate.
- Nearly 952,000 women were under the care, custody, or control of correctional agencies. Eighty-five percent of these women were under the supervision of probation or parole agencies.
- These women were the mothers of about 1.3 million minor children.
- Nearly two-thirds of the women confined in jails and prisons were women of color. Nearly two-thirds of the women under probation supervision were White.
- Nearly six out of ten women in state prisons had experienced sexual or physical abuse in the past. About a third of imprisoned women had been abused by an intimate; just under a fourth had been abused by a family member.
- Eleven women out of 1,000 will be incarcerated in their lifetime: five out of 1,000 White women; fifteen out of 1,000 Hispanic women; and thirty-six out of 1,000 African American women.

Source: Bureau of Justice Statistics Special Report, "Women Offenders," December 1999.
Note: Statistics are for 1998.

experiences of battered women. Even so, it is still very difficult for women to convince a jury that they were being abused, and there are many women in prison suffering very long sentences for these acts. In addition, among men and women who kill in self-defense during a rape where the assailant is a man, men who kill are more likely to be acquitted than women who kill. Likewise the crimes of passion that men commit on discovering an adulterous wife are viewed more sympathetically than when women kill adulterous men. The reading by Nina Siegal, "Stopping Abuse in Prison" explores the inhumane treatment of some women prisoners and the widespread sexual abuse that they experience.

Another example of the double standard concerning women as victims is U.S. asylum law that provides protection for immigrants fleeing their country if they are being persecuted because of race, religion, nationality, political opinion, or membership in a social group. As the reading by Anna Shelton "Battered Women: A New Asylum Case" explains, although there have been important advancements in asylum law that have protected women fleeing abusive husbands and gays and lesbians who fear persecution in their country, protection for battered women under these circumstances is still difficult to obtain.

THE MILITARY

The military, a branch of government that is constituted to defend against foreign and domestic conflict, is a central component of the state and political system. As mentioned in Chapter 2, the military has strong ties to the economic system through a military-industrial complex that supports industries that manufacture weapons. The Pentagon has connections to other branches of the state, especially the government and its representatives. The military is a very male-dominated

Active Duty Military Strength

- In 1998, 1,406,830 Americans were on active duty in the military.
- Of active duty personnel, 85.9 percent were men and 14.1 percent were women.
- Of military officers, 86.13 percent were men and 13.87 percent were women.
- Women were 18.01 percent of active duty Air Force personnel, 14.83 percent of Army personnel, 13.26 percent of Navy personnel, and 5.65 percent of Marine personnel.
- Women were 16.65 percent of Air Force officers, 14.14 percent of Navy officers, 13.21 percent of Army officers, and 4.77 percent of Marine officers.
- Women were 16.37 percent of Air Force cadets, 15.55 percent of Navy midshipmen, and 14.88 percent of Army cadets.

Note: Statistics are from the Department of Defense, September 1998.

arena, not only in terms of actual personnel who serve but in terms of the ways it is founded upon so-called masculine cultural traits like violence, aggression, hierarchy, competition, and conflict. The military uses misogynistic and homophobic attitudes to enforce highly masculine codes of behavior. In the mid-1990s women made up about 12 percent of active military forces.

Throughout most of history, women were not allowed to serve in the military except in such auxiliary forces as nursing. It was not until World War II that women who served in any military capacity were given formal status and not until 1976 that women were allowed into the military academies. In terms of race, the armed forces were officially segregated until 1948. Currently about 30 percent of the armed forces are people of color, and about 14 percent are women (with the Air Force having the highest proportion of women at 18 percent). Of women who serve, 38 percent are women of color. These figures are disproportionate compared to the general population and reflect the lack of opportunities for people of color in the civilian realm. Despite their relative high numbers of service, people of color are less likely than Whites proportionately to be found in leadership positions. This is true for women of all races as well.

In 1981 the Supreme Court reaffirmed that it is constitutional to require registering men but not women for the draft. Men at this point are subject to conscription if a draft is in process and women are not, although women are allowed to serve if they wish. The rationale for the 1981 decision centered on the fact that women were not allowed in combat positions, although it also involved the notion that women have responsibilities in the home and family. After women's service in the Gulf War in 1991, the pressure was on for President Clinton in 1993 to order a repeal of the ban on women in combat positions, and now most Navy and Air Force positions are open to women. The Army and Marines still prevent women from combat positions in field artillery, armor, and infantry.

In recent years the treatment of women in the military has received considerable public attention. Take, for example, the story of Shannon Faulkner who attempted to attend the all-male military academy the Citadel. Even though a court demanded the Citadel accept women, it still is a very inhospitable place for women cadets. Similarly, in 1991 the Tailhook scandal revealed that in this gathering of high-ranking Navy flying personnel, considerable sexual harassment had been an ongoing practice. The report from the Defense Department described men wearing t-shirts with inscriptions like "Women Are Property" as well as engaging in rowdy and misogynous behavior. A 1997 Army report found widespread harassment aimed at women personnel.

Finally, the military has a long history of homophobia that has included the execution, persecution, and dismissal of gay soldiers. Arguments in favor of such prejudice mirror those proposing racial segregation in earlier times: The morale and fighting spirit of military personnel will drop if openly gay and lesbian personnel are present, and gays and lesbians pose a national security threat. Through the 1980s, more than 15,000 military personnel were discharged because of homosexuality. By the mid-1990s President Clinton had created the "don't ask, don't tell" policy, which was supposed to be a compromise, although it has few supporters. Discharges are still allowed under the policy, and, as one study reports, dismissals increased after the initiation of the policy. In addition, lesbians were disproportionately discharged. In this way, the government policy on lesbians and gays in the military illustrates how the state has differential effects on some groups compared to others.

The state is a very powerful institution that has enormous effects upon women's everyday lives. It is important to understand how gender, race, and class mold and shape government, law, and policy and how these institutions reflect and promote the needs of some groups over others.

Constitutional Argument

Susan B. Anthony

Friends and Fellow-Citizens:—I stand before you under indictment for the alleged crime of having voted at the last presidential election, without having a lawful right to vote. It shall be my work this evening to prove to you that in thus doing, I not only committed no crime, but instead simply exercised my citizen's right, guaranteed to me and all United States citizens by the National Constitution beyond the power of any State to deny.

Our democratic-republican government is based on the idea of the natural right of every individual member thereof to a voice and a vote in making and executing the laws. We assert the province of government to be to secure the people in the enjoyment of their inalienable rights. We throw to the winds the old dogma that government can give rights. No one denies that before governments were organized each individual possessed the right to protect his own life, liberty and property. When 100 or 1,000,000 people enter into a free government, they do not barter away their natural rights; they simply pledge themselves to protect each other in the enjoyment of them through prescribed judicial and legislative tribunals. They agree to abandon the methods of brute force in the adjustment of their differences and adopt those of civilization. Nor can you find a word in any of the grand documents left us by the fathers which assumes for government the power to create or to confer rights. The Declaration of Independence, the United States Constitution, the constitutions of the several States and the organic laws of the Territories, all alike propose to *protect* the people in the exercise of their God-given rights. Not one of them pretends to bestow rights.

All men are created equal, and endowed by the Creator with certain inalienable rights. Among these are life, liberty and the pursuit of happiness. To secure these, governments are instituted among men, deriving their just powers from the consent of the governed.

Here is no shadow of government authority over rights, or exclusion of any class from their full and equal enjoyment. Here is pronounced the right of all men, and "consequently," as the Quaker preacher said, "of all women," to a voice in the government. And here, in this first paragraph of the Declaration, is the assertion of the natural right of all to the ballot; for how can "the consent of the governed" be given, if the right to vote be denied? Again:

> Whenever any form of government becomes destructive of these ends, it is the right of the people to alter or abolish it, and to institute a new government, laying its foundations on such principles, and organizing its powers in such form, as to them shall seem most likely to effect their safety and happiness.

Surely the right of the whole people to vote is here clearly implied; for however destructive to their happiness this government might become, a disfranchised class could neither alter nor abolish it, nor institute a new one, except by the old brute force method of insurrection and rebellion. One-half of the people of this nation today are utterly powerless to blot from the statute books an unjust law, or to write there a new and a just one. The women, dissatisfied as they are with this form of government, that enforces taxation without representation—that compels them to obey laws to which they never have given their consent—that imprisons and hangs them without a trial by a jury of their peers—that robs them, in marriage, of the custody of their own persons, wages and children—are this half of the people who are left wholly at the mercy of the other half, in direct violation of the spirit and letter of the declarations of the framers of this government, every one of which was based on the immutable principle of equal rights to all. By these declarations, kings, popes, priests, aristocrats, all were alike dethroned and placed on a common level, politically, with the lowliest born subject or serf. By them, too, men, as such, were deprived of their divine right to rule and placed on a political level with women. By the practice of these declarations all class and caste distinctions would be abolished, and slave, serf, plebeian, wife, woman, all alike rise from their subject position to the broader platform of equality.

The preamble of the Federal Constitution says:

> We, the people of the United States, in order to form a more perfect union, establish justice,

insure domestic tranquillity, provide for the common defence, promote the general welfare and secure the blessings of liberty to ourselves and our posterity, do ordain and establish this Constitution for the United States of America.

It was we, the people, not we, the white male citizens, not we, the male citizens; but we, the whole people, who formed this Union. We formed it not to give the blessings of liberty but to secure them; not to the half of ourselves and the half of our posterity, but to the whole people—women as well as men. It is downright mockery to talk to women of their enjoyment of the blessings of liberty while they are denied the only means of securing them provided by this democratic-republican government—the ballot. . . .

READING 78

Women and Family Law
Marriage and Divorce

M. Margaret Conway, David W. Ahern, and Gertrude A. Steuernagel

LAWS AND PUBLIC POLICIES GOVERNING MARRIAGE

American public policy regarding marriage is rooted in English common law. The common law doctrine that had the most serious economic and legal consequences for women was coverture; by the act of marriage, a woman in effect committed legal suicide. Under this doctrine, a woman's legal identity was suspended during marriage. As Supreme Court Justice Hugo Black aptly but disapprovingly described coverture, the husband and wife became one, but the husband was the one.[1]

When her legal identity merged with that of her husband (symbolized by the assumption of

his surname), the wife's ownership and control of her property, including her earnings, passed to him. She lost the right to enter into contracts; without it, she could not engage in a business or profession. Nor could she bring suit.

At various times throughout the second half of the nineteenth century, state legislators removed many of these disabilities stemming from coverture. These statutes, which were collectively known as the Married Women's Acts, varied in content from state to state, but most conferred on wives the right to own and control property, to conduct a business, to enter into contracts, and to sue. The acts were egalitarian in theory, and were an improvement over the common law doctrine of coverture, but they did not make married women their husbands' equals. If a woman followed tradition and worked inside the home (as an unpaid housekeeper and childbearer) rather than outside the home, her new right to own property, for example, had little practical significance because few women had money or property of their own. Even if a woman worked outside the home, her wages were likely to be a small fraction of her husband's. More fundamentally, coverture had reflected society's attitude that women were subordinate socially, economically, and legally, and that attitude was affected by the Married Women's Acts. Nonetheless, they represented the most important changes that would be made in the status of married women until the 1970s.

As noted, most family law in the United States is state law. States establish the conditions for the legal recognition of a marriage. Currently, fifteen states and the District of Columbia recognize common law marriage, sometimes referred to as nonceremonial marriage. Although the definition of common law marriage varies among those states that recognize it, in general a common law marriage occurs between two individuals of the opposite sex who live together for a significant period of time and represent themselves as a married couple or who intend to be married. Couples within a common law marriage can file joint tax returns and enjoy all of the benefits of a conventional marriage. A formal divorce is needed to end a common law marriage.[2]

Marital Property Law

Two kinds of marital property law govern spousal rights of ownership, control, and disposition of property acquired during marriage: separate property law and community property law. *Separate property law* is derived from English common law; its fundamental principle is that each spouse owns and controls all property that he or she acquires during the marriage. *Community property law* is derived from the civil law of France and Spain; its principal tenet is that the "community," consisting of husband and wife, owns everything acquired during the marriage. Forty-two states are separate property law states; the other eight (Arizona, California, Idaho, Louisiana, Nevada, New Mexico, Texas, and Washington) are community property law states.

With passage of the Married Women's Acts in the nineteenth century, married women in separate property law states acquired the right to own and control the property they brought to the marriage and that which they acquired during marriage. The husband would, as before, own what he brought to the marriage as well as that which he acquired during the marriage. And because the husband owned his earnings and everything bought with his money, he had the legal right to control the family assets, since the wife, in her traditional role, had no assets. Many separate property law states offered some legal protection to the non-wage-earning spouse, however; they prohibited either spouse from selling the family home without the consent of the other. Further, most of these states gave a widow (or widower) a share (one-third to one-half) of the estate of a deceased spouse. In addition, the law in these states permitted joint ownership of property. If spouses chose joint ownership, each had equal control over the assets of both.

In community property law states, property acquired during marriage is considered to belong to the community and thus to both spouses; a bank account in the name of one spouse belongs to the community and thus to both. Until the reforms of the 1970s, however, the law authorized the husband to control the assets of the community.

Beginning in the 1970s, the community property law states experimented with various techniques to increase the wife's managerial control. One technique was to give each spouse control over his or her earnings; control over the remaining property resided with both. Another was to permit each spouse to manage the community property, subject to the restriction that neither could commit more than one-half of that property without the consent of the other.

...

Marital Rape

Traditionally, a husband was immune from prosecution for raping his wife. One justification for this exemption stems from the pronouncement of the seventeenth-century English jurist Lord Chief Justice Matthew Hale that marriage implies consent to sexual intercourse. According to this theory, marriage is a contract, under the terms of which a husband has the absolute power to determine the time, place, and manner of sexual intercourse. The husband is authorized to enforce the contract unilaterally, by force if he deems that necessary.

In the 1970s, some states either modified the marital exemption rule or abolished it. Whereas the exemption traditionally was absolute, these states denied immunity if the parties were divorced, living apart, or legally separated; if force was used; if there was fear of bodily harm; or if physical injury was inflicted.[3] By the late 1990s, most states had abolished the marital defense in rape cases, although variations among the states remained. Two states, for example, continue a marital exception for lesser cases but deny it for forcible rape. Two other states retain a spousal exception for rape but have adopted new spousal sexual assault laws.[4]

Social Security Benefits

The social security retirement benefits received by women, on average, are lower than those received by men. The disparities are both long-term and contemporary.[5] In part, the reason is simply that women earn less than men; for every dollar a man earns, a woman earns between 58 cents and 74 cents: in the 1930s, women's earnings were 58 percent of men's; in the 1970s, this proportion was 59 percent; in the

1980s, it increased to 64 percent; and in the early 1990 it was 74 percent, probably because of the increasing number of younger women entering higher-paying, male-dominated professions. Because benefits are related to earnings, the benefits received by working women who are now of retirement age are lower than those received by working men of retirement age. Indeed, many married retired women workers have chosen to receive spousal benefits rather than benefits on the basis of their earnings alone because the former are higher.

Many women receive retirement benefits that are lower than those received by men because they never held a paying job; their benefits are thus dependent upon their husband's earnings. Spousal benefits, however, do not equal those of the retired wage earner. A retired wage earner receives 100 percent of the benefits to which he or she is entitled, but the dependent spouse over the age of sixty-five receives an amount equal to 50 percent of those benefits. Widows over the age of sixty-five receive the 100 percent to which their husbands would have been entitled. If widows start receiving benefits before age sixty-five, however, the amount is 71.5 percent. An older nonworking woman whose husband dies before she reaches age sixty-five frequently has little choice but to accept the lower benefit at an earlier age. Divorced older women who never worked outside the home during marriage receive retirement benefits that are equal to or less than spousal benefits. If the marriage lasted less than ten years (the requirement was less than twenty years until 1979), she receives no benefits on the basis of her husband's earnings; now she receives 50 percent if the marriage lasted more than ten years.

The social security system offers no protection to widowed homemakers under the age of sixty unless they are disabled or have minor children. Benefits cease when the child reaches the age of eighteen. The widow is not entitled to receive benefits again until age sixty. This "widow's gap" leaves many middle-aged dependent homemakers who lack job skills or work experience with no source of income. If the widowed homemaker is disabled, there are no benefits until she reaches age fifty.

One proposal aimed at reducing the economic insecurity of older married women who never worked outside the home is to assign a monetary value to homemaking and child rearing. To finance such a program, either homemakers would pay taxes on the assigned value of their services in the home, or paid workers would pay more taxes. Another suggestion intended to protect married women is an "earnings sharing" plan under which each person's benefits would be based on his or her earnings when single plus one-half of the total earnings of the married couple. For a one-income family, the worker's earning on which benefits would be based would be split 50-50; the earnings credits would be divided if the couple were to divorce or when one spouse reached age sixty-two.

Most of the economic disadvantages suffered by married women under the social security system are unrelated to specific gender-based distinctions but are rather a result of the different economic and domestic roles and pay scales of men and women. The Social Security Act was replete with such distinctions, but the most obvious ones have been changed by Congress or invalidated by the Supreme Court—although those that were invalidated by the Court discriminated primarily against men, not women. In 1975, for example, the Supreme Court invalidated a provision authorizing benefits for widows with minor children but denied benefits to similarly situated widowers.[6] In 1977 it invalidated a provision that authorized benefits for surviving widows over the age of sixty but denied benefits to similarly situated widowers unless they had received at least one-half of their support from their wives.[7]

Neither judicial nor legislative changes in social security legislation provide economic security for women who had spent most or all of their adult lives as homemakers or in low-paying or part-time jobs. The social security

system was not originally intended to be the sole source of retirement income; it was designed to supplement other resources, including private pension plans provided by employers. But married women fare no better under these plans for much the same reason that they suffer under the social security system. As a result of the efforts of such groups as the Older Women's League, the plight of older women is beginning to receive the attention of the nation's lawmakers. The proposed economic equity act, which deals with a variety of issues of interest to women (such as child care), seeks greater equity in both the social security system and private pension plans. Until both married and single women routinely enter the work force and earn as much as men, older women who have to rely on their own pensions are likely to continue to be economically insecure.

LAWS AND PUBLIC POLICIES GOVERNING DIVORCE

Public policy regarding divorce was traditionally based on the assumption that marriage is a lifelong arrangement. Grounds for divorce were both limited and gender based. Almost 50 percent of all marriages now end in divorce. In the 1970s, most states moved toward acceptance of divorce on demand. In 1970, California inaugurated no-fault divorce when it adopted an "irreconcilable differences" standard. Irreconcilable differences are those which a court determines "to be substantial reasons for not continuing the marriage and which make it appear that the marriage should be dissolved." No-fault divorce is now available in some form in all of the states. Whatever grounds are statutorily specified, most states in effect allow unilateral divorce on demand. Although no-fault divorce was initially viewed as benefiting both men and women because it would lessen the recriminations associated with divorce, the reform may have further disadvantaged economically dependent women because they can no longer use the refusal to agree to a divorce as a bargaining chip to obtain a larger property settlement or alimony payment.[8]

A state's interest in the preservation of marriage may have dwindled, but its interest in related problems (property division, alimony, child custody, child support) certainly has not. Changes in these areas in the name of equality were precipitated by the no-fault movement. Early indications are that the newer egalitarian reforms, like the nineteenth-century Married Women's Property Acts, when superimposed on the unchanged social and economic roles of husbands and wives, will fail to bring about the equality sought by their advocates. On the basis of an in-depth ten-year study (1974–1984) of the postreform status of women and children in California, one scholar concluded that California's no-fault divorce, in combination with changed rules governing property division and spousal support, accounted for a post-divorce decline of 73 percent in the living standard of women and children and a rise of 42 percent in that of men.[9]

Some states, including Idaho, Michigan, and Iowa, are considering what supporters see as "pro-family" changes in divorce law. These range from extending the waiting period for the divorce to become finalized to educating parents concerning the effects of divorce on children to a return to fault-based divorces. In 1997, Louisiana enacted a law giving couples the option of "covenant marriage." If couples choose a covenant marriage—and they are not required to do so—they agree to seek counseling if problems develop in their marriage and are entitled to seek divorce or legal separation for a very limited set of reasons, including adultery, abandonment, and physical or sexual abuse of the spouse or children. Couples may petition to have their marriages retroactively designated as covenant marriages.

Interestingly, 84 percent of attorneys responding to an American Bar Association survey indicated they do not favor a return to fault-based divorces. The attorneys did not see fault-based divorce as a solution to the problems of no-fault, including the financial dispar-ity between husbands and wives that often leads to women faring poorly in divorce.[10]

Property Division

Lorna Jorgenson Wendt and Gary Wendt, childhood sweethearts, were married thirty-two years. While Gary advanced in his career, eventually becoming chairman of GE Capital Services, Lorna stayed home with the couple's two daughters. Lorna became the quintessential "corporate wife." She entertained her husband's business associates, traveled with him on business trips, and represented him in a number of community and charitable groups. Although Lorna had studied to become a teacher and had taught while Gary went to Harvard Business School, she gave this up to become a full-time wife and mother. The couple prospered financially and went from very few assets to a marital estate worth as much as $100 million. Unfortunately, the marriage did not last. Gary offered Lorna an $11 million settlement, but she refused it, arguing that she was entitled to not only half of what they had accumulated during their marriage, but also half of what Gary would receive when he retired. This would include stock options, bonuses, and unvested pension benefits. Gary claimed Lorna had not contributed to his successes; she claimed she did. The judge ruled in Lorna's favor, and argued that the marriage was indeed a partnership. Lorna and Gary were divorced in Connecticut, a state that does not have community property laws but does give judges latitude in deciding who gets what in divorce cases.[11]

The basic issues to be decided in dividing property are which property is to be divided, how it is to be divided, and what factors are to be considered in making the division. Historically, in most states the title and acquisition source have been decisive in determining which property acquired during marriage is subject to division. The law itself was gender neutral; however, in a traditional marriage in which the husband worked outside the home for money and the wife worked either inside the home without monetary compensation or outside the home as well, at a lower paying job, the wife was clearly at a disadvantage.

In separate property law states, titled property (such as a house or a car) acquired by the husband with his earnings and held in his name belonged to him; it was not subject to division, even if the wife contributed financially to the acquisition of property held in his name. He could take it with him when he left the marriage. The court might order him to pay alimony, but the property remained his. The acquiring spouse—usually presumed to be the husband—also owned untitled family assets such as household goods. Further, the husband's earning capacity and his retirement benefits—frequently a family's most valuable assets—were considered his alone and thus not subject to division. Even if the wife worked in the home as well as at a low-paying job to help support the family and to put her husband through school, she traditionally would not reap any benefit from her labors if the couple divorced. The husband took his earning capacity, as well as any pension rights he acquired during the marriage, with him when he left the marriage. If the wife were the innocent party, that fact might enable her to obtain some of what the law deemed to be her husband's property. Nonetheless, for traditional homemakers, termination of a long marriage could spell economic disaster.

Responding to the organized efforts of women's groups, legislatures began to reform marital property laws in the 1970s. As a result, title and monetary contribution to the acquisition of family assets in separate property law states have been of decreasing importance with regard to property division at the time of divorce. Instead, most of these state legislatures have expanded the definition of marital property subject to division to include all property acquired during the marriage regardless of title or whose income paid for such property. Property acquired by gift or inheritance is still not subject to division nor, in some states, is property that the couple agrees to exclude by prenuptial agreement.

. . .

Formal equality of property division, whether in a separate property law state or a community property law state, might not achieve real equality. Since few couples amass many divisible assets (the average has been estimated to be $20,000, usually a house), equal division frequently requires sale of the house and the award of one-half of the proceeds to the husband and one-half to the wife. Eminently fair on its face, such a division might be unequal in fact if one-half goes to the husband and one-half goes to the wife and the children, for whom she must provide primary care in addition to perhaps finding a low-paying job with flexible hours while she prepares to move from the family home. If she is not awarded, or cannot collect, child support, her descent into poverty is not forestalled by equal property division. For an older traditional housewife without minor children but with few job prospects, equal property division rarely permits continuation of the living standard she enjoyed during marriage because that standard was dependent on her former husband's earnings, which he takes with him.

. . .

Award and Payment of Alimony

Historically, payment of alimony was based on the common law duty of a husband to support his wife. In theory, this obligation continued after divorce if the husband was at fault. In fact, the award of alimony has been the exception, not the rule. From the late nineteenth century to the early 1970s, alimony was awarded in only 10 to 15 percent of all divorces.

In the 1970s, states began revising their alimony laws. Alimony statutes were made gender neutral, thus permitting awards to husbands. Short-term "rehabilitative" awards (temporary payments to permit acquisition of job skills) began to replace long-term alimony obligations. The enactment of no-fault divorce laws meant that the "guilty" party was no longer required to pay alimony to the "innocent" party. In determining whether and how much alimony is to be awarded, courts consider such factors as the dependent spouse's need (alimony is usually not awarded if the judge decides that the dependent spouse is able to work; a short-term award is made to those without job skills), the wage earner's ability to pay, the length of the marriage (an award of alimony is rare in short-term marriages), the age of the partners (alimony is usually not awarded to a young or middle-aged spouse if the judge decides that he or she is capable of self-support), and the contributions (including homemaking activities) of the dependent spouse. Whether the dependent or lower-paid spouse receives alimony or a sufficient amount depends on whether the judge makes a realistic assessment of such factors as the ability of a traditional housewife to enter or reenter the job market and earn a living wage if she does. Frequently both are overestimated, with the result that the dependent spouse's income and living standard decline.

The anti-alimony trend of the 1970s has perhaps worked to the disadvantage of a few women; it probably has had little effect on most of the others, who, under the old, for-cause-only divorce laws, would have received little or nothing—although wives of "guilty" well-to-do men who wanted a divorce might have been able to extract alimony from them. About 15 percent of all divorced women are awarded alimony.

Today, many states use the Uniform Marriage and Divorce Act (UMDA) as a model for alimony awards. But the award of alimony and its payment are two different things. In 1978, only two-thirds of the women awarded alimony actually received some payment. The average amount received was only $2,850. In the 1980s, the average amount was not even $4,000—less than half the poverty level. In 1981, the figure was $3,000; in 1983, it was $3,980; and in 1985, it was $3,733. Of the 19.1 million divorced and separated women in 1985, 840,000 were entitled to alimony but 616,000 actually received payment.[12]

The infrequency of alimony awards and the small amounts that are awarded and received account for some of the poverty faced by traditional housewives who become divorced in middle age and by young custodial parents who receive little or no child support yet have responsibility for child care. The seemingly exorbitant alimony extracted from a few wealthy men, such as in the case of Gary and Lorna Wendt, grabs the public's attention, but the reality is that just as few men are rich, few women are awarded alimony and fewer still receive alimony payments above the poverty level. If the partners are economic and domestic equals (they divide responsibilities for child care and housework), elimination of a long-term alimony obligation is simply an acknowledgement of an egalitarian marriage and does not spell economic hardship. But because roles continue to differ in many marriages, many spouses who were dependent during marriage become poorer after divorce if alimony is not ordered or received.

Child Support

Change is the only constant in descriptions of America's families. American households are becoming more and more diverse, requiring us to rethink the meaning of "family." In 1970, for example, there were 5.6 million families maintained by women with no husband present. By 1995, that number had more than doubled to 12.2 million.[13] The reasons for this jump include increases in divorce, separation, and out-of-wedlock births. What is important to remember, however, is that many children residing in female-headed households live in poverty. Indeed, a child living in a single-parent household—be that parent a mother, father, or some other adult—is much more likely than a child in a two-parent household to be poor. Today, almost 25 percent of American children live in poverty. Policy makers agree that nonpayment of child support is a major contributing factor to childhood poverty. Many also feel that parents, rather than the government, should be responsible for children's financial situation. To that effect, Congress created in 1975 the Child Support Enforcement (CSE) program. This program is charged with establishing and enforcing support obligations of noncustodial parents.[14] The Office of Child Support Enforcement within the Administration for Children and Families of the Department of Health and Human Services oversees the program. Although it does succeed in collecting some child support, the program has not been an unqualified success. In its first year, it collected $700,000, and by 1996 the program had secured more than $12 billion.[15] Yet many children continued to receive little or no support. In 1991, for example, payments were awarded to only 46 percent of custodial parents, and only 75 percent of those actually received payment.[16] In 1991, the most recent year for which comprehensive data are available on both paid and unpaid support, a total of $11.9 billion was paid in child support. This was $5.8 billion less than what was owed.[17] As a result, Congress took action. The welfare reform act known as the Personal Responsibility and Work Opportunity Reconciliation Act of 1996 provided for a major overhaul of the CSE program. Under the revised program, there are now a number of state and federal databases available to those trying to locate noncustodial parents, an important first step in collecting child support. CSE staff also has access to motor vehicle databases, public utilities records, and state and local tax records. In addition, access to IRS information has been simplified. The new law also increases the tools available to those responsible for collecting child support. For example, drivers licenses and professional, occupation, and recreational licenses may be revoked for nonpayment of child support. There are also provisions in the new law to help correct the problem of a parent moving to a different state to avoid payment.

It is too early to determine the effectiveness of these reforms. Some of the issues surrounding child support, however, may be beyond the scope of what public policy can do, and some policies intended to correct a problem may actually make it worse or result in undesirable consequences. Those who work in the domestic abuse area, for example, fear that increased pressure on women to name fathers and pursue child support collection may result in more violence against these women. Ironically, then, welfare reform designed to help women and children may actually place them at greater risk of physical assault.[18] There are also problems with implementation. Computerization, the so-called "magic bullet" of child support enforcement, has not proceeded smoothly. In 1988 a law was passed that required states to computerize child support collection; the 1996 welfare law called for enhancement of these systems. Unfortunately, as of July 1997 only fifteen states, comprising just 14 percent of the child support caseload, were certified or conditionally certified as having met the computerization requirements contained in the original 1988 law. Congress has continually extended the deadline for computerization, and only one state met the original 1995 target date.[19] There was little for the 1996 welfare reform requirements to build on.

Child Custody

On July 5, 1991, Sharon Lynne Bottoms gave birth to a baby boy she named Kenneth Tyler Doustou. "Tyler," as he came to be known, was naturally unaware he would soon become the center of a heated court battle between his mother and his grandmother, Pamela Key Bottoms. When Tyler was two years old, his grandmother learned that her daughter was a lesbian. As a result, she sought legal custody of the boy, and in 1993 a county court in Virginia ruled in her favor. This decision was subsequently upheld by the circuit court, with the judge in that case stating that lesbians are never fit to be parents. Sharon was permitted only limited visitation with Tyler and never in the presence of her partner, April Wade. In 1994 the Virginia court of appeals ruled that Sharon was a fit parent, but a subsequent 1995 decision by the Virginia Supreme Court returned custody to Tyler's grandmother. The decision, although not equating lesbianism with unfitness to parent, did claim that Tyler would be stigmatized if raised by a lesbian mother. Legal battles continue over Sharon's visitation arrangements with her son.[20]

The case of Sharon Bottoms is one example of the emotional, legal, and financial costs of child custody issues, all of which are complicated by the fact that Sharon Bottoms is a lesbian. Each year, more than one million children are affected by their parents' divorce.[21] They join the swelling ranks of children who are living with the impact of divorce. Even children whose parents never married can find themselves affected by custody issues.

In the matter of child custody, changes in public policy have kept pace with cultural changes. Under the common law that prevailed in the early days of this country, fathers automatically received custody of children. Since most family law, including questions of custody, is determined by individual states, changes in this practice began to occur on a state-by-state basis. In the early to middle nineteenth century, courts began to award custody of young children to mothers. This came to be known as the "tender years doctrine," referring to the age of the children in question. In the 1970s, some states abandoned the tender years doctrine in favor of a gender neutral standard, although many courts continued to award custody of very young children to mothers.[22] Today, courts in twenty states award sole or joint legal custody and sole or joint physical custody. Courts in most states favor joint legal

custody, while joint physical custody continues to be unusual.[23]

. . .

CONCLUSION

The common law doctrine of coverture established the legal inferiority of married women to their husbands. By the end of the nineteenth century, state legislatures had removed many of the disabilities stemming from coverture. Married women acquired the rights to own property, to sue, and to enter into contracts. Such legal changes did not bring about equality, however. If a woman played the traditional role of wife and mother, she had few legally enforceable rights. If the marriage ended, the law tended to favor men in all areas other than child custody. A lower standard of living, if not poverty, awaited many divorced women. Not only did they emerge from marriage with few of the assets acquired during marriage, they either were not awarded or did not receive alimony or child support payments.

As a result of the women's movement, legislatures began to increase married women's rights. The new legislation directed judges to divide marital property equally or equitably. Both Congress and the states have concentrated their efforts on forcing the noncustodial parent to make child support payments. In many states, the female partner in a nonmarital relationship has been given the opportunity to prove that she is entitled to some of the property acquired during cohabitation.

Because many of these changes are relatively recent, their long-term effect is difficult to assess, but there is some indication that they have not improved the status of women, particularly those whose marriages end in divorce. Even no-fault divorce and equal or equitable property division, which seemed to hold so much promise, have rebounded to the disadvantage of some, especially women who receive little or no alimony or child support and have a lower earning capacity because they have been restricted to childbearing and housekeeping roles. Whether women will in fact become equal partners in a marriage as well as after its dissolution will depend in part on judicial and legislative capacity to adapt the new laws to these realities and to change the laws found wanting.

NOTES

1. Dissenting in *United States v. Yazell*, 382 U.S. 341, 361 (1966).
2. The states that recognize common law marriage are Alabama, Colorado, Georgia, Idaho (if created before January 1, 1996), Iowa, Kansas, Montana, New Hampshire (for inheritance purposes only), Ohio (if created before October 10, 1991), Oklahoma, Pennsylvania, Rhode Island, South Carolina, Texas, and Utah.
3. See Leigh Bienen, "Rape III: National Developments in Rape Reform Legislation," *Women's Rights Law Reporter* 6 (Spring 1980): 170–213. See also Dennis Drucker, "The Common Law Does Not Support a Marital Exception for Forcible Rape," *Women's Rights Law Reporter* 5 (Winter–Spring 1979): 181–200.
4. Neil Miller, "Domestic Violence Legislation Affecting Policy and Prosecutor Responsibilities in the United States: Inferences from a Fifty-State Review of State Statutory Codes," presented to the Fifth International Family Violence Conference, University of New Hampshire, June 30, 1997 (revised September 2, 1997), available at the Institute for Law and Justice web site at http://www.ilj.org/dv/vawa.htm (July 1998).
5. U.S. Department of Health, Education, and Welfare, *Social Security and the Changing Roles of Men and Women* (Washington, D.C.: Government Printing Office, 1979). For an overview of the variations, see U.S. Department of Commerce, Bureau of the Census, "Social Security (OASI) Retirement Benefits, by Sex: 1960 to 1981"; and U.S. Department of Commerce, Bureau of the Census, *Statistical Abstract of the United States, 1996* (Washington, D.C.: Government Printing Office, 1997), 374.
6. *Weinberger v. Wiesenfeld*, 420 U.S. 655 (1975).
7. *Califano v. Goldfarb*, 430 U.S. 199 (1977).
8. Lenore J. Weitzman, *The Divorce Revolution: The Unexpected Social and Economic Consequences for Women and Children in America* (New York: Free Press, 1985).
9. Ibid., 323. Although few dispute that the economic status of most divorced women has declined, not everyone attributes that decline to no-fault divorce. See, for example, Annamay T. Sheppard, "Women, Families, and Equality," *Women's Rights Law Reporter* 12 (Fall 1990): 143–152.
10. For a discussion of the survey results, see "Family Law Attorneys Reject Return to Fault-Based Divorce Finds ABA Survey," the American Bar Association web site at http://www.abanet.org/media/oct96/faulrrel.html (July 1998). For a discussion of Louisiana's covenant marriage law, see "Louisiana's Covenant Marriage Law" at Bob Walker's Official New Orleans Area Wedding Guide at http://206.104.52.1/walker/covenant_marriage.html (July 1998).
11. Sharon Walsh and Devon Spurgeon, "Divorce Means an Equal Split, Judge Rules in Big-Money Case." *Washington Post*, December 4, 1997, E1.
12. Stuart S. Nagel and Lenore J. Weitzman, "Women as Litigants," *Hastings Law Journal* 23 (November 1971): 171–198. See also U.S. Department of Commerce, Bureau of the Census, *Divorce, Child Custody, and Child Support* (Washington, D.C.: Government Printing Office, 1979); *Child Support and Alimony: 1981* (1983), *Child Support and Alimony: 1983* (1986), and *Child Support and Alimony: 1985* (1987); Weitzman, *The Divorce Revolution;* Citizens Advisory Council on the Status of Women, *The ERA and Alimony and Child Support Laws,* CACSQ 23-N-1972 (Washington, D.C.: Department of Labor, 1972); Andrea H. Beller, "Trends in Child Support Payments," *Proceedings, First Annual Women's Policy Research Conference*, Washington, D.C., May 19, 1989, 52–57, Demie Kurz, "Divorce and Inequality: The Case of Child Support," *Proceedings, Second Annual Women's Policy Research Conference*, Washington, D.C., June 1–2, 1990, 32–39; Mimi Hall, "Child Support: States Pay if Parents Don't" *USA Today*, March 28, 1994, 10A; J. Hanna, "Divorce Law: A Debate About to Happen Again," *Chicago Tribune*, January 7, 1996, sec. 2, 1.
13. "Changing Family Composition," the Administration for Children and Families, Department of Health and Human Services at http://www.acf.dhhs.gov/ACFPrograms/CSE/new/magazine.html#9708h.
14. Ibid.
15. Ibid.

16. U.S. Department of Commerce, Bureau of the Census, *Statistical Abstract of the United States, 1996* (Washington, D.C.: Government Printing Office, 1997), 385.

17. "Who Receives Child Support?" Economics and Statistics Administration. U.S. Department of Commerce, at http://www.census.gov/socdemo/www/chldsupp.html (May 1995).

18. See Paula Roberts, "Pursuing Child Support: More Violence?" the Electronic Policy Network at http://epn.org/clasp/970916.html (May 1997).

19. Center for Law and Social Policy, "Child Support: Computer Systems Snags" at http://www.handsnet.org/handsnet2/Articles/art.876165029.html (October 6, 1997).

20. "ACLU Fact Sheet: Chronology of Bottoms v. Bottoms, A Lesbian Mother's Fight for Her Son" at the American Civil Liberties web site at http://www.aclu.org/news/n050797c.html (July 1998). In a few states, including Alaska, California, New Mexico, and Pennsylvania, a parent's sexual orientation cannot technically be used to deny custody. See the 'Lectric Law Library web site at http://www.lectlaw.com/files/fam08 (July 1998).

21. U.S. Department of Commerce, Bureau of the Census, *Statistical Abstract of the United States, 1996*, p. 105.

22. Anne P. Mitchell, "The Hypocrisy of 'Equality' in a Family Law Context" at her web site at http://central.co.nz/~stokem/fare/dads.html (1991).

23. "Types of Child Custody" at the DivorceSource web site at http://www.divorcesource.com/AL/info/cctypes.html (July 1998). States that don't distinguish between legal and physical custody use "custody" to refer to both sets of arrangements. See the Nolo Press web site at http://www.nolo.com/ChuckPC/PC.index.html#2 (July 1998).

CHRONOLOGY

1881 In *Chapman v. Phoenix National Bank,* a New York state court interprets common law as requiring a married woman to adopt her husband's surname as her own.

1945 In *People ex. rel. Rago v. Lipsky,* an Illinois state court rules that under common law, a married woman's legal surname is that of her husband.

1952 In *Hill v. Estate of Westbrook,* a California court dismisses a dependent cohabitant's attempt to obtain a share of the estate of her deceased partner on the grounds that a nonmarital sexual union confers no rights on the dependent partner.

1966 In *United States v. Yazell,* the Supreme Court recognizes the power of a state to restrict the right of married women to enter into contracts regarding their separate property.

1971, 1972 In *Forbush v. Wallace,* a federal district court holds that Alabama can constitutionally require a married woman to adopt her husband's surname as her legal name. The Supreme Court affirms that holding.

1972 In *Stuart v. Board of Supervisors of Elections for Howard County,* Maryland's highest court holds that the common law rule that individuals have the right to choose their own legal name applies to married women; thus, a married woman has the legal right to be known by her maiden name rather than the surname of her husband.

1972 In *Sillery v. Fagan and Fagan,* New Jersey's highest court throws out the common law rule that a husband is legally obligated to support his wife on the grounds that it is an unconstitutional gender distinction and holds that both the wife and the husband are legally liable for debts incurred by the wife.

1973 In *Green v. Commissioner,* a Massachusetts state court holds that the old common law rule that a wife's domicile follows that of her husband is outmoded and therefore will no longer be enforced.

1975 In *Weinberger v. Wiesenfeld,* the Supreme Court invalidates a provision of the Social Security Act that provides benefits for widows, but not widowers, with minor children.

1976 In *Marvin v. Marvin,* the California Supreme Court holds that property division agreements between cohabitants are judicially enforceable.

1977 In *Califano v. Goldfarb,* the Supreme Court invalidates a provision in the Social Security Act that authorizes retirement benefits for surviving widows, but not widowers.

1979 In *Kozlowski v. Koslowski,* the New Jersey Supreme Court upholds a lower court's enforcement of an agreement between cohabitants concerning financial support when the relationship ends.

1979 In *Hewitt v. Hewitt,* Illinois's highest court refuses to permit judicial enforcement of property division agreements between cohabitants.

1980 In *Trammel v. United States,* the Supreme Court abandons the traditional rule in federal courts that a person cannot testify against his or her spouse without the consent of the defendant spouse.

1981 In *Condore v. Prince George's General Hospital,* Maryland's highest court holds that the common law rule requiring a husband to support his wife violates the state's equal rights amendment.

1981 In *McCarty v. McCarty,* the Supreme Court holds that military pensions are not community property subject to division at the time of divorce. Congress rejects this interpretation and enacts legislation permitting states to consider such retirement benefits to be divisible at the time of divorce.

1982 In *Artiss v. Artiss,* a Hawaii court awards a dependent cohabitant a share of property acquired during cohabitation.

1993 In *Bottoms v. Bottoms,* the Virginia Supreme Court grants custody of a lesbian mother's son to the boy's grandmother.

1996 The Personal Responsibility and Work Opportunity Reconciliation Act (P.L. 104-193), popularly known as "welfare reform," provides for more aggressive collection of child support.

1996 The Defense of Marriage Act (P.L. 104-199) allows states not to recognize same sex marriages if legalized by another state.

1997 Louisiana enacts its Covenant Marriage Law aimed at making divorce more difficult to obtain.

READING 79

The Crime that Had No Name

Mary Frances Berry

When lesbians and gay men began to disclose their relationships in child custody, contract, and property disputes, they asked the public and the courts to adopt the new stories of acceptance to displace the old stories of sickness and sin. They wanted not only to redefine sex, . . . but also to redefine the family—the gateway to acceptance in civil society—to gradually include homosexual relationships. The courts recognized that a redefinition of acceptable sex involved a redefinition of the family. Judges interpreted standard legal doctrines and chose between the old and evolving stories in deciding the issues.

In child custody cases, early gay claimants were summarily rejected. In 1952, the same year in which the Pennsylvania legislature made homosexuality eligible for psychiatric treatment as an alternative to incarceration, a gay father's suit to remove conditions on his joint custody of his children came before the state supreme court. Luther Bachman and Catherine Bachman, of Lehigh County, divorced in 1946 after nine years of marriage and the birth of two children. Catherine and the children continued to live in the same house where she and Bachman had resided; he paid child support. Bachman was a businessman and active in community affairs. She was "a devoted mother," but Luther received shared custody after the divorce, which continued during Catherine's remarriage. Three years after the divorce, Bachman tried to eliminate a restriction on his custody that forbade anyone except his mother from being present with him and the children. He claimed the condition was "impractical," "embarrassing" to him, and "perplexing" to the children. At the hearing concerning his request, Catherine told the judge that she objected to the children staying with Bachman overnight because they were "too young" and because, since he "admitted his homosexual tendencies," she did not want the children exposed to his gay acquaintances.

At trial, Bachman admitted only that he was "bi-erotic" and he was "as much attracted to male friendships" as to "female friendships." The trial court found that he lived in a newly built, "pretentious" house with his mother and a male friend. The friend could have afforded his own apartment but, after moving from New York City, had lived with Bachman since about six months before the hearing. The friend also appeared "qualified and capable," but had no job, other than employment by Bachman. The court thought Bachman's "propensities were abnormal and his conduct immoral." Furthermore, a "convicted sodomist" formerly in Bachman's employ "testified that he had had relations with him on four occasions." Bachman had not remarried and displayed his gay lifestyle openly.

The trial court left the shared custody arrangements intact. However, the state supreme court decided to make a change in "the best interests and permanent welfare of the children." Although no "untoward incidents involving the children [had] occurred," the judges thought "harmful influences" might be met with. Because of Bachman's homosexuality, the justices awarded full custody to their mother. She could grant him "such limited visitation" as she thought in the best interests of the children. Bachman essentially lost even shared custody because, in the view of the court, he wanted more than toleration; he wanted acceptance of his homosexual lifestyle.

Judges in *Bachman* and other child custody disputes involving gays reflected the public's adherence to the old story of appropriate family behavior. In this old story, homosexuality remained a perversion. In 1980, the Kentucky appellate court, finding a homosexual parent's behavior too open and threatening, agreed to consider a father's suit to void a custody order

granted to his wife when they divorced. The court noted that the couple's daughter was less than a year old at the time of the divorce. Soon the father learned that the mother had begun a lesbian relationship and worked at a lesbian bar. Her lover lived with her and the child, and the two women had exchanged vows and rings in a commitment ceremony. The court agreed that the mother's new lifestyle could harm the infant. The evidence included a court-appointed psychologist's opinion that "there is a social stigma attached to homosexuality," so the child would "have additional burdens to bear in terms of teasing, possible embarrassment and internal conflicts." Also, research on the effects of parental modeling on children indicated that she might "have difficulties in achieving a fulfilling heterosexual identity of her own in the future." The court, still enmeshed in the old story, perceived the possibility of positive attitudes toward homosexual relationships as too far removed to counter any negative effects on children.

In the same year, however, a Massachusetts court decided to develop a new legal narrative about sexual orientation. The new story treated homosexual and heterosexual families as similar: both faced difficulties, but could function equally well.

Brenda King Bezio was a lesbian who, admittedly, had led an unstable life and had suffered long-standing financial and physical problems. A trial court decided that a permanent guardian should keep her children, because of her lesbianism and her former inability to care for them. The appellate judges disagreed, finding no evidence that the sexual preference of adults in the home had "any detrimental impact on children," and concluding that her earlier problems were resolved. Furthermore, the record included no proof that children "who are raised with a loving couple of the same sex are any more disturbed, unhealthy, maladjusted than children raised with a loving couple of mixed sex." Therefore, the state could not take children away from their parents "simply because their households fail to meet the ideals approved by the community . . . [or] simply because the parents embraced ideologies or pursue life-styles at odds with the average." Dr. Alexandra Kaplan, a clinical psychologist and professor of psychology at the University of Massachusetts, testified: "There is no evidence at all that sexual preference of adults in the home has any detrimental impact on children." Many factors influence child rearing, and "sexual preference per se is typically not one of them." Dr. Kaplan also testified that a parent's homosexual relationship would not necessarily cause a child to become a homosexual instead of a heterosexual: "Most children raised in a homosexual situation become heterosexual as adults." Furthermore, she explained, the sexual orientation of the parent "is irrelevant to [the child's] mental health." Psychologist David Johnson, a defense witness who had seen the children in play therapy, concurred with Dr. Kaplan. The Massachusetts court accepted the new stories gays and lesbians had been telling for nearly a decade, and also acknowledged the evidence provided for those new stories. The court rejected as unfounded the myths of the past.

However, the work of undermining the stories of danger to children and perversion in a homosexual family was not yet done. Proof of this lay in the decisions of other courts that rejected the *Bezio* decision. The conflicting perspectives in the Kentucky and Massachusetts cases were at issue in Virginia's disposition of Sharon Bottoms's fight for custody of her three-year-old son. One court, adopting the Massachusetts view, found no evidence that the child would be harmed if Bottoms was awarded custody. The Virginia Supreme Court overturned the decision in 1995, preferring the rationale of harm and confused identity used in the Kentucky decision. Professor Nancy Polikoff, of the American University law school, argued that the court had given a "blueprint to any judge who wants to deny custody to a gay or lesbian parent." All such a judge had to do was selectively quote expert opinion and emphasize the stigma attached to homosexuality.

Homosexual-parent custody disputes remain caught between new and old stories. By 1995, eight states had denied custody to a homosexual parent and five had not. In 1996, the Washington State Supreme Court extended the new positive stories. On the basis of expert testimony, the justices concluded that restrictions on either parent's sexual behavior with partners other than the former spouse were inappropriate: "Problems with adjustment are the normal response to any breakup of a family. But restrictions on a parent's conduct designed to artificially ameliorate changes in a child's life are not permissible. If the problem is adjustment, the remedy is counseling."

Courts in child custody cases could not avoid considering whether an acceptable family meant only a family that practiced heterosexual sex. To decide property and contract disputes between gays, the courts had to acknowledge the reality of a same-sex relationship; however, they could avoid confronting directly whether the relationship constituted a family. Much like courts that relied on due process concerns in deciding sodomy cases, they took refuge in legal stories. They upheld the validity of standard contract and property rules, so important to every enterprise in society, without regard to the parties' sexuality. In Arkansas, Benjamin Selman bought a house in the name of his companion, James Bramlett, with an oral agreement that Bramlett would transfer it to Selman once he obtained his divorce. Selman and Bramlett had been lovers and lived together for about a year. In 1980, the state supreme court concluded that Bramlett knew the title was temporary and must convey it back to Selman. He could not gain a "windfall" by taking advantage of their relationship, "by claiming the stigma of homosexuality." According to this and other decisions, to reinforce standard contract doctrines did not undermine family values.

Similarly, a dispute between tennis champion Martina Navratilova and her lover Judy Nelson was interpreted so as to require no sanction of their lesbian relationship. The matter, the parties agreed, rested solely on the validity of a contract. Nelson, a forty-five-year-old divorced mother of two, began living with Navratilova in July 1984, and traveled with her to tournaments around the world. Nelson and Navratilova signed a "non-marital cohabitation agreement" in 1986. Nelson sued Navratilova upon receiving formal notification from her in April 1991 that their relationship was over. Nelson wanted to enforce the cohabitation agreement, which provided that if they parted they would divide assets accrued since they began living together. Nelson's lawsuit was settled out of court in 1992. However, despite the public awareness of the affair, the legal result avoided sanction of homosexuality and relied solely on contract law.

The law punished homosexual behavior when it became categorized as homosexuality. As gays sought public recognition they became a threat to gender prescriptions. Judicial opinions mirrored public concern about gender roles and were influenced by race and class narratives. Gay men, lesbians, and African American homosexuals were regarded very differently. Gay males evoked a negative response because they represented the dominant group. Gay male sex was a threat to the image of males as patriarchs and heads of families, who exercised power over women and children. Lesbians were harassed in bars and on the streets, but sex between women was not the target of the sodomy statutes. Further, lesbians did not solicit sex from strangers in public restrooms and other venues, behavior that exposed men to criminal charges. African American men were peripheral to power. However, African American gays faced homophobia within the black community, because of widely accepted fundamentalist religious stories. They also were harassed by the legal system because they defied the image of the sexually consumed African American man. This image was important to white men who defined themselves as the opposite, a civilized other.

Homosexuality in the courts traveled a long and convoluted route, from being an outlawed offense with no story to tell, to being an outlawed offense enveloped in medical stories of sin and illness, to become a story in itself, one of affirming relationships and positive values. Gays and lesbians are still elaborating newer stories in an attempt to gain societal acceptance and displace the old ones that linger in the public mind. Because the old stories change, homosexuals' experiences and self-images change, and hence so do the stories they tell. Languages, stories, and identities are protean dynamic forces, just like the society they reflect or tell about. Indeed, the story about gay men and lesbians has changed enough for a federal Employer Non-Discrimination Act to receive serious consideration. It has also changed sufficiently for domestic partnerships to gain recognition from a few employers. The old story still protects the definition of marriage as a union of one man and one woman, and still appears in child custody arrangements. The work of imprinting new stories has yet to be fully accomplished. Until the work is done, gay and lesbian relationships will be regarded as a major challenge to gender roles—just as interracial marriage was considered a major challenge to racial subordination before the 1960s.

It's a Family Affair
Women, Poverty, and Welfare

Randy Albelda and Chris Tilly

Hating poor women for being poor is all the rage—literally. Radio talk show hosts, conservative think tanks, and many elected officials bash poor single mothers for being too "lazy," too "dependent," and too fertile. Poor mothers are blamed for almost every imaginable economic and social ill under the sun. Largely based on anecdotal information, mythical characterizations, and a recognition that the welfare system just isn't alleviating poverty, legislatures across the land and the federal government are proposing and passing draconian welfare "reform" measures.

It is true that current welfare policies do not work well—but not for the reasons usually presented. Welfare "reform" refuses to address the real issues facing single-mother families, and is heavily permeated by myths.

Aid to Families with Dependent Children (AFDC), the government income transfer program for poor non-elder families in the United States, serves only about 5 percent of the population at any given time, with over 90 percent of those receiving AFDC benefits being single mothers and their children. In 1993, 14 million people (two-thirds of them children) in the United States received AFDC. That same year, just under 40 million people were poor. Despite garnering a lion's share of political discussion, AFDC receives a minuscule amount of funding: It accounts for less than 1 percent of the federal budget and less than 3 percent of the state budgets.

Single mothers work. Not only do they do the unpaid work of raising children, they also average the same number of hours in the paid labor force as other mothers do—about 1,000 hours a year (a full-time, year-round job is about 2,000 hours a year).[1] And while close to

80 percent of all ADFC recipients are off in two years, over half of those return at some later point—usually because their wages in the jobs that got them off welfare just didn't match the cost of health care and childcare needed so they could keep the jobs. In fact, most AFDC recipients "cycle" between relying on families, work, and AFDC benefits to get or keep their families afloat.[2] That means that, for many single mothers, AFDC serves the same function as unemployment insurance does for higher-paid, full-time workers.

And, contrary to a highly volatile stereotype, welfare mothers, on average, have fewer kids than other mothers. And once on AFDC, they are less likely to have another child.

POVERTY AND THE "TRIPLE WHAMMY"

Poverty is a persistent problem in the United States. People without access to income are poor. In the United States, most people get access to income by living in a family with one or more wage-earners (either themselves or others). Income from ownership (rent, dividends, interest, and profits) provides only a few families with a large source of income. Government assistance is limited—with elders getting the bulk of it. So wages account for about 80 percent of all income generated in the United States. Not surprisingly, people whose labor market is limited, or who face discrimination, are the people most at risk for poverty. Children, people of color, and single mothers are most likely to be poor. . . .

In 1993, 46 percent of single-mother families in the United States were living in poverty, but only 9 percent of two-adult families with children were poor.[3]

Why are so many single-mother families poor? Are they lazy, do they lack initiative, or are they just unlucky? The answer to all of these is a resounding "No." Single-mother families have a very hard time generating enough income to keep themselves above the poverty line for a remarkably straight-forward reason: One female adult supports the family—and one female adult usually does not earn enough to provide both childcare expenses and adequate earnings.

To spell it out, single mothers face a "triple whammy." First, like all women, when they do paid work they often face low wages—far lower than men with comparable education and experience. In 1992, the median income (the midpoint) for all women who worked full-time was $13,677. That means that about 40 percent of all working women (regardless of their marital status) would not have made enough to support a family of three above the poverty line. Even when women work year-round full-time, they make 70 percent of what men do.

Second, like all mothers, single mothers must juggle paid and unpaid work. Taking care of healthy and, sometimes, sick children, and knowing where they are when at work, requires time and flexibility that few full-time jobs afford. All mothers are more likely to earn less and work less than other women workers because of it.

Finally, *unlike* married mothers, many single mothers must juggle earning income and taking care of children without the help of another adult. Single-mother families have only one adult to send into the labor market. And that same adult must also make sure children get through their day.

. . .

DENYING THE REAL PROBLEMS

The lack of affordable childcare, the large number of jobs that fail to pay living wages, and the lack of job flexibility are the real problems that face all mothers (and increasingly everyone). For single mothers, these problems compound into crisis.

But instead of tackling these problems head on, politicians and pundits attack AFDC. Why? One reason is that non-AFDC families themselves are becoming more desperate, and resent the limited assistance that welfare provides to the worst-off. With men's wages falling over the last 30 years, fewer and fewer families can get by with only one wage earner. The government is not providing help for many low-income families who are struggling but are still above the AFDC eligibility threshold. This family "speed-up" has helped contribute to the ideas that if both parents in a two-parent household can work (in order to be poor), then all AFDC recipients should have to work too.

Instead of facing the real problems, debates about welfare reform are dominated by three dead ends. First, politicians argue that single mothers must be made to work in the paid labor market. But most single mothers already work as much as they can. Studies confirm that AFDC recipients already do cycle in and out of the labor force. Further, as surveys indicate, mothers receiving AFDC would like to work. The issue is not whether or not to work, but whether paid work is available, how much it pays, and how to balance work and childcare.

Second, there is a notion of replacing the social responsibilities of government assistance with individual "family" responsibilities: Make men pay child support, demand behavioral changes of AFDC recipients, or even pressure single women to get married. While child support can help, for most single mothers it offers a poor substitute for reliable government assistance. Penalizing women and their children for ascribed behaviors (such as having more children to collect welfare) that are supported by anecdotes but not facts is at best mean-spirited.

Third, there is an expectation that people only need support for a limited amount of time—many states and some versions of federal welfare reform limit families to 24 months of aid over some period of time (from a lifetime to five years). Yet limiting the amount of time women receive AFDC will not reduce or limit the need for support. Children do not grow up in 24 months, nor will many women with few skills and little education necessarily become job ready. But more important, many women who do leave AFDC for the workplace will not make enough money to pay for childcare or the health insurance they need to go to work.

In short, welfare "reform" that means less spending and no labor market supports will do little beyond making poor women's lives more miserable.

BEYOND WELFARE REFORM

What could be done instead? Welfare reform in a vacuum can solve only a small part of the problem. To deal with poverty among single-mother families, to break the connection between gender and poverty, requires changing the world of work, socializing the costs of raising children, and providing low-wage supports.

If we as a nation are serious about reducing the poverty of women and children, we need to invest in seven kinds of institutional changes:

- *Create an income-maintenance system that recognizes the need for full-time childcare.* Policies that affect families must acknowledge the reality of children's needs. To truly value families means to financially support those (women or men) who must provide full-time childcare at home or to provide dependable, affordable, and caring alternative sources of childcare for those who work outside the home.
- *Provide support for low-wage workers.* If leaving welfare and taking a job means giving up health benefits and childcare subsidies, the loss to poor families can be devastating. Although high-salary workers receive (or can afford) these benefits, low-wage workers often don't. Government should provide these supports; universal health

care and higher earned income tax credits (EITC) are a first step in the right direction.
- *Close the gender pay gap.* One way to achieve pay equity is to require employers to re-evaluate the ways that they compensate comparable skills. Poor women need pay equity the most, but all women need it. Another way to close the pay gap is to increase the minimum wage. Most minimum-wage workers are women. An increase from the current $4.25 an hour to $5.50 would bring the minimum wage to 50 percent of the average wage.
- *Create jobs.* Create the opportunity to work, for poor women and poor men as well. Full employment is an old idea that still makes sense.
- *Create jobs that don't assume you have a "wife" at home to perform limitless unpaid work.* It's not just the welfare system that has to come to terms with family needs; it's employers as well. With women making up 46 percent of the workforce—and men taking on more childcare responsibilities as well—a change in work styles is overdue.
- *Make education and training affordable and available for all.* In an economy where the premium on skills and education is increasing, education and training are necessary for young people and adults, women and men.
- *Fix the tax structure.* Many of these proposals require government spending consistent with the ways our industrial counterparts spend money. Taxes must be raised to pay for these programs: the alternative—not funding child allowances, health care, and training—will prove more costly to society in the long run. But it is critically important to make the programs universal, and to fund them with a *fairer* tax system. Federal, state, and local governments have taxed middle- and low-income families for too long without assuring them basic benefits. Taxes paid by the wealthiest families as a percentage of their income have fallen dramatically over the last 15 years, while

the burden on the bottom 80 percent has risen; it's time to reverse these trends.

The changes proposed are sweeping, but no less so than those proposed by the Republican Contract with America. With one out of every four children in this nation living in poverty, all our futures are at stake.

NOTES

1. These data, and others throughout the paper, were calculated by the authors using current population survey tapes.
2. Five recent studies have looked at welfare dynamics and all come to these conclusions. LaDonna Pavetti, "The Dynamics of Welfare and Work: Exploring the Process by Which Young Women Work Their Way Off Welfare," paper presented at the APPAM Annual Research Conference, 1992; Kathleen Harris, "Work and Welfare Among Single Mothers in Poverty," *American Journal of Sociology* vol. 99 (2), September 1993, pp. 317–52; Roberta Spalter-Roth, Beverly Burr, Heidi Hartman, and Lois Shaw, "Welfare That Works: The Working Lives of AFDC Recipients," Institute for Women's Policy Research, 1995; Rebecca Blank and Patricia Ruggles, "Short-Term Recidivism Among Public Assistance Recipients," *American Economic Review,* vol. 84 (2), May 1994, pp. 49–53; and Peter David Brandon, "Vulnerability to Future Dependence Among Former AFDC Mothers," Institute for Research on Poverty discussion paper DP1005-95, University of Wisconsin, Madison, Wis., 1995.
3. U.S. Department of Commerce, Census Bureau, "Income, Poverty and Valuation of Noncash Benefits," *Current Populations Reports,* 1995, pp. 60–188, p. D-22.

READING 81

I Was a *Welfare Mom*

Cindy Ballard (as told to Tracy Thompson)

I remember that warm spring morning so vividly: I woke up feeling like I was coming down with the flu, and it was all I could do to feed my 4-month-old daughter without throwing up. So I told my husband, Kent, I was too sick to make his lunch before he left for work. He was furious: He yelled that I was lazy, that the house was a pigsty. Then he saw our other child, 5-year-old Jason, sucking his thumb and started to spank him. For me, it was the last straw, Watching my son sobbing, I thought: *We cannot live this way anymore.*

Looking back, I see that our marriage had been straining at the seams for some time. I had married Kent at age 20, just months after meeting him. Jason was born nine months later. Although I'd worked through Jason's childhood, selling ads for a radio station, we were constantly behind with the bills. I resented how Kent insisted on controlling the purse strings even though, at times, I was the main breadwinner. When I was pregnant with Sara, our fights got worse, and his criticisms of me escalated. When Sara was born, Kent showed little interest in her. Meanwhile, Jason was turning into a tense, unhappy little boy.

That day, I gathered my resolve. When Jason got home from kindergarten, I sat down with him at the kitchen table. "If I told you we could leave here, but that you couldn't take any of your toys, just some clothes, what would you say?" I asked. Jason didn't hesitate. "Mommy, let's leave," he said. Quickly, I packed as many of our clothes as I could, and Jason, Sara, and I got ourselves to a local women's shelter. It was there, three days later, that I learned why I'd felt so nauseated that morning. I was pregnant.

I had stopped working when Sara was born, at Kent's insistence. Now, my morning sickness made job hunting all but impossible. Before long, I ended up on welfare, and began a journey that changed me profoundly. I used to think of welfare moms as mostly minority women who stayed on the dole for decades and just didn't try hard enough to find work. Now I know the reality: A large percentage of welfare recipients are, in fact, white, and only a minority stay on assistance for more than two or three years. In my own case, I got off welfare through sheer stubbornness—and the strength I learned from my mom, who had worked to support her own children after ending a difficult marriage with my father.

I called her from the women's shelter and cried and cried. She didn't have any money to give us, but she tried to comfort me, saying that I was smart and resourceful—that I would find a way. Later she told me that she used to lie awake at night wondering what on earth was going to happen to us.

Applying for welfare and food stamps was the last thing I wanted to do, but I had no choice. It was degrading. When you ask the state to give you money, you give up any pretense of privacy. They asked me everything: how much money Kent made, whether he was the father of my children, how much money we had in savings.

Then there was the grocery store: There's nothing like buying groceries with food stamps. People get a certain look on their faces when you hand them over—one of contempt, or pity, or this careful blank expression that they imagine hides what they're thinking. But you know, I felt like a complete zero. It had come to this: I was one of those welfare moms I had always held in such disdain.

We stayed at the women's shelter for three weeks. Then, with the help of a counselor there, I got a court order requiring Kent to move out of our house, and the children and I moved back in. Kent was so angry that at one point the police sent a cruiser to the house to tell me they

feared for my safety. The kids and I went to stay with Kent's brother for a week until things cooled down.

I'd left my husband in May 1992. In August, I filed a petition for child support, and in November, the Circuit Court of Frederick County, MD, ordered Kent to pay $45 a week. He fell behind in his payments almost immediately. For five months, Jason, Sara, and I got by on $377 a month in welfare payments (which went immediately to pay our $375 rent bill), $300 a month in food stamps, and $1,500 that I'd taken out of our savings account when I left. When we finally got a chance to move into subsidized housing, things got a little easier.

I still hoped Kent and I would be able to patch things up somehow. He sought counseling to try to deal with his anger and was with me when Sam was born. But he never took enough responsibility for his part in our marital troubles. In fact, he blamed the counselors at the women's shelter for breaking up our marriage. And he continued to fall behind in his child-support payments. At one point, he disappeared for almost a year. When he came back to town, he had a girlfriend and a newborn baby. In 1995, when Sam turned 2, I filed for divorce.

After awhile, I developed a love-hate relationship with welfare. Strange as it sounds, it actually had some good points. For one thing, it gave me a way to stay home with my children when they were young. It also forced me to create a household budget and stick to it. I planned our meals carefully, and I became the best yard-sale bargain-hunter east of the Mississippi. You'd never have known from looking at me or my kids that we were wearing other people's castoffs. I even found bargains for my neighbors, other single moms with kids.

But as time passed, getting those monthly checks started to erode my already tattered self-esteem. When you're on public assistance, working people seem better or smarter than you. You get the feeling that life is a game, and only dummies like you don't know how to play.

I stopped thinking of myself as a person who could earn her own living—even though I'd had several jobs in my life. I didn't talk to anybody except other women in my situation and kids. Anytime I was in a place where people were all polished and self-confident and dressed up, I was extremely conscious of how different I looked and felt.

So I started to procrastinate. At first I was going to get off welfare right away. Then I told myself I'd take a little longer, maybe wait a year. Then it was when Sam got into kindergarten. But then, when Sam was 3, my caseworker told me my time was up. I had to start looking for a job or my benefits would expire. It was welfare reform, she said. New rules. Suddenly I was as petrified about getting off welfare as I'd been about getting on it.

Finding day care was the first challenge. Then there was transportation. I was driving a beat-up, rusty old station wagon; even if I could find a job, I wasn't sure it could get me there reliably. My last job seemed as if it had happened in another lifetime. But just when things seems impossible, I thought of my mom: She'd made her life better on her own, and I would too.

The job counselors advised me to take the first job I could get, but I knew I wanted to be in communications. No, they said, you can't be so picky. But I knew I needed more than minimum wage: I needed a job with a future. Eventually I found a position as a sales rep for a direct-mail marketing firm, making $200 a week. That's when the financial pressure really started.

The minute I started bringing in money, my welfare check was cut and my rent went up. For awhile, I was bringing home less money by working than if I had just continued to take assistance, because I had to buy gas for the car and clothes to wear to work. I did get day-care vouchers, which were essential, but finding good day care was harder than I thought it would be. I went through four providers in that first year: the kids were in a constant state of upheaval. Then, to top it off, the engine of my

station wagon blew up. If it hadn't been for someone at my church who gave me their old clunker, I would have failed right then and there.

Every day was a marathon. I'd roll out of bed in the morning, get myself and the kids dressed, get them off to school and day care, work all day—then pick the kids up, go home, cook dinner, help them with their homework, put them to bed, and try to get the house picked up. I missed having another adult around to talk to, and I worried constantly about making ends meet. Late at night, I'd stare at the walls and think, *My God, I have to do all this all over again tomorrow.* But I was too scared of what would happen to me and the kids to quit.

The feeling of incompetence that you have when you're on welfare can be reinforced by a lot of other people, I discovered. My new employer second-guessed everything I did, as if I were a teenager. Once she even made a hair appointment for me, without asking. (My hairstyle was frumpy, I admit, but I'd rather have decided that for myself.) After nine months, I was so frustrated, I did something crazy for a woman with three kids to support: I quit. My welfare counselor said she could put me back on welfare while I looked for a new job, but I said no, afraid it would be even harder to get off a second time. Somehow, my panic focused me. I knew I wanted to go back to my old line of work, selling ads for a radio station, and I even knew where: oldies station 106.9 in Hagerstown, MD. They'd already turned me down once. But now I went back, more determined than ever.

It was a strange interview; the owner did most of the talking. But I managed to squeeze in the critical question: "When do you want me to start?"

"Oh, why don't you start Monday," he said, like it was no big deal. I couldn't believe it. It was hard for me to sit there and look professional when I felt like jumping up and down. The job paid $18,000 a year. That's only $1,950 above the poverty level for a family of four. But

I still qualified for child-care vouchers, and by then, Jason was 11 and could take care of himself after school. This wasn't the best arrangement, but it was the only thing I could afford. I wouldn't be able to get health insurance for myself, but my kids could still get it through the state. All I had to do was stay healthy and work like crazy.

At first, I didn't tell my employers I'd been on welfare and was still getting a state child-care subsidy. I didn't want anything to color their assessment of my work. But after I'd been at the station for ten months, I was lured out of the closet.

My former caseworker called with a request: The county office of the Maryland Department of Human Services was setting up a luncheon to encourage local business leaders to hire people from the welfare-to-work program I'd been in. Would I mind speaking? My first reaction was, are you crazy? The people I'd be talking to were the same ones I was trying to sell ads to every day. But then I reconsidered. Getting a job had so helped my self-confidence that I wanted to share what I had learned about moving from welfare to work with others.

It was no fancy speech; I just told my story. I told them that rich people wind up in bad marriages too; they just have more of a financial cushion when things don't work out. I told them what it was like to feed your kids on $300 a month, and how scared I'd been to go looking for work after nearly four years on welfare. I told them there were plenty of times when I was still afraid—afraid that I'd get sick or be in a car wreck or that something would happen to my kids while I was putting in long hours at work.

Later, I heard that some people had tears in their eyes by the time I had finished. The local newspaper ran a story about the luncheon and my speech, and the next thing I knew, I got a call from a person named Connie Tolbert, from the state office of Human Services. She wanted to see if I was interested in making a video about my experience on welfare and how I was working my way off. As it turned out, Connie and I had a lot in common, even though it didn't seem that way at first. She's from New York City; I'm a farm girl from Pennsylvania. She's black; I'm white. But Connie was a former welfare mom too. Her marriage had foundered because of money trouble and her husband's drug problem. She spent 11 years on welfare, raising four kids in inner-city Baltimore. Unlike me, she had to try several times to get off welfare before she finally succeeded. Now she was working for the agency that had once signed her checks.

Looking at Connie, I saw somebody who had managed to make the journey from total dependency to self-sufficiency, and who was now helping other people along the same path. And I thought, *I would like to do that too.* Today, the video we made is used throughout Maryland as an educational tool for women who are trying to make the transition.

My own transition, it seems, is finally complete. I've been off welfare for more than three years now, and though life isn't perfect, it's pretty good. I will always regret that my kids didn't get to have their father around much. But all three are doing great. Jason has been on the honor roll at school, and my younger two are well-adjusted and confident. Last year, I was even able to buy a new car. My next goal is to buy a house. I'm talking to a real estate agent about finding one in our price range. I know it's going to be tough, but I think I can do it.

Not long ago, another radio station made me a job offer. I actually turned it down; I think I have more of a future where I am. Who would have thought I'd ever have the luxury of doing that?

READING 82

Battered Women
A New Asylum Case

Anna Shelton

A battered immigrant from the Congo calls collect from a pay phone at the 300-bed detention center in Elizabeth, New Jersey. She has been waiting there since March 1998 to be granted asylum in the United States. She goes only by her initials, D.K. In hurried French, she describes the history of her relationship with her abusive husband in her home country. She says she endured threats and harassment from the beginning of their marriage twenty-five years ago. After twenty-one years together, she claims, her husband began to abuse her physically in front of her four children.

"He beat me," she says. "He kicked me. He dragged me on the ground. He threatened me with a gun." Once she had an operation on her eye after he beat her badly, she says. Her husband is a major in the military and has friends among the police. These connections, she says, "made it difficult for me to do anything."

Then, in January 1998, her husband beat her almost to death, she says. Her son saved her, dragging her out of the house and taking her to the home of her brother. She was unconscious for four days.

While she recovered, her brother and a friend began making plans to send her to the United States, where they understood she would be protected. Using her sister's passport, she left the Congo in March 1998.

"My brother told me that when I got to the United States, I just needed to explain my story and they would understand," she says. "So I explained it to somebody in the airport, and they saw my face, which was deformed after the beating and was sort of twisted. My cheek was sagging a little bit." Instead of gaining protection, D.K. was taken to Manchester, Massachusetts, where she was processed as an illegal immigrant because she had used her sister's passport.

"I would like for the United States to protect women like me," she says. "Neither my family nor my government can protect me in my country. There are women who die because of these things. I lived it—I saw it with my own eyes. There was one policeman whose wife wanted to leave him, and so he killed her. I just want to emphasize that if I go back to the Congo, I cannot divorce my husband because he'll never agree to it. He'll kill me. I'm absolutely positive he'll kill me."

D. K. is not alone. Dozens of battered women from around the world have applied for asylum in the United States, but they are finding it much more difficult to obtain than they ever anticipated.

Under current U.S. law, you can gain asylum only if you have a "credible fear" of persecution because of your race, religion, nationality, political opinion, or membership in a social group. Advocates for battered women argue that some women fleeing domestic violence should be granted asylum as well. Canada began offering protection to battered women seeking asylum in 1993.

In 1994, U.S. Immigration Judge Paul Nejelski granted protection to a Jordanian woman who was fleeing thirty years of domestic violence in her home country. It was the first time an immigration judge granted asylum for someone fleeing spousal abuse. "The respondent has been harmed and threatened on account of two of the five grounds," Nejelski ruled, "political opinion and membership in a particular social group." He determined that "these two grounds are not mutually exclusive.

The respondent believes in Western values. The respondent's social group consists of those women who espouse Western values and who are unwilling to live their lives at the mercy of their husbands, their society, their government."

The next big step forward occurred in 1995, when the Immigration and Naturalization Service (INS) issued gender guidelines for asylum officers considering the cases of women who have been persecuted because of their sex. The guidelines state that "rape (including mass rape in, for example, Bosnia), sexual abuse and domestic violence, infanticide, and genital mutilation are forms of mistreatment primarily directed at girls and women, and they may serve as evidence of past persecution on account of one or more of the five grounds."

In 1997, Fauziya Kassindja of Togo was the first to file a successful claim, citing fear of genital mutilation. Adelaide Abankwah of Ghana was the second. Her similar claim was just granted on August 13.

Asylum guidelines have also been broadened in recent years to grant protection to gays and lesbians who fear persecution in their home countries. Dusty Aráujo, asylum program coordinator at the International Gay and Lesbian Human Rights Commission in San Francisco, says that the commission knows of about 250 cases of asylum granted in the United States on the basis of sexual orientation since 1994. "Around the world, gays, lesbians, transgendered, and HIV-positive people are denied their rights on a daily basis," says Aráujo. "In many countries, people are jailed just because someone thinks they are gay, and are tortured, blackmailed, and threatened with psychiatric treatment." People persecuted because of their sexual orientation should be regularly granted asylum in the United States, Aráujo says.

Despite these landmark extensions of asylum, protection in the United States for women fleeing domestic violence is hard to come by. In late June, the Board of Immigration Appeals, which is part of the Department of Justice, denied asylum to a Guatemalan woman who said she was seeking protection from an abusive husband in her home country.

Rodi Alvarado Peña, now thirty-three years old, told authorities she was kicked, pistol-whipped, and raped by her husband until she hemorrhaged, *The Washington Post* reported. Like D.K., Alvarado said that she was beaten by her husband so badly she lost consciousness. Alvarado told the *Post* that when she sought protection from police, they told her "they couldn't insert themselves in the matter of a couple." After years of abuse, Alvarado fled to the United States to seek help.

Originally, Alvarado was told that she could stay. In 1996, Immigration Judge Mimi Yam granted her asylum claim. But the INS appealed the decision, and the Board of Immigration Appeals overturned Yam 10 to 5. The majority stated that her claim "does not lie in our asylum laws as they are currently formulated." That decision sets a bad precedent for pending domestic-violence-related cases, including D.K.'s. Alvarado is appealing the decision.

Congressman Luis Gutierrez, Democrat of Illinois, is leading a campaign to draw attention to Alvarado's case. The Congressional Hispanic Caucus, with Gutierrez as chairman of its task force on immigration, presented a letter to Attorney General Janet Reno in July asking her to step in and reverse the Alvarado ruling.

"We are deeply troubled by this decision and find it to be inconsistent with a growing body of precedent in the U.S.," the letter says, calling the decision "a wrong and unacceptable step backwards."

Neil Nolen, staff attorney with Ayuda, a nonprofit advocacy organization for refugees and victims of domestic violence, was also outraged by the denial. "This decision seems to be in direct conflict with INS's own instructions," he says. "As national advocates, we're demanding that both the INS and the Clinton Administration be consistent in their defense of women's rights."

But INS spokesman Daniel Kane contends that the Board acted appropriately. "Although gender-related claims can raise hard questions, the INS remains committed to their fair adjudication and to seeing the law surrounding them develop in a fair way," he said. "Gender guidelines are one manifestation of this commitment."

Advocates for battered immigrants are trying to seek relief not just for the women who come to the United States, but for those undocumented and abused women who are already living here. The Violence Against Women Act, passed in 1994, makes it possible for battered immigrants living within the United States to petition for residency status by themselves. Usually, U.S. citizens and permanent residents must file for a visa in order for their spouses to gain status in America. But abusive husbands who are working legally in the United States sometimes refuse to file for their spouses in order to maintain control over them. The option that allows these battered wives to gain status is called the self-petition. Since the processing system was established in September 1996, says Violence Against Women Act program officer Karen FitzGerald, the INS has received 8,080 self-petitions and has approved 4,323.

"Jennifer" came to the United States from Mexico when she was ten years old, she says, crossing the border illegally to join her mother. When she was fifteen, she "got kind of in love" with a twenty-one-year-old man who was renting a room in her mother's house. He had a green card. The two were married when she was sixteen years old. The abuse started, she says, with what she thought were playful pinches and little punches on her arm. But one evening, she says, he slapped her on the face because she could not get their baby daughter to stop crying. Another day, when he was drunk, he beat her savagely, she says. "He got on top of me, and he got a perfume bottle and smashed it on my head. He wouldn't stop. I said, 'What are you doing? You don't even know who I am! I'm your wife. Don't do this. Love me better.' And then he got a brass knob that was on the bedpost and he smashed it, first on my face and second on my head." Jennifer

ran outside as he threatened to beat her with a belt, and someone in the neighborhood called the police, she says.

When she finally did manage to leave him, he found her, kidnapped her and their three children, and took them to Mexico. Once across the border, he put them in an isolated house with dirt floors. He kept them there for eight months without letting them out, she says. But one morning, she managed to flee with her children.

Jennifer took a taxi to Tijuana, where she stayed in a homeless shelter and worked as a cashier for six months. This spring, she returned illegally to the United States with her children. Her self-petition is pending.

But because of defects in the Violence Against Women Act, some abused immigrant women find it difficult to self-petition.

Currently, the law requires women to return to their home countries for final processing. This may sound like an innocuous requirement, but it can lead to a disastrous outcome for women who lived illegally in the United States with their partners. Once these women leave the United States, they could be barred from reentering because they were at one time unlawfully present. The irony is that in order to be eligible to petition in the first place, they must have been undocumented.

This fall, Congress has the opportunity to pass the Violence Against Women Act II, which would correct the defect and make the petitioning process more flexible for women seeking protection.

Those who oppose broader immigration fear the floodgates will open by extending asylum to abused women and by expanding the self-petitioning process. They also contend that we are losing sight of the original reasons for an established set of international asylum laws.

"Asylum law was written to prevent genocide and ethnic cleansing of large groups of people based on race, ethnicity, or national origin," says David Ray, associate director of the anti-immigration group Federation for American Immigration Reform. "Asylum law was certainly never written to address domestic inequalities or problems such as abuse in marriages. If you make family problems one of the reasons to qualify for asylum, you would completely undermine the program. If you encourage addressing domestic problems by mass exodus, you're going to be creating more problems on top of it."

But Shirley Tang, D. K.'s pro bono attorney at the New Jersey-based law firm Friedman Siegelbaum, disagrees.

"We're not asking that every battered women apply for asylum in the United States," she says. "We're not asking that at all. What we're asking for is that very small sliver of the world population where the woman is beaten by her husband; where there are no mechanisms within the country that provide for women's groups, shelters, or safe houses; where the law of the country itself prohibits the woman from free access to go on with her life and start over. That's when the United States should be the safe haven that it represents itself to be."

"Isabel" is a teacher from Guatemala who is currently seeking asylum in the United States on the basis of domestic abuse. She married her boyfriend when she was just sixteen and very much in love. One night in 1982, when she was seven months pregnant with their first child, her husband got drunk and threw her on the bed, breaking her arm, she says. He proceeded to rape her.

Isabel wanted to get a divorce, but that can take a long time in Guatemala, and her husband would not agree to it. She says he called and threatened to kill her and their three children: "He said, 'You know who this is. If you go to court, when you come back to your house, you'll find your children dead. You'll have to pick up the pieces, and you'll have to put the pieces in different boxes because they won't be recognizable or identifiable.'"

The death threats continued. In October 1996, her husband told her mother that Isabel would be killed the following March. She left her children with her mother and fled to the United States that fall.

"In my country," Isabel says, "when you seek help, when you are a married woman and you are abused, it doesn't matter what kind of education you have. When one looks for help, the police say, 'This is a domestic problem. Go home and solve it.' Even if they see the man killing his wife, they tell you, 'Go home and solve your problem there.'"

Domestic violence is widespread in Guatemala, Isabel says, and the effects are devastating. "In my country, many women choose the quick way out, the shortcut—they are committing suicide. They can no longer put up with it, and this is their only way out.

Isabel was lucky and escaped. But it has been three years since she last saw her children, who are now ten, fifteen, and seventeen years old. They are living with their grandmother, yet they see their father sometimes, and they say that he has been treating them badly, hitting them and insulting them. Her husband sends messages to Isabel through her children, saying he knows where she is and could hurt her.

When her kids ask when they will be able to see her again, she doesn't know how to answer. She has not heard whether she will be granted asylum, and she is worried, especially in light of the Alvarado decision.

"Sometimes I think I will be able to accomplish it, bringing my children here," she says. "But now, with this decision, I feel that at any moment, this will all end with a letter that says that I have to return to my country."

READING 83

Stopping Abuse in Prison

Nina Siegal

Widespread abuses of women behind bars barely received notice until seven or eight years ago. Across the country, there were incidents of prison or jail staff sexually molesting inmates with impunity. Slowly but surely, the nation's correctional facilities are responding to this abuse.

"Ten years ago, I think we knew it was going on, but we hadn't named it," says Brenda Smith, a Practitioner-in-Residence at Washington College of Law at American University. "Until you raise it as a problem, and until people start coming forward and talking about it, it is not perceived as a problem."

The changes are the result of several landmark legal cases, a shift in government policy, and the attention of human-rights groups. Still, problems remain. Guards continue to rape women inmates. But now there's a process to bring them to justice.

The stories were too consistent to be ignored. Numerous female inmates in three Washington, D.C., prison and jail facilities said they had been awakened at two or three in the morning for a "medical visit" or a "legal visit" only to be led into the kitchen, the clinic, the visiting hall, or a closet to have sex. Many inmates were becoming pregnant in a system that allowed no conjugal visits.

"There were a lot of places where people could have sex," says Smith. "A lot of it was in exchange for cigarettes." Prison employees offered other deals: "'I will give you phone calls, I will make sure you get a better job assignment, I'll give you drugs if you have sex with me.' The sex involved not just correctional officers. It involved chaplains, administration, deputy wardens, contractors, and food-service workers. It involved not just male staff but female staff as well," Smith says.

In 1993, the National Women's Law Center and a District of Columbia law firm filed a class-action suit, *Women Prisoners vs. District of Columbia Department of Corrections,* in U.S. District Court. The suit alleged a pattern of discrimination against women in the jail, the Correctional Treatment Facility, and the Lorton Minimum Security Annex, a D.C. facility in Lorton, Virginia. A large portion of the case focused on issues of sexual misconduct, based on evidence that the law firm had collected during an investigation. The following year, a judge found that there was a pattern of practice of misconduct so severe that it violated the Eighth Amendment protection against cruel and unusual punishment. The decision was appealed and is still in court.

As extreme as the D.C. situation was, it was not unique.

Lawyers in Georgia had been preparing a class-action suit on behalf of men and women in the state's prisons for almost ten years when they began to come across striking charges of sexual misconduct in the Georgia Women's Correctional Facility in Milledgeville and the nearby camp, Colony Farm. The alleged activities included rape, criminal sexual contact, leering, and abusive catcalling of inmates. One lieutenant had sex with at least seven prisoners from 1987 to 1991, directing women to meet him in various locations in the prisons for sex.

In 1992, the lawyers for the suit, *Cason v. Seckinger,* amended their complaint to add allegations of sexual abuse that had taken place over a period of fourteen years. Seventeen staff members were indicted. None were convicted, though several were dismissed from their jobs as a result of the lawsuit. The suit resulted in a number of federal court orders requiring the department to rectify many of its practices. It also influenced the department to close

Milledgeville and move all the female inmates to a different facility.

These two suits—and the criminal prosecutions that ensued—were the first major legal attempts to address a problem that had been plaguing the criminal justice system for decades.

One of the biggest cases for the rights of women prisoners was settled last year. The case (*Lucas vs. White*) involved three inmates of a federal facility in Pleasanton, California, called FCI Dublin, who were sold as sex slaves to male inmates in an adjoining facility. Inmates paid guards to allow them into the cells of female inmates who were being held in the men's detention center, which is across the street from Dublin.

The plantiffs settled their civil suit against the Federal Bureau of Prisons for $500,000 and forced the agency to make dramatic changes in the way it handles allegations of misconduct. According to the settlement, the Bureau of Prisons was to set up a confidential hotline, or some other reporting mechanism, so that inmates and staff can inform the authorities of problems inside. It was also supposed to provide medical and psychological treatment for inmates who have been victimized and establish new training programs for staff and inmates.

Geri Lynn Green, one of the two attorneys for the Lucas case, has been monitoring the changes at the prison since the case settled. After the lawsuit and the subsequent training, she says, "it appears there was a tremendous impact."

Brett Dignam, clinical professor of law at Yale University, agrees that the *Lucas* case made a big difference: "More prison staff members are resigning over issues of sexual misconduct."

Human rights advocates, too, have taken up the cause. In 1996, the Women's Rights Project at Human Rights Watch issued "All Too Familiar: Sexual Abuse of Women in U.S. Prisons."

The 347-page report detailed problems in California, Washington, D.C., Michigan, Georgia, and New York. "We have found that male correctional employees have vaginally, anally, and orally raped female prisoners and sexually assaulted and abused them," says the report. "We found that in the course of committing such gross misconduct, male officers have not only used actual or threatened physical force, but have also used their near total authority to provide or deny goods and privileges to female prisoners to compel them to have sex, or, in other cases, to reward them for having done so."

Last June, the United Nations sent a special rapporteur, Radhike Coomaraswamy, to the United States to investigate sexual misconduct in the nation's women's facilities. She argued that stronger monitoring was needed to control widespread abuses.

"We concluded that there has been widespread sexual misconduct in U.S. prisons, but there is a diversity—some are dealing with it better than others," Reuters reported her saying in December. "Georgia has sexual misconduct but has set up a very strong scheme to deal with it. In California and Michigan, nothing has been done and the issue is very prevalent." In April, Coomaraswamy will give a final report to the U.N. Commission on Human Rights.

This March, Amnesty International released its own report, "'Not Part of My Sentence': Violations of the Human Rights of Women in Custody," which includes a section on sexual abuse. "Many women inmates are subjected to sexual abuse by prison officials, including: sexually offensive language, observation by male officers while showering and dressing, groping during daily pat-down searches, and rape." In addition to the problems detailed in the Human Rights Watch report, Amnesty investigators found problems in Illinois, Massachusetts, New Hampshire, Texas, West Virginia, and Wyoming.

Lawyers and human rights groups have won some important reforms. In 1990, only seventeen states had a law on the books defining sexual misconduct in prisons as either a misdemeanor or a felony offense. Today, there are only twelve states left that do not criminalize sexual relations between staff and inmates—Alabama, Kentucky, Massachusetts, Minnesota, Missouri, Montana, Nebraska, Oregon, Utah, Vermont, West Virginia, and Wisconsin—according to Amnesty International, which is campaigning to get all these states to pass their own laws.

The U.S. Justice Department is also taking a more active role. It has filed two suits charging that the correctional systems in Michigan and Arizona were responsible for violations of prisoners' constitutional rights. The suits cite numerous allegations of abuse, including rape, lack of privacy, prurient viewing, and invasive pat searches. Both cases are still pending.

Meanwhile, state prison systems are training personnel. Andie Moss was a project director with the Georgia Department of Corrections in 1992 when the department was asked to help interview inmates for the class-action lawsuit. She ended up culling information from women who said they had been subjected to misconduct over a fourteen-year period. Today, Moss works with the National Institute of Corrections, part of the Bureau of Prisons. Her primary responsibility is to develop training programs to educate both staff and inmates about sexual misconduct, the new laws, and their rights.

Since her program, "Addressing Staff Sexual Misconduct," was initiated in early 1997, Moss and her team have provided training for more than thirty state correctional systems, and she expects to complete training for all fifty states by the end of 1999.

The training involves four basic elements: clarifying the departments' sexual misconduct policy, informing inmates and staff of the law in their state, telling inmates and staff how to report abuse that they witness, and giving examples of how people have intervened in the past.

"We know it's still an issue. We know corrections departments still need to work diligently on this," says Moss. "It's a constant effort because it is a cultural change. But if you could

follow the change in the law, the change in policy and practice, there's been an amazing effort in the last three years."

Despite all the positive steps, however, women are still being abused in America's prisons and jails. Investigators from a number of California-based law firms who recently visited the Valley State Prison for Women in Chowchilla, California, heard stories of at least a dozen assaults by specific guards. They also found "a climate of sexual terror that women are subjected to on a daily basis," says Ellen Barry, founding director of Legal Services for Prisoners with Children, based in San Francisco.

"The instances of both physical and sexual abuse are much higher than any other institution where I've interviewed women," she says. "The guards are really brutalizing women in a way that we really haven't seen before."

Valley State Prison inmate Denise Dalton told investigators that a doctor at the facility groped her and conducts inappropriate pelvic exams. "If I need Tylenol, all I need to do is ask him for a pelvic and he will give me whatever I want," she said.

But most of the abusive conduct was of the type that, Barry says, made for "a climate of sexual terror" in the prison. Coreen Sanchez, another inmate, said that in December, she entered the dayroom at the facility and asked a correctional officer if the sergeant had come in, and he responded by saying, "Yeah, he came in your mouth." She also reported seeing correctional officers flaunt their erections in front of inmates.

Advocates of prisoners say there still needs to be a dramatic cultural shift within the system before women are safe from the people who guard them behind bars.

"I think we have to keep in perspective the limitations of litigation and advocacy work for truly making a change in this arena," says Barry.

One problem that advocates cite is the recalcitrance of the unions that represent prison guards. "The people we really have to win over are not legislators, but the unions," says Christine Doyle, research coordinator for Amnesty International U.S.A. "Guards look at this as a workplace violation, as something fun to do on the job. They don't look at these women as human beings. The message that these are human beings they are exploiting isn't getting through."

For them to get that message, says Doyle, corrections officers will have to hear it from within the unions, and not from any set of codes, procedures, or laws. "We have states that have legislation, and some of them are just as bad, if not worse, than states without legislation," Doyle says. "So, obviously, that doesn't work. If it comes from within, and the unions themselves say, 'We can do this internally,' workers will respond better."

Human rights groups, for now, are focusing on legislative solutions. In 1996, Human Rights Watch recommended that Congress require all states, as a precondition of receiving federal funding for prisons, criminalize all sexual conduct between staff and inmates. It also urged the Department of Justice to establish secure toll-free telephone hotlines for reporting complaints.

Amnesty International's new report takes an additional step, arguing that the role of male staff be restricted in accordance with the United Nations' Standard Minimum Rules for the Treatment of Prisoners, which state that "women prisoners shall be attended and supervised only by women officers."

Debra LaBelle, a civil rights attorney who filed a class-action suit on behalf of abused women inmates in Michigan, says she would like to see men taken out of women's institutions altogether.

"I resisted going there for a long time, but I don't know another solution," she says. "When we started out, they didn't do any training, much supervision, investigation. In the last three years, they've changed countless policies and yet it is still happening. Get them out of there. It's not like they're losing employment opportunities. There are, unfortunately, many more facilities that men can work in."

Sheila Dauer, director of the Women's Human Rights Program for Amnesty International, says the group's report aims to persuade the final thirteen states without laws against sexual misconduct to initiate legislation, starting with eight state campaigns this year. She says the campaign will also lend support to a federal bill that would do the same thing.

Amnesty's report, she says, is designed to "wake up the American public to the horrible abuses that women inmates are suffering in prison and stop the suffering."

DISCUSSION QUESTIONS FOR CHAPTER ELEVEN

1. What are some of the ways the state maintains social inequality? Have you experienced discrimination by the state in any way?

2. How does the early American assumption that citizens were White men perpetuate contemporary social inequities?

3. Do you believe that full equality can be achieved under our present system of democracy and capitalism? Why or why not?

4. What myths that maintain inequity do you see operating in the state, the law, and social policies?

5. What changes do you believe should be made in order to create a more just state?

SUGGESTIONS FOR FURTHER READING

Arneil, Barbara. *Politics and Feminism: An Introduction.* Malden, MA: Blackwell, 1999.

Baer, Judith A. *Our Lives Before the Law: Constructing a Feminist Jurisprudence.* Princeton, NJ: Princeton University Press, 1999.

Enloe, Cynthia. *Maneuvers: The International Politics of Militarizing Women's Lives.* Berkeley: University of California Press, 2000.

Forrell, Caroline, and Donna Matthews. *A Law of Her Own: The Reasonable Woman as a Measure of Man.* New York: New York University Press, 2000.

Katzenstein, Mary Fainsod, and Judith Reppy, eds. *Beyond Zero Tolerance: Discrimination in Military Culture.* Lanham, MD: Rowman and Littlefield, 1999.

Woods, Harriet. *Stepping Up to Power: The Political Journey of American Women.* Boulder, CO: Westview, 2000.

CHAPTER TWELVE

Religion and Spirituality in Women's Lives

Religion is a complex and complicating feature of many women's lives. Although many women feel empowered by religion because it offers them a place of belonging, comfort, acceptance, and encouragement, others feel oppressed by religion because it excludes and sometimes denigrates women. In this way, as this chapter will explore, religion remains a significant personal and political force in women's lives. Many of the social and cultural battles raging in American society are cast in religious terms—abortion, gay marriage, sex education, racial violence, domestic violence, to name a few—and many women organize their lives around their religious convictions.

The Southern Baptist controversy illustrates the experiences of many women in religious traditions. Throughout the 1980s and early 1990s, Southern Baptists, the nation's largest Protestant denomination with more than 14 million members, were embroiled in a controversy between fundamentalist and moderate leaders. The Baptist battles began over the issue of inerrancy (the notion that the Bible is without error in history, science, or doctrine) but quickly expanded to include, and then emphasize, social issues such as abortion, homosexuality, and the role of women in the home and church. As the fundamentalists grew in political power, they led the Southern Baptist Convention to pass resolutions excluding women from pastoral leadership in the churches and encouraging wives to submit to their husbands. Fundamentalist victory, however, did not come without a long, bitter conflict in which many women, particularly women in ministry, left the denomination. Other women decided to stay and focus their efforts on the autonomous local churches that carried on in the Baptist tradition of dissent, unbound by convention resolutions. Many became involved in alternative Baptist organizations that grew out of the controversy and promised women more visibility, opportunity, and support as seminary professors and denominational leaders. The women who found positions as seminary professors often faced resistance from students and misunderstanding from colleagues. Numbers of women became associate pastors in moderate Baptist churches, but very few were offered senior pastor positions. Women in the pews heard the rhetoric of equality, but it came from the lips of the men who held the top positions in the churches and newly formed Baptist organizations.

The willingness of so many moderate Southern Baptist women to stay in Baptist churches despite the anti-woman actions of the Southern Baptist Convention indicates the powerful pull of religion. Even women who strongly opposed the policy of the Southern Baptist Convention often became active participants in other Christian denominations: few left Christianity entirely. This simultaneous push and pull of religion, as exemplified by the experience of Southern Baptist women, merits careful feminist analysis. As both a force that can oppress and empower, religion has a dramatic potential to work politically—either to continue women's oppression or to support women's liberation. Understanding this complex dynamic involves a close reading of the discourse of religion.

RELIGION AS OPPRESSIVE TO WOMEN

Southern Baptists are not alone in Christianity, nor is Christianity alone in world religions, in functioning as an oppressive force to women. Central to religion's oppressive function is the notion of a divinely ordained order of creation in which woman is deemed inferior. This notion is often supported by creation myths that embed woman's inferior status in the religious community's narrative of identity; these are the stories a religious community tells about itself in order to make itself known to both members and the outside community. For example, a common interpretation of the second Hebrew myth of creation (although feminist biblical scholars take issue with this interpretation) is that Eve is created after Adam because she is to serve him and be his inferior. Later in the Christian testament, one writer argues that woman's secondary status is a result of Eve's role as temptress in the fall of humanity. As Elizabeth Cady Stanton pointed out in her "Introduction to *The Woman's Bible* over a hundred years ago, the Bible has most often been used to maintain the oppression of women by excluding them from particular roles in church, family, and society.

Women's second-class status is further maintained by excluding women from sacred rituals. Women have not been allowed to celebrate the Eucharist, pray in public, dance sacred dances, hear confession, make sacrifices, baptize, enter the holy of holies, read sacred scriptures aloud in public, preach, or teach men. One argument for the exclusion of women from priesthood has been that the priest stands as a representative of God, and a woman cannot represent God because she is female. The underlying assumption is that men are more Godlike than women. When worshippers see only men as representatives of God, it reinforces the notion that men are more Godlike, and women's exclusion continues.

Furthermore, religions maintain women's oppression very directly through church laws that require wives to submit to their husbands, that regulate women's sexuality, and that create highly defined gender roles for women and men. For example, these laws may keep women in abusive relationships. Women are often told by church authorities that their role in the home is to be the support person for the husband and to submit to his divinely ordained authority in the home. Then, when abuse occurs, a woman may be told that she is to continue to submit because that is her role, and God will change her husband because of her obedience to God's commandments. The husband's abusive behavior then becomes the wife's responsibility because his changing is contingent upon her submission. This situ-

> ## Ideas for Activism
>
> - Invite a group of women pastors, ministers, priests, and rabbis to participate in a panel discussion of women in ministry.
> - Organize a women's spirituality group.
> - Organize an educational event to explore women in the world's religions. If possible, invite practitioners of various faiths to speak about women in their religious tradition.
> - Investigate the official stance of your own religious tradition on women's roles and women's issues. Where there is room for improvement, write religious leaders to express your opinion.
> - Organize an event to commemorate the women who died in the "burning times."

ation is exacerbated by a prohibition on divorce in some denominations, which prevents women from permanently leaving abusive marriages.

Historically and currently, religions also exercise control over women through church and state sanctioned persecution. In the "burning times" (between the eleventh and fourteenth centuries) millions of women in Europe were murdered as witches. For many of these women, "witchcraft" was simply the practice of traditional healing and spirituality and the refusal to profess Christianity. For other women, the charge of witchcraft had nothing to do with religious practices and everything to do with accusations rooted in jealousy, greed, and fear of female sexuality. But in the frenzy of the times, defending oneself against an accusation of witchcraft was practically impossible, and an accusation alone generally meant death.

At various times, Christian imperialism has proved especially destructive for women and men of color and has reinforced racism and ethnocentrism. For example, the genocide of Native Americans was conducted with the underlying belief that it was the God-given destiny of Europeans to conquer the native peoples of the Americas. Without understanding African cultures, Christian missionaries insisted indigenous African peoples adopt Western ways. The legacy of Christian racism continued in the American South, where many Christians defended slavery based on their reading of scripture. Following reconstruction, hate groups such as the Ku Klux Klan arose, calling for the continued dominance of the White, anglo, Christian race. In Germany, thousands of Christians joined in Hitler's plan to build a master race and contributed directly to the genocide of 6 million Jews. In the 1950s and 1960s, while many Christians worked tirelessly for the civil rights movement and African American churches in particular became sites of resistance to racism, many others defended segregation and participated in acts of racial hatred. Only in 2000 did Bob Jones University, a fundamentalist institution of higher education in South Carolina, repeal its rule against interracial dating. Despite the many advances in the twentieth century, the twenty-first century began with the continuing problems of racism and intolerance by many who profess Christianity. But, as Elizabeth Cook-Lynn suggests in "A Visit from Reverend Tileston," Christian inability to listen to others may ultimately prove harmful to Christianity itself.

Learning Activity: That Old-Time TV Religion

Watch several episodes of religious programming on television, such as the *700 Club* and two or three televised worship services. Who are the key personalities? What is their message? In the worship services, who is speaking? Who is singing? Who is leading? What messages about gender are conveyed, not only in the words themselves but also in the roles played by different people? What messages about race, class, sexual orientation, and/or ability are conveyed? Do you think these shows are helpful to people? Why or why not? Are they helpful to women? Who do you think benefits from these shows? Are there ways in which these shows reinforce the subordination of women and other nondominant groups? Keep a log of your observations to share with your classmates.

In India, many Hindu women are raised to see self-immolation as a high form of religious commitment. Sati, the act by which a wife throws herself on the burning pyre with her dead husband, was considered a great act of honor by the codifiers of Hindu law and became glorified in Hindu legends told to little girls. In the nineteenth century, the British who occupied and colonized India outlawed sati. Nonetheless, as recently as 1987, 18-year-old Roop Kanwar was burned alive on her husband's funeral pyre. Karen McCarthy Brown relates the story of Roop Kanwar to fundamentalism in her essay titled "Fundamentalism and the Control of Women."

Currently the Religious Right, a political movement of religious ultraconservatives in the United States, is attempting to exert control over women by influencing the American legal system. Already the Religious Right has managed to chip away at abortion rights by convincing lawmakers to pass various restrictions on abortion. At the end of the twentieth century and the beginning of the twenty-first, the Religious Right's agenda began to focus on the gains made by the gay and lesbian rights movement. A particularly telling example of the power of the Religious Right to influence American politics came in the Defense of Marriage Act (DOMA), mentioned in Chapter 11, which allows states not to recognize gay unions performed in other states. At the time the law passed, no state even allowed gay marriage. DOMA was a significant departure from precedent in which every state recognized the legal contracts entered into by other states. By mid-2000, more than two-thirds of the states had passed state laws refusing to recognize gay marriages performed in other states.

The Muslim practice of wearing the veil (*hijab*) presents an especially complex example of the simultaneously oppressive and empowering role of religion in women's lives. From a Western perspective, the practice of veiling is often viewed as absolutely oppressing. In particular, recent media images of forced veiling of women in Afghanistan by the Taliban regime offer powerful evidence of the oppressiveness of this religious practice. Although many Muslim women criticize the coercion exercised in Afghanistan, they also see choosing to wear the veil as an empowering practice of ethnic and cultural identity in the face of Western influence. Nadia Hijab argues this point in "Islam, Social Change, and the Reality of Arab Women's Lives." Muslim women often explain that they feel safer when veiled in public. The veil indicates that a woman is devout and virtuous, and therefore

Muslim men will not objectify and sexualize a veiled woman. In fact, very often these women express sympathy for American women who must constantly fear sexual assault in public places. The veil, they claim, protects them and therefore allows them the freedom to move about publicly without fear.

RELIGION AS EMPOWERING TO WOMEN

Despite religion's long history of oppressing women, women have also experienced profound support, encouragement, and satisfaction in religion. For many women, religion provides a place in which they find a sense of worth as a valued child of God. Also, for many women religion provides an environment in which they experience real community with other women. Women in traditional marriages who work in the home may find their only real social outlet in the church. Here they build connections with other women and participate in personally meaningful experiences in a community context.

Sometimes religion provides women, particularly those in traditional families, with opportunities for building and exercising leadership skills that they might not learn otherwise. For example, although Southern Baptists have generally excluded women from pastoral leadership in the churches, the Woman's Missionary Union (WMU), auxiliary to the Southern Baptist Convention, has provided thousands of women with the opportunity to become lay leaders in their churches, as well as in associational, state, and national WMU organizations. WMU is a missions education organization for women. In local church WMU organizations, women plan, budget, and implement programs for education and action. WMU curriculum materials teach young girls that they can do anything God calls them

Learning Activity: Women of Faith

Interview three women who actively participate in a religious community. Ask about their experiences as women in their faith. Use the following questions or develop your own interview protocol.

- What is your religious community's stance on women's roles in home, society, and the religious community itself?
- What roles do women fulfill in your religious community?
- In what activities do you participate in your religious community?
- In what ways has your religious community been empowering for you as a woman? Has your religious community ever been oppressive to you as a woman?
- What do you gain by your participation in your religious community?
- How might your religious community better serve women?

Gather the data obtained by several other students in your class and examine your findings. Do you see any common themes arising from your interviews? What do your data suggest about these women's experiences in their faith communities? Can you make any generalizations from the data about how women experience religion as both empowering and oppressive?

Activist Profile: Nannie Helen Burroughs

Nannie Helen Burroughs was only 21 years old when she delivered her stirring speech, "How the Sisters Are Hindered from Helping" at the 1900 National Baptist Convention in Richmond, Virginia. This speech proved to be instrumental in the formation of the Women's Convention Auxiliary to the National Baptist Convention, the largest African American women's organization in the country at that time. The Women's Convention promptly elected Burroughs its corresponding secretary and continued to re-elect her every year from 1900 to 1948. In 1948, she became the convention's president and served in that role until her death in 1961.

Burroughs was also a tireless activist—challenging lynching and segregation, denouncing employment discrimination, opposing European colonization of Africa, and promoting women's suffrage. After the Nineteenth Amendment was passed, she founded the National League of Republican Colored Women and worked to encourage African American women to become politically involved. She also established the Women's Industrial Club, which offered short-term housing to African American women and taught them basic domestic skills. The club also offered moderately priced lunches for downtown office workers. During the Depression, Burroughs formed Cooperative Industrial, Inc., which provided free facilities for a medical clinic, hair salon, and variety store.

One of Burroughs's driving passions was the education of African American women. In 1909, with the support of the National Baptist Convention, she opened the National Trade and Professional School for Women and Girls in Washington, DC, and served as the institution's president. The school emphasized a close connection between education and religion. Its curriculum focused on the development of practical and professional skills and included a program in Black history in which every student was required to take a course. Burroughs's motto for the school was "We specialize in the wholly impossible." In 1964, the school was renamed the Nannie Burroughs School. In 1975 Mayor Walter E. Washington proclaimed May 10 Nannie Helen Burroughs Day in the District of Columbia in recognition of Burroughs's courage in advocating for education for African American women despite societal norms.

to do. The subversive power of this message is clear in talking to Southern Baptist women in ministry. Many of them report first experiencing their call to ministry in a WMU organization. Similarly, Catholic women have been empowered through convent experiences, in which they exercise leadership and enjoy community with other women.

In Santeria, a Caribbean religion, women who are healers or *santeras* have great personal power and hold immense social power in their communities. These women willingly enter into altered states of consciousness and allow the spirits to use them to bring about healing. When a person visits a *santera,* the *santera* sees all the spirits with that person, and the *santera* is often able to reveal to the person what she or he needs to do. This ability puts the *santera* in an extremely powerful position, especially when the person consulting her is a politician or government official, as is often the case. Furthermore, as Caribbean women visit

Learning Activity: How Well Do You Know the Goddess?

Match the Goddess to her name.

_____ 1. Odudua

_____ 2. Coatlicue

_____ 3. Izanami-no-kami

_____ 4. Demeter

_____ 5. Tho-og

_____ 6. Kali

_____ 7. Astarte

_____ 8. Kokyan Wuhti

_____ 9. Freyja

_____ 10. Haumea

_____ 11. Po Ino Nogar

_____ 12. Hathor

_____ 13. Anu

_____ 14. Asherah

_____ 15. Artemis Ephesus

a. Egyptian mother Goddess and Goddess of the underworld, the queen of heaven and mother of light.

b. "Queen of Heaven." Assyrian creator of life, mother and guardian. Goddess of fertility, love, sexuality, and justice.

c. Celtic creator of life. Mother Goddess of the earth and moon. The mother of all heroes or deities.

d. Scandinavian creator of life. Leader of the Valkyries.

e. "Great, Invincible, and Magnificent Founder and Savior, Commander and Guide, Legislator and Queen." Creator and mother Goddess of Anatolia.

f. The mother of Hawaii. Mother and guardian, mother of Pele and the Hawaiian people.

g. Creator of life who brings fertility and love. Goddess of the Yoruba people of Nigeria.

h. Tibetan primordial being. The eternal mother who is self-formed. She is the preexisting space.

i. "The Great Mother Goddess." Mesopotamian Goddess of justice, earth, nature, and goodness.

j. Hindu Goddess. She who gives life and also destroys it. The symbol of eternal time.

k. "Spider Grandmother." Hopi creator of life. Beneficent deity who created humans, plants, and animals.

l. "Serpent Skirt." Mother Goddess of all Aztec deities of Mexico, the ruler of life and death.

m. Greek mother and guardian. One of the twelve great Greek Olympian deities. She has power over the productivity of the earth and the social order of humans.

n. "Female-Who-Invites." Japanese creator of life, earth and nature, heaven and hell.

o. "Great One." Vietnamese creator of life. World fertility Goddess who brings rice to the people and protects the fields and harvests.

Answers: 1. g 2. l 3. n 4. m 5. h 6. j 7. b 8. k 9. d 10. f 11. o 12. a 13. c 14. i 15. e

Source: Martha Ann and Dorothy Myers Imel. *Goddesses in World Mythology: A Biographical Dictionary.* New York: Oxford University Press, 1993.

santeras, they see women who wield power in their culture and who can act as role models for them.

Religion has also often played an important role in empowering women to become engaged in social action. Jesse Daniel Ames helped organize the antilynching movement in the early part of the twentieth century by working through women's missions organizations in Methodist and Baptist churches in the South. Black churches were at the heart of the 1950s and 1960s civil rights movement in which many early leaders of second wave feminism had their first experiences of political organizing. A key component of Judaism is social justice, and Jewish women have long been actively involved in anti-Semitic, anti-racist, anti-sexist, and anti-heterosexist work. Ernestine Louise Rose, who fought for women's rights and against slavery during the 1840s and 1850s, challenged New York state lawmakers in 1854 to allow women to retain their own property and have equal guardianship of children with their husbands. When male politicians urged women to postpone their quest for suffrage and focus on the rights of former slaves, Rose declared, "Emancipation from every kind of bondage is my principle." She also spoke out against anti-Semitism and set the tone for twentieth-century Jewish feminists' critique of Judaism's traditional attitudes toward women.

In the late twentieth century, many women have participated in revivals of ancient woman-centered religions. Wicca, or witchcraft, is a Goddess and nature-oriented religion whose origins pre-date both Judaism and Christianity. Current Wiccan practice involves the celebration of the feminine, connection with nature, and the practice of healing. As Starhawk suggests in "Witchcraft and Women's Culture," witchcraft encourages women to be strong, confident, and independent and to love the Goddess, the earth, and other human beings. This notion of witchcraft is very different from the cultural norms associated with witches that are propagated at Halloween.

WOMEN AND GOD-LANGUAGE

Many theorists contend that one of the most powerful influences in molding gender and maintaining gender oppression is language. The language religions use to talk about God is especially powerful in shaping the ways we think about men and women. Any language we use to talk about God is of necessity metaphorical. We create images that can only partially represent the full reality of the concept of God. Unfortunately, those images sometimes become understood in literal rather than metaphorical ways. So instead of thinking of God *as* Father, we may come to think God *is* Father. Throughout Jewish and Christian history, the preponderance of images for God have been masculine—Father, King, Lord, Judge, Master—and the effect has been that many people believe that God is male.

In ancient times, the image of the Great Mother Goddess was primary in many cultures, but as war-centered patriarchal cultures developed, the life-giving Goddess had to be defeated by the warring God. In ancient Babylonian mythology, Tiamat was the Great Mother, but she was eventually slaughtered by her son Marduk, the God of war. Yahweh, the God of the ancient Israelites, was originally a consort of the Canaanite Mother Goddess, but, as the Israelites moved toward a pa-

Learning Activity: Exploring New Metaphors for Deity

Metaphors are images drawn from familiar human experiences, used in fresh ways to help explore realities that are not easily accessible in our everyday experience. All language about deity is metaphorical because no one image or analogy can capture the essence of deity. Throughout the history of Jewish and Christian faiths, in particular, deity has been variously imaged as Father, Shepherd, King, Lord, and Master. Originally, these metaphors helped many people explore and grapple with different aspects of the nature of deity. Many contemporary theologians, however, suggest the need for new metaphors for deity, shocking metaphors that will cause people to think about deity in new ways. Theologian Sallie McFague contends, "The best metaphors give both a shock and a shock of recognition." In good metaphors, we see something about reality, and we see it in new ways.

What are some of the metaphors for deity with which you are familiar? In what ways have those metaphors been helpful? In what ways are those metaphors limiting? What do you perceive as the consequences of taking these metaphors literally? Are there some metaphors you think have outlived their usefulness?

Following are a number of new metaphors for deity that are being utilized in current theological discussion. What do you think of these metaphors? In what new ways do they cause you to think about deity? What new ideas about deity do they suggest to you? In what ways do they call you to reappraise images of deity?

- God as mother
- God as lover
- God as companion
- God as gambler
- The earth as God's body

Can you think of any shocking new metaphors that help you think about deity in original ways?

triarchal monotheism (belief in just one God), Yahweh became prominent as the Great Father God, and worship of the Goddess was harshly condemned by Yahweh's priests. The prominence of a single masculine image of deity then became reflected in the exclusion of women from the priesthood and eventually from the concept of Israel itself.

In response to the hegemony of masculine images of God, feminist theologians have constructed alternative feminine images of deity. Some theologians, such as Virginia Mollenkott, have returned to the Jewish and Christian testaments to point out the existence of feminine images within scripture. Other theologians, such as Sallie McFague, have challenged people to develop new models of God such as God as mother, God as love, and God as companion. And yet other women have returned to the ancient images of the Goddess herself. In "Grandmother of the Sun," Paula Gunn Allen explains Native American feminine images of deity.

The political nature of the decision to challenge normative God-language does not go unnoticed by traditionalists wishing to cling to male images. The Southern Baptist Convention issued a statement declaring that God is not *like* a father, but

God *is* Father. And a group of mainline churchwomen created a furor within their denominations when at a conference they chose to call God "Sophia," a biblical, but feminine name, for deity.

REINTERPRETING AND RECONSTRUCTING TRADITIONS

For those feminist women who have chosen to remain in religious traditions, the task of reworking oppressive elements has been great. Theology itself has been constructed with male experience as normative and has not taken into account the experiences of both men and women. Since the 1960s, feminist theologians have undertaken the task of rethinking traditional theological notions from the perspective of women's experiences. For example, the traditional notion of sin expressed in the story of the Fall in Genesis is that of pride and the centrality of the self. Redemption in the Christian testament then involves the restoration of what man lacks—sacrificial love. Yet the normative experience for women is not pride and self-centeredness, given that women are generally socialized to be self-negating for the sake of their families, and, in fact, encouraging women to be self-sacrificing as a form of redemption simply exacerbates women's situation. Feminist theology, as Alicia Ostriker suggests in her poem "Everywoman Her Own Theology," brings women's experiences to the center and reconstructs theological concepts in keeping with those experiences.

Because of the predominance of Christianity in the United States, the Bible and its various interpretations play a large role in shaping women's lives. Given this importance, feminist re-examinations of religion are on a continuum from reinterpretation to reconstruction. *Reinterpretation* involves recognizing the passages that are particularly problematic for women and highlighting and reintegrating the passages that extol equality between women and men. Proponents of such reinterpretation include Christian feminists who maintain a positive view of scripture as they continue to accept scripture as an authority in their lives. The goal of *reconstruction*, however, is to move beyond reinterpretation and recognize the patriarchal underpinnings of various interpretations and the ways they have been used to oppress women.

As an example of a reconstructionist account, Christian testament scholar Elisabeth Schüssler Fiorenza encourages readers of scripture to look for the presence of women in the margins and around the edges of the text. She calls for biblical readers to re-create the narratives of women that were left out of but hinted at in the text. In a similar fashion, the reading "Standing Again at Sinai" by Jewish feminist scholar Judith Plaskow calls for a reconceptualization of notions of God, Torah, and Israel that are inclusive of women. Other reconstructions of scripture include "womanist" biblical interpretations of women of color that analyze the Bible in light of both sexism and racism. In these accounts the Bible itself is subject to scrutiny in terms of its expressions of justice and injustice. Readers of the Bible with this perspective focus on the moral and ethical imperatives of justice contained therein and with an eye toward struggle for liberation for women of color.

"... and so, then I said, 'You think that just because I'm a woman I can't preach, just because I'm a woman I can't hold office in the convention, just because I'm a woman I can't do evangelism, just because I'm a woman I can't teach theology!' And he said, 'Yes.'"

Reprinted with permission from Norma Young.

Women have begun to challenge and reconstruct religious traditions as well as scripture. For example, Jewish women have developed feminist haggadahs, texts containing the ritual for celebrating the Passover seder. These feminist haggadahs commemorate the women of the Exodus, the liberation of the Israelites from slavery in Egypt. In one haggadah, the four sons of the traditional ceremony become four daughters, and the lives of the women celebrating Passover are inserted in the ceremony to create a living history and a new story.

Perhaps one of the most contentious reconstructions of religious traditions is the ordination of women. Although feminist church historians have recovered a long tradition of women as rabbis, priests, pastors, bishops, and evangelists, most Christian denominations did not ordain women until the latter part of the twentieth century. Many still do not. One exception to this is the Quakers. Quakers have a long and unique history of women's equality in the congregation. Although Quakers do not ordain anyone, some groups of Quakers do record ministers, and women have always been among the recorded. In silent Quaker meetings, women as well as men are assumed to be able to receive and speak a word from God. Beginning in the 1960s, many mainline Protestant churches began to ordain women ministers, although men still make up the larger percentage of senior pastors in almost every denomination. Roman Catholics still prohibit women from becoming priests, although there is a growing movement within Catholicism, particularly American Catholicism, to change this policy. Only the United Church of Christ ordains openly gay and lesbian people, as does the Unitarian Universalist Association.

CREATING NEW SPIRITUAL TRADITIONS

Although some feminists believe in the reinterpretation and reconstruction of scriptures and choose to work within existing denominations, others prefer to create their own empowering religious texts and organizations. For some, traditional religious scriptures are so essentially androcentric that they can only reproduce patriarchal social relations. They see no possibility of liberation for women in scripture because even reconstruction of biblical texts cannot change the patriarchal core of, for example, the Bible. Rather, these reconstructions simply perpetuate the patriarchal order. Feminist philosopher Mary Daly argues that patriarchal language is not accidental or incidental to the Bible but is an essential element of it, rendering the Bible useless in the liberation of women. These women look beyond traditional scripture for their spiritual insights and understandings.

In this way, although many women have expressed their spirituality within formal religious traditions, many others have created forms of spiritual expression outside churches, synagogues, and mosques. Women's spirituality is an empowering force that has taken such various forms as meditation, poetry, art, prayer, ritual, and social action. Spirituality enables women to experience connection with creation, with other human beings, and with the divine within themselves.

For many feminists, spirituality is a central force in their politics. The awareness of the interconnectedness of all things motivates feminist action toward justice and peace and encourages women to work together across differences. Nature-based spiritualities affirm the connections among all living things and seek to protect the natural environment on which we all depend. Feminist spirituality values and affirms the diversity that makes up the unity of creation, and it challenges women to restructure the systems of power that create and maintain injustice. As Marge Piercy writes:

> Praise our choices, sisters, for each doorway
> open to us was taken by squads of fighting
> women who paid years of trouble and struggle,
> who paid their wombs, their sleep, their lives
> that we might walk through these gates upright.
> Doorways are sacred to women for we
> are the doorways of life and we must choose
> what comes in and what goes out. Freedom
> is our real abundance.*

---

*"The Sabbath of Mutual Respect," *The Moon Is Always Female*. New York: Knopf, 1980.

Introduction to *The Woman's Bible*

Elizabeth Cady Stanton

From the inauguration of the movement for woman's emancipation the Bible has been used to hold her in the "divinely ordained sphere," prescribed in the Old and New Testaments.

The canon and civil law; church and state; priests and legislators; all political parties and religious denominations have alike taught that woman was made after man, of man, and for man, an inferior being, subject to man. Creeds, codes, Scriptures and statutes, are all based on this idea. The fashions, forms, ceremonies and customs of society, church ordinances and discipline all grow out of this idea.

. . .

The Bible teaches that woman brought sin and death into the world, that she precipitated the fall of the race, that she was arraigned before the judgment seat of Heaven, tried, condemned and sentenced. Marriage for her was to be a condition of bondage, maternity a period of suffering and anguish, and in silence and subjection, she was to play the role of a dependent on man's bounty for all her material wants, and for all the information she might desire on the vital questions of the hour, she was commanded to ask her husband at home. Here is the Bible position of woman briefly summed up.

. . .

These familiar texts are quoted by clergymen in their pulpits, by statesmen in the halls of legislation, by lawyers in the courts, and are echoed by the press of all civilized nations, and accepted by woman herself as "The Word of God." So perverted is the religious element in her nature, that with faith and works she is the chief support of the church and clergy; the very powers that make her emancipation impos-

sible. When, in the early part of the Nineteenth Century, women began to protest against their civil and political degradation, they were referred to the Bible for an answer. When they protested against their unequal position in the church, they were referred to the Bible for an answer.

This led to a general and critical study of the Scriptures. Some, having made a fetish of these books and believing them to be the veritable "Word of God," with liberal translations, interpretations, allegories and symbols, glossed over the most objectionable features of the various books and clung to them as divinely inspired. Others, seeing the family resemblance between the Mosaic code, the canon law, and the old English common law, came to the conclusion that all alike emanated from the same source; wholly human in their origin and inspired by the natural love of domination in the historians. Others, bewildered with their doubts and fears, came to no conclusion. While their clergymen told them on the one hand, that they owed all the blessings and freedom they enjoyed to the Bible, on the other, they said it clearly marked out their circumscribed sphere of action: that the demands for political and civil rights were irreligious, dangerous to the stability of the home, the state and the church. Clerical appeals were circulated from time to time conjuring members of their churches to take no part in the anti-slavery or woman suffrage movements, as they were infidel in their tendencies, undermining the very foundations of society. No wonder the majority of women stood still, and with bowed heads, accepted the situation.

Fundamentalism and the Control of Women

Karen McCarthy Brown

Religious fundamentalism is very difficult to define; yet many of us—scholars and journalists in particular—think we know it when we see it. For those attuned to gender as a category of analysis, a stab of recognition is often occasioned by the presence of high degrees of religiously sanctioned control of women. In conservative religious movements around the world, women are veiled or otherwise covered; confined to the home or in some other way strictly limited in their access to the public sphere; prohibited from testifying in a court of law, owning property, or initiating divorce; and they are very often denied the authority to make their own reproductive choices.

I propose to take up the thread of the control of women and follow it into the center of the maze of contemporary fundamentalism. Yet I will not argue, as might be expected, that the need to control women is the main motivation for the rise of fundamentalism, but rather that aggravation of this age-old, widespread need is an inevitable side effect of a type of stress peculiar to our age.

I will suggest that the varieties of fundamentalism found throughout the world today are extreme responses to the failed promise of Enlightenment rationalism. Fundamentalism, in my view, is the religion of the stressed and the disoriented, of those for whom the world is overwhelming. More to the point, it is the religion of those at once seduced and betrayed by the promise that we human beings can comprehend and control our world. Bitterly disappointed by the politics of rationalized bureaucracies, the limitations of science, and the perversions of industrialization, fundamentalists seek to reject the modern world, while nevertheless holding onto its habits of mind: clarity, certitude, and control. Given these habits, fundamentalists necessarily operate with a limited view of human activity (including religious activity), one confined largely to consciousness and choice. They deny the power of those parts of the human psyche that are inaccessible to consciousness yet play a central role in orienting us in the world. Most of all they seek to control the fearsome, mute power of the flesh. This characteristic ensures that fundamentalism will always involve the control of women, for women generally carry the greater burden of human fleshliness.

This essay is an exploratory one. Its topic is huge and it ranges widely, crossing over into several academic disciplines other than my own. Occasionally I am forced to paint with a broad stroke and a quick hand. Writing that is preliminary and suggestive can be risky, but the connections I see between religious fundamentalism and other, larger aspects of our contemporary world seem compelling enough to lead me to take that risk. My argument begins close to home, in the United States, with Christian anti-abortion activism.

THE ANTI-ABORTION MOVEMENT IN THE UNITED STATES

The "pro-life movement" emerged in the 1970s as a new type of religio-political organization. It was a bottom-up movement that used sophisticated, top-down technology. In the early stages of the movement, the organizing work was done around kitchen tables. But the envelopes stuffed at those tables were sent to addresses on computer-generated mailing lists, the product of advanced market-research techniques. This blend of grass-roots organization and advanced technology quickly brought a minority movement[1] to a position of significant political power. The combination of traditional and modern methods also reveals an ambivalence toward the ways of the modern world that I will later argue is characteristic of fundamentalist movements.

Many observers have noted an inconsistency in the pro-life position. The very groups who launch an emotional defense of the fetus's right to life are curiously indifferent to children outside the womb. As a rule pro-lifers do not support social programs focused on issues such as child abuse, day care, foster care, or juvenile drug use. They oppose welfare programs in general and have taken no leadership in educational reform beyond concern with sex education, public school prayer, and the theory of evolution. Furthermore, their so-called pro-life argument is deeply compromised by staunch support for increased military spending and for the death penalty. It seems clear that the pro-life position is not a consistent theological or philosophical stance. A quite different kind of consistency emerges from the full range of this group's social policy positions. Their overriding concern is that of maintaining strong and clear social boundaries—boundaries between nation-states, between law-abiding citizens and criminals, between the righteous and the sinful, between life and death, and not coincidentally, between men and women. This is a group centrally concerned with social order and social control.

Beyond the trigger of the 1973 Supreme Court decision in *Roe* v. *Wade*, stresses with a broader historical range have contributed to a focus on boundary maintenance in the anti-abortion movement. The upheavals of the 1960s created the immediate historical context of the anti-abortion movement of the 1970s. Student activists of the 1960s questioned the authority of parents, educators, and politicians. Black activists challenged the cherished American myths of equal opportunity and equal protection under the law. And the Vietnam War not only raised questions about U.S. military

prowess but also planted doubts about the moral valence of the international presence and policy of the United States. These are very specific reasons why Americans in the 1970s might have felt that the social and moral orders were becoming dangerously befuddled.

. . .

A WORLD SUDDENLY TOO BIG

From the mid-nineteenth century into the early decades of the twentieth, the writings of travelers, missionaries, and, eventually, anthropologists were popular bedside reading materials in the United States. Americans were fascinated by exotic "others." They were concerned about their own place in this expanding, newly complex world. Most of these books did more than titillate. With their implicit or explicit social Darwinism, they also carried deeply comforting messages of progress and of Western superiority. Such messages, coming from many sources, infused an air of optimism into an otherwise disorienting age. During the same general time span, the seeds of American fundamentalism were sown and came to fruition.

Some of the social forces that shaped this period—expanding knowledge of and contact with the larger world, and increased communication—had emerged over a relatively long period of time. Others, such as the burgeoning of cities, the dramatic increase in immigrant populations, and a series of shifts in women's roles, had occurred more recently.[2] All of these forces came together in the second half of the nineteenth century to contribute to a general sense of vertigo; the world was becoming too big, too complicated, and too chaotic to comprehend. Most important, each individual's own place in it was uncertain. Religion, given its basic orientational role in human life, emerged as a natural arena for dealing with the resulting stress.

From that period until this in the United States, conservative Christians have come under a double attack. On one level, they have had to deal with the general stress of the times; and on the other, with the direct challenge of Enlightenment rationalism in the form of biblical higher criticism and evolutionary theory. The reaction of some groups of Christians has been ironic: they have responded to the threat by mimicking Enlightenment rationalism. The religion-versus-science debate pits against one another groups who share a common intellectual style: each claims to possess the truth. Believers, like rationalists, stress consciousness, clarity, and control.[3] Morality is codified; sacred narratives are taken literally and sometimes attempts are made to support them with "scientific evidence"; all sorts of truths are listed and enumerated; scripture becomes inerrant. Furthermore conscious consent to membership in the community of belief, on the model of "making a decision for Christ," becomes increasingly important.

These are the religious groups we call fundamentalists. Their central aim is to make of their religion an Archimedean point in the midst of a changing world. But to do so, they must limit their religion's responsiveness to its social environment; and as a result they are left with little flexibility to respond to the complexity of their own feelings or to the challenge of a changing world. Sometimes they fall into aggressively defending brittle truths. This is what makes fundamentalism in the contemporary world problematic and, in some cases, dangerous.

. . .

FUNDAMENTALISM CROSS-CULTURALLY

Up to this point, I have been concerned with Christian fundamentalism in the United States, but in the process I have focused on dimensions of the story that serve, without denying the significance of local variations, to characterize fundamentalism around the globe. Religious fundamentalism is born in times and places where, for a variety of reasons, the world suddenly seems too complex to comprehend; and one's place in it, too precarious to provide genuine security.

One example is modern India, where the cult that developed around the recent immolation of a young woman on her husband's funeral pyre has been described as an instance of fundamentalism. John Hawley demonstrates that the background for the *sati* of Roop Kanwar was emerging Hindu nationalism in India augmented by a multitude of local destabilizing forces in Deorala, the site of the immolation. Furthermore, as Hawley and other authors have pointed out, Deorala is not a truly deprived area, and its residents are not traditionalists out of contact with the larger realities of modern India. I would therefore suggest, along with Hawley, that fundamentalism is not primarily a religion of the marginalized, as some have argued. Its more salient feature is that it develops among people caught off balance. Hence, fundamentalist groups often arise in situations where social, cultural, and economic power is up for grabs; many, like these groups now being referred to as Hindu fundamentalists, arise in postcolonial situations. Far from being essentially marginal to the societies in which they exist, fundamentalists are often directly involved in the political and economic issues of their time and place. And they often have a significant, if precarious, stake in them.

For the Rajputs in Deorala, traditional sources of pride and authority are being challenged by increasing contact with the cities of Jaipur and Delhi, and through them, all of India. These Rajputs are experiencing the disorientation of having to depend on economic and political systems beyond their control. Marwari merchants and industrialists, financial backers of the cult of the goddess Sati, are destabilized in another way. As their economic role expands throughout India, they risk their livelihood in a wider, less familiar, and less predictable world than the one in which earlier generations operated. The Marwari focus on the district around Jhunjhunu with its important Sati shrine gives them their emotionally saturated Archimedean point. The case of the Marwari businessmen suggests, even more directly than does that of the Rajputs, that fundamentalism is not a religion of the marginalized, but of the disoriented.

In the contemporary Indian context, rallying around the *sati* of Roop Kanwar (like anti-abortion activity in the United States) reasserts social control and demonstrates moral worth. It strengthens gender boundaries and provides an example of undiluted, innocent virtue that vicariously underwrites the virtue of Rajputs and Marwaris in general. Furthermore, as in the United States, insecurity about social control and moral rectitude is displaced onto the body of a woman. But in the *sati* ritual described by Hawley, the drive to kill the devouring, fleshly goddess and to enshrine the pure, spiritual one is much more painfully literal.

Both men and women attended the *sati* of Roop Kanwar, and both men and women subsequently revere her. At first glance this may seem difficult to understand, but the complicity of Indian women in the practice of *sati* has to be considered on more than one level. At the deepest level its explanation lies in the fear of women's will and women's flesh that men and women share, and in the relief that both feel when these forces are kept in check. But on another level there are explanations of a much more practical nature. Most Indian women's economic security heavily depends on marriage. A woman doing homage at a Sati shrine thus signals to her husband and to the world at large, as well as to herself, that she intends to be good and to do good, according to her society's standards. Thus she chooses to ignore any anger or fear she might feel about the practice, in the name of living a secure and ordered life. It is a herculean task for women to try to define the meaning and worth of their lives in terms different from those that prevail in their community. So some security can always be

found in surrendering to, and even helping to strengthen, the accepted gender norms.

. . .

THE FAILED PROMISE OF ENLIGHTENMENT RATIONALISM

Modern communications, transnational economic pressures, and wars waged from the opposite side of the globe have brought many populations intimate knowledge of the vastness and complexity of their worlds. In the late twentieth century, the others in relation to whom we must define ourselves are more available to our experience and imagination than ever before; yet few if any of us have a satisfactory model for understanding ourselves within this complex, stressful world.

We all live in and are defined by a world too big and unstable for intellect or belief to comprehend, and we all react to intimations—as well as a few pieces of hard evidence[4]—of the failed promise of the Enlightenment. Academics, politicians, and ordinary folk the world over are immersed in this challenge and most commonly react to it (as fundamentalists do) by assuming that, with sufficient effort, the chaos can be first comprehended and then managed. In this way fundamentalists are simply extreme versions of the rest of us.

An emphasis on the control of women is characteristic of fundamentalism, but there is some of it everywhere in the world. The anti-abortion movement in the United States arises out of a much broader context in which, among other signals of misogyny, public power and authority have been denied to women for centuries. And the Sati cult could not have become an issue in Indian nationalism if in general Indian women were not seen as sources of pollution as well as of blessing—as a result of which they have been subject to a variety of social controls through the ages. When the mind and the spirit are cut off from the body, women become magnets for the fear raised by everything in life that seems out of control. The degree to which control is exercised over women is therefore a key to the profundity of stresses felt by most persons and groups. Fundamentalism is a product of extreme social stress.

Religion, whose primary function is to provide a comprehensible model of the world and to locate the individual safely and meaningfully within it, is an obvious place for this type of stress to express itself and seek redress. But as long as religions deal with this stress by positing a world that can be directly known, and in which it is possible to determine one's own fate, they only reinforce the controlling tendencies of enlightenment rationalism and do nothing to move us beyond it to whatever comes next. We should be suspicious of any religion that claims too much certainty or draws the social boundaries too firmly. In this period marked by the gradual breakdown of Enlightenment rationalism and Euro-American hegemony in the world, something more is necessary. We need help in accepting ourselves as organic creatures enmeshed in our world rather than continuing to posture as cerebral masters granted dominion over it. This requires that we learn to trust the wisdom of our mute flesh and accept the limitations inherent in our humanity. If we could do this, it would radically diminish our scapegoating of women and all the other "others" who provide a convenient screen on which to project fears.

The resurgence of religion that we are experiencing at the turn of this millennium should not be viewed in an entirely negative light. If any system of orientation in the world can help us now, it seems likely to be a religious one.

There is no small comfort in knowing that, as the grand ambitions spawned by the Enlightenment falter in the present age, what is likely to emerge is not what several generations of social scientists predicted. It is not civilization marching toward increasing secularization and rationalization. What is slowly being revealed is the hubris of reason's pretense in trying to take over religion's role.

NOTES

1. From the beginning of the anti-abortion movement to the present, opinion polls have consistently shown that the majority of people in the United States favor a woman's right to have an abortion.
2. Betty A. DeBerg, *Ungodly Women: Gender and the First Wave of American Fundamentalism* (Minneapolis: Fortress Press, 1990), has an excellent discussion of the general changes—and particularly the changes in women's roles—attendant to the formation of fundamentalism in the United States. . . .
3. Often the only kind of control that fundamentalists can exercise over a chaotic and threatening world rests in their claim to have a privileged understanding of the deeper meaning of the chaos. Fundamentalists who engage in "end-time" thinking thus sometimes find themselves in the position of welcoming the signs of modern social decay because these signal the approach of the time when God will call home the chosen few.
4. The growing ecological crisis is one of the most tangible pieces of this evidence; it also reinforces the point that reason alone is an insufficient problem-solving tool, because we are incapable of holding in consciousness the full range of the interconnectedness of things.

Grandmother of the Sun
The Power of Woman in Native America

Paula Gunn Allen

There is a spirit that pervades everything, that is capable of powerful song and radiant movement, and that moves in and out of the mind. The colors of this spirit are multitudinous, a flowing, pulsing rainbow. Old Spider Woman is one name for this quintessential spirit, and Serpent Woman is another. Corn Woman is one aspect of her, and Earth Woman is another, and what they together have made is called Creation, Earth, creatures, plants, and light.

At the center of all is Woman, and no thing is sacred (cooked, ripe, as the Keres Indians of Laguna Pueblo say it) without her blessing, her thinking.

> . . . In the beginning Tse che nako, Thought Woman finished everything, thoughts, and the names of all things. She finished also all the languages. And then our mothers, Uretsete and Naotsete said they would make names and they would make thoughts. Thus they said. Thus they did.[1]

This spirit, this power of intelligence, has many names and many emblems. She appears on the plains, in the forests, in the great canyons, on the mesas, beneath the seas. To her we owe our very breath, and to her our prayers are sent blown on pollen, on corn meal, planted into the earth on feather-sticks, spit onto the water, burned and sent to her on the wind. Her variety and multiplicity testify to her complexity: she is the true Creatrix for she is thought itself, from which all else is born. She is the necessary precondition for material creation, and she, like all of her creation, is fundamentally female—potential and primary.

She is also the spirit that informs right balance, right harmony, and these in turn order all relationships in conformity with her law.

To assign to this great being the position of "fertility goddess" is exceedingly demeaning: it trivializes the tribes and it trivializes the power of woman. Woman bears, that is true. She also destroys. That is true. She also wars and hexes and mends and breaks. She creates the power of the seeds, and she plants them. As Anthony Purley, a Laguna writer, has translated a Keres ceremonial prayer, "She is mother of us all, after Her, mother earth follows, in fertility, in holding, and taking again us back to her breast."[2]

The Hopi account of their genatrix, Hard Beings Woman, gives the most articulate rendering of the difference between simple fertility cultism and the creative prowess of the Creatrix. Hard Beings Woman (Huruing Wuhti) is of the earth. But she lives in the worlds above where she "owns" (empowers) the moon and stars. Hard Beings Woman has solidity and hardness as her major aspects. She, like Thought Woman, does not give birth to creation or to human beings but breathes life into male and female effigies that become the parents of the Hopi—in this way she "creates" them. The male is Muingwu, the god of crops, and his sister-consort is Sand Altar Woman who is also known as Childbirth Water Woman. In Sand Altar Woman the mystical relationship between water, worship, and woman is established; she is also said to be the mother of the katsinas, those powerful messengers who relate the spirit world to the world of humankind and vice versa.[3]

Like Thought Woman, Hard Beings Woman lived in the beginning on an island which was the only land there was. In this regard she resembles a number of Spirit Woman Beings; the Spirit genatrix of the Iroquois, Sky Woman, also lived on an island in the void which only later became the earth. On this island, Hard Beings Woman is identified with or, as they say, "owns" all hard substances—moon, stars, beads, coral, shell, and so forth. She is a sea goddess as well, the single inhabitant of the earth, that island that floats alone in the waters of space. From this meeting of woman and water, earth and her creatures were born.[4] . . .

Contemporary Indian tales suggest that the creatures are born from the mating of sky father and earth mother, but that seems to be a recent interpolation of the original sacred texts. The revision may have occurred since the Christianizing influence on even the arcane traditions, or it may have predated Christianity. But the older, more secret texts suggest that it is a revision. It may be that the revision appears only in popular versions of the old mythic cycles on which ceremony and ritual are based; this would accord with the penchant in the old oral tradition for shaping tales to reflect present social realities, making the rearing and education of children possible even within the divergent worlds of the United States of America and the tribes.

According to the older texts (which are sacred, that is, power-engendering), Thought Woman is not a passive personage: her potentiality is dynamic and unimaginably powerful. She brought corn and agriculture, potting, weaving, social systems, religion, ceremony, ritual, building, memory, intuition, and their expressions in language, creativity, dance, human-to-animal relations, and she gave these offerings power and authority and blessed the people with the ability to provide for themselves and their progeny.

Thought Woman is not limited to a female role in the total theology of the Keres people. Since she is the supreme Spirit, she is both Mother and Father to all people and to all creatures. She is the only creator of thought, and thought precedes creation.[5]

Central to Keres theology is the basic idea of the Creatrix as She Who Thinks rather than She Who Bears, of woman as creation thinker and female thought as origin of material and non-material reality. In this epistemology, the perception of female power as confined to maternity is a limit on the power inherent in femininity. But "she is the supreme Spirit, . . . both Mother and Father to all people and to all creatures."[6] . . .

In Keres theology the creation does not take place through copulation. In the beginning existed Thought Woman and her dormant sisters, and Thought Woman thinks creation and sings her two sisters into life. After they are vital she instructs them to sing over the items in their baskets (medicine bundles) in such a way that those items will have life. After that crucial task is accomplished, the creatures thus vitalized take on the power to regenerate themselves— that is, they can reproduce others of their kind. But they are not in and of themselves self-sufficient; they depend for their being on the medicine power of the three great Witch creatrixes, Thought Woman, Uretsete, and Naotsete. The sisters are not related by virtue of having parents in common; that is, they are not alive because anyone bore them. Thought Woman turns up, so to speak, first as Creatrix and then as a personage who is acting out someone else's "dream." But there is no time when she did not exist. She has two bundles in her power, and these bundles contain Uretsete and Naotsete, who are not viewed as her daughters but as her sisters, her coequals who possess the medicine power to vitalize the creatures that will inhabit the earth. They also have the power to create the firmament, the skies, the galaxies, and the seas, which they do through the use of ritual magic.

. . .

THE HEART OF POWER

. . .

Pre-Conquest American Indian women valued their role as vitalizers. Through their own bodies they could bring vital beings into the world—a miraculous power whose potency does not diminish with industrial sophistication or time. They were mothers, and that word did not imply slaves, drudges, drones who are required to live only for others rather than for themselves as it does so tragically for many modern women. The ancient ones were empowered by their certain knowledge that the power to make life is the source of all power and that no other power can gainsay it. Nor is that power simply of biology, as modernists tendentiously believe. When Thought Woman brought to life the twin sisters, she did not give birth to them in the biological sense. She sang over the medicine bundles that contained their potentials. With her singing and shaking she infused them with vitality. She gathered the power that she controlled and focused it on those bundles, and thus they were "born." Similarly, when the sister goddesses Naotsete and Uretsete wished to bring forth some plant or creature they reached into the basket (bundle) that Thought Woman had given them, took out the effigy of the creature, and thought it into life. Usually they then instructed it in its proper role. They also meted out consequences to creatures (this included plants, spirits, and katsinas) who disobeyed them.

The water of life, menstrual or postpartum blood, was held sacred. Sacred often means taboo; that is, what is empowered in a ritual sense is not to be touched or approached by any who are weaker than the power itself, lest they suffer negative consequences from contact. The blood of woman was in and of itself infused with the power of Supreme Mind, and so women were held in awe and respect. The term *sacred*, which is connected with power, is similar in meaning to the term *sacrifice*, which means "to make sacred." What is made sacred is empowered. Thus, in the old way, sacrificing meant empowering, which is exactly what it still means to American Indians who adhere to traditional practice. Blood was and is used in sacrifice because it possesses the power to make something else powerful or, conversely, to weaken or kill it.

Pre-contact American Indian women valued their role as vitalizers because they understood that bearing, like bleeding, was a transformative ritual act. Through their own bodies they could bring vital beings into the world—a miraculous power unrivaled by mere shamanic displays. They were mothers, and that word implied the highest degree of status in ritual cultures. The status of mother was so high, in fact, that in some cultures Mother or its analogue, Matron, was the highest office to which a man or woman could aspire.

The old ones were empowered by their certain knowledge that the power to make life is the source and model for all ritual magic and that no other power can gainsay it. Nor is that power really biological at base; it is the power of ritual magic, the power of Thought, of Mind, that gives rise to biological organisms as it gives rise to social organizations, material culture, and transformations of all kinds—including hunting, war, healing, spirit communication, rain-making, and all the rest. . . .

A strong attitude integrally connects the power of Original Thinking or Creation Thinking to the power of mothering. That power is not so much the power to give birth, as we have noted, but the power to make, to create, to transform. Ritual means transforming something from one state or condition to another, and that ability is inherent in the action of mothering. It is the ability that is sought and treasured by adepts, and it is the ability that male seekers devote years of study and discipline to acquire. Without it, no practice of the sacred is possible, at least not within the Great Mother societies.

And as the cultures that are woman-centered and Mother-ritual based are also cultures that value peacefulness, harmony, cooperation, health, and general prosperity, they are systems of thought and practice that would bear deeper study in our troubled, conflict-ridden time.

NOTES

1. Anthony Purley, "Keres Pueblo Concepts of Deity," *American Indian Culture and Research Journal* 1 (Fall 1974): 29. The passage cited is Purley's literal translation from the Keres Indian language of a portion of the Thought Woman story. Purley is a native-speaker Laguna Pueblo Keres.
2. Ibid., 30–31.
3. Hamilton A. Tyler, *Pueblo Gods and Myths,* Civilization of the American Indian Series (Norman, OK: University of Oklahoma Press, 1964), 37. Evidently, Huruing Wuhti has other transformative abilities as well. Under pressure from patriarchal politics, she can change her gender, her name, and even her spiritual nature.
4. Ibid., 93.
5. Purley, "Keres Pueblo Concepts," 31.
6. Ibid.

READING 87

Islam, Social Change, and the Reality of Arab Women's Lives

Nadia Hijab

For more than a hundred years, Arab women have been engaged in the public debate on their role in a rapidly changing society. Both women and men have conducted the debate within an Islamic framework; they have turned to the Quran, the sharia (Islamic law), the sayings of the Prophet Muhammad, and the lives of his companions to define women's rights in the modern age. While modernists have argued for the most liberal interpretation of Islam possible, the conservatives have used the same sources to argue for restrictions on women's roles.

SOCIAL CHANGE

The debates make frequent references to the centrality of Arab women in maintaining family ties and community solidarity and in transmitting cultural values across generations. This was best captured in the document prepared by the Economic and Social Commission for Western Asia for the 1985 United Nations World Conference on Women, which was held in Nairobi. The document declared:

> Constitutions, charters, and legislation in the region have asserted the role of the family as the nucleus of social organization in Arab societies. It is necessary, therefore, to make available to the family the economic, social, cultural, and psychological conditions that would ensure its stability and satisfy its needs.

Therefore, the document accorded "priority to the work of women who devote their time to family and home affairs and hence ensure the continuity of generations, the cultivation of values, and the transmittal of knowledge and expertise from one generation to another."

Hitherto, Arab women themselves have assigned a great deal of value to their traditional roles within the family. This is partly because they are accorded a great deal of respect. As the social scientist Nadia Haggag Youssef noted, women's status can be seen as having two different components:

> the *rights* given to women and the *respect* given to them. Confusion ensues because the two distinct factors are erroneously used interchangeably, when in reality they are often inversely correlated. Thus, women receive great respect in certain societies that give them few rights; they receive equality of rights in societies in which they compete with men but have relatively low respect.

Today, Arab women are in the unenviable position of having to choose between rights and respect. Neither women nor men want to lose the warmth and security that the extended Arab family traditionally provided, particularly at a time of rapid social and economic change. However, modernization efforts by the state have steadily eroded traditional support and mediation systems, and women now are increasingly reliant on state legislation and institutions to protect their rights. Yet in the crucial area of relations within the family, the law in the Arab world does not provide for equal rights between men and women. This has occurred because the debate on women's roles has been conducted within the Islamic framework.

LAW AND THE ISLAMIC FRAMEWORK

The constitutions of the Arab nations, in those countries that have them, provide for nondiscrimination based on race, sex, or creed as called for in international law and United Nations conventions. Thus they provide equal political rights for Arab women, who can vote and stand for election in all the Arab countries that have parliaments (except in Kuwait). Arab labor laws that have been legislated during this century also compare well to international standards.

However, family laws, which regulate rights and responsibilities in marriage, divorce, child custody, and inheritance, do not provide for equality between the sexes because they have been developed within the Islamic framework in all Arab countries. Because the legislation has been developed independently, there is a wide range in interpretation. While Tunisia has almost achieved equality between men and women within the Islamic framework, Egyptian law provides for "equivalence" rather than equality. In Bahrain, which has not passed a state law regulating family relations, the disposition of legal opinion has been delegated to the judges to interpret the sharia directly as they see fit.

Thus, in effect, most family laws, as they currently stand, contradict the provisions of the constitutions and labor laws that have been decreed. For instance, in some Arab countries the constitution may guarantee the right to work and the labor law may be fair, yet the family law may allow a husband to stipulate that his wife must have his consent to work outside the home.

Egypt is one of the Arab countries that has ratified the United Nations Convention on the Elimination of All Forms of Discrimination Against Women (CEDAW), which is the most far-reaching international instrument providing for equality between men and women. Such ratification of a United Nations convention is seen as the governments' commitment to bring their national laws into line with the convention, unless they have stipulated reservations to specific articles. As was the case with many other countries around the world, Egypt had reservations. These included the following reservation to Article 16:

> concerning the equality of men and women in all matters relating to marriage and family relations during marriage and upon its dissolution. This must be without prejudice to the Islamic sharia provisions whereby women are accorded rights equivalent to those of their spouses so as to ensure a just balance between them. This is out of respect for the sanctity deriving from firm religious beliefs which govern marital relations in Egypt and which may not be called in question.

The reservation explained that, in the Egyptian context, the husband was obliged to support the wife financially and to provide support in case of divorce, while the wife had no such obligation; "the sharia therefore restricts the wife's rights to divorce by making it contingent on a judge's ruling, whereas no such restriction is laid down in the case of the husband." Thus, on the one hand, women should be entitled to full equality with men since Egypt has ratified the Convention. On the other hand, when it comes to the detailed application of the Convention, women's rights are restricted on grounds that no one "may call into question." In effect, the fact that family law has evolved within an Islamic framework means that Arab women can be equal outside the home but not within it.

This is being increasingly questioned by Arab feminists, who hold Tunisia up as a model, noting that it has evolved its family law within an Islamic framework, but has interpreted sharia law in such a way that it provides for equality between men and women.

ISLAM AND IDENTITY

It is clear that the Islamic framework continues to be of great importance and to have a strong hold when it comes to defining women's roles within the family. This attitude is reinforced by the fact that the region is still engaged in shaping its identity vis-à-vis other parts of the world, an exercise that has proven to be quite painful because memories of Western colonialism in the region are still fresh. In many Arab countries, independence was only won in the 1950s or 1960s—and in the case of the Palestinians it has yet to be achieved. The quest for independence was charged by the desire to express national identity without external interference. Thus the contentious question of what constituted an authentic Arab identity surfaced after independence. To date, it has not been satisfactorily resolved, nor have other questions that were a by-product of colonialism, such as how independent Arab state systems should relate to non-Arabs living within their societies.

The effort to define an authentic identity in postcolonial societies gave culture and heritage a more important and prominent role than they might otherwise have had. The extreme example is Algeria, perhaps one of the most

harshly colonized Arab countries, where the French sought to stamp out Islamic religion and culture. After independence in 1962, therefore, there was great emphasis on defining Algerian identity in terms of the country's "Arab–Islamic heritage." This had an appreciable impact on defining women's rights and responsibilities. Indeed, one reason why it took the country nearly twenty years to pass a family law at all was because of the complexity (if not impossibility) of forging consensus on what an "Arab–Islamic heritage" is and how this translates into rights and responsibilities for men and women. The family law that was eventually passed was much closer to the conservative interpretation of Islamic law than the liberal one enshrined in Tunisian law.

The question of identity is thus complicated by the need to define "the self" in opposition to the former colonialists, which is, in the final analysis, a defensive position. As Leila Ahmed has pointed out:

> the Islamic civilisation is not only a civilisation unambiguously on the defensive, emphasizing and reaffirming old values, but also a civilisation that finds itself reaffirming them the more intransigently and dogmatically and clinging to them perhaps the more obstinately because it is reaffirming them against [an old enemy—the West].

What makes the challenge even more acute is the fact that, in the postindependence era, many Arabs feel that economic and cultural colonialism has replaced political colonialism, and that there is all the more reason to adhere to indigenous culture and tradition in response. Efforts to redefine women's roles in society are often seen, rightly or wrongly, as an extension of Western efforts at cultural domination. During the Lebanese civil war (1975–1990), a Lebanese woman writer, Mona Fayyad Kawtharani, argued strongly that the *hijab* (Islamic headcovering) was a form of resistance to cultural and by extension economic domination. In an article in the daily newspaper *As Safir* in 1985, she said that the West had found that:

> [the] best way to control us was by destroying our cultural and religious beliefs, so that the believer came to be defined as a "fanatic." And this was done to enable the West to invade our lands and to penetrate with its consumer commodities, to transform our countries into markets. This led to political and economic dependency, and to loss of cultural identity, which was replaced by "modernisation." The Easterner would not buy these diverse commodities—clothes, cars, electrical appliances, processed foods, furniture, etc.—unless he was convinced that he was in need of a culture other than his own, and that this culture represented "modernity" whereas his own represented backwardness.

Kawtharani went on to defend the veil as a symbol of opposition to political, economic, and cultural domination. In fact, the notable increase in the use of the veil over the last decade is a multifaceted phenomenon. Some people support it for reasons of cultural authenticity, others for reasons of piety, and still others because it enables them to study and work outside the home without fear of harassment.

The search for an authentic (Arab–Islamic) identity, the incomplete separation of religion and state (particularly when it comes to family law), and the sense that the West continues to dominate cultural and economic development, all mean that it is wiser—indeed safer—to articulate proposals for change in Islamic rather than Western terms. This is why, as Ahmed pointed out:

> reformers and feminists repeatedly try to affirm (with remarkable tenacity and often too with ingenuity) that the reforms they seek involve no disloyalty to Islam, that they in fact are in conformity with it, and if not in conformity with the letter and actual text of the culture's central formulation, then in conformity with what nevertheless is still there somehow, in the spirit not quite caught by the words.

Thus, the debate on women's roles in the Arab world is not only a debate about women's roles within the family. It is also linked to the debate on the role of Islam in the state, and is closely bound with the Arab search for political independence, economic self-reliance, and an authentic identity. . . .

Standing Again at Sinai

Judith Plaskow

EXPLORING THE TERRAIN OF SILENCE

. . . The central Jewish categories of Torah, Israel, and God are all constructed from male perspectives. Torah is revelation as men perceived it, the story of Israel told from their standpoint, the law unfolded according to their needs. Israel is the male collectivity, the children of a Jacob who had a daughter, but whose sons became the twelve tribes. God is named in the male image, a father and warrior much like his male offspring, who confirms and sanctifies the silence of his daughters. Exploring these categories, we explore the parameters of women's silence.

In Torah, Jewish teaching, women are not absent, but they are cast in stories told by men. As characters in narrative, women may be vividly characterized, as objects of legislation, singled out for attention. But women's presence in Torah does not negate their silence, for women do not decide the questions with which Jewish sources deal. When the law treats of women, it is often because their "abnormality" demands it. If women are central to plot, the plots are not about them. Women's interests and intentions must be unearthed from texts with other purposes, for both law and narrative serve to obscure them.

The most striking examples of women's silence come from texts in which women are most central, for there the normative character of maleness is especially jarring. In the family narratives of Genesis, for example, women figure prominently. The matriarchs of Genesis are all strong women. As independent personalities, fiercely concerned for their children, they often seem to have an intuitive knowledge of God's plans for their sons. Indeed, it appears from the stories of Sarah and Rebekah that they understand God better than their husbands. God defends Sarah when she casts out Hagar, telling Abraham to obey his wife (Gen. 21:12). Rebekah, knowing it is God's intent, helps deceive Isaac into accepting Jacob as his heir (Gen. 25:23; 27:5–17). Yet despite their intuitions, and despite their wiliness and resourcefulness, it is not the women who receive the covenant or who pass on its lineage. The establishment of patrilineal descent and the patriarchal family takes precedence over the matriarch's stories. Their relationship to God, in some way presupposed by the text, remains an undigested element in the narrative. What was the full theophany to Rebekah, and how is it related to the covenant with Isaac? The writer does not tell us; it is not sufficiently important. And so the covenant remains the covenant with Isaac, while Rebekah's experience floats at the margin of the story.

The establishment of patrilineal descent and patriarchal control, a subtext in Genesis, is an important theme in the legislation associated with Sinai. Here again, women figure prominently, but only as objects of male concerns.

The laws pertaining to women place them firmly under the control of first fathers, then husbands, so that men can have male heirs they know are theirs. Legislation concerning adultery (Deut. 22:22, also Num. 5:11–31) and virginity (Deut. 22:13–21) speaks of women, but only to control female sexuality to male advantage. The *crime* of adultery is sleeping with another man's wife, and a man can bring his wife to trial even on suspicion of adultery, a right that is not reciprocal. Sleeping with a betrothed virgin constitutes adultery. A man who sleeps with a virgin who is not betrothed must simply marry her. A girl whose lack of virginity shames her father on her wedding night can be stoned to death for harlotry. A virgin who is raped must marry her assailant. The subject of these laws is women, but the interest behind them is the purity of the male line.

The process of projecting and defining women as objects of male concerns is expressed most fully not in the Bible, however, but in the Mishnah, an important second-century legal code. Part of the Mishnah's Order of Women (one of its six divisions) develops laws discussed in the Torah concerning certain problematic aspects of female sexuality. The subject of the division is the transfer of women—the regulation of women who are in states of transition, whose uncertain status threatens the stasis of the community. The woman who is about to enter into a marriage or who has just left one requires close attention. The law must regularize her irregularity, facilitate her transition to the normal state of wife and motherhood, at which point she no longer poses a problem. But it is not even the contents of the order, male-defined as they are, that trumpet most loudly women's silence. In a system in which a division of Men would be unthinkable nonsense, the fact of a division Women is sufficient evidence of who names the world, who defines whom, in "normative" Jewish sources.

Thus Torah—"Jewish" sources, "Jewish" teaching—puts itself forward as *Jewish* teaching but speaks in the voice of only half the Jewish people. This scandal is compounded by an-

other: The omission is neither mourned nor re-
gretted; it is not even noticed. True, the rabbis
were aware of the harshness of certain laws
pertaining to women and sought to mitigate
their effects. They tried to find ways to force a
recalcitrant husband to divorce his wife, for example. But the framework that necessitated
such mitigations went unquestioned. Women's
Otherness was left intact. The Jewish passion
for justice did not extend to Jewish women. As
Cynthia Ozick puts it, one great "Thou shalt
not"—"Thou shalt not lessen the humanity of
women"—is missing from the Torah.

For this great omission, there is no historical
redress. Indeed, where one might expect redress, the problem is compounded. The
prophets, those great champions of justice,
couch their pleas for justice in the language of
patriarchal marriage. Israel in her youth is a devoted bride, subordinate and obedient to her
husband/God (for example, Jer. 2:2). Idola-
trous Israel is a harlot and adulteress, a faith-
less woman whoring after false gods (for example, Hos. 2,3). Transferring the hierarchy of
male and female to God and his people, the
prophets enshrine in metaphor the legal subordination of women. Those who might have
named and challenged women's marginalization thus ignore and extend it.

The prophetic metaphors mark an end and a
beginning. They confront us with the injustice
of Torah; they link that injustice to other central
Jewish ideas. If exploring Torah means exploring a terrain of women's silence, this is no less
true of the categories of Israel or God.

Israel, the bride, the harlot, the people that
is female (that is, subordinate) in relation to
God is nonetheless male in communal self-
perception. The covenant community is the
community of the circumcised (Gen. 17:10),
the community defined as male heads of
household. Women are named through a filter
of male experience: that is the essence of
their silence. But women's experiences are not
recorded or taken seriously because women are
not perceived as normative Jews. They are part
of but do not define the community of Israel.

The same evidence that speaks to women's
silence in the tradition, to the partiality of
Torah, also reflects an understanding of Israel
as a community of males. In the narratives of
Genesis, for example, the covenant moves from
father to son, from Abraham to Isaac to Jacob to
Joseph. The matriarchs' relation to their husbands' God is sometimes assumed, sometimes
passed over, but the women do not constitute
the covenant people. Women's relation to the
community is also ambiguous and unclear in
biblical legislation. The law is couched in male
grammatical forms, and its content too presupposes a male nation. "You shall not covet
your neighbor's wife" (Ex. 20:17). Probably we
cannot deduce from this verse that women are
free to covet! Yet the injunction assumes that
women's obedience is owed to fathers and husbands, who are the primary group addressed.

The silence of women goes deeper, however,
than who defines Torah or Israel. It also finds its
way into language about God. Our language
about divinity is first of all male language; it is
selective and partial. The God who supposedly
transcends sexuality, who is presumably one
and whole, comes to us through language that
is incomplete and narrow. The images we use
to describe God, the qualities we attribute to
God, draw on male pronouns and experience
and convey a sense of power and authority that
is clearly male. The God at the surface of Jewish
consciousness is a God with a voice of thunder,
a God who as lord and king rules his people
and leads them into battle, a God who forgives
like a father when we turn to him. The female
images that exist in the Bible and (particularly
the mystical) tradition form an underground
stream that occasionally reminds us of the inadequacy of our imagery without transforming
its overwhelmingly male nature.

This male imagery is comforting and familiar—comforting because familiar—but it is
an integral part of a system that consigns
women to the margins. Since the experience of
God cannot be directly conveyed in language,
imagery for God is a vehicle that suggests what
is actually impossible to describe. Religious

experiences are expressed in a vocabulary drawn from the significant and valuable in a particular culture. To speak of God is to speak of what we most value. In attributing certain qualities to God, we both attempt to point to God and offer God's qualities to be emulated and admired. To say that God is just, for example, is to say both that God acts justly and that God demands justice. Justice belongs to God but is also ours to pursue. Similarly with maleness, to image God as male is to value the quality and those who have it. It is to define God in the image of the normative community and to bless men—but not women—with a central attribute of God.

But our images of God are not simply male images; they are images of a certain kind. The prophetic metaphors for the relation between God and Israel are metaphors borrowed from the patriarchal family—images of dominance softened by affection. God as husband and father of Israel demands obedience and monogamous love. He repays faithfulness with mercy and loving-kindness, but punishes waywardness, just as the wayward daughter can be stoned at her father's door (Deut. 22:21). When these family images are combined with political images of king and warrior, they reinforce a particular model of power and dominance. God is the power over us, the One out there over against us, the sovereign warrior with righteousness on his side. Family and political models of dominance and submission are recapitulated and rendered plausible by the dominance and submission of God and Israel. The silence and submission of women becomes part of a greater pattern that makes it appear fitting and right.

. . .

Clearly, the implications of Jewish feminism reach beyond the goal of equality to transform the bases of Jewish life. Feminism demands a new understanding of Torah, Israel, and God. It demands an understanding of Torah that begins by acknowledging the injustice of Torah and then goes on to create a Torah that is whole. The silence of women reverberates through the tradition, distorting the shape of narrative and skewing the content of the law. Only the deliberate recovery of women's hidden voices, the unearthing and invention of women's Torah, can give us Jewish teachings that are the product of the whole Jewish people and that reflect more fully its experiences of God.

Feminism demands an understanding of Israel that includes the whole of Israel and thus allows women to speak and name our experience for ourselves. It demands we replace a normative male voice with a chorus of divergent voices, describing Jewish reality in different accents and tones. Feminism impels us to rethink issues of community and diversity, to explore the ways in which one people can acknowledge and celebrate the varied experiences of its members. What would it mean for women *as women* to be equal participants in the Jewish community? How can we talk about difference without creating Others?

Feminism demands new ways of talking about God that reflect and grow out of the redefinition of Jewish humanity. The exclusively male naming of God supported and was rendered meaningful by a cultural and religious situation that is passing away. The emergence of women allows and necessitates that the long-suppressed femaleness of God be recovered and explored and reintegrated into the Godhead. But feminism presses us beyond the issue of gender to examine the nature of the God with male names. How can we move beyond images of domination to a God present *in* community rather than over it? How can we forge a God-language that expresses women's experience?

Everywoman Her Own Theology

Alicia Ostriker

I am nailing them up to the cathedral door
Like Martin Luther. Actually, no,
I don't want to resemble that *Schmutzkopf*
(See Erik Erikson and N. O. Brown
On the Reformer's anal aberrations,
Not to mention his hatred of Jews and
    peasants),
So I am thumbtacking these ninety-five
Theses to the bulletin board in my kitchen.

My proposals, or should I say requirements,
Include at least one image of a god,
Virile, beard optional, one of a goddess,
Nubile, breast size approximating mine,
One divine baby, one lion, one lamb,
All nude as figs, all dancing wildly,
All shining. Reproducible
In marble, metal, in fact any material.

Ethically, I am looking for
An absolute endorsement of loving-kindness.
No loopholes except maybe mosquitoes.

Virtue and sin will henceforth be discouraged,
Along with suffering and martyrdom.
There will be no concept of infidels;
Consequently the faithful must entertain
Themselves some other way than killing
    infidels.

And so forth and so on. I understand
This piece of paper is going to be
Spattered with wine one night at a party
And covered over with newer pieces of paper.
That is how it goes with bulletin boards.
Nevertheless it will be there.
Like an invitation, like a chalk pentangle,
It will emanate certain occult vibrations.

If something sacred wants to swoop from the
    universe
Through a ceiling, and materialize,
Folding its silver wings,
In a kitchen, and bump its chest against mine,
My paper will tell this being where to find me.

Witchcraft and Women's Culture

Starhawk

From earliest times, women have been witches, *wicce*, "wise ones"—priestesses, diviners, midwives, poets, healers, and singers of songs of power. Woman-centered culture, based on the worship of the Great Goddess, underlies the beginnings of all civilization. Mother Goddess was carved on the walls of paleolithic caves, and painted in the shrines of the earliest cities, those of the Anatolian plateau. For her were raised the giant stone circles, the henges of the British Isles, the dolmens and cromlechs of the later Celtic countries, and for her the great passage graves of Ireland were dug. In her honor, sacred dancers leaped the bulls in Crete and composed lyric hymns within the colleges of the holy isles of the Mediterranean. Her mysteries were celebrated in secret rites at Eleusis, and her initiates included some of the finest minds of Greece. Her priestesses discovered and tested the healing herbs and learned the secrets of the human mind and body that allowed them to ease the pain of childbirth, to heal wounds and cure diseases, and to explore the realm of dreams and the unconscious. Their knowledge of nature enabled them to tame sheep and cattle, to breed wheat and corn from grasses and weeds, to forge ceramics from mud and metal from rock, and to track the movements of moon, stars, and sun.

Witchcraft, "the craft of the wise," is the last remnant in the west of the time of women's strength and power. Through the dark ages of persecution, the covens of Europe preserved what is left of the mythology, rituals, and knowledge of the ancient matricentric (mother-centered) times. The great centers of worship in Anatolia, Malta, Iberia, Brittany, and Sumeria are now only silent stones and works of art we can but dimly understand. Of the mysteries of Eleusis, we have literary hints; the poems of Sappho survive only in fragments. The great collections of early literature and science were destroyed by patriarchal forces—the library of Alexandria burnt by Caesar, Charlemagne's collection of lore burnt by his son Louis "the Pious," who was offended at its "paganism." But the craft remains, in spite of all efforts to stamp it out, as a living tradition of Goddess-centered worship that traces its roots back to the time before the triumph of patriarchy.

The old religion of witchcraft before the advent of Christianity was an earth-centered, nature-oriented worship that venerated the Goddess, the source of life, as well as her son-lover-consort, who was seen as the Horned God of the hunt and animal life. Earth, air, water, fire, streams, seas, wells, beasts, trees, grain, the planets, sun, and most of all, the moon, were seen as aspects of deity. On the great seasonal festivals—the solstices and equinoxes, and the eves of May, August, November, and February,—all the countryside would gather to light huge bonfires, feast, dance, sing, and perform the rituals that assured abundance throughout the year.

When Christianity first began to spread, the country people held to the old ways, and for hundreds of years the two faiths coexisted quite peacefully. Many people followed both religions, and country priests in the twelfth and thirteenth centuries were frequently upbraided by church authorities for dressing in skins and leading the dance at the pagan festivals.

But in the thirteenth and fourteenth centuries, the church began persecution of witches, as well as Jews and "heretical" thinkers. Pope Innocent the VIII, with his Bull of 1484, intensified a campaign of torture and death that would take the lives of an estimated 9 million people, perhaps 80 percent of whom were women.

The vast majority of victims were not coven members or even necessarily witches. They were old widows whose property was coveted by someone else, young children with "witch blood," midwives who furnished the major competition to the male-dominated medical profession, free-thinkers who asked the wrong questions.

An enormous campaign of propaganda accompanied the witch trials as well. Witches were said to have sold their souls to the devil, to practice obscene and disgusting rites, to blight crops and murder children. In many areas, the witches did worship a Horned God as the spirit of the hunt, of animal life and vitality, a concept far from the power of evil that was the Christian devil. Witches were free and open about sexuality—but their rites were "obscene" only to those who viewed the human body itself as filthy and evil. Questioning or disbelieving any of the slander was itself considered proof of witchcraft or heresy, and the falsehoods that for hundreds of years could not be openly challenged had their effect. Even today, the word *witch* is often automatically associated with "evil."

With the age of reason in the eighteenth century, belief in witches, as in all things psychic and supernatural, began to fade. The craft as a religion was forgotten; all that remained were the wild stories of broomstick flights, magic potions, and the summoning of spectral beings.

Memory of the true craft faded everywhere except within the hidden covens. With it, went the memory of women's heritage and history, of our ancient roles as leaders, teachers, healers, seers. Lost, also, was the conception of the Great Spirit, as manifest in nature, in life, in woman. Mother Goddess slept, leaving the world to the less than gentle rule of the God-Father.

The Goddess has at last stirred from sleep, and women are reawakening to our ancient power. The feminist movement, which began as a political, economic, and social struggle, is opening to a spiritual dimension. In the process, many women are discovering the old religion, reclaiming the word *witch* and, with it, some of our lost culture.

Witchcraft, today, is a kaleidoscope of diverse traditions, rituals, theologies, and structures. But underneath the varying forms is a basic orientation common to all the craft. The outer forms of religion—the particular words said, the signs made, the names used—are less important to us than the inner forms, which cannot be defined or described but must be felt and intuited.

The craft is earth religion, and our basic orientation is to the earth, to life, to nature. There is no dichotomy between spirit and flesh, no split between Godhead and the world. The Goddess is manifest in the world; she brings life into being, *is* nature, *is* flesh. Union is not sought outside the world in some heavenly sphere or through dissolution of the self into the void beyond the senses. Spiritual union is found in life, within nature, passion, sensuality—through being fully human, fully one's self.

Our great symbol for the Goddess is the moon, whose three aspects reflect the three stages in women's lives and whose cycles of waxing and waning coincide with women's menstrual cycles. As the new moon or crescent, she is the Maiden, the Virgin—not chaste, but belonging to herself alone, not bound to any man. She is the wild child, lady of the woods, the huntress, free and untamed—Artemis,

Kore, Aradia, Nimue. White is her color. As the full moon, she is the mature woman, the sexual being, the mother and nurturer, giver of life, fertility, grain, offspring, potency, joy—Tana, Demeter, Diana, Ceres, Mari. Her colors are the red of blood and the green of growth. As waning or dark moon, she is the old woman, past menopause, the hag or crone that is ripe with wisdom, patroness of secrets, prophecy, divination, inspiration, power—Hecate, Ceridwen, Kali, Anna. Her color is the black of night.

The Goddess is also earth—Mother Earth, who sustains all growing things, who is the body, our bones and cells. She is air—the winds that move in the trees and over the waves, breath. She is the fire of the hearth, of the blazing bonfire and the fuming volcano; the power of transformation and change. And she is water—the sea, original source of life; the rivers, streams, lakes and wells; the blood that flows in the rivers of our veins. She is mare, cow, cat, owl, crane, flower, tree, apple, seed, lion, sow, stone, woman. She is found in the world around us, in the cycles and seasons of nature, and in mind, body, spirit, and emotions within each of us. Thou art Goddess. I am Goddess. All that lives (and all that is, lives), all that serves life, is Goddess.

Because witches are oriented to earth and to life, we value spiritual qualities that I feel are especially important to women, who have for so long been conditioned to be passive, submissive and weak. The craft values independence, personal strength, *self*—not petty selfishness but that deep core of strength within that makes us each a unique child of the Goddess. The craft has no dogma to stifle thought, no set of doctrines that have to be believed. Where authority exists, within covens, it is always coupled with the freedom every covener has, to leave at any time. When self is valued—in ourselves—we can see that self is everywhere.

Passion and emotion—that give depth and color and meaning to human life—are also valued. Witches strive to be in touch with feelings, even if they are sometimes painful, because the joy and pleasure and ecstasy available to a fully alive person make it worth occasional suffering. So-called negative emotion—anger—is valued as well, as a sign that something is wrong and that action needs to be taken. Witches prefer to handle anger by taking action and making changes rather than by detaching ourselves from our feelings in order to reach some nebulous, "higher" state.

Most of all, the craft values love. The Goddess' only law is "Love unto all beings." But the love we value is not the airy flower power of the hippies or the formless, abstracted *agape* of the early Christians. It is passionate, sensual, personal love, *eros*, falling in love, mother-child love, the love of one unique human being for other individuals, with all their personal traits and idiosyncrasies. Love is not something that can be radiated out in solitary meditation—it manifests itself in relationships and interactions with other people. It is often said "You cannot be a witch alone"—because to be a witch is to be a lover, a lover of the Goddess, and a lover of other human beings.

READING 91

A Visit from Reverend Tileston

Elizabeth Cook-Lynn

Fifty miles from the nearest town of any size, deep in the Bend of the Missouri River where the Dakotapi had made history for generations, lived the Family: Father, a first-born son whose eyes bore the immutable and unspoken agony of his generation, handsome and strong, a cattleman not so much from choice as from necessity; Mother, a fine quill artist, small boned and stout, a woman with one crooked elbow caused by a childhood accident, a good cook, accomplished at the piano, guitar and harmonica, talents she had learned at the government boarding school; Uncle, the Mother's younger brother, a truck driver sometimes, a drunk increasingly often whenever those inexplicable waves of grief washed over him; Grandmother, Grandfather and five children ranging in ages from 3 to 15 years. Uncle's son often lived with the Family as did the Grandmother's half sister and her husband and their two granddaughters. The Family was part of a small community which has reassembled itself at this place after the violent Diaspora and Displacement which was endured by this ancient tribe for several generations, the Family all the more closely knit because of this tragedy of recent history as well as the more practical problem of long distances to the few sparse surrounding towns settled a hundred years before by whites anxious to possess land and become rich. The year was 1935 and this was a place where strangers, though alien and undesirable, even called *to' ka*, were largely unthreatening and often ignored, and where strange events were witnessed with inexplicable but characteristic tolerance.

From the gravelled road which followed the course of the river, the small three-room frame house in which the Family now lived, built by the U.S. Government for Bureau of Indian Affairs employees in early reservation days and abandoned in later times, looked strangely remote and ageless. It seemed to stare listlessly toward the river's loop, and in winter its long-windowed eyes would be the first to catch a glimpse of the landing of the Canadian geese on the cold shores of the whitened, timeless river. It turned its back on the ludicrously inexpedient pyramid-shaped, steel-roofed icehouse which had once afforded Bureau employees from the East the luxury of iced drinks in the summer as they came to this blistering Dakotah prairie to work "in the Indian Service." The ice-house was abandoned now, also, too big and deep to be of any use to the Family except for the summer drying of the pounded meat and berry patties, *wasna*, which would be laid out upon its roof in the sun. During this drying process the children would be set to fanning the flies away with long willows, a task which held attention a surprisingly brief time. Bored, they would run off in pursuit of more imaginative pastimes only to be called back as soon as Grandmother discovered their absence.

Also at the rear of the house was a large tipi, the color of smoke at the top, streaked with rain, lined with cow hides, comfortable, shaded in late afternoon by the lone pine tree which was, itself, a stranger to the hot plains country of the Dakotah, itself a survivor of the days when Bureau employees lived there. The children imagined that the tree was brought there by a medicine man and was used in his cures but it was not a cedar, just a scraggly pine tree which had barely survived hard times. There was a tall hand pump set in the middle of the yard where Grandmother would kneel to wash the paunch during butchering times and also a corral set some distance away in the tall pasture grass at the foot of a small rise in the prairie landscape. A huge mound of earth covered a man-made cave which was complete with wooden steps and a slanting door which had to be picked up and drawn aside. A very large bull-snake often found refuge from the blistering sun under one of the wooden steps, stretching himself full length in the soft, cool black earth.

Just beyond the cave was the small white outdoor toilet, another survivor of former times, a product of imaginative Public Health Service officials who set about dotting Indian reservations with these white man's conveniences during the early part of the century. Across the road from the house a gray stuccoed Catholic church, St. Anne's, sat with a closed, tight-lipped visage as though shielding itself from the violent summer prairie storms which came intermittently, pounding the gravel and the stucco, flattening the prairie grass. To the rear of the church lay the remains of the ancestors in a cemetery which, years later, was said to be occupied by a den of rattlesnakes.

In summer evenings, the air was often still and quiet, heavy with moisture. After a late meal, the quiet deepened. The only sound was Grandmother's soft footsteps as she went back and forth to the kitchen carrying dishes from the table. Her ankle length black dress hid her bowed legs and her head was covered, always, with a black scarf, her long white braids lying on her breast. Every now and then she stopped to wipe her smooth face with a white cloth, breathlessly.

"Grandmother, we should cook outside, tomorrow," said the Youngest Daughter, disheveled and hot, bearing a load too heavy for her to the kitchen.

The Mother simply sat, one arm outstretched on the table, the crooked one fanning her face and hair with a handkerchief. For her it had been a long day as she and her sister had spent the afternoon picking wild plums and buffalo berries along the river.

As the evening came on, the children could be heard outside running and chasing one another around the house and yard, trying to touch each other on the back, stretching away, laughing, now and again falling and crashing into the bushes near the pump. The dogs barked loudly. It was a game the boys never seemed to tire of even as the sun started to glow in the west and Uncle went outside to begin his nightly summer ritual of starting a smoke-fire, a smudge, to keep the mosquitoes away for the evening.

"*Hoksila kin tuktel un he?*" muttered Uncle as he looked around for one of his nephews to help him gather firewood. "He's never around when you need him."

"Go get some of that wood over there by the back porch," he directed his voice toward the hapless Youngest Daughter who wrinkled up her nose, but went, dutifully, to get the wood. Uncle bent down on one knee to place the sticks and dead leaves just right to produce a heavy smoke. He carefully touched a match to the soft underbrush and as the smoke rose he watched, one thumb hooked in his belt. In a few moments smoke filled the air and members of the Family began to gather for the evening.

They might even see man-being-carried in the sky, thought Uncle, and then he could tell a story if the children felt like listening and could stay awake long enough for the stars to show themselves clearly.

When he straightened up, he was surprised to see a small black sedan some distance down the road, making its way slowly toward them. He kept his eyes on the road to see if he could recognize in the dusk who its occupants were. He stepped up on the porch and lit a cigarette, the match illuminating the fine, delicate bones of his deeply pocked, scarred face.

Holding the match close for a moment, Uncle said, to no one in particular, "A car's coming."

Cars were rarely seen here on this country road this late in the evening.

As Uncle stood watching, he heard church music, faintly at first, and later, blaring, and he realized after a few long moments that it was coming from the loudspeaker positioned on top of the sedan.

"On-ward, Christian so-o-o-l-diers," sang the recorded voices of an entire church choir into the quiet evening light as the car came slowly into the river's bend, "with the cross of J-e-e-e-sus going on before."

Uncle stood with the cigarette in his mouth, his hands in his pockets as his brother-in-law came out of the house and sat down on the porch step with a cup of coffee. They watched the car approach and listened to the music, now blaring loud enough to get the attention of the children who stopped running and stood gazing at the strange-looking vehicle.

They stood, transfixed, as the car approached slowly and came to a stop. The loudspeaker fell silent as the driver of the sedan parked the car on the side of the road near the mailbox and, with great cheer, stepped from the car, waving and smiling. He was a man of about forty with a broad, freckled face. He was perspiring heav-

ily and he made his way down the short path from the road to the house. Behind him came two women dressed in blue white-flowered dresses, brown stockings and flat brown shoes; their faces, like pale round melons, were fixed with broad smiles. They all carried black leather-bound Bibles, the kind with red-tipped pages.

"Boy, it's hot!" said the fortyish freckled man as he held out his hand in greeting. The Father did not look at him nor did he get up. He put the cup to his lips and sipped coffee quietly, ignoring the intrusion with sullen indifference. Uncle kept his hands in his pockets and with his tongue he shifted his cigarette to the other side of his mouth.

Ignoring what was clearly a personal affront by the two men on the steps, the freckled man said, "Say, that's a good trash burning operation there," turning to the children standing beside the smudge. The children looked first at the smudge and then back at the perspiring man and, silently, they shook hands with him. Grasping the unwilling hand of the Youngest Daughter standing a few feet away, the man, in a loud voice asked, "Is your mommy home, honey?" Nearly overcome with embarrassment she said, "Yeh, she's in there," and gestured toward the door.

"Well," the man said as he turned and walked up the steps slowly, avoiding the Father and the Uncle still mutely positioned there, "we've come a long way with the message of hope and love we've got right here," and he patted the black leather-bound book he carried. As he tapped on the screen door, the Mother appeared and the freckled man quickly opened the door, stepped inside and held it open for the two smiling women who accompanied him to squeeze inside and in front of him.

"I'm Sister Bernice," began the plumper of the two women, "and this is Sister Kate . . . ?" Her voice trailed off as if she had asked a question. When there was no response, she turned to the freckled man and, putting her hand on his elbow she said, "And we're here with Reverend Tileston."

Taking a deep breath, the Reverend said to the Mother in his kindliest voice, "Ma-a'aam, we'd like to pray with you," and there in the middle of the room he knelt and began paging through his Bible, motioning for the women to join him as he knelt. His two companions quickly dropped to their knees and the plump one said to the Mother, "Please pray with us, sister," and the Mother, after a brief, uncertain moment, also knelt. Espying the Grandmother and her half sister peering at them curiously from the kitchen doorway, the Reverend quickly got up and led them to the middle of the room saying, "Come on with us, Granny, pray with us," and the two old women, too, with great effort, got to their knees. The Youngest Daughter, having followed the astonishing trio into the house, stood beside her Grandmother and looked expectantly at the perspiring freckled man as he fell to reading from the leather-bound book:

"With ALL our energy we ought to lead back ALL men to our most MER-ci-ful Re-DEEE-mer," he read. His voice rose:

"He is the Divine Conso-o-o-oler of the afflicted"; Youngest Daughter hung her head, copying the attitude of the visitors.

"To rulers and subjects alike He teaches lessons of true holiness,"
the Reverend sucked in air:

"unimpeachable justice and,"
he breathed again,

"generous charity."
The Reverend's voice seemed to fill the cramped little room and Sisters Bernice and Kate, eyes tightly closed, murmured "Amen" louder and louder with each breath the minister took.

Youngest Daughter glanced first at her Mother, then her Grandmothers who were kneeling shoulder to shoulder, faces impassive, eyes cast to the floor. Then, the Reverend closed the book, raised his arms and recited from memory, PROVERBS:

"Hear, O Children, a father's instruction," he shouted. "Be attentive, that you may gain understanding! Yea, excellent advice I give you; my teaching do not forsake."

One of the dogs, hunching itself close to the screen door, began to whine.

The Reverend continued to shout: "When I was my father's child, frail, yet the darling of my mother, he taught me, and said to me: 'Let your heart hold fast my words! Keep my commands, do not forget; go not astray from the words of my mouth.'"

His arms fell and his voice softened as he uttered the last phrase, opened his eyes and looked, unseeing, at the little girl, his gaze moist and glittering. The dog's whine became more persistent, his tone now pitched higher to match the Reverend's and he began to push his nose against the screen door, causing it to squeak loudly.

The Reverend Tileston looked into the passive faces of the Mother and the Grandmothers and he said, "The beginning of wisdom is: get wisdom; at the cost of ALL-L-L-L you have," his arm swung dangerously close to the unfortunate dog who flattened his ears and pushed himself closer to the door.

"Get understanding," Reverend Tileston urged. "Forsake her not and she will preserve you; love her, and she will safeguard you; extol her, and she will exalt you; she will bring you honors if you embrace her; she will put on your head a graceful diadem; a glorious crown will she bestow upon you."

The words seemed to roll from his tongue and Youngest Daughter imagined shining crowns placed upon the heads of her Mother and her Grandmothers still kneeling stiffly and impassively. She was thrilled with the sound of the English words though she knew she didn't comprehend their meaning. It was like the time when Felix Middle Tent, the well-known Dakotah orator, made his speeches at the tribal council meeting she sometimes attended with her father, when he used his most eloquent and esoteric Dakotah vocabulary, oftentimes derisively referred to by Uncle as "jawbreakers."

As the Reverend's hefty arm again swept the room, the whining dog lurched backward and fell against a large pail of buffalo berries which Mother had left on the porch that late afternoon. Terrified, the dog leapt into the second pail of plums, scattering them wildly, then he dashed under the porch where he set up a mournful howl. The boys who had been listening at the side window fled into the bushes, laughing and screaming.

The Mother and Grandmothers, surprised and shocked at this turn of events but bent upon retrieving the day's pickings, swept past the astonished, speechless minister, shouting abuse at the now thoroughly miserable dog, and the screen door slammed behind them. Youngest Daughter was left looking into the disappointed faces of the Reverend and his companions. She smiled.

Forced by these circumstances to admit that the spiritual moment was lost, the Reverend Tileston got to his feet and ushered Sisters Bernice and Kate out of the house, carefully picking a path through the berries covering the porch. He was relieved that the Father and Uncle were nowhere to be seen and he turned at the last step and made a final effort, saying,

"Meditate, Mothers, on the Scriptures, have knowledge of them for they are the food which sustains men during times of strife."

The women, engrossed in saving the berries, didn't hear him.

His final proselytical gesture, the attempted distribution of printed pamphlets, was also ignored.

Their composure now completely shattered, the trio which bore God's word into this obscure bend in the river found its way, falteringly, to the sedan, switched on the loudspeaker, and drove slowly away.

Youngest Daughter looked after them as they ventured deeper into the curve along the river and the faint echo of "With the Cross of Jee-e-sus . . ." rang in her ears. After a moment she went to find Uncle who would tell her a story about the star people and how the four blanket carriers once helped him find his way home from a long and difficult journey.

She hoped that the Reverend knew about the blanket carriers.

DISCUSSION QUESTIONS FOR CHAPTER TWELVE

1. Why do you think the control of women is a central component in many religions?

2. How do you think religion has been both empowering and oppressive for women?

3. How do you think the availability of a greater variety of images of God might impact religion and religion's influence on social life?

4. How might women work toward reform from within religious traditions? Why might some women feel the need to abandon religious traditions completely?

5. How have negative stereotypes of witchcraft served to perpetuate the oppression of women? Why do you think practices of women's spirituality were (and still are) perceived as such a threat?

6. How do nondominant religious traditions challenge the influence of hegemonic Christianity in U.S. society?

SUGGESTIONS FOR FURTHER READING

Christ, Carol, and Judith Plaskow, eds. *Womanspirit Rising: A Feminist Reader in Religion.* San Francisco: HarperCollins, 1992.

Gross, Rita M. *Feminism and Religion: An Introduction.* Boston: Beacon, 1996.

Isasi-Diaz, Ada Maria, and Yolanda Tarango. *Hispanic Women: Prophetic Voice in the Church.* San Francisco: Harper & Row, 1988.

King, Ursula, ed. *Women in the World's Religions: Past and Present.* New York: Paragon, 1987.

Mollenkott, Virginia. *Sensuous Spirituality: Out from Fundamentalism.* New York: Crossroad, 1992.

Reis, Elizabeth, ed. *Spellbound: Women and Witchcraft in America.* Wilmington, DE: Scholarly Resources, 1998.

Spretnak, Charlene. *The Politics of Women's Spirituality: Essays by Founding Mothers of the Movement.* New York: Anchor, 1982.

CHAPTER THIRTEEN

Activism, Change, and Feminist Futures

THE PROMISE OF FEMINIST EDUCATION

In Chapter 1 we discussed the objectives of women's studies as a discipline. These objectives include, first, an understanding of the social construction of gender and the intersection of gender with other systems of inequality in women's lives; second, a familiarity with women's status, contributions, and individual and collective actions for change; and third, an awareness of ways to improve women's status. A fourth objective of women's studies is that you will start thinking about patterns of privilege and discrimination in your own life and understand your position vis-à-vis systems of inequality. We hope you will learn to think critically about how societal institutions affect individual lives—especially your own. We hope you will gain new insights and confidence and that new knowledge will empower you.

Feminist educators attempt to give students more inclusive and socially just forms of knowledge and to support teachers using their power in nonexploitive ways. Women's studies usually involve nonhierarchical, egalitarian classrooms where teachers respect students and hope to learn from them as well as teach them. The focus is on the importance of the student voice and experience and encouraging both personal and social change. Most women's studies classes, however, are within colleges that do not necessarily share the same goals and objectives. Many feminist educators operate within the social and economic constraints of educational institutions that view "counter-hegemonic" education—that is, education that challenges the status quo—as problematic and/or subversive. Despite these constraints, feminist education, with its progressive and transformative possibilities, is an important feature on most campuses.

For many students, and perhaps for you too, the term *feminism* is still problematic. Many people object to the political biases associated with feminist education and believe knowledge should be objective and devoid of political values. It is important to emphasize that all knowledge is associated with power, as knowledge arises from communities with certain positions, resources, and understandings of the world. This means that all knowledge (and not just feminist knowledge) is ideological in that it is in some way associated with history and politics. To declare objectivity or value-neutrality is to mask the workings of power within knowledge. Although feminist education is more explicit than other forms of knowledge in speaking of its relationship to power in society, this does not mean it is more biased or ideological than other forms of knowledge. As civil rights activists declared, "If you're not part of the solution, then you're part of the problem." In other words, whether you are part of the problem or part of the solution (however you define problem and solution), you are equally political.

Many people support the justice-based goals of feminism but do not identify with the label. The reading by Lisa Maria Hogeland titled "Fear of Feminism: Why Young Women Get the Willies" addresses this issue. She also looks in depth at continuing resistance to feminism as politics and as a way of life. She makes the important distinction between *gender consciousness* and *feminist consciousness,* explains why one does not necessarily imply the other, and discusses the fear of reprisals and consequences associated with a feminist consciousness.

ACTIVISM

We live in a complex time. White women have made significant progress over the past decades and have begun the twenty-first century integrated into most societal institutions. Although the progress of women of color lags behind the gains made by White women, they too are beginning to be heard. Yet, the big picture is far from rosy, as society has not been transformed in its core values as feminists throughout the last century would have wanted. An equitable sharing of power and resources in terms of gender, race, class, and other differences has not been actualized. In addition, as women receive more public power, they are encouraged to internalize more private constraints concerning the body and sexuality.

These times at the turn of the century have been touted as prosperous even while the gap between the rich and the poor in the United States is the largest among industrialized nations and is increasing. Most people are working harder than ever so that they may enjoy this prosperity, and large numbers of people (especially non-White children) are living in poverty. Violence is increasing in our society in all walks of life; women, people of color, and gays and lesbians are frequently the target of hate and hostility; and the balance of power in the world seems fragile and in the hands of relatively few (often egocentric, delusional) men. The picture is one of great optimism and yet simultaneous despair.

In the reading "Taking the High Road," Suzanne Pharr writes that violence, bigotry, and hatred are related in important ways to the alienation and disconnection felt by some people in contemporary society. She encourages us to address the rage, cynicism, and mean-spiritedness of this historical moment and come up with a transformational politics that encourages a consciousness shift and extends generosity and compassion toward others. In other words, any movement for justice-based equalities must have a strong moral foundation based upon love and human dignity, and community.

As Audre Lorde, one of the most eloquent writers of the feminist second wave once declared, "Silence will not protect you." Lorde wrote about the need to be part of social change efforts, and she encouraged us to speak out and address the problems in our lives and communities. And, as the reading by Michael Kimmel, "Real Men Join the Movement," implies, speaking out and addressing inequities involves learning how to be an ally to people who are different from you and who

Size Does Matter and Nine Other Tips for Effective Protest

- *Size does matter.* The most memorable protests—and the ones the media tends to cover—are the big ones: Think of the 1968 March on Washington and the Million Man March in 1995. The best way to put masses of people on the streets? Forge coalitions in order to broaden your base of potential protesters.
- *Get organized.* A large crowd is not, ipso facto, an effective performance. In November 1997, the Disney/Haiti Justice Campaign pulled together a sizable number of protesters outside the Disney Store in Times Square to denounce the company's Haitian sweatshops, but organizers failed to start a picket line or lead energetic chants. Many in the crowd simply milled around with their hands in their pockets or sipping coffee.
- *Location, location, location.* Many large, well-organized protests happen outside corporate headquarters or foreign consulates. Unfortunately, those tend to be on side streets with little pedestrian traffic and no adjoining public spaces. Simply relocating the event to a busy nearby corner can increase the audience tenfold.
- *Distinguish yourself.* In December 1997, the East Timor Action Network marched up Madison Avenue to the Indonesian Consulate to protest the occupation of East Timor. Only a few carried signs; the rest were indistinguishable from other pedestrians on the crowded street. Solution? Form a picket line or sit down en masse on the busy sidewalk.
- *Get the crowd involved.* Successful protests encourage audience participation—appearing exclusive is a sure way to alienate onlookers from your cause. At a 1997 World AIDS Day vigil in New York, for example, organizers handed out chalk to passersby and asked them to write on a nearby fountain the names of loved ones who had died of AIDS.
- *Put it down on paper.* A simple, clearly written leaflet that explains who is protesting, why, and how to get involved is crucial. Sure, it may end up in the nearest trash can, but some people will read it, and a few might show up at the next event.
- *Manage the media.* Of course, the biggest prize for any protest is media coverage. Inform local newspapers and TV and radio stations (not just "progressive" media) a few days in advance.
- *Above all, be spectacular.* Eye-catching costumes, a sea of candles in a dark plaza, limp bodies being carried from a street to a police van—these telegenic images make for good press. At an August 1997 march prompted by the police beating of Haitian immigrant Abner Louima, many waved toilet plungers—the tool with which Louima was allegedly beaten and sodomized—transforming an ordinary object into an unforgettable symbol of violent racism.
- *Meteorology matters.* A wet and cold protester is usually a demoralized one. Plan for foul weather by establishing an alternative day; if timing is critical, find a nearby indoor or protected space to which protesters can retreat. To be sure, there are exceptions: A dedicated group braving the elements can convey a profound sense of commitment to a cause—assuming, of course, that someone's watching.
- *Use protest to beget protest.* Any single march or demonstration should be one link in a larger chain. Most political movements, after all, must endure for years to attain their goals. So think about the morning after: How can the momentum generated (if any) be maintained? How soon is too soon for the next protest? What worked, what didn't? Protests should be carefully crafted performances designed to be unforgettable and moving for audiences and participants alike. Only meaningful and memorable protests can effectively challenge people to think differently and motivate still further protest in the days and years ahead.

Source: Jeff Goodwin, *Mother Jones,* March/April 1990.

do not enjoy the privileges you enjoy. Kimmel emphasizes the necessity of men joining with women to make this world better for everyone. In this sense, coalitions are a central aspect of social change efforts.

In the past four decades there has been significant resistance to the status quo in U.S. society, despite enormous backlash from the conservative right and other groups. Response to this backlash is the focus of Ruth Rosen's article in the readings, "Epilogue: Beyond Backlash." The strength of justice-based resistance has been its multiissue and multistrategic approach. *Multiissue* means organizing on many fronts over a variety of different issues that include political, legal, and judicial changes; educational reform; welfare rights; eliminating violence; reproductive issues; and workplace reform. *Multistrategic* means relying on working coalitions that mobilize around certain shared issues and involve different strategies toward a shared goal.

As discussed in Chapter 1, some liberal or moderate activists have worked within the system and advocated change from within. Their approach locates the source of inequality in barriers to inclusion and advancement and has worked to change women's working lives through comparable worth, sexual harassment policy, and parenting leaves. Legal attacks on abortion rights have been deflected by the work of liberal feminists working within the courts, and affirmative action and other civil rights legislation have similarly been the focus of scholars, activists, and politicians working in the public sphere. These organizations tend to be hierarchical with a centralized governing structure (president, advisory board, officers, and so forth) and local chapters around the country. Other strategies for change take a more radical approach (for example, radical or cultural feminism) and attempt to *transform* the system rather than to adapt the existing system. Together these various strategies work to advocate justice-based forms of equality.

Although differences in strategy are sometimes a source of divisiveness among activists and feminists, they are also a source of strength in being able to work on multiple issues from multiple approaches. Indeed, any given issue lends itself to both reformist and radical approaches. Lesbian and gay rights, for example, is something that can be tackled in the courts and in the voting booths as organizations work toward legislation to create domestic partner legislation or community civil protections. At the same time, consciousness-raising activities and grassroots demonstrations, such as candlelight vigils for victims of hate crimes and Queer Pride parades, work on the local level. As the reading by Marj Schneider on the movement for disability rights, "From Personal Tragedy to Group Consciousness,"

Learning Activity: Feminist.com

Visit the website of feminist.com at *www.feminist.com* and follow the link to the activism page. There you'll find links to action alerts and legislative updates for a number of feminist organizations, including the National Organization for Women (NOW), Sisterhood Is Global, Women Organizing for Change, and Planned Parenthood. Follow these links to learn what actions you can take. Also, check out the link to the "outrage of the month" to see what outrageous things are happening in the world and what you can do about them. The website also offers links to government resources and voter education and other activist resources.

Ideas for Activism

- Organize an activism awareness educational event on your campus. Invite local activists to speak about their activism. Provide opportunities for students to volunteer for a wide variety of projects in your area.
- Find out about your school's recycling program. If there's not one in place, advocate with administrators to begin one. If one is in place, try to find ways to help it function more effectively and to encourage more participation in recycling. If recycling services are not provided in your local community, advocate with city and county officials to begin providing these services.
- Find out what the major environmental issues are in your state and what legislative steps need to be taken to address these concerns. Then organize a letter-writing campaign to encourage legislators to enact laws protecting the environment.
- Identify a major polluter in your community and organize a nonviolent protest outside that business demanding environmental reforms.
- Sponsor a workshop on conflict management and nonviolence for campus and community members.

explains, change occurs as a result of group consciousness that challenges old ways of thinking as well as laws and institutional reforms (such as the Americans with Disabilities Act). Together, the different strategies improve the quality of life.

One important aspect to consider is that simply increasing women's participation and leadership does not necessarily imply a more egalitarian or feminist future. As you know, there are women and people of color who are opposed to strategies for improving the general well-being of disenfranchised peoples. Changing the personnel—replacing men with women, for example—does not necessarily secure a different kind of future. Although in practice liberal feminism is more sophisticated than, for example, simply considering female candidates merely because they are women, it has been criticized for promoting women into positions of power and authority irrespective of their stance on the social relations of gender, race, class, and other differences.

Contemporary feminism is concerned with issues that are increasingly global. These concerns have resulted in the sponsorship of numerous international conferences and have promoted education about women's issues all over the world. And, as communication technologies have advanced, the difficulties of global organization have lessened. International feminist groups have worked against militarism, global capitalism, and racism, as well as supporting issues identified by indigenous women around the world. This activism culminated in 1995 with the United Nations Fourth World Conference on Women held in Beijing, China (the first conference was held in Mexico City in 1975, the second in Copenhagen in 1980, and the third in Nairobi in 1985). More than 30,000 women attended the Beijing conference and helped create the internationally endorsed Platform for Action. This platform is a call for concrete action involving human rights of women and girls as part of universal human rights, the eradication of poverty of women, the removal of obstacles to women's full participation in public life and decision making, the elimination of all forms of violence against women, the

Activist Profile: Indigo Girls, Emily Saliers and Amy Ray

In many ways Indigo Girls Emily Saliers and Amy Ray exemplify contemporary feminist activism. With a comprehensive understanding of injustice and a commitment to work for equality on all fronts, Saliers and Ray have consciously worked to make a difference in the world, using their status as rock stars to advocate for the world's disadvantaged.

The duo started playing together in high school as the B Band and then Saliers and Ray, becoming Indigo Girls in 1985 while at Emory University in Atlanta. They were signed by Epic Records in 1988 and released their self-titled album to critical acclaim. By September 1989, the album had gone gold, and Indigo Girls was nominated for a Grammy as Best New Artist and won a Grammy for the Best Contemporary Folk Recording of 1989. Since then, Indigo Girls has released eight albums. They have sold over 7 million albums worldwide, including one double platinum disc, three platinum, and four gold, and have earned six Grammy nominations.

Beyond their talent as musicians, Saliers and Ray stand out because of their integrity and the way they have lived their convictions. Although many of their songs deal with relationships and heartbreak, many also deal with political issues such as poverty, homelessness, discrimination, and homophobia. More importantly, Saliers and Ray have used their wealth and influence to bring about change in the music industry and in the world at large. In 1990, in appreciation for the help provided to Indigo Girls by other Atlanta and Athens musicians, Ray founded Daemon Records, an independent label focusing on Atlanta-area bands. Indigo Girls has participated in three Lilith Fair concert series (initiated by musician Sarah McLaughlan to highlight women musicians), and in 1998 they started the Suffragette Sessions Tour, described by Ray as "a socialist experiment in rock and roll—no hierarchy, no boundaries."

(continued)

Activist Profile: Indigo Girls, Emily Saliers and Amy Ray (*continued*)

In 1995 and 1997, Indigo Girls headlined a series of concerts called Honor the Earth to benefit Indigenous activists. They have also been involved in supporting a number of other justice causes such as Greenpeace; the Zapatistas in Chiapas, Mexico; and AIDS research.

In 1994, both Ray and Saliers openly acknowledged their sexuality. In 1999, five high schools in South Carolina and Tennessee canceled scheduled Indigo Girls concerts. But the shows were rebooked in clubs, and the students came anyway.

The activism of Indigo Girls Amy Ray and Emily Saliers offers a powerful model for feminist activism. Recognizing the adage "injustice anywhere is a threat to justice everywhere," Ray and Saliers practice a multifaceted activism, challenging oppression wherever it is found. As their song "Hammer and a Nail" states, "Now I know a refuge never grows from a chin in a hand in a thoughtful pose, gotta tend the earth if you want a rose."

assurance of women's access to educational and health services, and actions to promote women's economic autonomy. The text of the Platform for Action is included in the readings and also discussed in the reading by Ruth Rosen.

FUTURE VISIONS

How might the future look? How will our knowledge of gender, race, and class-based inequalities be used? Does our future hold the promise of prosperity and peace or economic unrest and increased militarization? Will technology save us or quicken our destruction? Will feminist values be a part of future social transformation? Many who write about the future emphasize that future visions are metaphors for the present; we anticipate the future in light of how we make sense of the present and have come to understand the past. This approach encourages us to look at the present mindfully, so that we are aware of its politics, and creatively, so that we can see the possibility for change. In her playful poem "Warning," Jenny Joseph looks to the future to offer some guidance in the present.

There are some social trends that have implications for the future. Given the higher fertility rates among the non-White population as well as immigration figures, Whites will eventually become a relatively smaller percentage of the population until they are no longer a majority in the United States. In addition, the rise in births between 1946 and 1960 (the baby boomer cohort) and the decline through the 1970s will mean a large percentage of the population will be over 65 years old within the next couple of decades. And, although some people have always lived to be 80, 90, and 100 years old, this number will grow in response to better nutrition and health care among certain segments of the population. As the baby boomers age, they will create stress on medical and social systems. They might also influence family systems as several generations of aged family members could require care at the same time. This is complicated by the fact that families are becoming smaller, and divorce and remarriage rates will probably continue at current rates. Ties between stepfamilies and other nonfamilial ties are most likely going to become more important in terms of care and support.

In our society where the profit motive runs much of our everyday lives, where citizens have lost respect for political and governmental institutions, and where people are working longer hours and becoming more disconnected from families and communities, the issue of integrity is something to consider. The definition of integrity is two part: one, a moral positioning about the distinction between right and wrong, and two, a consistent stance on this morality such that we act out what we believe and attempt to live our ideals. "Do as I say and not as I do" is an example of the very opposite of integrity. What might it mean to live with feminist-inspired integrity as well as envision a future where feminist integrity is central? We'll discuss seven implications here.

First, it is important to set feminist priorities and keep them. In a society where sound bytes and multiple, fragmented pieces of information vie to be legitimate sources of knowledge, we must recognize that some things are more important than others. Priorities are essential. Postmodernism might have deconstructed notions of truth to the point where some argue that there is no such thing as the truth; yet, some things are truer than others. Figure out your truths and priorities based upon your own values, politics, and/or religion.

Second, it is important that we live and envision a society that balances personal freedom and identity with public and collective responsibility. Suzanne Pharr writes about this in "Taking the High Road" when she says that transformational politics calls for living with communal values by which we learn how to honor the needs of the individual as well as the group. The United States is a culture that values individualism very highly and often forgets that although the Constitution says you have the right to do something, I also have the right to criticize you for it. Similarly, we must question the limitations associated with certain rights. Is your right still a right if it violates my rights or hurts a community? And, just because the Constitution says something is your right, that does not necessarily make that act a moral choice. Although the Constitution exists to protect choices and rights, it does not tell us which choices and rights are best.

Third, recognize that corporate capitalism does not function in everybody's interests. In this sense, *economic* democracy must not be confused with *political* democracy. Many of us have learned that capitalist societies are synonymous with democracies and that other economic systems are somehow undemocratic in principle. We live in a society that attempts a political democracy at the same time that economic democracy, or financial equity for all peoples, is limited. Unfortunately, capitalism has had deleterious effects on both physical and human environments, and consumerism has changed families and communities by encouraging people to accumulate material possessions beyond their immediate needs. Perhaps a motto for the future might be "pack lightly."

Fourth, a present and future with a core value of feminist integrity is one that understands the limitations of technology as well as its liberating aspects. This means being in control of technology so that it is used ethically and productively. This is related to the previous point about capitalist expansion. Corporations have invested heavily in new technologies that do not always work for the collective good.

Principles of Environmental Justice

1. Environmental justice affirms the sacredness of Mother Earth, ecological unity and the interdependence of all species, and the right to be free from ecological destruction.
2. Environmental justice demands that public policy be based on mutual respect and justice for all peoples, free from any form of discrimination or bias.
3. Environmental justice mandates the right to ethical, balanced, and responsible uses of land and renewable resources in the interest of a sustainable planet for humans and other living things.
4. Environmental justice calls for universal protection from nuclear testing, extraction, production and disposal of toxic/hazardous wastes and poisons that threaten the fundamental right to clean air, land, water, and food.
5. Environmental justice affirms the fundamental right to political, economic, cultural, and environmental self-determination of all peoples.
6. Environmental justice demands the cessation of the production of all toxins, hazardous wastes, and radioactive materials, and that all past and current producers be held strictly accountable to the people for detoxification and containment at the point of production.
7. Environmental justice demands the right to participate as equal partners at every level of decision making, including needs assessment, planning, implementation, enforcement, and evaluation.
8. Environmental justice affirms the right of all workers to a safe and healthy work environment, without being forced to choose between an unsafe livelihood and unemployment. It also affirms the right of those who work at home to be free from environmental hazards.
9. Environmental justice protects the right of victims of environmental injustice to receive full compensation and reparations for damages as well as quality health care.
10. Environmental justice considers governmental acts of environmental injustice a violation of international law, the Universal Declaration on Human Rights, and the United Nations Convention on Genocide.
11. Environmental justice must recognize a special legal and natural relationship of Native Peoples to the U.S. government through treaties, agreements, compacts, and covenants affirming sovereignty and self-determination.
12. Environmental justice affirms the need for urban and rural ecological policies to clean up and rebuild our cities and rural areas in balance with nature, honoring the cultural integrity of all our communities, and providing fair access for all to the full range of resources.
13. Environmental justice calls for the strict enforcement of principles of informed consent and a halt to the testing of experimental reproductive and medical procedures and vaccinations on people of color.
14. Environmental justice opposes the destructive operations of multinational corporations.
15. Environmental justice opposes military occupation; repression and exploitation of lands, peoples and cultures, and other life forms.
16. Environmental justice calls for the education of present and future generations that emphasizes social and environmental issues, based on our experience and an appreciation of our diverse cultural perspectives.
17. Environmental justice requires that we, as individuals, make personal and consumer choices to consume as little of Mother Earth's resources and to produce as little waste as possible; and make the conscious decision to challenge and reprioritize our lifestyles to ensure the health of the natural world for present and future generations.

Source: People of Color Environmental Leadership Summit, 1991. *www.umich.edu/~jrazer/nre/whatis.html.*

Women Working for Peace

The International Peace Bureau (IPB) is the world's oldest and most comprehensive international peace federation. Founded in 1892, the organization won the Nobel Peace Prize in 1910. Its role is to support peace and disarmament initiatives. Current priorities include the abolition of nuclear weapons, conflict prevention and resolution, human rights, and women and peace. To learn more about the IPB, visit the website at *www.ipb.org*.

The Women's International League for Peace and Freedom (WILPF), founded in 1915 to protest the war in Europe, suggests ways to end war and to prevent war in the future; as well, it seeks to educate and mobilize women for action. The goals of the WILPF are political solutions to international conflicts, disarmament, promotion of women to full and equal participation in all society's activities, economic and social justice within and among states, elimination of racism and all forms of discrimination and exploitation, respect of fundamental human rights, and the right to development in a sustainable environment. For more information, including action alerts and readings, visit the WILPF homepage at *www.wilpf.org*.

Female Nobel Peace Laureates

Ten women have been honored with the Nobel Peace Prize for their work for justice. They are:

Baroness Bertha Von Suttner (1905) Austrian honored for her writing and work opposing war.

Jane Addams (1931) International President, Women's International League for Peace and Freedom.

Emily Greene Balch (1946) Honored for her pacifism and work for peace through a variety of organizations.

Betty Williams and Mairead Corrigan (1976) Founders of the Northern Ireland Peace Movement to bring together Protestants and Catholics to work for peace together.

Mother Teresa (1979) Honored for her "work in bringing help to suffering humanity" and her respect for individual human dignity.

Alva Myrdal (1982) Honored with Alfonso Garcia Robles for their work with the United Nations on disarmament.

Aung San Suu Kyi (1991) Burmese activist honored for nonviolent work for human rights in working for independence in Myanmar.

Rigoberta Menchú Tum (1992) Honored for her work for "ethno-cultural reconciliation based on respect for the rights of indigenous peoples."

Jody Williams (1997) Honored for her work with the International Campaign to Ban Landmines.

Source: *http://womenshistory.about.com/education/womenshistory/msubnobelpeace.htm*

Fifth, feminist integrity requires advocating a sustainable physical environment. There is only one world and we share it; there is an interdependence of all species. Given this, it makes no sense to destroy our home through such behaviors as global climate change, environmental pollution, and species eradication. Sustainable environmental practices start with addressing issues associated with capitalist global expansion and technological development, as discussed previously.

Also associated is the need for environmental justice because the poor and communities of color have suffered disproportionately in terms of environmental pollution and degradation. Environmental justice calls for protection from nuclear testing, extraction, production, and disposal of toxic and hazardous wastes and poisons that threaten the fundamental right to clean air, land, water, and food. It also demands that workers have the right to safe and healthy work environments without being forced to choose between unsafe livelihood and unemployment.

Sixth, a peaceful and sustainable future is one that respects human dignity, celebrates difference and diversity, and yet recognizes that diversity does not necessarily imply equality. It is not enough to be tolerant of the differences among us, although that would be a good start; it is necessary to recognize everyone's right to a piece of the pie and work toward equality of outcome and not just equality of access. We believe we must create social movements that derive from an ethic of caring, empathy, and compassion.

Seventh and finally, we believe it is important to have a sense of humor and to take the time to play and celebrate. As socialist labor reformer Emma Goldman once said, "If I can't dance, I don't want to be part of your revolution."

A justice-based politics of integrity embraces equality for all peoples. It is an ethic that has the potential to help create a peaceful and sustainable future, improving the quality of our lives and the future of our planet. An ethic that respects and values all forms of life and seeks ways to distribute resources equitably is one that moves away from dominance and uses peaceful solutions to environmental, societal, and global problems. As a blueprint for the future, a focus on justice and equality has much to offer. As Rosen writes in the reading "Epilogue: Beyond Backlash," in her reference to the movement for women's human rights, the struggle has begun and there is no end in sight!

READING 92

Fear of Feminism
Why Young Women Get the Willies

Lisa Maria Hogeland

I began thinking about young women's fear of feminism, as I always do in the fall, while I prepared to begin another year of teaching courses in English and women's studies. I was further prodded when former students of mine, now graduate students elsewhere and teaching for the first time, phoned in to complain about their young women students' resistance to feminism. It occurred to me that my response—"Of course young women are afraid of feminism"—was not especially helpful. This essay is an attempt to trace out what that "of course" really means; much of it is based on my experience with college students, but many of the observations apply to other young women as well.

Some people may argue that young women have far less to lose by becoming feminists than do older women: they have a smaller stake in the system and fewer ties to it. At the same time, though, young women today have been profoundly affected by the demonization of feminism during the 12 years of Reagan and Bush—the time when they formed their understanding of political possibility and public life. Older women may see the backlash as temporary and changeable; younger women may see it as how things are. The economic situation for college students worsened over those 12 years as well, with less student aid available, so that young women may experience their situation as extremely precarious—too precarious to risk feminism.

My young women students often interpret critiques of marriage—a staple of feminist analysis for centuries—as evidence of their authors' dysfunctional families. This demonstrates another reality they have grown up with: the increased tendency to pathologize any kind of oppositional politics. Twelve years of the rhetoric of "special interests versus family values" have created a climate in which passionate political commitments seem crazy. In this climate, the logical reasons why all women fear feminism take on particular meaning and importance for young women.

To understand what women fear when they fear feminism—and what they don't—it is helpful to draw a distinction between gender consciousness and feminist consciousness. One measure of feminism's success over the past three decades is that women's gender consciousness—our self-awareness as women—is extremely high. Gender consciousness takes two forms: awareness of women's vulnerability and celebration of women's difference. Fear of crime is at an all-time high in the United States; one of the driving forces behind this fear may well be women's sense of special vulnerability to the epidemic of men's violence. Feminists have fostered this awareness of violence against women, and it is to our credit that we have made our analysis so powerful; at the same time, however, we must attend to ways this awareness can be deployed for nonfeminist and even antifeminist purposes, and most especially to ways it can be used to serve a racist agenda. Feminists have also fostered an awareness of women's difference from men and made it possible for women (including nonfeminists) to have an appreciation of things pertaining to women—perhaps most visibly the kinds of "women's culture" commodified in the mass media (soap operas and romance, self-help books, talk shows, and the like). Our public culture in the U.S. presents myriad opportunities for women to take pleasure in being women—most often, however, that pleasure is used as an advertising or marketing strategy.

Gender consciousness is a necessary precondition for feminist consciousness, but they are not the same. The difference lies in the link between gender and politics. Feminism politicizes gender consciousness, inserts it into a systematic analysis of histories and structures of domination and privilege. Feminism asks questions—difficult and complicated questions, often with contradictory and confusing answers—about how gender consciousness can be used both for and against women, how vulnerability and difference help and hinder women's self-determination and freedom. Fear of feminism, then, is not a fear of gender, but rather a fear of politics. Fear of politics can be understood as a fear of living in consequences, a fear of reprisals.

The fear of political reprisals is very realistic. There are powerful interests opposed to feminism—let's be clear about that. It is not in the interests of white supremacy that white women insist on abortion rights, that women of color insist on an end to involuntary sterilization, that all women insist on reproductive self-determination. It is not in the interests of capitalism that women demand economic rights or comparable worth. It is not in the interests of many individual men or many institutions that women demand a nonexploitative sexual autonomy—the right to say and mean both no and yes on our own terms. What would our mass culture look like if it didn't sell women's bodies—even aside from pornography? It is not in the interests of heterosexist patriarchy that women challenge our understandings of events headlined MAN KILLED FAMILY BECAUSE HE LOVED THEM, that women challenge the notion of men's violence against women and children as deriving from "love" rather than power. It is not in the interests of any of the systems of domination in which we are enmeshed that we see how these systems work—that we understand men's violence,

male domination, race and class supremacy, as systems of permission for both individual and institutional exercises of power, rather than merely as individual pathologies. It is not in the interests of white supremacist capitalist patriarchy that women ally across differences.

Allying across differences is difficult work, and is often thwarted by homophobia—by fears both of lesbians and of being named a lesbian by association. Feminism requires that we confront that homophobia constantly. I want to suggest another and perhaps more subtle and insidious way that fear of feminism is shaped by the institution of heterosexuality. Think about the lives of young women—think about your own. What are the arenas for selfhood for young women in this culture? How do they discover and construct their identities? What teaches them who they are, who they want to be, who they might be? Our culture allows women so little scope for development, for exploration, for testing the boundaries of what they can do and who they can be, that romantic and sexual relationships become the primary, too often the only, arena for selfhood.

Young women who have not yet begun careers or community involvements too often have no public life, and the smallness of private life, of romance as an arena for selfhood, is particularly acute for them. Intimate relationships become the testing ground for identity, a reality that has enormously damaging consequences for teenage girls in particular (the pressures both toward and on sex and romance, together with the culturally induced destruction of girls' self-esteem at puberty, have everything to do with teenage pregnancy). The feminist insistence that the personal is political may seem to threaten rather than empower a girl's fragile, emergent self as she develops into a sexual and relational being.

Young women may believe that a feminist identity puts them out of the pool for many men, limits the options of who they might become with a partner, how they might decide to live. They may not be wrong either: how many young men feminists or feminist sympathizers do you know? A politics that may require making demands on a partner, or that may motivate particular choices in partners, can appear to foreclose rather than to open up options for identity, especially for women who haven't yet discovered that all relationships require negotiation and struggle. When you live on Noah's ark, anything that might make it more difficult to find a partner can seem to threaten your very survival. To make our case, feminists have to combat not just homophobia, but also the rule of the couple, the politics of Noah's ark in the age of "family values." This does not mean that heterosexual feminist women must give up their intimate relationships, but it does mean that feminists must continually analyze those pressures, be clear about how they operate in our lives, and try to find ways around and through them for ourselves, each other, and other women.

For women who are survivors of men's violence—perhaps most notably for incest and rape survivors—the shift feminism enables, from individual pathology to systematic analysis, is empowering rather than threatening. For women who have not experienced men's violence in these ways, the shift to a systematic analysis requires them to ally themselves with survivors—itself a recognition that *it could happen to me.* Young women who have not been victims of men's violence hate being asked to identify with it; they see the threat to their emergent sense of autonomy and freedom not in the fact of men's violence, but in feminist analyses that make them identify with it. This can also be true for older women, but it may be lessened by the simple statistics of women's life experience: the longer you live, the more likely you are to have experienced men's violence or to know women who are survivors of it, and thus to have a sense of the range and scope of that violence.

My women students, feminist and nonfeminist alike, are perfectly aware of the risks of going unescorted to the library at night. At the same time, they are appalled by my suggesting that such gender-based restrictions on their access to university facilities deny them an equal education. It's not that men's violence isn't real to them—but that they are unwilling to trace out its consequences and to understand its complexities. College women, however precarious their economic situation, and even despite the extent of sexual harassment and date rape on campuses all over the country, still insist on believing that women's equality has been achieved. And, in fact, to the extent that colleges and universities are doing their jobs—giving women students something like an equal education—young women may experience relatively little overt or first-hand discrimination. Sexism may come to seem more the exception than the rule in some academic settings—and thus more attributable to individual sickness than to systems of domination.

Women of all ages fear the existential situation of feminism, what we learned from Simone de Beauvoir, what we learned from radical feminists in the 1970s, what we learned from feminist women of color in the 1980s: feminism has consequences. Once you have your "click!" moment, the world shifts, and it shifts in some terrifying ways. Not just heterosexism drives this fear of political commitment—it's not just fear of limiting one's partner-pool. It's also about limiting oneself—about the fear of commitment to something larger than the self that asks us to examine the consequences of our actions. Women fear anger, and change, and challenge—who doesn't? Women fear taking a public stand, entering public discourse, demanding—and perhaps getting—attention. And for what? To be called a "feminazi"? To be denounced as traitors to women's "essential nature"?

The challenge to the public-private division that feminism represents is profoundly threatening to young women who just want to be left alone, to all women who believe they can hide from feminist issues by not being feminists.

The central feminist tenet that the personal is political is profoundly threatening to young women who don't want to be called to account. It is far easier to rest in silence, as if silence were neutrality, and as if neutrality were safety. Neither wholly cynical nor wholly apathetic, women who fear feminism fear living in consequences. Think harder, act more carefully; feminism requires that you enter a world supersaturated with meaning, with implications. And for privileged women in particular, the notion that one's own privilege comes at someone else's expense—that my privilege *is* your oppression—is profoundly threatening.

Fear of feminism is also fear of complexity, fear of thinking, fear of ideas—we live, after all, in a profoundly anti-intellectual culture. Feminism is one of the few movements in the U.S. that produce nonacademic intellectuals—readers, writers, thinkers, and theorists outside the academy, who combine and refine their knowledge with their practice. What other movement is housed so substantially in bookstores? All radical movements for change struggle against the anti-intellectualism of U.S. culture, the same anti-intellectualism, fatalism, and disengagement that make even voting too much work for most U.S. citizens. Feminism is work—intellectual work as surely as it is activist work—and it can be very easy for women who have been feminists for a long time to forget how hard-won their insights are, how much reading and talking and thinking and work produced them. In this political climate, such insights may be even more hard-won.

Feminism requires an expansion of the self—an expansion of empathy, interest, intelligence, and responsibility across differences, histories, cultures, ethnicities, sexual identities, othernesses. The differences between women, as Audre Lorde pointed out over and over again, are our most precious resources in thinking and acting toward change. Fear of difference is itself a fear of consequences: it is less other women's difference that we fear than our own implication in the hierarchy of differences, our own accountability to other women's oppression. It is easier to rest in gender consciousness, in one's own difference, than to undertake the personal and political analysis required to trace out one's own position in multiple and overlapping systems of domination.

Women have real reasons to fear feminism, and we do young women no service if we suggest to them that feminism itself is safe. It is not. To stand opposed to your culture, to be critical of institutions, behaviors, discourses—when it is so clearly *not* in your immediate interest to do so—asks a lot of a young person, of any person. At its best, the feminist challenging of individualism, of narrow notions of freedom, is transformative, exhilarating, empowering. When we do our best work in selling feminism to the unconverted, we make clear not only its necessity, but also its pleasures: the joys of intellectual and political work, the moral power of living in consequences, the surprises of coalition, the rewards of doing what is difficult. Feminism offers an arena for selfhood beyond personal relationships but not disconnected from them. It offers—and requires—courage, intelligence, boldness, sensitivity, relationality, complexity, a sense of purpose, and, lest we forget, a sense of humor as well. Of course young women are afraid of feminism—shouldn't they be?

Real Men Join the Movement

Michael Kimmel

Cory Shere didn't go to Duke University to become a profeminist man. He was going to be a doctor, covering his bets with a double major in engineering and premed. But his experiences with both organic chemistry and feminist women conspired to lead this affable and earnest 20-year-old Detroit native in a different direction. Now in his junior year, he still has a double major—women's studies and psychology. And he works with a group of men to raise awareness about sexual assault and date rape.

Eric Freedman wasn't profeminist either, when he arrived at Swarthmore College three years ago. A 20-year-old junior literature major from Syracuse, New York, he became involved in a campus antiracism project, and began to see the connections among different struggles for equality. At an antiracism workshop he helped organize, he suddenly found himself speaking about male privilege as well as white privilege. This fall, he's starting a men's group to focus on race and gender issues.

Who are these guys? And what are they doing in the women's movement?

They are among a growing number of profeminist men around the country. These aren't the angry divorcés who whine about how men are the new victims of reverse discrimination, nor are they the weekend warriors trooping off to a mythopoetic retreat. They're neither Promise Keepers nor Million Man Marchers vowing to be responsible domestic patriarchs on a nineteenth-century model.

You might think of profeminist men as the "other" men's movement, but I prefer to consider it the "real" men's movement, because by actively supporting women's equality on the job or on the streets and by quietly changing their lives to create that equality at home, profeminist men are also transforming the defini-

tion of masculinity. Perhaps this is the movement about which Gloria Steinem rhapsodized when she wrote how women "want a men's movement. We are literally dying for it."

Profeminist men staff the centers where convicted batterers get counseling, organize therapy for rapists and sex offenders in prison, do the workshops on preventing sexual harassment in the workplace, or on confronting the impact of pornography in men's lives. On campus, they're organizing men's events during Take Back the Night marches; presenting programs on sexual assault to fraternities, dorms, and athletic teams; taking courses on masculinity; and founding campus groups with acronyms like MAC (Men Acting for Change), MOST (Men Opposed to Sexist Tradition), MASH (Men Against Sexual Harassment), MASA (Men Against Sexual Assault), and, my current favorite, MARS (Men Against Rape and Sexism). Maybe John Gray was right after all—real men *are* from Mars!

FEMINISM AND MEN'S LIVES

I first met Cory, Eric, and about a dozen other young profeminist men in April at the Young Feminist Summit, organized by NOW, in Washington, D.C. They were pretty easy to spot among the nearly one thousand young women from colleges all over the country. As we talked during an impromptu workshop, I heard them describe both the exhilaration and isolation of becoming part of the struggle for women's equality, the frustrations of dealing with other men, the active suspicions and passive indifference of other students.

It felt painfully familiar. I've spent nearly two decades in feminist politics, first as an activist in antirape and antibattery groups, and later helping to organize the National Organization for Men Against Sexism (NOMAS), a network of profeminist men and women around the country. More recently, I've tried to apply the insights of academic feminist theory to men's lives, developing courses on men, debating with Robert Bly and his followers, and writing a history of the idea of manhood in the United States.

Of course, men like Cory and Eric are a distinct minority on campus. They compete with the angry voice of backlash, those shrill interruptions that scream "Don't blame me, I never raped anyone! Leave me alone!" They compete with that now familiar men-as-victims whine. Men, we hear, are terrified of going to work or on a date, lest they be falsely accused of sexual harassment or date rape; they're unable to support their scheming careerist wives, yet are vilified as bad fathers if they don't provide enough child support to keep their ex-wives in Gucci and Donna Karan after the divorce.

In the public imagination, profeminist men also compete with the mythopoetic vision of the men's movement as a kind of summer-camp retreat, and the earnest evangelical Promise Keepers with their men-only sports-themed rallies, and the Million Man March's solemn yet celebratory atonement. All offer men solace and soul-work, and promise to heal men's pain and enable them to become more nurturing and loving. All noble goals, to be sure. But to profeminist men, you don't build responsibility and democracy by exclusion—of women, or of gays and lesbians.

And profeminist men compete with the most deafening sound coming from the mouths of American men when the subject is feminism: silence. Most men, on campus and off, exude an aura of studied indifference to feminism. Like the irreverent second child at the Passover seder, they ask, "What has this to do with me?"

A lot. Sure, feminism is the struggle of more than one half of the population for equal rights.

But it's also about rethinking identities, our relationships, the meanings of our lives. For men, feminism is not only about what we *can't* do—like commit violence, harassment, or rape—or *shouldn't* do, like leave all the child care and housework to our wives. It's also about what we *can* do, what we *should* do, and even what we *want* to do—like be a better father, friend, or partner. "Most men know that it is to all of our advantage—women and men alike—for women to be equal," noted NOW President Patricia Ireland, in her Summit keynote address. Far from being only about the loss of power, feminism will also enable men to live the lives we say we want to live.

This isn't the gender cavalry, arriving in the nick of time to save the damsels from distress. "Thanks for bringing this sexism stuff to our attention, ladies," one might imagine them saying. "We'll take it from here." And it's true that some men declare themselves feminists just a bit too effortlessly, especially if they think it's going to help them get a date. (A friend calls it "premature self-congratulation," and it's just as likely to leave women feeling shortchanged.)

In part, this explains why I call them "profeminist men" and not "feminist men" or "male feminists." As an idea, it seems to me, feminism involves an empirical observation—that women are not equal—and the moral position that declares they should be. Of course, men may share this empirical observation and take this moral stance. And to that extent men support feminism as an ideal. But feminism as an identity also involves the felt experience of that inequality. And this men do not have, because men are privileged by sexism. To be sure, men may be oppressed—by race, class, ethnicity, sexuality, age, physical ability—but men are not oppressed *as men*. Since only women have that felt experience of oppression about gender, it seems sensible to make a distinction in how we identify ourselves. Men can support feminism, and can call ourselves "antisexist" or "profeminist." I've chosen profeminist because, like feminism, it stresses the positive and forward-looking.

In a sense, I think of profeminist men as the Gentlemen's Auxiliary of Feminism. This honorable position acknowledges that we play a part in this social transformation, but not the most significant part. It's the task of the Gentlemen's Auxiliary to make feminism comprehensible to men, not as a loss of power—which has thus far failed to "trickle down" to most individual men anyway—but as a challenge to the false sense of entitlement we have to that power in the first place. Profeminism is about supporting both women's equality and other men's efforts to live more ethically consistent and more emotionally resonant lives.

. . .

The routes taken by today's profeminist men are as varied as the men themselves. But most do seem to have some personal experience that made gender inequality more concrete. For some, it involved their mother. (Remember President Clinton describing how he developed his commitment to women's equality when he tried to stop his stepfather from hitting his mother? Of course, one wishes that commitment had facilitated more supportive policy initiatives.) Max Sadler, a 17-year-old senior at Trinity High School in New York City, watched his professional mother hit her head on the glass ceiling at her high-powered corporate job—a job she eventually quit to join a company with more women in high-level positions. Max shared her frustration, and also felt ashamed at the casual attitudes of her male colleagues.

Shehzad Nadeem, a 19-year-old student at James Madison University in Virginia, remembered the way his older sister described her experiences. "I could barely believe the stories she told me, yet something deep inside told me that they were not only true, but common. I realized that we men are actively or passively complicit in women's oppression, and that we have to take an active role in challenging other men." Shehzad joined MOST (Men Opposed to

Sexist Tradition), which has presented workshops on violence and sexual assault at Madison dorms.

. . .

Or perhaps it was having a feminist girlfriend, or even just having women friends, that brought these issues to the fore for men. "I grew up with female friends who were as ambitious, smart, achieving, and confident as I thought I was—on a good day," recalls Jason Schultz, a founder of MAC at Duke, who now organizes men's programs to combat campus sexual assault. "When I got to college, these same women began calling themselves feminists. When I heard men call women 'dumb chicks' I knew something was wrong."

. . .

THE PROFEMINIST "CLICK!"

But there has to be more than the presence of feminist role models, challenges from girlfriends, brilliant assignments, or challenging support from professors. After all, we all have women in our lives, and virtually all of those women have had some traumatic encounter with sexism. There has to be something else.

Feminists call it the "click!"—that moment when they realize that their pain, fears, confusion, and anger are not theirs alone, but are shared with other women. Do profeminist men have "clicks!"? Yes, but they don't typically come from righteous indignation or fear, but rather from guilt and shame, a gnawing sense of implication in something larger and more pervasive than individual intention. It's that awful moment when you hear women complain about "men" in general and realize, even just a little bit, that you are what they're talking about. (Much of men's reactive defensiveness seems to be a hedge against these feelings of shame.)

Suddenly, it's not those "bad" men "out there" who are the problem—it's all men. Call it the Pogo revelation: "We have met the enemy, and he is us."

That's certainly the way it felt for Jeff Wolf (not his real name). A sexually naive college sophomore, he found himself growing closer and closer to a woman friend, Annie, during a study date. They talked long into the night, and eventually kissed. One thing began to lead to another, and both seemed eager and pleased to be with the other. Just before penetration, though, Jeff felt Annie go limp. "Her eyes glazed over, and she went kind of numb," he recalled, still wincing at the memory.

This is the moment that many a college guy dreams of—her apparent surrender to his desire, even if it was induced by roofies or alcohol. It's a moment when men often space out, preferring to navigate the actual encounter on automatic pilot, fearing that emotional connection will lead to an early climax.

As Annie slipped into this mental coma, though, Jeff stayed alert, as engaged emotionally as he was physically. "What had been so arousing was the way we had been connecting intellectually and emotionally," he said. After some patient prodding, she finally confessed that she'd been raped as a high school sophomore, and ever since, had used this self-protective strategy to get through a sexual encounter without reliving her adolescent trauma. Jeff, it seemed, was the first guy who noticed.

. . .

Others say their "click!" experience happened later in life. In the 1970s, psychologist David Greene was deeply involved in political activism, when he and his wife had a baby. "Not that much changed for me; I still went around doing my thing, but now there was a baby in it." On the other hand, his wife's life was totally transformed by the realities of round-the-clock child care. She'd become a mother. "After several weeks of this, she sat me down and confronted me," he recalls. "The bankruptcy of my politics quickly became clear to me. I was an oppressor, an abuser of privilege—I'd become the enemy I thought I was fighting against." The couple meticulously divided housework and child care, and David learned that revolu-

tions are fought out in people's kitchens as well as in the jungles of Southeast Asia. Terry Kupers, a 54-year-old psychiatrist, and author of *Revisioning Men's Lives,* remembers his first wife initiating some serious talks about the "unstated assumptions we were making about housework, cooking, and whose time was more valuable." Not only did Kupers realize that his wife was right, "but I also realized I liked things better the new way."

. . .

PROFEMINISM TODAY—AND TOMORROW

And just as sisterhood is global, so too are profeminist men active around the world. Men from nearly 50 countries—from Mexico to Japan—regularly contribute to a newsletter of international profeminist scholars and activists, according to its editor, Oystein Holter, a Norwegian researcher. Scandinavian men are working to implement a gender equity mandated by law. Liisa Husu, a senior advisor to Finland's gender equity commission, has developed a parliamentary subcommittee of concerned men. (When I met with them last fall, we spent our day discussing our mutual activities, after which they whisked me off to an all-male sauna resort on the shore of an icy Baltic Sea for a bit of male-bonding as a follow-up to all that equity work.) Scandinavian men routinely take parental leave; in fact, in Sweden and Norway they've introduced "Daddy days," an additional month of paid paternity leave for the men to have some time with their newborns after the mothers have returned to work About half of Swedish men take paternal leave, according to fatherhood expert Lars Jalmert at the University of Stockholm.

The world's most successful profeminist organization must be Canada's White Ribbon Campaign. Begun in 1991 to coincide with the second anniversary of the Montreal Massacre—when a young man killed 14 women engineering students at the University of Montreal on December 6, 1989—its goal was to publicly and visibly declare opposition to men's violence against women by encouraging men to wear a white ribbon as a public pledge. "Within days, hundreds of thousands of men and boys across Canada wore a ribbon," noted Michael Kaufman, one of the campaign's founders. "It exceeded our wildest expectations—even the prime minister wore a ribbon." This year, WRC events are also planned for Norway, Australia, and several U.S. colleges; in Canada, events include an Alberta hockey team planning a skating competition to raise money for a local women's shelter. WRC organizers have also developed curricula for secondary schools to raise the issue for boys.

But just as surely, some of the most important and effective profeminist men's activities are taking place in American homes every day, as men increasingly share housework and child care, reorganize their schedules to be more responsive to the needs of their families, and even downsize their ambitions to develop a family strategy that does not revolve exclusively around *his* career path. "Housework remains the last frontier" for men to tame, argues sociologist Kathleen Gerson in her book *No Man's Land.* . . .

But the payoff is significant. If power were a scarce commodity or a zero-sum game, we might think that women's increased power would mean a decrease in men's. And since most men don't feel very powerful anyway, the possibilities of further loss are rather unappealing. But for most men, all the power in the world does not seem to have trickled down to enable individual men to live the lives we say we want to live—lives of intimacy, integrity, and individual expression. By demanding the redistribution of power along more equitable lines, feminism also seeks a dramatic shift in our social priorities, our choices about how we live, and what we consider important. Feminism is also a blueprint for men about how to become the men we want to be, and profeminist men believe that men will live happier, healthier, and more emotionally enriched lives by supporting women's equality.

Part of profeminist men's politics is to visibly and vocally support women's equality, and part of it is to quietly and laboriously struggle to implement that public stance into our own lives. And part of it must be to learn to confront and challenge other men, with care and commitment. "This cause is not altogether and exclusively woman's cause," wrote Frederick Douglass in 1848. "It is the cause of human brotherhood as well as human sisterhood, and both must rise and fall together."

From Personal Tragedy to Group Consciousness
The Movement for Disability Rights

Marj Schneider

For over 30 years the disability rights movement has pushed for equal treatment and opportunities in education, employment and community life. In recent years, the situation faced by disabled people has changed dramatically. Prior to the 1970s, there was little legal recourse for a disabled person denied education, housing or a job, and no laws mandating that buildings and public transit systems be usable by people in wheelchairs (Johnson, 1988: 46). Many states had large institutions that passed for home for thousands of people labeled mentally retarded. During the seventies and eighties, most of these warehousing institutions were closed. Residents moved into smaller facilities or group homes, allowing some developmentally disabled people to participate more in their communities (Trent, 1993: 264–65). Today, most disabled children are educated in regular classrooms along with their peers (Kerzner Lipsky & Gartner, 1989: 3–24). Computers adapted for use by blind, learning disabled and physically disabled persons, and faster, light-weight wheelchairs are examples of technological advancements, unavailable in the past, that promote independence (Shapiro, 1993: 211–236).

A new group consciousness on the part of disabled people challenges old ways of thinking about disability, but long-held, unexamined beliefs and attitudes of nondisabled society are slow to change. Disabled people have long maintained that societal fears, prejudices and stereotypes often present more problems than the limitations imposed by the disability itself (Shapiro, 1993: 9).

. . .

THE MEDICAL MODEL

During the twentieth century, increasing numbers of nondisabled professionals have promoted a medicalized view of disability, casting the disabled individual into the perpetual role of patient. In this role, patients depend upon professionals rather than participate in decision-making regarding their physical care and other needs. (Funk, 1987: 13).

Historian Paul Longmore (1992) says that the goal of professional intervention has been, if not to cure people, then at least to correct the functional consequences of a disability enough to enable them to participate in society. The emphasis is on "normalization," to try to be as much like nondisabled people as possible. Longmore (1992) states: "Within this medical model lurks considerable ambivalence about people who look different or function differently. . . . Fundamentally, this is a paternalistic

ideology that regards the objects of its concern as incompetent to manage their own lives, sometimes as even dangerous to society and as needing supervision."

. . .

EARLY ACTIVISM

Challenges to the medical model began when blind and deaf people founded their own organizations to advocate for legislation and policies to address their particular needs (Funk, 1987: 13). The development of a broader disability rights movement started in the 1960s, and was profoundly influenced by the black civil rights and women's movements. Ideas such as integration and equality of opportunity took hold among disabled people who began talking about how society needed to change rather than how they as individuals needed to "overcome their handicaps." There was a growing comprehension that they had rights, could make their own choices and could be full and equal participants in society.

In 1972, the incorporation of the Berkeley Center for Independent Living was the first instance of severely disabled individuals designing a program to meet their own needs as they saw them. Over the next decade, more than 200 programs run by disabled people were established throughout the country modeled on the Berkeley Center. These centers created services to facilitate disabled people's living in the community, giving hope and dignity. The new concept of independent living had a tremendous impact on disability professionals, law makers and disabled people around the world (Funk, 1987: 15).

Other coalitions and organizations evolved as well that cut across differing disabilities to focus on issues of common concern. The decades of the sixties and seventies saw significant growth in organizing and advocacy efforts by disabled people and parents of disabled children. Traditional disability programs and policies were challenged in the courts and legislatures, based on constitutional rights. By 1979, there were class action suits on behalf of institutionalized mentally disabled people in 17 states. Advocates demanded that individuals be provided with alternatives for living in the community (Funk, 1987: 15–16).

In 1973, Congress passed a Rehabilitation Act that included Section 504, which banned discrimination against disabled people by programs receiving federal funds. However, Section 504 wasn't implemented until 1977 when activists occupied the offices of the Department of Health Education and Welfare for 28 days, demanding that the rules governing this law be signed. Since Section 504 affected only programs getting federal dollars, activists began working for passage of state access laws and adding disabled people as a protected group under state civil rights statutes. Some communities with active disability organizations slowly became more accessible, but it was rare to find one being totally barrier-free (Johnson, 1988: 47).

In 1975, the Education for All Handicapped Children Act (today called the Individuals with Disabilities Education Act, IDEA) mandated that all children, regardless of the severity of their disabilities, receive a free appropriate public education. The word *appropriate* in the law means that a child's needs should be met in ways that work best for the individual, not on the basis of category of disability. The law reflected the belief that a disability didn't necessarily mean a child should be removed from the regular classroom, though some children might require specialized services (Kerzner Lipsky & Gartner, 1989: 5).

. . .

THE CURRENT SITUATION

In the late eighties, disability activism re-emerged on the national level when advocates drafted and began lobbying for the passage of the Americans With Disabilities Act (ADA). The ADA is a comprehensive piece of civil rights legislation extending the provisions of Section 504 to cover all businesses and public facilities. Activists organized a grassroots campaign that included visits to every member of Congress from constituents with compelling stories of discrimination (Shapiro, 1994: 125). But opposition to the proposed act came from transportation and business groups resulting in compromises before the bill was passed and signed into law on July 26, 1990 (Dardick, 1993: 99).

The ADA has four titles that cover employment, government programs, public accommodations, transportation and telecommunications. Civil rights protection for other minorities also entails expense to implement and enforce, but they do not require the obvious financial outlay of making busses and subways physically accessible, or providing disability-related accommodations on the job or in government services. Some businesses resist complying with the law, assuming costs will be prohibitive, and that only a few people will benefit.

. . .

The public accommodations provisions of Title III of the ADA require that businesses building new, or remodeling old facilities must make them physically accessible. Businesses cannot discriminate in providing goods or services to patrons with disabilities. Implementation of this part of the act has had the most visible impact on all Americans. These access requirements have provided needed impetus in communities that had no building access codes prior to the ADA. Curb-cuts are now common-place. Malls and hotels are built with access in mind. Old, heavy doors are being replaced with light-weight or automatic ones. Of course thousands of older buildings still only have steps leading to them, or remain difficult to negotiate inside for mobility-impaired people. Even completed modifications may still be inadequate, poorly designed or broken (Woodward, 1995: 28).

Title I prohibits discrimination in employment for businesses with 15 or more employees. An employer cannot refuse to hire an otherwise qualified disabled person, and employers must make "reasonable accommodations" so a disabled person can perform a job. This could mean putting an amplifier on a telephone, lowering a desk or modifying a work schedule. Employers aren't required to hire disabled persons over other applicants, nor are they required to provide accommodations if the cost would pose an "undue hardship." There are incentives in the law to encourage businesses to comply with the ADA such as tax deductions for the removal of architectural barriers (Dardick, 1993: 100). According to the University of West Virginia's Jobs Accommodation Network, 69% of accommodations cost $500 or less (Johnson, 1993: 102).

However, John Woodward, writing in the *Disability Rag*, (1995: 28) believes that Title I is not serving the long-term unemployed disabled population it was supposed to benefit. This section of the law is enforced by the Equal Employment Opportunity Commission (EEOC), an agency of the Federal government that makes determinations on all types of discrimination claims related to employment. Since Title I of the ADA went into effect, 50% of the 34,877 complaints filed with the EEOC were from individuals with back injuries. A much smaller number of claims came from persons with other kinds of conditions covered under the law such as emotional/psychological impairment, neurological impairments or mobility impairments. Some 89% of discrimination claims are over issues of firing, benefits and promotions, rather than the refusal to hire disabled applicants.

. . .

Legislative and policy changes are not the only arenas where disabled activists push for social change. However, under the current anti-big government political climate, the ADA has come under attack, and supporters must not only work to ensure its enforcement, but must also monitor attempts to amend or repeal the act. The ADA has become a favorite target of conservatives who want to see government stop protecting civil rights.

. . .

OTHER KEY ISSUES

Many disabled individuals are living successful, fulfilling lives because of the progress that has been made in building and transportation access, medical treatment and technology, education, and opportunities to participate in work and community life. Yet there are crucial needs that continue to be unmet for many, and each disability group has particular issues of concern.

The United States is almost the only industrialized country in the world that does not have a national health insurance program. According to the US Census Bureau's 1993 Population Survey, 39.7 million Americans have no insurance to cover the high cost of doctors visits or hospital stays. When Congress debated health care reform in 1993 and 1994, the voices of disabled people were part of the discussion. This issue is more compelling for us because many of us confront medical problems and daily living situations that neither private insurance nor the government's medicare/medicaid programs deal with adequately. Writing in *Mainstream,* William Stothers says, "Those of us with disabilities are at greatest risk, not because we're sick, most of us aren't, but because we're at the edge. A common cold or flu can create serious ramifications quickly. Our need for health care services keeps many of us dependent upon government support programs" (Stothers, 1994: 46). Congress has failed to pass any health care reform measures, in part due to vehement opposition from the powerful insurance industry that wants to keep its profits high. This issue hasn't gone away. The crisis is deepening despite its becoming a dead issue for the media.

Assistance from a personal care attendant is essential for individuals who need help with activities of daily living like getting in and out of bed, dressing, bathing, eating, going to the bathroom, shopping, and cleaning. Some states have programs to provide attendant care to those who need it for at least a few hours each day. But other states have no attendant services at all, and older people as well as young people and children with severe disabilities are forced to live in nursing homes or other large institutions. The World Institute on Disability estimates that 7.7 million people in the US require assistance from another person to accomplish everyday tasks. Three million of these people are not getting the help they need and must rely on volunteers. About one third of these live in institutions and could live in the community if support services were available. On the average, nursing home care costs $30,000 per person per year. Attendant care costs half this much or less (ADAPT, 1995). Currently, most long-term care funds through Medicaid are funneled into nursing homes and are not being directed into more cost-efficient attendant programs. ADAPT (Americans Disabled for Attendant Programs Today) holds highly visible protest actions around the country against this practice. They are demanding that 25% of Medicaid money that goes to nursing homes be redirected to community-based alternatives.

. . .

CONCLUSION

Before the beginning of the movement for disability rights, disabled people wouldn't have been part of the decision-making process about attendant services or health care reform. For the first time, we are present at the table, advocating for ourselves on the issues that affect our lives. At times we still aren't invited, but we make a place at the table for ourselves, sharing knowledge gained through personal experience. Even though advocates repeat the advantages of programs that meet people's disability-related needs and laws that create opportunities, many politicians refuse to notice and continue to discredit and slash resources for human services.

The support of nondisabled allies who have learned from disabled people is crucial to hold on to our gains and continue to make progress. Anyone can become disabled either through accident or illness. Then questions about rights and choices become immediate and very real. It's not just those who are disabled now who benefit from opportunities for education and jobs. It's not just those who are disabled now who benefit from inclusion in family and community life. All of us benefit when disabled people are participants, not burdens who've been locked away and forgotten.

The disability-rights movement is challenging priorities in American society: promoting passage and enforcement of laws like the ADA; protesting and lobbying for adequate health care and attendant services; and demanding public resources go to individuals not institutions. The needs are so obvious and the benefits so clear.

REFERENCES

ADAPT. (1995, May). *Facts Sheet.*

Dardick, G. (1993) "Moving Towards Independence: The Americans With Disabilities Act and What it Means." *The Whole Earth Review,* Fall, 1992, reprinted in the *Utne Reader,* March/April, issue 56, pp. 98–100.

Frum, D. & Brennan, J. (1993, April 26) "Oh My Aching . . . You Name It." *Forbes Magazine,* pp. 52–54.

Funk, R. J. "Disability Rights: From Caste to Class in the Context of Civil Rights." (1989). In Gartner, A. & Joe, T. (Eds.), *Images of the Disabled, Disabling Images.* pp. 7–339. New York: Praeger.

Gill, C. J. (1987, Spring). "A New Social Perspective on Disability and its Implications for Rehabilitation." *Occupational Therapy and Health Care,* vol. 7, no. 1, pp. 49–55.

Goldman, C. D. (1995). "Legal Access: Another Dumb Act? ADA at the Crossroads." *Horizons,*

July 1995, reprinted in the *Braille Forum,* July, pp. 16–19.

Gwin, L. (1995, July–August). "This Just In." *Mouth Magazine,* p. 4.

Johnson, M. (1988). "Disability Rights Movement: Overcoming the Social Barriers." *The Nation Magazine,* April 9, reprinted in *Reporting on Disability: Approaches and Issues.* Johnson and Elkins. (Eds.), pp. 46–48.

Johnson, M. (1993). "Pushing for Access: Loopholes in the ADA Present Continuing Obstacles." *The Progressive,* August 1991, reprinted in the *Utne Reader.* March–April 56, pp. 101–103.

Kerzner Lipsky, D. & Gartner, A. "The Current Situation." (1989) in Kerzner Lipsky D. & Gartner A. (eds.), *Beyond Separate Education: Quality Education for All.* Baltimore, Paul H. Brooks, pp. 3–24.

Longmore, P. (1992). "Subverting the Dominant Paradigm." Lecture, University of Minnesota, October 5.

Rifkin, J. (1995, May–June). "After Work: a Blueprint for Social Harmony in a World Without Jobs." *The Utne Reader,* pp. 51–62.

Rosen, S. L. (1980, November). "A Survivor's Manual." *Disability Rag,* pp. 6–7.

Shapiro, J. P. (1994). "Disability Policy and the Media: A Stealth Civil Rights Movement Bypasses the Press and Defies Conventional Wisdom." *Journal of Social Policy,* 22(1) pp. 123–133.

Shapiro, J. P. (1993). *No Pity: People with Disabilities Forging a New Civil Rights Movement.* New York: Times Books.

Stothers, W. G. (1994, April). "There's a Crisis All Right and It's Bad for our Health." *Mainstream,* p. 46.

Trent, J. W. (1994). *Inventing the Feeble Mind: A History of Mental Retardation in the United States.* Berkeley: University of California Press.

Woodward, J. R. (1995, July–August). "The ADA at 5." *Disability Rag,* pp. 27–31.

READING 95

The Beijing Declaration and Platform for Action

Beijing Declaration

1. We, the Governments participating in the fourth World Conference on Women,

2. Gathered here in Beijing in September 1995, the year of the fiftieth anniversary of the founding of the United Nations,

3. Determined to advance the goals of equality, development and peace for all women everywhere in the interest of all humanity,

4. Acknowledging the voices of all women everywhere and taking note of the diversity of women and their roles and circumstances, honouring the women who paved the way and inspired by the hope present in the world's youth,

5. Recognize that the status of women has advanced in some important respects in the past decade but that progress has been uneven, inequalities between women and men have persisted and major obstacles remain, with serious consequences for the well-being of all people,

6. Also recognize that this situation is exacerbated by the increasing poverty that is affecting the lives of the majority of the world's people, in particular women and children, with origins in both the national and international domains,

7. Dedicate ourselves unreservedly to addressing these constraints and obstacles and thus enhancing further the advancement and empowerment of women all over the world, and agree that this requires urgent action in the spirit of determination, hope, cooperation and solidarity, now and to carry us forward into the next century.

We reaffirm our commitment to:

8. The equal rights and inherent human dignity of women and men and other purposes and principles enshrined in the Charter of the United Nations, to the Universal Declaration of

Human Rights and other international human rights instruments, in particular the Convention on the Elimination of All Forms of Discrimination against women and the Convention on the Rights of the Child, as well as the Declaration on the Elimination of Violence against Women and the Declaration on the Right to Development.

9. Ensure the full implementation of the human rights of women and of the girl child as an inalienable, integral and indivisible part of all human rights and fundamental freedoms;

10. Build on consensus and progress made at previous United Nations conferences and summits—on women in Nairobi in 1985, on children in New York in 1990, on environment and development in Rio de Janeiro in 1992, on human rights in Vienna in 1993, on population and development in Cairo in 1994 and on social development in Copenhagen in 1995 with the objective of achieving equality, development and peace;

11. Achieve the full and effective implementation of the Nairobi Forward-looking Strategies for the Advancement of Women;

12. The empowerment and advancement of women, including the right to freedom of thought, conscience, religion and belief, thus contributing to the moral, ethical, spiritual and intellectual needs of women and men, individually or in community with others and thereby guaranteeing them the possibility of realizing their full potential in society and shaping their lives in accordance with their own aspirations.

We are convinced that:

13. Women's empowerment and their full participation on the basis of equality in all spheres of society, including participation in the decision-making process and access to power, are fundamental for the achievement of equality, development and peace;

14. Women's rights are human rights;

15. Equal rights, opportunities and access to resources, equal sharing of responsibilities for the family by men and women, and a harmonious partnership between them are critical to their well-being and that of their families as well as to the consolidation of democracy.

16. Eradication of poverty based on sustained economic growth, social development, environmental protection and social justice requires the involvement of women in economic and social development, equal opportunities and the full and equal participation of women and men as agents and beneficiaries of people-centered sustainable development;

17. The explicit recognition and reaffirmation of the right of all women to control all aspects of their health, in particular their own fertility, is basic to their empowerment;

18. Local, national, regional and global peace is attainable and is inextricably linked with the advancement of women, who are a fundamental force for leadership, conflict resolution and the promotion of lasting peace at all levels.

19. It is essential to design, implement and monitor, with the full participation of women, effective, efficient and mutually reinforcing gender-sensitive policies and programmes, including development policies and programmes, at all levels that will foster the empowerment and advancement of women;

20. The participation and contribution of all actors of civil society, particularly women's groups and networks and other non-governmental organizations and community-based organizations, with full respect for their autonomy, in cooperation with Governments, are important to the effective implementation and follow-up of the Platform for Action;

21. The implementation of the Platform for Action requires commitment from Governments and the international community. By making national and international commitments for action, including those made at the Conference, Governments and the international community recognize the need to take priority action for the empowerment and advancement of women.

We are determined to:

22. Intensify efforts and actions to achieve the goals of the Nairobi Forward-looking

Strategies for the Advancement of Women by the end of this century;

23. Ensure the full enjoyment by women and the girl child of all human rights and fundamental freedoms and take effective action against violations of these rights and freedoms;

24. Take all necessary measures to eliminate all forms of discrimination against women and the girl child and remove all obstacles to gender equality and the advancement and empowerment of women;

25. Encourage men to participate fully in all actions toward equality;

26. Promote women's economic independence, including employment, and eradicate the persistent and increasing burden of poverty on women by addressing the structural causes of poverty through changes in economic structures, ensuring equal access for all women, including those in rural areas, as vital development agents, to productive resources, opportunities and public services;

27. Promote people-centered sustainable development, including sustained economic growth, through the provision of basic education, lifelong education, literacy and training, and primary health care for girls and women;

28. Take positive steps to ensure peace for the advancement of women and, recognizing the leading role that women have played in the peace movement, work actively towards general and complete disarmament under strict and effective international control, and support negotiations on the conclusion, without delay, of a universal and multilaterally and effectively verifiable comprehensive nuclear-test-ban treaty which contributes to nuclear disarmament and the prevention of the proliferation of nuclear weapons in all its aspects;

29. Prevent and eliminate all forms of violence against women and girls;

30. Ensure equal access to and equal treatment of women and men in education and health care and enhance women's sexual and reproductive health as well as education;

31. Promote and protect all human rights of women and girls;

32. Intensify efforts to ensure equal enjoyment of all human rights and fundamental freedoms for all women and girls who face multiple barriers to their empowerment and advancement because of such factors as their race, age, language, ethnicity, culture, religion, or disability, or because they are indigenous people;

33. Ensure respect for international law, including humanitarian law, in order to protect women and girls in particular;

34. Develop the fullest potential of girls and women of all ages, ensure their full and equal participation in building a better world for all and enhance their role in the development process.

We are determined to:

35. Ensure women's equal access to economic resources, including land, credit, science and technology, vocational training, information, communication and markets, as a means to further the advancement and empowerment of women and girls, including through the enhancement of their capacities to enjoy the benefits of equal access to these resources, *inter alia*, by means of international cooperation;

36. Ensure the success of the Platform for Action, which will require a strong commitment on the part of Governments, international organizations and institutions at all levels. We are deeply convinced that economic development, social development and environmental protection are interdependent and mutually reinforcing components of sustainable development, which is the framework for our efforts to achieve a higher quality of life for all people. Equitable social development that recognizes empowering the poor, particularly women living in poverty, to utilize environmental resources sustainably is a necessary foundation for sustainable development. We also recognize that broad-based and sustained economic growth in the context of sustainable development is necessary to sustain social development and social justice. The success of the Platform for Action will also require adequate mobilization of resources at the national and

international levels as well as new and additional resources to the developing countries from all available funding mechanisms, including multilateral, bilateral and private sources for the advancement of women; financial resources to strengthen the capacity of national, subregional, regional and international institutions; a commitment to equal rights, equal responsibilities and equal opportunities and to the equal participation of women and men in all national, regional and international bodies and policy-making processes; and the establishment or strengthening of mechanisms at all levels for accountability to the world's women;

37. Ensure also the success of the Platform for Action in countries with economies in transition, which will require continued international cooperation and assistance;

38. We hereby adopt and commit ourselves as Governments to implement the following Platform for Action, ensuring that a gender perspective is reflected in all our policies and programmes. We urge the United Nations system, regional and international financial institutions, other relevant regional and international institutions and all women and men, as well as non-governmental organizations, with full respect for their autonomy, and all sectors of civil society, in cooperation with Governments, to fully commit themselves and contribute to the implementation of this Platform for Action.

. . .

PLATFORM FOR ACTION

Critical Areas of Concern

41. The advancement of women and the achievement of equality between women and men are a matter of human rights and a condition for social justice and should not be seen in isolation as a women's issue. They are the only way to build a sustainable, just and developed society. Empowerment of women and equality between women and men are prereq-

uisites for achieving political, social, economic, cultural and environmental security among all peoples.

42. Most of the goals set out in the Nairobi Forward-looking Strategies for the Advancement of Women have not been achieved. Barriers to women's empowerment remain, despite the efforts of Governments, as well as non-governmental organizations and women and men everywhere. Vast political, economic and ecological crises persist in many parts of the world. Among them are wars of aggression, armed conflicts, colonial or other forms of alien domination or foreign occupation, civil wars and terrorism. These situations, combined with systematic or de facto discrimination, violations of and failure to protect all human rights and fundamental freedoms of all women, and their civil, cultural, economic, political and social rights, including the right to development and ingrained prejudicial attitudes towards women and girls are but a few of the impediments encountered since the World Conference to Review and Appraise the Achievements of the United Nations Decade for Women: Equality, Development and Peace, in 1985.

43. A review of progress since the Nairobi Conference highlights special concerns—areas of particular urgency that stand out as priorities for action. All actors should focus action and resources on the strategic objectives relating to the critical areas of concern which are, necessarily, interrelated, interdependent and of high priority. There is a need for these actors to develop and implement mechanisms of accountability for all the areas of concern.

44. To this end, Governments, the international community and civil society, including non-governmental organizations and the private sector, are called upon to take strategic action in the following critical areas of concern:

- The persistent and increasing burden of poverty on women
- Inequalities and inadequacies in and unequal access to education and training

- Inequalities and inadequacies in and unequal access to health care and related services
- Violence against women
- The effects of armed or other kinds of conflict on women, including those living under foreign occupation
- Inequality in economic structures and policies, in all forms of productive activities and in access to resources
- Inequality between men and women in the sharing of power and decision-making at all levels
- Insufficient mechanisms at all levels to promote the advancement of women

- Lack of respect for and inadequate promotion and protection of the human rights of women
- Stereotyping of women and inequality in women's access to and participation in all communication systems, especially in the media
- Gender inequalities in the management of natural resources and in the safeguarding of the environment
- Persistent discrimination against and violation of the rights of the girl-child

---

READING 96

Taking the High Road

Suzanne Pharr

In the mid-1990s, we are seeing a rapid rise of mean-spiritedness, fed by radio and television, the rhetoric of cynical politicians, and the embittered disillusionment of people whose hopes and dreams have been destroyed and whose lives feel threatened. It is a mean-spiritedness that seems to feed upon itself, seeking everywhere someone to blame, someone who is the cause of this pain, this disappointment, this failure to succeed. The airwaves are filled with rancor and anger, cynicism and accusation. Recently, I have been asking people to describe the mood of the country. They respond, "depressed, angry, overwhelmed, feeling isolated and cut off, mistrustful, mean, hurt, fearful." To succeed, our organizing must address these feelings.

As progressive and moderate voices are excluded or silenced or mimic this rage and cynicism, I worry about our better selves diminishing from lack of nurturance and support. I think of our better selves as that place where

compassion, sympathy, empathy, tolerance, inclusiveness, and generosity reside.

All of our strategies for social change will mean very little if we do not have access to that place inside us where generosity, for example, lives. Much of our work has to be focused on nurturing the life of the spirit, on keeping the door to our better selves as wide open as possible.

Cultural work offers one of our best means of nurturing the individual spirit and our sense of connection to others. It is through the creation of art and culture that the spirit is fed and kept alive and our common humanity is expressed and exposed.

Yet in much of our social change work, we incorporate art and culture only as "add-ons"— the concert after a conference, the song or poem at the beginning of the meeting. We rarely see cultural organizing as social change work. One reason is that we are often stuck in the same old methods of organizing and do not question how people learn, what moves us to change. Another reason is that we can sometimes become too focused on a single goal or issue and do not consider the wholeness of ourselves and our constituency. In building a movement, eating and singing together may be as important as handing out leaflets. Being able to involve our families with us in our work may be as important as recruiting new members. The basis for successful organizing work is people who are connected, not separated, people who feel whole, not fragmented.

Storytelling is one of the strongest cultural expressions; it helps us feel whole and connected. Nothing is more critical than storytelling to defining our humanity. When telling our stories, we assert both our individuality and our connection to others, and we make others aware of our identity and history. What better way to counter gross stereotyping, demonizing, and dehumanization than by presenting a multiplicity of voices and experiences, each individualized, each unique, and each connected to a common history?

In the early days of the women's antiviolence movement, women met in groups to tell the story of the violence that had occurred in their lives. For many, it was the first time they had told anyone what happened—the rape, incest, battering, torture—and telling the story to others brought them out of isolation and gave them connection to a group. But what followed next was the foundation for a women's antiviolence movement: after women heard each others stories, they came to recognize the great similarities among them. Through discussing these commonalities, they created an analysis of the relationship between the perpetrator of violence and its target, and they recognized that though the victim is frequently blamed for the violence, the fault lies with the perpetrator and the society that accepts the violence. Those desiring to end violence against themselves and other women then moved to take action: creating safe homes and battered women's shelters, hotlines and support groups, working with police, changing laws, confronting batterers and rapists, providing political education and changing public policy.

For whatever reasons, progressive people have not always talked a great deal about the strong moral convictions underlying why we do this work of social justice: *it is because we believe every person counts, has human dignity, and deserves respect, equality, and justice.* This morality is the basis for our vision, and all our work flows from this basic belief.

We are living in a time in which people are crying out for something to believe in, for a moral sense, for purpose, for answers that will bring some calm to the chaos they feel in their lives. I believe it is our moral imperative to help each other make connections, to show how everyone is interrelated and belongs in community. It is at our peril if we do work that increases alienation and robs meaning from life. Today's expressions of violence, hatred, and bigotry are directly related to the level of alienation and disconnection felt by people. For our very survival, we must develop a sense of common humanity.

It may be that our most important political work is figuring out how to make the full human connection, how to engage our hearts as well as our minds, how to heal the injuries we have suffered, how to do organizing that transforms people as well as institutions.

We have to think about our vision of change.

I am not arguing that we should give up direct action, civil disobedience, issue campaigns, political education, confrontation, membership and voter drives, et cetera. We need to do these things and much more. I am suggesting that we rethink the meaning of social change and learn how to include the long-term work of transforming people as we work for social justice. We must redefine "winning." Our social change has to be more than amassing resources and shifting power from the hands of one group to another. We must seek a true shift in consciousness, one that forges vision, goals, and strategies from belief, not just from expediency, and allows us to become a strong political force.

The definition of transformational politics is fairly simple: it is political work that changes the hearts and minds of people; supports personal and group growth in ways that create healthy, whole people, organizations, and communities; and is based on a vision of a society where people—across lines of race, gender, class, and sexuality—are supported by institutions and communities to live their best lives.

It calls for living with communal values. We face a daunting challenge here because our culture glorifies individualism. Creating community requires seeing the whole, not just the parts, and understanding how they interrelate. However, the difficult part is learning how to honor the needs of the individual as well as those of the group, without denying the importance of either. It requires a balance between identity and freedom on the one hand and the collective good and public responsibility on the other. It requires ritual and celebration and collective ways to grieve and show anger; it requires a commitment to resolve conflict.

Building connection and relationship demands that we give it time, not just in meetings but in informal opportunities surrounding meetings, structured and unstructured. Our communities are where our moral values are expressed. It is here that we are called upon to share our connection to others, our interdependence, our deepest belief in what it means to be part of the human condition, where people's lives touch one another, for good or for bad. It is here where the rhetoric of belief is forced into the reality of living. It is from this collection of people, holding within it smaller units called families, that we build and live democracy—or, without care and nurturance, where we detach from one another and destroy our hope for survival.

It is one thing for us to talk about liberation politics; it is of course another to live it. We lack political integrity when we demand liberation for one cause or one group of people and act out oppression or exploitation toward others. In our social change organizations in particular we can find ourselves in this dangerous position: where we are demanding, for example, liberation from sexism but within the organization we act out racism, economic injustice, and homophobia. Each is reflected in who is allowed to lead, who makes the highest and lowest salaries, who is allowed to participate in the major decision-making, who decides how resources are used. If the organization does not have a vision and a strategy that also include the elimination of racism, sexism, economic injustice, and homophobia (as well as oppressions relating to age, physical ability, et cetera), then internal conflict is inevitable.

. . .

I believe that all oppressions in this country turn on an economic wheel; they all, in the long run, serve to consolidate and keep wealth in the hands of the few, with the many fighting over crumbs. Without work against economic injustice, against the dehumanizing excesses of capitalism, there can be no deep and lasting work on oppression. The theocratic Right has been successful in driving wedges between oppressed groups because there is little common understanding of the linkages common to all oppressions. Progressives have contributed to these divisions because, generally, we have dealt only with single pieces of the fabric of injustice. Often we have no knowledge of a shared history. We stand ready to be divided. Our challenge is to learn how to use the experiences of our many identities to forge an inclusive social change politics. The question that faces us is how to do multi-issue coalition-building from an identity base. The hope for a multiracial, multi-issue movement rests in large part on the answer to this question.

If women are treated as people undeserving of equality within civil rights organizations, or lesbians and gay men are, how can those organizations demand equality? If women of color and poor women are marginalized in women's rights organizations, how can those organizations argue that women as a class should be moved into full participation in the mainstream? If lesbian and gay organizations are not feminist and antiracist in all their practices, what hope is there for the elimination of homophobia and heterosexism in a racist, sexist society? It is an issue of integrity.

When we grasp the value and interconnectedness of our liberation issues, then we will at last be able to make true coalition and begin building a common agenda that eliminates oppression and brings forth a vision of diversity that shares both power and resources.

READING 97

Epilogue
Beyond Backlash

Ruth Rosen

"If you're on the right track, you can expect some pretty savage criticism," veteran feminist Phyllis Chesler warned young women at the close of the twentieth century. "Trust it. Revel in it. It is the truest measure of your success." Words of wisdom from one of the pioneer activists who understood the meaning of a fierce backlash.

No movement could have challenged so many ideas and customs without threatening vast numbers of women and men. Some activists viewed the backlash as either a political conspiracy or a media plot hatched to discredit feminists. But the backlash, in fact, reflected a society deeply divided and disturbed by rapid changes in men's and women's lives, at home and at work.

Abortion genuinely polarized American women. Working women, as sociologist Kristin Luker discovered, tended to support abortion rights, while homemakers, who depended on a breadwinner's income, were more likely to regard children as a means of keeping husbands yoked to their families and so opposed it. The backlash, which had grown alongside the women's movement, gained strength in 1973 after the Supreme Court, in its *Roe v. Wade* decision, made abortion legal. The Catholic Church—and later the evangelical Christian Right—quickly mobilized to reverse that decision. By 1977, Congress had passed the Hyde

Amendment, which banned the use of taxpayers' money to fund abortions for poor women. By 1980, the New Right had successfully turned abortion into a litmus test for political candidates, Cabinet officials, and Supreme Court justices. By 1989, the Supreme Court's *William L. Webster v. Reproductive Health Services* decision began the process of chipping away at women's right to abortion.

A long, drawn-out struggle over the Equal Rights Amendment also helped consolidate opposition to the women's movement. Passed quickly by Congress in a burst of optimism in 1972, the ERA needed to be ratified by thirty-eight state legislatures in order to become a part of the Constitution. Within a year, the ERA received swift ratification or support from thirty states, but then it stalled, and in 1978, proponents extracted a reluctant extension from Congress. By 1982, the ERA, unable to gain more state ratifications, had been buried, a victim of the rising symbolic politics of a triumphant political movement of the Right.

The ten-year battle over the ERA and the escalating struggle over abortion helped mobilize conservative women. Ironically, women of the Right learned from the women's movement, even if in opposition to it. In a kind of mirror-image politicking, they began to form their own all-female organizations, including Happiness of Motherhood Eternal (HOME),

Women Who Want to Be Women (WWWW), American Women against the Ratification of the ERA (AWARE), Females Opposed to Equality (FOE), and the Eagle Forum. Soon, they engaged in their own kinds of local and national consciousness-raising activities. Their tactics, like those of the women's movement, included polite protest and lobbying in Washington, as well as more militant rallies and protests. But unlike the women's movement, the fringes engaged in actual terrorism at abortion clinics.

The political struggle also catapulted several conservative women to national prominence. Among them was Phyllis Schlafly, a shrewd attorney who nonetheless—like Betty Friedan almost two decades earlier—described herself as "just a housewife," and founded Stop ERA, which she credited with defeating the ERA. An influential if little-known member of the conservative Right, Schlafly had written a book, *The Power of the Positive Woman* (1977), which attacked feminists for their negative assessments of women's condition in the United States. Schlafly also blamed "limousine liberals," "the cosmopolitan elite," and "chic fellow travelers" for living in a rarefied world that cared little about the traditional family and its values. Schlafly used her antifeminism as a vehicle for reinventing herself as a national celebrity. Thanks to the media, her name soon became a household word.

The growing engagement of women in the religious and secular New Right legitimated an increasing fusillade of attacks on feminism by right-wing male religious and political leaders. In *The New Right: We're Ready to Lead,* Richard Viguerie, one of those leaders, announced that the New Right had to fight "anti-family organizations like the National Organization for Women and to resist laws like the Equal Rights Amendment that attack families and individuals." Schlafly, Viguerie, and other leaders of the New Right blamed the hedonistic values of American culture on feminists. For them, an independent woman was by definition a selfish, self-absorbed creature who threatened the nation's "traditional values."

Support for the growing backlash came from many directions, including many women who were not members of any New Right organization. Some of those disgruntled women now felt overwhelmed by the double responsibilities they bore at home and at work; they blamed feminism for their plight. The media took its cue from such women. A new formulaic narrative appeared in the print media, that of the repentant career woman who finally realizes that feminism had very nearly ruined her life. Editors began to dispatch reporters in search of professional women who had quit their high-status jobs and returned home with great sighs of relief to care for their husbands and children.

Like the "first woman" stories of the 1970s, these cautionary tales of the 1980s obscured the actual lives of the vast majority of women in the labor force, for whom there was no choice but to get up every morning and go to work. Most working mothers labored at low-paid jobs, and husbands generally avoided even a reasonable share of the housework from their now-employed spouses. So women daily returned home to what sociologist Arlie Hochschild dubbed the "second shift." Even successful professional women were discovering that they, too, had no choice but to enter careers on men's terms. Their new employers expected them to be available "25 hours a day, seven days a week" and their husbands, too, expected the same services they would have received from an unemployed wife. To secure promotions, career women—but not men—felt compelled to choose whether to dedicate their prime childbearing years to their careers and remain childless, or to face the daunting prospect of trying to do it all.

Despite the difficulties women and men experienced as they tried to adjust to this newly configured home life, it's important to recognize that the women's movement did not invariably pit men against women. This was not a battle between the sexes; it was part of the highly gendered and racialized cultural wars that polarized Americans in the wake of the

1960s. Men and women fought *together* on both sides of the divide, for this was a struggle between social and cultural ideals.

. . .

Feminist responses to the backlash began to appear in literature as well. During the heady years of the 1970s, feminist utopian novels had become the *genre du jour*. Some of the most prominent novels—Marge Piercy's *Woman on the Edge of Time* or Ursula Le Guinn's *The Left Hand of Darkness*—had played with gender and sexual identity and optimistically imagined new ways of achieving gender equality. In the wake of the backlash, the Canadian novelist Margaret Atwood published a bleak dystopian novel, *The Handmaid's Tale* (1986), which quickly became a best-seller. This chilling novel took the destructive potential of the religious backlash seriously and offered a scary answer to the question: "What if the religious Right actually gained political power?"

Despite the sense of gloom and defeat that many feminists experienced at the time, American women were, in fact, increasingly embracing the goals of the women's movement. Reasons were not hard to fathom. Growing numbers of women were falling into poverty. Diana Pearce's 1978 phrase "the feminization of poverty" caught a startling and unexpected reality of American life. Divorce rates, which had doubled since 1965, had created a new cohort of women who joined the poor when their marriages ended. By 1984, working women began to outnumber women who worked at home and the glamorization of the superwoman and her career choice had eroded the prestige of homemaking. The growing tendency of middle-class women to postpone marriage and motherhood, combined with an increase in single mothers and divorced mothers, created a critical mass of women who now wondered how they were going to support themselves and their children. Polls steadily revealed what the much-publicized backlash obscured, that a majority of women now looked favorably upon the goals of the women's movement.

Women's attitudes had, in fact, changed rapidly. In a 1970 Virginia Slims opinion poll, 53 percent of women cited being a wife and mother as "one of the best parts of being a woman." By 1983, that figure had dropped to 26 percent. In 1970, very few women expressed concern over discrimination. By 1983, one-third of women agreed that "male chauvinism, discrimination, and sexual stereotypes ranked as their biggest problem"; while 80 percent agreed that "to get ahead a woman has to be better at what she does than a man." Nor did women still believe they lived privileged lives, as they had in 1975, when one-third of Americans viewed men's lives as far more difficult. By 1990, nearly half of all adults assumed that men had the easier life.

At the height of the backlash, in short, more American women, not fewer, grasped the importance of the goals of the women's movement. In 1986, a Gallup poll asked women, "Do you consider yourself a feminist?" At a time when identifying yourself as a feminist felt like a risky admission, 56 percent of American women were willing to do so (at least privately to Gallup's pollsters). Women of all classes were also becoming aware of the ways in which gender shaped their lives. Sixty-seven percent of all women, including those who earned under $12,500 *and* those who made more than $50,000, favored a strong women's movement. Pollsters consistently found that more African-American women approved of the goals of the women's movement than did white women. A 1989 poll found that 51 percent of all men, 64 percent of white women, 72 percent of Hispanic women, and 85 percent of African-American women agreed with the statement: "The United States continues to need a strong women's movement to push for changes that benefit women."

In 1989, *Time* magazine ushered in a new decade with yet one more pronouncement of the death of feminism. Its cover story, "Women Face the '90s," bore the subtitle "During the '80s, they tried to have it all. Now they've just plain had it. Is there a future for feminism?"

But, inside, the reader discovered quite a different story. Feminism was endangered, *Time* magazine suggested, not because it had failed, but precisely because it had been so successful. "In many ways," the article declared,

> feminism is a victim of its own resounding achievements. Its triumphs—in getting women into the workplace, in elevating their status in society and in shattering "the feminine mystique" that defined female success only in terms of being a wife and a mother—have rendered it obsolete, at least in its original form and rhetoric.

The growth of gender consciousness had, in fact, altered society and culture in countless ways. In August 1980, a *New York Times* editorial declared that the women's movement, once viewed as a group of "extremists and troublemakers," had turned into an "effective political force." The editorial concluded that "the battle for women's rights is no longer lonely or peripheral. It has moved where it belongs; to the center of American politics." In 1984, commenting on legislation that would grant child support for all families and give wives access to their husbands' pensions, the *Times* editorialized that "'Women's Issues' have already become everyone's." And so they had. Perhaps the important legacy was precisely that "women's issues" had entered mainstream national politics, where they had changed the terms of political debate.

Everyday life had changed in small but significant ways. Strangers addressed a woman as Ms.; meteorologists named hurricanes after *both* men and women; schoolchildren learned about sexism before they became teenagers; language became more gender-neutral; popular culture saturated society with comedies, thrillers, and mysteries that turned on changing gender roles; and two decades after the movement's first years, the number of women politicians doubled. Even more significantly, millions of women had entered jobs that had once been reserved for men.

Although women had not gained the power to change institutions in fundamental ways, they had joined men in colleges and universities in unprecedented numbers. In the 1950s, women had constituted only 20 percent of college undergraduates, and their two most common aspirations, according to polls of the time, were to become the wife of a prominent man and the mother of several accomplished children. By 1990, women constituted 54 percent of undergraduates and they wanted to do anything and everything. Women had also joined men in both blue collar and professional jobs in startling numbers. In 1960, 35 percent of women had worked outside the home; by 1990, that figure had jumped to 58 percent. During the same period, the number of female lawyers and judges leaped from 7,500 to 108,200; and female doctors from 15,672 to 174,000.

The cumulative impact of decades of revelations, education, debates, scandals, controversies, and high-profile trials raised women's gender consciousness, which in turn eventually showed up in a long-awaited political "gender gap." In 1871, Susan B. Anthony had prematurely predicted that once women got the right to vote, they would vote as a bloc. A gender gap did not appear until 1980, when more men than women voted for Ronald Reagan, whose opposition to the Equal Rights Amendment and abortion may have moved some women into the Democratic column. More important was Reagan's pledge to dismantle the welfare state, which nudged even more women toward the Democrats, the party more likely (theoretically) to preserve the safety net. Eventually, the gender gap would cause at least a temporary realignment of national politics. In 1996, 16 percent more women than men voted for Bill Clinton for president. Some political analysts now believed that women were voting their interests as workers, family caregivers, or as single or divorced mothers.

Gender gap or not, the rightward tilt of American politics led to the demonization of poor women and their children. As some middle-class women captured meaningful and well-paid work, ever more women slid into poverty and homelessness, which, on balance, the women's movement did too little, too late, to change. On the other hand, the lives of many ordinary working women, who had not become impoverished, improved in dramatic ways. In 1992, a *Newsweek* article described how twenty years of the women's movement had changed Appleton, Wisconsin (the hometown of Joseph McCarthy and the John Birch Society). Women, the magazine reported, had taken on significant roles in local politics. In addition, the article observed,

> There are women cops and women firefighters, and there are women in managerial jobs in local business and government. There is firm community consensus, and generous funding with local tax dollars, for Harbor House, a shelter for battered women. And there is an active effort, in the Appleton public schools, to eliminate the invidious stereotyping that keeps young women in the velvet straitjacket of traditional gender roles.

GLOBAL FEMINISM

As ideas from the Western women's movement traveled across the Atlantic, American feminists learned more than they taught. On October 25, 1985, President Vigdis Finnbogadottir of Iceland joined tens of thousands of women who had walked off the job in a twenty-four-hour protest against male privilege on the island. She also refused to sign a bill that would have ordered striking flight attendants back to work. Iceland's telephone system collapsed, travel came to a halt, and groups of men crowded into hotels for the breakfast their wives refused to cook for them.

As feminism began spreading beyond industrialized nations, American feminists also encountered new definitions of "women's issues." Sometimes "freedom" meant better access to fuel and water, toppling a ruthless dictator, or ending a genocidal civil war. The gradual emergence of global women's networks made such encounters and confrontations inevitable.

Many of these networks grew out of the United Nation's 1975 International Women's Year. At the first World Conference on Women in Mexico, delegates urged the UN to proclaim the years between 1975 and 1985 "The Decade for Women." At each subsequent UN conference, there were two parallel meetings—one for delegates who represented their governments and another for women who participated in the nongovernmental organization (NGO) meetings. The numbers of NGO participants mushroomed. Six thousand women participated in the second conference, held in 1980 at Copenhagen; fourteen thousand attended the third in 1985 in Nairobi; and a startling thirty thousand arrived in Huairou, China, for the fourth in 1995.

What President Kennedy's Commission on the Status of Women had done for American women activists, the UN's World Conferences now did at a global level. Proximity bred intimacy and spread knowledge. The thousands of women rubbing shoulders or debating in Mexico, Denmark, Kenya, or China were learning from and teaching each other about their lives. Aside from their differences, they were also discovering the ubiquity of certain kinds of shared oppression—violence and poverty that had once seemed local, rather than global. And, in the process, they were nurturing and legitimating a global feminism, which was quite literally being born at UN conferences as they watched.

That didn't mean that women everywhere interpreted the information newly available to them in the same way. From the start, the NGO forum meetings witnessed serious clashes between "First" and "Third" World women, and between women whose nations were at war. Over time, the atmosphere began to improve. Western feminists began to *listen,* rather than *lecture,* and women from developing countries, who had formerly viewed Western concerns over clitoridectomies, dowry deaths, wife-beatings, and arranged marriages as so many instances of cultural imperialism—the urge of developed countries to impose their values and customs on underdeveloped nations—began the painful process of redefining their own customs as crimes.

Here was the essence of global feminism—addressing the world's problems *as if women mattered.* Human rights organizations, for instance, had traditionally focused exclusively on state-sanctioned violence against political activists. But most women encountered violence not in prison or at protests, but in their homes and communities. Viewed as customs rather than crimes, wife-beating, rape, genital excision, dowry deaths, and arranged marriages had never been certified as violations of women's human rights.

At a 1993 UN World Conference on Human Rights in Vienna, women from all over the globe movingly testified to the various forms of violence that had devastated their lives. Feminists successfully made their case; the conference passed a resolution that recognized violence against women and girls as a violation of their human rights. One immediate consequence of this historic redefinition of human rights was that Western nations could now grant *political* asylum to women fleeing certain violence or death from husbands or other relatives.

Two years later, at a 1995 UN Conference on Development and Population in Cairo, feminists criticized accepted development policies that promoted massive industrial or hydroelectric projects as *the* way to improve the standard of living of developing nations. Such projects, they argued, irreversibly damaged the human and natural ecology, provided work for indigenous men, but not for women, and undermined women's traditional economic role and social authority. Instead, they advocated small-scale cottage industries, through which women could earn money for their education. They also attacked those population experts who took it, as an article of faith, that population growth automatically declined when industrial development lifted people out of poverty. Citing the failure of such policies, feminists coun-

tered that educating women and giving them control over their reproductive decisions was a far more effective way of controlling population growth. As one reporter wrote, "The deceptively simple idea of a woman making a decision about her future is one of the cornerstones of the emerging debate on global population policy."

The "Platform for Action," the document that emerged from the Beijing conference in 1995, asked the nations of the world to see social and economic development through the eyes of women. Although the "Platform" recognized the differences that separated women, it also emphasized the universal poverty and violence that crippled the lives of so many of the world's women. In addition to affirming women's rights as human rights, the conference also declared three preconditions for women's advancement; equality, development, and peace. To many participants, the event seemed like a miracle, a moment existing out of time, when the world's women imagined a different kind of future, even if they had little power to implement it.

By publicizing even more gender consciousness, the 1995 Fourth World Conference on Women probably encouraged greater numbers of the world's women to challenge traditional forms of patriarchal authority. In the years following the conference, feminist activists and scholars began the process of redefining rape (when it occurred during a military conflict) as a war crime, publicizing the particular plight of refugees (most of whom were women), and rethinking the role women might play in reconstructing societies ravaged by war.

At the same time, women in both developed and developing nations began debating the impact of feminism itself on global culture and economics. Was feminism yoked only to concepts of individual rights? Was it simply an inevitable by-product of Western consumer capitalism, whose effects would rupture the ties that bound families and communities together—and to the land? Or could feminism help protect the rights of women as they left family and land behind and entered the global wage economy? Could women's rights, redefined as human rights, provide a powerful new stance from which to oppose totalitarian societies of both the Right and the Left? Many theories proliferated, heated debates took place, but the answers—even many of the questions—lay in the future.

There is no end to this story. Over a hundred years ago, the suffragist Matilda Gage turned her gaze toward the future. The work of her generation of activists, she wrote, was not for them alone,

> nor alone for the present generation, but for all women of all time. The hopes of posterity were in their hands, and they were determined to place on record for the daughters of 1976, the fact that their mothers of 1876 had thus asserted their equality of rights, and thus impeached the government of today for its injustice towards women.

Nearly a century later, veteran feminist Robin Morgan, along with thousands of other twentieth-century "daughters," took up the unfinished agenda left by the suffrage movement. Morgan, too, realized that she struggled for future daughters and worried that her generation might squander precious opportunities.

> I fear for the women's movement falling into precisely the same trap as did our foremothers, the suffragists: creating a bourgeois feminist movement that never quite dared enough, never questioned enough, never really reached out beyond its own class and race.

As women in developing countries become educated and enter the marketplace as wage-earners, they will invariably intensify existing cultural conflicts between religious and secular groups, and between those sectors of society living under preindustrial conditions and those who connect through cyberspace in a postmodern global society. Like small brushfires, these cultural wars may circle the globe, igniting a wild and frightening firestorm. Inevitably, some women will feel defeated as they encounter wave after wave of backlash. But in the darkness of their despair, they should remember that resistance is not a sign of defeat, but rather evidence that women are challenging a worldview that now belongs to an earlier era of human history.

Each generation of women activists leaves an unfinished agenda for the next generation. First Wave suffragists fought for women's citizenship, created international organizations, dedicated to universal disarmament, but left many customs and beliefs unchallenged. Second Wave feminists questioned nearly everything, transformed much of American culture, expanded the idea of democracy by insisting that equality had to include the realities of its women citizens, and catapulted women's issues onto a global stage. Their greatest accomplishment was to change the terms of debate, so that women mattered. But they left much unfinished as well. They were unable to change most institutions, to gain greater economic justice for poor women, or to convince society that child care is the responsibility of the whole society. As a result, American women won the right to "have it all," but only if they "did it all."

It is for a new generation to identify what they need in order to achieve greater equality. It may even be their solemn duty. In the words of nineteenth-century suffragist Abigail Scott Duniway:

> The young women of today, free to study, to speak, to write, to choose their occupation, should remember that every inch of this freedom was bought for them at a great price. It is for them to show their gratitude by helping onward the reforms of their own times, by spreading the light of freedom and truth still wider. The debt that each generation owes to the past it must pay to the future.

The struggle for women's human rights has just begun. As each generation shares its secrets, women learn to see the world through their own eyes, and discover, much to their surprise, that they are not the first, and that they are not alone. The poet Muriel Rukeyser once asked, "What would happen if one woman told the truth about her life?" Her answer: "The world would split open." And so it has. A revolution is under way, and there is no end in sight.

READING 98

Warning

Jenny Joseph

When I am an old woman I shall wear purple
With a red hat which doesn't go, and doesn't
  suit me.
And I shall spend my pension on brandy and
  summer gloves
And satin sandals, and say we've no money
  for butter.
I shall sit down on the pavement when I'm
  tired
And gobble up samples in shops and press
  alarm bells

And run my stick along the public railings
And make up for the sobriety of my youth.
I shall go out in my slippers in the rain
And pick the flowers in other people's gardens
And learn to spit.

You can wear terrible shirts and grow more fat
And eat three pounds of sausages at a go
Or only bread and pickle for a week
And hoard pens and pencils and beermats and
  things in boxes.

But now we must have clothes that keep us
  dry
And pay our rent and not swear in the street
And set a good example for the children.
We must have friends to dinner and read the
  papers.
But maybe I ought to practise a little now?
So people who know me are not too shocked
  or surprised
When suddenly I am old, and start to wear
  purple.

DISCUSSION QUESTIONS FOR CHAPTER THIRTEEN

1. How has your experience in a feminist classroom had on impact on you?

2. What do you consider important factors for building a "beloved community"?

3. How do you envision a just future? How do you think we can get there?

4. What does integrity mean to you? How does integrity affect your work for justice?

5. What impact might a "transformational politics" have on our society?

6. Why are peace and the environment important women's issues?

7. What will you take away from this class to help you make your way in the world?

SUGGESTIONS FOR FURTHER READING

Daly, Mary. *Quintessence . . . Realizing the Archaic Future: A Radical Elemental Feminist Manifesto.* Boston: Beacon, 1999.

Clare, Eli, and Suzanne Pharr. *Exile and Pride.* Boston: South End, 1999.

Mellor, Mary. *Feminism & Ecology.* New York: New York University Press, 1998.

Naples, Nancy A. *Community Activism and Feminist Politics: Organizing Across Race, Class, and Gender.* New York: Routledge, 1997.

———. Grassroots Warriors: *Activist Mothering, Community Work, and the War on Poverty.* New York: Routledge, 1998.

Ryan, M. J., ed. *The Fabric of the Future: Women Visionaries of Today Illuminate the Path to Tomorrow.* Berkeley: Conari, 2000.

Credits

Index of Authors, Titles, and Subjects